INDEX TO BLACK POETRY

DOROTHY H. CHAPMAN

G. K. HALL & CO., 70 LINCOLN STREET, BOSTON, MASS. 1974

5/1975
Gen.
(Given)

This publication is printed on permanent/durable acid-free paper.

Library of Congress Cataloging in Publication Data

Chapman, Dorothy.
    Index to Black poetry.

    1. Negro poetry--Indexes. 2. Negroes--Poetry--
Indexes. I. Title.
PN1025.C5   811'.008   74-8838
ISBN 0-8161-1143-X

To my daughters Dessalyn Renee and Karen Adele Chapman,
my sisters, Mary Will, Lorraine Bigelow and Vangie Wright,
my late parents, Rosker and Irene Hilton
and two lovely girls, Billye and Michelle Baines.

Contents

Foreword

Building on the earlier work of Dorothy Porter, this index undertakes to bring into one volume for the first time a complete reference of black poems and poets. Black poetry is here defined in the broadest manner, rather than in the more exact sense scholars have more recently employed. References are included for the work not only of black poets but also of those poets who have in some way dealt with the black experience or written within the black tradition, regardless of their racial origins. It includes Blake's "Little Black Boy" as well as Dunbar's "Little Brown Baby," and as such is a broadly defined poetic reference of black subject matter, styles and authors.

The appearance of this volume is highly significant; it is symbolic of the growing recognition of the creative work of black poets. A generation ago, few were known to any sizeable portion of the reading public. It is true many in the black community grew up on Dunbar's "Lias! Lias! Bless De Lawd!" and Langston Hughes' "I've Known Rivers" and some of the other well known poems of the Renaissance, but the range was not wide and the readership relatively limited. For the majority of the white population, the black writer was best epitomized by W. E. B. Dubois' famous metaphor of a man crying out, unheard and unnoticed, as though behind a glass wall. This index marks the newly recognized importance of the black poetic voice, providing a reference for both the older body of poetry and for the dramatic explosion of black poetry in the sixties and early seventies. This development has added a new dimension to black literature and life and, as a new phenomenon on the national scene, is commanding increasing attention.

In one of the first important anthologies, The Book of American Negro Poetry, James Weldon Johnson spoke prophetically of the black poets' contribution as creators and shapers of culture. This has become a substantial reality, although not in the sense that Johnson foresaw. Despite the increased recognition that the poetry has gained, it has scarcely been the persuasive agent in white attitudinal change that Johnson contemplated. It has, on the other hand, developed an identity, a direction, a scope and a function of its own. This Index will serve as a valuable guide for those seeking to understand this development.

For countless years black poets have had more than the usual problems in getting published. There were few poets who could print entire volumes, or even appear in noted anthologies. As a number of critics, both black and white, have pointed out, the latter were in reality anthologies of white American poets. The individual black poets who did manage to squeeze into the published pages found their work scattered in many, and often obscure, volumes. This Index offers in one volume the usually dispersed locations of the work of particular authors, with the practical consequence of making some of them accessible for the first time. The Index may also aid the individual inquirer to assess the comparative usefulness of the increasing number of anthologies of black poetry. Narrowing the search for needed poems is an enormous help for the scholar or other interested reader.

Glancing through the Title and First Line Index one can gain much insight about the history, breadth, style and concerns of the black artist. The origins of the poetry in the folk lore and the oral tradition become evident. The spiritual emphasis and the reliance upon the eighteenth century classical traditions can be picked out in many of the first lines of Phyllis Wheatley, James Corrothers and Frances Harper. The plantation dialect Dunbar made famous cannot help but catch the eye. The rhythms and stylistic impulses of the twenties and the Renaissance are evident in the first lines of Countee Cullen and Claude McKay. And the new directions of the sixties and seventies may unnerve some readers with lines like: "aaaaaaaaaaaaaaaaaaaaha haaha ahah aaheehe heeeeheeaahaahneeahh." Generational distance is more sharply apparent in "Why Fades a Dream," by Dunbar, followed hard on by "Why i don't get high on shit" by Sonia Sanchez. It is not only the distinct styles of generations that are noteworthy; the novice would be fooled if he or she relied simply on style to categorize black poets within time periods. "Camptown Ladies Sing Dis Song" by Imamu Baraka (here, under LeRoi Jones) does not belong with the early dialect poems. This fact suggests two striking characteristics of much of black poetry--the great flexibility in the use of sources and the strong reliance upon origins.

The Index, particularly the Subject Index, affords a broad perspective of the themes which have absorbed black poets over the centuries, from the eighteenth century pieties of Phyllis Wheatley to the drum beat of revolt and nation building of the sixties and early seventies. As with poets everywhere, it is clear that black poets have been much occupied with thoughts of love, death, religion, "man," "woman," but they reflect also a special concern for Africa and, in the sixteen and one half pages of titles and first lines starting with the pronoun "I", probably a stronger than usual exploration of the question of identity. As is no doubt the case with all such reference volumes, there are occasional lapses. A number of important additional subject headings suggest themselves and those included offer a beginning reference point rather than a critical analysis or evaluation of a theme.

The Author Index with its listing of each author's poems is a useful tool in identifying and locating the poet and his poems. It also serves to remind us that many figures prominent in other fields, such as Daniel Payne, educator and religious leader of the nineteenth century, were in addition poets of more than negligible merit. There is an occasional listing of an African or Caribbean poet, but the entries are much too few for those cultural areas to be deemed included. The volume overwhelmingly concerns itself with black poetry in the United States. This it does, for the most

part, well. This is a highly worthwhile pioneer effort which, for some time
to come, should prove to be a uniquely useful tool for those interested in
black poetry.

SAMUEL W. ALLEN
DEPARTMENT OF ENGLISH
BOSTON UNIVERSITY

Preface

This work attempts to provide the first index devoted solely to black poetry. Ninety-four books and pamphlets by individual poets are indexed as well as thirty-three anthologies. The major portion of the books indexed were selected from The Negro in the United States, A Selected Bibliography by Dorothy Porter (Library of Congress, Washington, D.C., 1970) and North American Poets, A Bibliographical Checklist of Their Writings, 1760-1944 also by Dorothy Porter (Hattiesburg, Mississippi, Book Farm 1945.). The poetry section of the Heartman Collection of the Texas Southern University Library (Houston, Texas) provided a wealth of sources and works.

I should like to extend my thanks to Ms. Rebecca Richard who urged me to undertake and compile this work, Mrs. Mattie Kirkling for her patience in securing books through interlibrary loan, and the students at Texas Southern University for indicating by their interest the need for such an index.

Explanatory Notes

There are three major sections: the Title and First Line Index, the Author Index and the Subject Index. Arrangement is alphabetical throughout.

The Title and First Line Index contains bibliographic information for the author, the book in which the work is to be found and the page. The main words of the title are capitalized. Where the title and first line are the same, only the title is given, followed by two asterisks. One asterisk next to an entry indicates a non-black author.

For a full list of books indexed with abbreviations refer to the Key to Abbreviations for Books Indexed.

The Author Index includes a list of titles arranged alphabetically under each author; the Subject Index indicates general, key word descriptions for the poems and each subject is followed by a list of authors and titles.

Key to Abbreviations for Books Indexed

AFR   Afrodisia; new poems. Ted Joans. New York: Hill & Wang (c.1970)
          150p.

AfW   African Wings. Craig Williamson. New York: Citadel Press (c.1969)
          53p.

AKOR   Another Kind of Rain. Gerald W. Barrax. Pittsburgh: University of
          Pittsburgh Press (c.1970) 86p. (paperback)

AmNP   American Negro Poetry. Arna Bontemps, ed. New York: Hill & Wang
          (c.1963) 197p.

AnA   Annie Allen. Gwendolyn Brooks. New York: Harper (c.1949) 60p.

ANP   Anthology of Negro Poetry, An. By Negroes and Others. New Jersey:
          Works Progress Administration, n.d. 140p.

ATB   Against the Blues. Alvin Aubert. Detroit: Broadside Press (c.1972)
          30p.

AVAN   Anthology of Verse by American Negroes. Newman Ivey White, ed.
          Durham, N.C.: Moore Publishing Co. (c.1968) 250p.

BANP   Book of American Negro Poetry, The. James Weldon Johnson, ed. New
          York: Harcourt, Brace & World (c.1922, 1950, 1958, 1971) 300p.

BCF   'Bout Cullud Folkses. Lucy Mae Turner. New York: Henry Harrison
          (c.1938) 64p.

BFBTBJ   Black Feeling Black Talk Black Judgement. Nikki Giovanni. New York:
          William Morrow (1970) 98p.

BFM   Blues For Momma and Other Low Down Stuff. John Raven. Detroit:
          Broadside Press (c.1971) 31p.

BlC   Black Christ, The; and Other Poems. Countee Cullen. New York:
          Harper & Bros. (1929) 110p.

BLIA   Black Literature in America. Houston A. Baker, Jr. ed. New York:
          McGraw-Hill Book Co. (1971) 443p.

BlSp   <u>Black Spirits; a Festival of New Black Poets in America</u>. Woodie King, ed. New York: Random House (c.1972) 252p.

BlW   <u>Black Wisdom</u>. Frenchy Jolene Hodges. Detroit: Broadside Press (c.1971) 30p.

BlWo   <u>Black Words</u>. Arthur Boze. Detroit: Broadside Press (c.1972) 22p.

BMP   <u>Black Magic Poetry, Sabotage Target Study Black Art; Collected Poetry 1961-1967</u>. LeRoi Jones. Indianapolis: Bobbs-Merrill Co. (c.1969) 225p.

BOG   <u>Band of Gideon, The, and Other Lyrics</u>. Joseph S. Cotter, Jr. Boston: The Cornhill Company (1918) 29p.

BOL   <u>Black Out Loud</u>. Arnold Adoff, ed. New York: Macmillan (c.1969) 86p.

BOR   <u>Ballad of Remembrance, A</u>. Robert E. Hayden. London: Paul Breman (1962) 72p.

BPW   <u>Black Pow-wow; Jazz Poems</u>. Ted Joans. New York: Hill and Wang (c.1969) 120p.

BrT   <u>Broadside Treasury, A</u>. Gwendolyn Brooks, ed. Detroit: Broadside Press (c.1971) 188p.

BTB   <u>Beyond the Blues</u>. Rosey E. Pool, ed. Lympne, Kent, Hand and Flower Press (c.1962) 188p.

BTh   <u>Brown Thrush, The; Anthology of Verse by Negro Students at Talladega College</u>. Lillian W. Voorhees and Robert W. O'Brien, eds. Bryn Athyn, Penna.: Lawson-Roberts Pub. Co. (c.1932) 67p.

CaD   <u>Caroling Dusk</u>. Countee Cullen, ed. New York: Harper (1927) 237p.

CCC   <u>Color</u>. Countee Cullen. New York: Harper and Bros. (1925) xvii, 108p.

ChG   <u>Christmas Gif'</u>. Charlemae H. Rollins, ed. Chicago: Follett Pub. Co. (c.1963) 119p.

CLT   <u>Candle-Lightin' Time</u>. Paul Laurence Dunbar. New York: Dodd, Mead (c.1901) 127p.

CNAW   <u>Cavalcade Negro American Writing from 1760 to the Present</u>. Arthur P. Davis, ed. Boston: Houghton Mifflin Co. (c.1971) 905p.

CPJSC   <u>Collected Poems</u>. Joseph S. Cotter, Sr. New York: Henry Harrison (c-1938) 78p.

CPPLD   Complete Poems of Paul Laurence Dunbar, The. New York: Dodd, Mead & Co. (1913, 1962) 479p.

CpS   Copper Sun. Countee Cullen. New York: Harper & Bros. (1927) 89p.

DaR   Dark Rhapsody. William Lorenzo Morrison. New York: Henry Harrison (c.1945) 62p.

DCS   Don't Cry, Scream. Don L. Lee. Detroit: Broadside Press (c.1969) 64p.

DJDC   Dear John Dear Coltrane. Michael S. Harper. Pittsburgh: University of Pittsburgh Press (c.1970) 88p.

DSNP   Directionscore: Selected and New Poems. Don L. Lee. Detroit: Broadside Press (c.1967, 1968, 1969, 1970, 1971) 208p.

DYTB   Don't You Turn Back. Langston Hughes. New York: Alfred A. Knopf (c.1967, 1969) 78p.

EBAP   Early Black American Poets. William H. Robinson, ed. Dubuque, Iowa: W. C. Brown Co. Pub. (c.1969) 275p.

EbR   Ebony Rhythm, an anthology of Contemporary Negro Verse. Beatrice M. Murphy, ed. New York: Exposition Press (c.1948) 162p.

FaP   Family Pictures. Gwendolyn Brooks. Detroit: Broadside Press 23p.

FCTJ   Fine Clothes to the Jew. Langston Hughes. New York: Knopf (1927) 89p.

FHOF   From the Heart of a Folk. Waverly Turner Carmichael. Boston: The Cornhill Co. (c.1918) 60p.

FMP   For My People. Margaret Walker. New Haven: Yale University Press (1942) 58p.

FNP   Four Negro Poets. The Pamphlet Poets. New York: Simon & Schuster (c.1927) 31p.

FoM   For Malcolm; Poems on the Life and the Death of Malcolm X. Dudley Randall and Margaret G. Burroughs eds. Detroit: Broadside Press (c.1969) 126p.

FOW   Fields of Wonder. Langston Hughes. New York: Alfred A. Knopf (1947) 114p.

FYOP   Fifty Years and Other Poems. James Weldon Johnson. Boston: The Cornhill Co. (c.1917) 92p.

FYSS   For Your Sweet Sake. James E. McGirt. Philadelphia: John C. Winston Co. (c.1906) 79p.

KEY TO ABBREVIATIONS FOR BOOKS INDEXED

GANIV   Great American Negroes in Verse, 1723-1965. Eloise Crosby Culver. Washington, D.C.: Associated Pub. Inc. (c.1966) 80p.

GoS   Golden Slippers, an anthology of Negro Poetry for young readers. Arna Bontemps, ed. New York: Harper & Bros. (c.1941) 220p.

GoT   God's Trombones. James Weldon Johnson. New York: Viking Press (c.1927) 56p.

GuW   Guerilla Warfare; newer poemes. Ahmed Akinwole Alhamisi. Detroit: Black Arts Publications, Distributed by Broadside Press (1970) 16p.

HaG   Harlem Gallery. Melvin B. Tolson. Book 1, The Curator. New York: Collier-MacMillan (c.1965) 155p. (paperback)

HaS   Harlem Shadows. Claude McKay. New York: Harcourt, Brace & World (c.1922) 95p.

HeD   Heralding Dawn, an Anthology of Verse by Selected and Edited with a Historical Summary on the Texas Negroes' verse-making. John Mason Brewer. Dallas: Superior Typesetting Co. (c.1936) 45p.

HFL   House of Falling Leaves, The. William S. Braithwaite. Boston: John W. Luce & Co. (1908) Reprinted by Mnemosyne (1969) 112p.

HSITD   Heart-Shape in the Dust. Robert E. Hayden. Detroit: The Falcon Press (c.1940) 63p.

HWOP   Heart of a Woman and Other Poems, The. Georgia Douglas Johnson. Boston: The Cornhill Co. (1918) 62p.

IABW   I Am a Black Woman. Mari Evans. New York: William Morrow & Co. (c.1938, 1964, 1967, 1968, 1969, 1970) 95p.

IADB   I Am the Darker Brother; an anthology of modern poems by Negro Americans. Arnold Adoff. New York: Macmillan (c.1968) 128p.

InL   In Love. Gordon Parks. Philadelphia: J. B. Lippincott Co. (c.1971) unpaged.

ITBLA   Introduction to Black Literature in America. Lindsay Patterson, comp. & ed. New York: Publishers Comp. Inc. (1968) 302p.

ITM   In the Mecca. Gwendolyn Brooks. New York: Harper & Row (c.1968) 54p.

JGM   Just Give Me a Cool Drink of Water 'Fore I Diiie. Maya Angelou. New York: Random House (c.1971) 48p.

JHANP   Jupiter Hammon, American Negro poet. Oscar Wegelin, ed. New York: Ninety-nine copies printed for C. F. Heartman (1915) 51p.

KAL   Kaleidoscope; poems by American Negro poets. Robert E. Hayden, comp. New York: Harcourt, Brace & World (c.1967) xxiv, 231p.

LATP   Look at the People. Bernie Casey. Garden City, New York: Doubleday & Co. (1969) 92p.

LiG   Li'l' Gal. Paul Laurence Dunbar. New York: Dodd, Mead & Co. (1904) 123p.

LiS   Life Styles. Marion Nicholes. Detroit: Broadside Press (1971) 22p.

LLL   Lyrics of Life and Love. William S. Braithwaite. Boston: H. B. Turner & Co. (1904) 80p.

LOF   Links of Friendship. Joseph S. Cotter, Sr. Louisville, Ky.: The Bradley & Gilbert Co. (1898) 64p.

LOLL   Lyrics of Lowly Life. Paul Laurence Dunbar. New York: Arno Press (1969) xx, 208p.

LoY   Love You. Dubley Randall. London: Paul Breman (1970) 16p.

LRL   Libretto for the Republic of Liberia. Melvin B. Tolson. New York: Collier Books (c.1953) unpaged.

LUP   Lincoln University Poets. Waring Cuney, Langston Hughes, and Bruce M. Wright, eds. New York: Fine Editions Press (c.1954) 72p.

MASP   Medea and Some Poems, The. Countee Cullen. New York: Harper & Bros. (1935) 97p.

MBP   Magic of Black Poetry, The. Raoul Abdul, ed. New York: Dodd, Mead & Co. (c.1972) 118p.

MyH   My House. Nikki Giovanni. New York: William Morrow & Co. (1972) 69p.

NBP   New Black Poetry, The. Clarence Majors, comp. New York: International Publishers (c.1969) 156p.

NNPUSA   New Negro Poets U.S.A. Langston Hughes, ed. Bloomington, Indiana: University Press (c.1964) 127p.

ONC   Once. Alice Walker. New York: Harcourt, Brace & World (c.1968) 81p.

OTIS   On These I Stand. Countee Cullen. New York: Harper & Bros. (c.1927, 1929, 1935, 1940, 1947) 197p.

OWT   One-Way Ticket. Langston Hughes. New York: Alfred A. Knopf (1949) 136p.

PAL   Poems and Letters. Phillis Wheatley. New York: C. F. Heartman (c.1915) Mnemosyne Reprint (c.1969) 111p.

PAOP   Poet and Other Poems, The. Raymond Garfield Dandridge. Cincinnati, Ohio

PAS   Poems After Slavery. Zachary Withers. San Francisco: Pacific Coast Appeal Pub. Co. (1905) 47p.

PATL   Panther and the Leash, The. Langston Hughes. New York: Alfred A. Knopf (1967) 101p.

PBFH   Poems. Frances E. W. Harper. Philadelphia

PBK   Poems by Kali. Kali Grosvenor. New York: Doubleday (1970) 62p.

PeP   Penciled Poems. Ray Garfield Dandridge. Cincinnati, Ohio

PFND   Prophets for a New Day. Margaret Walker. Detroit: Broadside (1970) 32p.

PLL   Powerful Long Ladder. Owen Dodson. New York: Farrar, Straus (1946) 103p.

P1S   Plantation Songs for my Lady's Banjo and other Negro Lyrics & Monologue. Eli Shepperd. New York: R. H. Russell Pub. (1901) 150p.

PoN   Poetry of the Negro, 1746-1949. Langston Hughes and Arna Bontemps, Garden City, N. Y.: Doubleday (1949) xviii, 429p.

PoNe   Poetry of the Negro, 1746-1970. Langston Hughes and Arna Bontemps, eds. Garden City, N. Y.: Doubleday (1970) 645p.

PONS   Plea of the Negro Soldier and a Hundred Other Poems. Charles Fred White. East Hampton, Mass.: Press of Enterprise Printing Co. (c.1900).

PPW   Poems. Phillis Wheatley. Julian D. Mason, Jr., ed. Chapel Hill: University of North Carolina Press (1966) lviii, 113p.

RHY   Rhyming, A. Joseph S. Cotter, Sr. Louisville, Kentucky: The New South Pub. Co. (c.1895) 32p.

RWA   Rendezvous with America. Melvin B. Tolson. New York: Dodd, Mead & Co. (1944) 121p.

SAM   Symptoms & Madness. Clarence Major. New York: Corinth Books (1971) 76p.

SCh   Some Changes. June Jordan. New York: E. P. Dutton & Co. (1971) 86p.

KEY TO ABBREVIATIONS FOR BOOKS INDEXED

SFD   <u>Songs From the Dark</u>. Nick Aaron Ford. Boston: Meador Pub. Co. (1940) 40p.

SIH   <u>Shakespeare in Harlem</u>. Langston Hughes. New York: Alfred A. Knopf (1942) 124p.

SNA   <u>Snaps</u>. Victor Hernandez Cruz. New York: Random House (c.1968, 1969) 135p.

SOC   <u>Songs of Creation</u>. Marion Cuthbert. New York: Woman's Press National Board of the Women's Christian Association (c.1949) 46p.

SOMP   <u>Songs of my People</u>. Charles Bertram Johnson. Boston: The Cornhill Co. (c.1918) 55p.

SoR   <u>Southern Road</u>. Sterling A. Brown. New York: Harcourt, Brace & Co. (1932) xv, 135p.

SoS   <u>Soulscript, Afro-American Poetry</u>. June Jordan, ed. Garden City, New York: Doubleday (c.1970) 146p.

SPCM   <u>Selected Poems</u>. Claude McKay. New York: Bookman Associates (1953) 109p.

SPPH   <u>Sequel to the "Pied Piper of Hamelin" and other poems</u>. Joseph S. Cotter, Sr. New York: Henry Harrison (c.1939) 93p.

SPRH   <u>Selected Poems</u>. Robert Hayden. New York: October House, Inc. (c.1966) 79p.

SPWSB   <u>Selected Poems</u>. William S. Braithwaite. New York: Coward-McCann, Inc. (c.1948) 96p.

SVH   <u>Still Voice of Harlem</u>. Conrad Kent Rivers. London: Paul Breman (1968) 24p.

TGWL   <u>To Gwen with Love</u>. Patricia L. Brown, ed. Chicago: Johnson Pub. Co. (1971) 149p.

TNV   <u>Today's Negro Voices</u>. Beatrice M. Murphy, ed. New York: Julian Messner (1970).

TYBP   <u>3000 Years of Black Poetry</u>. Alan Lomax and Raoul Aboul, eds. New York: Dodd, Mead (1970) 261p.

VER   <u>Verses</u>. William C. Braithwaite. London: Swarthmore Press, Ltd. (c.1922) 128p.

WABP   <u>We a BaddDDD People</u>. Sonia Sanchez. Detroit: Broadside Press (c.1970) 72p. (paperback).

WeB   <u>Weary Blues, The</u>. Langston Hughes. New York: Alfred A. Knopf (1926) 109p.

WGC   <u>Walk, God's Chillun</u>. Lucile D. Goodlett. Dallas: The Kaleidograph Press (c.1933) 74p.

WLOV   <u>We Lift Our Voices and other Poems</u>. Mae V. Cowdery. Philadelphia: Alpress (1936) 68p.

WMS   <u>When Malindy Sings</u>. Paul Laurence Dunbar. New York: Dodd, Mead & Co. (c.1896, 1903) 144p.

WSBO   <u>White Song, A, and a Black One</u>. Joseph S. Cotter, Sr. Louisville, Ky.: The Brawley & Gilbert Co. (1900) 64p.

WWW   <u>We Walk the Way of the New World</u>. Don L. Lee. Detroit: Broadside Press (c.1970) 71p.

ZaP   <u>Zalka Peetruza and other Poems</u>. Raymond Garfield Dandridge. Cincinnati: The McDonald Press (1928) 107p.

ZJP   <u>Ziba</u>. James Pipes.* Norman, Oklahoma: University of Oklahoma Press (1943) 188p.

* Non-Black

TITLE AND FIRST LINE INDEX

aaaaaaaaaaaaaaaaaaaha haaha ahah aaneene neeeeneeaahaaahneeahh. LeRoi Jones.
    BMP p.151
A is awful unhappy. Ted Joans. AFR p.109
A. L. Imes. Raymond Garfield Dandridge. PAOP p.37
A. N. Marquis has erased your song. Percy Edward Johnston. CNAW p.771
Aardvard. Julia Fields. BOL p.33
Abandoned Baby. June Jordan. SCh p.12
Abe Lincoln was a poor man's son. Eloise Culver. GANIV p.33
Ablaze with candles sconced. Robert Hayden. SPRH p.16
About June. John Raven. BFM p.30
About me young and careless feet linger along the garish street. Claude
    McKay. FNP p.8; HaS p.12; SPCM p.67
About Soho we went before the light. Claude McKay. HaS p.78
Above a rough altar coarse cement all. Charles F. Pressoir. PoN p.361
Abraham Lincoln, Great Emancipator, 1809-1865. Eloise Culver. GANIV p.33
Abraham Lincoln. John W. Fentress. EbR p.63
Abraham Lincoln. Ray Garfield Dandridge. PeP p.26
Abraham Lincoln shit he never walked nowhere to read a book. June Jordan.
    SCh p.75
Absence. Claude McKay. AVAN p.20; HaS p.64; SPCM p.93
Absence. Nick Aaron Ford. SFD p.15
Absence. Paul Laurence Dunbar. CPPLD p.147
Absent in Spring. William S. Braithwaite. SPWSB p.35
Absolute Pain. Bernie Casey. LATP p.67
Accident. Maya Angelou. JGM p.15
Accidental far into the longer light, or smoking clouds. June Jordan. SCh
    p.38
Accountability. Paul Laurence Dunbar. CPPLD p.6; LOLL p.6
Ache you feel is an evil spirit hiding between your teeth, The. Ted Joans.
    AFR p.50
Across the dewy lawn she treads. Jonathan Henderson Brooks. BTh p.19; CsD
    p.195
Across the hill and down the narrow ways. Paul Laurence Dunbar. CPPLD
    p.192
Across the Ho Chi Minh trail. Ahmed A. Alhamisi. GuW p.8
Across the Sea.** William C. Braithwaite. VER p.68
Acrostic for Julia Shepard, An. George Moses Howard. CNAW p.35
Addenda to an Unfinished Poem. Albert Aubert. ATB p.20
Address to Miss Phillis Wheatley (sic) Ethiopian Poetess ... Jupiter Hammon.
    EBAP p.9; JHANP p.32

Afrodisia. Ted Joans. AFR p.71
After. Maya Angelou. JGM p.17
After. Naomi Long Madgett. BTB p.147
After a Visit. Paul Laurence Dunbar. CPPLD p.64; LOLL p.91; MASP p.67;
    OTIS p.141
After All. Donald Jeffrey Hayes. CaD p.191
After all and after all. Donald Jeffrey Hayes. CaD p.191
After an interminable wait you came. Gordon Parks. InL unpaged
After england-france-belgium & germany had run over. Ted Joans. AFR p.59
After five minutes of argument. Waring Cuney. LUP p.15
After Harvest. William S. Braithwaite. LLL p.71
After her man had left her for the sixth time that year (an uncommon occur-
    rence). Don L. Lee. DSNP p.160; WWW p.36
After Impression Came Soul. Tommy Whitaker. TNV p.134
After Many Days. Paul Laurence Dunbar. CPPLD p.441
After Many Springs. Langston Hughes. WeB p.92
After our fierce loving in the brief time we found to be together. Dudley
    Randall. BrT p.128
After the Ball. LeRoi Jones. BMP p.17
After the baths and bowel-work, he was dead. Gwendolyn Brooks. AnA p.8
After the cloud embankments. Arna Bontemps. AmNP p.80; BLIA p.217; KAL p.81
After the Dancing for Pamela. Victor Hernandez Cruz. SNA p.49
After the good fairy. Quandra Prettyman. BOL p.18
After the illness and fever had fled, and you lay as cold as stone on your
    bed. Naomi Evans Vaughn. EbR p.150
After the Operations. Michael S. Harper. DJDC p.70
After the Quarrel. Paul Laurence Dunbar. CaD p.5; CPPLD p.62; LOLL p.88
After the Winter. Claude McKay. BANP p.171; HaS p.26; IADB p.104; PoN
    p.327; PoNe p.96; SPCM p.30
After they put down their overalls.** Lenrie Peters. TYBP p.170
After While. Paul Laurence Dunbar. CPPLD p.81; LOLL p.120
After Winter. Sterling A. Brown. BTB p.58; GoS p.171; PoN p.86; PoNe p.165;
    SoS p.50; SoR p.79
Aftermath. Michael S. Harper. DJDC p.773
Afternoon grew darkening from the West, The. William S. Braithwaite. HFL
    p.55
Afternoon Off. Lucia M. Pitts. EbR p.121
Afterwards, They Shall Dance. Bob Kaufman. PoNe p.409
Afterword: for Gwen Brooks, An (the search for the new-song begins with the
    old). Don L. Lee. DSNP p.204
Again he strode forward and they waited. David Llorens. Brt p.22; FOM p.19
Again that perverse entity of relays and my number. Gerald W. Barrax. AKOR
    p.48
Again the day. Samuel Adams. IADB p.83; NNPUSA p.85
Again we meet--a flashing glance. Georgia D. Johnson. HWAOP p.60
Against Boldness. Joseph S. Cotter, Sr. LOF p.41; SPPH p.80
Against our puny sound and sight. Countee Cullen. BlC p.32; OTIS p.89
Against that Day. Sterling A. Brown. SoR p.132
Against the day of sorrow. Georgia D. Johnson. AmNP p.21
Against this wrong of the Teutonic night. William S. Braithwaite. PoN p.45;
    SWWSB p.86

Against what light is false what breath sucked, for deadness. LeRoi Jones.
    CNAW p.648
Agile bit of baby girl, An. Raymond Dandridge. ZaP p.55
Agonies confirm this hour. Robert Hayden. BOR p.43; SPRH p.61
Agony and the Bone, The. Delores Kendrick. TGWL p.60
Agony as now, An. LeRoi Jones. SoS p.124
Ah, children dear, the hour draws near. Ann Plato. ANP p.12
Ah Christ I love you rings to the wild sky. Allen Tate. PoNe p.520
Ah! Dead! What! Dead! my favorite prince! Charles Fred White. PONS p.105
Ah, Douglass, we have fall'n on evil days. Paul Laurence Dunbar. CPPLD
    p.339
Ah, how poets sing and die. Anne Spencer. BANP p.218; CaD p.50; KAL p.37
Ah! How the wind raves this bitter night. Lauretta Holman Gooden. HeD p.15
Ah, I have changed, I do not know. Paul Laurence Dunbar. CPPLD p.448
Ah, I know what happiness is .... Blanche Taylor Dickinson. ANP p.130;
    CaD p.107
Ah, little road all whirry in the breeze. Helene Johnson. AmNp p.101; BANP
    p.280; CaD p.221; GoS p.176; PoN p.154; PoNe p.266
Ah, love, my love is like a cry in the night. Paul Laurence Dunbar. CPPLD
    p.361
Ah me, it is cold and chill. Paul Laurence Dunbar. CPPLD p.299
Ah, my Black one thou art not beautiful. Langston Hughes. WeB p.65
Ah, no respect for church or state. Eli Shepperd. PlS p.13
Ah, Nora, my Nora, the light fades away. Paul Laurence Dunbar. CPPLD p.99;
    LOLL p.146
Ah-So! Ted Joans. AFR p.95
Ah, yes, 'tis sweet still to remember. Paul Laurence Dunbar. CPPLD p.49;
    LOLL p.78
Ah, yes, the chapter ends to-day. Paul Laurence Dunbar. AVAN p.57; CPPLD
    p.161
Ah, you are cruel. Anne Spencer. CaD p.47
Ah! you're quite a jolly girl I see where are you from? Charles Fred White.
    PONS p.20
Ah'm bowed down but God's gwine raise me. Lucy Mae Turner. BCF p.46
Ah'm sick, docter-man-Ah'm sick. John Wesley Holloway. AVAN p.186; BANP
    p.135
Aimless O.k'd. Joseph S. Cotter, Sr. SPPH p.71
Ain't been in Market Street for nothing. Margaret Walker. PFND p.7
Aint Got. Ted Joans. BPW p.31
Ain't got time for a bite to eat. Mari Evans. IABW p.55
Aint it nice to have a mammy. Paul Laurence Dunbar. BLIA p.115; CPPLD
    p.388
Ain't nobody nevah tol' you not a wo'd a-tall. Paul Laurence Dunbar. CPPLD
    p.291
Air. Clarence Major. SoS p.96
Air. LeRoi Jones. BMP p.87
Air a-gittin' cool an' coolah. Paul Laurence Dunbar. CNAW p.211; CPPLD
    p.122; LOLL p.182
Air is dark, the sky is gray, The. Paul Laurence Dunbar. CPPLD p.103; LOLL
    p.153
Air is Dirty, The.** Glen Thompson. SoS p.10

Air of stale milk, I was under the influence of power flow. Clarence Major.
    SAM p.12
Al Fitnah Muhajir. Nazzam Al Sudan. NBP p.127
Alabama. Julia Fields. PoNe p.420
Alabama Earth (At Booker Washington's Grave). Langston Hughes. DYTB p.23;
    GoS p.164
Alarm and time clock still intrude too early. M. Carl Holman. AmNP p.148;
    PoN p.205; PoNe p.364
Alarm Clock, The. Mari Evans. BOL p.6; IABW p.59
Alarm clock sure sound loud. Mari Evans. BOL p.6; IABW p.59
Alas! and am I born for this. George Moses Horton. ANP p.13; CNAW p.37;
    ITBLA p.93; KAL p.16; PoN p.9; PoNe p.11
Alas, the willing hands are stilled in death. Ray Garfield Dandridge. PeP
    p.13
Albert Ayler: eulogy for a decomposed saxophone player. Stanley Crouch.
    B1Sp p.42
Albert! Hey Albert! Langston Hughes. DYTB p.13; FCTJ p.61
Aleta mentions in her tender letters. Claude McKay. HaS p.18; SPCM p.26
Alexander Crummell - Dead. Paul Laurence Dunbar. CPPLD p.181
Alfonso, Dressing to Wait at Table. Claude McKay. HaS p.7
Alfonso is a handsome bronze-hued lad. Claude McKay. HaS p.7
Alfred Tennyson. Joseph S. Cotter, Sr. LOF p.18
Algernon Charles Swinburne. Joseph S. Cotter, Sr. CPJSC p.63; WSBO p.23
Ali is our prince. Lloyd M. Corbin, Jr. BOL p.26
Ali. Lloyd M. Corbin, Jr. BOL p.26
Alice. Paul Laurence Dunbar. CPPLD p.61; LOLL p.87
Alien. Bernie Casey. LATP p.17
Alien. Donald Jeffrey Hayes. AmNP p.93
All-conquering death by the resistless pow'r. Phillis Wheatley. PAL p.47;
    PPW p.55
All day subdued, polite, kind, thoughtful to the faces that are white.
    Langston Hughes. OWT p.70
All day Sunday didn't even dress up. Langston Hughes. SIH p.7
All day the Zulu hunters and their chief tracked in the bushland. Melvin
    Tolson. RWA p.69
All de night long twell de moon goes down. Paul Laurence Dunbar. CPPLD
    p.415
All deep there stirs the throb of spring. Georgia D. Johnson. HWAOP p.54
All earth is a circus groud. Raymond G. Dandridge. PeP p.7; ZaP p.5
All Earth is a Poet. Joseph S. Cotter, Sr. CPJSC p.63; WSBO p.23
All garbed in grave farewell - attire his steed exhaling zigzag fire.
    J. Henderson Brooks. BTh p.38
All God's spades... got shades and some of God's spades (you'll never know
    which one has got long-sharp protective blades). Ted Joans. BTB p.131;
    BPW p.78
All god's spades wear dark shades. Ted Joans. TYBP p.248
All Hail! Thou truly **noble chief**. James M. Whitfield. EBAP p.49
All Heaven in a Grain of Sand. William S. Braithwaite. SPWSB p.17
All hot and Grimy from the road. Paul Laurence Dunbar. CPPLD p.366
All I wanted was your love. Mari Evans. IABW p.20

All In One. Ted Joans. AFR p.107
All life is built from song. Charles B. Johnson. SOMP p.14
All Lives, All Dances and All is Loud. Anonymous. MBP p.11
All Nashville is a Chill, and Everywhere. George Marion McLlellan. EBAP
    p.122
All night I walked among your spirits, Richard. Conrad Kent Rivers. SVH p.9
All night they whine upon their ropes and boom. Arna Bontemps. BANP p.263;
    PoNe p.224
All night, through the eternity of night. Claude McKay. HaS p.94; SPCM
    p.107
All night we danced upon our windy hill. Countee Cullen. CCC p.19
All of them are six. June Jordan. SCh p.49
All over the road the no-winged geese swim in beams. Michael S. Harper.
    DJDC p.34
All praise be to Allah. Mari Evans. IABW p.82
All Ready. All Right. LeRoi Jones. BMP p.52
All that I can see of you are your swift strong hands resting lightly on the
    porch railing. Countess W. Twitty. EbR p.148
All that night I prayed for eyes to see again. Alice Walker. ONC p.39
All that night I walked alone and wept. Arna Bontemps. CaD p.159
All that ragtime behind glass. Albert Aubert. ATB p.10
All the Clocks. Carolyn Rodgers. BlSp p.184
All the clocks are off or have stopped in the Black ghetto. Carolyn Rodgers.
    BlSp p.184
All The Dead. Countee Cullen. CCC p.73
All the pretty baubles spread are not the answer to my need. **Georgia Douglas**
    Johnson. ANP p.87
All the Things. LeRoi Jones. BMP p.91
All the time they were praying. Waring Cuney. CaD p.208; PoN p.147
All the Tom-toms of the jungles beat in my blood. Langston Hughes. WeB
    p.102
All the World is hatred. LeRoi Jones. BMP p.66
All the World Moved.** June Jordan. Sch p.24
All the World moved.** June Meyer. NBP p.89
All the world of deep desire loves your song. William S. Braithwaite. HFL
    p.99
All things a beam of glory shed. Charles R. Dinkins. AVAN p.113
All things confirm me in the thought that dust. Countee Cullen. CoS p.55
All things come to pass when they do. Keorapetse Kgositsile. BlSp p.112
All This Review. Owen Dodson. PLL p.81
All through an empty place I go. Countee Cullen. PoN p.131
All thru last year they sang. Victor Hernandez Cruz. SNA p.99
All white on Europe Sist-nine Western Front. Ted Joans. AFR p.62
All who have and have all can cry: "Peace!" Russell Atkins. NBP p.24
All yesterday it poured. Claude McKay. HaS p.66; SPCM p.16
All you violated ones with gentle hearts you violent dreamers whose cries
    shout heartbreak. Margaret Walker. FoM p.32; PFND p.18
Allah is the most high. Anonymous. MBP p.61
Allegro. Robert E. Hayden. HSITD p.32
Allegro con Rocks. LeRoi Jones. BMP p.215

America   TITLE AND FIRST LINE INDEX

And on this shore. M. Carl Holman. AmNP p.148; PoN p.205; PoNe p.364
And once again: pain. William Browne. BTB p.64
And one morning while in the woods I stumbled suddenly upon the thing.
    Richard Wright. AmNP p.103; IADB p.78; PoN p.156
And One Shall Live in Two. J. Henderson Brooks. BTh p.21; PoN p.135; PoNe
    p.239
And our tree grew as trees do (up). Paulette Jones. TGWL p.58
And Sampson cried out terrified and afraid. Owen Dodson. PLL p.98
And several strengths from drowsiness campaigned. Gwendolyn Brooks. ITM
    p.49
And she shall be the friend of youth for age. Angelina Grimke. ANP p.87
And she was brown and she always wore and dressed in brown. Ted Joans. BPW
    p.79; BTB p.132
And silence which proves but a referent to my disorder. LeRoi Jones. AmNP
    p.181; BTB p.135; SoS p.76
And So It Is With Love. Mae V. Cowdery. WLOV p.39
And so this is the way it rains in Carolina 22 Sept. 69. Gerald W. Barrax.
    AKOR p.55
And so Tomorrow. Samuel E. Boyd. EbR p.8
And so we lick our chop at Birmingham and say "see!" Langston Hughes.
    PATL p.74
And so we Talk. Countess W. Twitty. EbR p.147
And so, when the time came. Frank A. Collymore. PoN p.347
And so you like this gay banjo? Eli Shepperd. PlS p.38
& Stuff Like That. Victor Hernandez Cruz. SNA p.19
And the Greatest of These is War. James Weldon Johnson. FYOP p.37
And the hotel room held only him.** Mari Evans. IABW p.37
... And the old women gathered.** Mari Evans. KAL p.175; NNPUSA p.79
And the subway gives such refinement. Conrad Kent Rivers. KAL p.207
And the voices dropped from the ashy ceiling. Walter Bradford. BrT p.177
And the sun exploded in my soul. Katherine L. Cuestas. BTB p.76
And there are those. James Thompson. BlSp p.210
And there they were: with fire everywhere. S. E. Anderson. NBP p.23
And they were mostly all blk/ S. Sanchez. WABP p.34
And this silly wire (which some consider essential, connected us and we came
    together). Nikki Giovanni. BFBTBJ p.12
And thou art one - one with th' eternal hills. Joseph S. Cotter, Jr. BOG
    p.18
... and two bird-chidren harmonized far inside a yellow field... Joseph
    Major. NBP p.88
And we came that sun day etheride & i to that quiet / looooking / street.
    Sonia Sanchez. TGWL p.86; WABP p.58
And what do I have to make me smile. Frenchy J. Hodges. BlW p.7
And what shall you say? Joseph S. Cotter, Jr. ANP p.34; AVAN p.182; BANP
    p.186; BOG p.13; CaD p.103; PoN p.72; PoNe p.135
And what would I do in Heaven, pray. Countee Cullen. CCC p.89; FNP p.18;
    OTIS p.39
And when I come to see you again, I will bring my gifts. Mae V. Cowdery.
    WLOV p.43
And when I have beat the enemy and he has fled. Bruce McM. Wright. LUP
    p.57

Are You Too, Able? Ted Joans. AFR p.149
Aren't We all? Norman Hills Stateman. EbR p.133
Areytos. Jean Brierre. EbR p.9
Arise. Raymond Garfield Dandridge. PAOP p.39; ZaP p.97
Arise, my soul, on wings enraptur'd, rise. Phillis Wheatley. EBAP p.101;
    PPW p.19; PAL p.42
Arise! O humble undertrodden wight. Raymond Garfield Dandridge. ZaP p.97
Arise! ye humble undertrodden wight. Raymond G. Dandridge. PAOP p.39
"An Aristotelian Elegy." Donald E. Bogle. TNV p.21
Arm yourself Africa! Ted Joans. AFR p.31
Around each empty nest by subtle memory stirred. Charles B. Johnson. SOMP
    p.6
Around me roar and crash the pagan isms. Claude McKay. SPCM p.49
Around the council-board of hell, with satan at their head. James Weldon
    Johnson. FYOP p.37
Arrow rides upon the sky, An. Samuel Evans. NNPUSA p.18
Arsenal of the Lord, The. William S. Braithwaite. PoN p.45; SPWSB p.86
Arson and Cod Lace (or how: yearn to burn bay burn). Worth Long. NBP p.84
Art of a Poet, The. George Moses Horton. EBAP p.24
Arthur Mitchell. Marianne Moore. PoNe p.506
Arthur Ridgewood, M.D. Frank Marshall Davis. KAL p.106
Artic Tern in a Museum. Effie Lee Newsome. PoN p.56; PoNe p.71
Artist looked up from his painting and saw in his doorway there a tiny maid
    with pecan-colored skin and a mass of black tangled hair. Constance
    Nichols. EbR p.110
As a Black child I was a dreamer. Conrad Kent Rivers. AmNP p.176; BLIA
    p.356; PoNe p.404
As a child I bought a red scarf and women told me how beautiful it looked.
    Conrad Kent Rivers. IADB p.105; NNPUSA p.10; PoNe p.404; SVH p.18
As a goldfish sees the world. L. Doretha Lowery. BTh p.63
As a new-made bride at the altar-stair. William S. Braithwaite. HFL p.75
As a Possible Lover.** LeRoi Jones. AmNP p.180; SoS p.78
As a quiet little seedling. Paul Laurence Dunbar. CPPLD p.17; LOLL p.22
As a youth I knew the venom of Watts. Robert Reedburg. TNV p.108
As Critic. Margaret Danner. TGWL p.29
As day burned out in the smouldering west. Bruce McM. Wright. LUP p.59
As Don Took Off at Dawn. Ted Joans. AFT p.51
As I blew the second chorus of Old Man River. Ted Joans. BPW p.124; FOM
    p.25
As I Grew Older. Langston Hughes. BANP p.240; DYTB p.67; WeB p.55
As I lie in bed. Joseph S. Cotter, Jr. BANP p.185; BOG p.6
As I look into each different face. Owen Dodson. KAL p.128
As I look on the drear day, from which the warmth of sun has flown. Charles
    Fred Ford. PONS p.45
As I stood beside the ocean. Joseph S. Cotter, Sr. RHY p.6
As I talk with learned people, I have heard a strange remark. Walter Everett
    Hawkins. AVAN p.149
As I was going to town. Lula Lowe Weeden. CaD p.22
As if it were some noble thing she spoke of song at war. Langston Hughes.
    PATL p.53

As if the trucks were slaves, and slobbered over their chains. LeRoi Jones.
    BMP p.77
As in some dim baronial hall restrained. Paul Laurence Dunbar. CPPLD p.150
As It Is. Joseph S. Cotter, Sr. CPJSC p.28; WSBO p.22
As Keats' old honeyed volume of romance. William S. Braithwaite. LLL p.37
As Lise however my mother was white. Oswald Durand. P1N p.352
As lone I sat one summer's day. Paul Laurence Dunbar. AVAN p.6; CPPLD
    p.195
As long as people. William J. Harris. BOL p.70
As much as my eyes may be said to be open it was you who opened them.
    A. B. Spellman. TGWL p.91
As one who hath been dreaming all night long. William S. Braithwaite. HFL
    p.89
As one who stands beside a magic pool and cries to every nymph that lifts its
    head. Joseph S. Cotter, Sr. LOF p.57
As one would rob a reptile of its sting. Joseph S. Cotter, Sr. LOF p.47
As-Salaam-alaikum my black princes the morning awaits u. Sonia Sanchez
    B1Sp p.188
As Seen By Disciplines. Gwendolyn Brooks. ITM p.44
As silent through the world she goes.** William S. Braithwaite. HFL p.94
As simile to myth and myrrh. Joseph S. Cotter, Sr. CPJSC p.23
As some rapt gazer on the lowly earth. Paul Laurence Dunbar. CPPLD p.169
"As surely as I hold your hand in mine." Countee Cullen. CCC p.5
As the Old Year Passed. William Moore. ANP p.60
As the word was given to prophets of old. Margaret Walker. BrT p.150;
    PFND p.22
As things be/come let's destroy. Nikki Giovanni. BFBTBJ p.39; BOL p.9
As we all probably realize on some level, people are basically selfish.
    Nikki Giovanni. BFBTBJ p.87
As We Love, So Are We Loved. Charles Fred White. PONS p.156
As we pass along life's highway day by day. W. Clarence Jordan. ANP p.126
As We Should Be. Charles Fred White. PONS p.95
As when Emotion Too Far Exceeds Its Causes. Elizabeth Bishop. G. C. Oden.
    KAL p.183
As ye cast your eyes around you. William F. Brooks. LUP p.3
As you go dreaming, sure a dream for me. James (Nakisaki) Christopher.
    EbR p.35
As You Leave Me. Etheridge Knight. BrT p.80
As you may brush your clothes at times so that no grain of dust remain.
    Charles Fred White. PONS p.115
Ascendency. Herbert A. Simmons. NBP p.120
Ascension. William S. Braithwaite. SPWSB p.11
Ashamed of my race? Joseph S. Cotter, Jr. ANP p.34; BOG p.5
Ashes Lord--But warm still from the fire that cheered us. Albert Aubert.
    ATB p.29
Ashes Of Love. Raymond Garfield Dandridge. PoP p.33
Ashes to Ashes, dust unto dust. Paul Laurence Dunbar. AVAN p.88; CPPLD
    p.164
Asked And Answered. Countee Cullen. B1C p.33
Aspiration. James C. Hughes. ANP p.123
Aspiration. Langston Hughes. SIH p.33

At The Ebony Circle. Helen G. Quigless. TNV p.94
At the Etoile Cat the Unknown Soldier's Grave in Paris. Countee Cullen.
   B1C p.12
At the feet o' Jesus. Langston Hughes. DYTB p.35; FCTJ p.47; FNP p.28;
   ITBLA p.159
At the golden gate of song. Paul Laurence Dunbar. CPPLD p.288
At the Lincoln Monument in Washington, August 28, 1963. Margaret Walker.
   PFND p.16
At the outer edge of the world. William S. Braithwaite. LLL p.44
At the Post House. Dudley Randall. LoY p.13
At The Tavern. Paul Laurence Dunbar. CPPLD p.370
At The Wailing Wall in Jerusalem. Countee Cullen. CpS p.75; OTIS p.70
At times me feel like me. Ted Joans. BPW p.20
At twenty-one Jupe ran away.** Hodding Carter. PoNe p.540
At war. Russell Atkins. AmNP p.169
Atheist jews double crossers stole our secrets crossed the white desert.
   LeRoi Jones. BMP p.205
Athlete, The. Ted Joans. BPW p.18
Athlete's Tomb, The. William C. Braithwaite. VER p.14
Athwart the sky the great sun sails. Georgia Douglas Johnson. HWOP p.21
Atlantic City Waiter. Countee Cullen. CCC p.10
Atlantic Moonrise. Vivian L. Virtue. PoN p.326
Atlantic, they teach and tell us. Ted Joans. AFR p.31
Atrocities. Nikki Giovanni. MyH p.54
Attend my lays, ye ever honour'd nine. Phillis Wheatley. ANP p.10; CNAW
   p.12
Attention. Attention.** LeRoi Jones. BMP p.135
Audubon Drafted (for Linda). LeRoi Jones. KAL p.213; TYBP p.250
Auf Wiedersehen. Donald Jeffrey Hayes. CaD p.189
August 'twas the twenty fifth. Lucy Terry. EBAP p.4; ITBLA p.27; PoN p.3;
   PoNe p.3
Aunt Chloe's Lullaby. Daniel Webster Davis. EBAP p.238
Aunt Jane Allen. Fenton Johnson. GoS p.162; IADB p.7; PoN p.62; PoNe p.89
Aunt Jamima Dead. Kali Grosvenor. B1Sp p.106
Aunt Martha bustles from room to room. Melvin Tolson. RWA p.26
Aunt Sue has a head full of stories. Langston Hughes. ANP p.102; DYTB p.4;
   WeB p.57
Aunt Sue's Stories. Langston Hughes. ANP p.102; DYTB p.4; WeB p.57
Autobiography. Mbella Sonne Di Poro. TYBP p.142
Autumn Chorus. Owen Dodson. PLL p.55
Autumn Leaf, The. William C. Braithwaite. VER p.125
Autumn leaves are too heavy with color, The. Langston Hughes. WeB p.45
Autumn Song. William Allyn Hill. LUP p.22
Autumn trees bend and sway. William Allyn Hill, LUP p.22
Autumnal. Robert E. Hayden. HSITD p.9
Ave and Vale. William S. Braithwaite. HFL p.51
Averroes' Tempo. LeRoi Jones. BMP p.16
Awake. Raymond Garfield Dandridge. PeP p.21
Awake all night with loving. Langston Hughes. SIH p.112
Awake! arise oh, men of my race. George Marion McLlelan. EBAP p.126

Bacon. Joseph S. Cotter, Sr. LOF p.45
Bad Case of the Flying Pussy of Perry Street, The. Ted Joans. AFR p.144
Bad Luck Card. Langston Hughes. FCTJ p.60
Bad Man. Langston Hughes. FCTJ p.21
Bad-man Stagolee. Margaret Means. FMP p.35
Bad Morning. Langston Hughes. OWT p.98
Bahá 'u' lláh in the Garden of Ridwan. Robert Hayden. SPRH p.61
Baker's boy delivers loaves, The. Effie Lee Newsome. CaD p.58; GoS p.26
Baker's Boy, The. Effie Lee Newsome. CaD p.58; GoS p.26
Balances. Nikki Giovanni. BFBTBJ p.90
Ballad. Paul Laurence Dunbar. CPPLD p.91; LOLL p.135
Ballad for Sterling Street, A. Sonia Sanchez. BrT p.146; WABP p.66
Ballad of Birmingham. Dudley Randall. BLIA p.337; BrT p.124
Ballad of Gin Mary. Langston Hughes. FCTJ p.35
Ballad of Late Annie, The. Gwendolyn Brooks. AnA p.10
Ballad of Margie Polite, The. Langston Hughes. OWT p.75
Ballad of Nat Turner, The. BOR p.68; SPRH p.72
Ballad of Remembrance, A. Robert Hayden. AmNP p.109; BLIA p.252; BOR p.6;
    IADB p.32; PoN p.164; PoNe p.291; SPRH p.39
Ballad of Rudolph Reed, The. Gwendolyn Brooks. SoS p.46
Ballad of Sue Ellen Westerfield, The. (For Clyde). Robert Hayden. KAL
    p.113; SPRH p.21
Ballad of the Brown Girl, The. Countee Cullen. OTIS p.175
Ballad of the Brown Girl. Alice Walker. ONC p.72
Ballad of the Fortuneteller. Langston Hughes. SIH p.84
Ballad of the Free, The. Margaret Walker. PFND p.10
Ballad of the Girl whose Name is Mud. Langston Hughes. SIH p.91
Ballad of the Gypsy. Langston Hughes. SIH p.93
Ballad of the Hoppy-Toad. Margaret Walker. PFND p.29
Ballad of the Killer Boy. Langston Hughes. SIH p.87
Ballad of the Lame Man and the Blind Man. Waring Cuney. LUP p.14; PoN p.149
Ballad of the Lighteyed Little Girl, The. Gwendolyn Brooks. AnA p.41
Ballad of the Man Who's Gone. Langston Hughes. SIH p.97
Ballad of the Morning Streets. LeRoi Jones. BMP p.166
Ballad of the Pawnbroker. Langston Hughes. SIH p.95
Ballad of the Rattlesnake, The. Melvin Tolson. RWA p.53
Ballad of the Sinner. Langston Hughes. SIH p.85
Ballad to the Anonymous. James Patterson. FoM p.77
Ballada O Neizbestnosti. James Patterson. FoM p.76
Ballade. Paul Laurence Dunbar. CPPLD p.331
Ballade of Macheral. William C. Braithwaite. VER p.62
Ballade of One Who Died Before His Time. Benjamin Brawley. AVAN p.159
Ballade of Ships. William C. Braithwaite. VER p.60
Ballit of de Boll Weevil, De. Anonymous. ITBLA p.121
Balm for Weary Minds, A. James E. McGirt. FYSS p.71
Ban the spears, arrows, and clubs. Ted Joans. BPW p.67
Bananas ripe and green, and ginger-root. Claude McKay. AmNP p.28; ANP p.71;
    AVAN p.204; BTB p.145; FNP p.11; GoS p.131; HaS p.8; KAL p.47; PoN p.327;
    PoNe p.95; SPCM p.31; TYBP p.118
Banbury Bells. William C. Braithwaite. VER p.97

Bed. Ted Joans. AFR p.80
Bed if you could speak. Ted Joans. AFR p.80
Bed Time. Langston Hughes. SIH p.5
Bedbug. Anonymous. GoS p.15; MBP p.41
Bedtime's come fu' little boys. Paul Laurence Dunbar. CPPLD p.230; GoS
    p.191
Bee that was searching for sweets one day, A. Paul Laurence Dunbar. CPPLD
    p.29; LOLL p.39
Beehive. Jean Toomer. IADB p.79; PoN p.69; TYBP p.211
Been workin' on de levee. Langston Hughes. SIH p.46
Beer is bitter but better than vapour. Percy Johnston. BTB p.133
Beetles, noisy bumbles. Tom Dent. ITBLA p.274; NNPUSA p.80
Before a Monument. Alexander Young. EbR p.161
Before a monument to one unknown and martyred Negro soldier once I stood.
    Alexander Young. EbR p.161
Before a Painting. James Weldon Johnson. FYOP p.27
Before i could sit down to eat my lunch i knew we both knew. Bernie Casey.
    LATP p.39
Before I Could Explain. Gordon Parks. InL (unpaged)
Before I kill one man more I will say no. Craig Williamson. AfW p.51
Before I sink to sleep below. **William S. Braithwaite.** SPWSB p.53
Before Lovin. John Raven. BFM p.18
Before the bells of yankee capital. Melvin Tolson. LRL p.19
Before the Feast of Shushan. Anne Spencer. BANP p.213; CNAW p.269
Before the wind, in wisps of smoke, the curdled sand is swept to sea.
    William C. Braithwaite. VER p.84
Beggar Boy. Langston Hughes. WeB p.85
Beggars' Will. J. Henderson Brooks. BTh p.64
Beginning of A Long Poem on Why I Burned the City. Lawrence Benford. CNAW
    p.762; NBP p.26; TYBP p.257
Behind the Arras. Paul Laurence Dunbar. CPPLD p.150
Behind the Gun. Clarence Major. SAM p.18
Behold a prophet will bring plans of liberation in the world again. Ahmed
    Akinwold Alhamisi. GuW p.11
Behold nothing surpasses books. Anonymous. MBP p.i
Behold! the living thrilling lines. Georgia Douglas Johnson. HWOP p.46
Beige sailors with large noses. Langston Hughes. OWT p.45
Bein' Back Home. Paul Laurence Dunbar. CPPLD p.427
Being Different. Clarence Major. BlSp p.132
Being exit in the World.** Calvin C. Hernton. BTB p.118
Being walkers with the dawn and morning. Langston Hughes. DYTB p.26
Being you, you cut your poetry from wood. Gwendolyn Brooks. BTB p.51
Beings. Clarence Major. SAM p.21
Belated Oriole, A. George Marion McClellan. AVAN p.97
Belated wanderer of the ways of spring. Paul Laurence Dunbar. CPPLD p.288
Belfry of Isone, The. William C. Braithwaite. VER p.34
Belief Brings Relief. Ted Joans. AFR p.50
Believe me chaste as is spring water. William C. Braithwaite. SPWSB p.29
Believe You Me! Ted Joans. BPW p.115
Belle - De - Nuit. Ignance Nau. PoN p.355

Bells of Notre Dame, The. Benjamin Brawley. AVAN p.158
Beloved, there have been starless time when I have longed to join the alien
    hosts of death. Robert Hayden. HSITD p.31
Belsen,Day of Liberation (For Rosey). Robert Hayden. BTB p.112; SPRH p.18
Bend willow, willow bend down deep. Herbert Clark Johnson. PoN p.161;
    PoNe p.285
Beneath the bare-boughed Cambridge elms to-day. William C. Braithwaite.
    HFL p.82
Benedicite. William C. Braithwaite. VER p.113
Benediction. Bob Kaufman. PoNe p.412
Benediction. Donald Jeffrey Hayes. AmNP p.91; PoN p.140; PoNe p.248
Benediction. Georgia Douglas Johnson. GoS p.187
Benjamin Banneker (Astronomist, Surveyor, Inventor, 1731-1806, Maryland).
    Eloise Culver. GANIV p.13
Berck-Plage. William C. Braithwaite. VER p.83
Berkeley's Blue Black. Edward S. Spriggs. FoM p.74
Bernice said she wanted a diamond or two. Langston Hughes. SIH p.87
Beside the road in youth I sat in slumber. James E. McGirt. FYSS p.53
Beside the ungathered rice he lay.** Henry Wadsworth Longfellow. PoN p.234;
    PoNe p.459
Beside the waters of the bay the hurrying crows keep holiday. William C.
    Braithwaite. VER p.72
Bessie. Alvin Aubert. ATB p.7
Bessie. Sterling A. Brown. SoR p.41
Bessie Smith's Funeral. Alvin Aubert. ATB p.8
Best blues singer I know is doin' life. John Raven. BFM p.17
Best laughter of all. Waring Cuney. LUP p.13
Best of It, The. Raymond Garfield Dandridge. PeP p.15
Beta. Melvin Tolson. HaG p.19
Better the heart should yield and fall, have done. Robert Hayden. HSITD
    p.33
Between lines (in a little book P.P.). Raymond Garfield Dandridge. PAOP
    p.40
Between the World and Me. Richard Wright. AmNP p.103; IADB p.70; PoN p.156
Beverly Hills, Chicago (and the people live till they have white hair.)
    Gwendolyn Brooks. AnA p.48
beware: do not read this Poem. Ishmael Ree. SoS p.64
bewildered souls i've looked upon, condemned. Stephen Kwartler. SoS p.4
Beyond earth's vanity that vanisheth. William C. Braithwaite. VER p.127
Beyond the Shadows. William L. Morrison. DaR p.33
Beyond the turning sea's far foam. Russell Atkins. AmNP p.169
Beyond the Years.** Paul Laurence Dunbar. CPPLD p.63; LOLL p.90
Biafra Blues. Michael S. Harper. DJDC p.87
Bible Belt. Langston Hughes. PATL p.38
Bien loin de tes parens, sur la rive ètrangère. Armand Lanusse. EBAP p.157;
    translated EBAP p.158
Big. Ted Joans. AFR p.82
Big Bell in Zion, The. Theodore Henry Shackelford. BANP p.209
Big Ben, I'm gonna bust you bang up side the wall. Langston Hughes. SIH p.6
Big Black Three, The.* Ted Joans. BPW p.125
Big Daddy Lipscomb who used to help them up.* Randall Jarrell. PoNe p.567

TITLE AND FIRST LINE INDEX

Black America! in Fame's Hall go place this group. Raymond Garfield
    Dandridge. PeP p.45; ZaP p.34
Black and Tan. J. Farley Ragland. EbR p.124
Black and White. Tony Rutherford. BrT p.174
Black Angel, The. Michael S. Harper. DJDC p.29
Black Angel Child. Sterling D. Plumpp. TGWL p.81
Black Art. LeRoi Jones. BLIA p.396; BMP p.116
Black Bourgeoisie. LeRoi Jones. BMP p.111
Black boy, let me get up from the white man's table of fifty sounds. Melvin
    Tolson. HaG p.136; CNAW p.364
Black Brother, think you life so sweet you would like at any price? Raymond
    Garfield Dandridge. ANP p.91; PAOP p.16; ZaP p.23
Black, brown, yellow, red and white mix them together. Ritten Edward Lee.
    EbR p.99
Black Cameo on Pink Quartz. John W. Burton. EbR p.18
blk/chart (to be sed everyday, slowly). Sonia Sanchez. WABP p.33
Black Children. Carole Gregory Clemmons. TGWL p.20
Black Christ, The. Countee Cullen. BlC p.69; OTIS p.104
Black Christ, The. Don L. Lee. DSNP p.60
Black Church on Sunday. Joseph M. Mosley, Jr. NBP p.91
Black Consciousness. Bruce Walton. TGWL p.96
Black Cowboys. Arthur Boze. BlWo p.17
Black Cowerie, The. Ted Joans. AFR p.49
Black Crispus Attucks taught us how to die. Melvin Tolson. AmNP p.37; BLIA
    p.239; PoN p.72; PoNe p.136; RWA p.37
Black Dada Nihilismus. LeRoi Jones. CNAW p.648
Black Faces. Anita Scott Coleman. EbR p.51
Black faces lifted to the Heavens ... searching. Thelma Parker Cox. TNV
    p.28
Black February Blood Letting. Ted Joans. BPW p.65
Black Finger, The. Angelina Weld Grimké. AmNP p.17; PoN p.49
Black Fire. Craig Williamson. AfW p.48
Black First, A. Ted Joans. AFR p.13
Black Gabriel, Riding. Robert Hayden. HSITD p.23
Black Gal. Langston Hughes. FCTJ p.66
Black Gauntlet. William Cousins. EbR p.53
Black Girl Black Girl. Dudley Randall. BOL p.5; LoY p.9; NBP p.103
Black Girl Goes By, A. Emile Roumer. TYBP p.90
Black girl with a pink hula hoop. Albert Aubert. ATB p.26
Black Haiku. Frenchy J. Hodges. BlW p.22
Black is. Kali Grosvenor. BlSp p.104
Black Is Beautiful. Townsend T. Brewster. TNV p.25
Black Is Best.* Larry Thompson. BOL p.2
Black is Black. Kali Grosvenor. PBK p.15
Black is not all inclusive. Don L. Lee. BlSp p.117; BrT p.105; DCS p.61;
    DSNP p.127; SoS p.92
Black is something to laugh about. Kali Grosvenor. BlSp p.104
Black Is Soul. Joseph White. IADB p.94
Black is what the prisons are. Bruce McM. Wright. AmNP p.144; LUP p.60;
    PoN p.201; PoNe p.347

Black jam for dr. negro. Mari Evans. IABW p.77
Black Judgments. Nikki Giovanni. BrT p.60; BFBTBJ p.98; TNV p.33
Black Lady's Inspiration. Alfred Diggs. TGWL p.31
Black Light. Ted Joans. BPW p.83
Black Lotus / a Prayer. Alicia Ley Johnson. NBP p.74
Black Madonna, The. Albert Rice. CaD p.177; ChG p.99
Black Magdalens. Countee Cullen. BANP p.230; BLIA p.158; CCC p.9; OTIS p.6
Black Magic. Dudley Randall. LoY p.9
Black Magic. Sonia Sanchez. BrT p.137
Black Magician, The. Ariel Williams Holloway. BTh p.31
Black Majesty (after reading John W. Vandercook's Chronicle of Sable Glory).
    Countee Cullen. BlC p.64; OTIS p.101
Black Mammies. John Wesley Holloway. BANP p.138
Black Mammy, The. James Weldon Johnson. BLIA p.135; FYOP p.12
Black man: I'm a black man. Michael S. Harper. DJDC p.3
Black Man is Making New Gods, The. LeRoi Jones. BMP p.205
Black man is not worried yet, The. LeRoi Jones. BMP p.181
Black man talks of reaping, A. Arna Bontemps. AmNP p.75; ANP p.127; BANP
    p.262; CaD p.165; CNAW p.332; IADB p.76; ITBLA p.161; KAL p.83; PoN p.110;
    PoNe p.209
Black Mane. Ted Joans. AFR p.37
Black Man's Feast. Sarah Webster Fabio. PoNe p.393
Black Man's Son, The. Oswald Durand. PoN p.352; TYBP p.91
Black Maria. Langston Hughes. SIH p.121
Black Memorial Day. Frenchy Hodges. BlW p.25
Black militant man in structured white power. Clarence Major. FoM p.26
Black Mother Praying. Owen Dodson. PLL p.8
Black Muslim Boy in a Hospital. James A. Emanuel. PoNe p.375
Black Narcissus. Gerald William Barrax. KAL p.203
Black 99th, The. Arthur Boze. BlWo p.18
Black Ode. Maya Angelou. JGM p.37
Black Panther. Langston Hughes. PTAL p.19
Black Pascal. Craig Williamson. AfW p.12
blk / people are we CIA agents. Sonia Sanchez. WABP p.19
Black People. Doughtry Long, Jr. TNV p.66
Black people! LeRoi Jones. BLIA p.397; BMP p.225
Black people. Ted Joans. BPWL p.75
Black People Think. Don L. Lee. BOL p.2; BrT p.85; DSNP p.46
Black people: this is our destiny. LeRoi Jones. BMP p.199
Black Pierrot, A. Langston Hughes. WeB p.61
Black Poetry Day, A. Alicia Ley Johnson. BOL p.13
Black poets should live - not leap. Etheridge Knight. BrT p.161
Black Power. Nikki Giovanni. BFBTBJ p.37; BrT p.53
Black Prince, The. Alice Walker. ONC p.69
Black reapers with the sound of steel on stones. Jean Toomer. CaD p.94;
    FNP p.13; KAL p.52; SoS p.63
Black Recruit. Georgia Douglas Jonson. EbR p.94
Black Repeater. Ted Joans. AFR p.63
Black revolution is passing you bye. Nikki Giovanni. BFBTBJ p.24; BrT p.50

Body, rupa, Body, rupa, Body, rupa, Body, rupa, matter a body flies. LeRoi
    Jones. BMP p.136
Bohemian, The. Paul Laurence Dunbar. CPPLD p.147
Bold champion of a noble race. Benjamin Clark. EBAP p.177
Bold Nat Turner by the blood of God rose up preaching on Virginia's sod.
    Margaret Walker. PFND p.10
Boll-weevil's coming, and the winter's cold. Jean Toomer. CaD p.99; FNP
    p.13; SoS p.121
Bombardment and Aftermath. John Henrik Clarke. EbR p.44
Bombings in Dixie. Langston Hughes. PATL p.48
Bombs they dropped on you were wrapped in an American dream.
    BlSp p.200
"Bon soir, monsieur," they called to me. Countee Cullen. BlC p.56
Bone a prominent reflecting thing, The. Clarence Major. SAM p.51
Bones a-gittin' achy. Paul Laurence Dunbar. ChG p.58; CPPLD p.246
Boogah Man, The. Paul Laurence Dunbar. CPPLD p.298; WMS p.65
Boogie-Woogie Ballads.* St. Clair McKelway. PoN p.300; PoNe p.534
Book of Love, The. William C. Braithwaite. NFL p.98
Booker T. and W.E.B. Dudley Randall. BrT p.127; BTB p.165; CNAW p.774;
    KAL p.131; MBP p.84
Booker T. Washington. John Wesley Fentress. EbR p.62
Booker T. Washington. Paul Laurence Dunbar. CPPLD p.341
Booker T. Washington. Raymond Garfield Dandridge. PeP p.13; ZaP p.22
Booker T. Washington. Waverly T. Carmichael. FHOF p.24
Booker T. Washington, pioneer in Industrial Education, 1865-1915. Virginia.
    Eloise Culver. GANIV p.43
Book's Creed, The. Joseph S. Cotter, Sr. CPJSC p.77
Book's Message, The. Joseph S. Cotter, Sr. CPJSC p.59
Boooo! I'm a spook toooo! John Raven. BFM p.21
Borcovicus. William C. Braithwaite. VER p.17
Border Ballad, A. Paul Laurence Dunbar. CPPLD p.73; LOLL p.108
Border Line. Langston Hugnes. FOW p.13; ITBLA p.160
Born down in Georgia, die in Tennessee. Frenchy J. Hodges. BlW p.17
Born like the Pines.** James E. McGirt. FYSS p.1
Born of the sorrowful heart. Countee Cullen. CaD p.186; CCC p.70; FNP p.20;
    GoS p.169; KAL p.102; OTIS p.37
Born to be Burned. Victor Hernandez Cruz. SNA p.85
Borne. Daniel Walter Owens. TNV p.82
Borne across rivers of grey, life forces. Daniel Walter Owens. TNV p.82
Boston Roller Coaster, The. Victor Hernandez Cruz. SNA p.95
Boston Tea. David Wadsworth Cannon, Jr. EbR p.24
Bottled: New York. Helene Johnson. CaD p.221; GoS p.126
"Bottoms," The. Nick Aaron Ford. SFD p.25
Bound No'th Blues. Langston Hughes. AmNP p.65; CNAW p.308; FCTJ p.87
Bouquets of painted tin. Robert Hayden. BOR p.51
'Bout Cullud Folkses. Lucy Mae Turner. BCF p.7
'Bout de Moon. Lucile D. Goodlett. WGC p.23
Bow down my soul in worship very low. Claude McKay. AmNP p.29; CaD p.87;
    KAL p.49; PoN p.334; SPCM p.84
Boy Breaking Glass. Gwendolyn Brooks. ITM p.36

Boy should have an open fireplace. Herbert Clark Johnson. PoN p.161; PoNe
     p.283
Boyhood Etchings. Walter Adolphe Roberts. PoN p.311
Boy's Need, A. Herbert Clark Johnson. PoN p.161; PoNe p.283
Boy's Summer Song, A. Paul Laurence Dunbar. CPPLD p.381
Braggard, The. Raymond Garfield Dandridge. PeP p.34
Braggart, The. Melvin Tolson. RWA p.68
Brain Washing Dramatized. Don Johnson. PoNe p.436
Brass Spittoon. Langston Hughes. AmNP p.61; BANP p.234; FCTJ p.28; BLIA
     p.197
Bread. Ted Joans. BPW p.33
Bread and Wine. Countee Cullen. CCC p.83
Bread, cast on the water, will return ... Nell Chapman. EbR p.29
Bread On The Water. Nell Chapman. EbR p.29
"Break me my bounds, and let me fly." Paul Laurence Dunbar. CPPLD p.471
Break me no bread however white it be. Countee Cullen. CoS p.64; OTIS p.66
Breakfast Time. Charles B. Johnson. SOMP p.41
Breaking dead leaves 'neath my feet, The. Georgia Douglas Johnson. HWOP p.6
Breaking The Charm. Paul Laurence Dunbar. CPPLD p.240
Breakthrough. John Sinclair. NBP p.122
Breast under breast when you shall lie. Countee Cullen. B1C p.50; OTIS p.96
Breath of life imbued those few dim days, The. Jessie Fauset. CaD p.70
Breath of ripe September after rain, The. William C. Braithwaite. VER p.106
breathing the breath clearance. Clarence Major. SoS p.96
Breaths. Birago Diop. TYBP p.139
Breeze a-sighin' and blowin. James Weldon Johnson. FYOP p.64
Breeze flew in at the window, A. Joseph S. Cotter, Sr. SPPH p.44
Breeze sets my face all a-tingle, The. William C. Braithwaite. VER p.63
Breezes blowin' middlin' brisk. Paul Laurence Dunbar. ChG p.60; CPPLD p.125;
     LOLL p.186
Brer Rabbit, you's de cutes' of 'em all. James Weldon Johnson. FYOP p.81
Br'er Rabbit's Christmas Trick. Charles B. Johnson. SOMP p.49
Bress mah life! why, dis hain't Trussey & James D. Corrothers. EBAP p.247
Bridal Measure, A. Paul Laurence Dunbar. CPPLD p.154
Bridge Party or Gaps in Teeth ain't New. Marion Nichols. LiS p.21
Brief Encounter. Langston Hughes. SIH p.42
Brief Procession, The. Albert Aubert. ATB p.8
Bright Bindings. Countee Cullen. B1C p.49; OTIS p.96
Bright sun flower yellow tiger was at my bedroom door, A. Nikki Giovanni.
     MyH p.56
Brightly now the sun is shining on this Easter Sabbath morn. Charles Fred
     White. PONS p.35
Brightness Moved us Softly, The. Dudley Randall. LoY p.12
Bring down the elements into your snare. Oliver LaGrone. BTB p.139
Bring me all of your dreams. Langston Hughes. DYTB p.39; WeB p.94
Bring me the livery of no other man. Paul Laurence Dunbar. CPPLD p.14
Bring me those needles, Marthe. Owen Dodson. KAL p.123
British said to Azikiwe, we're tired of you running round loose. Langston
     Hughes. LUP p.29

Bruddah Mocking Bird. James D. Corrothers. EABP p.246
Bruised and Battered. Frank Marshall Davis. GoS p.137
Brushes and paints are all I have. Gwendolyn B. Bennett. CaD p.155
Brute Will. Joseph S. Cotter, Sr. SPPH p.68
Bubbling Wine. Abu Zakariya. TYBP p.46
Buck Dancer's Choice. James Dickey. PoNe p.579
Buckle. Ted Joans. BPW p.101
Bud, The. W. Blanche Nivens. BTh p.60
Bud bursting from a tomb. Countee Cullen. B1C p.20
"Build me a house" said the master. Frances Harper. PBFH p.25
"Build me a nation," said the Lord. Frances Harper. PBFH p.75
Building, The. Frances Harper. PBFH p.25
Bumi. LeRoi Jones. BMP p.196
Bumble-bee, too full with sweets falls from the flower and futile beats.
    Charles B. Johnson. SOMP p.40
Burden. Langston Hughes. FOW p.16
Burdens of All, The. Frances Harper. PBFH p.90
Burial of a Young Love. Waring Cuney. BANP p.285; OTIS p.48; PoN p.146
Burial of Sarah. Frances Harper. PBFH p.61
Burial of the Past, The. Charles F. White. PONS p.120
Burial. Paulin Joachim. TYBP p.146
Burly Facing One, The.* Robert Hayden. BOR p.16; SPRH p.45
Burning General, The. LeRoi Jones. BMP p.27
Burnished glow of the old-gold moon, The. Joseph S. Cotter, Jr. BOG p.20
Bury me in a free land. Frances Harper. ANP p.17; AVAN p.42; CNAW p.103;
    EBAP p.36
bus driver say move back! Mari Evans. IABW p.24
Bus Window. June Jordan. SCh p.63
Bus window show himself a wholesale florist. June Jordan. SCh p.63
But can see better there, and laughing there. Gwendolyn Brooks. AnA p.14;
    KAL p.157; PoNe p.336
But ever stand through the ages of humanity's ebb and flow. Nannie M.
    Travis. EbR p.143
But He Was Cool. Don L. Lee. B1S p.114; BrT p.92; DCS p.21; DSNP p.91
But I had called the office. Nikki Giovanni. BFBTBJ p.14
But in the crowding darkness not a word did they say. Gwendolyn Brooks.
    AmNP p.140; PoN p.190
But in the saying let not despair. Pinkie Gordon Lane. TGWL p.66
But now old dew hints best to wait. Eli Shepperd. P1S p.74
But the whole thing is a miracle--see?   Nikki Giovanni. BrT p.53;
    BFBTBJ p.37
But when daylight begins to creep across the earth that's half asleep. Eli
    Shepperd. P1S p.20
Butterflies: 1965. Gerald W. Barrax. AKOR p.38
Butterfly in Church. George Marion McClellan. ANP p.92; BANP p.97
Butterfly, The. Nikki Giovanni. MyH p.18
Buy and Buy. Ted Joans. AFR p.46
Buy it. Ted Joans. BPW p.66
Buzzard, The. Joseph S. Cotter, Sr. CPJSC p.40
Buzzard's sailing in the early morning, The. Joseph S. Cotter, Sr. CPJSC
    p.40

TITLE AND FIRST LINE INDEX

Chasm that spans the peerless void between life and after death is but a
    silken strand. William L. Morrison. DaR p.48
Chaucer. Benjamin Brawley. AVAN p.158; BANP p.151
Check Up Blues. Ted Joans. AFR p.123
Checkers. Sterling A. Brown. SoR p.75
Cheery Good-Day, A. William L. Morrison. DaR p.36
Chestnut colt appreciates the green, The. Michael S. Harper. DJDC p.8
Chi. Melvin Tolson. HaG p.130
Chic Freedom's Reflection. Alice Walker. ONC p.37
Chicago Defender Sends a Man to Little Rock, Fall 1957. Gwendolyn Brooks.
    AmNP p.142; BTB p.52; CNAW p.521
Chicago, Illinois. Joseph S. Cotter, Sr. CPJSC p.15; WSBO p.26
Chicago mistress of the lakes. Charles Fred White. PONS p.146
Chicago Picasso, The. Gwendolyn Brooks. ITM p.40
Chicago sharks ... hung along the lake. Delores Kendrick. TGWL p.60
Chicken, she chided early should not wait. Gwendolyn Brooks. AnA p.7
Chickitten Gitten. Ted Joans. AFR p.116
Child, The. Erskine Hayes. BTh p.29
Child, The. Joseph S. Cotter, Sr. CPJSC p.12; WSBO p.25
Child Elsie. William C. Braithwaite. LLL p.50
Child is like the sculptor's clay be he dark or fair. Erskine Hayes. BTh
    p.29
Childhood. Margaret Walker. BOL p.73; FMP p.53; KAL p.145
Childhood games, played without innocence. Michael S. Harper. DJDC p.29
Childhood rememberances are always a drag if you're Black. Nikki Giovanni.
    BFBTBJ p.58; NBP p.53; SoS p.22
Children of the Mississippi. Sterling A. Brown. BLIA p.220; SoR p.67
Children of the Poor. Gwendolyn Brooks. AnA p.35
Children of the Sun. Fenton Johnson. ANP p.39; BANP p.141
Children Today - Tomorrow - Men! Georgia Douglas Johnson. GoS p.51
Children's Children. Sterling A. Brown. SoR p.107
Children's Rhymes. Langston Hughes. BOL p.43; PATL p.49
Child's Nightmare, A. Bobb Hamilton. BrT p.168
Chill, the rain falls, chill. Charles B. Johnson. AVAN p.189; SOMP p.12
Chilled into a serenity. Blanche Taylor Dickinson. CaD p.110
Chillen Get Shoes. Sterling A. Brown. SoR p.110
Chillun uv de Dus', dat's a wide road leadin' down to de city. Lucile D.
    Goodlett. WGC p.37
Chilly Willie. John Raven. BFM p.28
Chippy. Langston Hughes. FOW p.67
Chittlins and pig feet, hog head and sow's meat. Bernie Casey. LATP p.83
Choice, A. Joseph S. Cotter, Sr. SPPH p.71
Choice, A. Paul Laurence Dunbar. AVAN p.87; CPPLD p.201
Choicy. Lawrency Carlyle Tatum. HeD p.40
Chops are flyin. Stanley Crouch. NBP p.42
Choucoune. Oswald Durand. PoN p.350
Chrismus Is A-Comin'. Paul Laurence Dunbar. ChG p.58; CPPLD p.246
Chrismus On The Plantation. Paul Laurence Dunbar. CNAW p.312; CPPLD p.219
Christ In Alabama. Langston Hughes. PATL p.37
Christ is a nigger, beaten and Black: oh bare your back! Langston Hughes.
    PATL p.37

City of tense and stricken faces. Margaret Walker. PFND p.12; BrT p.151
City rises in color, The. LeRoi Jones. BTB p.136
City: San Francisco. Langston Hughes. GoS p.133
City used to be a thing apart. Joseph S. Cotter, Sr. SPPH p.71
City's Love. Claude McKay. BLIA p.166; HaS p.16; SPCM p.66
Civil Rights Poem. LeRoi Jones. BMP p.140
Civil Service. Constance Nichols. EbR p.109
Civil war was over, The. Eloise Culver. GANIV p.42
Clairvoyance. Norman Jordan. BlSp p.96
Clark's Way West: Another Version. Michael S. Harper. DJDC p.36
Classified Ad. Tomi Carolyn Tinsley. EbR p.142
Clean de ba'n an' sweep de flo'. James Edwin Campbell. BANP p.67
Clean the spittoons, boy. Langston Hughes. AmNP p.61; BANP p.234; BLIA
    p.197; FCTJ p.28
Clever mother mother divine cleverness. Alicia L. Johnson. TGWL p.55
Click Chick, The. Ted Joans. AFR p.29
Cliffs of Etretat, the white cliffs, the white cliffs. William C. Braith-
    waite. VER p.78
Cliffy crack me mornin' with a whistle. Larry O. Stone. BTB p.171
Clift is revealed; and below its cragged ledge I see waters sweet and a
    maiden on its ledge. William L. Morrison. DaR p.21
Climax of passion, the dancers are trembling. Jose Zacarias Tallet. TYBP
    p.102
Climb high, black boy, climb high. Samuel A. Haynes. EbR p.82
Clock on Hancock Street. June Jordan. SCh p.70
Clogged and soft and sloppy eyes. Gwendolyn Brooks. AnA p.6
Close Mouf. Raymond Garfield Dandridge. PeP p.18; ZaP p.66
Close of Day. Wesley Curtwright. CaD p.225
Close your eyes! Arna Bontemps. AmNP p.76; CaD p.171; KAL p.79; PoN p.116;
    PoNe p.218
Closed window looks down on a dirty court yard, A. LeRoi Jones. BMP p.146
Closed windows on all the six floors. Victor Hernandez Cruz. SNA p.7
Closing Time. Langston Hughes. FCTJ p.32
Clothed with a mantle of the night. Zachary Withers. PAS p.43
Cloud fell down from the heavens, A. Paul Laurence Dunbar. CPPLD p.477
Cloud looked in at the window, The. Paul Laurence Dunbar. CPPLD p.115;
    LOLL p.171
Clouds are shedding tears of joy. Raymond Garfield Dandridge. PAOP p.54
Clouds are swirling, clouds are straying. Alexander Pushkin. MBP p.63
Clouds hit the delicately balanced mountains. LeRoi Jones. BMP p.71
Clouds of slavery cast their gloom, The. Zachary Withers. PAS p.10
Clouds that linger just kind a stay, The. William L. Morrison. DaR p.59
Clouds weave a shawl, The. Langston Hughes. GoS p.175
Club baron got niggas goin juga jug. Clarence Reed. BlSp p.171
Clubwoman. Mary Carter Smith. PoNe p.388
C'mon godamya c'mon gimme that pussy! Ted Joans. AFR p.116
Coal. Audre Lorde. BTB p.141; SoS p.95
Coast-Guard Path.** William C. Braithwaite. VER p.85
Cocaine Galore 1. Victor Hernandez Cruz. SNA p.21
Codicil. Albert Aubert. ATB p.19

Cover him over with daisies white. Paul Laurence Dunbar. CPPLD p.426
Crab Man. Anonymous. ITBLA p.125
Cracker is not to be played with, The. Sonia Sanchez. WABP p.50
Cracker Man. Charles L. Anderson. BTB p.41
Craftsman, The. Marcus B. Christian. EbR p.35; PoN p.83; PoNe p.156
Craftsman of Ex-scham. Melvin B. Tolson. LUP p.48; RWA p.88
Crag and misty summit ye are ours to win. William C. Braithwaite. VER p.43
Crap Game. Langston Hughes. FCTJ p.34
Craving of Samuel Rouse for clearance to create, The. Margaret Danner.
     AmNP p.157
Crawl Into Bed.** Quandra Prettyman. BOL p.74
Crazy Woman, The. Gwendolyn Brooks. MBP p.28
Creation. Carter Webster. EbR p.153
Creation, The. James Weldon Johnson. ANP p.42; BANP p.117; CaD p.19; GoS
     p.55; ITBLA p.120; SoS p.60
Creation fires my tongue! George Moses Horton. AVAN p.35
Creation of Man, The. Anonymous. MBP p.7
Creature slender as a reed, A. Countee Cullen. CCC p.51
Creatures of gauze and velvet wings. George Marion McClellan. AVAN p.95
Creditor to His Proud Debtor, The. George Moses Horton. CNAW p.35
Credo.* Walter Everette Hawkins. ANP p.67
Creed. Anne Spencer. CaD p.51
Creed. Walter Lowenfels. PoNe p.516
Creole Girl. Leslie M. Collins. PoN p.172; PoNe p.297
Crescendo. Dorothy F. Blackwell. EbR p.6
Cricket and the Star, The. Effie Lee Newsome. GoS p.75
Criminals Investigating Americans (C.I.A.) Faggots Bullying Indirectly
     (F.B.I.). Ted Joans. BPW p.89
Crimson Rose, A. Thelma T. Clement. BTh p.54
Crimson Rose at twilight sighed, A. Thelma T. Clement. BTh p.54
Crisis, The. Paul Laurence Dunbar. AVAN p.55; CPPLD p.179
Crisis in the Midlands: St. Louis, Missouri. Michael S. Harper. DJDC p.21
Crispus Attucks. George Hannibal Temple. AVAN p.104
Crispus Attucks, Revolutionary War Hero about 1723-1770 Massachusetts.
     GANIV p.11
Critics cry unfair, The. Conrad Kent Rivers. BOL p.20; SVH p.22
Crocuses, The. Frances Harper. PHFH p.4
Cross. Langston Hughes. AmNP p.62; BANP p.236; CNAW p.304; FNP p.26; IADB
     p.6; PoN p.103; WeB p.52
Cross legged on his bed. James A. Emanuel. PoNe p.377
Crossing. Langston Hughes. SIH p.69
Crossing A Creek. Herbert Clark Johnson. PoN p.161; PoNe p.284
Crouched in its towering green the Indian hid. Dudley Randall. BTB p.167
Crow Jane in High Society. LeRoi Jones. CNAW p.647
Crowd was very still but tense, The. Eloise Culver. GANIV p.73
Crowns and Garlands. Langston Hughes. PATL p.6
Crucifixion. Carter Webster. EbR p.154
Crucifixion. Waring Cuney. BANP p.285; GoS p.60
Crucifixion, The. James Weldon Johnson. GoT p.39
Cruisin. John Raven. BFM p.30

Crust of bread and a corner to sleep in, A. Paul Laurence Dunbar. AmNP p.6;
    ANP p.26; AVAN p.89; CaD p.5; CPPLD p.9; LOLL p.11
... Crystalline snow falling. Jack H. Dawley. LUP p.18
Cuba, disheveled, naked to the waist. Walter Adolphe Roberts. PoN p.316;
    TYBP p.116
Cuddle down, Ma Honey in yo' bed. James Weldon Johnson. FYOP p.83
Cultural Awareness. Nikki Giovanni. BFBTBJ p.87
Cultural Exchange. Langston Hughes. PATL p.81; PoNe p.203
Cum listen w'ile yore Unkel sings. Raymond Garfield Dandridge. BANP p.191;
    FAOP p.25; ZaP p.20
Cuntinent. Ted Joans. AFR p.72
Cup of Knowledge, The. Charles B. Johnson. SOMP p.28
Cure All, The. Don L. Lee. BrT p.85; DSNP p.52
Curious twists and bent turns of pain, The. Ernie Nikalimoto. NBP p.90
Curiosity. Paul Laurence Dunbar. CPPLD p.394; LiG p.27
Curiosity am a painful disease. Lucy Mae Turner. BCF p.49
Curiosity. Lucy Mae Turner. BCF p.49
Curious. Langston Hughes. OWT p.97
Curtain. Paul Laurence Dunbar. CPPLD p.65; LOLL p.93
Curtains of twilight are drawn in the west, The. Georgia D. Johnson. HWOP
    p.41
Custer's Last Ride. Albert A. Whitman. EBAP p.220; ITBLA p.94
Customs & Culture. Ted Joans. BPW p.99
Cut out the insides. LeRoi Jones. BMP p.23
Cuz it says nigger. Sonia Sanchez. WABP p.57
Cycle, The. Calvin H. Raullerson. LUP p.41
Cycle. Langston Hughes. GoS p.180
Cymbals clash. William Browne. AmNP p.173; BTB p.65
Cynic. Tomi Carolyn Tinsley. EbR p.141

- D -

Dada Zodji. LeRoi Jones. BMP p.61
Daddy drinks lots of beer. Charles Cooper. BOL p.8
Daddy knows a whole lot o' tales. Charles B. Johnson. SOMP p.49
Daddy-O Buddy-O works at the foundry. Langston Hughes. OWT p.125
Dago Red. Askia Muhammad Toure. BlSp p.223
Daih's a moughty soothin' feelin'. Paul Laurence Dunbar. CPPLD p.302; WMS
    p.139
Daily Grind, The. Fenton Johnson. AmNp p.25
Daily Prayer, A. Waverly T. Carmichael. FHOF p.40
Dali Fantasy. Countess W. Twitty. EbR p.148
Damascus Blade. Melvin B. Tolson. LUP p.48; RWA p.88
Dance. Lula Lowe Weeden. CaD p.229
Dance, The. Paul Laurence Dunbar. CPPLD p.274
Dance Committee, (Concerning Jean-Leon Destine), The. Nikki Giovanni.
    BFBTBJ p.43
Dance Finale. Samuel E. Boyd. EbR p.7
Dance for Ma Rainey, A. Al Young. NBP p.134
Dance of Love, The. Countee Cullen. CCC p.19

Dar's a lazy, sort ah hazy. Ray Garfield Dandridge. BANP p.192; PAOP p.28;
    ZaP p.38
Dar's blood on de clouds and de moon's shickle is sharp. Eli Shepperd.
    PLS p.43
Dar's mighty thing, a-gwine on. Daniel Webster. AVAN p.101
Dar's one flower by de brook. Eli Shepperd. PlS p.28
Dar's War in de worl', O my brothers. Eli Shepperd. PlS p.134
Dat ar tr'flin' trash ain' nothin', with no sence ob decencee. Raymond Gar-
    field Dandridge. PeP p.20; ZaP p.91
Dat Gal O' Mine. James Weldon Johnson. FYOP p.77
Dat Ol' Mare O' Mine. Paul Laurence Dunbar. CLT p.21; CPPLD p.30
Dave Garroway's Mr. J' Fred Muggs often thumps. Owen Dodson. KAL p.126
David Copperhead. LeRoi Jones. BMP p.39
David dug genesis. Amus Mor. BlSp p.134
David Morton Sonnet Analyzed. Joseph S. Cotter, Sr. CPJSC p.21
Dawn. Georgia Douglas Johnson. HWOP p.7
Dawn. Paul Laurence Dunbar. AmNP p.5; CPPLD p.10; GoS p.3; LOLL p.153;
    PoN p.34
Dawn came at six today. Alice Walker. ONC p.49
Dawn Cities. Mae V. Cowdery. WLOV p.7
Dawn in New York. Claude McKay. HaS p.43; SPCM p.65
Dawn in the heart of Africa. Patrice Emery Lumumba. TYBP p.150
Dawn Patrol: Chicago. Richard V. Durham. GoS p.134
Dawn Song. Linwood D. Smith. TNV p.116
Dawn! The dawn! the crimson-tinted comes, The. Claude McKay. HaS p.43;
    SPCM p.65
Dawn of Love, The. Henrietta Cordelia Ray. EBAP p.142
Dawnbreaker. Robert Hayden. SPRH p.16
Dawn's Awake! Otto Leland Bohanan. BANP p.20
Dawn's Carol. Henrietta Cordelia Ray. AVAN p.152; ANP p.129
Day. Paul Laurence Dunbar. CPPLD
Day after day I sit and write, and thus the moments spend. Ann Plato. ANP
    p.11
Day and Night. Lewis Alexander. CaD p.129
Day Break (from path of Dreams, 1916). George Marion McLlelan. EBAP p.126
Day Breaker. Arna Bontemps. AmNP p.76; CaD p.171; GoS p.181; IADB p.66;
    PoN p.119; PoNe p.223
Day brought confusion and night brought despair, The. John Henry Owens.
    EbR p.111
Day goes on with maddening whir, it's kill, and cut and grind and stir, The.
    Eli Shepperd. PlS p.89
Day is a Negro, The. Lewis Alexander. CaD p.129
Day is mild, the spring is here, The. Charles Fred White. PONS p.43
Day of Freedom. Waverly T. Carmichael. FHOF p.17
Day of joy, a week of pain, A. Waverly Carmichael. ANP p.30; ANP p.124;
    FHOF p.10
Day of Repentance, The. Waverly T. Carmichael. FROF p.52
Day of Rest, The. Charles Fred White. PONS p.114
Day of the Dead. Robert Hayden. BOR p.46
Day passeth day in sunshine or shadow. Joseph S. Cotter, Jr. BOG p.9

Day with Bo, A. Victor Hernandez Cruz. SNA p.91
Daybreak. Langston Hughes. SIH p.6
Daybreak in Alabama. Langston Hughes. DYTB p.78; OWT p.83; PATL p.101
Days. Raymond Garfield Dandridge. AVAN p.192; PAOP p.28; ZaP p.39
Days After. Helen Quigless. FoM p.65
Days are short, the air is cold, The. Charles Frew White. PONS p.63
Days git wa'm an' wa'mah. Paul Laurence Dunbar. CPPLD p.390; WMS p.131
Day's Recreation, A. J. C. Stevenson. HeD p.36
Day's Work, The. Joseph S. Cotter, Sr. SPPH p.66
De Angels wings is white as snow. Langston Hughes. FCTJ p.52
De axes has been ringin' in de woods de blessid day. Paul Laurence Dunbar.
   CPPLD p.229
De big bell done rung dat bigges' big one. Eli Shepperd. PlS p.145
De breeze / is blowin' 'cross de bay. Paul Laurence Dunbar. CPPLD p.234;
   LiG p.116
De 'cession's stahted on de gospel way. Paul Laurence Dunbar. CPPLD p.314
De Creed. (Matthew 2:15). Raymond Dandridge. PAOP p.29
De Critter's Dance. Paul Laurence Dunbar. CPPLD p.291
De Cunjah Man. James Edwin Campbell. BANP p.65; EBAP p.234
De da'kest hour, day allus say. Paul Laurence Dunbar. CPPLD p.265
De dog go howlin' 'long de road. Paul Laurence Dunbar. CPPLD p.40
De Drum Majah. Raymond Garfield Dandridge. BANP p.92; PAOP p.58; ZaP p.10
De Gospel train com er scootin' down de rail. Eliot B. Henderson. EBAP
   p.245
De Gustibus. James Worley. FoM p.26
De hardes' ob hard rows we hoes fo' little pay, de goo' Lawd knows. Raymond
   Garfield Dandridge. PAOP p.53; ZaP p.37
De Innah Part. Raymond Garfield Dandridge. PAOP p.41; ZaP p.68
De Lady I work for told her husband she wanted a robe O' Love. Langston
   Hughes. SIH p.30
De Lawd! Mucy Mae Turner. BCP p.62
De Lawd is a spirit, great, glorious, and strong. Lucy Mae Turner. BCP p.62
De Little Pickaninny's Gone to Sleep. James Weldon Johnson. FYOP p.83
De Lord He hardened Pharoah's heart because he would not bow. Eli Shepperd.
   PlS p.135
De mystic's banks I held my dream. Paul Laurence Dunbar. CPPLD p.331
De night creep down erlong de lan'. Paul Laurence Dunbar. CPPLD p.267;
   WMS p.53
De ol' time's gone, de new time's hyeah. Paul Laurence Dunbar. CPPLD p.312
De peopl' call me a conger. James E. McGirt. FYSS p.17
De Preacher Kyo Siam. Lucile D. Goodlett. WGC p.61
De Profundis. Albert Aubert. ATB p.11
De Railroad Bridge's. Langston Hughes. CaD p.147; FCTJ p.24
De Reverend is Gwine to be Big 'Soc'ation.** Lucy Mae Turner. BCF p.56
De river is a-glistenin' in de moon light. James Weldon Johnson. FYOP p.69
De Sight of Unc' Sol. Eli Shepperd. PlS p.10
De Signs O' Spring. Waverly T. Carmichael. FHOF p.8
De Speretual 'Oman. Lucile D. Goodlett. WGC p.55
De sun hit shine an' de win'hit blow. Paul Laurence Dunbar. CPPLD p.421
De Tar Paper Bungalow. Lucy Mae Turner. BCF p.40

De Tes'. Ray Garfield Dandridge. PeP p.44; ZaP p.82

De times is mighty stirrin' 'mong de people up ovah way. Paul Laurence Dunbar. AVAN p.76; CPPLD p.255

De trees is bendin' in de sto'm. Paul Laurence Dunbar. CPPLD p.313

De turkey good, de turkey fat, and ole Brer' Possum fatter. Eli Shepperd. P1S p.90

De Way T'ings Come. Paul Laurence Dunbar. CPPLD p.367

De win' is blowin' wahmah. Paul Laurence Dunbar. CPPLD p.383

De win' is hollahin' "daih you" to de shuttahs an' de fiah. Paul Laurence Dunbar. ChG p.66; CPPLD p.280

De wind whine, 'de fiah blow. Lucile Goodlett. WGC p.56

De wintah black an de wintah bittah. Lucile Goodlett. WGC p.35

De winter days are drawin' nigh. Waverly T. Carmichael. BANP p.163; FHOF p.57

Deacon Jones' Grievance. Paul Laurence Dunbar. CPPLD p.58; LOLL p.83

Dead. Paul Laurence Dunbar. CPPLD p.115; LOLL p.172

Dead-Day: Malcolm, Feb. 21. Michael S. Harper. DJDC p.82

Dead Fires. Jessie Redmond Fauset. ANP p.89; BANP p.207; PoN p.66; PoNe p.68

Dead, he died in Detroit, his beard was filled with lice. Etheridge Knight. BrT p.83

Dead Leaves. Georgia Douglas Johnson. HWOP p.6

Dead men are wisest, for they know, how far the roofs of flowers go. Countee Cullen. CCC p.95; OTIS p.40; PoN p.126; PoNe p.230

Dead 'Oman's Eyes. Lucile Goodlett. WGC p.53

Dead Soldier. Nicolas Guillen. PoN p.376; TYBP p.105

Deadly eyes are stars!, The. LeRoi Jones. BMP p.142

Dear Benedict, to you I bring on this your happy natal day. Nick Aaron Ford. SFD p.30

Dear Cassie: yes I got your letter. Langston Hughes. SIH p.10

Dear critic, who my lightness so deplores. Paul Laurence Dunbar. CPPLD p.30; KAL p.19; MBP p.33

Dear daughter dear son if you are in there growing inch by inch. Ted Joans. AFR p.90

Dear Death: I got your message that my son is dead. Langston Hughes. PATL p.55

Dear Exerter, I fare thee well! Charles Fred White. PONS p.99

Dear Father Brown, the great the good, the noble leader of our race. James McGirt. FYSS p.36

Dear Friend, my teacher for the bygone term, accept this token of my love for thee. Charles Fred White. PONS p.92

Dear Friends and Gentle Hearts. Countee Cullen. OTIS p.163

"Dear God, the earth is bright." William C. Braithwaite. VER p.119

Dear God, when you send your angels out to do their chores tonight, bid one of them to dust well my star of hope. Myrtle Campbell Gorham. EbR p.71

Dear heart, good night! Paul Laurence Dunbar. CPPLD p.36; LOLL p.51

Dear heart, what tho' I press the heedless throng. William C. Braithwaite. LLL p.65

Dear heart, who rules and ever in my breast. William C. Braithwaite. VER p.121

Defiant in the cannon's mouth. Albery Allson Whitman. EBAP p.223
Definition. Marion Nicholes. LiS p.14
Definition. Owen Dodson. PLL p.99
Deft easily above the ship's gleam levels in the far place. Samuel Allen.
    TGWL p.11
Del Cascar. William Stanley Braithwaite. BANP p.103; CaD p.33; CNAW p.225;
    SPWSB p.19
Delay and Truth. Joseph S. Cotter, Sr. SPPH p.71
Delay in anger bit the sphere of truth. Joseph S. Cotter, Sr. SPPH p.71
Delinquent, The. Paul Laurence Dunbar. CPPLD p.102; LOLL p.151
Delphy. See Echoes of Childhood
Delta. Margaret Walker. FMP p.20
Delta. Melvin Tolson. HaG p.26
Deluge. Georgia Douglas Johnson. HWOP p.57
Dely. Paul Laurence Dunbar. CPPLD p.238; LiG p.119
"Dem Phillupeeners." Joseph S. Cotter, Sr. CPJSC p.16; WSBO p.54
Demagogue, The. Joseph S. Cotter, Sr. LOF p.37; SPPH p.78
Demagogue is grave and gay, The. Joseph S. Cotter, Sr. LOF p.37; SPPH p.78
Democratic order such things in twenty years I understand, The. Alice
    Walker. ONC p.43
Democracy. Langston Hughes. OWT p.87
Democracy will not come. Langston Hughes. OWT p.87
Demystify. Ted Joans. BPW p.42
Den come along niggers, play yo' pranks to-day. Eli Shepperd. PlS p.63
Denial. Mae V. Cowdery. WLOV p.53
Departure, The. Robert Hayden. HSITD p.50
Departure, The. Waverly T. Carmichael. FHOF p.47
Departure of Pierrott, The. William S. Braithwaite. LLL p.39
Der ain't no use in sayin' de Lord won't answer prah. James Weldon Johnson.
    AVAN p.178; FYOP p.75
Der Fiddle Is My Comfort. Waverly T. Carmichael. FHOF p.36
Der Rabbitt's Foot. James O. Corrothers. EBAP p.243
Der ain't no 'arthly use I hol' in totin' 'roun er gun. Joseph S. Cotter,
    Sr. CPJSC p.22; WSBO p.53
Dere wouldn't a been no village. Lucy Mae Turner. BCF p.15
Der's no use bein' scared o' cungers. James E. McGirt. FYSS p.28
Des a little cabin. Charles B. Johnson. BANP p.198; SOMP p.29
Des Fo' Day. James E. McGirt. FYSS p.6
Descarga. Victor Hernandez Cruz. SNA p.123
Descarga en cueros. Victor Hernandez Cruz. SNA p.77
Description of a Kentucky School House. Joseph S. Cotter, Sr. RHY p.18
Desert. Langston Hughes. FOW p.27; KAL p.91
Deserted Cabin, The. Lucy Mae Turner. BCF p.32
Deserted Plantation, The. Paul Laurence Dunbar. AVAN p.71; CPPLD p.107;
    LOLL p.158
Deserted Village. Peter Wellington Clark. EbR p.38
Deserter, The. Joseph S. Cotter, Jr. CaD p.102; BOG p.7
Desire. Constance Nichols. EbR p.110
Desire. Gordon Parks. InL (unpaged)
Desire. Langston Hughes. FOW p.55

Desire. Thelma T. Clement. BTh p.23
Desire to us was like a double death. Langston Hughes. FOW p.55
Desolate City. Claude McKay. CaD p.88; SPCM p.52
Desolation. Charles Fred White. PONS p.126
Despair. Georgia Douglas Johnson. HWOP p.41
Despair. Paul Laurence Dunbar. CPPLD p.431
Despite his caricatures of poets and poetasters hide ho's joy was hasidic
    among the lives and works of the masters. Melvin Tolson. HaG p.130
Despite the strange noises from the empty apartment next door. Norman Jor-
    dan. BlSp p.95
Despondency. Charles Fred White. PONS p.49
Destiny. Joseph S. Cotter, Sr. AVAN p.147; SPPH p.44
Destruction of America, The. John Sinclair. FoM p.58
Detached, The. Maya Angelou. JGM p.13
Devastation. Georgia Douglas Johnson. HWOP p.53
Devil and Sis Viney, The. J. Mord Allen. AVAN p.117; EBAP p.250
Devil and the Higher Criticism, The. Joseph S. Cotter, Sr. CPJSC p.37; LOF
    p.21
Devil sat with the Sons of God, The. Joseph S. Cotter, Sr. CPJSC p.37; LOF
    p.21
Dew. J. Mason Brewer. HeD p.4
Dew. William L. Morrison. DaR p.42
Dew-drunken poises beck and call. Raymond Garfield Dandridge. ZaP p.54
Dew is on the grasses, dear, The. Georgia Douglas Johnson. BANP p.182; GoS
    p.77; HWOP p.24; PoN p.57; PoNe p.74
Dey been speakin' at de cou'thouse. Paul Laurence Dunbar. CPPLD p.332
Dey greets you wid a nod an' smile. Raymond Garfield Dandridge. PAOP p.46;
    ZaP p.70
Dey had a great big pahty down to Tom's de othah night. Paul Laurence Dunbar.
    AmNP p.8; CPPLD p.134; LOLL p.199
Dey is snow upon de meddahs, dey is snow upon de hill. Paul Laurence Dunbar.
    CPPLD p.271
Dey is times in life when nature. Paul Laurence Dunbar. BANP p.61; CNAW
    p.210; CPPLD p.89; LiG p.48; LOLL p.132
Dey lynched him, shore dey lynched him. Ernest J. Wilson, Jr. PoNe p.370
Dey sent John Thomas to a one-room school. Sterling A. Brown. SoR p.32
Dey think I is "set" an' fo' gee, an' dey lub to sneer an' laff. Raymond
    Garfield Dandridge. PAOP p.60; ZaP p.52
Dey was hard times jes fo Christmas round our neighborhood one year. James
    David Corrothers. AVAN p.164; BANP p.77; PoN p.22; PoNe p.27
Dey was oncet a auful quoil 'twixt de skillet an' de pot. Paul Laurence
    Dunbar. CPPLD p.445
Dey was talkin' in de cabin, dey was talkin' in de' hall. Paul Laurence
    Dunbar. CLT p.81; CPPLD p.293
Dey's a so't o' threatenin' feelin' in de blowin' of de breeze. Paul Lau-
    rence Dunbar. CPPLD p.275; LiG p.68
Deze eatin' folks may tell me ub de gloriz ub spring lam'. Daniel Webster
    Davis. BANP p.83; AVAN p.100
Dialect Quatrain. Marcus B. Christian. AmNP p.53
Dialogue. Countee Cullen. CCC p.97

Disgrace. Anonymous. MBP p.27
Dishonored eyes in the man I explicitly see walking. Clarence Major. SAM
    p.18
Disillusion. Langston Hughes. WeB p.104
Disillusion. Lillian G. Brown. BTh p.63
Disloyal to my native land? Joseph S. Cotter, Sr. LOF p.50
Dismal Moment, Passing. Clarence Major. SAM p.9
Dispatcher. Albert Aubert. ATB p.27
Dispute Over Suicide, A. Anonymous. TYBP p.26
Distance Between Me and Tomorrow, The. Clarence Major. SAM p.56
Distances. William S. Braithwaite. LLL p.33
Distress separate bodies not people. Keorapetse Kgositsile. BlSp p.108
Distant Drum, The. Calvin C. Hernton. BOL p.19; BTB p.117; NNPUSA p.101;
    SoS p.97; TYBP p.250
Distant grew the summer's green. William L. Morrison. DaR p.23
Distant Hearts, Come Closer, in the Smash of Night. LeRoi Jones. BMP p.223
Distinction. Paul Laurence Dunbar. CPPLD p.183
Disturbed by consciousness god created creation. Gayl Jones. SoS p.15
Disturber, The. Paul Laurence Dunbar. CPPLD p.208
Diu desideravimus. John M. Williams. LUP p.55
Diver, The. Robert Hayden. BTB p.112; CNAW p.385; KAL p.109; SPRH p.1
Dives and Laz'us. Anonymous. TYBP p.197
Divided. William S. Braithwaite. LLL p.15
Djellaba-headed hustlers haunting raggedly headed hippys. Ted Joans. AFR
    p.60
Do. Melvin Tolson. LRL p.42
Do' a-stan'in' on a jar, fiah a-shin' thoo. Paul Laurence Dunbar. CPPLD
    p.317; WSM p.79
Do I love you? Raymond Patterson. BOL p.71
"Do not cheer, men are dying," said Capt. Phillips in the Spanish American
    War.** Frances Harper. PBFH p.88
Do not hold my years against me. Alice Walker. ONC p.61
Do not mistake me and consider that I would tamper with or touch or twist or
    frolic in the wheels of time. Gordon Heath. BTB p.115
Do not sell me out, baby. Langston Hughes. SIH p.49
Do not speak to me of martyrdom. Sonia Sanchez. BrT p.25; FoM p.38
Do not stifle me with the strange scent. Donald Jeffrey Hayes. AmNP p.93
Do Subways Race.** Kali Grosvenor. PBK p.56
Do tell me, where is yesterday? Raymond Garfield Dandridge. AVAN p.192;
    PAOP p.28; ZaP p.39
Do; the first note in the scale from Libretto for the Republic of Liberia.
    LRL p.13; PoNe p.143
Do they miss me? (a parody).** Benjamin Clark. EBAP p.181
Do unto white others as they do. Ted Joans. BPW p.67
Do you also hear the silence between us? David Llorens. TNV p.60
Do you blame me that I loved him? Frances Harper. CNAW p.104; EBAP p.27;
    PBFH p.12
Do you know my home, my home on Lathwaite Green. William C. Braithwaite.
    VER p.48
Do you know what it is to dance? James Weldon Johnson. FYOP p.34

Do you love me?** Gordon Parks. InL (unpaged)
Do you mind the news while we eat? P. M. Sherlock. PoN p.320
"Do you not wish to renounce the devil?" Armand Lanusse. MBP p.30; PoN p.12;
    PoNe p.13; TYBP p.96
Do you remember. Frank Horne. BTB p.94; GoS p.94
Do you remember. Melvin Tolson. KAL p.65
Do you remember how you won that last race? **Frank Horne.** BTB p.121; PoN
    p.82; PoNe p.154
Do you remember, love. William S. Braithwaite. LLL p.45
Do you see this grain of sand. Frances Harper. PBFH p.3
Dr. Booker T. Washington to the Negro Business League. Joseph S. Cotter, Sr.
    CPJSC p.71; WSBO p.39
Dr. Carter G. Woodson Father of Negro History, 1875-1950 Virginia. Eloise
    Culver. GANIV p.55
Dr. Charles R. Drew Father of the Blood Bank, Washington, D.C., 1905-1950.
    Eloise Culver. GANIV p.67
Dr. Daniel Hale Williams, Pioneer in Heart Surgery, 1858-1931, Pennsylvania.
    Eloise Culver. GANIV p.41
Dr. George Washington Carver, Botanist, 1864-1943, Missouri. Eloise Culver.
    GANIV p.45
Dr. Mary M. Bethune, Founder of Bethune-Cookman College, 1875-1955, South
    Carolina. Eloise Culver. GANIV p.52
Dr. Mason. Raymond Garfield Dandridge. PeP p.31
Doctor turned away his head, The. Joseph McMillan. HeD p.32
Dr. W. E. B. DuBois, Dean of Historians, 1868-1963, Massachusetts. Eloise
    Culver. GANIV p.47
Does a jazz-band ever sob? Langston Hughes. WeB p.29
Does man love art? man visits art, but squirms. Gwendolyn Brooks. ITM p.40
Dog Catcher, The. Lucy Mae Turner. BCF p.42
Dog Catcher's a mean old man, The. Lucy Mae Turner. BCF p.42
Dog lover, a lover of dogs in a land where poodles eat, A. Don L. Lee.
    BrT p.109; DSNP p.161; WWW p.37
Dogwood Blossoms. George Marion McClellan. BANP p.96
Doll, don't be too proud of those eyes. Darwin T. Turner. PoNe p.401
Dollar speaks to the young Negro, The. Joseph S. Cotter, Sr. SPPH p.88
Dolly sits a-quilting by her mother, stitch by stitch. Paul Laurence Dunbar.
    CPPLD p.391
Dominicaine, The. H. Binga Dismond. EbR p.58
Don' know my name? Joseph S. Cotter, Sr. SPPH p.75; WSBO p.53
Done are the toils and the wearisome marches. Paul Laurence Dunbar. CPPLD
    p.35; LOLL p.49
Don't be too quick to condemn me. Charles P. Wilson. ANP p.93
Don't Care Negro, The. Joseph S. Cotter, Sr. CPJSC p.16; WSBO p.48
Don't Cry, Scream. Don L. Lee. BrT p.93; DCS p.27; DSNP p.94
Don't go down into the bottoms tonight. Nick Aaron Ford. SFD p.25
Don't know why I. Langston Hughes. BTB p.127; PATL p.64; TYBP p.230
Don't Let the Minute Spoil the Hour. Ted Joans. AFR p.141
Don't let them die out all these old / blk / people. Sonia Sanchez. WASP
    p.67
Don't love me, my sweet. Flavien Ranaivo. TYBP p.154

Dust Bowl. Robert A. Davis. GoS p.151; IADB p.31
Dust in de sunshine an' lint on de air. Lucile D. Goodlett. WGC p.20
Dust, through which proud blood once flowed. Waring Cuney. CaD p.210
Dust unto dust returns. Raymond Garfield Dandridge. ZaP p.57
Dutch Treatment. Ted Joans. AFR p.42
Dutiful, underpaid bearer of burden (although as oxen your past roles were
     cast). Raymond Garfield Dandridge. PAOP p.30; ZaP p.42
Duty. Zachary Withers. PAS p.9
Duty For a Beauty. John Raven. BFM p.25
Dying Bondman, The. Frances Harper. CNAW p.102; ITBLA p.93; PBFH p.117
Dying Water-Moccasin, The. Joseph S. Cotter. CPJSC p.36
Dykes of the world are united. Nikki Giovanni. BFBTBJ p.45
Dylan, Who is Dead. Samuel Allen. BTB p.76
Dynamite black girl fucking in the halls. LeRoi Jones. BMP p.84
Dynamite Transported From Canada to New York City. Clarence Major. SAM p.46

- E -

E. O. Blues, The. John Raven. BFM p.23
Each known mile comes ·late. Conrad Kent Rivers. IADB p.89
Each Morning. LeRoi Jones. IADB p.21; NNPUSA p.75
Each Night. Mae V. Cowdery. WLOV p.38
Each spring even when she'd lippedpast eighty she scopped her winter drapes.
     Albert Aubert. ATB p.25
Eagerly like a woman hurrying to her lover. Frank Marshall Davis. AmNP p.91;
     PoN p.141; PoNe p.250
Eagle now has stirred the next, The. Edna Mae Weiss. BTh p.53
Early blue evening lights ain't come on yet. Langston Hughes. DYTB p.59
Early Evening Quarrel. Langston Hughes. SIH p.113
Early in the mornin.** Mari Evans. IABW p.6
Early in the voyage we discovered idolatry among the passengers. Gerald W.
     Barrax. AKOR p.86
Early Morning, to America. Craig Williamson. AfW p.37
Early on one Sunday morning ere the autumm had grown old. Charles Fred
     White. PONS p.122
Earth. Askia Muhammad Toure. BrT p.172
Earth is our mother, but thou, thou art father of us and of time, The.
     William S. Braithwaite. AVAN p.145; HFL p.33; SPWSB p.55
Earth-Meaning, The. Langston Hughes. FOW p.43
Earth-Quake. Waring Cuney. BTB p.82
Earthlog: Final Entry. Gerald W. Barrax. AKOR p.86
Earthlog I. Gerald W. Barrax. AKOR p.59
Earthsong. Langston Hughes. FOW p.106
Ease. Raymond Garfield Dandridge. PAOP p.25; ZaP p.81
Easter. Raymond Garfield Dandridge. ZaP p.27
Easter Flower. Claude McKay. AVAN p.204; HaS p.3; SPCM p.14
Easter Morn, An. Charles Fred White. PONS p.35
Easter Morn'. Raymond Garfield Dandridge. PeP p.39
Easy-Goin' Feller. Paul Laurence Dunbar. CPPLD p.74; LOLL p.109
Easy on Your Drums. Arna Bontemps. GoS p.101

End. Langston Hughes. FOW p.28

End is the real world, The. Don L. Lee. BrT p.116; DSNP p.182; WWW p.58

End of Man is His Beauty, The. LeRoi Jones. AmNP p.181; BTB p.135; SoS p.76

End of the Chapter, The. Paul Laurence Dunbar. AVAN p.57; CPPLD p.161

Ending. Norman Jordan. PoNe p.423

Endless Chant, The. Eli Shepperd. PlS p.145

Endymion, your star is stedfast now. Countee Cullen. BTB p.79; CpS p.76; OTIS p.71

Enemy, The. Alice Walker, ONC p.46

Energy. Victor Hernandez Cruz. SNA p.61

Energy for a New Thang (e equals blackness squared). Ernie Mkalimoto. NBP p.90

Engagement. Owen Dodson. PLL p.77

England cannot thy shores boast bards as great. Arbery Allson Whitman. AVAN p.52; EBAP p.222

Enigma. Jessie Redmond Fausel. PoN p.65; PoNe p.66

Enigmas. William S. Braithwaite. HFL p.95

Enigmatic Moon has it ... Leslie Collins. BTB p.73

Ennui. Langston Hughes. DYTB p.21

Enough! enough thy catalog of woe. H.A.B. Jones-Quartey. LUP p.36

Enough of love! let break its every hold. James Weldon Johnson. FYOP p.25

Enslaved. Claude McKay. HaS p.32; SPCM p.42

Enter harlem to walk from the howling cave called the "A" train. David Henderson. BlSp p.82

Entreaty. Walter G. Arnold. EbR p.2

Envoi. Raymond Patterson. BTB p.158

Ephemera, The. George Marion McClellan. AVAN p.95

Epigram. Armand Lanusse. MBP p.30; PoN p.12; PoNe p.13; TYBP p.96

Epigram. Iola M. Brister. EbR p.13

Epilogue. Countee Cullen. CpS p.77; OTIS p.72

Epilogue. Langston Hughes. WeB p.109

Epilogue. Stephen Kwartler. SoS p.4

Epilogue (To the Browning Centenary, May 12, 1912). William S. Braithwaite. SPWSB p.63

Epistrophe. LeRoi Jones. ITBLA p.272; KAL p.210; NNPUS p.73

Epitaph, An. Countee Cullen. CpS p.60

Epitaph for a Badman. John Raven. BFM p.13

Epitaph for a Bigot. Dorothy Vena Johnson. EbR p.91; PoN p.120; PoNe p.226

Epitaph for a Negro Woman. Owen Dodson. PoN p.174; PoNe p.301

Epitaph in April (1968). Craig Williamson. AfW p.50

Epitaph to a Man. In Memory of Dr. Martin Luther King, Jr. Robert Reedburg. TNV p.104

Epsilon. Melvin Tolson. HaG p.30

Equality. Herman L. McMillan. TNV p.73

Equipment. Paul Laurence Dunbar. CPPLD p.455

Ere sleep comes down to soothe the weary eyes. Paul Laurence Dunbar. AVAN p.59; BANP p.54; CaD p.2; CPPLD p. 3; ITBLA p.96; LOLL p.1; PoN p.39; PoNe p.43

Ere yet the morn its lovely blushes spread. Phillis Wheatley. PAO p.34; PPW p.7

Escape. Mari Evans. IABW p.42
Escort, The. Waverly Carmichael. FHOF p.13
Esperanto. Melvin Tolson. RWA p.30
Essay on Beauty. Robert Hayden. HSITD p.29
Essie Mae. David Nelson. B1Sp p.154
Esthete in Harlem. Langston Hughes. BANP p.239
Estimable Mable. Gwendolyn Brooks. FaP p.20
Eta. Melvin Tolson. HaG p.38
etc. etc. etc. Dorothy C. Parrish. TNV p.87
Eternal Desire. William L. Morrison. DaR p.12
Eternal Desire. William L. Morrison. DaR p.60; EbR p.109
Eternal God our souls simply at thy rich fountain kneeling bow. Zachary
    Withers. PAS p.27
Eternal Self, The. AVAN p.141; HFL p.56
Eternal spirit of dead dried autumn leaves. Alicia Ley Johnson. NBP p.74
Eternities before the firstborn day. James Weldon Johnson. AVAN p.179;
    EFOP p.22
Eternities - now numbering six or seven. James Weldon Johnson. KAL p.27
Eternity. George Marion McLlelan. EBAP p.123
Eternity. Raymond Garfield Dandridge. PAOP p.48; ZaP p.25
Ethiopia Saluting the Colors from Drumtops.* Walt Whitman. ANP p.134; PoN
    p.214; PoNe p.470
Ethiopian Sonnet. William L. Morrison. DaR p.15
Etretat. William C. Braithwaite. VER p.78
Etta Moten's Attic. Margaret Danner. BrT p.39
Eulogy to the Brave. Zachary Withers. PAS p.40
Europe on Five Dollars a Day. Ted Joans. BPW p.23
Eva Brown. Bernie Casey. LATP p.63
Eva Brown she said her name was eva brown. Bernie Casey. LATP p.63
Evah feal a sicknin' fright. Raymond Garfield Dandridge. PeP p.21; ZaP p.87
Evahbody's Got Trubbles.** Lucy Mae Turner. BCF p.31
Evaluation of the mysteries by the sons of all experience, The. LeRoi Jones.
    BMP p.38
Evanescent Love. Eugene Redmond. TNV p.99
Eve. Lucy Mae Turner. BCF p.26
Eve of the garden magnificent mother. Lucy Mae Turner. BCF p.26
Even as late as this long narrow rut, the way I have falsely penciled light
    onto the quality in the mind. Clarence Major. SAM p.71
Even as the earth thirsts for rain. Mae V. Cowdery. WLOV p.39
Even as we kill let us not forget that it is only so we may be more human.
    Julius Lester. SoS p.24
Evenin' Air Blues. Langston Hughes. SIH p.38
Evening. Paul Laurence Dunbar. CPPLD p.456
Evening. William S. Braithwaite. LLL p.23
Evening in Haiti. Emile Roumer. MBP p.48
Evening Rush Hour in Mid-July. John Raven. BFM p.30
Evening Song. Jean Toomer. CaD p.94; PoN p.70
Evening star that in the vaulted skies, The. Pierre Dalcour. MBP p.24;
    PoN p.12; PoNe p.16; TYBP p.97
Evening sun beams not upon me as I sit in silent shade. Charles Fred White.
    PONS p.65

Evening Thought, a salvation by Christ, with potential cries, An. Jupiter
    Hammon. ANP p.8; EBAP p.7; ITBLE p.27; JHANP p.29; PoN p.4; PoNe p.3
Eventide. Georgia Douglas Johnson. HWOP p.22
Eventide. Waverly T. Carmichael. FROF p.56
Even and over anon. James Edwin Corrothers. BANP p.75
Ever been kidnapped by a poet. Nikki Giovanni. BrT p.66
Ever notice how it's only the ugly honkies who hate. Nikki Giovanni.
    BFBTBJ p.81
Every day the old Negro moves the sprinkler. Gerald W. Barrax. AKOR p.75
Every Lover. Countee Cullen. MASP p.73
Every man has a night to his thoughts. William L. Morrison. DaR p.62
Every Man Heart Lay Down. Lorenz Graham. ChG p.82
Everybody Half-Pint Gin? Langston Hughes. CNAW p.303; WeB p.27
Everybody Out. LeRoi Jones. BMP p.109
Everybody passed the drummer. Victor Hernandez Cruz. SNA p.133
Everyone says: fate is a bad number. Owen Dodson. PLL p.99
Everything is stopped. Allen Polite. NNPUSA p.72
Everything was wrong, the local slaves were smiles. Seldon Rodman. PoN
    p.245; PoNe p.545
Everytime you flush the toilet twenty-two litres of drinking water goes down
    the toilet's drain. Ted Joans. AFR p.99
Everywhere. Raymond Garfield Dandridge. PAOP p.53; ZaP p.78
Everywhere everywhere there are people. Kali Grosvenor. PBK p.17
Everywhere I go. Robert Hayden. HSTID p.51
Evicted. Beatrice M. Murphy. TNV p.140
Evidence of Happenstance. Bernie Casey. LATP p.77
Evil. Langston Hughes. SIH p.15
Evil Morning. Langston Hughes. SIH p.118
Evil Nigger Waits for Lightnin'. LeRoi Jones. BMP p.129
Evil Woman. Langston Hughes. FCTJ p.62
Evolution. Thelma Parker Cox. TNV p.28
Ex-Judge at the Bar, An. Melvin Tolson. RWA p.19
Excerpt from A Sea-Chantey. Derek Walcott. TYBP p.111
Excerpt from I Have a Dream. Martin Luther King, Jr. TYBP p.249
Exchange in Greed the Ungraceful Signs. Etheridge Knight. BLIA p.423;
    BrT p.81
Excuse. Alice Walker. ONC p.75
Execution. James Randall. BrT p.129
Exercise in Quits. June Jordan. SCh p.71
Exercises on Themes From Life. Alice Walker. ONC p.79
Exhortation: Summer, 1919. Claude McKay. CaD p.84; HaS p.49
Exiled from places of honor about the throne of grace in Saint Mary's Cathe-
    dral. Joseph M. Mosley, Jr. NBP p.91
Exit. William S. Braithwaite. BANP p.101
Exits. Langston Hughes. FOW p.65
Expectancy. William Moore. ANP p.61
Expectation. Paul Laurence Dunbar. AVAN p.74; CPPLD p.209; LiG p.93
Experience. Eldon George McLean. EbR p.107
Experience. James E. McGirt. FYSS p.40
Explanation. James Weldon Johnson. FYOP p.82

Exultation. Mae V. Cowdery. WLOV p.26
Eye Heart and Voice of the Nation, The. James S. Cotter, Sr. SPPH p.33
Eye of the land has a piercing stare, The. Joseph S. Cotter, Sr. SPPH p.33
Eye that pierces with wide precision, The. Helen H. King. TGWL p.63
Eye Uptown and Downtown (three days, The. Victor Hernandez Cruz. SNA p.109
Eyes and Ears of the World. LeRoi Jones. BMP p.218
Eyes Come Back. LeRoi Jones. BMP p.59
Eyes of Johanna, The. Craig Williamson. AfW p.28
Eyes Gentled at the Corners So. Mari Evans. IABW p.85
Eyes of my Regret. Angelina Weld Grimké. CaD p.37
Eyes that are frozen from not crying. Langston Hughes. FOW p.69
Eyes that rolled on the floor. Victor Hernandez Cruz. SNA p.21

- F -

Feeeeeeeeeeeeeeeeeeeeee feeeeeeeeeeeeeeeeeeeee Feeeeeeeeeeeeeeeeeeee EEE EEE
    EEE EEE EEE EEE. LeRoi Jones. BMP p.189
F.B.I. came by my house three weeks ago, The. Nikki Giovanni. MyH p.59
Fa. Melvin Tolson. LRL p.21
Fabulous Mosaic Log, A. Melvin Tolson. LRL p.21
Face. Jean Toomer. CaD p.98; FNP p.13
Face of Poverty. Lucy Smith. NNPUSA p.45; PoNe p.267
Face of War is my face, The. Langston Hughes. PATL p.59
Faces and more remember. Maya Angelou. JGM p.32
Faces. Dudley Randall. LoY p.107
Faces. Maya Angelou. JGM p.32
Faces. Ted Joans. BPW p.102
Faces, not only crocus faces or fresh-snowfall faces. Dudley Randall.
    LoY p.10
Faces of Americans sit open hating each other, The. LeRoi Jones. BMP p.29
Facial. Gwendolyn Brooks. AnA p.53
Facts. Raymond Garfield Dandridge. PAOP p.47; ZaP p.24
Fade in the sound of summer music. M. Carl Holman. AmNP p.151; KAL p.163;
    PoN p.203; PoNe p.36
Failure in a crown of Sorrow. William S. Braithwaite. HFL p.79
Faint is the speech of the tired heart. William C. Braithwaite. LLL p.71
Fair Alabama, "Here we rest," thy name. George Marion McLlelan. EBAP p.125
Fair morn unbars her gates of gold. Henrietta Cordelia Ray. AVAN p.152;
    ANP p.129
Fairest lips are those we kiss, The. Georgia Douglas Johnson. HWOP p.43
Fairford Windows. William C. Braithwaite. VER p.102
Faith. Joseph S. Cotter, Sr. LOF p.43
Faith. Paul Laurence Dunbar. CPPLD p.400
Faith. Raymond Dandridge Garfield. PeP p.39
Faith is essential to prosperity. Joseph S. Cotter, Sr. LOF p.43
Faithful One. Langston Hughes. FOW p.85
Falcon, The. Robert Hayden. HSITD p.13
Fall To. Howard Jones. NBP p.77
Fallacy. Ricardo Weeks. EbR p.157
Fancy bore me on her wing far away. Raymond Garfield Dandridge. PeP p.19;
    ZaP p.9

Fancy halts my feet at the way-side well, A. Joseph S. Cotter, Sr. ANP p.33;
    CaD p.15; CPJSC p.44; PoN p.14; PoNe p.18
Fantasy. Georgia Douglas Johnson. HWOP p.48
Fantasy. Gwendolyn B. Bennett. CaD p.158
Fantasy in Purple. Langston Hughes. BANP p.242; CaD p.148; WeB p.46
Fantasy Under the Moon. Emanuel Boundzekei-Dongala. TYBP p.148
Far above the strife and striving. Benjamin Griffith Brawley. AVAN p.157
Far better take the word of man. Joseph S. Cotter, Sr. SPPH p.71
Far Cry From Africa. Derek Walcott. TYBP p.114
Far down, down through the city's great gaunt gut. Claude McKay. HaS p.54;
    SPCM p.75
Far From Africa: Four Poems. Margaret Danner. AmNP p.153; NNPUSA p.29
Far from this foreign Easter damp and chilly. Claude McKay. AVAN p.205;
    HaS p.3; SPCM p.14
Far from your native hills although you roam. Vivian L. Virtue. PoN p.326
Far in a vale among the mountains blue. Arbery Allson Whitman. EBAP p.214
Far in the night I hear the freight roll in with a load of fog. William L.
    Morrison. DaR p.40
Far up in the cathedral so they tell. Benjamin Griffith Brawley. AVAN p.158
Farewell. Isaac Toussaint L'Ouverture. PoN p.353; TYBP p.89
Farewell, The.* John Greenleaf Whittier. PoN p.236; PoNe p.46
Farewell, A. Langston Hughes. WeB p.72
Farewell. Mae V. Cowdery. WLOV p.29
Farewell to America (1773) To Mrs. S.W. Phillis Wheatley. PAL p.49; PPW
    p.57
Farewell to Arcady. Paul Laurence Dunbar. CPPLD p.198
Farewell to His Mother. Placido. BANP p.294; PoN p.383
Farewell to Morocco. Claude McKay. SPCM p.88
Farewell to My Mother (In the Chapel). Placido. BANP p.293; TYBP p.99
Farewell, ye halls of red and gray! Charles Fred White. PONS p.83
Farm Child's Lullaby, The. Paul Laurence Dunbar. CPPLD p.401
Farmer scatters grain with lavish hand, The. Joseph S. Cotter. CPJSC p.39
Fat black bucks in a wine barrel room.* Vachel Lindsay. PoN p.250; PoNe
    p. 484
Father and Mother, authors of my birth. Daniel A. Payne. EBAP p.51
Father, Father, Abraham. (On the Anniversary of Lincoln's Birth).** James
    Weldon Johnson. FYOP p.13
Father John's bread was made of rye. William S. Braithwaite. CaD p.31;
    SPWSB p.25
Father Missouri takes his own. Sterling A. Brown. PoN p.89; PoNe p.170;
    SoR p.73
Father, Son and Holy Ghost. Audre Lord. BTB p.140
Father, unto Thee thanksgiving. William C. Braithwaite. VER p.114
Favorite Diet, The. Waverly T. Carmichael. FHOF p.37
Fayfriends. Ted Joans. BPW p.91
Fear. Edward Richards. EbR p.125
Fear not the dog's howl. Joe C. Brown. EbR p.15
Feast. Mae V. Cowdery. WLOV p.62
Federico. Nicolas Guilén. PoN p.381
Feeding the Lions. Norman Jordan. BOL p.45; NBP p.78

First fight, then fiddle.** Gwendolyn Brooks. PoNe p.337
First Lady. Edna L. Harrison. EbR p.79
First, suicide notes should be (not long) but written. Alice Walker. ONC
    p.74
First, the color black. Don L. Lee. BLIA p.421; DSNP p.69
First the melody, clean and hard, and the flat slurs are faint. Lance
    Jeffers. BTB p.130
First warmth is in her smile, The. Edna L. Harrison. EbR p.79
Fish does ... hip, The. Anonymous. MBP p.11
Fisher Child's Lullaby, The. Paul Laurence Dunbar. CPPLD p.399
Fishermen. James Emanuel. BrT p.45
"Fishers of Men." Frances Harper. PBFH p.82
Fishes and the poet's Hand, The. Frank Yerby. AmNP p.134; PoNe p.332
Fishin'. Lucile D. Goodlett. WGC p.29
Fishing. James Cunningham. TGWL p.23
Fishing. Paul Laurence Dunbar. CLT p.63; CPPLD p.276
Fishy Poem, A. Nikki Giovanni. MyH p.9
Five Father Divine women circling a cadillac on the last day of the year.
    LeRoi Jones. BMP p.172
Five gleaming crows are big, black forms. Peter Clarke. MBP p.38
Five-part Invention. Gerald W. Barrax. AKOR p.27
Five Sonnets of Freedom. William C. Braithwaite. VER p.10
Five Winters Age.** David Henderson. SoS p.27
Fixed in the fireplace gaslit square with brick lining the iron frame.
    Michael S. Harper. DJDC p.11
Flags. Gwendolyn Brooks. AmNP p.141; PoN p.190
Flame-flower, day-torch, mauna loa. Anne Spencer. AmNP p.18; CaD p.52;
    CNAW p.272; ITBLA p.155; PoN p.53; PoNe p.64
Flame-Heart. Claude McKay. AmNP p.30; BANP p.174; CaD p.85; HaS p.9; PoN
    p.234; PoNe p.104; SPCM p.13; ITBLA p.156
Flames. Mari Evans. IABW p.79
Flap my sole, bim bam. Dorothy Rosenberg. PoNe p.571
Flash of lightning does not satisfy thirst, A. Anonymous. TYBP p.59
Flat Ride, A. Michael S. Harper. DJDC p.78
Fledgling Bard and the Poetry Society, The. George Reginald Margetson. BANP
    p.108
Flesh chase night, weather booming and dark host of fear pushing the windows
    even in plastic land. LeRoi Jones. BMP p.31
Flesh Line, the Space. Clarence Major. SAM p.47
Fleshdamp fragrance of such moments of coupling thrusts in the dew-soft cove,
    The. Gordon Parks. InL (unpaged)
Flickering shadows of the eve grow fainter as the sun goes down. William L.
    Morrison. DaR p.46
Flight. Langston Hughes. OWT p.55
Flight or a Warrant is Issued for Malcolm X. Joe Goncalves. FoM p.40
Fling off de back step. Lucile D. Goodlett. WGC p.41
Flirt, The. Ted Joans. AFR p.119
Flirt is like the filth the dirt that one gets under finger nails, The. Ted
    Joans. AFR p.119
Flirtation. Claude McKay. HaS p.21; SPCM p.100

Float Up. Clarence Major. SAM p.58
Float up without anchor like a child with wrist against wall. Clarence
    Major. SAM p.58
Flood-Tide. William L. Morrison. DaR p.22
Floodtide (for the Black tenant Farmers of the South). Askia Muhammad Toure.
    PoNe p.424
Floor is man-made. H.A.B. Jones-Quartey. LUP p.35
Florence to Her Cathedral Builders. William C. Braithwaite. VER p.27
Florida Night, A. Paul Laurence Dunbar. CPPLD p.310; LiG p.79
Florida Road Workers. Langston Hughes. GoS p.33; OWT p.91; PATL p.4
Flotsam. Ricardo Weeks. EbR p.155
Flow on, O charming stream of life. Zachary Withers. PAS p.28
Flower, The. Waverly Carmichael. FHOF p.27
Flower and Root. William S. Braithwaite. SPWSB p.23
Flower of Love. Claude McKay. HaS p.75; SPCM p.97
Flowers are Dead, The. Ted Joans. BPW p.32
Flowers of Darkness. Frank Marshall Davis. AmNP p.96; IADB p.12; PoN p.143;
    PoNe p.255
Flukum couldn't stand strain. Etheridge Knight. BrT p.82
Flushed with the hope of high desire. Benjamin Brawley. BANP p.150; PoN
    p.50; PoNe p.59
Flyin'. Lucy Mae Turner. BCF p.48
Flyolfloyd, i know from harringer he used to be the daredevil sex playing
    loves of the old sod. LeRoi Jones. BMP p.186
Fo Yoreself. Raymond Garfield Dandridge. PeP p.10; ZaP p.62
Folding and unfolding, A. Welton Smith. PoNe p.372
Folks ain't got no right to censuah othah folks about dey havits. Paul Lau-
    rence Dunbar. CPPLD p.6; LOLL p.6
Folks, I come up north cause they told me de north was fine. Langston
    Hughes. SIH p.38
Folks is talkin' 'bout de money, 'bout de silvah an' de gold. Paul Laurence
    Dunbar. CPPLD p.216; BLIA p.117
Fondle me carress and cradle me. Mari Evans. IABW p.32
Food For a Savage. William L. Morrison. DaR p.56
Food Poisoning. Marion Nicholes. LiS p.17
Foolin' Wid De Seasons. Paul Laurence Dunbar. CPPLD p.222
Foolish Heart, The. Countee Cullen. B1C p.30; OTIS p.88
Fool's Get Away. Michael S. Harper. DJDC p.34
Fools say, i've sd it. LeRoi Jones. BMP p.143
Football spirals straight up, The. Gerald W. Barrax. AKOR p.86
For a Black Poet. Gerald W. Barrax. AKOR p.68
For a cause that is loving and timely and just. Joseph S. Cotter, Sr.
    SPPH p.35
For A Child. Naomi Long Madgett. CNAW p.772; BTB p.148
For a Fatalist. Countee Cullen. CCC p.63
For a Fool. Countee Cullen. CCC p.60
For A Lady I Know. Countee Cullen. CaD p.187; CCC p.50; CNAW p.326; FNP
    p.19; GoS p.166; IADB p.84; KAL p.100; MBP p.27; OTIS p.33; PoN p.128;
    PoNe p.231
For A Lady i Know. LeRoi Jones. BMP p.119

For   TITLE AND FIRST LINE INDEX

For A Lady of Pleasure Now Retired. Nikki Giovanni. BrT p.67
For A Lovely Lady. Countee Cullen. CCC p.51
For A Magician. Countee Cullen. CCC p.55
For A Mouthy Woman. Countee Cullen. CCC p.57; MBP p.28; OTIS p.35
For A New Mother. Mae V. Cowdery. WLOV p.46
For A Pessimist. Countee Cullen. CCC p.56; OTIS p.34
For A Poet. Countee Cullen. CCC p.45; GoS p.197; MBP p.109; OTIS p.31;
    PoN p.125; PoNe p.229; TYBP p.234
For A Poet I Know. Nikki Giovanni. BFBTBJ p.91
For A Preacher. Countee Cullen. CCC p.66
For A Singer. Countee Cullen. CCC p.48
For A Skeptic. Countee Cullen. CCC p.62
For A Spin.* William C. Braithwaite. VER p.90
For a thousand years, you, African, suffered like a beast. Patrice Emery
    Lumumba. TYBP p.150
For A Virgin. Countee Cullen. CCC p.49
For A Wanton. Countee Cullen. CCC p.65
For All Matter. LeRoi Jones. BMP p.181
For An Anarchist. Countee Cullen. CCC p.54
For An Atheist. Countee Cullen. CCC p.52
For An Evolutionist and His Opponent. Countee Cullen. CCC p.53
For An Intellectual Audience. Nikki Giovanni. BFBTBJ p.35
For Andy Goodman - Michael Schwerner - and James Chaney. Margaret Walker.
    BrT p.152; PFND p.18
For Beautiful Mary Brown Chicago Rent Strike Leader. June Jordan. SCh p.49
For Billie Holiday. Langston Hughes. EbR p.87
For Black People. Don L. Lee. BrT p.112; DSNP p.178; WWW p.54
For Black Poets Who Think of Suicide. Etheridge Knight. BrT p.161
For Brother Malcolm. Edward S. Spriggs. BrT p.30; FoM p.73
For Brother you know who you are. Marion Nicholes. LiS p.19
For Bud. Michael S. Harper. DJDC p.18
For careless heart I crave, and a glad mind. William C. Braithwaite. VER
    p.126
For Christopher. June Jordan. SCh p.39
For Daughters of Magdalen. Countee Cullen. CCC p.64
For Dead Mimes. Langston Hughes. FOW p.37
For Eusi, Ahy Kwei & Gwen Brooks. Keorapetse W. Kgositsile. TGWL p.62
For ever and ever and ever, beyond time and space, never, never, never will
    peace know my face. Lucia M. Pitts. EbR p.120
For Fifty Years. James Weldon Johnson. FYOP p.29
For five hours the two dents of your face will not disappear. Michael S.
    Harper. DJDC p.25
For forty years I shunned the lust. Countee Cullen. CCC p.49
For gardens I have never seen and birds and winds and water. Mae V. Cowdery.
    WLOV p.22
For Gwen. Maxine Hall Elliston. TGWL p.33
For Gwen. Sharon Scott. TGWL p.89
For Gwen - 1969. Margaret Walker. TGWL p.95
For Gwendolyn Brooks. Helen H. King. TGWL p.63
For Gwendolyn Brooks. Nikki Giovanni. TGWL p.48

For Gwendolyn Brooks. Zack Gilbert. TGWL p.46
For gwendolyn brooks - a whole & beautiful spirit. Johari. Amini. TGWL
    p.12
For Hazel Hall, American Poet. Countee Cullen. CCC p.69
For He Lumumba perhaps Lumumba like their johnbrown made hasty hurry ups.
    Ted Joans. BPW p.16
For Helen Keller. Countee Cullen. BlC p.32; OTIS p.89
For I am Rightful Fellow of their band. Gwendolyn Brooks. KAL p.156; PoN
    p.191
For I have been bitten by more than a viper fang. Ritten Edward Lee. EbR
    p.100
For Jim Easter Eve. Anne Spencer. AmNP p.17; PoN p.54; PoNe p.65
For John Keats. Countee Cullen. CaD p.186; CCC p.68; KAL p.101; OTIS p.36
For John Moses / PFC. Albert Aubert. ATB p.28
For Joseph Conrad. Countee Cullen. CCC p.71
For lighter, whiter skin in just ten days. Don Johnson. PoNe p.436
For Lionel Hampton. Oliver La Grone. BTB p.139
For Love of the Sea, Child Elsie. William S. Braithwaite. LLL p.50
For Lover Man, and all the Other Young Men Who Failed to Return from World
    War II. Mance Williams. NNPUSA p.56
For Malcolm. Joyce Whitsitt Lawrence. BrT p.33; FoM p.20
For Malcolm, a Year After. Etheridge Knight. FoM p.43
For Malcolm: After Mecca. Gerald W. Barrax. AKOR p.85
For Malcolm X. Nanina Alba. FoM p.39
For Malcolm X. Julia Fields. FoM p.33
For Malcolm X. Margaret Walker. FoM p.32; PFND p.18
For Malcolm's eyes, when they broke the face of some dumb white man. LeRoi
    Jones. BANP p.112; BrT p.28; FoM p.61
For Malik. Bobb Hamilton. FoM p.43
For Mary McLeod Bethune. Margaret Walker. PoN p.188; PoNe p.326
For Me Again. Ted Joans. BPW p.39
For Mother in Paradise. Malcolm Christian Conley. HeD p.12
For My Grandmother. Countee Cullen. CaD p.186; CCC p.46; GoS p.67; OTIS
    p.32
For My Mother. June Jordan. SCh p.3
For my mother I would write a list. June Jordan. SCh p.3
For My People. Margaret Walker. AmNP p.128; BLIA p.261; CNAW p.527; FMP
    p.13; IADB p.107; ITBLA p.219; KAL p.138; PoN p.186; PoNe p.314
For my people everywhere singing their slave songs repeatedly. Margaret
    Walker. AmNP p.128; BLIA p.261; CNAW p.527; FMP p.13; IADB p.107; ITBLA
    p.219; KAL p.138; PoN p.186; PoNe p.314
For Myself. Countee Cullen. CCC p.72
For Nina Simone. Kali Grosvenor. PBK p.44
For O - Two Hung Up. Carolyn Rodgers. BlSp p.182
For once the earth had failed to thaw. William L. Morrison. DaR p.38
For one brief golden moment rare like Wine. Claude McKay. BLIA p.166; HaS
    p.16; SPCM p.66
For one bright moment heavenly goddess shine. Phillis Wheatley. PPW p.86
For one profound disturbing dream. William S. Braithwaite. SPWSB p.11
For One Who Died Singing Of Death. Countee Cullen. CCC p.67

For   TITLE AND FIRST LINE INDEX

For One Who Gayly Sowed His Oats. Countee Cullen. CCC p.61
For Our American Cousins. Reginald Wilson. FoM p.35
For Our Lady. Sonia Sanchez. WABP p.41
For Our Land Called America. S. E. Anderson. BlSp p.11
For Paul Laurence Dunbar. Countee Cullen. CaD p.186; CCC p.70; FNP p.20;
     GoS p.160; KAL p.102; OTIS p.37
For Saundra. Nikki Giovanni. BFBTBJ p.88; BrT p.57; TNV p.34; TYBP p.256
For Some Poets. Mae Jackson. BOL p.16
For Somebody to Start Singing. June Jordan. SCh p.19
For spreading plain and peak that towers we give Thee Thanks. Raymond Gar-
     field Dandridge. ZaP p.50
For Stokely Carmichel. Kali Grosvenor. PBK p.45
For the brothers resurrected from the nod. S. E. Anderson. BlSp p.10
For The Candle Light. Angelina Weld Grimke. CaD p.45; PoN p.47; PoNe p.55
For the death of life leaps of the Middle Passage. S. E. Anderson. BlSp
     p.10
For the dim regions whence my fathers came. Claude McKay. AmNP p.28; HaS p.
     45; ITBLA p.156; SPCM p.41
For the honey bee Queen and her poets. W. D. Wandick. TGWL p.97
For the little white poem, the big painting blue, and the swinging music in
     hot red. Ted Joans. AFR p.141
For The Man Who Fails. Paul Laurence Dunbar. CPPLD p.190
For the sun that shone at the dawn of spring. Edward Smyth Jones. AVAN
     p.154; BANP p.148
For the Truth. Edward S. Spriggs. BrT p.162
For the Viet Congo. Ted Joans. BPW p.13
For their clean bodies, and malcolm's eyes I walk the streets confused and
     half sick. LeRoi Jones. BMP p.85
For Theresa. Nikki Giovanni. BFBTBJ p.93
For they who fashion songs must live too close to pain. Frank Yerby. AmNP
     p.136
For this peculiar tint that paints my house. Claude McKay. CaD p.92
For three hours (too short for me) I sat in your home. Nikki Giovanni.
     BFBTBJ p.6
For Tiny. Victor Hernandez Cruz. SNA p.87
For Tom Postell, Dead Black Poet. LeRoi Jones. BMP p.153
For who a girl named Barbra ... what is this. Victor Hernandez Cruz. SNA
     p.35
For William Edward Brughardt Du Bois on His Eightieth Birthday. Betty
     Latimer. PoN p.208
Force that guides the ideal thought, the power that doth control, The.
     Zachary Withers. PAS p.26
Force was he in the thoroughfare, A. Joseph S. Cotter, Sr. CPJSC p.30;
     WSBO p.17
Ford ain't hirin. Robert E. Hayden. HSITD p.42
Foreclosure. Sterling A. Brown. SoR p.73; PoN p.88; PoNe p.170
Foredoom. Georgia Douglas Johnson. HWOP p.39
Forest Greeting, The. Paul Laurence Dunbar. CPPLD p.385
Forever. Paul Laurence Dunbar. CPPLD p.392
Forever pointing heavenward, and when. William S. Braithwaite. SPWSB p.84

Forever shall not burn his tongue. Countee Cullen. B1C p.19
Forget? Ah, never! Joseph S. Cotter, Jr. BOG p.26
Forget me not. Ann Plato. EBAP p.116
Forget me not. Waverly T. Carmichael. FHOF p.34
Forgiveness. Will Smallwood. EbR p.130
Forgotten, The. Raymond Patterson. BTB p.157
Forgotten Dreams. Edward Silvera. LUP p.42; PoN p.150; PoNe p.259
Form is Emptiness. LeRoi Jones. BMP p.155
Formerly a slave.* Herman Melville. PoN p.246; PoNe p.466
Formula. Carolyn J. Ogletree. TNV p.78
Forseen in Eve's desire. William S. Braithwaite. HFL p.18
Forth on the fatal morn. Albery A. Whitman. IEBAP p.220; ITBLA p.94
Fortune teller look in my hand. Langston Hughes. OWT p.18
47,000 Windows. June Jordan. SCh p.66
Forward. Raymond Garfield Dandridge. PeP p.14
Forward, every son and daughter born of Ethiopia's hue. Raymond Garfield
    Dandridge. PeP p.14
Fossil, Fuchsia, Mantis, Man. Robert Hayden. BOR p.40; SPRH p.59
Fo'ty acres jes fo' me! David Wadsworth Cannon, Jr. PoN p.160; PoNe p.281
"Foun' dis rabbit's foot, you see. James D. Corrothers. EBAP p.243
Found in the blackest corner with a tail making perfect circles. Clarence
    Major. SAM p.64
Found Star, The. Charles B. Johnson. SOMP p.13
Fount of Tears, The. Paul Laurence Dunbar. CPPLD p.366
Four Epitaphs. Countee Cullen. AmNP p.88; CaD p.186
Four Glimpses of Night. Frank Marshall Davis. AmNP p.97; MBP p.103; PoN
    p.141; PoNe p.250
Four great walls have hemmed me in. Blanche Taylor Dickinson. CaD p.110
Four hundred years ago a tangled waste. Paul Laurence Dunbar. CPPLD p.72;
    LOLL p.105
Four-Leaf Clover. Wesley Cartwright. GoS p.78
Four Little Girls. Arthur Boze. B1Wo p.9
Four little girls who went to Sunday School that day. Langston Hughes. PATL
    p.46; PoNe p.200
Four Little girls with dark eyes. Arthur Boze. B1Wo p.9
Four Odd Bodkins For My Analist. Bruce Wright. BTB p.183
Four Questions Addressed to His Excellency the Prime Minister. James P.
    Vaughn. AmNP p.167
Four Poems--After the Japanese. Mae V. Cowdery. WLOV p.12
Four sheets to the wind and a one-way ticket to France. Conrad Kent Rivers.
    AmNP p.176; BLIA p.356; IADB p.105; NNPUSA p.107; PoNe p.404; SVH p.18
Four Walls. Blanche Taylor Dickinson. CaD p.110
Four Walls Can Hold. Langston Hughes. FOW p.66
Four Walls. Malcolm Christian Conley. HeD p.13
Fourth Dance Poem. Gerald W. Barrax. AKOR p.78
4th Dimension. David Henderson. B1Sp p.87
Fox Fiah. Lucile D. Goodlett. WGC p.52
Fox flees like a lamb before a hungry pack of wolves, The. Ricardo Weeks.
    EbR p.157
Foxey Lady. Phillip Solomon. SoS p.4
Foxey lady walkin' down the street. Phillip Solomon. SoS p.4

Fragile fabric of our dream, The. Georgia Douglas Johnson. HWOP p.27
Fragile, tiny, just a sprite. Georgia Douglas Johnson. HWOP p.23
Fragility. James Edgar Smith. EbR p.130
Fragment. H.A.B. Jones-Quartey. LUP p.35
Fragment. James Weldon Johnson. FYOP p.17
Fragment. Jessie Fauset. CaD p.70
Fragment: Biographic, A. William S. Braithwaite. SPWSB p.69
Fragments. Langston Hughes. FOW p.26
Frail Children of Sorrow, dethroned by a hue. Georgia Douglas Johnson.
   CaD p.75
France! how shall we call her Belle again? Countee Cullen. OTIS p.170
Francs amis demandent un rondeau. Nichole Riquet. EBAP p.164; Trans. EBAP
   p.165
Frankie and Johnny. Sterling A. Brown. SoR p.34
Frankie was a half **white**, Johnny **was a nigger**. Sterling A. Brown. SoR p.34
Freckles tickle your nose. Gregory J. Ford. TNV p.31
Frederick Douglass. Joseph Seaman Cotter. EBAP p.185; LOF p.17
Frederick Douglass. Paul Laurence Dunbar. CPPLD p.7; LOLL p.8
Frederick Douglass. Robert Hayden. AmNP p.119; BOR p.71; CNAW p.392; IADB
   p.45; ITBLA p.220; KAL p.117; MBP p.83; PoN p.171; PoNe p.296; SPRH p.78;
   SoS p.41; TYBP p.237
Frederick Douglass: 1817-1895. Langston Hughes. PATL p.31
Frederick Douglass, Freedom Seeker, 1817-1895, Maryland. Eloise Culver.
   GANIV p.30
Free Man. Langston Hughes. SIH p.31
Free me from the memories of the shackle. Eldon George McLean. EbR p.107
Free Spirit. Victor Hernandez Cruz. SNA p.71
Free Wine on Communion Day. Linwood D. Smith. TNV p.117
Freedom. Leslie Pinckney Hill. AVAN p.197
Freedom. Langston Hughes. PATL p.89
Freedom. Charles L. Reason. ANP p.11; AVAN p.44
Freedom ain't that a word?* James Pipes. ZJP p.173
Freedom in mah soul. David Wadsworth Cannon, Jr. PoN p.160; PoNe p.281
Freedom Is A Word.* James Pipes. ZJP p.173
Freedom is just frosting on somebody else's cake. Langston Hughes. PATL
   p.84
Freedom is not the surfeit of greedy maw. William C. Braithwaite. VER p.10
Freedom Rider: Washout. James Emanuel. BrT p.44
Freedom Triumphant. Zachary Withers. PAS p.7
Freedom will break the tyrant's chain. Thomas S. Sidney. EBAP p.260
Freedom will not come today, this year not ever through compromise and fear.
   Langston Hughes. PATL p.89
Freedom's Snare. Ritten Edward Lee. EbR p.99
Fren' Ship. Raymond Garfield Dandridge. PAOP p.32; ZaP p.100
French Leave. Claude McKay. HaS p.86; SPCM p.68
Friday. LeRoi Jones. BMP p.52
Friday Ladies of the Pay Envelope, The. Mari Evans. IABW p.49
Friend of mine told me he'd risen above jazz, A. Michael S. Harper. DJDC
   p.5
Friends, amid my rhymings gay of fellowship and holiday. William C. Braith-
   waite. VER p.9

Friendship true is rare indeed, A. Charles Fred White. PONS p.122
Frightened bartender hit their heads on the South bronx, The. Victor Hernan-
    dez Cruz. SNA p.115
Frightened Flowe. William J. Harris. BOL p.69
Frolic, A. Paul Laurence Dunbar. AVAN p.75; CPPLD p.325
From a Black Perspective. Don L. Lee. DCS p.34; DSNP p.102
From a Bus. Joyce Whitsitt Lawrence. NBP p.130
From a Fellow Who's Been Out Drinking With the Boys Till 2 AM. John Raven.
    BFM p.23
From a Logical Point of View. Nikki Giovanni. BFBTBJ p.71
From a vision red with war I awoke and saw the Prince of Peace hovering over
    no man's Land. BANP p.42
From all we are yet cannot be. Robert Hayden. BOR p.57; SPRH p.36
From America. James M. Whitfield. EBAP p.40
From an 18 year old poet with a raggedy face. Prentiss Taylor, Jr. TGWL
    p.93
From Austriad. Juan Latino. TYBP p.65
From blue-grey mist and river haze the day is born. Mae V. Cowdery. WLOV
    p.7
From bright West Indies' sunny seas. James M. Whitfield. EBAP p.48
From Carma. Jean Toomer. KAL p.53
From: Cities #8. Victor Hernandez Cruz. BOL p.68
From Congo's wastes and Egypt's Nile she comes with Eden's heart and guile.
    Joseph S. Cotter, Sr. CPJSC p.48
From dark abodes to fair ethereal light. Phillis Wheatley. ITBLA p.28; PAL
    p.88; PPW p.10
From death of star to new star's birth. Countee Cullen. CCC p.83
From: Glimpses # xii. Lawrence McGaugh. BOL p.74
From Harlem Gallery. Melvin B. Tolson. KAL p.63; TYBP p.213
From her writing I infuse two months of imprecise bleeding. Michael S.
    Harper. DJDC p.16
From ivory towers they come. Austin Black. NBP p.29
From Karintha. Jean Toomer. KAL p.51
From Leelah Misled. Albery Allson Whitman. EBAP p.197
From Les Salaziennes. Auguste La Caussade. TYBP p.69
From Letters Found Near a Suicide. Frank Horne. KAL p.65
From Miscellaneous Poems Hymn to the Nation. Arbery Allson Whitman. EBAP
    p.216
From Montgomery to Memphis, he marches. Margaret Walker. PFND p.25
From my personal album two photos. Nanina Alba. FoM p.39
From near the sea, like Whitman my great predecessor. Frank O'Hara. PoNe
    p.58
From on the fugitive slave law. Elymas Payson Rogers. EBAP p.60
From out the rosy dawn the sun comes forth. James McGirt. FYSS p.44
From Return to my native land. Aime Cesaire. TYBP p.123
From Riot Rimes: USA. Raymond Patterson. SoS p.108
From Rome's palaces and villas gaily issued forth a throng. Frances Harper.
    PBFH p.66
From Selma. Langston Hughes. EbR p.88
From Some Far-Fringing Wood.** William C. Braithwaite. VER p.105

From   TITLE AND FIRST LINE INDEX

Full Hope, The. William S. Braithwaite. HFL p.65
Full many lift and sing. Charles Bertram Johnson. ANP p.38; BANP p.199;
    SOMP p.9
Full moon rising on the waters of my heart. Jean Toomer. CaD p.94; PoN p.70
Full Moon. Robert Hayden. BTB p.111; KAL p.112; SPRH p.15
Full Price to Pay (to get away). Ted Joans. AFR p.36
Full September moon sheds floods of light, The. George Marion McLlelan.
    EBAP p.124
Funeral. Langston Hughes. OWT p.120
Funeral. Sterling A. Brown. SoR p.111
Funeral of Martin Luther King, Jr., The. Nikki Giovanni. BFBTBJ p.56; BOL
    p.30; BrT p.54; TNV p.37
Funeral Poem. LeRoi Jones. BMP p.175
Funeral Poem on the Death of C.E. an Infant of Twelve Months, A. Phillis
    Wheatley. PPW p.31
Funky Marie. John Raven. BFM p.21
Funny Company (or) Why Ain't Him and His Girls on T.V.? Arthur Pfister.
    B1Sp p.160
Furlough, The. Melvin Tolson. RWA p.23
Futile of me to offer you my hand. Langston Hughes. PATL p.57
Futile to chide the stinging shower. Dudley Randall. AmNP p.121
Futility. Claude McKay. HaS p.93; SPCM p.106

- G -

G. I. John Raven. BFM p.17
Gabriel. Robert Hayden. HSITD p.23
Gaily we ride by the river. Charles Fred White. PONS p.56
Gailgone. Michael S. Harper. DJDC p.80
Gain and Loss. Joseph S. Cotter, Sr. SPPH p.65
Gale winds ripen the cheeks which splice broken blood vessels. Michael S.
    Harper. DJDC p.27
Gallant Castle Builders. William C. Braithwaite. VER p.70
Galleon ages drift beyond the beyond, The. Melvin Tolson. RWA p.73
Gallows, The. Melvin Tolson. LUP p.45; RWA p.60
Gal's Cry For A Dying Lover. Langston Hughes. FCTJ p.82
Game of Game, The. Nikki Giovanni. BrT p.65
Games. Conrad Kent Rivers. SVH p.10
Games, you say! Conrad Kent Rivers. SVH p.10
Gamma. Melvin Tolson. HaG p.23
Gamut, The. Maya Angelou. JGM p.4
Gang Girls. Gwendolyn Brooks. ITM p.47
Gang girls are sweet exotics. Gwendolyn Brooks. ITM p.47
Gao in and out windows flies and mosquitos. Ted Joans. BPW p.89
Garden is very quiet tonight, The. William Moore. BANP p.85
Garden of Life, The. Raymond Garfield Dandridge. PeP p.41
Garden of Shushan. Anne Spencer. BANP p.213; CNAW p.269
Garden Sanctuary. William Morrison. DaR p.41
Garden Scene. Albert Aubert. ATB p.15
Garmet. Langston Hughes. GoS p.175

Glory of the day was in Her Face.**James Weldon Johnson. BANP p.127; CaD
    p.18; FYOP p.24; IADB p.15; PoN p.30
Gnarled and knotty iron-wrought hands fashioned for the spade and plow.
    Anita Scott Coleman. EbR p.50
Go count the stars. Fenton Johnson. AmNP p.27
Go down death (a Funeral Sermon). James Weldon Johnson. AmNP p.2; BLIA
    p.191
Go Down, Moses.** Anonymous. BLIA p.41; MBP p.79
"Go Down, Moses!" Marcus B. Christian. EbR p.34
Go Down, Old Hannah. Anonymous. TYBP p.200
Go Forth, My Son. Georgia Douglas Johnson. GoS p.187
Go Look for Beauty Where you Least. Countee Cullen. CpS p.67; OTIS p.67
Go Slow. Langston Hughes. PATL p.90
Go Slow, They Say. Langston Hughes. PATL p.90
Go tell it on the Mountain.** Anonymous. ChG p.93; ITBLA p.97; MBP p.69
Go through the gate with closed eyes. Arna Bontemps. AmNP p.76; CaD p.171;
    KAL p.79; PoN p.116; PoNe p.218
Go' way from me an le' me 'lone. Waverly T. Carmichael. FHOF p.26
Go' Way From My Window.** Anonymous. MBP p.51
Go Work in my vineyard.** Frances Harper. PBFH p.31
Goal, The. Joseph S. Cotter, Jr. AVAN p.181; BOG p.25
Goal. Mae V. Cowdery. WLOV p.18
God (a Folk Sermon). Anonymous. MBP p.1
God and the devil still are wrangling. Countee Cullen. CCC p.57; MBP p.28;
    OTIS p.35
God Blame America!! Ted Joans. AFR p.79
God bless our country. James E. McGirt. FYSS p.32
God bless our home, land of the free. James E. McGirt. FYSS p.32
God Bless Our Native Land.**Frances Harper. PBFH p.23
God called from out the dark. Charles B. Johnson. SOMP p.19
God give the yellow man an easy breeze at blossom time. Arna Bontemps. ANP
    p.126; BANP p.267; CaD p.172; PoNe p.225
God fashioned you an autumn birch standing stately on a hill. Gertrude
    Parthenia McBrown. EbR p.104
God give to men. Arna Bontemps. ANP p.126; BANP p.267; CaD p.172; PoNe
    p.225
God gives man bent of will and scope of vision. Joseph S. Cotter, Sr. SPPH
    p.39; WSBO p.52
God has his plans and what if we. Paul Laurence Dunbar. CPPLD p.130; LOLL
    p.193
God Having a Hemorrhage. Langston Hughes. WeB p.76
God in the Garden. William C. Braithwaite. VER p.110
God is a woman in the dark morning of Africa. Craig Williamson. AfW p.1
God is an Indian. Anita Scott Coleman. EbR p.50
God is Kind.** Mae V. Cowdery. WLOV p.15
God is Tall Trees.** Craig Williamson. AfW p.10
God is the most high. Bilal Carab. TYBP p.43
God is the old repair man. Fenton Johnson. AmNP p.27; ITBLA p.218
God knows we have our troubles too. Langston Hughes. CNAW p.310
God Macbeth, A? Charles Fred White. PONS p.161

God made this world a **garden**.   Eloise Culver.   GANIV.p.77
God must have scanned the Heavens, said, "It needs just one more light.
    Eloise Culver.   GANIV p.48
God spoke once that made your girdle fall, The.*   **Selden Rodman.** PoN
    p.293; PoNe p.543
God the Father, God the Son. George Reginald Margetson. AVAN p.169
God was **poring over the** world the other day. Waring Cuney. BTB p.82
God wrought you **flesh and hair and eyes.** William S. Braithwaite. LLL p.76
Goddam if we move and water crystalizes. Gerald W. Barrax. AKOR p.15
Goddess of Love.** Dudley Randall. LoY p.5
God's angry with the world again. Robert Hayden. SPRH p.13
Gods. Countee Cullen. CCC p.101; FNP p.19
God's glory and my country's shame. Countee Cullen. B1C p.69; OTIS p.104
God's gonna Set Dis World on Fire.**Anonymous. ITBLA p.97
God's gwine to Take All My Trubbles Away. Lucy Mae Turner. BCF p.46
Gods in Vietnam. Eugene Redmond. NBP p.108
God's Christmas Tree. Eve Lynn. ChG p.98
God's Masterpiece. J. Henderson Brooks. BTh p.45
God's placid heavens mother you. Raymond Garfield Dandridge. PAOP p.16
Goin' down the road, Lawd. Langston Hughes. AmNP p.65; CNAW p.308; FCTJ
    p.87
Going East. Frances Harper. PBFH p.63
Going Uptown to Visit Miriam. Victor Hernandez Cruz. SNA p.47
Gold of heaven, The. Tom Dent. NNPUSA p.71
Golden Day, A. Paul Laurence Dunbar. ANP p.24; CPPLD p.411
Golden girl in a golden gown. Langston Hughes. LUP p.25
Golden Hair. William S. Braithwaite. HFL p.90
Golden Moon Rise. William S. Braithwaite. AVAN p.142; HFL p.27
Golden State, The. Zachary Withers. PAS p.44
Golden Stove, The. Gene Holmes. EbR p.83
Golgotha Is A Mountain. Arna Bontemps. AmNP p.77; PoN p.117; CaD p.173;
    PoNe p.219
Goliath of Gath. Phillis Wheatley. PAL p.101; PPW p.13
Gone are the sensuous stars, and manifold. Benjamin Brawley. AVAN p.158;
    BANP p.151
Gone, gone, gone, gone, gone - dead fer days fore I knew you dead. Michael
    S. Harper. DJDC p.51
Gone, Gone - sold and gone.** John Greenleaf Whittier. PoN p.236; PoNe p.461
Gone West. Raymond Garfield Dandridge. PAOP p.50
Gonna Git High. Robert Hayden. HSITD p.44
Goo' By, Jinks, I got to hump. Paul Laurence Dunbar. CPPLD p.102; LOLL
    p.151
Good After All. Waverly T. Carmichael. FHOF p.38
Good Assassination Should Be Quiet, A. Mari Evans. B1Sp p.70; IABW p.84
Good Bye Honey - Good Bye. Elliot B. Henderson. EBAP p.243
"Good-Bye." I said to my conscience. Paul Laurence Dunbar. CPPLD p.48;
    LOLL p 69
Good evening PUBIK PAK listeners! Ted Joans. AFR p.138
Good Everywhere. Raymond Garfield Dandridge. PeP p.10
Good glory, give a look at sporting Beasley. Sterling A. Brown. KAL p.76;
    SoR p.113

Grave is all too weak a thing, A. Countee Cullen. CCC p.105
Grave. Waring Cuney. PoN p.148
Graveyard is the cheapest boarding houses, The. Langston Hughes. OWT p.119
Gray dawn on the mountain top. Paul Laurence Dunbar. CPPLD p.406
Gray-yard. Langston Hughes. FOW p.21
Gray Day, A. Raymond Garfield Dandridge. PAOP p.48
Gray is the palace where she dwells. Paul Laurence Dunbar. CPPLD p.288
Gray of the sea, and the gray of the sky, The. Paul Laurence Dunbar.
    CPPLD p.148
Great amazon of God behold your bread. Margaret Walker. PoN p.188; PoNe
    p.326
Great biologist said: The semen of change crawls upward from the simple to
    the complex, The. Melvin Tolson. LUP p.45; RWA p.59
Great Civil Rights Law (A.D. 1964), The. Mari Evans. IABW p.66
Great event seeks an author, A. Juan Latino. TYBP p.66
Great gift, we thought, even for us the error was co los sal. Gerald W.
    Barrax. AKOR p.59
Great in the riches the world-brain has wrought. Joseph S. Cotter, Sr.
    SPPH p.36; WSBO p.24
Great Laws, The. Marian Cuthbert. SOC p.25
Great Lonely Hills. Langston Hughes. FOW p.5
Great Pax Whitie, The. Nikki Giovanni. BFBTBJ p.60
Great swart check and the gleam of tears, A. Otto Leland Bohana. BANP
    p.204
Great teacher set the last bag of grain under the shed roof. Marion Cuth-
    bert. SOC p.25
Great Truths. Marion Cuthbert. SOC p.37
Greatness. Zachary Withers. PAS p.6
Greek Room, The. James W. Thompson. BTB p.174
Green lawn a picket fence flowers. Alice Walker. ONC p.23
Green swirling neon snow. LeRoi Jones. BMP p.20
Green the grass is on the campus, but the leaves are turning brown. Charles
    Fred White. PONS p.110
Green Valley. Dorothy Vena Johnson. PoN p.120; PoNe p.226
Greeness. Angelina Weld Grimké. ANP p.86; CD p.36
Greens and fat back pickled pig tails. Marion Nicholes. LiS p.17
Greetings, Master, take from me. William S. Braithwaite. HFL p.45
Grey Dawn. William S. Braithwaite. HFL p.91
Gri-gris. Ted Joans. BPW p.117
Grief. Langston Hughes. FOW p.69
Grief lays down its law. Gordon Parks. InL (unpaged)
Grievance, A. Paul Laurence Dunbar. CPPLD p.303
Grill Room. Jesse Franklin Patterson. EbR p.114
Grim monarch! see, deprived of vital breath. Phillis Wheatley. PAL p.38;
    PPW p.12
Grim monarch! see depriv'd of vital breath. Phillis Wheatley. PPW p.71
Grits and Rice Grains. Mari Evans. IABW p.48
Group, The. Victor Hernandez Cruz. SNA p.99
"Grow in Hope and Grace." Barbara Anne Baker. TNV p.15
Growin' Gray. Paul Laurence Dunbar. CPPLD p.129; LOLL p.192

Hail! ye heroes who yet stand. Charles Fred White. PONS p.42
Hain't you see my Mandy Lou. Paul Laurence Dunbar. CPPLD p.278; WMS p.73
Hail - Silver - gray. Jean Toomer. CaD p.98; FNP p.13
Half a page From Square Business. Victor Hernandez Cruz. SNA p.3
Half in the dim light from the hall. William S. Braithwaite. LLL p.75
Half of his body hung in the air. Victor Hernandez Cruz. SNA p.119
Hallelujah Queens. Craig Williamson. AfW p.21
Hallowe'en. Charles Fred White. PONS p.93
Hamlet Rives Us, A. Melvin Tolson. ITBLA p.218; RWA p.63
Hand of fate cannot be stayed, The. James Weldon Johnson. FYOP p.17
Hands. Anita Scott Coleman. EbR p.50
Hands. LeRoi Jones. BMP p.78
Hands. Glen Thompson. SoS p.9
Hands of all nations stretching to pull one another together. Glen Thompson.
    SoS p.9
Hanging out in the music. David Henderson. BlSp p.85
Hangs whipped blood striped mean pulled clothes ripped slobber. LeRoi Jones.
    BMP p.124
Happiness in Heaven. Charles Fred White. PONS p.149
Happy Fool Year! Ted Joans. AFR p.19
Happy Hymn. Eli Shepperd. PlS p.150
Hard burst (heart, a word before, had heart bursts. LeRoi Jones. BMP p.76
Hard Daddy. Langston Hughes. BANP p.238; FCTJ p.86
Hard is A Horse To Ride.** Herbert G. Pickett. BTh p.627
Hard Luck. Langston Hughes. FCTJ p.18
Hard Rock Returns to Prison From the Hospital For the Criminal Insane.
    Etheridge Knight. BLIA p.422; BrT p.78
Hard Rock was known not to take no shit. Etheridge Knight. BLIA p.422;
    BrT p.78
Hard Time Blues. Waring Cuney. LUP p.10
Harder Blood-Blizzards. LeRoi Jones. BMP p.51
Hark! I hear the sound of singing. Charles Fred White. PONS p.48
"Hark! strange, rest your weary self ... Herman J. Carter. EbR p.27
Hark to the call of the August morn. William C. Braithwaite. VER p.91
Harlem. Jean Brierre. EbR p.11; PoN p.369; TYBP p.93
Harlem. Langston Hughes. ITBLA p.158; PoNe p.199; PATL p.4
Harlem Dance Hall. Langston Hughes. FOW p.94
Harlem Dancer, The. Claude McKay. BANP p.169; BLIA p.167; FNP p.8; HaS
    p.42; SPCM p.61
Harlem Gallery, an Afric Pepper bird, awakes me at a people's dusk of dawn.
    Melvin Tolson. HaG p.17
Harlem Hopscotch. Maya Angelou. JGM p.48
Harlem is vicious modernism. LeRoi Jones. BMP p.108
Harlem Night Club. Langston Hughes. WeB p.32
Harlem Night Song. Langston Hughes. WeB p.62
Harlem sent him home. Langston Hughes. OWT p.116
Harlem Shadows. Claude McKay. AVAN p.205; BANP p.170; CNAW p.293; HaS p.22;
    PoN p.331; PoNe p.99; SPCM p.60
Harlem: Sidewalk Icons. Oliver Pitcher. BTB p.160; CNAW p.773
Harlem Sounds: Hallelujah Corner. William Browne. AmNP p.173; BTB p.65

Harlem Street Walkers. Sterling A. Brown. SoR p.112
Harlem Sweeties. Langston Hughes. PoN p.101; PoNe p.190; SIH p.18; TYBP
    p.227
Harlem to Picasso. Ted Joans. AFR p.61
Harlem Vignettes Read, I felt I should make (like Hide Ho) a second Harlem
    marriage bed. Melvin Tolson. HaG p.119
Harlem Wine. Countee Cullen. CCC p.13
Harlem's night upon the world. Don L. Lee. DSNP p.154; WWW p.30
Harpers Ferry.* Seldon Rodman. PoN p.245; PoNe p.545
Harriet Beecher Stowe. Paul Laurence Dunbar. CPPLD p.191; KAL p.18
Harriet Tubman. Margaret Walker. PoN p.181; PoNe p.320
Harriet Tubman, freedom Fighter About 1823-1913, Maryland. Eloise Culver.
    GANIV p.23
Harvest, The. Zachary Withers. PAS p.31
Harvest Song. Jean Toomer. ITBLA p.156
Has a gold tooth, sits long hours on a stool thinking about money. LeRoi
    Jones. BMP p.111
Hat, The. Ted Joans. BPW p.110
Hatched in the orange story beds of old Ngoni fires. Craig Williamson.
    AfW p.2
Hate and love, hate and love, circles still remain. Roslyn Greer. TNV p.44
Hatred. Gwendolyn B. Bennett. AmNP p.73; BANP p.246; CaD p.160
Haunted. Mae V. Cowdery. WLOV p.54
Haunted Oak, The. Paul Laurence Dunbar. BANP p.58; CPPLD p.356; KAL p.21
"Haunting Music of the Ocean's Call, The." William C. Braithwaite. VER p.58
Havana Dreams. Langston Hughes. FOW p.34; GoS p.135; PoN p.100; PoNe p.189
Have Mercy, Lord! Langston Hughes. FCTJ p.53
Have the poets left a single spot for a patch to be sewn. Antar. TYBP p.37
Have you been sore discouraged in the fight. James Weldon Johnson. FYOP
    p.10
Have you dug the spill of Sugar Hill? Langston Hughes. PoN p.101; PoNe
    p.190; SIH p.18; TYBP p.227
Have you ever seen the moon. Lula Lowe Weeden. CaD p.228
Have you ever watched an ant work. Bernie Casey. LATP p.35
Have you noticed how black is for utility. Marion Nicholes. LiS p.20
Have You Seen It. Lula Lowe Weeden. CaD p.228
Have you seen the way people look at me. Bernie Casey. LATP p.12
Haven. Donald Jeffrey Hayes. AmNP p.92; PoN p.138; PoNe p.245
Having attained success in business. Frank Marshall Davis. KAL p.105; PoN
    p.143; PoNe p.254
Having Had You. Mae V. Cowdery. WLOV p.27
Having had you once and lost you. Mae V. Cowdery. WLOV p.27
Having heard the word provincial he looked it up and settled down. Albert
    Aubert. ATB p.27
Having reached my boiling point. Yvette Johnson. TNV p.55
Hawg Killin'. Lucile D. Goodlett. WGC p.21
He breathed the hot room alive with jazz and vivid colors. David Henderson.
    BlSp p.85
He calls them out with a musical shout. William S. Braithwaite. HFL p.85

He came, a dark youth singing in the dawn. James David Corrothers. ANP p.36; AVAN p.167; BANP p.73; CNAW p.190; PoN p.21; PoNe p.25

He came back and shot. LeRoi Jones. BMP p.118

He came from a dead-end world of under breed. Melvin Tolson. RWA p.17

He came in silvern armour trimmed with black. Gwendolyn B. Bennett. AmNP p.71; CaD p.160; ITBLA p.218; PoN p.109; PoNe p.206

He came to see her. Milas Love. BTh p.13

He carries his own strength and his own laughter. Langston Hughes. WeB p.77

He could not tell the way he came. William S. Braithwaite. AVAN p.144; BANP p.102

He dark and cold and chilled in vein. Zachary Withers. PAS p.24

He debated whether as a poet. Frank Marshall Davis. KAL p.106

He did not know that loving beauty is loving God. Isabelle McClellan Taylor. EbR p.134

He didn't say wear yr/ blackness in outer garments. Don L. Lee. BrT p.98; DCS p.33; DSNP p.100; FoM p.64

He dines alone surrounded by reflections of himself. Robert Hayden. AmNP p.110; BOR p.18; SPRH p.47

He doan care how po' I am. Raymond Garfield Dandridge. PAOP p.56; ZaP p.76

He does not think I blindly plod along some strange misleading way. Raymond Garfield Dandridge. ZaP p.41

He dwelt within a little hut. Joseph S. Cotter, Sr. SPPH p.58

He entered with the authority of politeness.* Karl Shapiro. PoN p.284; PoNe p.565

He felt the child-heart throb beside his own. Joseph S. Cotter, Sr. SPPH p.40; WSBO p.20

He glides so swiftly. Langston Hughes. FOW p.7

He grew up being curious. Gwendolyn Brooks. AnA p.vi

He had a dream.** Arthur Boze. BlWo p.15

He had a dream e x p loded down his throat. Mari Evans. BlSp p.70; IABW p.84

He had a whim and laughter it out. William S. Braithwaite. VANP p.101

He Had His Dream.** Paul Laurence Dunbar. CPPLD p.96; LOLL p.145

He had never lost the common touch. William L. Morrison. DaR p.43

He "had not where to lay his head." Frances Harper. PBFH p.30

He had a girl who has flaxen hair. Nikki Giovanni. BFBTBJ p.4

He has been many places. Langston Hughes. FOW p.76

He has gone too far...... Ted Joans. BPW p.74

He has no enemies, you say. Benjamin Clark. EBSP p.183

"He has no gain who never had a loss." Joseph S. Cotter, Sr. SPPH p.65

He heard the four winds and the seven seas. William S. Braithwaite. HFL p.96; SPWSB p.88

He is a weakling whose brute will is not. Joseph S. Cotter, Sr. SPPH p.68

He is firm and strong. Anonymous. TYBP p.11

He is foredoomed whose questing lips have known. Robert Hayden. HSITD p.11

He is found with homeless dogs. Robert Hayden. SPRH p.35

He is murdered upright in the day. Myron O'Higgins. IADB p.51; KAL p.161

"He is not fore doomed." Robert Hayden. HSITD p.11

He is Shaka the unshakable. Anonymous. TYBP p.16

He is very busy with his looking. Gwendolyn Brooks. FaP p.14

He is wasted now. Samuel Allen. BTB p.176

He jumped me while I was assailant. John Raven. BFM p.3; BrT p.134

He lifted up his pleading eyes and scanned each cruel face. Frances Harper. PBFH p.49

He looks back to me from life. Michael S. Harper. DJDC p.41

He loved her, and through many years. Paul Laurence Dunbar. CPPLD p.205

He mocks the God invisible. J. Henderson Brooks. BTh p.14

He never spoke a word to me. Countee Cullen. AmNP p.89; CCC p.14; FNP p.20; ITBLA p.158; OTIS p.8; PoN p.125; TYBP p.235;

He now is old, but he once was young. Joseph S. Cotter, Sr. CPJSC p.70

He prayed for patience, care and sorrow came. Clara Ann Thompson. AVAN p.133

He ran faster he jumped higher. Ted Joans. BPW p.18

He rode across like a cavalier. Countee Cullen. CCC p.17

He said a real revolution to change the structure of the society. Clarence Major. FoM p.8

He said in America would i like California? Bernie Casey. LATP p.9

He sang of life, serenity sweet. Paul Laurence Dunbar. CPPLD p.309; KAL p.20

He sat upon the rolling deck. Langston Hughes. DYTB p.63; GoS p.102

He saw life masquerade in Babylon. Joseph S. Cotter, Sr. CPJSC p.54

He scans the world with the world with calm and fearless eyes. James Edward McCall. BTB p.142; CaD p.34

He scrubbles some in prose and verse. Paul Laurence Dunbar. CPPLD p.76; LOLL p.112

He see the brussels lawn. Melvin Tolson. RWA p.32

He Sees through Stone.** Etheridge Knight. NBP p.80

He sits in the corner of late winter. Raymond Patterson. BTB p.157

He sits on a hill. Langston Hughes. FOW p.84

He snuggles his fingers. Sterling A. Brown. BTB p.58; GoS p.171; PoNe p.165; SoR p.79; SoS p.50

He spoke his love so bashfully. Joseph S. Cotter, Sr. SPPH p.69

He Spy. Ted Joans. BPW p.51

He stood before my heart's closed door. Frances Harper. PBFH p.58

He stood before the sons of Heth. Frances Harper. PBFH p.61

He strolled from door to door. B. Felton. BrT p.173

He thinks in black. Lucian Watkins. ANP p.121

He thought his race to labor and wait. John Wesley Fentress. EbR p.62

He threads his pink paws on the landing. Michael S. Harper. DJDC p.55

He tilled the old deserted fields with zeal. Joseph S. Cotter. EBAP p.191; LOF p.45

He took three big gulps.* Mason Jordan Mason. PoNe p.524

He volunteered his life and health to go to cruel War. Charles Fred White. PONS p.58

He walked tall. Albert Aubert. ATB p.28

He walks the land where hate has trod the path of brotherhood. Conrad Kent Rivers. SVH p.4

He was a good man. Waring Cuney. BANP p.285

He was a man who lived a peaceful life. Joseph S. Cotter, Sr. EBAP p.186; LOF p.26

He was born in Alabama. Gwendolyn Brooks. CNAW p.516; PoN p.189

He was free, the patriarch of our house! Dio Lewis. EbR p.102

He was fretful it happened again it was forced this time. Clarence Major.
    SMA p.44

He was, in truth, a man whose genius dwelt. Joseph S. Cotter, Sr. LOF p.45

He was married for a short time. Don L. Lee. BrT p.87

He was my teacher a continent of years ago. Melvin Tolson. LUP p.45; RWA
    p.60

He was shot, you see shot, you see. Patricia. FoM p.32

He was there this day in Tunisia. Ted Joans. AFR p.37

He went there. Rui Nogar. TYBP p.187

He went to being called a colored man after answering to "hey nigger." Maya
    Angelou. JGM p.43

He who has lost all. David Diop. TYBP p.138

He who has rolled his pants up to his knees. Herbert Clark Johnson. PoN
    p.161; PoNe p.284

He who laughed last, laughed best. Charles Fred White. PONS p.128

He who lives by the sword dies by the sword. John Sinclair. NBP p.122

He who saved Ankoma oh nature. Anonymous. TYBP p.14

He who thinks immortality flaming with furious fidelity could be dead has no
    head. Keorapetse W. Kgositsile. BrT p.75

He whose might you sang so well. Countee Cullen. CCC p.67

He wore a white shirt and bow tie. Don L. Lee. DSNP p.73

He wore clean white cotton cloth pants. Ted Joans. BPW p.69

He wore his coffin for a hat. Countee Cullen. CCC p.56; OTIS p.34

He would slump to his knees, now that his agonies. Robert Hayden. BOR p.37

He wrote upon his heart. Donald Jeffrey Hayes. CaD p.188

Head of Lincoln looks down from the wall, The. Langston Hughes. OWT p.46

Headline, The. Arthur Boze. BlWo p.16

Headline read "Black people have shootout with Klan in South Carolina."
    Arthur Boze. BlWo p.16

Heah ole ooman! Heah me. Joseph S. Cotter, Sr. CPJSC p.66; WSBO p.58

Heahd er sermon tudder night. Joseph S. Cotter, Sr. CPJSC p.41; WSBO p.62

Healer of the New Day. Marion Nicholes. LiS p.22

Healing power is not found in Sterling White. Marion Nicholes. LiS p.22

Hear me, white brothers. Robert Hayden. HSITD p.27

Hear the prayer from a Plaquemine Jail. Margaret Walker. PFND p.27

Hear the sound it is unlike any other. Charles Patterson. NBP p.98

Hear Uncle Roger as he sings of old-time, half-forgotten things. Eli
    Shepperd. P1S p.52

Hear ye! Hear ye! Starting July 4th is bring in yr/ gun/ down/ to/ yr/
    hearest/ po/ lice/ station. Sonia Sanchez. WABP p.28

Heard de owl a hootin'. Langston Hughes. FCTJ p.82

Heard you that shriek? It rose. Frances Harper. AVAN p.41; EBAP p.31

Heart. Langston Hughes. FOW p.31

Heart claws out into the street. LeRoi Jones. BMP p.42

Heart free, hand free. William Stanley Braithwaite. AVAN p.49; ANP p.40;
    BANP p.105; CNAW p.225; HFL p.61; SPWSB p.49

Heart has need of some deceit, The. Countee Cullen. MASP p.72

Heart I hold is mine, The. LeRoi Jones. BMP p.126

Heart of a Woman, The. Georgia Douglas Johnson. ANP p.86; BANP p.181; CaD
    p.81; HWOP p.1; PoN p.57; PoNe p.73
Heart of a woman goes forth with the dawn, The. Georgia Douglas Johnson.
    ANP p.86; BANP p.181; CaD p.81; HWOP p.1; PoN p.57; PoNe p.73
Heart of my Heart, the day is chill. Paul Laurence Dunbar. CPPLD p.337
Heart of the soft, wild rose. William S. Braithwaite. LLL p.19
Heart of the South, my little girl is as hard and rigid as stone. Charles
    Fred White. PONS p.116
Heart of the Southland heed me pleading now. Paul Laurence Dunbar. CPPLD
    p.352
Heart of the Woods. Wesley Curtright. PoN p.159; PoNe p.280
Heart-Song. William S. Braithwaite. LLL p.65
Heartbroken. Raymond Garfield Dandridge. PeP p.34
Hearts of America, The. Charles Fred White. PONS p.116
Heather, high upon the hill, The. William C. Braithwaite. VER p.46
Heaven. Langston Hughes. DYTB p.38; FOW p.3; GoS p.144; LUP p.24
Heaven is the place. Langston Hughes. LUP p.24
Heaven is the place where **happiness is everywhere. Langston Hughes.** FOW
    p.3; GoS p.144
Heaven is the place where happiness is everywhere. Langston Hughes. DYTB
    p.38; FOW p.3; FOW p.115; GoS p.144; LUP p.24
Heaven: the City Called Heaven. Langston Hughes. GoS p.144
He'd play, after the bawdy songs and blues. Sterling A. Brown. AmNP p.55;
    SoR p.12
Heel and toe, heel and toe. Paul Laurence Dunbar. CPPLD p.274
Hegel. LeRoi Jones. BMP p.23
Hegira. Mari Evans. IABW p.31
Height overhead to the deeps. William S. Braithwaite. LLL p.80
Heights of Arlington were wrapped in snow, The. William S. Braithwaite.
    HFL p.80
Hell, Mary. Jon Eckels. BrT p.43
Hell, Mary Bell Jones, full of groans, the slum lord is on you. Jon Eckels.
    BrT p.43
Hello are u the suicide man? Sonia Sanchez. WABP p.12
Hello, Central, what's the matter with this line? W. C. Handy. GoS p.87
Hello dar, Miss Melerlee! John Wesley Holloway. BANP p.134; PoN p.17; PoNe
    p.19
Hello, ole man, you're a-gittin' gray. Paul Laurence Dunbar. CPPLD p.129;
    LOLL p.192
Hello, Sailor boy, in from the sea! Langston Hughes. WeB p.74
Help a brother, you never can tell. Milas Love. BTh p.50
"Help from Denis cease to crave." William C. Braithwaite. VER p.77
Help me O Lord, to face the coming foes. Waverly T. Carmichael. FHOF p.40
Help me to make my heart's a citadel. Ruby Berkley Goodwin. EbR p.67
Hemingway. Conrad Kent Rivers. SVH p.14
Henry O. Tanner, Painter, 1859-1937, Pennsylvania. Eloise Culver. GANIV
    p.49
Henry Wadsworth Longfellow, 1807-1882, Maine. Eloise Culver. GANIV p.34
Her bosom blossomed like a flower. William L. Morrison. DaR p.11
Her Christmas Gift. Charles Johnson. SOMP p.54

Her dark brown face is like a withered flower. Langston Hughes. WeB p.34
Her eyes? Dark pools of deepest shade. George Leonard Allen. CaD p.204
Her eyes gave forth a light that suffered so. Joseph S. Cotter, Sr. LOF
   p.47
Her eyes, marvelous sunrises. Sterling D. Plumpp. TGWL p.81
Her Eyes Twin Pools.** James Weldon Johnson. FYOP p.53
Her face is a meditative frown. Nora Blakely. TGWL p.14
Her face was a fair olive hue. William S. Braithwaite. HFL p.87
Her first, first three was a husband. Clarence Major. SAMP p.50
Her friends all call her "Skeeter." Eloise Culver. GANIV p.75
Her granmother called her from the playground. Nikki Giovanni. MyH p.5
Her great adventure ended. Langston Hughes. OWT p.33
Her life was dwarfed and wed to blight. Georgia Douglas Johnson. HWOP p.39
Her love is true I know. Waring Cuney. CaD p.213
Her mind was always happy. Tejumola Ologhoni. TGWL p.77
Her neon sign blared two Harlem blocks. Melvin Tolson. HaG p.38
Her nose on the draperies. LeRoi Jones. CNAW p.647
Her panties hang limp and wet. Ted Joans. AFR p.124
Her parents and her dolls destroyed. Robert Hayden. BTB p.112; SPRH p.18
Her room grows in her stale building. Clarence Major. BlSp p.131
Her skin is like dusk on the Eastern Horizon. Jean Toomer. KAL p.51
Her sleeping head with its great gelid mass. Robert Hayden. BOR p.38;
   SPRH p.58
Her teeth wore yellow socks with green tops. Ted Joans. BPW p.29
Her Thought and His. Paul Laurence Dunbar. CPPLD p.148
Her Way is The World's Ways. Joseph S. Cotter, Sr. RHY p.20
Here Africa take this gift of me. Ted Joans. AFR p.24
Here and now. Catharine Cater. AmNP p.148; PoN p.102; PoNe p.340
Here at the crossroads is the night so black. William Ellery Leonard. PoNe
   p.259
Here beneath a place of comfort time warns the blood of some dead seeker.
   Conrad Kent Rivers. FoM p.66
Here comes the Seventh Avenue. John Raven. BFM p.30
Here frowns the cruel thor stone on the slope. William C. Braithwaite. VER
   p.94
Here He Comes Again. LeRoi Jones. BMP p.54
Here hold I converse with some spirit pure. William C. Braithwaite. VER
   p.102
Here - Hold My Hand.** Mari Evans. IABW p.25
Here I come! Langston Hughes. PATL p.79
Here I set with a bitter old thought. Langston Hughes. SIH p.3
Here I sit with my shoes mismated. Langston Hughes. OWT p.98
Here in a Chicago museum, these small bells of Benin. Margaret Danner.
   BrT p.39
Here in the newspaper--the wreck of the East Bound. Russell Atkins. AmNP
   p.171; SoS p.98
Here in the wombed room. Maya Angelou. JGM p.5
Here in this ancient, dusty room. William C. Braithwaite. HFL p.92
Here is a place that is no place. Calvin C. Hernton. IADB p.17; ITBLA p.276;
   KAL p.197; NNPUSA p.102; PoNe p.403; SoS p.81

Hey, loser!   John Raven.   BFM p.31
Hey moon faced female with your under wear on upside down!   Ted Joans.   BPW
    p.114
Hey Ninny Neigh!   Langston Hughes.   SIH p.111
Hey Picasso aren't those moorish eyes you have.   Ted Joans.   AFR p.61
Hey there Nigger!   V. A. Reese.   BTh p.25
Hey there poleece.   Bobb Hamilton.   TYBP p.255
Hey Willie, how's ya doing?   Arthur Boze.   BlWo p.6
Hey you know where to eat.   Victor Hernandez Cruz.   SNA p.91
Hi! Miss Liza's got er banjer.   Daniel Webster Davis.   EBAP p.236
Hid in a close and lowly nook.   William S. Braithwaite.   LLL p.31
Hide Ho Heights and I, like the brims of old hats, slouched at a sepulchured
    table in the Zulu Club.   Melvin Tolson.   HaG p.64
Hideout Heights, a Black Gigas, **ghosted above us** in a fun vaulting of awkward
    age lights and shadows.   Melvin Tolson.   HaG p.71
Hidesong.   Aig Higo.   TYBP p.159
High above the city streets he swings.   Ricardo Weeks.   EbR p.156
High amid gothic rocks the altar stands.   Robert Hayden.   BOR p.52; SPRH p.32
High Tide.   Countess W. Twitty.   EbR p.146
High To Low.   Langston Hughes.   CNAW p.310
High Top!   James Pipes.   ZJP p.81
High upon a mountain top a lonely laurel pined.   William L. Morrison.   DaR
    p.13
High/ yellow / black/ girl walken like the sun u be.   Sonia Sanchez.   BlSp
    p.190
High-yellow of my heart, with breasts like tangerines.   Emile Roumer.   PoN
    p.361 TYBP p.90
Highway of Blood.   Victor Hernandez Cruz.   SNA p.93
Hills, The.   Frenchy Jolene Hodges.   BlW p.8
Hills are calling, The.   Frenchy Jolene Hodges.·   BlW p.8
Hills are wroth; the stones have scored you bitterly, The.   Arna Bontemps.
    CaD p.165; KAL p.82
Hills of Sewanee, The.   George Marion McClellan.   BANP p.95
His Answer.   Clara Ann Thompson.   AVAN p.133
His blond magnificence keyed his vanity.   Melvin Tolson.   RWAp.68
His Body Is An Eloquence.   Pinkie Gordon Lane.   TGWL p.66
His brother after dinner once a year would play the piano.   June Jordan.
    SCh p.13; SoS p.28
His clothes were thrown out into the snow.   John Raven.   BFM p.15
His country seared its conscience through its gain.   Joseph S. Cotter.
    CPJSC p.45; WSBO p.19
His desires, growing from timid heights.   Sarah Webster Fabio.   PoNe p.393
His Excellency General Washington.   Phillis Wheatley.   EBAP p.108; KAL p.5;
    PAL p.51; PoN p.6; PoNe p.7; PPW p.89
His feet were bad / bad 'er than he was.   Ted Joans.   BPW p.60
His fingers leaned forcefully against the neck of a broken gin bottle.   Don
    L. Lee.   DSNP p.175; WWW p.51
His friends went off and left him dead.   J. Henderson Brooks.   AmNP p.95;
    CaD p.193; PoN p.133; PoNe p.236
His guiding star cast our shadows quietly behind us.   Edward Richards.   EbR
    p.125

His headstone said. Nikki Giovanni. BFBTBJ p.56; BOL p.30; BrT p.54; TNV
    p.37
His lips move unceasingly. Flavien Ronalvo. MBP p.38
His moods are sorrow's cenotaph. Joseph S. Cotter, Sr. CPJSC p.69
His spirit in smoke ascended to high heaven. Claude McKay. AVAN p.206;
    BANP p.168; BLIA p.166; HaS p.51; IADB p.64; SPCM p.37
Historic Episodes. Peter Wellington Clark. EbR p.39
Historic Moment, An. William J. Harris. BOL p.15
Historical Footnote to Consider Only When All Else Fails (for Barbara
    Crosby). Nikki Giovanni. BFBTBJ p.16
Historical Review, A. Charles Fred White. PONS p.66
History. Langston Hughes. PATL p.69
History As Process. LeRoi Jones. BMP p.38
History of blacklife is put down in the motions of mouths and blackhands
    with fingering lips and puckered raven fingers. S. E. Anderson. BlSp
    p.6
History of the Poet As A Whore (to all Negro Poets Who Deal in Whi-te Parono-
    masia). Don L. Lee. DCS p.40; DSNP p.106
Hit me! Jab me! Langston Hughes. OWT p.130; PATL p.18
Hit's been drizzlin' an' been sprinklin'. Paul Laurence Dunbar. AVAN p.67;
    CPPLD p.290; WMS p.17
Ho! Cra-ab Man! Anonymous. ITBLIA p.125
Ho! Growler. James Pipes. ZJP p.51
Hoboes in the hoboes jungle are supping on gruel, The.* Mason Jordan Mason.
    PoNe p.527
Hoc erat in votis. William S. Braithwaite. HFL p.53
Hog-Killin' Times in Dixie land. Eli Shepperd. PlS p.70
Hog Meat. Daniel Webster Davis. AVAN p.100; BANP p.83
Hokku Poems. Richard Wright. AmNP p.104; IADB p.87
"Hol' on what you mean by walkin' wid a man? Waverly T. Carmichael. FHOF
    p.6
Hol' up yo' haid, ol' mule, I say! John Wesley Holloway. AVAN p.185
Hold Fast to dreams. Langston Hughes. DYTB p.44; GoS p.194
Hold me she told me. LeRoi Jones. BMP p.36
Hold my rooster, hold my hen. Anonymous. GoS p.16; TYBP p.198
Hold up, chil'en, de ole man 'bleeged to rest. Eli Shepperd. PlS p.44
Holidays, The. Charles Fred White. PONS p.30
Holland again to holler loud again. Ted Joans. AFR p.42
Hollow eye sees moons dance music in the pupil as it studies the changing
    world. LeRoi Jones. BMP p.121
Holly Berry and Mistetoe. William S. Braithwaite. LLL p.63
Holy Days. Larry Neal. BlSp p.148
Holy Easter, God-sent solace. Raymond Garfield Dandridge. ZaP p.27
Holy the days of the old prune face junkie men. Larry Neal. BlSp p.148
Holyghost woman an ol nomad moving thru the south. Clarence Major. SAM
    p.19; SoS p.52
Homage is Thine Because for Sooth, Thy Face. Joseph S. Cotter, Sr. LOF p.50
Homage to the Empress of the Blues. Robert Hayden. BOR p.15; PoN p.164;
    PoNe p.290; SPRH p.44
Home. Raymond Garfield Dandridge. PeP p.19; ZaP p.9

Home. Ted Joans. AFR p.20
Home Agin, an' home to stay. Paul Laurence Dunbar. CPPLD p.427
Home and Mother. Raymond Garfield Dandridge. PeP p.28
Home Instruction. Waverly T. Carmichael. FHOF p.31
"Home Sick." James E. McGirt. FYSS p.4
Home Sweet Home. Frances Harper. PBFH p.26
Home Thoughts. Claude McKay. BLIA p.168; GoS p.76; HaS p.11; SPCM p.21
Homecoming. Gordon Parks. InL (unpaged)
Homesick Blues. Langston Hughes. CaD p.147; FCTJ p.24
Homing. Arna Bontemps. CaD p.172
Homing Swallows. Claude McKay. HaS p.15; SPCM p.18
Honey and Roses. William L. Morrison. DaR p.11
Honey Babe. Langston Hughes. OWT p.40
Honey Babe, you braid your hair too tight. Langston Hughes. OWT p.40
Honey is sweet, and the Queen Bee knows it. Joseph S. Cotter, Sr. CPJSC
    p.65
Honey people murder mercy U.S.A. June Jordan. SCh p.15; SoS p.115
Honey, pepper, leaf-green limes. Agnes Maxwell-Hall. MBP p.43; PoN p.310;
    TYBP p.117
Honey when de man call out de las train. Sterling Brown. AmNP p.53; BLIA
    p.218; BTB p.56; CNAW p.404; GoS p.159; PoN p.92; PoNe p.174; SoR p.48
Honey, whin de dusk creep long de piney hill. Lucile D. Goodlett. WGC p.52
Honey Whut's you askin'? Joseph S. Cotter, Sr. CPJSC p.26; WSBO p.51
Honkies always talking 'bout Black Folks. Nikki Giovanni. BFBTBJ p.21
Hope. Joseph S. Cotter, Sr. LOF p.22
Hope. Paul Laurence Dunbar. CPPLD p.403
Hope. Langston Hughes. DYTB p.19; SIH p.16
Hope. Georgia Douglas Johnson. CaD p.75
Hope, and the love of life that's in it. Jesse Franklin Patterson. EbR p.
    p.113
Hope is a crushed stalk. Pauli Murray. AmNP p.107
Hopeless useless the sound makes me tremble. Victor Hernandez Cruz. SNA
    p.25
Hosea. Margaret Walker. PFND p.27
Hospital / poem (for Etheridge, 9/26/69). Sonia Sanchez. WABP p.29
Host of loves is the City, A: LeRoi Jones. BMP p.28
Hot Blood/ Bad Blood. Felipe Luciano. BlSp p.124
Hot blood/ bad blood you a machete and a pyramid. Felipe Luciano. BlSp
    p.124
Hot ice, in this car my sister drives like mad. Clarence Major. SAM p.49
Hounded slave that flags in the race leans by the fence blowing cover'd with
    sweet, The.* Walt Whitman. PoN p.213; PoNe p.468
Houndi. LeRoi Jones. BMP p.7
"Hour To Spend, An."** William C. Braithwaite. VER p.115
Hour with the red letter stumbles in, The. Melvin Tolson. HaG p.51
House catch on fire. Anonymous. BLIA p.48; ITBLA p.124
House Cleaning. Nikki Giovanni. BrT p.61
House In Taos, A. Langston Hughes. CaD p.152; FOW p.73; LUP p.30
House of Death, The. William S. Braithwaite. HFL p.58
House of Falling Leaves. William S. Braithwaite. HFL p.13; PoN p.42; PoNe
    p.47

House of falling leaves we entered in. William S. Braithwaite. HFL p.13;
   PoN p.42; PoNe p.47
House of Time, The. William Cousins. EbR p.53
How Can I Forget?** Alice Robinson. BTh p.46
How can you forget? Langston Hughes. CNAW p.309
How can you sing, America. John Henrik Clarke. EbR p.43
How Come Dat? Lucy Mae Turner. BCF p.26
How cool beneath this stone the soft moss lies. PoN p.174; PoNe p.301
How dare you question him, or doubt. Raymond Garfield Dandridge. PAOP p.53;
   ZaP p.78
How Death Came. Anonymous. TYBP p.5
How desolate is life for those who live within the wall of woes. Charles
   Fred White. PONS p.126
How did it happen that we quarreled? Jessie Fauset. CaD p.65
How did You Feel Mary. May Miller. BTB p.151
How Do You Want Yours? Ted Joans. BPW p.6
How envied, how admired a male. Countee Cullen. OTIS p.189
How far have i yet to go. Bernie Casey. LATP p.17
How have I found this favor in your sight. Countee Cullen. B1C p.33
How I can lie to you. Maya Angelou. JGM p.21
How like the consummation and despair. Robert Hayden. PoN p.167
How long, baby, how long. Anonymous. BLIA p.48; ITBLA p.124
How Long Blues. Anonymous. BLIA p.48; ITBLA p.124
How Lucy Backslip. Paul Laurence Dunbar. AVAN p.76; CPPLD p.255
How many bullets does it take to kill a fifteen-year-old kid? Langston
   Hughes. PATL p.15
How many days and weeks and years. Zachary Withers. PAS p.20
How many death songs will we write? Mari Evans. IABW p.85
How many of u niggers watched ted kennedy on tv yesterday. Sonia Sanchez.
   WABP p.24
How Many Silent Centuries Sleep in My Sultry Veins?** Margaret Walker. PFND
   p.15
How many years since 1619 have I been singing spirituals? Margaret Walker.
   FMP p.26
How much living have you done? Georgia Douglas Johnson. AmNP p.22
How oft inflated hope carries us on. Joseph S. Cotter, Sr. LOF p.22
How often as we trudge along. Joseph S. Cotter, Sr. SPPH p.77
How old brown took Harper's Ferry.* Edmund Clarence Stedman. PoN p.239;
   PoNe p.493
How placidly this silent river rolls. William S. Braithwaite. HFL p.23
How quiet it is in this sick room. Langston Hughes. WeB p.88
How Rich the Moon. Lance Jeffers. BTB p.130
How sad it must be to love so many women. Sonia Sanchez. BrT p.139; WABP
   p.14
How Shall I Woo Thee.** Paul Laurence Dunbar. CPPLD p.479
How soft and bright at break of day. Lucy Mae Turner. BCF p.45
How still, how strangely still the water is today. Langston Hughes. DYTB
   p.56; WeB p.75
How strange the fairest pearls are found deep in the ocean's womb. Peter
   Wellington Clark. EbR p.36

How sweet the music sounded. Paul Laurence Dunbar. CPPLD p.470
How tender the heart grows. Una Marson. PoN p.325
How thin and sharp is the moon tonight! Langston Hughes. DYTB p.55; MBP
    p.4; WeB p.44
How this car broke down. Victor Hernandez Cruz. SNA p.45
How those loose rocks got piled up here like this. Ed. Roberson. PoNe p.430
How to Change The U.S.A. Harry Edwards. NBP p.48
How to describe fall from now on. Clarence Major. SAM p.25
How true, dear, my love is. James E. McGirt. FYSS p.33
How, well I still remember it was at flood-tide that we met. William L.
    Morrison. DaR p.22
How would you have us, as we are? James Weldon Johnson. FYOP p.5
How you Feel. Victor Hernandez Cruz. SNA p.89
Howcome de fools have a spcial day and de wise dey have nose? Eli Shepperd.
    P1S p.52
"Howdy, Honey Howdy!" Paul Laurence Dunbar. CPPLD p.317; WMS p.777
Howdy, sister Mandy! Richard T. Hamilton. HeD p.18
How's a man to write a sonnet, can you tell. Paul Laurence Dunbar. AVAN
    p.89; CPPLD p.182
Hu! Hu! some fo'ks won't take nuffin. Lucy Mae Turner. BCF P.11
Huddled there on the sidewalk is heartbreak. **Beatrice M. Murphy.** TNV p.140
Human Soul. Rene Maran. TYBP p.71
Human to Spirit Humanism for animals.** LeRoi Jones. BMP p.201
Humility. Anita Scott Coleman. EbR p.51
Humility of the Soul. Zachary Withers. PAS p.27
Humor. Charles B. Johnson. SOMP p.34
Humorous Verse. Abu Dolama. TYBP p.43; MBP p.33
Hump, The. Ted Joans. AFR p.122
Hunchback Girl: She Thinks of Heaven. Gwendolyn Brooks. KAL p.151; ITBLA
    p.217
Hunger. Anonymous. TYBP p.156
Hunger. Countee Cullen. CpS p.64; OTIS p.66
Hunger. Frances Merrill Foster. EbR p.64
Hunger makes a person climb up to the ceiling. Anonymous. TYBP p.156
Hungry Cancer will not let him rest, A. Countee Cullen. B1C p.39; OTIS
    p.91
Hunted. Una Marson. PoN p.324
Hunted hare seeks out some dark retreat, The. Una Marson. PoN p.324
Hunting Song. Paul Laurence Dunbar. CPPLD p.242
Hurt was the nation with a mighty wound. Paul Laurence Dunbar. CPPLD p.295
Hurry, Hurry. Bernie Casey. LATP p.64
Hush, Chillun. Lucile D. Goodlett. WGC p.51
Hush! I hyeah a mighty singin' over on de hill. **Waverly T. Carmichael.**
    FHOG p.35
Hush is over all the teeming lists, A. Paul Laurence Dunbar. CPPLD p.7;
    LOLL p.8
Hush Little Lily. Sterling A. Brown. SoR p.110
Hush! my baby; stop yer fuss. James Edwin Campbell. EBAP p.238
Hush Now. Dorothy C. Parrish. TNV p.88
Hush now baby, not a peep. Dorothy C. Parrish. TNV p.88

Hush now, Mammy's baby scaid. Waverly T. Carmichael. FHOF p.3
Hush! tis a voice I heah afar. Waverly T. Carmichael. FHOF p.44
Hushaby, Hushaby, dark one at my knee. Countee Cullen. OTIS p.165
Hushed By the Hands of Sleep.** Angelina Weld Grimké. CaD p.36
Hyeah come Caesar Higgins. Paul Laurence Dunbar. BLIA p.111; CPPLD p.232
Hyeah dat singin' in de medders. Paul Laurence Dunbar. CPPLD p.339; LiG
    p.88
Hyena. Anonymous. TYBP p.9
Hymn. Alice Walker. ONC p.41
Hymn. Paul Laurence Dunbar. CPPLD p.106; LOLL p.157
Hymn, A. Paul Laurence Dunbar. AVAN p.61; CPPLD p.156
Hymn. Paul Laurence Dunbar. CPPLD p.213
Hymn Chune, A. Eli Shepperd. P1S p.127
Hymn for the Slain in Battle. William S. Braithwaite. LLL p.78
Hymn for Zion's Centennial. Joseph S. Cotter, Sr. LOF p.46
Hymn of Counsel, A. Charles Fred White. PONS p.60
Hymn of Freedom. Eli Shepperd. P1S p.140
Hymn of Rejoicing. Eli Shepperd. P1S p.132
Hymn of Repentence. Eli Shepperd. P1S p.117
Hymn of Safety. Eli Shepperd. P1S p.139
Hymn of the Dead. Eli Shepperd. P1S p.112
Hymn of the Winds. Eli Shepperd. P1S p.134
Hymn of Time. Eli Shepperd. P1S p.146
Hymn to Humanity, An. (To S.P.G. Esq.). Phillis Wheatley. PAL p.62; PPW
    p.45
Hymn to the Evening, An. Phillis Wheatley. ANP p.10; CNAW p.13; PAL p.83;
    PPW p.26
Hymn to the Morning, An. Phillis Wheatley. CNAW p.12
Hymn to the Morning, A. Phillis Wheatley. ANP p.10
Hymn to the Sun, The. Anonymous. TYBP p.21
Hymn Written after Jeremiah Preached to me in a Dream. Owen Dodson. AmNP
    p.124; KAL p.122
Hymns of the Black Belt. Eli Shepperd. P1S p.111

- I -

I, a circus battleships carrying heavy laughter. Clarence Major. AmNP
    p.182
I acknowledge I did wrong, I stayed in de wilderness mos' too long. Eli
    Shepperd. P1S p.141
I ain't gonna mistreat ma good gal any more. Langston Hughes. FCTJ p.62
I ain't gonna work no mo' no mo'. V. A. Reese. BTh p.25
I ain't no wagon, ain't no dray. Anonymous. GoS p.17
I ain't seen no poems stop a .38. Don L. Lee. BrT p.86
I ain't seen the light till I saw the night black ass of Georgia White.
    Everett Hoagland. BrT p.71
I aint Turn Susie Out. Waverly Turner Carmichael. FHOF p.6
I always like summer. Nikki Giovanni. BFBTBJ p.65; BrT p.55; BOL p.58
I always liked house cleaning. Nikki Giovanni. BrT p.61
I always sought to fill the days I knew. Alpheus Butler. EbR p.20

I always think that when I see you. Gwendolyn Brooks. FaP p.20
I always wanted to be a bridesmaid. Nikki Giovanni. MyH p.13
I am a black pierrot. Langston Hughes. WeB p.61
I Am a Black Woman. Mari Evans. BLIA p.349
I am a boy. Helen Morgan Brooks. PoNe p.277
I am a child of the valley. Margaret Walker. FMP p.20
I am a Cowboy in the Boat of Ra.** Ishamel Reed. NBP p.109
I Am A Negro. Muhammad Al-Fituri. TYBP p.54
I am a Negro. Langston Hughes. ANP p.104; DYTB p.71; WeB p.19
I am a part of this. Owen Dodson. PLL p.89
I am a reaper whose muscles set at sundown. All my oats are cradled. Jean
    Toomer. ITBLA p.156
I am a rover ever wandering far into the hidden places of a soul. Alpheus
    Butler. EbR p.21
I am a sincere man. Jose Marti. TYBP p.100
I am a slave born Black. Anonymous. MBP p.54
I am a soul in the world. LeRoi Jones. AmNP p.179; CNAW p.647
I am a Spiritual Alcoholic.* Anonymous. BTB p.42
I am afraid to laugh! Ariel Williams. BTh p.17
I am Africa. Nick Aaron Ford. SFD p.38
I am always lonely fer things I've never had. Nikki Giovanni. BFBTBJ p.11
I am an American. Leslie M. Collins. BTB p.70
I am an iconoclast. Walter Everette Hawkins. ANP p.67
I am an inter-citian, I am Black as you can see. Yillie Boy, TNV p.18
"I am Antar!" he chants. Anonymous. MBP p.66
I am as fond of fun and jokes as other real red-blooded folks. Raymond Gar-
    field Dandridge. PAOP p.26
I Am Black. Kali Grosvenor. PBK p.15
I am Black and I have seen Black hands, millions and millions of them.
    Richard Wright. PoN p.154; SoS p.112
I am Black but still if I die let God take my soul. Kali Grosvenor. PBK
    p.16
"I am but clay," the sinner plead. Paul Laurence Dunbar. CPPLD p.183
"I am Casper, I have brought Frankincense. Ruben Darion. MBP p.74
I am drowsy, having drunk two deeply of the silence of the night. Joseph S.
    Cotter, Sr. SPPH p.66
I am driven mad with the printed word. Allen Polite. NNPUSA p.103
I am drunk with beauty. Mae V. Cowdery. WLOV p.62
I am feelin' kind o' sad 'bout my mother dear. Waverly T. Carmichael. FHOF
    p.47
I am for sleeping and forgetting. Countee Cullen. CCC p.108; OTIS p.43
I am glad day long.** William S. Braithwaite. AmNP p.15; BANP p.106; GoS p.4;
    LLL p.13; SPWSB p.65
I am going back. Ted Joans. BPW p.115
I am going to rise. Mari Evans. BOL p.50; CNAW p.765; IABW p.70
I am Happy Today.** William H. Green. BTh p.46
I am Here to Announce.** Ronda Davis. BlSp p.48
I Am Hungry. Ted Joans. BPW p.84
I am hurting because I am hungry. Ted Joans. BPW p.84
I am Indian. Anita Scott Coleman. EbR p.48

I been t'inkin' 'bout de preachah; whut he said de othah night. Paul Lau-
    rence Dunbar. BLIA p.111; CPPLD p.346
I be'n down in ole Kentucky. Paul Laurence Dunbar. CPPLD p.64; LOLL p.91
I Blow You A Kiss.** William S. Braithwaite. LLL p.73
I Break the Sky. Owen Dodson. PLL p.84
I breathe the lyric of my love. Georgia Douglas Johnson. HWOP p.48
I broke ma heart this mornin'. Langston Hughes. FCTJ p.58
I buried you deeper last night. Frank Horne. AmNP p.56; BANP p.277; CaD
    p.113
I Called Them Trees. Gerald W. Barrax. AKOR p.40
I called you through the silent night. Georgia Douglas Johnson. HWOP p.30
I came as a shadow. Lewis Alexander. PoN p.84; PoNe p.158
I came from somewhere. Jose Craveirinha. MBP p.106; TYBP p.186
I came in the blinding sweep of **ecstatic pain.** Frank Horne. BTB p.120;
    CaD p.115; **PoN p.79; PoNe p.151**
I came to the **crowd seeking friends.** Nikki Giovanni. BFBTBJ p.5
I came upon him first chance he was awake. Charles B. Johnson. SOMP p.31
I **Can No Longer Sing.**** Mari Evans. IABW p.23
I can be alone by myself. Nikki Giovanni. BrT p.65
I can be the beautiful Black man. LeRoi Jones. BMP p.177
I can clear a beach or swimming pool without touching water. Don L. Lee.
    BrT p.85; DSNP p.32
I can hey on water. Langston Hughes. SIH p.52
I can remember when I was a little young girl. Jessie Fauset. ANP p.89;
    AVAN p.194; BANP p.207
I can remember wind-swept streets of cities. Margaret Walker. FMP p.56
I can see your house, babe. Langston Hughes. OWT p.97
I cannot be hurt anymore. Henry Dumas. BOL p.7
I cannot fight a memory. Countess W. Twitty. EbR p.146
I cannot hold my peace, John Keats. Countee Cullen. BANP p.226; CCC p.102;
    CaD p.184; CNAW p.329; OTIS p.41
I cannot tell how high my soul takes wing. William S. Braithwaite. LLL p.56
I care not for the clash of steel. Raymond Garfield Dandridge. PeP p.42
I care not how soon I leave here. Charles Fred White. PONS p.49
I catch the pattern. Langston Hughes. FOW p.47
I Celebrate the Sons of Malcolm.** June Jordan. SCh p.78
I **climbed towards** you on a ray of moonlight. Emmanuel Boundzekei-Dongala.
    TYBP p.148
I **Closed my Shutters Late Last Night.**** Georgia Douglas Johnson. PoN p.59;
    PoNe p.79
I continued to walk backwards with no balance. Clarence Major. BlSp p.132
I could love her with a love so warm. Fenton Johnson. AmNP p.26
I Could Not Know. Lois Royal Hughes. EbR p.90
I could take the Harlem night. Langston Hughes. IADB p.14; LUP p.26
I could tell you if I wanted to. Langston Hughes. PATL p.85
I crossed the Sahara. Ted Joans. AFR p.13
I crushed a little flower. James Edgar Smith. EbR p.130
I did not know my place. Ruby Berkley Goodwin. EbR p.68
I did not know she'd take it so. Countee Cullen. ChG p.101; CpS p.89; GoS
    p.81

I did not know that life could be so sweet. Paul Laurence Dunbar. CPPLD
    p.414
I didn't live in rat filled tenements. Arthur Boze. BlWo p.4
I do not ask for love, ah! no. Georgia Douglas Johnson. CaD p.77
I do not care for sleep, I'll wait awhile. William Moore. ANP p.61
I do not expect the spirit of Penelope. Etheridge Knight. BrT p.81
I do not hate you. Langston Hughes. WeB p.106
I do not know the ocean's song. James McGirt. FYSS p.2
I do not long to be a king. Nick Aaron Ford. SFD p.13
I do not want to turn away. Robert J. Abrams. BTB p.35; NNPUSA p.111
I don' ker' 'bout yo' cake an' pie. Waverly T. Carmichael. FHOF p.37
I don' know no proper words fo t' say up heah. Lucile D. Goodlet. WGC p.33
I done got 'uligion, honey, an' I's happy ez a king. Paul Laurence Dunbar.
    AVAN p.83; CPPLD p.235
I don't believe in 'ristercrats. Paul Laurence Dunbar. AmNP p.6; CPPLD
    p.223
I don't like girls named Shirley. John Raven. BFM p.31
I don't love you. LeRoi Jones. BMP p.55
I doubt not God is good, well-meaning, kind. Countee Cullen. AmNP p.88;
    BANP p.231; BLIA p.153; BTB p.78; CaD p.182; CCC p.3; CNAW p.324; IADB
    p.88; ITBLA p.158; OTIS p.3; PoN p.132; PoNe p.233; SoS p.128; TYBP p.235
I drank Dubonnet and began to meditate - out loud. Don L. Lee. DSNP p.36
I Dream a World.** Langston Hughes. AmNP p.71
I Dream of War.** Ricardo Weeks. EbR p.156
I dreamed all my fortitude screamed. M. Carl Rowan. AmNP p.150; PoN p.204;
    PoNe p.204
I dreamed that I was a rose. James Weldon Johnson. FYOP p.54
I drink to your glory my god. Tehicaya U Tam'si. TYBP p.149
I entreated ... "O beloved death. Mae V. Cowdery. WLOV p.38
I fast and pray and go to church. Countee Cullen. CCC p.101; FNP p.19
I fear all. Stanley F. Morris. BTB p.156
I feel myself in need. George Moses Horton. ANP p.14; CNAW p.36; KAL p.9
I feel ridiculous. Leon Damas. TYBP p.121
I fell in love. Ted Joans. BPW p.48
I felt this itching all over my skin. Raymond Patterson. SoS p.108
I felt today within me life. Marion Nicholes. LiS p.16
I 'fess Ise ugly, big an' ruff. Raymond Garfield Dandridge. PAOP p.41; ZaP
    p.68
I find myself in bed. Ted Joans. AFR p.133
I find the world viewed as a whole. Doretta Lowery. BTh p.63
I first read his work in June 1942. Ted Joans. BPW p.13
I forgotten who I is. LeRoi Jones. BMP p.196
I found you and I lost you. Paul Laurence Dunbar. ANP p.24; CPPLD p.411
I fucked your mother on top of a house. LeRoi Jones. BMP p.105
I gazed sadly from my window. Eugene Redmond. TNV p.99
I Give You thanks my God.** Bernard Dadie. TYBP p.44
I got a friend named Percy. Glenny Myles. NBP p.92
I Got a Home in Dat Rock.** Anonymous. ITBLA p.98
I got a job now. Langston Hughes. FCTJ p.38
I got me a question. Sterling A. Brown. SoR p.25

I got my eyes, ears, mouth, nose and toes. Ted Joans. BPW p.117

I Got the Blues. Anonymous. TYBP p.203

I got those little white schoolhouse blues.* Florence Beeker Lennon. PoNe
   p.514

I got those sad old weary blues. Langston Hughes. OWT p.102

I greet you son, with joy and winter rue. Jonathan Brooks. PoN p.135; PoNe
   p.240

I grew a rose once more to please mine eye. Paul Laurence Dunbar. CPPLD
   p.19; LOLL p.24

I grew a rose within a garden fair. Paul Laurence Dunbar. LOLL p.23

I grieve to think of you alone. Donald Jeffrey Hayes. PoN p.131; PoNe
   p.243

I hab been to many a meetin. Clarence F. Carr. HeD p.9

I had a dream a varied dream. Frances Harper. PBFH p.82

I had a gal, she was driving alone. Langston Hughes. SIH p.115

I had a rail good, easy job, valet fo' Mr. Lee. Raymond Garfield Dandridge.
   PeP p.29

I had a rendezvous with love. Lois Royal Hughes. EbR p.89

I had know winters for so long. Mae V. Cowdery. WLOV p.45

I had ma clothes cleaned. Langston Hughes. FCTJ p.65; GoS p.117

I had no need to be Juliet's deatheyed boy. Gerald W. Barrax. AKOR p.27

I had no thought of violets of late. Alice Dunbar Nelson. ANP p.84; BANP
   p.164; CaD p.72; PoN p.41; PoNe p.46

I had not known before. Paul Laurence Dunbar. CPPLD p.392

I had some cards printed. Langston Hughes. OWT p.7

I had thought of putting an altar here in the house. Isabella Maria Brown.
   NNPUSA p.61; PoNe p.341

I had to kick their law into their teeth in order to save them. Gwendolyn
   Brooks. KAL p.152

I had two braids and a rubber Ball. Linda Brown. BTB p.54

I had two husbands. Langston Hughes. OWT p.24

I had wanted to see you sleeping. Gerald W. Barrax. AKOR p.35

"I had always laked good eatin's. James D. Corrothers. EABP p.238

I has been er backwoods teacher in my day. Joseph S. Cotter, Sr. CPJSC
   p.31; WSBO p.43

I has hyeahd o' people dancin' an' I's hyeahd o' people singin'. Paul Lau-
   rence Dunbar. CPPLD p.252

I hate to die this way with the quiet. Langston Hughes. SIH p.66

I hate to lose something. Maya Angelou. JGM p.8

I have a dream, my vision is long. Frenchy J. Hodges. BlW p.16

I have a dream of where when I grew old having no further joy to take in lip
   or limb. Countee Cullen. MASP p.91; OTIS p.156

I have a dream that one day on the red hills of Georgia. Martin Luther King.
   TYBP p.249

I have a friend.** Anne Spencer. CaD p.47

I have a rendezvous with life. Countee Cullen. CaD p.180

I have a rendezvous with life. Nick Aaron Ford. SFD p.28

I have a river in mind. Owen Dodson. PoN p.172; PoNe p.298

I have a song that few will sing. Leslie Pinckney Hill. AVAN p.195

I have arrived. Mari Evans. BLIA p.348; IABW p.68; IADB p.92

I have   TITLE AND FIRST LINE INDEX

I have awakened from the unknowing to the knowing. Bette Darcie Latimer.
    PoN p.208; PoNe p.392
I have been alive but dying. Gerald W. Barrax. AKOR p.45
I have been alive since Friday but in my room studying and writing. Gerald
    W. Barrax. AKOR p.44
I have been seeking what I have never found. Langston Hughes. PATL p.44
I have been to the desert. Ted Joans. AFR p.64
I have built my tower on the wings of a spider. Nikki Giovanni. MyH p.45
I have come, as it were, from nowhere. Charles Fred White. PONS p.32
I have come to catch birds. Anonymous. TYBP p.28
I have denied my body and my soul. Robert Hayden. HSITD p.38
I have done so little. Langston Hughes. LUP p.29
I have escaped.** William C. Braithwaite. VER p.65
I have filched a mite ob time. Raymond Garfield Dandridge. PAOP p.32; ZaP
    p.100
I have forgotten you as one forgets at dawning. Helen Morgan Brooks. NNPUSA
    p.104; PoNe p.278
I have found joy. Joseph S. Cotter, Jr. AVAN p.181; BOG p.25
I have gone back in boyish wonderment. Sterling A. Brown. CaD p.139; ITBLA
    p.161; SoR p.129
I have grown weary of this carnal bard. David Wadsworth Cannon, Jr. EbR
    p.25
I have heard thee, o life, in the tumblings of nature and questioned the good
    thereof. Joseph S. Cotter, Sr. SPPH p.87
I have in anguish sought to comprehend the deep persistent folly of the rich
    man's way. Theodore Stanford. EbR p.132
I have just seen a beautiful thing slim and still. Angelina Weld Grimké.
    AmNP p.17; PoN p.49
I have known nights rain-washed and crystal-clear. Frank Yerby. AmNP p.136
I have named you Malaguena. William S. Braithwaite. HFL p.73
I have never been contained. Mari Evans. IABW p.18
I have nine guppies there were ten but the mother died shortly. Nikki Gio-
    vanni. MyH p.9
I have no fancy for that ancient cant. Paul Laurence Dunbar. CPPLD p.149
I have no words, no words for this. Robert Hayden. BTB p.114
I have not ever seen my father's grave. Audre Lord. BTB p.140
I have not loved you in the noblest way. Countee Cullen. MASP p.80; OTIS
    p.149
I have people. Kali Grosvenor. PBK p.20
I have seen a lovely thing. Arna Bontemps. BANP p.264; CaD p.170
I Have Seen Black Hands. Richard Wright. PoN p.154; SoS p.112
I have seen full many a sight. Paul Laurence Dunbar. CLT p.15; CPPLD p.305
I have seen the smallest minds of my generation. Ray Durem. NBP p.47
I have seen them at many hours. Julia Fields. PoNe p.417
I have seen you suffer in the midst of winter. Jean Brierre. EbR p.11; PoN
    p.369; TYBP p.93
I have sown beside all waters in my day. Arna Bontemps. AmNP p.75; ANP
    p.127; BANP p.262; CaD p.165; CNAW p.332; IADB p.76; ITBLA p.151; KAL
    p.83; PoN p.110; PoNe p.209
I have swung to the uttermost reaches of pain. Georgia Douglas Johnson.
    HWOP p.56

I have tasted alien mouths and felt the sinews of an arm. Mari Evans. IABW
    p.30
I have the greatest fun at night. Effie Lee Newsome. CaD p.58
I have the shape of cotton typewriters. Ted Joans. AFR p.104
I have washed you in my tears. Malcolm Christian Conley. HeD p.12
I have watched you dancing in the streets of Daker. Elton Hill-Abu Ishak.
    NBP p.71
I have wrapped my dreams in a silken cloth. Countee Cullen. CCC p.48; GoS
    p.197; MBP p.109; OTIS p.31; PoN p.126; PoNe p.229; TYBP p.234
I hear a voice that speaks to me. William S. Braithwaite. LLL p.14
I hear in your voice the birth of the world. Jean Brierre. EbR p.12
I hear the halting footsteps of a lass. Claude McKay. AVAN p.205; BANP
    p.170; CNAW p.293; HaS p.22; PoN p.331; PoNe p.99; SPCM p.60
I hear the little Black cricket. Effie Lee Newsome. GoS p.75
I hear the man downstairs slapping the hell out of his stupid wife again.
    Ted Joans. BPW p.9; NNPUSA p.83
I hear the stars still singing.** James Weldon Johnson. FYOP p.27
I Heard a Young Man Saying.** Julia Fields. BTB p.107; NNPUSA p.110
I heard an organ pealing a soft refrain. Mae V. Cowdery. WLOV p.24
I heard the train's shrill whistle call.** John Greenleaf Whittier. ANP
    p.139
I heard your heart's soft tears. Helen C. Harris. EbR p.78
"I heeard de ole folks talkin' in our house da other night. Alex Rogers.
    BANP p.158
I held my heart so far from harm. Paul Laurence Dunbar. CPPLD p.420
I helped to build this great America. Marcus B. Christian. EbR p.31
i here within myself centuries of self hate that know no way to destruct
    that know no way to break loose. Mae Jackson. BlSp p.91
I hold not with the fatalist creed. Countee Cullen. CpS p.70; OTIS p.69
I hold the book of life in my hands. William S. Braithwaite. HFL p.98
I hold the splendid daylight in my hands. George Campbell. PoN p.317
I hooked my hopes on a shooting star. Ritten Edward Lee. EbR p.100
I hope ma chile'll never love a man. Langston Hughes. FCTJ p.81
I hope that when I am dead that I shall lie. Jessie Redmond Fauset. ANP
    p.89; BANP p.208; PoN p.67; PoNe p.69
I hope when I have sung my rounds. Countee Cullen. BlC p.31
I humbly bow beneath my cross. Lucy Mae Turner. BCF p.46.
I hunt the black puritan. LeRoi Jones. BMP p.18
I is allus very happy. Lucy Mae Turner. BCF p.7
I is fifty more or less, an' it's cuttin' ter my pride. Joseph S. Cotter, Sr.
    CPJSC p.56; WSBO p.61
I is the total Black being spoken from the earth's inside. Audre Lord. BTB
    p.141; SoS p.95
I judge my soul eagle nor mole: a man is what he saves from rot. Melvin
    Tolson. RWA p.45
I just can't hate me any more. Bernie Casey. LATP p.19
I just turned a pan of scalding hot water on my arm. Isabella Maria Brown.
    PoNe p.342
I keeps er sharp eye on de folks I see. Joseph S. Cotter. CPJSC p.58;
    WSBO p.56

I kissed   TITLE AND FIRST LINE INDEX

I kissed a kiss in youth. William S. Braithwaite. AmNP p.15; BANP p.105;
    CaD p.31; CNAW p.226; SPWSB p.51
I kissed my lover in the storm. Thelma T. Clement. BTh p.22
I knew Blacks nobody else knew. Conrad Kent Rivers. SVH p.14
I knew not I a sister had with intellect so great. Charles Fred White. PONS
    p.51
I knew not who had wrought with skills so fine. James Weldon Johnson. FYOP
    p.27
I knock at the door of romance. Nicolas Guillen. PoN p.381
I know a girl from Oklahoma. Waring Cuney. CNAW p.376
I know a household made of pure delight. William S. Braithwaite. HFL p.28
I know a kindly bluff grey hill. William C. Braithwaite. VER p.52
I know a lover when I see one. Countee Cullen. BlC p.25
I Know A Man. Paul Laurence Dunbar. CPPLD p.382
I know I am the Negro problem being wined and dined. Langston Hughes. PATL
    p.73
I Know I'm Not Sufficiently Obscure.** Ray Durem. BTB p.103; SoS p.122
I Know Jesus Heard Me.** Charles L. Anderson. BTB p.41
I know my love is true. Paul Laurence Dunbar. CPPLD p.91; LOLL p.135
I Know My Soul. Claude McKay. HaS p.46; SPCM p.56
I know not why or whence he came. Joseph S. Cotter, Jr. BOG p.7; CaD p.102
I know now how a man whose blood is hot. Countee Cullen. MASP p.82; OTIS
    p.151
I know now that Notre Dame is in Paris. Langston Hughes. PoNe p.196
I know of all the words I speak or write. Countee Cullen. BlC p.43
I know what the caged bird feels, alas! Paul Laurence Dunbar. AmNP p.13;
    CaD p.8; CPPLD p.162; IADB p.81; ITBLA p.96; PoN p.33; PoNe P.34
I know with pain the me that is I. Mari Evans. IABW p.19
I know you Cambridge. Julian Bond. BTB p.45
I know you dig dark me. Ted Joans. BPW p.24
I laks yo' kin' of lovin'. Sterling A. Brown. BANP p.254; CaD p.134; SoR
    p.8
I Laughed When I Wrote It. (Don't You Think It's Funny?) Nikki Giovanni.
    MyH p.59
I lay in silence at her side. Countee Cullen. BlC p.55
I learned while in my teens of notes of chords. Alpheus Butler. EbR p.21
I leave their fields a stem entangles my hair. Charles F. Gordon. NBP p.54
I like best. Horace Mungin. BOL p.44
I like it here just fine and I don't want no bail. Margaret Walker. PFND
    p.8
I like the way you look at things. Catherine L. Findley. EbR p.64
I like things that are intense. Countess W. Twitty. EbR p.146
I like this quiet place of lawns and trees well kept. Mae V. Cowdery. WLOV
    p.44
I like to see you lean back in your chair. Gwendolyn Brooks. FaP p.16
I listened for the sounds of cannon, cries. Robert Hayden. BOR p.10
I Live in Subtraction.** June Jordan. SCh p.26
I live uptown in Harlem. Ted Joans. BPW p.35
I loathe defeat, whose keen-edged plow furrows deep my heart. James A.
    Emanuel. EbR p.61

I lobes you lak I used ter do? Joseph S. Cotter. CDJSC p.26
I lobes your hands gal, yes I do. Joseph S. Cotter, Sr. CPJSC p.34; WSBO
    p.49
I long not now, a little while at least. Countee Cullen. CaD p.181; CpS
    p.59; OTIS p.64
I long to fly vast feathers past your mouths or mine. June Jordan. SCh
    p.81
I look beyond my casement where, the snow the last March wind in hedge and
    fence had piled. Charles B. Johnson. SOMP p.37
I look in the kettle, the kettle is dry. Langston Hughes. SIH p.4
I look into the eyes of one returning from distant lands. Mary Wilkerson
    Cleaves. EbR p.45
I looked and I saw that man they call the law. Langston Hughes. PATL p.16;
    OWT p.73
I looked down 31st Street. Langston Hughes. SIH p.105
I looked over Jordan, and what did I see. Anonymous. GoS p.61
I Looked Up and Saw History Caught.** A. B. Spellman. NPB p.126
I love Black Faces. Anita Scott Coleman. EbR p.51
I love her Black butt. Ted Joans. BPW p.72
"I love my baby, but my baby don't love me. Gerald W. Barrax. AKOR p.77
I love old faces mellow wise. Charles Bertram Johnson. AVAN p.190
I love the way you do this and that. Ted Joans. AFR p.95
I love this arrogant young nation who parades her glory. John Henrik Clarke.
    EbR p.44
I Love those Little Booths at Benvenuti's. Gwendolyn Brooks. AnA p.46
I love to sit alone, and dream. James Weldon Johnson. FYOP p.40
I Love You. LeRoi Jones. BMP p.98
I Love you Don't.** Kali Grosvenor. PHK p.24
I love you for your browness. Gwendolyn Bennet. ANP p.128; BANP p.243; CaD
    p.157
I love you, my darling. H. A. B. Jones-Quartey. LUP p.36
I love your hands. Angelina Weld Grimké. CaD p.44
I loved my friends. Langston Hughes. DYTB p.24; WeB p.95
I loved the apple sweetness of the air. Owen Dodson. PLL p.88
I Loved You Once (from the Russian of Alexander Pushkin). Dudley Randall.
    AmNP p.122
I loved you once; love even yet, it may be. Dudley Randall. AmNP p.122
I loved you when we were young. Owen Dodson. PLL p.81
I mastered pastoral theology, the Greek of the Apostles. Fenton Johnson.
    KAL p.42
i mean i thought she was it. Don L. Lee. DSNP p.34
I mean it's only natural that if water seeks its own level. Nikki Giovanni.
    BFBTBJ p.71
i mean we bees real bad. Sonia Sanchez. BrT p.141; TGWL p.87; WABP p.52
i met a part time re vo lu tion ist too-day. Don L. Lee. DSNP p.68
I met a sustah the udder day. Ted Joans. AFR p.115
I might be a fool to say I'll give all my love each day. William L. Morrison.
    DaR p.54
I mind me how when first I looked at her. Countee Cullen. MASP p.76; OTIS
    p.148

I mused at Kelmscott by the stripling Thames. William C. Braithwaite. VER
    p.107
"I must be ready when he comes," she said. Countee Cullen. CpS p.49
I must not gaze at them although your eyes are dawning day. Claude McKay.
    BANP p.172; HaS p.13; SPCM p.80
I must say yes, sir. Langston Hughes. FCTJ p.39
I need a woman to love me madly. Ted Joans. AFR p.114
I need more than this crust of salt. Lance Jeffers. BrT p.72
I never did feel so blue. Lillian Tucker Lewis. HeD p.27
I never dreamed that we would drift apart. Francis Merrill Foster. EbR p.64
I never knew your loneliness and knowing now I die. Mari Evans. IABW p.43
I never shall furgit that night when father hitched up Dobbin. Paul Laurence
    Dunbar. CPPLD p.65; LOLL p.93
I often think the truly wise are such as seek through doubts and fears.
    Joseph S. Cotter, Sr. LOF p.41; SPPH p.80
I often wonder, Oscar, how it fares with you. Raymond Dandridge. PAOP p.50
I once went down to de races. Lucy Mae Turner. BCF p.26
I only want to be there to kiss you. Nikki Giovanni. MyH p.67
I Own A Dream. Will Smallwood. EbR p.129
I passed by the house of the young man who loves me. Anonymous. MBP p.25;
    TYBP p.30
I peeped once through a holly wreath. Charlemae Rollins. ChG p.68
I pick up my life. Langston Hughes. BLIA p.196; ITBLA p.159; OWT p.61
I pity you, now under scorn and sneers. J. Henderson Brooks. BTh p.59
I play it cool. Langston Hughes. CNAW p.309; PATL p.11; **PoNe p.202**; SoS
    p.118
I plucked a rose, a red rose rare. Raymond Garfield Dandridge. PAOP p.20;
    ZaP p.102
I plucked a rose from out a bower fair. Joseph S. Cotter, Jr. BOG p.29
I plucked a rose from the top of the bush. William S. Braithwaite. SPWSB
    p.23
I plucked my **soul out of it's secret place.**   Claude McKay. HaS p.46; SPCM
    p.56
I ply with all the cunning of my art. Marcus B. Christian. EbR p.35; PoN
    p.83; PoNe p.156
I ponder a death at the curb and think. Carmin Avid Goulbourne. FoM p.29
I promised her probable things. Gerald W. Barrax. AKOR p.29
I put my nickel in the raffle of the night. Langston Hughes. OWT p.107
I put salt water to my thirsty lip. Joseph S. Cotter, Sr. LOF p.56
I rather like old gloomy days. Maurine L. Jeffrey. HcD p.23
I reach from pain to music great enough to bring you back. Michael S.
    Harper. DJDC p.64
I read a sonnet from the magic pen. Joseph S. Cotter, Sr. CPJSC p.38
I rebel not because of poverty. Robert T. Sye. TNV p.124
I Remember. Nikki Giovanni. MyH p.19
I Remember.** Mae Jackson. BOL p.35
I remember Chaffee, Missouri. J. Henderson Brooks. BTh p.20
I remember distinctly the tired tumult of my urges. Bruce McM. Wright. LUP
    p.56; PoN p.200; PoNe p.355
I remember from your life the senior laughter. Owen Dodson. PLL p.65

I remember learning you jump in your sleep. Nikki Giovanni. MyH p.19

I remember the boy. Albert Aubert. ATB p.13

I remember those seasonless tears flowing until your way was granted. Conrad Kent Rivers. SVH p.11

I remember Wednesday was the day. Myron O'Higgins. PoN p.196; PoNe p.350

I, Remembering. Roger Mais. PoN p.323

I, remembering how light love has a soft footfall. Roger Mais. PoN p.323

I rented once a house of clay. William S. Braithwaite. LLL p.62

I rest my deep within the wood. Georgia Douglas Johnson. HWOP p.9

I retrace your path in my bare feet. S. Carolyn Reese. BrT p.170

I return the bitterness. Lewis Alexander. CaD p.124; PoN p.85; PoNe p.160

I rise at 2 a.m., these mornings, to polish my horn. Ishmael Reed. PoNe p.415

I rise up in de mornin' early in the Spring. James E. McGirt. FYSS p.14

I said, in drunken pride of youth and you. Sterling A. Brown. CaD p.138; ITBLA p.161; SoR p.126

I said: now will the poets sing. Countee Cullen. MASP p.96; OTIS p.160

I said to my baby, baby, take it slow. Langston Hughes. BLIA p.199

I sailed in my dreams to the land of night. Gwendolyn B. Bennett. CaD p.158

I sang me a song, a tiny song. Joseph S. Cotter, Sr. RHY p.32

I sat beneath a stately elm. Charles Fred White. PONS p.96

I sat there in the midst of ten thousand folk or more. Eloise Culver. GANIV p.68

I sat there singing her songs in the dark. Langston Hughes. FOW p.50

I sat up in my attic high. Lucy Mae Turner. BCF p.33

I saw a brown-skin maiden beside a lonely pool. William S. Morrison. DaR p.18

I saw a forlorn creek that flowed down from the hill. William L. Morrison. DaR p.28

I saw a man today. Bernie Casey. LATP p.13

I saw a shooting star. Clifford Miller. BTB p.150

I saw Butch. Victor Hernandez Cruz. BOL p.68

I saw her in a cluttered basement store. Melvin Tolson. RWA p.66

I saw him faltering toward me in the street. Melvin Tolson. ITBLA p.218; RWA p.63

I saw myself leaving. Carl Gardner. NNPUSA p.98

I saw the falcon like a seimitar. Robert Hayden. HSITD p.13

I saw the picture of your face woven in the rain. William S. Braithwaite. HFL p.78

I saw two urchins a Negro and a Jew. Joseph S. Cotter, Sr. SPPH p.24

I saw you smile and heard the thunder. Bernie Casey. LATP p.80

I saw you today.** Gordon Parks. InL (unpaged)

I saw your hands on my lips like blind needles. Audre Lorde. NNPUSA p.106

I search each troubled night for you. Gordon Parks. InL (unpaged)

I search the iridescent faces. Herman L. McMillan. TNV p.74

I See And Am Satisfied. Kelly Miller. ANP p.110

I see Black people. Ted Joans. BPW p.75

I see her on a lonely forest track. Walter Adolph Roberts. PoN p.317

I see him everywhere: the many-hued chameleon. H.A.B. Jones-Quartey. LUP p.37

I see   TITLE AND FIRST LINE INDEX

I see in your eyes. Albert Rice. CaD p.179
I see it. Anonymous. TYBP p.13
I see skies more bright and blue. Cora Ball Moton. GoS p.186
I see the blinding flash once more. Carlyle B. Hall. EbR p.76
I see the executioner. Samuel W. Allen. BTB p.178
I see the sun. Victor Hernandez Cruz. BOL p.64
I see them Puerto Ricans / Spanish niggers bronze farmers look silly being
    doormen. Felipe Luciano. BlSp p.122
i see wonder in little things. Nikki Giovanni. MyH p.14
I see you in the silver. Effie Lee Newsome. PoN p.56; PoNe p.71
I see you now standing tall. Christine C. Johnson. FoM p.3
I seed him on de corner dar. Joseph S. Cotter, Sr. CPJSC p.12; WSBO p.16
I Seek. Katherine Cuestas. BTB p.76
I seek integration. Don L. Lee. BOL p.56; DSNP p.51
I seek my beloved. Robert Hayden. HSITD p.35
I set a dreamin' boy wus here. Charles B. Johnson. SOMP p.55
I set in de window, oh, love, so sweet, whah de moon streams lak a silver
    sea. Charles B. Johnson. SOMP p.27
I sets on dese heah rottin' legs, I watch dis drove of pigs and hogs. Eli
    Shepperd. PlS p.35
I Shall Build a Music-box.** Bruce McM. Wright. LUP p.64
I shall come this way again. Donald Jeffrey Hayes. CaD p.189
I shall hate you. Gwendolyn Bennett. AmNP p.73; BANP p.246; CaD p.160
I shall knock at your kitchen window no more. H. Binga Dismond. EbR p.58
I shall make a song like your hair. Langston Hughes. CaD p.155
I shall not regard my swelled head as a sign of real glory. Anne Cesaire.
    TYBP p.123
I shall not sing a May song. Gwendolyn Brooks. MBP p.28
I shall recall. Sterling A. Brown. KAL p.74; SoR p.97
I shall remember. H. D. Carberry. PoN p.336
I Shall Return. Claude McKay. HaS p.33; SPCM p.32
I shall return again. Claude McKay. SPCM p.32; HaS p.33
I Shall Succeed. James E. McGirt. FYSS p.43
I shall succeed, although fate rules to-day. James E. McGirt. FYSS p.43
i shall tell my son one day how my granpa found so much solace. Prentiss
    Taylor, Jr. TGWL p.93
I shall want this rainy sound of leaves. Robert Hayden. HSID p.55
I sho' dislak a man dat feels lak he's a turnin' all de wheels. Raymond
    Garfield Dandridge. PeP p.34
I should like to creep. Angelina Weld Grimké. CaD p.42
I sing for the silent slain speak for the dogtagged dead. Frank Marshall
    Davis. EbR p.54
I Sing No New Songs. Frank Marshall Davis. PoN p.142; PoNe p.252
I sing the body electric.* Walt Whitman. ANP p.133
I sit athrone upon the times. Maya Angelou. JGM p.16
I Sit and Sew. Alice Dunbar Nelson. CaD p.73
I sit and sew - a useless task it seems. Alice Dunbar Nelson. CaD p.73
I Sit and Wait For Beauty. Mae V. Cowdery. WLOV p.41
I sit at the dusk of death. William Cousins. EbR p.53
I sit here by the fire and watch the dying embers. Carlyle B. Hall. EbR
    p.77

I sit upon the old sea wall. Paul Laurence Dunbar. CPPLD p.184
I sometimes feel that life contains nothing. Timothy Thomas Fortune. AVAN
    p.115
I sometimes take you in my dreams to a far off land I used to know. James
    Weldon Johnson. FYOP p.57
I sought consolation in the sorrow of your eyes. Frank Horne. CaD p.117
I speak to you, my colored boys, I bid you to be men. Irvin W. Underhill.
    ANP p.108
I spied a maid in lover's lane. Bruce McM. Wright. LUP p.58
I stand above the city's rush and din. Paul Laurence Dunbar. CPPLD p.454
I stand most humbly. Langston Hughes. FOW p.107
I stand on the mark, beside the shore.* Elizabeth Barrett Browning. PoN
    p.216; PoNe p.448
I stepped on the black winter seeds. Thurmond Snyder. NNPUSA p.88
I stood among the wanting many. Richard Thomas. PoNe p.432
I stood by the shore at the death of day. Paul Laurence Dunbar. CPPLD
    p.109; LOLL p.162
I stood in a meadow and all I could see was the green valley surrounding me.
    PoN p.120; PoNe p.227
I stood in the door of dawn. Charles B. Johnson. SOMP p.13
I stood still and was a mushroom on the forest green. Nikki Giovanni.
    BFBTBJ p.7; BrT p.48
I stood with old friend death awhile last night. William Moore. ANP p.60
I struck tomorrow square in the face. Aig Higo. TYBP p.159
I Substitute for the Dead Lecturer. LeRoi Jones. BLIA p.393; SoS p.110
I swear to God baby that it really makes me mad when sometimes it be that
    way. Ted Joans. BPW p.21
I take my freedom lest I die. Mari Evans. IABW p.75
I take my soul in my hand. William S. Braithwaite. HFL p.76
I take no deep concern in alien woes. J. Henderson Brooks. BTh p.49
I talked to a bird today. Bernie Casey. LATP p.51
I talked to a farmer one day in Iowa. Margaret Walker. FMP p.55; KAL p.144
I talked to old Lem. Sterling A. Brown. CBAW p.402; IADB p.68; PoN p.87;
    PoNe p.167; TYBP p.221
I tell yo' 'bout 'Unk' Enoch Mann. Lucile D. Goodlett. WGC p.57
I 'ten'ed a campane speakin' et de Town Hall uddah night. Raymond G.
    Dandridge. PeP p.24; ZaP p.88
I Thank Thee Lord.** Charles Fred White. PONS p.17
I that had found the way so smooth. Jessie Fauset. CaD p.70
I the traveler who crossed Les Halles at summer's end admiring the nude rear
    of a fur flower from Egypt. Ted Joans. AFR p.98
I think an impulse stronger than my mind. Countee Cullen. BlC p.17; OTIS
    p.85
I think God gave you everything but this. William S. Braithwaite. SPWSB
    p.91
"I Think I see Her." Jessie Fauset. BANP p.208; GoS p.165; AVAN p.194
I think I see her sitting bowed and Black. Jessie Fauset. AVAN p.194;
    BANP p.208; GoS p.165
I Think I See Him There.** Waring Cuney. CaD p.210
I Think I Thought a Lie. David Gatewood Thomas. EbR p.137

I think of surf coming quick. James Randall. BrT p.132

I think that man hath made no beauteous thing. George Leonard Allen. CaD
    p.204

I think that though the clouds be dark. **Paul Laurence Dunbar.** CPPLD p.81;
    LOLL p.120

I think there scarely can be given nobler harmonies in heaven. Leslie
    Pinckney Hill. AVAN p.202

I think we probably love each other since we can't stay apart. Carolyn
    Rodgers. BlSp p.182

I Think When Judas Mother Heard. Countee Cullen. CCC p.90

I thought I saw an angel flying low. Arna Bontemps. BTB p.47; BLIA p.215;
    BANP p.265; AmNP p.81; CaD p.166; CNAW p.333; PoN p.111; PoNe p.211

I Thought It Was Tangiers I Wanted. Langston Hughes. PoNe p.196

I Thought Of My True Love. Waring Cuney. LUP p.12

I Thought of You.** Bernie Casey. LATP p.31

I thought of you early morning. Victor Hernandez Cruz. SNA p.43

I thought that missing you would fall at close of every day. Lois Royal
    Hughes. EbR p.90

I told my child God could make worlds. Marion Cuthbert. SOC p.9

I, Too. Langston Hughes. AmNP p.64; ANP p.102; BLIA p.194; CaD p.145; DYTB
    p.74; FNP p.29; IADB p.75; ITBLA p.160; KAL p.86; PoN p.97; PoNe p.182;
    EeB p.109

I, Too, Hear America Singing.** Julian Bond. BTB p.44

I, Too, Know What I Am Not. Bob Kaufman. NBP p.79

I, too, shall dance the dance of death. Samuel E. Boyd. EbR p.7

I, Too, Sing America.** Langston Hughes. AmNP p.64; ANP p.102; BLIA p.194;
    CaD p.145; DYTB p.74; FNP p.29; IADB p.75; ITBLA p.160; KAL p.86; PoN
    p.97; PoNe p.182; WeB p.109

I took a peek for the first time at the tiny brown mite on the bed.
    Constance Nichols. EbR p.110

I took a train to be by your side. George B. Browne. EbR p.16

I Touch You. Bernie Casey. LATP p.32

I tried to pattern all my life like the petals of a rose. Lois Royal Hughes.
    EbR p.89

I turned my thoughts inward today. Mae V. Cowdery. WLOV p.33

I Use Ter Dress. Waverly T. Carmichael. FHOF p.29

I used to wonder. Langston Hughes. FOW p.13; ITBLA p.160

I Used to Wrap My White Doll.* Mae Jackson. BOL p.72

I usta wonder who I'd be when I was a little girl in Indianapolis. Nikki
    Giovanni. BFBTBJ p.68

I vision God standing on the heights of heaven. Anonymous. MBP p.1; TYBP
    p.196

I wait in this room. Marion Nicholes. LiS p.19

I Wake Up Screaming. Carlyle B. Hall. EbR p.76

I walked all over the Zoo and the park. Langston Hughes. OWT p.41

I walked de streets till de shoes wore off my feet. Langston Hughes. SIH
    p.40

I wandered, absently, into the wedding Euphoric world of white crystals.
    Arthur Boze. BlWo p.12

I want a little brown girl. Ted Joans. BPW p.127

I want, I shall, I must cross your body continent. Ted Joans. AFR p.72

I want to see faces of all races. Ted Joans. BPW p.102

I want my body bathed again by southern sons, my soul reclaimed again from southern land. Margaret Walker. FMP p.18

I want to be buried in an anonymous crater inside the moon. Bob Kaufman. TYBP p.253

I want to die while you love me.** Georgia Douglas Johnson. AmNP p.22; BANP p.183; CaD p.78; ITBLA p.155; KAL p.39

I want to see the slip palm trees. Gwendolyn B. Bennett. AmNP p.73; BANP p.245

I want to tell you 'bout that woman. Langston Hughes. SIH p.50

I want you to stop, think and say a prayer. Carolyn Ogletree. TNV p.78

I wanta say just gotta say something bout those beautiful beautiful outasight Black men. Nikki Giovanni. BFBTBJ p.77; BrT p.57

I wanted something, you know in what you thought sitting suns galunkah deray shun of plove. LeRoi Jones. BMP p.160

I wanted to be an artist in my youth. Askia Muhammad Toure. BlSp p.220

I wanted to know my mother when she sat looking. LeRoi Jones. BMP p.217

I wanted to take your hand and run with you. Nikki Giovanni. MyH p.25

I wanted to write. Nikki Giovanni. BFBTBJ p.88; BrT p.57; TNV p.34; TYBP p.256

I was a boy then. Langston Hughes. FOW p.60

I was a minuteman at Concord bridge. Melvin Tolson. RWA p.33

I was ared man one time. Langston Hughes. WeB p.100

I was a woman at war. Hazel L. Washington. EbR p.152

I was alive yesterday but sleeping late. Gerald W. Barrax. AKOR p.44

I was at the station. Waring Cuney. LUP p.12

I was captive to a dream. William S. Braithwaite. AVAN p.137; HFL p.63

I was christened Ebenezer. Lucy Mae Turner. BCF p.38

i was five when mom & dad got married. Don L. Lee. DCS p.52; DSNP p.117

I was kissed once by a beautiful man. Alice Walker. ONC p.51

I was lookin' for a sandwich, Judge. Langston Hughes. SIH p.42

I was not here when you called last night. Mari Evans. IABW p.31

I was not now I am--a few days hence. Paul Laurence Dunbar. CPPLD p.27; LOLL p.36

I was seventeen before I learned the stage had an apron. Albert Aubert. ATB p.16

I was so sick last night I didn't hardly know my mind. Langston Hughes. SIH p.44

I was spinning with earth and a foul wind was blowing. Charles L. Anderson. BTB p.39

I was trying to figure out what it was all about. Langston Hughes. FOW p.98

I was with you. Bernie Casey. LATP p.55

I wasn't born here man. Victor Hernandez Cruz. BOL p.65

I wasn't sure it was you yes. Clarence Major. SAM p.60

I Watch. Bernie Casey. LATP p.34

I Watch You. Bernie Casey. LATP p.71

I watch you your smile your look your you. Bernie Casey. LATP p.71

I watched them playing there upon the sand. Sidney Alexander. PoN p.294; PoNe p.559

TITLE AND FIRST LINE INDEX

I watched you through my window. Bernie Casey. LATP p.34
I Weep.** Angelina Weld Grimké. CaD p.45
I welcome ye, fine masters of today. Joseph S. Cotter, Sr. CPJSC p.75;
    WSBO p.25
I went back to my cabin home. Lucy Mae Turner. BCF p.32
I went down home. Waring Cuney. LUP p.10
I went down the road. Langston Hughes. SIH p.85
I went down the ways of the roses this noon. William S. Braithwaite. LLL
    p.67
I went down to the corner. Langston Hughes. OWT p.99
I went down to the river I set down on the bank. Langston Hughes. OWT p.38
I went hom' wid me gal las' night. Waverly T. Carmichael. FHOF p.13
I went out in the cold. LeRoi Jones. BMP p.82
I went out in the world. Frenchy J. Hodges. BlW p.10
I went to church de other night. Waverly T. Carmichael. FHOF p.14
I went to court last night. Fenton Johnson. CaD p.63; GoS p.89
I went to look for joy. Langston Hughes. MBP p.21; WeB p.48
I went to ma daddy. Langston Hughes. BANP p.238; FCTJ p.86
I went to Riis Beach and put my ear to the ocean. S. E. Anderson. BlSp p.7
I went to San Francisco. Langston Hughes. GoS p.132
I went to the gypsy's. Langston Hughes. SIH p.93
I went walkin' by de blue bayou. Langston Hughes. OWT p.53
I, who am used to rolling swell. Lucy Mae Turner. BCF p.34
I who employ a poet's tongue. Countee Cullen. CpS p.20
I who encompass millions. Mari Evans. IABW p.17
I whose magic could explore. Countee Cullen. CCC p.55
I will have you meet my friend Slick. Victor Hernandez Cruz. SNA p.10
I will hide my soul and its mighty love. George Marion McLlelan. EBAP p.123
I will not reason, wrestle here with you. Claude McKay. HaS p.82; SPCM
    p.101
I will not toy with it nor bend an inch. Claude McKay. HaS p.23; SPCM p.74
I will remember a time when "Amazing Grace" was all the rage in the South.
    Alice Walker. ONC p.41
I will slaughter the enemies of my father. LeRoi Jones. BMP p.197
I will suppose that grief is wise. Joseph S. Cotter, Sr. CPJSC p.15
I wish that you and I might have been friends. Alexander Young. EbR p.162
I wish the rent was heaven sent. Langston Hughes. SIH p.21
I wish your body were in the grave. Countee Cullen. CpS p.26; OTIS p.57
I, with a need afire for your body and mine to wed. Gordon Parks. InL (un-
    paged)
I woke up this mornin' 'bout half-past three. Langston Hughes. SIH p.67
I woke up this mornin' with the blues all around my bed. Anonymous. TYBP
    p.203
I Wonder. J. Farley Ragland. BTB p.164
I wonder how it feels to do cart wheels? Langston Hughes. SIH p.33
I wonder if, at the last day, when departed saints shall rise and start
    their heavenly journey toward the celestial skies. Cornelius V. Troup.
    EbR p.144
I wonder if you flowers know the happiness you bring to me. Charles Fred
    White. PONS p.117

I wonder what de thunder grumblin' about. Eli Shepperd. P1S p.121

I / Wonder Why.** Tom Poole. BOL p.57; NBP p.100

I wonder why the Negro should be hated. Charles Fred White. PONS p.26

I wore a baseball cap. Naomi Long Madgett. BrT p.169

I work all day, said Simple John. Langston Hughes. WeB p.67

I work days, (9 to 5) in the front office of a well known Chicago company.
     Don L. Lee. DSNP p.57

I worked for a woman she wasn't mean. Langston Hughes. OWT p.5

I works all day. Langston Hughes. FCTJ p.59

I Would Be a Painter Most Of All. Len Chandler. NBP p.34

I would be simple again. Langston Hughes. WeB p.104

I would be wandering in distant fields. Claude McKay. AVAN p.205; HaS p.28;
     SPCM p.39

I would give you the blue-violet dreams of clouds. Mae V. Cowdery. WLOV
     p.51

I would I could, as other poets have. Countee Cullen. MASP p.87

I would liken you to a night without stars. Langston Hughes. WeB p.64

I would not tarry if I could be gone. Joseph S. Cotter, Jr. BOG p.19

I Would Play. Bernie Casey. LATP p.14

I would play on sunny days in that yard so big. Bernie Casey. LATP p.14

I wrote about things I love. Ted Joans. AFR p.105

i wrote this poem because i feel there are very few flowers in this field we
     so dishonestly call life. Nikki Giovanni. BlSp p.74

Ibadan. John Pepper Clark. MBP p.44

Ibadan, running splash of rust and bold. John Pepper Clark. MBP p.44

Ice tinkled in glasses. Lerone Bennett. NNPUSA p.53

Icicles. Joseph S. Cotter, Sr. CPJSC p.40

Icicles on Trees. Catherine L. Finley. EbR p.63

Icy evil that struck his father down, The. Robert Hayden. BrT p.20; FoM
     p.14

I'd really hate to go to bed. Effie Lee Newsome. GoS p.193

Idea of Ancestry, The. Etheridge Knight. BrT p.79

Idle Chatter. Charles Cooper. BOL p.8

Idling pivot of the frigate bird, The. Derek Walcott. TYBP p.112

Idol (coatlicue, Aztec goodness). Robert Hayden. SPRH p.31

Idolatry. Arna Bontemps. AmNP p.79; PoN p.116; PoNe p.217; ITBLA p.161

Idols of the Tribe, The. Velvin Tolson. RWA p.97

Idols of the tribe, in voices as puissant as the rutting calls of a bull,
     crocodile. Melvin Tolson. HaG p.30

Idyl. Henrietta Cordelia Ray. EBAP p.143

If. Paul Laurence Dunbar. CPPLD p.121; LOLL p.177

If. Oswald Durand. PoN p.353

If a man had made you, straight and tall. William C. Braithwaite. VER p.99

If a thousand is not enough, I'll get more. Bernie Casey. LATP p.50

If ah evah git to glory, an' ah hope to mek it thoo. John Wesley Holloway.
     BANP p.138

If an eagle be imprisoned. Henry Dumas. BOL p.40

If blood is black then spirit neglects my unborn son. Conrad Kent Rivers.
     BrT p.24; FoM p.27

If Crispus Attuck's statue took life to walk, he would wink his owl-eyes part
     lips and talk. Dorothy Vena Johnson. EbR p.91

If dead men died abruptly by a blow. Margaret Walker. FMP p.56

If death should claim me for her own today. Paul Laurence Dunbar. CPPLD p.343

If ever a garden was Gethsemane. Anne Spencer. AmNP p.7; PoN p.54; PoNe p.65

If ever I'd known Italy. Oswald Durand. PoN p.353

If Ever You Should Walk Away.** Lucia M. Pitts. EbR p.121

If ev'ybody and ev'ything, I say would des be silly one single day. Eli Shepperd. PlS p.59

If for a day joy masters me. Countee Cullen. CpS p.8

If God hath willed that I should die - and thus your race name glorify. Charles Fred White. PONS p.50

If God is not, then who is He. Raymond Dandridge. PeP p.37

If here and now he but a timely span. Katharine Cater. AmNP p.140; PoN p.192; PoNe p.340

If homely virtues drawn from me a tune. James Weldon Johnson. FYOP p.93

If I could bend each yesterday and make it do my will. Frenchy J. Hodges. BlW p.11

If I could ever know the loneliness of silent falling star. David Wadsworth Cannon, Jr. EbR p.26

If I Could Fly.** Kali Grosvenor. PBK p.57

If i could, oh, mother of mine I would a thousand times. William L. Morrison. DaR p.17

If I Could Touch. William S. Braithwaite. LLL p.22

If I could touch your hand tonight. William S. Braithwaite. LLL p.22

If I do take somebody's word on it means I don't know. June Jordan. SCh p.36

... if i had a gun that would shoot.** Mari Evans. IABW p.36

If I had a heart of gold. Langston Hughes. PATL p.98

If I had caught the tears I cried since you first broke my heart. Deborah Fuller Wess. EbR p.159

If I had dug in one place all my life. Waring Cuney. BTB p.83

If I had given myself to you. Lucy Mae Turner. BCF p.37

If I had mighty wings to fly, I'd soar aloft in younder sky. Raymond Garfield Dandridge. PAOP p.57; ZaP p.7

If I had some small change I'd buy a mule. Langston Hughes. SIH p.32

If I have run my course and seek the pearls. Fenton Johnson. CaD p.64

If I Must Know. Mae V. Cowdery. WLOV p.21

If I must know sorrow to live then burden my soul. Mae V. Cowdery. WLOV p.21

If I should chance to spy love far at sea, with out stretched arm beckoning unto me. James E. McGirt. FYSS p.74

If I use scorn when love would be more kind. John Henry Owens. EbR p.112

If I was a sea-lion swimming in the sea. Langston Hughes. SIH p.22

If I was born a liar, lass. Countee Cullen. CpS p.23

If I was in de ballroom when de bridegroom come, if I was in de ballroom when he come! Eli Shepperd. PlS p.117

if i were a painter it would be easier. Carolyn M. Rodgers. TGWL p.84

If in the lists of life he bore him well. Countee Cullen. BlC p.12

If - ing. Langston Hughes. SIH p.32

If I've tried to act the way I feel I'm sorry I felt at all. William L. Morrison. DaR p.57

If life were but a dream, my love. Paul Laurence Dunbar. CPPLD p.121; LOLL p.179

If Love Be Staunch.** Countee Cullen. CpS p.30

If Love Could See.** James E. McGirt. FYSS p.75

If Loving Were Wooing.** James E. McGirt. FYSS p.20

If Margie Polite had of been white. Langston Hughes. OWT p.75

If men but knew my homely wit. William C. Braithwaite. VER p.62

If my garden oak spares one bare ledge. Anne Spencer. CaD p.51

If nature says to you. Fenton Johnson. AmNP p.25

If only the day need not come when I must tell you. Naomi Long Madgett. BTB p.148; CNAW p.772

if only the sun would shine tonight. Ted Joans. BPW p.128

If possible, sleep through the morning three-thirties of the world. Gwendolyn Brooks. FaP p.22

If that white Mother Hubbard comes down my Black chimney dragging his playful bag. Ted Joans. BPW p.54

If the generous God of fortune has delt you a sunny sky. Raymond Garfield Dandridge. PeP p.17

If the muse were mine to tempt it. Paul Laurence Dunbar. CPPLD p.77; LOLL p.114

If the oar of the canoe shames your skill with flounce and flout. Melvin Tolson. RWA p.21

If the Stars Should Fall. Samuel Allen. IADB p.83; NNPUSA p.95

If the unfortunate fate engulfing me. Placido. BANP p.294; PoN p.383; TYBP p.99

If the world looked in a looking glass. Vanessa Howard. SoS p.2

If there be sorrow.** Mari Evans. IABW p.16; KAL p.174; NNPUSA p.22; PoNe p.308

If there must be elaborate favors. Owen Dodson. PLL p.77

If there were not a war, I would smile at the acne-blemished kids with rifles on their backs. Julius Lester. SoS p.70

if they put you in a jack-in-the-box poet would you pop up poeming. Nikki Giovanni. BrT p.69

If they'd call us Black or we'd call us Black. Ted Joans. BPW p.55

If This Be Good-bye.** Ruby Berkley. EbR p.67

If this is peace, this dead and leaden thing. Jessie Fauset. ANP p.89; BANP p.207; PoN p.66; PoNe p.68

If this radio was good I'd get KDQ. Langston Hughes. SIH p.5

If This World Were Up Side Down.** Kali Grosvenor. PBK p.61

If thou hast ever heard on a May morn. William S. Braithwaite. HFL p.97; SPWSB p.87

If thro' the sea of night which here surrounds me. Paul Laurence Dunbar. CPPLD p.421

If Tiny. Victor Hernandez Cruz. SNA p.87

If today I follow death. Maya Angelou. JGM p.20

If 'Trane had only seen her body. Doughtery (Doc) Long Jr. TNV p.65

If 'twere fair to suppose. Paul Laurence Dunbar. CPPLD p.425

If we call to ourselves if we want to feel who we are. LeRoi Jones. BMP p.110

If We Had Wings. Nick Aaron Ford. SFD p.14
If we had wings to shield our souls from scars. Nick Aaron Ford. SFD p.14
If We Must Die. Claude McKay. AmNP p.31; BANP p.168; BLIA p.165; CNAW
    p.294; HaS p.53; IADB p.63; KAL p.48; PoN p.333; PoNe p.102; SoS p.135;
    SPCM p.36; TYBP p.118
If we must die, let it not be like hogs. Claude McKay. AmNP p.31; BANP
    p.168; BLIA p.165; CNAW p.294; HaS p.53; IADB p.63; KAL p.48; PoN p.333;
    PoNe p.102; SoS p.135; SPCM p.36; TYBP p.118
If We Part Now.** Mae V. Cowdery. WLOV p.42
If wishing were getting, ah! wouldn't it be fine? James E. McGirt. FYSS
    p.20
If you could sit with me beside the sea to-day. Paul Laurence Dunbar.
    CPPLD p.31; LOLL p.45
If you plant a row of corn you can't reap no wheat. Waverly T. Carmichael.
    FROF p.45
If you plant grain you get fields of flour. Nikki Giovanni. BrT p.68
If you sang songs I could make a request. Nikki Giovanni. BFBTBJ p.91
If You Saw a Negro Lady.** June Jordan. SCh p.17; SoS p.54
If You Should Go. Countee Cullen. OTIS p.38; CCC p.78
If You Should Lie to Me.** Melvin Tolson. RWA p.62
If you should see a man. Ted Joans. BPW p.1
If you shoud see / a man / walking. Ted Joans. AmNP p.172; KAL p.191; TYBP
    p.247
If You Would Have a Star for Noon. Gordon Parks. InL (unpaged)
If your reputation in the community is good don't snub the other fellow.
    Langston Hughes. SIH p.27
If you've had a dream broken without a single token. Nick Aaron Ford. SFD
    p.24
If you're not home, where are you? LeRoi Jones. BMP p.47
Ignore those seals. Owen Dodson. PLL p.80
I'll break a rose to fit her hair. William L. Morrison. DaR p.52
I'll build a house of arrogance. Donald Jeffrey Hayes. AmNP p.92; PoN
    p.138; PoNe p.245
I'll get more. Bernie Casey. LATP p.50
I'll leap to your desire. William S. Braithwaite. HFL p.53
I'll ne'er forget the day when I was young and gay. James E. McGirt. FYSS
    p.30
I'll Remember Lincoln. Jack H. Dawley. LUP p.18
"I'll tell him, when he comes," she said. Countee Cullen. CCC p.81
I'll Walk the Tightrope. Margaret Danner. BTB p.87; ITBLA p.219; KAL p.125
Ills I sorrow at, The. Countee Cullen. MASP p.70; OTIS p.144
Illumined fountain flashed in the pond, The. William S. Braithwaite. HFL
    p.54
Illusions. Georgia Douglas Johnson. HWOP p.50
I'm????? Ted Joans. AFR p.58
I'm a bad, bad man. Langston Hughes. FCTJ p.21
I'm a happy moile. Nikki Giovanni. BFBTBJ p.35
I'm a Round Town Gent. Anonymous. GoS p.17
I'm A-waiting and A-watching.** Joseph S. Cotter, Jr. BOG p.12
I'm all alone in this world, she said. Langston Hughes. SIH p.117

I'm back down in ole Georgy, w'ere de sun is shinin' hot. James Weldon John-
    son. FYOP p.73
I'm bound. Bound with a thousand cords - never to be free. Ruth Brownlee.
    EbR p.96
I'm deep in trouble. Langston Hughes. FCTJ p.51
I'm flying over Alabama with Black power in my lap. Ted Joans. BPW p.26
I'm folding up my little dreams. Georgia Douglas Johnson. BANP p.184; CaD
    p.79; GoS p.196; HWOP p.62; PoN p.60; PoNe p.81
I'm giving up on language. Nikki Giovanni. MyH p.31
I'm glad that Henry Wadsworth took pen in hand. Eloise Culver. GANIV p.34
I'm goin back down South to work. John Raven. BFM p.23
I'm goin' where de southern crosses top de C & O. Sterling A. Brown. SoR
    p.105
I'm going to be just like you, Ma. Al Young. NBP p.134
I'm gonna walk to de grave yard. Langston Hughes. FCTJ p.83; FNP p.24
I'm in love. Ted Joans. BPW p.56
I'm Kentucky born. Sterling A. Brown. SoR p.42
I'm leaving at five. Nikki Giovanni. MyH p.63
I'm makin' a road. Langston Hughes. GoS p.33
I'm Not Lonely. Nikki Giovanni. BFBTBJ p.32; BrT p.52
I'm on de road. Eli Shepperd. P1S p.46
I'm out to find the new, the modern school. George Reginald Margetson.
    BANP p.108
I'm proud of this **brown skin of mine.**   Norman Hills Stateman. EbR p.133
I'm sure that Spring is on the way. Beatrice M. Murphy. GoS p.25
I'm the best that ever done it. Maya Angelou. JGM p.30
I'm the dance you try to do. Ted Joans. AFR p.58
I'm thousan' dollar Charlie, the mercy man. James Pipes. ZJP p.123
I'm tired, days and nights to me. Georgia Douglas Johnson. HWOP p.31
I'm waiting for ma mammy. Langston Hughes. FCTJ p.76; FNP p.28
Image. Henry Dumas. BOL p.7
Imagine what Mrs. Haessler would say. Margaret Danner. NNPUSA p.30; PoNe
    p.163
Imitation Of Horace. William C. Braithwaite. VER p.100
Immortality. Marion Cuthbert. SOC p.43
Immortality. Frank Horne. BANP p.278
Impasse. Langston Hughes. **PATL p.85**
Impelled. Georgia Douglas Johnson. HWOP p.21
Imperfection of the world is a burden, The. LeRoi Jones. BMP p.92
Impossibility. Jamye H. Coleman. EbR p.52
Impression on Induction. R. Orlando Jackson. BTB p.128
In a backwoods town. James Weldon Johnson. FYOP p.43
In a far away wood there lived two monkeys. Lillian G. Brown. BTh p.63
In a few moments the song will set me free. Conrad Kent Rivers. SVH p.12
In a Foxhole. Albert Aubert. ATB p.14
In a geometry of pain what theorem hold, what answer heals? James Worley.
    FoM p.68
In a Grave-yard. William S. Braithwaite. AVAN p.136; LLL p.29
In a hill-bound and somewhat rustic pocket. Joseph S. Cotter, Sr. RHY p.18
In a little shanty town was on a night like this. Edward Braithwaite. MBP
    p.13

In a Period of Growth. Don L. Lee. DSNP p.45

In a small and lonely cabin out of noisy traffic's way. Paul Laurence Dunbar.
    CPPLD p.199

In a Sunken Pool.** William S. Braithwaite. SPWSB p.27

In a Time.** Maya Angelou. JGM p.11

In a Troubled Key. Lanston Hughes. SIH p.49

In a Washateria. Albert Aubert. ATB p.10

In accord with the spirit of morning, rejoicing o'er a newly born day.
    Raymond Dandridge. ZaP p.28

In Air. Peter Clarke. MBP p.38

In America. Bernie Casey. LATP p.9

In amoratas, with an approbation bestowed his title. Gwendolyn Brooks.
    CNAW p.516

In an age of napalmed children with words like the enemy is whatever moves.
    Nikki Giovanni. MyH p.54

In An English Garden. Paul Laurence Dunbar. CPPLD p.178

In an envelope marked: personal. Langston Hughes. AmNP p.66; FOW p.83;
    PoN p.100; PoNe p.188

In an idle mood I caught thee. William S. Braithwaite. SPWSB p.37

In ancient times we're told in rhymes that thrones and empires decayed.
    Zachary Withers. PAS p.7

In argoeies of gold we trust. William C. Braithwaite. VER p.116

In August. Paul Laurence Dunbar. CPPLD p.207

In autumn the barren trees. Herman L. McMillan. TNV p.75

In balm iconic prague I offered my bosom to a wandering Arab student. Alice
    Walker. ONC p.66

In Barcelona City they dance the night along the streets. Claude McKay.
    SPCM p.85; MBP p.46

In Bethlehem on a Christmas night all around the child shone a Holy light.
    Langston Hughes. ChG p.80

In Bethlehem on Christmas Morn. Countee Cullen. MBP p.70; OTIS p.168

In Between Time. (Transcience). Marsha Ann Jackson. TNV p.52

In Bondage. Claude McKay. AVAN p.205; HaS p.28; SPCM p.39

(In Boubon, consumption: a lack of bear sets in). Clarence Major. SAM
    p.25

"In Bounds Confined."** William C. Braithwaite. VER p.117

In calm fellowship they sleep. William S. Braithwaite. AVAN p.136; LLL
    p.29

In Chapala, Jal. Clarence Major. SAM p.31

In childhood's sunny days my heart was taught to love. Josephine D. (Hen-
    derson) Heard. EBAP p.262

In college once I climbed the tree. Owen Dodson. AmNP p.124

In Damascus, the pearl of the desert, near the pillars of Khan the Great and
    dialed to sunrise and sunset lies the wise call Straight. Melvin Tolson.
    RWA p.90

In de dead of night I sometimes. Paul Laurence Dunbar. CPPLD p.429

In de hour of death when all am still. Waverly T. Carmichael. FROF p.55

In de middle of de winter. Langston Hughes. FCTJ p.84; FNP p.23

In dead hours of night when my oil burns low, Jesus will pilot me. Raymond
    Garfield Dandridge. PeP p.13

In one   TITLE AND FIRST LINE INDEX

In one hand I hold tragedy. Langston Hughes. FN P p.25; WeB p.53
In 1 way I phrase. Clarence Major. SAM p.48
In order to do, he sat in his room at nights and asked the moon. David
    Henderson. BlSp p.87
In our little village when **elders** are around boys must not look at girls.
    Matei Markwei. MBP p.20
In our time there were musicspheres that made the sound for us to dance.
    Gerald W. Barrax. AKOR p.16
In places like Selma, Alabama. Langston Hughes. EbR p.88
In Quest. Georgia Douglas Johnson. HWOP p.44
In revolutionary day a struggling nation, young, sent out a call for volun-
    teers. Raymond Garfield Dandridge. PeP p.30
In Robert's early manhood his people were not news. Eloise Culver. GANIV
    p.50
In rude days pre-scientific man was sunk in mere paganity. William C.
    Braithwaite. VER p.38
In shades of ebony the scarlet orchids grow. William L. Morrison. DaR p.37
In some distant year should you come to me sons lovers. Tomi Carolyn
    Tinsley. EbR p.141
In Some Time Hence. Isabelle McClellan Taylor. EbR p.136
In sometime hence, in some well-doing year when we have done with war.
    Isabelle McClellan Taylor. EbR p.136
In Spite Of All This Much Needed Thunder.** Zack Gilbert. PoNe p.390
In Spite of Death. Countee Cullen. CpS p.55
In Stripes. Raymond Garfield Dandridge. PAOP p.49
In such an armor he may rise and raid. Gwendolyn Brooks. IADB p.16; ITBLA
    p.217
In Summer. Paul Laurence Dunbar. CPPLD p.144
In Summer Time. Paul Laurence Dunbar. CPPLD p.462
In sun-whetted morning. Robert Hayden. SPRH p.42
In that great day, people, in that great day, God's a-going to rain down
    fire. James Weldon Johnson. GoT p.53
In the age-dark cavern of the blood's treasured tomb. Craig Williamson. AfW
    p.16
In the American lexicon of race and color Black is imaged as ashes on new
    fallen snow. Arthur Boze. BlWo p.13
In the Athenaeum Looking Out On the Granary Burying Ground on a Rainy Day in
    November. William S. Braithwaite. HFL p.92
In The Beginning. Don L. Lee. BrT p.112; DSNP p.178; WWW p.54
In the beginning is the black fire. Craig Williamson. AfW p.48
In the beginning of my love wild hearts and trees. LeRoi Jones. BMP p.207
In the beginning was the sight. Johari Amini. TGWL p.12
In the beginning was the word. Nikki Giovanni. BFBTBJ p.60
In the Black crime hearts. LeRoi Jones. BMP p.145
In the chateau on Espagne of vanity, bones and flesh, Black keys and white
    keys - changs and Engs - argued themselves into apoplexy. Melvin Tolson.
    HaG p.48
In the church of stained glass. James Randall. BrT p.133
In the city of St. Francis they have taken down the statue of St. Francis.
    Bob Kaufman. PoNe p.409

In the cool of the day - God was walking - around in the garden of Eden.
   James Weldon Johnson. GoT p.31
In the cool waters of the river. Valente Goenha Mal Angatana. TYBP p.190
In the Courtroom. Sonia Sanchez. WABP p.34
In the crazy quilt! of many colors! Africa! Ted Joans. BPW p.101
In the dark before the tall moon came. Langston Hughes. FOW p.45; MBP p.99
In the dark corners of buildings were politicians and their gray men won't be
   caught dead. Victor Hernandez Cruz. SNA p.23
In the dark the elf who had inherited the material world sat in a dark room
   with only himself. LeRoi Jones. BMP p.156
In the dark tower, out side the big city. LeRoi Jones. BMP p.97
In The Days When I Was Extemporaneously Dead (Wid Joy). Clarence Major. SAM
   p.60
In the East a star is rising. George Reginald Margetson. ANP p.56
In the east the morning comes. Paul Laurence Dunbar. CPPLD p.323
In The Evening. Fenton Johnson. AVAN p.161
In the evening, love returns. Fenton Johnson. AVAN p.161
In the face of the pace of an on-rushing horde. Raymond Dandridge. ZaP
p.107
In the forenoon's restful quiet. Paul Laurence Dunbar. CPPLD p.150
In the Gold Mines. B. W. Vilakazi. TYBP p.176
In the great northwest, always, my grandmother warned me. LeRoi Jones. BMP
   p.8
In the Heart of a Rose. George Marion McLlelan. EBAP p.122
In the heart of the maze. Robert Hayden. BOR p.56; SPRH p.36
In the heavy earth the miner. Paul Laurence Dunbar. CPPLD p.172
In the high, high grass of Guinee. Jacques Roumain. PoN p.363
In the High Hills. William S. Braithwaite. LLL p.80
In the Hour of Death. Waverly T. Carmichael. FROF p.55
In the in the quarter. Langston Hughes. PATL p.81; PoNe p.203
In the interest of Black salvation. Don L. Lee. BrT p.88; DSNP p.58
In the lightness of the breeze I heard your heart's soft tears. Helen C.
   Harris. EbR p.78
In the Matter of Two Men. James David Corrothers. BANP p.76
In the Mecca. Gwendolyn Brooks. ITM p.5
In the merry days of Bluff King Hal, York fair was the place for festival.
   William C. Braithwaite. VER p.29
In the middle of the harbour. Derek Walcott. TYBP p.111
In the Midst of Life. Countee Cullen. B1C p.20
In the morning. Paul Laurence Dunbar. CPPLD p.307; GoS p.5; WMS p.113
In the morning the city. Langston Hughes. GoS p.133
In the narrow street. H. D. Carberry.PoN p.338
In the pit of their presumption encumbered yet with the weight of fear.
   Samuel W. Allen. CNAW p.617
In the Public Garden. William S. Braithwaite. HFL p.54
In the quarter of the Negroes. PATL p.81; PoNe p.203
In the rain she was singing. LeRoi Jones. BMP p.176
In the ribs of an ugly school building. H. Carl Holman. KAL p.165
In the silence of my heart. Paul Laurence Dunbar. CPPLD p.175
In the sombre garden close. Paul Laurence Dunbar. CPPLD p.342

Interne at Provident. Langston Hughes. OWT p.134
Interracial. Georgia Douglas Johnson. EbR p.93; PoN p.59; PoNe p.77; TYBP
    p.210
Interrogation. Walter G. Arnold. EbR p.3
Interview. Ted Joans. AFR p.88
Interview in Color. Delores Kendrick. TGWL p.61
Into Blackness Softly. Mari Evans. IABW p.26
Into fog-horned space the word was uttered. Carter Webster. EbR p.153
Into the furnace let me go alone. Claude McKay. AVAN p.206; FNP p.7; HaS
    p.52; PoN p.333; PoNe p.103; SPCM p.35
Into the garden of sorrow. Georgia Douglas Johnson. HWOP p.20
Into the moorland stream it fell. William C. Braithwaite. VER p.125
Into the sixties a trane came. Don L. Lee. BrT p.93; DCS p.27; DSNP p.94
Invention of Comics, The. LeRoi Jones. AmNP p.179; CNAW p.647
Invisible Man, The. Conrad Kent Rivers. BTB p.168; KAL p.20
Invisible reality like twist thrush ball jamming in the heavens. LeRoi
    Jones. BMP p.20
Invisible, saccharined, intoxicating stimulant I drank of you. Raymond
    Garfield Dandridge. PAOP p.42; ZaP p.6
Invitation, The. Waverly T. Carmichael. FHOF p.22
Invitation. Frenchy J. Hodges. BlW p.7
Invitation To Love. Paul Laurence Dunbar. CPPLD p.96; LOLL p.142
Invocation. Charles R. Dinkins. AVAN p.105
Invocation. Helene Johnson. AmNP p.102; BANP p.282; PoN p.153; PoNe p.265
Involv'd in clouds of wo, Maria mourns. Phillis Wheatley. PPW p.79
Ione. Paul Laurence Dunbar. CPPLD p.49; LOLL p.70
Iota. Melvin Tolson. HaG p.51
Iowa Farmer. Margaret Walker. FMP p.55; KAL p.144
Ipigenia. Owen Dodson. PLL p.94
Ira Aldridge, Shakespearean Actor, 1805-1867? New York. Eloise Culver.
    GANIV p.21
Iron Years: For Money. Clarence Major. SoS p.89
Ironic: LL.D. William S. Braithwaite. BANP p.104
Irritable Song. Russell Atkins. AmNP p.170
Is A Dead Man. Victor Hernandez Cruz. SNA p.25
I's a gittin' weary of de way dat people do. Paul Laurence Dunbar. CPPLD
    p.400
I's a produck ob de country whar de wimins wear thair clo'es. Raymond Gar-
    field Dandridge. ZaP p.2
Is a slender chick running drunkenly from her "nigger" mother taking hours to
    tell of her Blackness. Edward J. Spriggs. FoM p.74
I's always been a workin' girl. Langston Hughes. FCTJ p.66
I's boun' to see my gal to-night. Paul Laurence Dunbar. CPPLD p.227; LiG
    p.100
Is de grass a growin' up. Charles B. Johnson. SOMP p.47
Is Dunbar gone, forever and for aye? Charles Fred White. PONS p.101
I's feelin' kin' o' lonesome in my little room to-night. Paul Laurence
    Dunbar. CPPLD p.32; WMS p.123
I's got 'ligion--yes 'ndeed. Charles B. Johnson. SOMP p.52
Is it because I Am Black? Joseph S. Cotter, Jr. BOG p.14; BANP p.186

Is it not strange that East and West should meet. Melvin Tolson. RWA p.81
Is life itself but many ways of thought. Anne Spencer. CaD p.48
Is Macbeth a "God in Ruins?" Charles Fred White. PONS p.161
Is Natural Take Me In. Clarence Major. SAM p.30
Is red beans ray barretto banging away stem out the radio. Victor Hernandez
    Cruz. SNA p.61
I's sebenty-two an' feelin' good. Raymond Dandridge. PeP p.42
Is she the sage who will not slip. Georgia Douglas Johnson. HWOP p.16
Is something like the rest of our doubt. LeRoi Jones. BLIA p.394
Is that the Blackman can not be destroyed I sed. Jackie Earley. BlSp p.62
Is The Eternal Voice Coltrane Is. Larry Neal. NBP p.92
Is the moment conscious that (with public prescription). Delores Kendrick.
    TGWL p.60
Is there not a hand of power that can stay the wheel of fate? Charles Fred
    White. PONS p.85
Is this dancing sunlight. Frank Horne. AmNP p.51
Is This the Price of Love? Joseph S. Cotter, Jr. BOG p.8
Is yo eye so empty in the moonlight of yo smoke. Johari Amini. BlSp p.2
Is You Is. Bernie Casey. LATP p.70
Isaiah. Margaret Walker. PFND p.24
Isaiah LXIII: 1-8. Phillis Wheatley. PAL p.82; PPW p.27
Isaiah was a man of the court. Margaret Walker. PFND p.24
I'se Jes' Er Little Negro. Joseph S. Cotter. CPJSC p.58; WSDO p.56
Island. Langston Hughes. DYTB p.58
Isolated interests that you do not share. Ted Joans. AFR p.89
Isolation. Georgia Douglas Johnson. AVAN p.208; HWOP p.29
It Am That Way. Ted Joans. BPW p.21
It couldn't be so if we tried to make it. William S. Braithwaite. SPWSB
    p.47
It crawled away from 'neath my feet. Blanche Taylor Dickinson. CaD p.109
It does not happen that love, removes. LeRoi Jones. KAL p.213; TYBP p.250
It does not matter what the text may be. Joseph S. Cotter. CPJSC p.62
It had never struck me til once. Albert Aubert. ATB p.20
It had no dignity before. Langston Hughes. FOW p.94
It Happened in Montgomery. Phil W. Petrie. MBP p.86
It has been hard for you sapphire. Bernie Casey. LATP p.78
It is a blessed heritage to wear pain. Mae V. Cowdery. WLOV p.64
It is a blessed thing to look into. Joseph S. Cotter, Sr. LOF p.53
It is a clever pushbutton you have, Juan Trippe. Samuel Allen. PoNe p.344
It is a great temptation to behold. Joseph S. Cotter, Sr. LOF p.36
It is a new America. Jean Toomer. AmNP p.34; PoNe p.107; SoS p.72
It is a new day and the sun is not dead. Don L. Lee. BrT p.116; DSN p.182;
    WWW p.58
It is a story that it cannot tell. Joseph S. Cotter, Sr. CPJSC p.12; WSBO
    p.25
It is as if a silver chord. Paul Laurence Dunbar. CPPLD p.352
It is cold Tuesday. Victor Hernandez Cruz. SNA p.3
It is crystal clear. Ted Joans. BPW p.81
It is crystal clear. Ted Joans. BPW p.83
It is dangerous for a woman to defy the gods. Anne Spencer. AmNP p.19; CNAW
    p.270; ITBLA p.155; PoN p.51

It is   TITLE AND FIRST LINE INDEX

It is dark, now, and grave. Michael Echeruo.   TYBP p.163
It is fitting that you be here. Frank Horne.   BANP p.276; CaD p.112; PoN
    p.76; PoNe p.146; TYBP p.212
It is friday the eagle has flown. Amus Mor.   BlSp p.142
It is midnight. Sonia Sanchez.   BrT p.136
It is New Year's Day. Margaret Danner.   PoNe p.162
It is night, and like the others, I clean my weapons. Larry Neal.   TGWL
    p.74
It is no longer night. Raymond Dandridge.   ZaP p.49
It is not "peace at any price" to which the world now must aspire. Isabelle
    McClellan Taylor.   EbR p.136
It is not weariness. Langston Hughes.   FOW p.16
It is nothing to me, the beauty said. Frances Harper.   EBAP p.32; PBFH p.42
It is Ours. Ted Joans.   AFR p.137
It is quite evident by now that Kennedys are kill able easily assinated.
    Sonia Sanchez.   WABP p.25
It is said that many a king in troubled Europe would sell his crown. Fenton
    Johnson.   GoS p.141; PoN p.61; PoNe p.85
It is so good to be alive. William S. Braithwaite.   ANP p.52; AVAN p.139;
    HFL p.48
It is so important to record. Nikki Giovanni.   BFBTBJ p.66
It is strange that I should want? William S. Braithwaite.   SPWSB p.35
It is the Negro' tragedy I feel which binds me like a heavy iron chain.
    Claude McKay.   BLIA p.167; BTB p.145; SPCM p.50
It Is Time. Ted Joans.   KAL p.192; NNPUSA p.34
It is time for the United States to spend money on education so that every
    American would be hipper, thus no way! Ted Joans.   KAL p.192; NNPUSA p.34
It is time to call the Children. Robert Hayden.   HSITD p.52
It is writ in truth's eternal. Walter Everette Hawkins.   AVAN p.148
It Just Ain't Right.** Theresa Thorpe.   BTh p.62
It leads into a world where beauty sip. Joseph S. Cotter, Sr.   CPJSC p.21
It looks like to me. Langston Hughes.   OWT p.111
It may be misery not to sing at all. Paul Laurence Dunbar.   ANP p.28; AVAN
    p.90; CPPLD p.367
It must have been yesterday. Langston Hughes.   SIH p.118
It needs no heaven - inspired eye. Joseph S. Cotter, Sr.   LOF p.3; SPPH p.45
It Seems To Me. Edna L. Anderson.   EbR p.1
"It seems to me," said Booker T. Dudley Randall.   BrT p.127; BTB p.165; CNAW
    p.774; KAL p.131; MBP p.84
it sits there. Ted Joans.   BPW p.110
It started with an alto horn, and a young boy. Frank London Brown.   PoNe
    p.395
It starts with a hand reaching out in the night. Nikki Giovanni.   BFBTBJ
    p.15
It takes two hearts. Waring Cuney.   LUP p.7
It was a blue fly with wings of pomegranate gold. Joaquim Maria Machado De
    Assis.   TYBP p.81
It Was a Funky Deal.** Etheridge Knight.   BLIA p.425; BOL p.32; BrT p.83;
    FoM p.21
It was a long time ago. Langston Hughes.   BANP p.240; DYTB p.67; WeB p.55

It was a year ago. Victor Hernandez Cruz. SNA p.19
It was as if Gaugin had upset a huge paintpot. Margaret Danner. BrT p.39
It was Chrismus Eve, I mind hit fu' a mighty gloomy day. Paul Laurence Dun-
   bar. CNAW p.212; CPPLD p.219
It was early, early one mornin'. Anonymous. TYBP p.201
It was in the year of eighteen hundred and sixty-one. Anonymous. BLIA p.45;
   ITBLA p.123
It was no dream. Victor Hernandez Cruz. SNA p.85
It was on that night down by the bay on the road that leads to Bizoton.
   H. Binga Dismond. EbR p.58
It was on the top of a hill beneath the glittering stars that I saw you.
   Georgia Holloway Jones. EbR p.98
It was raining. Ted Joans. AFR p.114
It was running down to the great Atlantic. Lula Lowe Weeden. CaD p.228
It was Tiny's habit to go down to the Great White Way. David Henderson.
   NNPUSA p.76; PoNe p.437
It Was Not Fate.** William H. A. Moore. BANP p.87
It was one day 'bout one er clock. Waverly T. Carmichael. FHOF p.17
It was that lonely day, folks. Langston Hughes. SIH p.69
It was the silver, heart-enveloping view. Claude McKay. HaS p.19; SPCM
   p.25
It was Tiny's Habit. David Henderson. ITBLA p.273; KAL p.223
It was very pleasant not having you around this afternoon. Nikki Giovanni.
   MyH p.21
It was water I was trying to think of all the time. Donald Jeffrey Hayes.
   AmNP p.90; PoN p.138; PoNe p.246
It was wild the bullet hit high. Don L. Lee. BOL p.29; BrT p.97; DCS p.32;
   DSNP p.99
It was yesterday morning I looked in my box for mail. Langston Hughes. OWT
   p.96
It Were As If This World Were Paradise.** William S. Braithwaite. LLL p.52
It will rain tonight. Joseph E. Kariuki. TYBP p.171
It would be too bad if Jesus were to come back Black. Langston Hughes.
   PATL p.38
it wouldn't have been so bad if there had been a white rock group singing
   "steal away." Nikki Giovanni. MyH p.61
It wuz cole, de snow dun drifted hi' roun & 'bout de ole barn do'e. Raymond
   Garfield Dandridge. PAOP p.34; ZaP p.72
Itching Heels. Paul Laurence Dunbar. CPPLD p.362
It's A Long Way.** William S. Braithwaite. GoS p.195; LLL p.72
It's a New Kind of Day. Kali Grosvenor. PBK p.53
It's a way of keeping informed, I guess. Gerald W. Barrax. AKOR p.64
It's all a farce - these tales they tell. Paul Laurence Dunbar. CPPLD p.87;
   LOLL p.130
It's All Through Life. Waverly T. Carmichael. ANP p.30; ANP p.124; FHOF
   p.10
It's an earth song. Langston Hughes. FOW p.106
It's been so long. Victor Hernandez Cruz. SNA p.135
It's bin ni on two three years since mah goo' man, Sandy. Raymond Garfield
   Dandridge. PAOP p.64

It's Christmas Day, I did not get the presents that I hoped for. Gwendolyn Brooks. ChG p.102

Its cold concretly cold in stone cold killer cold NYC. Ted Joans. BPW p.27

Its Curtains. Ted Joans. BPW p.78; TYBP p.248

It's four-forty in the morning. W. D. Wandick. TGWL p.97

It's funny that smells and sounds return. Nikki Giovanni. MyH p.33

Its got a good shape. Ted Joans. BPW p.40

It's Here in The. Russell Atkins. AmNP p.171; SoS p.98

It's hot to-day. The bees is buzzing. Paul Laurence Dunbar. CPPLD p.460

It's just another thought I cannot grasp the significance of. William L. Morrison. DaR p.62

Its just no use, trying to be like them. James Randall. BrT p.129

It's moughty tiahsome layin' 'roun'. Paul Laurence Dunbar. CPPLD p.316

It's not enough to mourn and not enough to pray. Langston Hughes. PATL p.48

It's our anniversary. Lucia M. Pitts. EbR p.120

It's purfeck scanluss how de chillen pleges de oldah folks now days. Raymond Garfield Dandridge. PeP p.46; ZaP p.84

It's so hard to love people who will die soon. Nikki Giovanni. BFBTBJ p.33

It's such a bore. Langston Hughes. DYTB p.21

It's such a static reference looking. LeRoi Jones. ITBLA p.272; KAL p.210; NNPUSA p.73

Its sudden dash from the huddled trees. Gerald Barrax. KAL p.202

It's the long road to Guinea. Jacques Roumain. PoN p.365; TYBP p.92

It's time for bloody **Watusis** to romp through the streets wielding spears like burning crosses. Quentin Hill. NBP p.68

It's too dark to see Black in the windows of Woodward or Virginia Park. Michael S. Harper. DJDC p.76

'Ittle Touzle Head. Raymond Garfield Dandridge. BANP p.191; PAOP p.25; ZaP p.20

I've a humble little motto. Paul Laurence Dunbar. CPPLD p.69; LOLL p.102

I've always been a faithful man. Paul Laurence Dunbar. CPPLD p.441

I've been list'nin' to them lawyers. Paul Laurence Dunbar. CPPLD p.34; LOLL p.47

I've been scarred and battered. Langston Hughes. OWT p.49

I've been watchin' of 'em, Parson. Paul Laurence Dunbar. CPPLD LOLL p.83

I've come this far to freedom and I won't turn back. Naomi Long Madgett. NNPUSA p.39; PoNe p.38; SoS p.126

I've Got a Home In That Rock. Raymond Patterson. PoNe p.398

I've got to go now. Frenchy J. Hodges. BlW p.13

I've got two hundred dollars. Alice Walker. ONC p.72

I've journeyed 'roun' consid'able, a seein' men an' things. Paul Laurence Dunbar. CPPLD p.256

I've just done it to my woman. Ted Joans. AFR p.107

I've known rivers. AmNP p.63; ANP p.103; BANP p.241; BLIA p.193; CaD p.149; DYTB p.6; CNAW p.307; GoS p.52; FNP p.30; IADB p.24; ITBLA p.159; LUP p.33; PoN p.106; PoNe p.187; TYBP p.225; WeB p.51

I've Learned To Sing. Georgia Douglas Johnson. EbR p.93; GoS p.29

I've loved about all the people I can. John Sinclair. FoM p.56

I've often heard my mother say. Countee Cullen. CpS p.12; GoS p.150; OTIS p.51

I've often said, he is a poet, and a good one too. Adolphus Johnson. ANP p.53

I've seen my mother, again. Ted Joans. BPW p.39

I've stayed in the front yard all my life. Gwendolyn Brooks. IADB p.11

Ivory Masks in Orbit. Keorapetse Kgositsile. BrT p.76

- J -

J. C. in these sentences of three read by Stokely C. Allen G. & me. Ted Joans. BLIA p.388; BPW p.111

J.F.K. Blues (Just for Kicks). Ted Joans. BPW p.122

Jackson, Mississippi. Margaret Walker. BrT p.151; PFND p.12

J'ai Peur (The Coward Speaks). Lucy Ariel Holloway. BTh p.17

Jai e. Langston Hughes. FOW p.84

Jamaica Market. Agnes Maxwell-Hall. MBP p.43; PoN p.310; TYBP p.117

James Meredith, Courageous Student 1933- Mississippi. Eloise Culver. GANIV p.79

James Russell Lowell. William S. Braithwaite. LLL p.21

James Whitcomb Riley. Paul Laurence Dunbar. CPPLD p.475

Jamie's Puzzle. Frances Harper. PBFG p.34

Jane, drive the cows to the grassy hill. Joseph S. Cotter, Sr. RHY p.20

Jan E. Matzeliger, Inventor of Shoe Lasting Machine, 1852-1889, Dutch Guiana. Eloise Culver. GANIV p.39

January Dandelion, A. George Marion McLlelan. EBAP p.122

January First. Raymond Dandridge. ZaP p.51

January 16, 1967: 5:30 P.M. Gerald W. Barrax. AKOR p.43

Japanese Hokku. Lewis Alexander. CaD p.127

Jasmine. Claude McKay. BLIA p.167; HaS p.88; SPCM p.102

Jaw-Bone Town.** James Pipes. ZJP p.103

Jazz Anatomy. Ted Joans. AFR p.131

Jazz band in a Parisian cabaret. Langston Hughes. BANP p.239; FCTJ p.74

Jazz Fantasia.* Carl Sandburg. PoN p.287; PoNe p.483

Jazz Is My Religion.** Ted Joans. BPW p.71

Jazz Must Be a Woman.** Ted Joans. BPW p.76

Jazzonia. Langston Hughes. AmNP p.63; BANP p.236; BLIA p.198; FNP p.22; KAL p.87; WeB p.25

Jealous. Paul Laurence Dunbar. BLIA p.111; CPPLD p.232

Jealousy. William L. Morrison. DaR p.49

Jeff, Gene, Geronimo and Bop. Gwendolyn Brooks. ITM p.45

Jefferson in a Tight Place. George Moses Horton. CNAW p.39

Jello. Raymond Garfield Dandridge. PeP p.20; ZaP p.91

Jeremiah. Margaret Walker. PFND p.23

Jeremiah, prophet of Jerusalem, is now a man whose name is Benjamin. Margaret Walker. PFND p.23

Jericho is on the inside. Blanche Taylor Dickinson. CaD p.106

Jes' began a clump o' pines. John Wesley Holloway. AVAN p.187; BANP p.136

Jes' er settin' by de fire. J. Mord Allen. AVAN p.130

Jes' lak toddy wahms you thoo'. Paul Laurence Dunbar. CPPLD p.238; LiG p.120

Jes two strapin' he'lfee boys, Bob and me. Raymond Garfield Dandridge. PeP
    p.22; ZaP p.92
Jesse Owens, Olympic Star of 1936, 1913-   . Alabama. Eloise Culver. GANIV
    p.74
Jessie Rufus. Lucile D. Goodlett. WGC p.26
Jest finished readen a book. Sonia Sanchez. BrT p.146; WABP p.66
"Jest look at 'em 'e got on my dres'." Waverly T. Carmichael. FHOF p.11
Jester, The. Langston Hughes. FNP p.25; WeB p.53
Jésus, Estrella, Esperanza, Mercy. Robert Hayden. AmNP p.113; BLIA p.254;
    BOR p.66; CNAW p.388; IADB p.34; SPRH p.65
Jesus' mother never had no man. Waring Cuney. BANP p.284; MBP p.70; PoN
    p.145
Jesus, my gentle Jesus, walking in the dark of the garden. James Weldon
    Johnson. GoT p.39
Jesus My King in Thee I Trust. Waverly T. Carmichael. FHOF p.39
Jewels. Lucy Mae Turner. BCF p.54
Jilted. Paul Laurence Dunbar. CPPLD p.217
Jim Crow Car. Langston Hughes. PATL p.99
Jim is on the gang. Sterling A. Brown. SoR p.93
Jim never had no luck wid de women. Sterling A. Brown. SoR p.81
Jitney. Langston Hughes. OWT p.131
Jitterbugs. LeRoi Jones. BMP p.92
Jive Eschatology, A. Larry Neal. TGWL p.74
Joansizeven. Ted Joans. AFR p.121
Job of criminals (in our world) is to disrupt the living. BlSp p.24
Joe, drive slow. John Raven. FM p.30
Joe Louis. Boxing Champion, Alabama, 1914-   . Eloise Culver. GANIV p.73
Joel. Margaret Walker. PFND p.26
Joel A. Rogers. Historian. 1883-1966. Jamaica, B.W.I. Eloise Culver. GANIV
    p.60
Joel, that young prophet son of Pethuel. Margaret Walker. PFND p.26
Joggin' Er Long. Paul Laurence Dunbar. CPPLD p.265
Johann. Alice Walker. ONC p.63
John an' Mandy's prancin' 'long. Joseph S. Cotter, Sr. CPJSC p.55; WSBO
    p.50
John Brown in Kansas settled, like a steadfast yankee farmer.* Edmund
    Clarence Stedman. PoN p.239; PoNe p.493
John Brown's prayer from John Brown's body.* Stephen Vincent Benet. PoN
    p.243; PoNe p.517
John Coltrane. Alfred B. Spellman. NNPUSA p.57
John Henry. Anonymous. BLIA p.43; GoS p.34; ITBLA p.122; MBP p.81
John Henry In Harlem. Melvin Tolson. GoS p.38
Johnny Speaks. Paul Laurence Dunbar. CPPLD p.382
Johnny Thomas. Sterling A. Brown. SoR p.32
Johnny was smart and he was good. Joseph S. Cotter, Sr. LOF p.58; SPPH p.26
Johnny's Dream of Santa Claus. Joseph S. Cotter, Sr. LOF p.58; SPPH p.26
Jollity. Charles Fred White. PONS p.20
Jonathan's Song. Owen Dodson. PLL p.89
Journal, The. Michael S. Harper. DJDC p.16
Journey. Ted Joans. AFR p.103
Journey To A Parallel. Bruce McM. Wright. LUP p.56; PoN p.200; PoNe p.355

Journey To Versailles. Conrad Kent Rivers. SVH p.19
Joy. Clarissa Scott Delany. CaD p.140; PoN p.96; PoNe p.180
Joy. Langston Hughes. MBP p.21; WeB p.48
Joy. Georgia Douglas Johnson. HWOP p.25
Joy is given to me joy is given to me. Ahmed Akinwole Alhamisi. GuW p.4
Joy, like the morning, breaks from one divine. Georgia Douglas Moses Horton.
    CNAW p.35
Joy of the wave in this shell of delight is caught. William C. Braithwaite.
    VER p.66
Joy of the world is in a man's strength, The. William S. Braithwaite. HFL
    p.95
Joy or Sorrow. Leanna F. Johnson. EbR p.95
Joy shakes me like the wind that lifts a sail. Clarissa Scott Delany. CaD
    p.140; PoN p.96; PoNe p.180
Joyce Cadoo 27 st. marks place AL4-1407. LeRoi Jones. BMP p.73
Joyous nymph with childlike pride takes wings and flitters near my side.
    Jules Wynn Smith. EbR p.131
J's 'bout d'hk I com' hom' ploddin, tired and ro'sted from de sun. James E.
    McGirt. FYSS p.7
Juba Dance. Anonymous. MBP p.14
Juba jump and juba sing. Anonymous. MBP p.14
Judas Iscariot. Countee Cullen. CCC p.90
Judge Robert W. Bingham. Joseph S. Cotter, Sr. CPJSC p.13
Judge, who lives impeccably upstairs, The. Hervey Allen. PoN p.285; PoNe
    p.50
Judge Ye Not. Raymond Garfield Dandridge. PAOP p.44
Judgment Day. Langston Hughes. FCTJ p.45
Judgment Day, The. James Weldon Johnson. GoT p.53
Judgment day for Big Red the Darwinian Doge R.I.P. Kent Foreman. BrT p.26;
    FoM p.45
Judy-One. Don L. Lee. DSNP p.151; WWW p.27
Juice Joint: Northern City. Langston Hughes. OWT p.67
Juice Of A Lemon On The Trail of Little Yellow. June Jordan. SCh p.25
JuJu of my own, A. Lebert Bethune. PoNe p.414
Juke boy love song. Langston Hughes. IADB p.14; LUP p.26
Juliet. Langston Hughes. FOW p.58
July in Georgy. James Weldon Johnson. FYOP p.73
jump bigness upward like u jump clean. Don L. Lee. DSNP p.206
Jump down, turn around to pick a bale of cotton. Anonymous. ITBLA p.121
Juncture.* Rea Lubar Duncan. PoNe p.574
June Breezes and Roses. Joseph S. Cotter. CPJSC p.39
June breezes ramble through the orchard boughs. Joseph S. Cotter, Sr.
    CPJSC p.39
June-bug's got the golden wing, The. Anonymous. GoS p.15; MBP p.41
June night rain and thunder of our hearts together. Dudley Randall. LoY p.8
Jungle. Mary Carter Smith. PoNe p.389
Jungle colors fluted and starred. Marcella Caine. FoM p.8
Jungle drums beat out a rhapsody. William Lorenzo Morrison. DaR p.7
Jungle Flowers. Marcella Caine. FoM p.8
Jungle huddled in like dungeon walls, The. Melvin Tolson. RWA p.61
Jungle Taste. Edward S. Silvera. CaD p.214
Junior Addict. Langston Hughes. PATL p.12

Jus' Livin'. Julia Gaillard. BTh p.42
Just a few miles from Manilla Bay. James E. McGirt. FYSS p.22
Just a herd of Negroes driven to the field. Langston Hughes. SIH p.77
Just a New York Poem. Nikki Giovanni. MyH p.25
Just as you think you're "better now," Gwendolyn Brooks. FaP p.17
Just for a moment of your love I crave. Francis Merrill Foster. EbR p.64
Just for the sight of you. William S. Braithwaite. SPWSB p.94
Just give me something. Albert Aubert. ATB p.11
Just like a rose in early spring. Benjamin Clark. EBAP p.180
Just one year ago we broke camp in the distant Cuban plain. Charles Fred
    White. PONS p.74
Just Reward, A. Joseph S. Cotter, Sr. LOF p.64
Just Standing. Bernie Casey. LATP p.25
Just where that star above. William S. Braithwaite. LLL p.33
Just Whistle A Bit.** Paul Laurence Dunbar. CPPLD p.15
Justice. Langston Hughes. PATL p.45
Justice, has thou fled and left us in this cruel unkind land. Charles Fred
    White. PONS p.144
"Juvann - dam pang - go fam - dam pang. William C. Braithwaite. VER p.34

- K -

Ka 'Ba. LeRoi Jones. BMP p.146
Ka-choo!! Ted Joans. BPW p.100
Kappa. Melvin Tolson. HaG p.57
Karamojans. Alice Walker. ONC p.20
Karenge Ya Marenge. Countee Cullen. OTIS p.167
Karibu, mweupe, karibu. Craig Williamson. AfW p.18
Karma. LeRoi Jones. BMP p.210
Kassel B'ldin'. Raymond Garfield Dandridge. PAOP p.62
Katherine Ferguson Founder of a Sunday School, 1779-1854, New York. Eloise
    Culver. GANIV p.36
Kathleen Color of Now. Craig Williamson. AfW p.26
Kathleen shebeen queen, I thou your ebony eyes. Craig Williamson. AfW p.26
Katy-did, The. Joseph S. Cotter, Sr. LOF p.40
Keats Was an Unbeliever.** William S. Braithwaite. LLL p.27
Keep A-Pluggin' Away. Paul Laurence Dunbar. CPPLD p.69; LOLL p.102
Keep A Song Up On De Way. Paul Laurence Dunbar. CPPLD p.272
Keep Away From The Evil Gal.** John Raven. BFM p.28
Keep Me, Jesus, Keep Me. Waverly Turner Carmichael. BANP p.162; FHOF p.41
Keep me 'neath thy mighty wing. Waverly Turner Carmichael. BANP p.162;
    FHOF p.41
Kentucky Blues. Sterling A. Brown. SoR p.42
Kenyatta Listening to Mozart. LeRoi Jones. BMP p.14
Ketched Mis' Lucy's Chris'mas gif'. Charles B. Johnson. SOMP p.54
Key and bar, key and bar. Paul Laurence Dunbar. CPPLD p.327
Kid (Cuernauaca). Robert Hayden. SPRH p.35
Kid Sleepy. Langston Hughes. SIH p.24
Kiddies and the Christmas Tree, The. Joseph S. Cotter, Sr. SPPH p.19
Kidnap Poem. Nikki Giovanni. BrT p.66
Kidnaped. Paul Laurence Dunbar. CPPLD p.420
Kids in the street. Yvette Johnson. TNV p.58

Kidsnatchers. Ted Joans. AFR p.149
Kilimanjaro Vision. Craig Williamson. AfW p.18
Kin dat be Miss Mandy Jenkins cumin' yonday thoo de gate? Raymond Garfield
    Dandridge. PeP p.10; ZaP p.62
Kind of place for sale big cities where no gateways wide to greet or terminate
    the staying there persist, The. June Jordan. SCh p.73
King Is Dead, The. Paul Laurence Dunbar. CPPLD p.168
King of Chit, The. William C. Braithwaite. VER p.62
King of Spain had seven daughters, The. Countee Cullen. MASP p.78
Kingdoms and Heirs. William S. Braithwaite. HFL p.102
King's Daughter, The. William S. Braithwaite. SPWSB p.29
Kinsman of Alexander and the Christ. J. Henderson Brooks. BTh p.26
Kiss, A. William L. Morrison. DaR p.8
Kiss, The. Alice Walker, ONC p.51
Kiss me, Miami, Thou Most Constant One! Paul Laurence Dunbar. CPPLD p.457
Kissie Lee. Margaret Walker. FMP p.38
Kitchenette Building. Gwendolyn Brooks. PoN p.188; PoNe p.334
Kiver up yo' haid, my little lady. Paul Laurence Dunbar. CLT p.95; GoS
    p.191; CPPLD p.230
Knee Deep. Ted Joans. AFR p.85
Knell, The. Muhammad Al-Fituri. TYBP p.53
Knight, The. Paul Laurence Dunbar. CPPLD p.173
Knock is at her door, but she is weak, A. Paul Laurence Dunbar. CPPLD
    p.115; LOLL p.172
Knocking Donkey Fleas Off A Poet From the Southside of Chi. (for brother ted
    joans). Don L. Lee. DSNP p.170
Know then, that all your beauty's passionate burning. Robert Hayden. HSITD
    p.29
Know you, winds that blow your course. Paul Laurence Dunbar. CPPLD p.61;
    LOLL p.87
Knowed dat bird you's 'bout to cyarve. Joseph S. Cotter, Sr. SPPH p.89
Knowing all the ways Black men die. Gerald W. Barrax. AKOR p.23
Knowing her is not knowing her. Don L. Lee. DSNP p.204
Knowing the Christmas turkey. Joseph S. Cotter, Sr. SPPH p.89
Knoxville, Tennessee. Nikki Giovanni. BFBTBJ p.65; BOL p.58; BrT p.55
Ku Klux. Langston Hughes. PATL p.44; SIH p.81
Kyries in slow Swahili chanting. Craig Williamson. AfW p.6

- L -

LBJ: Rejoinder. June Jordan. SCh p.53
La. Melvin Tolson. LRL p.28
La Belle De Demerara. William S. Braithwaite. HFL p.87
La Belle, La Douce, La Grande. Countee Cullen. OTIS p.170
La caliente or how would we all talk if lips are left to us. Victor Hernan-
    dez Cruz. SNA p.127
La Corrida. Robert Hayden. BOR p.55; SPRH p.36
La Grande Granny. Ted Joans. BPW p.27
La Mambo Dans Le Hounfort. Charles F. Pressoir.PoN p.361
La Paloma in London. Claude McKay. HaS p.78
Labor and Management. LeRoi Jones. BMP p.141
Labor On. Waverly T. Carmichael. FHOF p.33

Labor w'le the sun is bright. Waverly T. Carmichael. FHOF p.33

Lacrimae Aethiopiae. Charles B. Johnson. SOMP p.3

Lad and Lass. Joseph S. Cotter, Sr. SPPH p.22

Ladder, flag and amplifier. Langston Hughes. PATL p.3

"The ladies of the D.A.R. meet here today at four for tea." David Wadsworth
    Cannon, Jr. EbR p.24

Ladies' Poem. Victor Hernandez Cruz. SNA p.35

Lady Bird.** Kali Grosvenor. PBK p.35

Lady Bug. LeRoi Jones. BMP p.102

Lady, don't dash away. John Raven. BFM p.23

Lady, my lady, come from out the garden. Sterling A. Brown. CaD p.136; SoR
    p.124

Lady Santa Ana why does the child cry? Anonymous. ChG p.81

Lady's Blues. Michael S. Harper. DJDC p.7

Lake's dark breast, The. Paul Laurence Dunbar. CPPLD p.11; LOLL p.13

Lamda. Melvin Tolson. HaG p.61; PoNe p.141

Lame Man and the Blind Man. Waring Cuney. LUP p.14; PoN p.149

Lame man said to the blind man. Waring Cuney. LUP p.14; PoN p.149

Lament. Countee Cullen. CpS p.28; OTIS p.58

Lament. Owen Dodson. PLL p.3

Lament For Dark People. Langston Hughes. WeB p.100

Lament of the Slave. Anonymous. MBP p.54

Lament Over Love. Langston Hughes. FCTJ p.81

Lamps. Mae V. Cowdery. WLOV p.16

Lancelot. Arna Bontemps. CaD p.169

Land Grave's gilded hall was all bedecked. George Marion McLlelan. EBAP
    p.132

Land-No-End. William L. Morrison. DaR p.39

Land of Avia, lovely is the scene, The. James E. McGirt. FYSS p.59

Land of Hope-To-Be, The. William S. Braithwaite. LLL p.30

Land of quiet distance, where grazed, A. William C. Braithwaite. VER p.81

Land, 'Twixt Severn and Cotswold.** William C. Braithwaite. VER p.104

Land wants me to come back, The. Langston Hughes. FOW p.15

Langston. Mari Evans. BOL p.27

Langston Hughes. Jacques Roumain. PoN p.364

Langston Hughes paid his dues in the Harlems of the U.S.A. Ted Joans. BPW
    p.44

Langston Hughes, Writer, Missouri, 1902-1967. Eloise Culver. GANIV p.65

Langston, I would like to tell you about your poems. Kali Grosvenor. PBK
    p.49

Language We Are, The. F. J. Bryant. NBP p.32

Lanthwaite Green. William C. Braithwaite. VER p.48

Lapse, The. Paul Laurence Dunbar. CPPLD p.195

Larger Life, A. Charles B. Johnson. SOMP p.24

Lark is silent in his nest. Paul Laurence Dunbar. CPPLD p.97; LOLL p.144

Las' dance gwine dance to-night down in Holly's gyarden. Eli Shepperd.
    PlS p.10

Las' Sunday mo'nin', ha'f pas' eight, wid fishin' pole an can ob bait. Ray-
    mond Garfield Dandridge. PeP p.32

Lass is leaning on a wicker gate, A. Joseph S. Cotter, Sr. SPPH p.22

TITLE AND FIRST LINE INDEX

Lawd, howdy boy! whar hab you bin? Raymond Garfield Dandridge. PeP p.16;
    ZaP p.58
Lawd, I'm goin' away for the summer. Anonymous. ITBLA p.121
Lawd is dead, The. Barbara Marshall. TNV p.70
Laws of Nature. Adolphus Johnson. ANP p.54
Lawyers' Ways, The. Paul Laurence Dunbar. CPPLD p.34; LOLL p.47
Lay all of it open. LeRoi Jones. BMP p.58
Lay him down gently, lay him down slow. Margaret Burroughs. FoM p.22
Lay me down beneaf de willers in de grass. Paul Laurence Dunbar. AVAN p.91;
    BANP p.62; CaD p.4; CPPLD p.228, PoNe p.42
Lay my love in morning shroud. Craig Williamson. AfW p.37
Lazily lifting with rarity upward. William Morrison. DaR p.12
Lazy. James Weldon Johnson. AVAN p.177; FYOP p.45
Lazy Day, A. Paul Laurence Dunbar. CPPLD p.408
Lazy, laughing South with blood on its mouth, The. Langston Hughes. WeB
    p.54
Lazy petals of magnolia bloom float down the sluggish river. John Gould
    Fletcher. PoNe p.503
Lazy Sam. Joseph S. Cotter, Sr. SPPH p.75; WSBO p.53
Le Fou de Banba. Ted Joans. AFT p.48
Lead gently, Lord, and slow. Paul Laurence Dunbar. AVAN p.61; CPPLD p.156
Leadbelly Gives An Autograph. LeRoi Jones. BMP p.25
Leader, A. Raymond Garfield Dandridge. PeP p.33
Leader of the pack. Marion Nicholes. LiS p.19
Leaders, The. Gwendolyn Brooks. ITM p.45
Leaf from freedom is golden chap let fair. Henrietta Cordelia Ray. EBAP
    p.139
Lear is gay ... Robert Hayden. BOR p.39
Learned sages, scan these pages. Raymond Garfield Dandridge. PAOP p.40
Learning to Read. Frances Harper. EBAP p.37; CNAW p.106
Leave him alone, sweet enemy. Kwesi Brew. TYBP p.166
Leave my eyes alone. June Jordan. SCh p.20
Leave-taking, I, A. William S. Braithwaite. LLL p.25
Leave-taking, II, A. William S. Braithwaite. LLL p.26
Leave Your Coras. Langston Hughes. LUP p.25
Leaves. Countee Cullen. ANP p.96; CpS p.84
Leaves Blow Backward. June Jordan. SCh p.40
Leaves blow backward with the wind behind them. June Jordan. SCh p.40
Leaves In the Wind. Robert Hayden. HSITD p.55
Legacies. Nikki Giovanni. MyH p.5
Legacy. LeRoi Jones. BMP p.19
Legacy: my South. Dudley Randall. BTB p.166; NNPUSA p.43; PoNe p.306
Legend of Versailles, A. Melvin Tolson. RWA p.65
Legs. Bernie Casey. LATP p.73
Legs long nice between them, The. Bernie Casey. LATP p.73
Lemme be wid Casey Jones. Sterling A. Brown. BANP p.248; CaD p.130; CNAW
    p.400; SoR p.5
Lemme roll 'em boy. Langston Hughes. FCTJ p.34
Lemme Tell You What My Black Is All About. Clarence Reed. BlSp p.168
"Lend me thy fire," I said to my soul. Joseph S. Cotter, Sr. LOF p.57
Length of Moon. Arna Bontemps. BTB p.114; PoN p.114; PoNe p.214; CaD p.168

Lenox Avenue. Sidney Alexander. PoN p.304; PoNe p.556
Lenox Avenue Bar. Langston Hughes. PATL p.10
Lenox Avenue: Midnight. Langston Hughes. WeB p.39
L'envoi. William S. Braithwaite. HFL p.111
Leopard. Edward Braithwaite. MBP p.36
Leroy. LeRoi Jones. BMP p.217
Lerve. LeRoi Jones. BMP p.150
Lesson. Countee Cullen. BlC p.55
Lesson, The. Paul Laurence Dunbar. CPPLD p.10; LOLL p.12
Lest any forward thought intrude. Countee Cullen. CpS p.66
Lester Young. Ted Joans. AmNP p.171; ITBLA p.273
Let all who will eat quietly the bread of shame. Langston Hughes. PATL p.39
Let America be America again.** Langston Hughes. PoN p.106; PoNe p.193
Let Amicitia in her ample reign. Phillis Wheatley. EBAP p.111
Let Bourbons fight for status quo. Binga Dismond. PoN p.67; PoNe p.93
Let de people know (unnh). Myron O'Higgins. PoN p.194; PoNe p.347
Let happy throats be mute. Donald Jeffrey Hayes. AmNP p.93
Let me be buried in the rain. Helene Johnson. AmNP p.102; BANP p.282; PoN
    p.153; PoNe p.265
Let me close the eyes of my soul. Paul Laurence Dunbar. CPPLD p.431
Let me crook my arm around them. Mari Evans. IABW p.47
Let me hip you to the streets. Maya Angelou. JGM p.27
Let me learn now where beauty is. Anne Spencer. CaD p.48
Let me Live With Marriage.** June Jordan. SCh p.35
Let me seek no statesman's mantle let me seek no victor's wreath. Walter
    Everette Hawkins. ANP p.68
Let me steal gently from the marts of men when the sun is sending forth her
    ray. Constantia E. Riley. EbR p.126
Let My People Go. James Weldon Johnson. GoT p.45
Let none ignobly Halt.** Joseph S. Cotter. EBAP p.192; LOF p.56
Let not sorrow burden you thoughts. Mae V. Cowdery. WLOV p.31
Let not the proud of heart condemn. Countee Cullen. BlC p.16; OTIS p.84
Let the knowing speak. Charles Enoch Wheeler. AmNP p.105; PoN p.158; PoNe
    p.272
Let the leaders of nations. Beatrice M. Murphy. TNV p.139
Let the Light Enter. Frances Harper. PBFH p.71; PoN p.11; PoNe p.15
Let the rain kiss you. Langston Hughes. DYTB p.14
Let the r(evolution) come, uh. Carolyn M. Rodgers. TNV p.112
Let them come to us. Lucia M. Pitts. EbR p.117
Let there be one word more. William S. Braithwaite. LLL p.25
Let this be scattered far and wide, laid low. Countee Cullen. BlC p.18;
    OTIS p.86
Let this the funeral of our difference be. Charles Fred White. PONS p.120
Let those who will stride on their barren roads. Paul Laurence Dunbar.
    CPPLD p.349
Let Us Begin the Real Word (for Elijah Muhammad who has begun).** Sonia
    Sanchez. BrT p.145; WABP p.65
Let us not turn for this aside to me. Countee Cullen. BlC p.46; OTIS p.94
Let us promise ourselves this: when this interlude grows stagnant. Will
    Smallwood. EbR p.130
Let us talk the two of us. Don L. Lee. DSNP p.33

"Life and art," said Doctor Nkomo, "beget incestuously (like Osiris and Isis)
    the talented of brush and pen. Melvin Tolson. HaG p.83
Life and Death. William S. Braithwaite. LLL p.62
Life And Death. Joseph S. Cotter, Sr. SPPH p.57
Life and Love. James E. McGirt. FYSS p.52
Life for him must be the shivering of a great drum. Langston Hughes. FCTJ
    p.40; FNP p.24
Life in our Village. Matei Markwei. MBP p.20
Life is a boundless sea, on which men float. James E. McGirt. FYSS p.52
Life is Action. Jamye H. Coleman. EbR p.52
Life is Fine. Langston Hughes. OWT p.38
Life is the Art of Drawing.** Carolyn Ogletree. TNV p.79
Life-Long, Poor Browning.** Anne Spencer. CaD p.49; PoN p.50; PoNe p.60
Life of God, The. Marion Cuthbert. SOC p.17
Life of Lincoln West, The. Gwendolyn Brooks. BrT p.33; FaP p.9
Life of the Spirit in the Natural World, The. Charles S. Conner. ANP p.118
Life/ Poem. Sonia Sanchez. BrT p.142; WABP p.55
Life Styles. Marion Nicholes. LiS p.11
Life to the bigot is a whip. Dorothy Vena Johnson. EbR p.91; PoN p.120;
    PoNe p.226
Life Ushers some as heirs-elect. Countee Cullen. CCC p.63
Life was mine full of the close concern. Paul Laurence Dunbar. CPPLD p.164
Life was trembling faintly trembling. Frances Harper. CNAW p.102; ITBLA
    p.93; PBFH p.17
Life's certainties doth build a span. Joseph S. Cotter. CPJSC p.13
Life's Circus. Raymond Dandridge. PeP p.7; ZaP p.5
Life's fibres we are won't to separate. Joseph S. Cotter, Sr. LOF p.45
Life's Tragedy. Paul Laurence Dunbar. ANP p.28; AVAN p.90; CPPLD p.367
Lift Every Voice and Sing. James Weldon Johnson. GoS p.69; ITBLA p.119;
    PoN p.32; PoNe p.32
Light flowed between black branches and new snow. Dudley Randall. LoY p.12
Light inside has flickered and died, The. Frenchy J. Hodges. BLW p.22
Light lady. Countee Cullen. B1C p.24
Light, light, light natural light. Edward Christmas. TGWL p.7
"Light! more light! the shadows deepen. Frances Harper. PBFH p.71; PoN
    p.11; PoNe p.15
Light of Victory. George Reginald Margetson. ANP p.56
Light - years and then a star. Dudley Randall. LoY p.11
Lights. W. Blanche Nivens. BTh p.44
Like a Strong Tree. Claude McKay. FNP p.7; SPCM p.45
Like a wild flame it leaps and speaks to the innermost portion of the soul.
    Dolores A. Brown. EbR p.15
Like Brothers we Meet. George Moses Horton. CNAW p.40
Like dives in the deeps of hell I cannot break this fearful spell. Frances
    Harper. PBFH p.40
Like heart-loving brothers we meet. George Moses Horton. CNAW p.40
Like how do you build on a tower of truths. Val Gray Ward. TGWL p.99
Like hungry birds searching a winter land. Carole Gregory Clemmons. TGWL
    p.20
Like I can't say that they're whatchacallits. Arthur Pfister. B1Sp p.160
Like i mean don't it all come down to e / co / no / mics. Sonia Sanchez.
    WABP p.22

Listen, I'se talkin' to you, lawd. Frenchy J. Hodges. BlW p.19
          Kid sleepy. Langston Hughes. SIH p.24
Listen Lord. James Weldon Johnson. BANP p.125
Listen, Masa Joel, I'se er callin' ter you. Joseph S. Cotter, Sr. SPPH p.84;
     WSBO p.14
Listen more often. Birago Diop. TYBP p.139
Listen, this here is what Charlie did to the blues. Waring Cuney. BTB p.83
Listen to big black at S.F. State. Sonia Sanchez. WABP p.48
Listen to me colored brothers. Ted Joans. BPW p.98
Listen to the soul sounds through paper thin walls. Ted Joans. BPW p.68
Listen to the tale. Sterling Brown. BANP p.256; SoR p.83
Listen to yo' prophets. Langston Hughes. DYTB p.32; FCTJ p.49
Listen, white man, listen well. Samuel A. Haynes. EbR p.80
Litany. George Campbell. PoN p.317
Litany. Robert Hayden. HSITD p.49
Litany. Gordon Parks. InL (unpaged)
Litany for Peppe. Nikki Giovanni. BFBTBJ p.57
Litany of Atlanta done at Atlanta in the Day of Death, 1906, A. William
     Edward Burghardt DuBois. ANP p.115; BANP p.90; CaD p.26; PoN p.18; PoNe
     p.20
Litany of the Dark People, The. Countee Cullen. CpS p.13; OTIS p.53
Little Anthony and the Imperials singer. Sonia Sanchez. WABP p.30
Little April Child. William L. Morrison. DaR p.10
Little Birches. Effie Lee Newsome. PoN p.8; PoNe p.72
Little birches haunt the hills, The. Effie Lee Newsome. PoNe p.72
Little bird sits in the nest and sings, The. Paul Laurence Dunbar. CPPLD
     p.106; LOLL p.158
Little bird with plumage brown, A. Paul Laurence Dunbar. CPPLD p.125; LOLL
     p.185
Little Black boy, The.* William Blake. PoN p.215; PoNe p.445
Little Black Boy. Frank Horne. BANP p.268; CaD p.120
Little Black Boy.** Barbara Marshall. TNV p.69
Little black falcons blazing through wide open skies. Arthur Boze. BlWo
     p.18
Little blonde Johnny in school reading Alice in Wonderland and the Arabian
     Knights. Arthur Boze. BlWo p.5
Little boy who sticks a needle in his arm and seeks an out in other worldly
     dreams. Langston Hughes. PATL p.12
Little boys playing in fields of ominous green. Bernie Casey. LATP p.47
Little brother, little brother, put your feet on the floor. Michael Brown.
     DJDC p.34
Little Brown Bitch Blues (or; I've got the sun in my soul). Ted Joans. BPW
     p.127
Little Brown Baby. Paul Laurence Dunbar. BANP p.53; CPPLD p.214; MBP p.100;
     PoN p.37; PoNe p.40
Little brown baby wif spa'klin' eyes. Paul Laurence Dunbar. BANP p.53;
     CPPLD p.214; MBP p.100; PoN p.37; PoNe p.40
Little Brown Boy. Helene Johnson. AmNP p.100; BANP p.279; CaD p.218; GoS
     p.112
Little brown face full of smiles. Paul Laurence Dunbar. CPPLD p.442
Little Brown Jug. LeRoi Jones. BMP p.134

Little   TITLE AND FIRST LINE INDEX

Little Cabin, A. Charles Bertram Johnson. BANP p.198; SOMP p.29
Little Child Shall Lead Them. Francis Harper. PBFH p.19
Little Child That Leads, The. Joseph S. Cotter, Sr. CPJSC p.37; WSBO p.26
Little children, I believe! Been long time waggin' wid de cross. Eli Shepperd. PlS p.11
Little Christmas Basket, A. Paul Laurence Dunbar. ChG p.66
Little Cousins. Victor Hernandez Cruz. BOL p.68
Little Dandelion, The. Lula Lowe Weeden. CaD p.229
Little David play on yo' harp. Anonymous. GoS p.63; MBP p.80
Little David was a shepherd boy. Anonymous. GoS p.63; MBP p.80
Little dreaming by the way, A. Paul Laurence Dunbar. AVAN p.88; CPPLD p.183
Little dreams of spring time. Langston Hughes. PATL p.95
Little firefly passed me by, A. Eleanor A. Thompson. BTh p.47
Little Girl. Raymond Garfield Dandridge. PeP p.45
Little girl was sitting near her mother's house one day, A. Eloise Culver. GANIV p.15
Little Green Tree. Langston Hughes. OWT p.111
Little Green Tree Blues. Langston Hughes. PoN p.99
Little Hour of Sunshine. Georgia Douglas Johnson. HWOP p.49
Little kittens in de coal-house. J. Mord Allen. AVAN p.128
Little lady at de do'. Paul Laurence Dunbar. CPPLD p.284; WMS p.99
Little Lucy Land Man. Paul Laurence Dunbar. CPPLD p.170
Little Lyric. Langston Hughes. SIH p.21
Little Old Letter. Langston Hughes. OWT p.96
Little People. Bernie Casey. LATP p.47
Little Poem, A. Linda Brown. BTB p.54
Little Robin Red Breast. Lula Lowe Weeden. CaD p.228
Little snail dreaming you go. Langston Hughes. DYTB p.47; FOW p.4; GoS p.149; MBP p.36
Little Son. Georgia Douglas Johnson. AVAN p.209; CaD p.76
Little Song, A. William S. Braithwaite. AVAN p.135; LLL p.20
Little Song. Langston Hughes. FOW p.82
Little Song for the Children of Antilles. Nicolas Guillen. MBP p.14
Little song ill worth your while, A. William S. Braithwaite. AVAN p.135; LLL p.20
Little Song on Housing. Langston Hughes. PATL p.79
Little Sonnet to Little Friends. Countee Cullen. BlC p.16; OTIS p.84
Little Southern Colored Child, A. Langston Hughes. FOW p.99
Little Space, A. William L. Morrison. DaR p.61
Little Sycamore, The. Anonymous. TYBP p.29
Little Things. Raymond Garfield Dandridge. PeP p.17
Little While Before Farewell.** William S. Braithwaite. HFL p.66
Little White Schoolhouse Blues. Florence Becker Lennon. PoNe p.514
Little Willie a hero in the American tradition. Don L. Lee. DCS p.38
Little yellow looked at the banana tree. June Jordan. SCh p.25
Live and love; live and love. Valerie Tarver. TNV p.127
Live Celebration. Sarah Webster Fabio. TGWL p.34
"Live like the wind" he said, "unfettered. Countee Cullen. CpS p.39
Living Grave, A. Joseph S. Cotter, Sr. SPPH p.68
Living is too much effort ... Mari Evans. IABW p.33
Liza May. Paul Laurence Dunbar. CPPLD p.442

Long time ago, we two set out. Paul Laurence Dunbar. CPPLD p.191
Long time past before your Papa live before him Papa live before him pa's
     papa live. Lorenz Graham. ChG p.82
'Long To'ds Night. Paul Laurence Dunbar. CPPLD p.302; WMS p.137
Long Trip. Langston Hughes. DYTB p.51; WeB p.73
Long View: Negro. Langston Hughes. PATL p.30
Long years ago, within a distant clime. Paul Laurence Dunbar. CPPLD p.166
Longing. Paul Laurence Dunbar. CPPLD p.33; LOLL p.45
Longing. Lillian Tucker Lewis. HeD p.27
Longings. Mae V. Cowdery. WLOV p.10
Look a-yonder! look-a-yonder! Eli Shepperd. P1S p.132
Look at me, I am Ishmael. H. A. Vaughan. PoN p.346
Look at me I am the great thespian. Calvin C. Hernton. BTB p.117
Look At That Gal.** Julian Bond. BTB p.45; PoNe p.434; TYBP p.253
Look at the rain. Bernie Casey. LATP p.92
Look For Me Dear Mother.** Ahmed A. Alhamisi. GuW p.12
Look for me in the whirlwind. Larry Neal. BLIA p.400
Look heah! is I evah tole you 'bout de curious way I won. James Weldon
     Johnson. FYOP p.84
Look heah! 'splain to me de reason. James Weldon Johnson. FYOP p.82
Look hear, Tunk! - now, ain't dis auful. James Weldon Johnson. FYOP p.66
Look Homeward, Malcolm. Conrad Kent Rivers. FoM p.66
Look like to me. Langston Hughes. PoN p.99
Look, look! day dies and the evening has come. Luc Grimard. PoN p.355
Look out across the blue-green sea. William S. Braithwaite. HFL p.109
Lookout Point: USS San Francisco. Michael S. Harper. DJDC p.27
Look See. Bernie Casey. LATP p.92
Look there at the star! Langston Hughes. ChG p.76; MBP p.73
Look Within. Claude McKay. SPCM p.44
Looking for Equality. Herman L. McMillan. TNV p.74
Looking-Glass, The. Paul Laurence Dunbar. CPPLD p.336; WMS p.27
Looking thru the commercial glass of the holiday or howard j's (i failed to
     make a distinction). Don L. Lee. DSNP p.105; WWW p.61
Looks like what drives me crazy. Langston Hughes. SIH p.15
Loose eyes of an old man, The. Maxwell Bodenheim. PoN p.272; PoNe p.508
Lord, being dark, I said, "I can not bear. Countee Cullen. CCC p.26; OTIS
     p.16
Lord but lends His precious flowers for one brief season they are ours.
     Raymond Garfield Dandridge. ZaP p.29
Lord, Girl She Dance, She Dance. Clarence Reed. BlSp p.170
Lord, give me a heart that is patient and strong. Nick Aaron Ford. SFD
     p.19
Lord, God, forgive white Europe. Leopold Sedar Senghor. TYBP p.135
Lord God, I turn on this Thanksgiving Day. James E. McGirt. FYSS p.47
Lord, God of all in life and death. William S. Braithwaite. LLL p.78
Lord God of Hosts, incline thine ear. Richard T. Hamilton. HeD p.20
Lord God of hosts, incline thine ear. James E. McGirt. FYSS p.11
Lord, let me not be silent while we fight. Claude McKay. SPCM p.44
Lord looked down from His Heaven on yesterday, The. J. Mason Brewer. HeD
     p.4
Lord made clay of spittle, The. Robert Reedburg. TNV p.104

Lord of angelic nations bright. Charles R. Dinkins. AVAN p.105
Lord of my life before whose will I yield. William S. Braithwaite. HFL p.65
Lord of the mystic star blown gleams. William S. Braithwaite. HFL p.111
Lord of wind and water. William S. Braithwaite. LLL p.51
Lord, our God and Father up in Heaven, we praise Thy name. Charles Fred
    White. PONS p.18
Lord, shall I find it in Thy Holy Church. Claude McKay. BTB p.144; SPCM
    p.46
Lord, who am I to teach the way. Leslie Pinckney Hill. ANP p.74; BANP p.156;
    PoN p.46; PoNe p.52
Lord's lost him his mockingbird. Robert Hayden. BOT p.23; SPRH p.50
Lorenzo Jones and his wife Bell, lived in hell. LeRoi Jones. BMP p.138
Loss of life or Both feet or both hands or both eyes............... The
    Principal Sum. LeRoi Jones. BMP p.133
Loss of Love, The. Countee Cullen. PoN p.131
Los Cigarilles. James Weldon Johnson. FYOP p.31
Lost Dream, A. Paul Laurence Dunbar. CPPLD p.448
Lost far beyond voice of recall. Raymond Garfield Dandridge. PeP p.33
Lost Illusions. Georgia Douglas Johnson. ANP p.86; BANP p.182
Lost Love. Herman L. McMillan. TNV p.75
Lost Moment. Hoyt W. Fuller. TGWL p.44
Lot of slaves was always full of grief and strife, The. Eloise Culver.
    GANIV p.16
Lottery Girl, The. James Weldon Johnson. FYOP p.33
Lottery, lottery. James Weldon Johnson. FYOP p.33
Loud Jazz Horns. Carter Webster. EbR p.154
Louie was dragging his legs on the floor. Victor Hernandez Cruz. SNA p.77
Louisberg Square. William S. Braithwaite. LLL p.41
Louise. Charles Fred White. PONS p.158
Louisiana Weekly #4, The. David Henderson. SoS p.103
L'Ouverture / Fort de Jeux. Albert Aubert. ATB p.12
Louvre Afrique. Ted Joans. AFR p.57
Love. Anonymous. MBP p.19; TYBP p.198
Love. Benjamin Clark. EBAP p.182
Love. Joseph S. Cotter, Jr. BOG p.21
Love. Raymond Garfield Dandridge. PAOP p.42; ZaP p.6
Love. Tom Dent. NNPUSA p.71
Love. Paul Laurence Dunbar. CPPLD p.164
Love. Kali Grosvenor. PBK p.26
Love. Langston Hughes. SIH p.124
Love. Ted Joans. AFR p.86
Love. James E. McGirt. FYSS p.49
Love. Lucy Mae Turner. BCF p.36
Love. Alice Walker. ONC p.17
Love. Charles Fred White. PONS p.39
Love Again Blues. Langston Hughes. SIH p.103
Love and Grief. Paul Laurence Dunbar. CPPLD p.163
Love Beauty Always. William S. Braithwaite. SPWSB p.67
Love Despoiled. Paul Laurence Dunbar. AVAN p.61; CPPLD p.195
Love hands hold the she-sun cradled, memoring the late red couch of dawn.
    Craig Williamson. AfW p.17

Love hath the wings o the butterfly. Paul Laurence Dunbar. AVAN p.62;
    CPPLD p.189
Love is a brown man's fist. Langston Hughes. FCTJ p.57
Love Is a Flame.** George Marion McLlelan. EBAP p.124
Love is a funny thing. Anonymous. MBP p.19; TYBP p.198
Love is a Star. William S. Braithwaite. LLL p.36
Love is a wild wonder. Langston Hughes. SIH p.124
Love is enough, I read some where. Countee Cullen. BlC p.15
Love is My Color. Kali Grosvenor. PBK p.18
Love is not love demanding all, itself. Countee Cullen. CpS p.46; OTIS p.62
Love is the light of the world, my dear. Paul Laurence Dunbar. CPPLD p.373
Love is the soothing voice of Gods. Joseph S. Cotter, Jr. BOG p.21
Love kisses spurned so long ago. George Douglas Johnson. HWOP p.58
Love Leads Home. William S. Braithwaite. HFL p.64
Love, leave me, like the light. Countee Cullen. CCC p.78; OTIS p.38
Love Letter, A. Paul Laurence Dunbar. CPPLD p.440
Love lines your eye-sun silver blue elizabeth gold. Craig Williamson. AfW
    p.32
Love lover beloved loved one. Dudley Randall. LoY p.14
Love-mad lark you sing of swooned, they said. Countee Cullen. BlC p.34
Love me, I care not what the circling years. Paul Laurence Dunbar. CPPLD
    p.141
Love me, pretty baby. John Raven. BFM p.25
Love note II: Flags. Gwendolyn Brooks. PoN p.190
Love of freedom is why the Third world fights. Ted Joans. BPW p.61
Love Poem, A. Etheridge Knight. BrT p.81
Love Poem. Dudley Randall. LoY p.14
Love poem (for real). Nikki Giovanni. BFBTBJ p.33
Love Song. Anonymous. TYBP p.28
Love Song. Anonymous. TYBP p.30
Love Song. Anonymous. TYBP p.30
Love Song. Anonymous. TYBP p.31
Love Song. Anonymous. TYBP p.31
Love Song. Paul Laurence Dunbar. CPPLD p.343
Love-Song, A. Paul Laurence Dunbar. CPPLD p.361
Love Song. Samuel Allen. NNPUSA p.18
Love Song, A. Raymond Patterson. BOL p.71
Love Song for Summer. Mae V. Cowdery. WLOV p.52
Love Song in Middle Passage. Larry Neal. BLIA p.398
Love the meaning of the love is what I know. Ted Joans. AFR p.137
Love The Night. Ted Joans. AFR p.86
Love their faces, O port, gather your heart. Robert Hayden. HSITD p.15
Love thy piano, oh girl. Frank Horne. CaD p.117; PoN p.80; PoNe p.152
Love Tight. Ted Joans. AFR p.118
Love Tree, The. Countee Cullen. CpS p.36; OTIS p.59
Love, unto me be song of bird. Countee Cullen. CpS p.86
Love Way. Ted Joans. AFR p.95
Love; what is love. Charles Fred White. PONS p.44
Love, why hast thou forsaken me?** William L. Morrison. DaR p.30
Love, you have lied. Ted Joans. AFR p.123
Love you right back. Gwendolyn Brooks. FaP p.21

Love Your Enemy. Yusef Iman. TYBP p.258
Lover of late yesteryear sent letters of love. Ted Joans. AFR p.117
Lovelight. Georgia Douglas Johnson. AmNP p.23
Lovely dainty Spanish needle. Claude McKay. GoS p.147; HaS p.24; SPCM p.24
Lovely, dark, and lonely one. Langston Hughes. FNP p.27
Lover and the Moon, The. Paul Laurence Dunbar. CPPLD p.46; LOLL p.66
Lover whom duty called over the wave, A. Paul Laurence Dunbar. CPPLD p.40;
    LOLL p.66
Lover's Farewell, The. George Moses Horton. EBAP p.19
Lover's Lament, A. Francis M. Foster. EbR p.64
Lover's Lane. Paul Laurence Dunbar. BANP p.56; CPPLD p.211; LiG p.105
Lover's Proposal, A. Charles Fred White. PONS p.168
Lover's Return. Langston Hughes. SIH p.119
Lover's Spat, The. Waverly T. Carmichael. FHOF p.19
Lovers speak to each other as if they were born this second. LeRoi Jones.
    BMP p.96
Lovers that burn and learnèd scholars cold. Countee Cullen. MASP p.95; OTIS
    p.159
Love's Acid Test. William L. Morrison. DaR p.59
Love's Apotheosis. Paul Laurence Dunbar. CPPLD p.141
Love's Castle. Paul Laurence Dunbar. CPPLD p.327
Love's Chastening. Paul Laurence Dunbar. CPPLD p.163
Love's Cost. William L. Morrison. DaR p.58
Love's Draft. Paul Laurence Dunbar. CPPLD p.414
Love's Good-night. Fenton Johnson. AVAN p.160
Love's Helplessness. Alexander Young. EbR p.162
Love's Humility. Paul Laurence Dunbar. CPPLD p.169
Love's Phases. Paul Laurence Dunbar. AVAN p.62; CPPLD p.189
Love's Picture. Paul Laurence Dunbar. CPPLD p.466
Love's Roses I gathered, all dewy in May. Georgia Douglas Johnson. HWOP
    p.36
Love's Seasons. Paul Laurence Dunbar. CPPLD p.351
Love's Tangle. Joseph S. Cotter, Sr. CPJSC p.23
Love's Tendril. Georgia Douglas Johnson. HWOP p.61
Love's Way. Countee Cullen. CpS p.46; OTIS p.62
Love's Wayfaring. William S. Braithwaite. LLL p.45
Loving Beauty Is Loving God. Isabelle McClellan Taylor. EbR p.134
Low beating of the tom-toms, The. Langston Hughes. WeB p.105
Low Down. Sterling A. Brown. SoR p.72
Low Down. LeRoi Jones. BMP p.74
Low Down Blues. Lucile D. Goodlett. WGC p.43
Low mean of a leaden-colored sea do I hear, The. Leondidas Gobbs. BTh p.35
Low To High. Langston Hughes. CNAW p.309
Lower south in bush live African Villages of the Afric tribe in Memphis.
    Ahmed Akinwole Alhamis. TGWL p.8
Lower the flags for the dead become alive. Langston Hughes. PATL p.42
Lowly Grasses and Little Hills. William C. Braithwaite. VER p.52
Lucid night effulent glows, The. John Boyd. EBAP p.152
Luck. Langston Hughes. FOW p.64
Lucy done gone back on me. Paul Laurence Dunbar. CPPLD p.217
Lucy Let Your Hair Hang.** Craig Williamson. AfW p.47
Lullaby. Paul Laurence Dunbar. CLT p.91; CPPLD p.230; GoS p.191

Lullaby   TITLE AND FIRST LINE INDEX

Lullaby. Marion Nicholes. LiS p.18
Lullaby. Quandra Prettyman. BOL p.75
Lullaby. (For a Black Mother). Langston Hughes. DYTB p.15
Lullaby, Go to Sleep. James E. McGirt. FYSS p.30
Lullaby to a Dream. James Christopher. EbR p.35
Lumumba Lives Lumumba Lives!! Ted Joans. BPW p.16
Lumumba was Black and he didn't trust the whores all powdered with uranium
    dust. Langston Hughes. PATL p.65
Lumumba was murdered and made a martyr. Ted Joans. BPW p.65
Lumumba's Grave. Langston Hughes. PATL p.65
Lure, The. Raymond Dandridge. ZaP p.54
Lust hearts stalk nights dreaming heroes of themselves. LeRoi Jones. BMP
    p.86
Lute of Afric Tribe, The. Arbery Allson Whitman. EBAP p.218
Lynched Negro.* Maxwell Bodenheim. PoN p.273; PoNe p.509
Lynching, The. Isabelle McClellan Taylor. EbR p.135
Lynching, The. Claude McKay. AVAN p.206; BANP p.168; BLIA p.166; HaS p.51;
    IADB p.64; SPCM p.37
Lynching Bee, The. William Ellery Leonard. PoN p.259
Lynching Song. Langston Hughes. OWT p.58
Lyric, A. Paul Laurence Dunbar. CPPLD p.478
Lyric, A. Katie Kelly. BTh p.55
Lyric Of Autumn. William S. Braithwaite. LLL p.58
Lyric: When the Still Sombre Evening Closes Down. William S. Braithwaite.
    LLL p.48
Lyrics to the Well-Beloved. H. A. B. Jones-Quartey. LUP p.36

                         - M -

Ma Jesus was a troubled man. Waring Cuney. BANP p.284; GoS p.59
Ma Lady's lips Am Like De Honey (Negro Love Song). James Weldon Johnson.
    FYOP p.64
Ma Lord. Langston Hughes. GoS p.64
Ma Lord ain't no stuck-up man. Anonymous. GoS p.64
Ma Man. Langston Hughes. FCTJ p.88
Ma Man's a gypsy. Langston Hughes. FCTJ p.22
Ma Rainey. Sterling A. Brown. BTB p.59; SoR p.62
Ma six string with the lonesome sound. Owen Dodson. PLL p.5
Ma seet good man has. Langston Hughes. FCTJ p.20
McDonogh Day In New Orleans. Marcus B. Christian. AmNP p.52; PoN p.84; PoNe
    p.157
Macee. Frances Harper. PBFH p.79
Macee dead! a thrilled sorrow through our hearts in sadness ran. Frances
    Harper. PBFH p.79
Madam and Her Madam. Langston Hughes. OWT p.5
Madam and Her Might-Have-Been. Langston Hughes. OWT p.24
Madam and the Census Man. Langston Hughes. OWT p.26
Madam and the Charity Child. Langston Hughes. OWT p.16
Madam and the Fortune Teller. Langston Hughes. OWT p.18
Madam and the Minister. Langston Hughes. OWT p.22
Madam and the Number Writer. Langston Hughes. OWT p.11
Madam and the Phone Bill. Langston Hughes. OWT p.13

Madam and the Rent Man. Langston Hughes. OWT p.9
Madam and the Wrong Visitor. Langston Hughes. OWT p.20
Madam could look in your hand. Langston Hughes. SIH p.59
Madam, You Are Astonished.** Bruce McM. Wright. LUP p.58
Madame of Dreams. (To John Russel Hayes). William S. Braithwaite. HFL p.28
Madam's Calling Card. Langston Hughes. OWT p.7
Madam's Past History. Langston Hughes. OWT p.3
Madhouse. Calvin C. Hernton. IADB p.17; ITBLA p.276; KAL p.197; PoNe p.403;
    NNPUSA p.102; SoS p.81
Madimba: Gwendolyn Brooks. Michael S. Harper. TGWL p.50
Madness. LeRoi Jones. BMP p.162
Madness of Cane, striked the dumb world again striked it, The. LeRoi Jones.
    BMP p.222
Madness one Monday evening. Julia Fields. BTB p.108
Madness One Morning. Julia Fields. ITBLA p.275; KAL p.221; NNPUSA p.78
Madrigal, A. Paul Laurence Dunbar. CPPLD p.476
Maecenas, you, beneath the myrtle shade. Phillis Wheatley. PAL p.89; PPW
    p.3
Mae's Rent Party. Ernest J. Wilson, Jr. PoNe p.371
Magalu. Helene Johnson. CaD p.223; PoN p.152; PoNe p.263
Maggie camp up from Spartanburg. Sterling A. Brown. SoR p.109
Magi Call Him King, The. (A Christmas Song). Effie Lee Newsome. ChG p.69
Magic dance of the Second Ave. ladies. LeRoi Jones. BMP p.17
Magic my man is you turning my body into a thousand smiles. Sonia Sanchez.
    BrT p.137
Magic of Black Poetry, The. Anonymous. MBP p.1
Magic of the day is the morning, The. LeRoi Jones. BMP p.166
Magic Pants. Ted Joans. AFR p.124
Magical sunbeams slanting fall. Raymond Dandridge. ZaP p.26
Magnets. Countee Cullen. MASP p.69; OTIS p.143
Magnolia Flowers. Langston Hughes. FCTJ p.70
Mah Dawg. Raymond Garfield Dandridge. PeP p.8; ZaP p.14
Mah depen'able fren'. Raymond Garfield Dandridge. PAOP p.56; ZaP p.76
Mah ruddah's brokin, an' mah sail. Raymond Garfield Dandridge. PAOP p.21;
    ZaP p.43
Mahalia Jackson Gospel Singer, Alabama, 1911-1972. Eloise Culver. GANIV
    p.71
Mahogany Leaves. William L. Morrison. DaR p.25
Maid and Violinist. Alpheus Butler. EbR p.21
Maiden wept and, as a comforter. Paul Laurence Dunbar. CPPLD p.16; LOLL
    p.21
Maine Landing. Michael S. Harper. DJDC p.23
Major Bowes' Diary. LeRoi Jones. BMP p.31
Make a garland of Leontynes and Lenas. Langston Hughes. PATL p.6
Make it with the man if you can. Marion Nicholes. LiS p.17
Make me a grave where'er you will. Frances Harper. ANP p.17; AVAN p.42;
    CNAW p.103; EBAP p.36
Make me a song O dark singer. Robert Hayden. HSITD p.14
Make not a law to rule another. Joseph S. Cotter, Sr. LOF p.63
Make way for the beast with chrome beast. Thurmond Snyder. NNPUSA p.87
Maker-of-Sevens in the scheme of things. Anne Spencer. ANP p.123; BANP
    p.216

Making Friends With Baby. Charles B. Johnson. SOMP p.31
Making of a Militant. Yillie Bey. TNV p.18
Malagueña. William S. Braithwaite. HFL p.73
Malcolm. Katie M. Cumbo. BOL p.34
Malcolm. Bill Frederick. FoM p.24
Malcolm. Sonia Sanchez. BrT p.25; FoM p.38
Malcolm Exsiccated. Theodore Horne. FoM p.67
Malcolm Spoke / Who Listened? Don L. Lee. BrT p.98; DCS p.33; DSNP p.100;
    FoM p.64
Malcolm X. Vernoy E. White. TNV p.49
Malcolm X, a lover of the grass roots. Margaret Danner. FoM p.6
Malcolm X - an Autobiography. Larry Neal. BrT p.17; FoM p.9; SoS p.42
Malcolm X. (For Dudley Randall). Gwendolyn Brooks. CNAW p.523; FoM p.3;
    ITM p.39; MBP p.88; TYBP p.236
Malcolm X spoke to me and sounded you. Ted Joans. BOL p.31; BPW p.96; BrT
    p.17; FoM p.5
Malcolm's Blues. Michael S. Harper. DJDC p.38
Malcontents, The. Dio Lewis. EbR p.101
Malevolence. Carlyle B. Hall. EbR p.76
Males carry the hormones that do the work I'm told. David Llorens. TGWL
    p.70
Malika what is this that burns within me. Marvin X. BrT p.155
Malik's flowers fade among the weeds. Edward S. Spriggs. FoM p.72
Mama. Nora Blakely. TGWL p.14
Mama and Daughter. Langston Hughes. OWT p.31
Mama Drum. Ted Joans. BPW p.97
Mama! fine foxy mamma wearing the thorny crown of Christ. David Nelson.
    BlSp p.154
Mama I found this soldier's cap. Langston Hughes. FOW p.109
Mama papa and us 10 kids lived in a single room. John Raven. BFM p.5; BrT
    p.135
Mama, please brush off my coat. Langston Hughes. OWT p.31
Mammy. Langston Hughes. FCTJ p.76; FNP p.28
Mammy hums.* Carl Sandburg. PoN p.287; PoNe p.482
Mammy Spread De Winder, an' she frown an' frown. Paul Laurence Dunbar. LiG
    p.30
Mammy's Baby Scared. Waverly T. Carmichael. FHOF p.3
Mammy's in de kitchen, an' de do' is shet. Paul Laurence Dunbar. CPPLD
    p.394
Man, A. Bernie Casey. LATP p.13
Man. Langston Hughes. FOW p.60
Man. Ritten Edward Lee. EbR p.99
Man and a Woman, A. Gerald W. Barrax. AKOR p.71
Man and Woman (for earnie, 1964). Don L. Lee. DSNP p.158; WWW p.34
Man does not know.** Joseph S. Cotter, Sr. CPJSC p.27; LOF p.34; RHY p.12
Man git his feet set in a sticky mud bank. Sterling A. Brown. SoR p.220
Man he'll see like all faggots do jay ain't around. Victor Hernandez Cruz.
    SNA p.31
Man Hunt, The. Madison Cawein. ANP p.131
Man I Thought You Was Talking Another Language That Day. Victor Hernandez
    Cruz. BOL p.65

Marrie dear the box is full. Mari Evans. AmNP p.164; ITBLA p.274
Marrow of My Bone. Mari Evans. IABW p.32
"Marse" Henry Watterson. Joseph S. Cotter, Sr. SPPH p.34; WSBO p.12
Martha Graham. Owen Dodson. PLL p.101
Martin Luther King, Jr. Gwendolyn Brooks. BOL p.28; BrT p.167
Martin Luther King, peaceful warrior for Civil Rights Nobel Peace Prize win-
    ner, 1929-1968, Georgia. Eloise Culver. GANIV p.77
Martyr of Alabama, The. Frances Harper. PBFH p.49
Martyrdom is not our course. John W. Burton. EbR p.20
Mary. Joseph S. Cotter, Sr. LOF p.55; RHY p.30
Mary, Mother of Christ. Countee Cullen. CCC p.96
Mascara and sun blurred her cheeks when those final words stammered from
    Mississippi. Durward Collins, Jr. BTB p.68
Mask. Clarissa Scott Delany. CaD p.143; PoN p.94; PoNe p.177
Masquerading. Raymond Garfield Dandridge. PAOP p.63
Mastah drink his ol' made 'a. Paul Laurence Dunbar. CPPLD p.347
Master Charlie read my story of the piper in his glory. Joseph S. Cotter,
    Sr. SPPH p.12; WSBO p.28
Master-Player, The. Paul Laurence Dunbar. CPPLD p.26; LOLL p.35
Masters, The. Paul Laurence Dunbar. CPPLD p.445
Matador, El. Robert Hayden. BOR p.56; SPRH p.36
Mate. Georgia Douglas Johnson. HWOP p.12
Mater Triumphalis. To Louise Imogen Guiney. William S. Braithwaite. HFL
    p.18
Matilda At the Tubs. Lucy Mae Turner. BCF p.20
Matters not what kin' o' bein'. Joseph S. Cotter, Sr. SPPH p.62
Mattie dear the box is full. Mari Evans. BTB p.105; IADB p.56
Maumee Ruth. Sterling A. Brown. CaD p.133; SoR p.10
Mausoleum of a Winter's day, The. Melvin Tolson. RWA p.67
Maxie Allen. Gwendolyn Brooks. AnA p.4
Maxie Allen always taught her. Gwendolyn Brooks. AnA p.4
Maxims. William C. Braithwaite. VER p.122
May Flowers Come and Keep my Watch. William L. Morrison. DaR p.27
May he have new life like the fall. Alfred B. Spellman. NNPUSA p.57
May I Not Love?** Daniel A. Payne. EBAP p.58
May I Return? Lucy Mae Turner. BCF p.40
Maybe The Birds. June Jordan. SCh p.14
Maybe the birds are worried by the wind. June Jordan. SCh p.14
Mazzini At Rome. William C. Braithwaite. VER p.37
Me Alone. Lula Lowe Weeden. CaD p.227
"Me an' ma baby's got two mo' ways. Langston Hughes. CNAW p.303; FNP p.23;
    WeB p.26
Me and the Mule. Langston Hughes. IADB p.3; SIH p.29
Me Too! Ted Joans. BPW p.74
Mea Culpa. Katherine L. Cuestas. BTB p.76
Meadow Lark, The. Paul Laurence Dunbar. CPPLD p.113; LOLL p.168
Mearch de fiff, nineteen and two, mah honey Baby: How does you do? Raymond
    Garfield Dandridge. PeP p.38
Measure, The. Georgia Douglas Johnson. HWOP p.33
Meating. Ted Joans. AFR p.92
Mecca. Sterling A. Brown. SoR p.109

Mecca art is a Babel city in the people's shiner with a hundred gates.
    Melvin Tolson. HaG p.23
Mechanical oracles in the sky. Eugene Redmond. NBP p.108
Mechanic probes the belly of the car, The. Melvin Tolson. RWA p.52
Medgar Evers. Gwendolyn Brooks. ITM p.38
Medicine. Alice Walker. ONC p.70
Meditation on a Cold Dark, and Rainy Night. George Moses Horton. AVAN p.34
Meditations of a European Farmer. John Henrik Clarke. EbR p.43
Meditations of a Negro's Mind, I. Charles Fred White. PONS p.21
Meditations of a Negro's Mind, II. Charles Fred White. PONS p.23
Meditations of a Negro's Mind, III. Charles Fred White. PONS p.26
Meditations of a Negro's Mind, V. Charles Fred White. PONS p.132
Meditations of a Negro's Mind, VI. Charles Fred White. PONS p.144
Meditations of a Negro's Mind, VII. Charles Fred White. PONS p.166
Medusa. Countee Cullen. MASP p.76; OTIS p.148
Meetin' Chant, A. Eli Shepperd. PlS p.122
Meeting. Dudley Randall. LoY p.11
Megalopolis. Victor Hernandez Cruz. SNA p.93
Melancholia. Paul Laurence Dunbar. CPPLD p.84; LOLL p.125
Melchisedee and Pushkin. Joseph S. Cotter, Sr. SPPH p.74
"Melchisedee, the earth-God. Joseph S. Cotter, Sr. SPPH p.74
Mellow Yellow. Ted Joans. BPW p.109
Melting Pot. Michael Echeruo. TYBP p.163
Members' Hymn. Eli Shepperd. PlS p.128
Memorandum. Rudy Gee Graham. PoNe p.441
Memorandum on my Martinique. Aime Cesaire. PoN p.370
Memorial. Claude McKay. HaS p.90; SPCM p.104
Memorial Day. Bobb Hamilton. FoM p.80
Memorial Day in Easthampton. Charles Fred White. PONS p.138
Memorial of Childhood, A. Charles Fred White. PONS p.135
Memorial to Ed Bland. Gwendolyn Brooks. AnA p.vi
Memorial Wreath. Dudley Randall. IADB p.50; NNPUSA p.59; PoNe p.305
Memoriam. Bruce McM. Wright. LUP p.59
Memories. Joseph S. Cotter, Jr. BOG p.20
Memories. Raymond Garfield Dandridge. PAOP p.26
Memory, A. William S. Braithwaite. LLL p.80
Memory. Charles B. Johnson. SOMP p.6
Memory. Georgia D. Johnson. HWOP p.46
Memory. Margaret Walker. FMP p.56
Memory in Winter, A. Craig Williamson. AfW p.44
Memory, let me go. Ruth Brownlee Johnson. EbR p.97
Memory of boxer Benny (kid) Paret (To Norman & Cary Blubm), The.* Frank Lima.
    PoNe p.587
Memory of June, A. Claude McKay. HaS p.79; SPCM p.99
Memory of Martha, The. Paul Laurence Dunbar. CPPLD p.315; WMS p.29
Memory of W. W. Brown. James E. McGirt. FYSS p.36
Memphis Blues. Sterling A. Brown. BANP p.252; CNAW p.405; SoR p.59
Men and women long ago, The. Gwendolyn Brooks. AnA p.44
Men may sing of their Havanas, elevating to the star. Paul Laurence Dunbar.
    CPPLD p.206
Men never know. Waring Cuney. CaD p.212

Men said thy hopes were buried in thy needs. Joseph S. Cotter. CPJSC p.35
Men stagger in any light, yet are too dull. Joseph S. Cotter, Sr. LOF p.27
Men! whose beast it is that ye come of fathers brave and free.* James
     Russell Lowell. ANP p.138; PoN p.238; PoNe p.464
Mention his name and they bristle or shake heads like steel, exhibiting a
     frowned face. Helen Quigless. FoM p.65
Mentors. Gwendolyn Brooks. KAL p.156; PoN p.191
Mercedes is a Jungle-lily in a death house. Langston Hughes. WeB p.90
Merry Autumn. Paul Laurence Dunbar. CPPLD p.87; LOLL p.130
Merry bell since daybreak pealed. Raymond Garfield Dandridge. PeP p.39
Merry-Go-Round, colored child at Carnival. Langston Hughes. DYTB p.73;
     ITBLA p.158; MBP p.94; PATL p.92; PoN p.104; PoNe p.192; SIH p.80
Merry Voices Chatterin'. Claude McKay. BANP p.176; GoS p.45
Message All Black People Can Die. Don L. Lee. BrT p.106; DCS p.63; DSNP
     p.129
Message From the NAACP. LeRoi Jones. BMP p.160
Message to Siberia (Russia). Alexander Pushkin. TYBP p.68
Messengers of Dreams. William S. Braithwaite. HFL p.21
Messianic. William S. Braithwaite. SPWSB p.21
Metagnomy. N. H. Pritchad. NBP p.100
Metal rumor of the skies, The. Robert Hayden. HSITD p.17
Mexican Market Woman. Langston Hughes. DYTB p.9; WeB p.91
Mi. Melvin B. Tolson. LRL p.19
Micah. Margaret Walker. PFND p.27
Micah was a young man of the people. Margaret Walker. PFND p.27
Mid-Day. William L. Morrison. DaR p.9
Mid-Day Dreamer, A. James Weldon Johnson. FYOP p.40
Mid the discordant noises of the day I hear thee calling. Claude McKay.
     HaS p.58; SPCM p.54
Middle Passage. Robert Hayden. AmNP p.113; BLIA p.254; BOR p.60; CNAW
     p.388; IADB p.34; SPRH p.65
Midnight. Henrietta Cordelia Ray. EBAP p.144
Midnight Bell. Owen Dodson. PLL p.78
Midnight Chippie's Lament. Langston Hughes. SIH p.105
Midnight is no time for poetry. Julia Fields. AmNP p.183; ITBLA p.275
Midnight Raffle. Langston Hughes. OWT p.107
Midnight wooed the morning-star, The. Paul Laurence Dunbar. CPPLD p.158
Midsummer Morn. Frank Marshall Davis. GoS p.7
Midway. Naomi Long Madgett. NNPUSA p.39; PoNe p.381; SoS p.126
Midwinter Blues. Langston Hughes. FCTJ p.84; FNP p.23
Might as well bury her. Sterling A. Brown. CaD p.133; SoR p.10
Mightier, The. Raymond Garfield Dandridge. ZaP p.30
Mighty sun had kept his steady course across the autumn sky of cold steel
     gray. Charles Fred White. PONS p.136
Migrant. Langston Hughes. OWT p.125
Migration. Langston Hughes. FOW p.99
Miles Davis said he would like a little boy. Ted Joans. PoNe p.396
Militant. Langston Hughes. PATL p.39
Militant is quietly armed and waiting, The. Marion Nicholes. LiF p.14
Mill Mountain. Sterling A. Brown. SoR p.133
Millennial. Countee Cullen. CpS p.74

Millennium age today, A. Roscoe Lee Browne. BTB p.62
Milton. Henrietta Cordelia Ray. EBAP p.139
Mind and soul after dark. Norman Jordan. BlSp p.97
Mine is long like the wile. Ted Joans. AFR p.122
Mine is no plea for beggar's alms. William Cousins. EbR p.53
Minister, The. Fenton Johnson. KAL p.42
Minnie Sings Her Blues. Langston Hughes. FCTJ p.64
Minor Chord of Life, The. Charles Fred White. PONS p.85
Minstrel Man. Langston Hughes. FNP p.25
Minutely Hurt. Countee Cullen. BlC p.22; OTIS p.87
Minutes swiftly throb and pass. Georgia Douglas Johnson. HWOP p.10
Miracle. Louise Blackman. EbR p.5
Miracle Demanded. Countee Cullen. BlC p.26
Miracles. Arna Bontemps. CNAW p.333; GoS p.68; PoN p.111; PoNe p.210
Mirrored. Georgia Douglas Johnson. HWOP p.14
Misanthropist, The. James M. Whitfield. EBAP p.43
Misapprehension. Paul Laurence Dunbar. CPPLD p.187
Miscellaneous Verses. Gustavus Vassa. EBAP p.14
Mise en scene: Newark, 1947. LeRoi Jones. BMP p.20
Miser stands beside the sea, A. Joseph S. Cotter, Sr. LOF p.23; SPPH p.37
Misery. Langston Hughes. FCTJ p.19
Miss Ann. Bernie Casey. LATP p.62
Miss Gardner's in her garden. Langston Hughes. SIH p.75
Miss Katy at de cake-walk--move des so! Eli Shepperd. **PlS p.16**
Miss Liza's Banter. Daniel Webster Davis. EBAP p.236
Miss Lucy she is handsome. Anonymous. GoS p.18
Miss Melerlee. John Wesley Holloway. AmNP p.134; PoN p.17; PoNe p.19
"Miss Moses" people called her. Eloise Culver. GANIV p.23
Miss Nancy's Geo'ge. Lucile D. Goodlett. WGC p.25
Miss Nancy's Geo'ge got a stugie down by de corners sto. Lucile D. Goodlett.
    WGC p.25
Miss Packard and Miss Giles. Owen Dodson. CNAW p.394; PLL p.28
Miss Samantha Wilson. Frank Marshall Davis. EbR p.57
Miss Scarlet, Mr. Rhett and Other Day Saints. Maya Angelou. JGM p.28
Mississippi. Langston Hughes. PATL p.43
Mississippi Levee. Langston Hughes. SIH p.46
Mist has left the greening plain, The. Paul Laurence Dunbar. CPPLD p.413
Mrs. Hobart-Constantine awakens. James P. Vaughn. NNPUSA p.63
Mrs. Johnson Objects. Clara Ann Thompson. AVAN p.133
Mrs. Williams' face was pleading when she **spoke** of her God to me. Lance
    Jeffers. BrT p.72
Mistah me! Lucy Mae Turner. BCP p.58
Mistah Skeeter. Lucy Mae Turner. BCF p.34
Mistah skeeter - jes' skeet, on away fum hyah! Lucy Mae Turner. BCF p.34
Mistakes. Naomi Evans Vaughn. EbR p.149
Mr. and Mrs. Guy Delaporte III, through the shifting maze of Harlem's Vanity
    Fair. Melvin Tolson. HaG p.57
Mister Backlash, Mister Backlash, just who do you think I am? Langston
    Hughes. PATL p.8
Mister Banjo. Anonymous. MBP p.52
Mr. Goody's Goat. Joseph S. Cotter, Sr. LOF p.52; RHY p.22; SPPH p.23

Moon lights the wooded death spot to the shame of the wide-spreading tree, The. Isabelle McClellan Taylor. EbR p.135
Moon rocks time with its gaze, The. Joseph S. Cotter, Sr. SPPH p.60
Moon, moon. Robert Hayden. HSITD p.16
Moon Poem. Saundra Sharp. MBP p.5
Moon saw blowing wind breathe cold upon their dripping boughs. Catherine L. Findley. EbR p.63
Moon song for Elizabeth. Craig Williamson. AfW p.32
Moon, they say, called mantis, The. Anonymous. TYBP p.5
Moondrops. William L. Morrison. DaR p.9
Moonlight Amid the Hills. Zachary Withers. PAS p.3
Moonlight breaks upon the city's domes. Claude McKay. PoN p.320; PoNe p.98; SPCM p.69
Moonlight Night: Carmel. Langston Hughes. DYTB p.52
Moonlight moonlight. Clarence Major. SoS p.94
Moonlight moonlight in Valdosta, Georgia on Moody Air Force Base. Clarence Major. SoS p.94
Moral, A. Zachary Withers. PAS p.21
Moratorium means well what you think it means you dense? June Jordan. SCh p.71
More Letters Found Near a Suicide. Frank Horne. BANP p.270
More real than the weak passing of your sigh. Michael S. Harper. DJDC p.22
More Than a Fool's Song. Countee Cullen. CpS p.67; OTIS p.67
Mornin' After, The. John Raven. BFM p.15
Morning. Paul Laurence Dunbar. CPPLD p.413
Morning. Bernette Golden. TNV p.39
Morning After. Langston Hughes. SIH p.44
Morning Hymn, A. William C. Braithwaite. VER p.114
Morning is a state of mind. Bernette Golden. TNV p.39
Morning Joy. Claude McKay. HaS p.34; SPCM p.70
Morning, Noon and Night. James Weldon Johnson. FYOP p.52
Morning poems is to dig any new change. LeRoi Jones. BMP p.215
Morning Purpose. LeRoi Jones. BMP p.15
Morning Raga for Malcolm. Larry Neal. BrT p.19; FoM p.19
Morning Song of Love. Paul Laurence Dunbar. CPPLD p.328
Morninglight (the dew-drier). Ellie Lee Newsome. AmNP p.19; CaD p.55; PoN p.55; PoNe p.70
Mornings. Alice Walker. ONC p.53
Morocco conquering homage paid to Spain. Claude McKay. SPCM p.87
Mortal Boundness. Clarence Major. SAM p.34
Mortality. Paul Laurence Dunbar. CPPLD p.164; AVAN p.88
Mortality. Naomi Long Madgett. NNPUSA p.23; PoNe p.382
Moscow. Claude McKay. SPCM p.83
Moscow for many loving her was dead. Claude McKay. SPCM p.83
Mose. Sterling A. Brown. KAL p.70; SoR p.77
Mose is Black and evil. Sterling A. Brown. SoR p.77
Most people in the world stumble or drive around 24 hours everyday on a treadmill. Quincy Troupe. BlSp p.238
Mother. Raymond Garfield Dandridge. PeP p.9
Mother America. Hazel L. Washington. EbR p.151
"Mother dear, nay I go downtown. Dudley Randall. BLIA p.337; BrT p.124
Mother Night. James Weldon Johnson. AVAN p.179; FYOP p.22

Mother, shed no mournful tears. James Weldon Johnson. FYOP p.23
Mother Speaks: the Algiers Motel Incident, Detroit, A. Michael S. Harper.
    DJDC p.76
Mother fuckin' heart, of the mother fuckin' day. LeRoi Jones. BMP p.102
Mother In Wartime. Langston Hughes. PATL p.53
Mother To Son. Langston Hughes. AmNP p.67; ANP p.103; CaD p.151; CNAW p.306;
    DYTB p.20; FNP p.26; GoS p.170; ITBLA p.160; LUP p.32; MBP p.97; PoN
    p.104; PoNe p.186; TYBP p.225; SoS p.19; WeB p.107
Mother true, a mother wise this is the name she bears, A. Waverly T. Car-
    michael. FHOF p.21
Mother was a wolf. Donald D. Govan. NBP p.55
Mother, what's a Red? H. Binga Dismond. EbR p.58
Mother with no Christmas gifts, large or small, anywhere, dreaming at mid-
    night, I give my child quite bare. Gabriela Mistral. ChG p.91
Motherhood. William S. Braithwaite. LLL p.59
Mothering Blackness, The. Maya Angelou. JGM p.18
Motherland. Langston Hughes. FOW p.97
Motherless Child. Anonymous. BLIA p.40
Mothers, The. Waring Cuney. LUP p.8
Mothers. Nikki Giovanni. MyH p.6
Mother's Farewell To Her Son, The. Waverly T. Carmichael. FHOF p.50
Mother's Gone A-visitin' to Spend a Month Er Two. Paul Laurence Dunbar.
    CPPLD p.127; LOLL p.189
Mothers pass, sweet watermelon in a baby carriage. Langston Hughes. OWT
    p.123
Mothers push the carriages, The. Waring Cuney. LUP p.8
Mother's Treasures. Frances Harper. PBFH p.56
Moths. See Poems: Birmingham 1962-1964. Julia Fields
Motion inside my stomach is at an angular distance, The. Clarence Major.
    SAM p.56
Motto. Langston Hughes. CNAW p.309; PATL p.11; PoNe p.202; SoS p.118
Mount Shasta. Zachary Withers. PAS p.30
Mountain Climber, The. Melvin Tolson. RWA p.15
Mountain In a Storm. Herman J. D. Carter. EbR p.29
Mountain is earth's mouth, A. Mae V. Cowdery. WLOV p.13
Mountain Song, A. William C. Braithwaite. VER p.43
Mountains. David Wadsworth Cannon, Jr. EbR p.23
Mountains. Robert Hayden. SPRH p.28
Mountain, The. Robert Hayden. HSITD p.25
Mountains at Night. Lucy Mae Turner. BCF p.53
Mountains cover me like rain. Countee Cullen. CCC p.52
Mountain lift their hoary heads on high, The. Lucy Mae Turner. BCF p.53
Mourner's Hymn, The. Eli Shepperd. P1S p.141
Mournful lute or the preceptor's farewell, The. Daniel A. Payne. EBAP p.51
Mourning Grace. Maya Angelou. JGM p.20
Mourning Letter From Paris, A. Conrad Kent Rivers. SVH p.9
Mourning Poem For the Queen of Sunday. Robert Hayden. BOR p.23; SPRH p.50
Mouth. Ted Joans. AFR p.132
Move! LeRoi Jones. B1Sp p.24
Move, into our own, not theirs into out. Don L. Lee. DSNP p.191; BrT p.117;
    WWW p.67

Move On. Waverly T. Carmichael. FHOF p.46
Move Un-noticed To Be Noticed: A Nationhood Poem. Don L. Lee. BrT p.117;
    DSNP p.191; WWW p.67
Movie. LeRoi Jones. BMP p.122
Movie Queen. James P. Vaughn. NNPUSA p.62
Moving. Victor Hernandez Cruz. SNA p.127
Moving Deep. Stephany. BrT p.147
Ms; Harlem vignettes was done up in a Mamba's skin, The. Melvin Tolson.
    HaG p.100
Mu. Melvin Tolson. HaG p.64
Mu'Allaqa of Antar, The. Antar. TYBP p.37
Mud of Vietnam. Julius Lester. SoS p.66
Muddah Wit. Raymond Garfield Dandridge. PeP p.40
Muhammedan Call To Prayer. Bilal. TYBP p.43
Mulatto. Langston Hughes. FCTJ p.71
Mulatto to His Critics, The. Joseph S. Cotter, Jr. ANP p.34; BOG p.5
Mule Mountain. James Pipes. ZJP p.51
Multi-colored Balloon. Herbert D. Greggs. MBP p.16
Murdered Lover, The. Paul Laurence Dunbar. CPPLD p.345
Murderers of Emmet Till. Oliver Pitcher. BTB p.161; KAL p.187
Muse in late November. J. Henderson Brooks. PoN p.135
Music. William L. Morrison. DaR p.8
Music makes tears I need not hide. William L. Morrison. DaR p.8
Musical, A. Paul Laurence Dunbar. CPPLD p.414
Musing on roses and revolution. Dudley Randall. BrT p.121
Must be the Black Maria that I see. Langston Hughes. SIH p.121
Must I shoot the white man dead. Conrad Kent Rivers. SVH p.15
Mwilu (or Poem for the Living) (For Charles & Latanga). Don L. Lee. DSNP
    p.206
My Ace of Spades. Ted Joans. BOL p.31; BPW p.96; BrT p.17; FoM p.5
My America. Oliver La Grone. NNPUSA p.36
My Angel. J. Henderson Brooks. PoN p.134; PoNe p.238
My Baby-Boy. William C. Braithwaite. VER p.118
My baby-boy with yellow hair. William C. Braithwaite. VER p.118
My Bag. Ted Joans. BPW p.48
My bag is here. Ted Joans. BPW p.48
My Beauty Wades.** Ted Joans. AFR p.102
My Black brothers in South Africa, I feel pain for you. Arthur Boze. BlWo
    p.20
My Black is about rhythm. Clarence Reed. BlSp p.168
My Black sisters and brothers are dieing. Kali Grosvenor. PBK p.25
My Blackness is the Beauty of This Land.** Lance Jeffers. NBP p.72
My blk / ness like poetry is not to be deceived. Alicia Johnson. CNAW
    p.769
My blood sang to the music of a pulsing heat when you came near me. Dorothy
    F. Blackwell. EbR p.6
My boat sails downstream. Anonymous. TYBP p.31
My body is opaque to the soul. Jean Toomer. ITBLA p.157
My Brother. Eloise Culver. GANIV p.80
My brother, Bigger Thomas, son of Poor Richard, father of poor lost Jimmy,
    locked together all of us. LeRoi Jones. BMP p.161
My Brother Malcolm. Christine O. Johnson. FoM p.3

My Childhood.   James Randall.   BrT p.133
My City.   James Weldon Johnson.   BANP p.125; CaD p.25; PoN p.32; PoNe p.31
My City Garden Plot.   Lucy Mae Turner.   BCF p.34
My City Slept.   Lawrence Benford.   CNAW p.762; NBP p.26; TYBP p.257
My Corn-cob Pipe.   Paul Laurence Dunbar.   CPPLD p.206
My cot was down by a cypress grove.   Paul Laurence Dunbar.   CPPLD p.10; LOLL
   p.12
My dad calls me on the telephone.   Ted Joans.   AFR p.125
My darlin' I sho' love you.   Waverly T. Carmichael.   FHOF p.19
My darling fiance you're the first to know.   John Raven.   BFM p.14
My days are filled with diets and charts.   Mae V. Cowdery.   WLOV p.48
My days were a thing for me to live.   Countee Cullen.   CCC p.61
My dear, sweet girl I fancy you.   Charles Fred White.   PONS p.168
My dearest child, I have no wealth to give you.   James E. McGirt.   FYSS p.57
My desk sits facing yours across the floor.   William Lorenzo Morrison.   EbR
   p.109
My ear a ground I hear a sound far off.   Charles B. Johnson.   SOMP p.35
My empty steps mashed your face in a mad rhythm of happiness.   Don L. Lee.
   BrT p.90; DSNP p.10
My father (back blistered) beat me because I could not stop crying.   Alice
   Walker.   ONC p.43
My father came in the darkness.   Anonymous.   TYBP p.9
My father is a quiet man.   Countee Cullen.   CCC p.241; OTIS p.14; PoN p.129;
   SoS p.20
My father, it is surely a blue place.   Gwendolyn Brooks.   ITBLA p.217; KAL
   p.151
My father lies Black and hushed.   Richard Thomas.   PoNe p.433
My father's hand.   Robert Hayden.   HSITD p.28
My favorite things is u / blowen yo' / favorite things.   Sonia Sanchez.   WABP
   p.69
My feet are like lead.   John Raven.   BFM p.12
My friend, you marvel how this thing can be.   J. Henderson Brooks.   BTh p.65
My galleon of adventure.   Walter Adolphe Roberts.   PoN p.313; PoNe p.82
My Gloriana my Bessie Smith, enable me.   Alvin Aubert.   ATB p.7
My **grand-grand-dad was a common slave.**   James Patterson.   FoM p.77
My grandmothers were strong.   Margaret Walker.   BOL p.59; FMP p.25; KAL
   p.141
My great God, you been a tenderness to me.   Owen Dodson.   PLL p.8
My Grievance.   Raymond Garfield Dandridge.   PAOP p.61
My Guilt.   Maya Angelou.   JGM p.42
My guilt is "slavery's chains," too long.   Maya Angelou.   JGM p.42
My hand by chance.   Robert Hayden.   BOR p.31; SPRH p.56
My Harvah rit me week fo' las'.   Raymond Garfield Dandridge.   PAOP p.38; ZaP
   p.80
My head is a trumpet.   Ted Joans.   AFR p.131
My heart can tell them, every one.   William S. Braithwaite.   HFL p.21
My heart gives thanks for many things.   William S. Braithwaite.   LLL p.61
My heart is barren as the burnt sands of the desert.   Eldon George McLean.
   EbR p.107
My heart is full of ghosts tonight.   Mae V. Cowdery.   WLOV p.54
My heart is incased in rubies of red that are full of the seeds of malice
   in man.   Martha E. Lyons.   EbR p.103

My heart that was so passionless. Jessie Fauset. CaD p.70
My heart to thee an answer makes. William S. Braithwaite. LLL p.70
My heart to thy heart. Paul Laurence Dunbar. CPPLD p.19; LOLL p.25
My Hero (To Robert Gould Shaw). Benjamin Brawley. BANP p.150; PoN p.50;
   PoNe p.59
My House. Claude McKay. CaD p.92
My House. Nikki Giovanni. MyH p.67
My intentions are colors. LeRoi Jones. BMP p.82
My joy leaps with your ecstasy. Georgia Douglas Johnson. HWOP p.4
My Lad. Joseph S. Cotter, Sr. SPPH p.24
My lad, if you want a story book just hie away to the bubbling brook. Joseph
   S. Cotter, Sr. SPPH p.21
My lady love lives far away. Paul Laurence Dunbar. CPPLD p.478
My lady of castle grand. Paul Laurence Dunbar. CPPLD p.289
My Lady of the Cloisters. Bruce McM. Wright. LUP p.63
My Life. Henrietta C. Parks. TNV p.84
My life aint nothin'. Langston Hughes. SIH p.103
My lips from this day forget how to smile. Auguste La Caussade. TYBP p.69
My little babe was two hours old. William S. Braithwaite. HFL p.86
My Little Cabin Home. Waverly T. Carmichael. FHOF p.18
My little dark baby. Langston Hughes. DYTB p.15
My Little Dreams. Georgia Douglas Johnson. BANP p.184; CaD p.79; GoS p.196;
   HWOP p.62; PoN p.60; PoNe p.81
My Little March Girl. Paul Laurence Dunbar. CPPLD p.193
My little one of ebony hue. Joseph S. Cotter, Sr. ANP p.32; CPJSC p.47
My little stone sinks quickly. Frank Horne. AmNP p.42; CaD p.114; PoNe
   p.151
My Lord, What a Morning. Waring Cuney. BTB p.81; MBP p.90; TYBP p.236
My Love. Ted Joans. AFR p.93
My love for you is not a trivial thing. William Allyn Hill. LUP p.22
My love has left me has gone from me. Dudley Randall. KAL p.135
My love is a lotus blossom. Anonymous. TYBP p.28
My love is live mountains of the moon. Ted Joans. AFR p.93
My love when this is past. Stephany. BrT p.140
My lover one is unique without a peer. Anonymous. TYPB p.31
My Lover is a Fisherman. Gertrude Davenport. BTh p.51
My loving son, my message is as I bid you goodbye. Waverly T. Carmichael.
   FHOF p.50
My man is Black, Golden amber. Maya Angelou. JGM p.6
My man let me pull your coat. Mari Evans. IABW p.82
My Mother. Kali Grosvenor. PBK p.43
My Mother. Claude McKay. HaS p.26; SPCM p.22
My Mother. Eleanor A. Thompson. BTh p.43
My mother bore me in the southern wild.* William Blake. PoN p.215; PoNe
   p.445
My mother is a never-failing light. Eleanor A. Thompson. BTh p.43
My mother is lovely. Kali Grosvenor. PBK p.43
My Mother's Kiss. Frances Harper. PBFH p.1
My mother's kiss, my mother's kiss, I feel its impress now. Frances Harper.
   PBFH p.1
My Muse. Joseph S. Cotter, Sr. LOF p.33
My muse, if one so thoughtless should deny. Delmar Bobo. BTh p.32

My muse, thou art a laggard by the way. Joseph S. Cotter, Sr. LOF p.33
My muvver's ist the nicest one. Paul Laurence Dunbar. CPPLD p.404
My name is Afrika. Keorapetse Kgositsile. BlSp p.112
My name is Johnson. Langston Hughes. OWT p.3
My needing, really, my own sweet good. Gwendolyn Brooks. AnA p.15
My neighbor lives on a hill. Paul Laurence Dunbar. CPPLD p.311
My old man's a white old man. Langston Hughes. AmNP p.62; BANP p.236; FNP
    p.26; CNAW p.304; IADB p.6; WeB p.52; PoN p.103
My old mule. Langston Hughes. IADB p.3; SIH p.29
My old time daddy came back home last night. Langston Hughes. SIH p.119
My own sweet good. Gwendolyn Brooks. AnA p.15
My path is Lighted By a Star.** Lucy Mae Turner. BCF p.55
My Path. Joseph S. Cotter, Sr. CPJSC p.15
My pathway lies through worse than death. Georgia Douglas Johnson. AmNP
    p.24
My People Are Black.** Kali Grosvenor. PBK p.23
My People. Kali Grosvenor. PBK p.20
My People. Langston Hughes. CaD p.150; DYTB p.3; ITBLA p.159; SoS p.18;
    WeB p.58
My People. Charles B. Johnson. SOMP p.38
My people are in centers who see columns and touch concrete. Clarence Major.
    SAM p.70
My people laugh and sing and dance to death. Charles B. Johnson. SOMP p.38
My Pilot. Raymond Garfield Dandridge. PeP p.13
My pleasure but tutors my pain. Joseph S. Cotter, Sr. SPPH p.57
My poem. Nikki Giovanni. BFBTBJ p.95; BOL p.23; BrT p.58; TNV p.35
My poor wealth had been spent, that afternoon off. Lucia M. Pitts. EbR
    p.121
My poverty and wealth. Joseph S. Cotter, Sr. EBAP p.192; LOF p.64; SPPH
    p.72
My Rainy Day. Maurine L. Jeffrey. HeD p.23
My relatives and friends had come bringing their sad faces. Joe Goncalves.
    FoM p.40
My roots are deep in southern life. Margaret Walker. FMP p.19
My rag is red, my couch, where on I deal. G. C. Oden. AmNP p.161; NNPUSA
    p.47; PoNe p.385
My sable land I dare not heed. Raymond Dandridge. ZaP p.30
My Sadness Sits Around Me.** June Jordan. SCh p.30
My Sea of Tears. Deborah Fuller Wess. EbR p.159
My Second Birth. Dudley Randall. LoY p.15
My second birth was when you came. Dudley Randall. LoY p.15
My sister and I. Helen Morgan Brooks. NNPUSA p.109; PoNe p.274
My Sisters. Charles Fred White. PONS p.113
My Sister is a Sister.** Kali Grosvenor. PBK p.47
My son prince of peace in war like raiment. Marion Nicholes. LiS p.18
"My son," said father, "you are young. Eloise Culver. GANIV p.21
My Song. Joseph S. Cotter, Sr. RHY p.32
My sons, sometimes I can. Gerald W. Barrax. AKOR p.3
My soul's at Rest. James E. McGirt. FYSS p.7
My South. Joseph S. Cotter, Sr. CPJSC p.35
My spirit is within the mountains. William L. Morrison. DaR p.60
My succubus smokes too much. Gerald W. Barrax. AKOR p.61

My sword I shook. Abu Bakr. TYBP p.44
My Sort O' Man. Paul Laurence Dunbar. AmNP p.6
My Soul and I. Melvin Tolson. LUP p.48; RWA p.18
My soul cried out to you. Marsha Ann Jackson. TNV p.53
My soul, lest in the music's mist. Paul Laurence Dunbar. CPPLD p.121; LOLL
    p.180
My South. Joseph S. Cotter, Sr. CPJSC p.35; WSBO p.11
My South. Don West. PoN p.297; PoNe p.547
My spirit is a pestilential city. Claude McKay. CaD p.88; SPCM p.52
My spirit wails for water, water now. Claude McKay. HaS p.94; SPCM p.108
My Sweet Brown Gal. Paul Laurence Dunbar. CPPLD p.282; WMS p.106
"My Sweet," you sang and "sweet," I sang. Countee Cullen. CCC p.84
My talent was an uptown where. Melvin Tolson. HaG p.101
My thirty years. Juan Francisco Manzano. TYBP p.98
My Thoughts Go Marching Like an Armed Host.** William S. Braithwaite.   HFL
    p.1
My thoughts tilted at the corners like long nepalese. Melvin Tolson. HaG
    p.33
My thoughts wander among the wombs of Virginal women. Don L. Lee. DSNP p.44
My time is nearly up. Vera E. Guerard. TNV p.46
My tower. Nikki Giovanni. MyH p.45
My Trip. Ted Joans. AFR p.64
My uncle is a sergeant in the army now. Deborah Fuller Wess. EbR p.159
My verses dream-rich and tender you've read. Christian Werleigh. PoN p.358
My window, opens out into the trees. Clarissa Scott Delany. AmNP p.59;
    CaD p.74; PoN p.94; PoNe p.178
My woman has picked all the leaves. Michael S. Harper. DJDC p.69
My words shall drip like molten lava. Mae V. Cowdery. WLOV p.18
My worthy hearers have you come tonight. Joseph S. Cotter. LOF p.28
Mysterious are the ways of Jehovah and of mouse. Dio Lewis. EbR p.101
Mystery, The. William S. Braithwaite. AVAN p.144
Mystery, The. Paul Laurence Dunbar. CPPLD p.27; LOLL p.36
Mystery, A. James McGirt. FYSS p.2
Mystic Drum, The.** Gabriel Okara. TYBP p.157
Mystic Sea, The. Paul Laurence Dunbar. CPPLD p.145
Myth, The. Arthur Boze. BlWo p.10
Myths of the Circumference. William S. Braithwaite. SPWSB p.21

- N -

Nadia Rodezvous. Ted Joans. BPW p.113
Naked scalding wet from the sea my soul stands wobbly on its hind legs.
    Norman Jordan. BlSp p.97
Naked woman, Black woman. Leopold Sedar Senghor. TYBP p.134
Name is lost; the athlete's deeds remain, The. William C. Braithwaite. VER
    p.14
Name of God's name! William E. B. DuBois. BTB p.99
Name of the beast is man. Sonia Sanchez. NBP p.114
Name of this poem is George Washington. June Jordan. SCh p.76
Names. John Raven. BFM p.31
Narcissus, The. Raymond Garfield Dandridge. PAOP p.55; ZaP p.101

Nat Turner, an Epitaph. Lucy Mae Turner. BCF p.64
Nat Turner in the Clearing. Albert Aubert. ATB p.29
Nat Turner was a slave who stood for a supreme great brotherhood. Lucy Mae
    Turner. BCF p.64
Natives of America, The. Ann Plato. EBAP p.118
Natcha. Langston Hughes. WeB p.79
Natcha, offering love. Langston Hughes. WeB p.79
Nation Is Like Ourselves, The.** LeRoi Jones. BlSp p.19
Nation's Neglected Child, The. Joseph S. Cotter, Sr. CPJSC p.64
Nativity. Aquah Laluah. CaD p.197; ChG p.20; PoN p.384; TYBP p.164
Natural. Ted Joans. BPW p.53
Naturally. Audre Lorde. SoS p.87
Nature. H. D. Carberry. PoN p.335
Nature and Art. Paul Laurence Dunbar. CPPLD p.80; LOLL p.118
Nature's Puzzle. Joseph S. Cotter, Sr. CPJSC p.72
Nauseating heat, traffic in the street. William L. Morrison. DaR p.9
Naw, naw, little brother u don't shoot no-brother! Ronda M. Davis. BrT
    p.181
Nay, why reproach each other, be unkind. Claude McKay. HaS p.83; SPCM p.100
Near Colorado. Michael S. Harper. DJDC p.8
Near de margin of de stream. Waverly T. Carmichael. FHOF p.9
Near the End of April.** William S. Braithwaite. LLL p.77; SPWSB p.59
Near White. Countee Cullen. CCC p.11
Nearing La Guaira. Derek Walcott. TYBP p.113
Neatness, madam, has nothing to do. William J. Harris. BOL p.15
Neber min' what's in your cran'um. Joseph S. Cotter, Sr. CPJSC p.17; WSBO
    p.48
Nedjé. Roussan Camille. PoN p.366
Ned's Psalm of Life for the Negro. Joseph S. Cotter, Sr. CPJSC p.14; WSBO
    p.40
Needed / poem / for my salvation, A. Sonia Sanchez. BrT p.140; WABP p.49
Negro, The. James A. Emanuel. BrT p.44; KAL p.171
Negro, The. Langston Hughes. ANP p.104; DYTB p.71; TYBP p.226
Negro (a pure product of Americanism), The. Don L. Lee. DSNP p.64
Negro Audience. Herman J. D. Carter. EbR p.29
Negro Child, The. Joseph S. Cotter, Sr. ANP p.32; CPJSC p.47
Negro Child and the Story Book, The. CPJSC p.18; WSBO p.45
Negro Church, A. Nick Aaron Ford. SFD p.20
Negro Dancers. Langston Hughes. CNAW p.303; FNP p.23; WeB p.26
Negro Depot. Michael S. Harper. DJDC p.49
Negro Girl, The. Charles B. Johnson. SOMP p.8
Negro girls like 12 years old in (enclaves). Clarence Major. SAMP p.36
Negro here. Gwendolyn Brooks. KAL p.152
Negro holds firmly the reins of his four horses, the block swags underneath
    on its tied-over chair.* Walt Whitman. PoN p.214; PoNe p.469
Negro in the cane fields. Nicolas Guillen. PoN p.374
Negro Love Song. Joseph S. Cotter, Sr. CPJSC p.34; WSBO p.49
Negro Love Song, A. Paul Laurence Dunbar. BANP p.52; CPPLD p.75; LiG p.41;
    LOLL p.110; MBP p.21; PoN p.34; PoNe p.36
Negro Mother's Lullaby, A. Countee Cullen. OTIS p.165
Negro Peddler Song, A. Fenton Johnson. AmNP p.26
Negro Poets. Charles Bertram Johnson. ANP p.38; BANP p.199; SOMP p.9

Negro Preacher, The. Joseph S. Cotter, Sr. CPJSC p.36
Negro serenade. James Edwin Campbell. BANP p.65; ITBLA p.94
Negro Servant. Langston Hughes. OWT p.70
Negro simply asks the chance to think, The. William S. Braithwaite. ANP
    p.32; AVAN p.147; CPJSC p.11; WSBO p.47
Negro Singer. James David Corrothers. AVAN p.165; BANP p.74; CNAW p.190
Negro Sings, A. Normal Sylvain. PoN p.359
Negro Soldiers, The. Roscoe Conklin Jamison. ANP p.109; BANP p.195
Negro Speaks of Night, A. Iola M. Brister. EbR p.14
Negro Speaks of Rivers. Langston Hughes. AmNP p.63; ANP p.103; BANP p.241;
    BLIA p.193; CaD p.149; CNAW p.307; DYTB p.6; FNP p.30; GoS p.52; IADB
    p.24; ITBLA p.159; LUP p.33; PoN p.105; PoNe p.187; TYBP p.225; WeB p.5
Negro spiritual. Perient Trett. PoN p.248; PoNe p.548
Negro Spirituals. Eloise Culver. GANIV p.19
Negro to America, The. Robert Hayden. HSITD p.26
Negro Volunteer, The. Charles Fred White. PONS p.58
Negro with the trumpet at his lips. Langston Hughes. BTB p.124; FOW p.91;
    LUP p.27
Negro Woman, The. Joseph S. Cotter, Sr. CPJSC p.48
Negro Woman. Lewis Alexander. CaD p.122
Negroes. Maxwell Bodenheim. PoN p.272; PoNe p.508
Negroes here: dark votaries of the sun. Robert Hayden. HSITD p.12
Negroes, labouring. Nicolas Guillen. MBP p.45; TYBP p.104
Negroes, sweet and docile, meek, humble, and kind. Langston Hughes. OWT
    p.86; PATL p.100
Negro's Christmas Prayer, The. Joseph S. Cotter, Sr. CPJSC p.68; WSBO p.4
Negro's Educational Creed, The. Joseph S. Cotter, Sr. ANP p.32; AVAN p.147;
    CPJSC p.11; WSBO p.47
Negro's Friend, The. Claude McKay. SPCM p.51
Negro's Loyalty, The. LOF p.50
Negro's New year prayer, The. Joseph S. Cotter, Sr. CPJSC p.46; WSBO p.49
Negro's Prayer, A. Richard T. Hamilton. HeD p.20
Negro's Tragedy, The. Claude McKay. BLIA p.167; BTB p.145; SPCM p.50
Neighbors. Anne Spencer. CaD p.47
Neighbors in lands afar our native bones and flesh. Melvin Tolson. RWA p.30
Neighbors Stood on the Corner.** Waring Cuney. LUP p.9
Neighter life / time / ebony / or look you are just telephone book. Ted
    Joans. BPW p.52
Neither the teacher of the class nor the priest with his catechism can. Aimé
    Césaire. PoN p.370
Neon glitter of night. Thurmond Snyder. NNPUSA p.54
Nerve, The. Clarence Major. SAM p.74
Never. Ted Joans. BPW p.86
Never again the sight of her? Joseph S. Cotter, Jr. BOG p.8
Never before, and twice in one week. Michael S. Harper. DJDC p.23
Never love with all your heart. Countee Cullen. B1C p.51; OTIS p.98
Never, never, never. Lucia M. Pitts. EbR p.120
Never no more will I try. William L. Morrison. DaR p.58
Never saw him. James E. Emanuel. BrT p.44; KAL p.171
Never the Final Stone. Countee Cullen. B1C p.23
Never would I seek to capture you with tempestous ardor. Mae V. Cowdery.
    WLOV p.50

Night, and on all sides only the folding quiet. Sam Duby R. Sutu. TYBP
    p.175
Night and the hood soft plain and rape that tears apart. Conrad Kent Rivers.
    SVH p.20
Night - blackbright with shadows that caress, The. Ebon. BrT p.160
Night creeps over the city. Richard V. Durham. GoS p.134
Night, Death, Mississippi. Robert Hayden. SPRH p.23
Night, Dim Night. Paul Laurence Dunbar. CPPLD p.371
Night, dim night, and it rains, my love, it rains. Paul Laurence Dunbar.
    CPPLD p.371
Night drops within Black America. Herman L. McMillan. TNV p.76
Night Fire, The. Claude McKay. HaS p.55
Night: Four Songs. Langston Hughes. FOW p.14
Night Frowned, The. Nick Aaron Ford. SFD p.36
Night grows no flower, Children. Herbert A. Simmons. NBP p.120
Night I Went To Church, The. Waverly T. Carmichael. FHOF p.14
Night Interpreted. Everett Hoagland. NBP p.70
Night is Beautiful, The. Langston Hughes. CaD p.150; DYTB p.3; ITBLA p.159;
    SoS p.18; WeB p.58
Night is dewey as a maiden's mouth. CPPLD p.101; LOLL p.149
Night is for sorrow and dawn is for joy. Paul Laurence Dunbar. CPPLD p.143
Night is raining, The. William L. Morrison. DaR p.9
Night John Henry is born an ax, The. Melvin B. Tolson. TYBP p.213
Night like purple flakes of snow. Donald Jeffrey Hayes. CaD p.189
Night of Death, The. Frances Harper. PBFH p.53
Night of Love. Paul Laurence Dunbar. CPPLD p.71; LOLL p.104
Night of the Shark, The. Ted Joans. AFR p.38
Night of the two moon. Langston Hughes. FOW p.14
Night on the Ol' Plantashum. Daniel Webster Davis. AVAN p.98
Night Slivers. Darwin T. Turner. NBP p.129
Night Song. Katharine Beverly. EbR p.3
Night Song. Langston Hughes. FOW p.45; MBP p.99
Night turned over in her sleep. Mae V. Cowdery. WLOV p.12
Night Walks Down the Mountain.** William Allyn Hill. LUP p.20
Night was made for rest and sleep. Clarissa Scott Delany. ANP p.129; CaD
    p.142; PoN p.96; PoNe p.181
Night winds drone in mournful lay. Raymond Garfield Dandridge. PAOP p.42;
    ZaP p.98
Night, you are upon us. Birdelle Wycoff Ransom. HeD p.34
Nightdreamer. Michael S. Harper. DJDC p.39
Nightfall. Una Marson. PoN p.325
Nightmares Again. Michael S. Harper. DJDC p.68
Nightmares again the uterus contracts. Michael S. Harper. DJDC p.68
Nikki-Reasa. Nikki Giovanni. BFBTBJ p.58; NBP p.53; SoS p.22
Nine Month Blues. Ted Joans. AFR p.90
Nine O'clock. Louis Simpson. PoN p.319
Nineveh, Tyre. Sterling A. Brown. BANP p.252; CNAW p.405; SoR p.59
Niobe in distress for her children slain by Apollo, from Ovid's metamor-
    phoses, Book VI, and From a view of the painting of Mr. Richard Wilson.
    Phillis Wheatley. PAL p.94; PPW p.47
Nitty Gritty. Ted Joans. BPW p.114

No!! Anywhere my father goes. William Alfred McLean, Jr. BOL p.53
No Blues With Eros. Ted Joans. BPW p.94
No boy chooses war. Owen Dodson. AmNP p.125
No, dere ain't no use er workin' in de blazin' summer time. James E. McGirt.
    FYSS p.38
No doubt dat you lak to know jes whut wuz ailin' us. Raymond Garfield Dan-
    dridge. AVAN p.192; PAOP p.51; ZaP p.74
No Enemies. Benjamin Clark. EBAP p.183
No engines shrieking rescue storm the night. Claude McKay. HaS p.55
No friend to wipe the sweat of death from off his face. Benjamin Clark.
    EBAP p.180
No, his exit by the gate. William Stanley Braithwaite. BANP p.101
No; I am neither seeking to change nor keep myself. J. Henderson Brooks.
    BTh p.27
No, I am not death wishes of sacred rapists, singing on candy gallows. Bob
    Kaufman. NBP p.79
No Images. Waring Cuney. AmNP p.98; BANP p.283; CaD p.212; CNAW p.377; GoS
    p.28; LUP p.9; TYBP p.236; PoN p.145
No kitchen is big enough. Waring Cuney. CNAW p.376; LUP p.15
No light entered the darkened room. Louise Blackman. EbR p.5
No longer throne of a goddess to whom we pray. Robert Hayden. BTB p.111;
    KAL p.112; SPRH p.15
No Loser, No Weeper. Maya Angelou. JGM p.8
No Love. Marion Nicholes. LiS p.15
No love baby dont speak to me of love. Marion Nicholes. LiS p.15
No Mad Talk. Ted Joans. BPW p.20
No man can shape his destiny. Raymond Garfield Dandridge. PAOP p.24
No match in the house. Michael S. Harper. DJDC p.20
No matter what you call it. Paul Laurence Dunbar. CPPLD p.475
No Mo' Kneegrow. Ted Joans. BPW p.26
No Mo Meetings Where U Folk Bout Whitey. Sonia Sanchez. WABP p.48
No Mo Space For Toms. Ted Joans. AFR p.35
No money to bury him. Langston Hughes. SIH p.97
No More. Ted Joans. BPW p.72
No More Auction Block.** Anonymous. ITBLA p.98
No more for you the city of thorny ways. HaS p.67
No more from out the sunset. William S. Braithwaite. ANP p.50; BANP p.102
No more from the sunset. William S. Braithwaite. AVAN p.144
No more marching. Don L. Lee. DSNP p.75
No more the feel uf your hand. Mae Cowdery. WLOV p.29
No more the flow'ry scences of pleasure rise. Phillis Wheatley. PAL p.64;
    PPW p.43
No no no no. Maya Angelou. JGM p.38
No, no! not tonight, my friend. R. Nathaniel Dett. ANP p.120
No one can communicate to you. Lucy Smith. NNPUSA p.45
No one could have a Blacker tail. Ed Roberson. PoNe p.429
No one should feel peculiar living as they do. June Jordan. SCh p.9
No one's been told that Black men went first to the moon. Michael S. Harper.
    DJDC p.57
No race has had such chilly days. Waverly T. Carmichael. FHOF p.23
No Reservations. Nikki Giovanni. BrT p.64

No rock along the road but knows the inquisition of his toes. Donald Jeffrey
   Hayes. AmNP p.92; PoN p.137; PoNe p.242
No, Rox Ann is not moved to tears. Eli Shepperd. PlS p.28
No servile little fear shall daunt my will. Claude McKay. HaS p.86; SPCM
   p.68
No sleep tonight, Sonia Sanchez. BrT p.138
No sooner than I heard them holler out in Harlem. Theodore Horne. FoM p.67
No sound falls from the moaning sky. Maya Angelou. JGM p.17
No Tears. John Henrik Clarke. EbR p.44
No the two legg'd beasts that walk like men. Maya Angelou. JGM p.38
No Time. Marion Nicholes. LiS p.17
No Time For Poetry. Julia Fields. AmNP p.183; ITBLA p.275
No Tomb in Arlington.** Olive La Grone. FoM p.75
No train of thought, April 4, 1969. June Jordan. SCh p.64
No Use in Signs. James E. McGirt. FYSS p.28
No venomous cobra's stab e'er stung. Raymond Garfield Dandridge. PAOP p.40;
   ZaP p.36
No Way Out. Linda Curry. SoS p.8
No word upon the boarded page. Countee Cullen. BlC p.58
Noblesse Oblige. Jessie Fauset. CaD p.67
Nobody cares when I am glad. Georgia Douglas Johnson. HWOP p.15
Nobody knows me. David Henderson. BOL p.69; SoS p.84
Nobody planted roses, he recalls. Robert Hayden. BOR p.26; KAL p.115; SPRH
   p.53
Nobody Riding the Roads Today.** June Jordan. SCh p.41
Nobody's Lookin' But De Owl and De Moon. James Weldon Johnson. FYOP p.69
Nocturnal. Herman McMillan. TNV p.76
Nocturne. Gwendolyn Bennett. ANP p.128; BANP p.244
Nocturne. Dorothy F. Blackwell. EbR p.6
Nocturne. Roussan Camille. TYBP p.94
Nocturne. Countee Cullen. CpS p.21
Nocturne. Ylessa Dubonee. EbR p.61
Nocturne. Donald Jeffrey Hayes. CaD p.190
Nocturne. H. A. Vaughan. PoN p.346
Nocturne at Bethesda. Arna Bontemps. AmNP p.81; BANP p.265; BLIA p.215;
   BTB p.47; CaD p.166; CNAW p.333; PoN p.11; PoNe p.211
Nocturne of the Wharves. Arna Bontemps. BANP p.263; PoNe p.224
Nocturne Varial. Lewis Alexander. PoN p.84; PoNe p.158
Noddin' by De Fire. Paul Laurence Dunbar. CPPLD p.326; WMS p.63
Noises in the Night. William L. Morrison. DaR p.40
Non-John Browns, The. Ted Joans. BPW p.61
Noon. Paul Laurence Dunbar. CPPLD p.368
Noon Tide. Henrietta Cordelia Ray. EABP p.143
Noonday April Sun, The. George Love. IADB p.103; NNPUSA p.68
Nora: a Serenade. Paul Laurence Dunbar. CPPLD p.99; LOLL p.146
Norris Dam.** Selden Rodman. PoN p.294; PoNe p.542
North and South. Joseph S. Cotter, Sr. CPJSC p.13
North and South. Claude McKay. FNP p.11; GoS p.154; HaS p.17; SPCM p.20
North Boun'. Ariel Holloway. BANP p.288; BTh p.11; CaD p.201; GoS p.152;
   PoN p.144
North Gloster Song. William C. Braithwaite. VER p.89
North Yank.* James Pipes. ZJP p.81

Nothing Makes Sense. Nikki Giovanni. MyH p.56
Nothing surprises me. LeRoi Jones. BMP p.16
Nothing will keep us young you know. Sonia Sanchez. WABP p.21
Nothing's too high to reach for. Alice D. Anderson. EbR p.1
Notice. Ted Joans. AFR p.41
Nous n' Irons Plus Au Bois ... Sterling A. Brown. SoR p.130
November. Joseph S. Cotter, Jr. BOG p.27
Novembah Dusk. Lucile D. Goodlett. WGC p.27
November Cotton Flower. Jean Toomer. CaD p.99; FNP p.13; SoS p.120
November Eventide, A. Charles Fred White. PONS p.136
November sabbath morn. Charles Fred White, PONS p.122
November sun invites me. Paul Laurence Dunbar. CPPLD p.465
Novitiates sing ave before the whipping post. Maya Angelou. JGM p.28
Now. Donald E. Bogle. TNV p.23
Now. Bernie Casey. LATP p.65
Now. Margaret Walker. PEND p.9
Now Aint That Love? Carolyn M. Rodgers. BrT p.180
Now, All You Children. Ray Durem. BTB p.104; SoS p.106
Now and Then. Charles B. Johnson. SOMP p.14
Now at the three-score year I turn. William S. Braithwaite. SPWSB p.69
Now begins the sleep, my friend. Countee Cullen. PLL p.73
Now dreams are not available. Langston Hughes. FOW p.112; LUP p.28; PATL
    p.63
Now, first, let each one estimate to what extent he owes it. Joseph S.
    Cotter, Sr. CPJSC p.61; LOF p.35
Now, firstly, from my text I stray. Joseph S. Cotter, Sr. LUP p.48; RHY
    p.31
Now full of hope and deep repentance too. George Marion McLlelan. EBAP
    p.135
Now here at a time. Donald E. Bogle. TNV p.23.
Now, I am afraid to die. Gerald W. Barrax. AKOR p.74
Now I am cooled of folly's heat. Countee Cullen. MASP p.77
Now I am young and credulous. Countee Cullen. CCC p.22; KAL p.99; OTIS p.13
Now in June, when the night is a vast softness filled with blue stars.
    Langston Hughes. WeB p.92
Now let all lovely things embark. Countee Cullen. CpS p.28; OTIS p.58
Now look hyah nickle. Lucy Mae Turner. BCF p.57
Now, Matt Dillon, love has come for me. Gerald W. Barrax. AKOR p.38
Now my songs she'll grow. William S. Braithwaite. HFL p.31
Now, pick up the sword. Ahmed A. Alhamisi. GuW p.11
Now Poem For Us. Sonia Sanchez. WABP p.67
Now probation's over, soul attained. William S. Braithwaite. SPWSB p.63
Now that all the twilight glimmers through the lane. William S. Braithwaite.
    HFL p.64
Now that our love has drifted to a quiet close. Waring Cuney. AmNP p.100;
    BANP p.285; ITBLA p.160; PoN p.446
Now that the story has moved out of the headlines. Norman Jordan. BlSp p.94
Now the dead past seems vividly alive. Claude McKay. HaS p.30; PoN p.328;
    SPCM p.29
Now the thing the Negro has got to do. Samuel Allen. BrT p.159
Now the thunder is real in the sky. Owen Dodson. PLL p.92
Now they are gone to sunset lands who told. J. Henderson Brooks. BTh p.48

TITLE AND FIRST LINE INDEX

Now they go forth to war. Lucia M. Pitts. EbR p.117
Now thread my voice with lies. Maya Angelou. JGM p.21
Now we know to bed we won't go. Ted Joans. AFR p.24
Now while in clouds of bloom the blackbirds sing. Robert E. Hayden. HSITD
    p.18
Now would I tread my darkness down. Owen Dodson. KAL p.120; PLL p.74
Now you are gone, and with your unreturning goes. Countee Cullen. B1C p.33;
    OTIS p.93
Now you, John Henry, 'tain't no use to stan' up daih an' mak no 'scuse. Paul
    Laurence Dunbar. LiG p.24
"Now you must die," the young one said. Dudley Randall. BrT p.123
Nowadays the Heroes. June Jordan. SCh p.8
Nowadays the heroes, go out looking for the cradle in the cold. June Jordan.
    SCh p.8
Nowhere are we safe. Owen Dodson. AmNP p.124; KAL p.122
Nowhere beyond the margined land. William S. Braithwaite. SPWSB p.22
Nu. Melvin Tolson. HaG p.69
Nude as Cassandra. Gerald W. Barrax. AKOR p.27
Nude With Apple. Gerald W. Barrax. AKOR p.28
Nude With Flowers. Gerald W. Barrax. AKOR p.29
Nude With Seaweed. Gerald W. Barrax. AKOR p.30
Nude With Tumblers. Gerald W. Barrax. AKOR p.35
Nude Young Dancer. Langston Hughes. FNP p.22; WeB p.33
#4. Doughtery (Doc) Long, Jr. TNV p.63
Number 5 - December. David Henderson. BOL p.69; SoS p.84
Number runner come to my door. Langston Hughes. OWT p.11
#20. Doughtry (Doc) Long, Jr. TNV p.54
#25. Doughtry (Doc) Long, Jr. TNV p.65
#28. Doughtry (Doc) Long, Jr. TNV p.66
Numbers, Letters. LeRoi Jones. BMP p.47
Nutting Song. Paul Laurence Dunbar. CPPLD p.465
Nympholepsy. William S. Braithwaite. HFL p.43

- O -

O.D. er. John Raven. BFM p.29
O.E.A., The. Claude McKay. PoN p.329
O African Children of the Afric Tribe. Ahmad A. Alhamisi. GuW p.11
O Allah ... receive him a morning god. Larry Neal. BrT p.19; FoM p.19
O Apple Blossoms. Lewis Alexander. CaD p.127
O Black and unknown bards of long ago. James Weldon Johnson. AmNP p.1; ANP
    p.46; AVAN p.175; BANP p.123; BLIA p.136; FYOP p.6; ITBLA p.119; PoN p.23;
    PoNe p.29; TYBP p.207
O Black and Unknown Bards. James Weldon Johnson. AmNP p.1; ANP p.46; AVAN
    p.175; BANP p.123; BLIA p.136; FYOP p.6; ITBLA p.119; PoN p.23; PoNe
    p.29; TYBP p.207
O brothers mine, take care! take care! James Weldon Johnson. CaD p.22;
    FYOP p.19
O brothers mine, today we stand. James Weldon Johnson. ANP p.44; AVAN p.173;
    BANP p.130; FYOP p.1; PoN p.25
O calender of the century. Melvin Tolson. LRL p.30

O chillen, run, de cunjan man. James Edwin Campbell. BANP p.65; EBAP p.234
O come while youth's bright rosy veil. Georgia D. Johnson. HWOP p.59
O come, you pious youth adore. Jupiter Hammond. EBAP p.9; JHANP p.32
O courier on pegasus. Etheridge Knight. TGWL p.65
O cruel death! thy lancer sharp. Joseph S. Cotter, Sr. LOF p.18
O cruel mob - destroying crew. Lauretta Holman Gooden. HeD p.16
O Daedalus Fly Away Home. Robert Hayden. BOR p.67; CNAW p.393; IADB p.26;
    SoS p.120; SPRH p.71; PoN p.163; PoNe p.288
O dainty bud, I hold thee in my hand. Eva Jessye. ANP p.80
O, de birds ar' sweetly singin'. Daniel Webster Davis. BANP p.81
O, de light-bugs glimmer down de lane. James Edwin Campbell. BANP p.65;
    ITBLA p.94
O' de wurl' ain't flat. Ariel Holloway. BANP p.288; BTh p.11; CaD p.200;
    GoS p.152; PoN p.144; PoNe p.257
O death has sealed thy eyes, dear lad. Joseph S. Cotter, Sr. SPPH p.44
O death! Whose sceptere trembling realms obey. Phillis Wheatley. PPW p.95
O Dunbar! the son of everlasting fame. Waverly T. Carmichael. FHOF p.25
O, eloquent and caustic sage! Joseph S. Cotter. EBAP p.185; LOF p.17
O England! Mother England! hast thou come. Joseph S. Cotter. CPJSC p.60;
    LOF p.49
O foolish me, in quest of ease. Raymond Garfield Dandridge. ZaP p.81
O freedom! Freedom! O! how oft thy loving children call on thee! Charles
    Reason. ANP p.11; AVAN p.44
O freedom, let thy perfect work be wrought. Leslie Pinckney Hill. AVAN
    p.197
O giant of Sierra's chain. Zachary Withers. PAS p.30
O God of love unbounded! Lord supreme! Placido. TYBP p.99
O Great Black Masque. Ted Joans. BPW p.5
O heavy Black woman of mother-confidence and life weight. Francois Clemmons.
    TGWL p.21
O, I wish that yesterday. Langston Hughes. OWT p.101
O let the music play a little longer. William S. Braithwaite. LLL p.38
O Liberty, what charm so great. James Madison Bell. ANP p.18
O li'l' lamb out in de col'. Paul Laurence Dunbar. CPPLD p.213
O Little David, Play on Your Harp.** Joseph S. Cotter, Jr. BOG p.15
O lonely heart so timid of approach. Claude McKay. HaS p.70; SPCM p.109
O Lord God, we are told that Thou sleepest not. Joseph S. Cotter, Sr.
    CPJSC p.20
O Lord, the hard won miles. Paul Laurence Dunbar. ANP p.25; CPPLD p.16;
    LOLL p.20
O Lord we come this morning. James Weldon Johnson. BANP p.125
O Lords of purity. Robert Hayden. HSITD p.43
O love, you have shorn me, and rifled my heart. Georgia Douglas Johnson.
    HWOP p.53
O lovely form that has lain so long beneath my heart. Mae V. Cowdery. WLOV
    p.46
O, mass of tone immaculate of harmony most intricate. Charles Fred White.
    PONS p.107
O master seer! O singer sweet of lyrics of the lowly race. Charles B. John-
    son. SOMP p.15
O mighty, powerful, dark-dispelling sun. James Weldon Johnson. FYOP p.51

O mistress of the world! heaven's own dear child! William S. Braithwaite.
   HFL p.68
O Mondays is o.k. Victor Hernandez Cruz. SNA p.13
O mongrel land. Olive LaGrone. NNPUSA p.36
O mother race! To thee I bring. Paul Laurence Dunbar. ANP p.27; AVAN p.64;
   CNAW p.208; CPPLD p.23; LOLL p.30
O mothers O fathers of newer spirits. Ahmed A. Alhamisi. GuW p.8
O my trust and thy trust. Joseph S. Cotter, Sr. SPPH p.44
O my way and thy way and life's joy and wonder. Joseph S. Cotter, Sr. AVAN
   p.147
O oak! long years the stress of storm and wind has made thy limbs exult in
   growing them. Charles B. Johnson. SOMP p.26
O pharoah! way down in Egypt land, gwine tell ole Pharoah's band - let dem
   people go! Eli Shepperd. P1S p.23
O, plain man, plain man, doubly manned. Joseph S. Cotter, Sr. SPPH p.43;
   WSBO p.27
O, poet gifted with the sight divine! Henrietta Cordelia Ray. EBAP p.139
O, rich young lord, thou ridest by. James Edwin Campbell. BANP p.70
O say can u see on the baseball diamond. Sonia Sanchez. WABP p.36
O shepherds, while you watch your flocks the wise men watch his star. Effie
   Lee Newsome. ChG p.69
O silent God, Thou whose voice afar in mist and mystery. William Edward
   Burghardt Du Bois. ANP p.115; BANP p.90; CaD p.26; PoN p.18; PoNe p.20
O silver tree! Langston Hughes. AmNP p.63; BANP p.236; BLIA p.198; FNP
   p.22; KAL p.87; WeB p.25
O sky god, ruler of sky and land, send us in our distress an ark of covenant.
   Gene Holmes. EbR p.83
O sleep, thou kindest minister to man. James Weldon Johnson. FYOP p.50
O soldier of every nation. Mae V. Cowdery. WLOV p.66
O somebody dead in the graveyard and somebody dead in the sea. Eli Shepperd.
   P1S p.112
O South Land!** James Weldon Johnson. FYOP p.8
O summer-bee in de willer tree. Eli Shepperd. P1S p.19
O. sweep of stars over Harlem streets. Langston Hughes. DYTB p.22; FOW
   p.101
O sweet are tropic lands for waking dreams! Claude McKay. FNP p.11; GoS
   p.154; HaS p.17; SPCM p.20
O tempera, what is man? Melvin Tolson. HaG p.19
O thou bright jewel in my aim I strive. Phillis Wheatley. PAL p.91; PPW p.4
O thou whose exit wraps in boundless woe. Phillis Wheatley. PAL p.79; PPW
   p.90
O tremble! O tremble, O tremble. Hart LeRoi Bibbs. NBP p.28
O, what would people say if you ate bitter-tasting ants. Agnes Maxwell
O whisper, o my soul. Claude McKay. BANP p.172; HaS p.44; SPCM p.79
O white-faced mimes. Langston Hughes. FOW p.37
O White Mistress.** Don Johnson. NNPUSA p.40
O whitened head entwined in turban gay. James Weldon Johnson. BLIA p.135;
   FYOP p.12
O Williston a countless debt I owe. Charles Fred White. PONS p.156
O word I love to sing.** Claude McKay. HaS p.63; SPCM p.43

O ye young and thoughtless youth. Jupiter Hammon. JHANP p.37
O, you can't find a buddy. Langston Hughes. FCTJ p.36
O you would clothe me in silker frocks. Claude McKay. CaD p.87; HaS p.21;
    SPCM p.28
Obits. Gerald W. Barrax. AKOR p.44
Obituary. Robert Hayden. HSITD p.28
Oblivion. Jessie Redmond Fauset. ANP p.89; BANP p.208; PoN p.67; PoNe p.69
Obo in open like a cowrie. Ted Joans. BPW p.41
Ocean. John Boyd. EBAP p.153
October. Paul Laurence Dunbar. CPPLD p.100; LOLL p.148
October is the tresurer of the year. Paul Laurence Dunbar. CPPLE p.100; LOLL
    p.148
October Journey. Margaret Walker. AmNP p.132; BTB p.180; IADB p.28; PoNe
    p.317; PoN p.176
October 16: the Raid. Langston Hughes. BOL p.36; PATL p.28; OWT p.89
October XXIX, 1795 (Keat's Birthday). William S. Braithwaite. CaD p.32;
    HFL p.40; SPWSB p.83
Octoroon, The. Georgia Douglas Johnson. AVAN p.209
Ode, An. Francis Williams. EBAP p.266
Ode for Memorial Day. Paul Laurence Dunbar. CPPLD p.35; LOLL p.49
Ode of Verses, An. Phillis Wheatley. PPW p.69
Ode on the birthday of Pompey Stockbridge. Phillis Wheatley. EBAP p.111
Ode: Salute to the French Negro Poets.* Frank O'Hara. PoNe p.581
Ode to Benedict College. Nick Aaron Ford. SFD p.30
Ode to Blackmen. Zachary Withers. PAS p.10
Ode to Blackwoman. Zachary Withers. PAS p.17
Ode to Booker Washington. Charles B. Johnson. SOMP p.19
Ode to Ethiopia. Paul Laurence Dunbar. ANP p.27; AVAN p.64; CNAW p.208;
    CPPLD p.23; LOLL p.30
Ode to John Coltrane. Quincy Troupe. BlSp p.230
Ode to John Howard Griffin. Arthur Boze. BlWo p.21
Ode to Neptune (1772) on Mrs. W_____'s Voyage to England. Phillis Wheatley.
    PAL p.46; PPW p.35
Ode to Tenechtitlan. Michael S. Harper. DJDC p.85
Odysseus at the Mast. Gerald W. Barrax. AKOR p.67
Odyssey of Big Boy. Sterling A. Brown. BANP p.248; CaD p.130; CNAW p.400;
    SoR p.5
O'er all my song, the image of a face. James David Corrothers. AVAN p.165;
    BANP p.74; CNAW p.190
O'er the wintry sea. William S. Braithwaite. LLL p.74
O'erwhelming sorrow now demands my song. Phillis Wheatley. PAL p.69; PPW
    p.38
Of a Woman Who Turns Rivers. David Llorens. TGWL p.70
Of all the grandeur that was Solomon's. Countee Cullen. CpS p.75; OTIS p.70
Of all things, lady, be not proud. Countee Cullen. CpS p.69; OTIS p.68
Of Bread and Wine. Oliver LaGrone. BTB p.138
Of De Witt Williams on his way to Lincoln Cemetery. Gwendolyn Brooks. CNAW
    p.516; PoN p.189
Of Dictators. Robert N. Perry, Jr. EbR p.116
Of Earth. Mae V. Cowdery. WLOV p.13
Of Faith: Confessional. June Jordan. SCh p.80; SoS p.70
Of Liberation. Nikki Giovanni. BFBTBJ p.45

Of Man and Nature. Horace Mungin. BOL p.44

Of the fire, or the red bursts, eyes hearts yellow girls explosive disillu-
sions. LeRoi Jones. BMP p.122

Of the furious who take today and jerk it out of joint have made new under
pinnings and a head. Gwendolyn Brooks. BrT p.37; FaP p.18

Of the three wise men who came to the king, one was a brown man, so they
sing. Langston Hughes. Ch G p.73

Of the tribe of the tribes to be the tribe. LeRoi Jones. BMP p.173

Of tropic sensations the worst. James Weldon Johnson. FYOP p.32

Of two great truths we need to be so deeply clear. Marion Cuthbert. SoC
p.37

Of what avail the tardy showers. Georgia Douglas Johnson. HWOP p.26

Of'en w'en de race I'm runnin', chil' my feet gits blistered so. James E.
McGirt. FYSS p.9

Off our New England coast the sea to-night. William S. Braithwaite. HFL
p.13

Off Shore. William S. Braithwaite. HFL p.109

Off the coast of Ireland as our ship passed by. Langston Hughes. DYTB p.64;
WeB p.78

Off the New England Coast (To John Daniel). William S. Braithwaite. HFL
p.33; SPWSB p.55

Office Building: Evening. Langston Hughes. PATL p.40

Official Notice. Langston Hughes. PATL p.55

Oft D Pig. Ishmael Reed. SoS p.90

Oft lengthy eulogies are read and solemn **parting bells are tolled.** Raymond
Garfield Dandridge. ZaP p.18

Ofttimes I go into the cupboard of my mind and find upon its shelf **a bowl of**
mistakes. Naomi Evans Vaughn. EbR p.149

Oftimes I wish that I could be like yonder rustling poplar tree. Mae V.
Cowdery. WLOV p.14

Oh! a ring dis year, and a ring las' yer. Eli Shepperd. PlS p.81

Oh Achilles of the moleskins and the gridiron. Frank Horne. CaD p.118;
PoN p.80; PoNe p.152

Oh beautiful, Black martyr, cut down by guns held in Black hands. Joyce
Whitsitt Lawrence. BrT p.23; FoM p.20

Oh brother mine, let this true herald cease. Joseph S. Cotter, Sr. CPJSC
p.12

Oh, captain of wide western seas. Tom Redcam. PoN p.309

Oh chained human being of Bamba with your turned up truth exposed. Ted Joans.
AFR p.48

Oh, come my brother of the fairer skin and lean on me. William Thompson
Goss. EbR p.72

Oh, come quit de open fiel'. Eli Shepperd. PlS p.150

Oh Cordelia Brown. Anonymous. MBP p.57

Oh country, 'tis to thee land of the lynching bee! Charles Fred White.
PONS p.25

Oh day! with sun glowing. Mae V. Cowdery. WLOV p.26

Oh, de cedar tree is a mighty fine tree. Eli Shepperd. PlS p.78

Oh, de clouds is mighty heavy. Paul Laurence Dunbar. CPPLD p.272

Oh, de elements open and de love come down. Eli Shepperd. PlS p.140

Oh, de grubbin'-hoe's a-rustin' in de co'nah. Paul Laurence Dunbar. AVAN
p.71; CPPLD p.107; LOLL p.158

Oh, de weathah it is balmy an' de breeze is sighin' low li'l' gal. Paul Laurence Dunbar. FNP p.8; CPPLD p.338; GoS p.85

Oh, Dem Golden Slippers. James Bland. GoS p.118

Oh, dere's lots o' keer an' trouble. Paul Laurence Dunbar. AVAN p.68; CPPLD p.30; LOLL p.42

Oh doctor, I have a pain in my heart. Anonymous. MBP p.31

Oh far away across the beach. William S. Braithwaite. HFL p.51

Oh, fields of wonder. Langston Hughes. FOW p.9

Oh! foolish one in quest of ease. Raymond Garfield Dandridge. PSOP p.35

Oh, For a Little While Be Kind.** Countee Cullen. CCC p.77

Oh for the breath of the briny deep. Paul Laurence Dunbar. CPPLD p.146

Oh, for the veil of my far away youth. Georgia Douglas Johnson. ANP p.86; BANP p.182

Oh, Freedom.** Anonymous. MBP p.53

Oh, full and soft, upon the orange trees. Walter Adolphe Roberts. PoN p.311

Oh! gentle sir, calm and secure. Benjamin Clark. EBAP p.182

Oh god! am i never to find myself? Bernie Casey. LATP p.48

Oh God, make me white and shining as a star. Mae V. Cowdery. WLOV p.47

Oh, God of dust and rainbows, help us see. Langston Hughes. KAL p.89

Oh have you heard de lates'. Anonymous. ITBLA p.121

Oh, how the sunset teases like faint honeysuckle breezes. William L. Morrison. DaR p.45

Oh, I am hurt to death, my love. Paul Laurence Dunbar. CPPLD p.114; LOLL p.169

Oh, I des received a letter fo'm de sweetest little gal. Paul Laurence Dunbar. CPPLD p.440

Oh I have asked, and found no answer yet. William S. Braithwaite. SPWSB p.90

Oh, I Have Heard Asked. William S. Braithwaite. SPWSB p.90

Oh, I have tried to laugh the pain away. Claude McKay. HaS p.93; SPCM p.106

Oh, I haven't got long to live, for we all. Paul Laurence Dunbar. CPPLD p.73; LOLL p.108

Oh, I shall meet your friends, and chatter on. Sterling A. Brown. SoR p.130

Oh, I'm so grateful for your germs. John Raven. BFM p.22

Oh, in dat awful day de moon in blood 'll drip away. Eli Shepperd. P1S p.137

Oh, let's fix us a jelep and kick us a houn'.* St. Clair McKelway. PoN p.300; PoNe p.534

Oh like Atlanta parking lots insatiable and still collected kindly by the night love lies. June Jordan. SCh p.35

Oh, little Christ, why do you sigh. Jessie Redmond Fauset. BANP p.206

Oh! little girl. Normil Sylvan. PoN p.359

Oh! Lord. Antoinette T. Payne. TNV p.92

Oh, Mary, Don't You Weep.* Anonymous. BLIA p.41; ITBLA p.97

Oh, Mary, what you gonna name that pretty little baby? Anonymous. ChG p.96; ITBLA p.97

Oh, me, another week. John Raven. BFM p.19

Oh mighty forester of my when I perceive death loom, I ask no greater state than some ancient verdal tomb. William L. Morrison. DaR p.25

Oh mother, mother, where is happiness? Gwendolyn Brooks. AnA p.32

Oh my beauty of night-close, close quick your robe. Ignace Nae. PoN p.353

Oh my boy, Jesus. Owen Dodson. BTB p.93; MBP p.72; TYBP p.238

Oh, my fancy teems with a world of dreams. Georgia Douglas Johnson. HWOP p.37

Oh, my golden slippers am laid away. James A. Bland. GoS p.118

Oh my Lord. Waring Cuney. BTB p.81; MBP p.90; TYBP p.236

Oh, my lover is a fisherman. Gertrude Davenport. BTh p.51

Oh, my mother's moaning by the river. Fenton Johnson. GoS p.66; PoN p.63; PoNe p.91

Oh My Oh Yes.** Waring Cuney. BTB p.82

Oh, one was Black of the wise men of the East. Claude McKay. SPCM p.48

"Oh, Sail With me!" William C. Braithwaite. VER p.61

Oh, shattered, shattered the carven crystal bell. Robert Hayden. HSITD p.53

Oh, silver tree! Langston Hughes. AmNP p.63; BANP p.236; BLIA p.198; KAL p.87; WeB p.25

Oh something just now must be happening there! Claude McKay. BLIA p.168; GoS p.76; HaS p.11; SPCM p.21

Oh, summer has clothed the earth. Paul Laurence Dunbar. CPPLD p.144

Oh, that last long ride is a ride everybody must take. Langston Hughes. SIH p.107

Oh, the blue blue bloom. Effie Lee Newsome. CaD p.56

Oh, the breeze is blowin' balmy. Paul Laurence Dunbar. CPPLD p.433

Oh, the day has set me dreaming. Paul Laurence Dunbar. CPPLD p.170

Oh, the fullback bows to the cheering crowd. Curtis Smith. BTh p.52

Oh, the little bird is rocking in the cradle of the wind. Paul Laurence Dunbar. CPPLD p.401

Oh, the poets may sing of their lady Irenes. CPPLD p.41; LOLL p.59

Oh the sea is deep. Langston Hughes. PoNe p.198

Oh, the tidal waves of our suffering reach up and shake the sky. Albert Haynes. NBP p.58

Oh, the winter's coming. James E. McGirt. FYSS p.21

Oh, this is the tale the grandams tell. Countee Cullen. OTIS p.175

Oh to have you in May. Paul Laurence Dunbar. CPPLD p.266

Oh, two white hosses standin' side and side, me and massa Gab'iel gwine for to ride. Eli Shepperd. PlS p.127

Oh, victorious queen, it's through thy loyal grace. James E. McGirt. FYSS p.51

Oh, wash-woman. Langston Hughes. GoS p.41

Oh, what shall I do? I am wholly upset. Paul Laurence Dunbar. CPPLD p.208

Oh, what sorrow! Langston Hughes. PATL p.43

Oh, what sound is that. Bobb Hamilton. BrT p.168

Oh when I think of my long-suffering race. Claude McKay. HaS p.32; SPCM p.42

Oh, when I was a sinner I run my race so well I soon come to find out I was hangin' over hell. Eli Shepperd. PlS p.128

Oh, who is the Lord of the land of life. Paul Laurence Dunbar. CPPLD p.445

Oh, who would be sad tho' the sky be a-graying. Paul Laurence Dunbar. CPPLD p.383

Oh wind of the spring-time, oh free wind of May. Paul Laurence Dunbar. CPPLD p.360

Oh wistful and heartrending earth, oh land of colors singing symphonies of life. Claude McKay. SPCM p.88

Oh, write it in the drifting snow, and let the wind. Robert Hayden. HSITD p.30

Oh you were quite the gypsy on that night. Langston Hughes. SIH p.93

Oh you who bore us in pain and joy. Mae V. Cowdery. WLOV p.9

Ohhh break love with white things. LeRoi Jones. BMP p.192

Okay "Negroes."** June Jordan. ScH p.48

Okay You are Afraid of Africa.** Ted Joans. AFR p.30

Ol' Doc' Hyar. James Edwin Campbell. BANP p.67; EBAP p.231

Ol' Tunes, The. Paul Laurence Dunbar. CPPLD p.82; LOLL p.122

Old Apple Tree, The. Paul Laurence Dunbar. CPPLD p.13; LOLL p.17

Old Belly. Craig Williamson. AfW p.2

Old Billy of Main Street fame. Joseph S. Cotter, Sr. RHY p.24

Old Black Men. Georgia Douglas Johnson. CaD p.77; PoN p.58; PoNe p.77

Old Cabin, The. Paul Laurence Dunbar. CPPLD p.429

Old Convict, The. H. A. Vaughan. PoN p.346

Old devil, when you come with horns and tail. James Weldon Johnson. FYOP p.41

Old Dream, An. William S. Braithwaite. LLL p.35

Old Friends. Charles Bertram Johnson. ANP p.37

Old Front Gate, The. Paul Laurence Dunbar. CPPLD p.322; CLT p.49

Old Glory, The. Gerald W. Barrax. AKOR p.83

Old Glory. Raymond Garfield Dandridge. PAOP p.16

Old guy cursed me for the coin I held, The. Raymond Patterson. SoS p.53

Old Haigman is the cheapest booze. John Raven. BFM p.27

Old homestead, The. Paul Laurence Dunbar. CPPLD p.467

Old Houses. Melvin Tolson. RWA p.26

Old King Cotton.** Sterling A. Brown. SoR p.65

Old Laughter. Gwendolyn Brooks. AnA p.44

Old Lem. Sterling A. Brown. CNAW p.402; IADB p.68; PoN p.57; PoNe p.167; TYBP p.221

Old Man, An. Bernie Casey. LATP p.10

Old Man Buzzard.** Sterling A. Brown. SoR p.29

Old Man Michael. Melvin Tolson. RWA p.16

Old man planted and dug and tended. Paul Laurence Dunbar. CPPLD p.95; LOLL p.141

Old man sat upon a stump to ponder his plight, An. Bernie Casey. LATP p.10

Old man sits on a bench in the sun, The. Waring Cuney. CNAW p.374

Old man walks to me, The. Lawrence McGaugh. BOL p.74

Old-Marrieds, The. Gwendolyn Brooks. AmNP p.141; PoN p.190

Old Marse John.** Anonymous. TYBP p.198

Old Memory, An. Paul Laurence Dunbar. CPPLD p.470

Old Mill, The. Waverly T. Carmichael. FHOF p.9

Old Mr. Goody had a goat. Joseph S. Cotter. LOF p.52; RHY p.22; SPPH p.23

Old Molly Means was a hag and a witch. Margaret Walker. AmNP p.130; FMP p.33; KAL p.141; PoN p.178; PoNe p.309

Old Negro minister concludes his sermon in his loudest voice. Langston Hughes. OWT p.35

Old Negro Soldier of the Civil War, The. Joseph S. Cotter, Sr. CPJSC p.70

Old Negro Teacher and the New, The. Joseph S. Cotter, Sr. CPJSC p.31; WSBO p.43

Old November, Sergeant Brown. Joseph S. Cotter, Jr. BOG p.27

On a red letter day pained by the sharp ache of a corn that protests a tight shoe. Melvin Tolson. HaG p.96

On a snug evening I shall watch her fingers. Gwendolyn Brooks. AmNP p.142; ITBLA p.217; KAL p.155; PoN p.192

On a street in Knoxville.* Kenneth Porter. PoN p.299; PoNe p.539

On a Suicide. Joseph S. Cotter, Sr. RHY p.31

On a summer's day as I sat by a stream. Paul Laurence Dunbar. CPPLD p.405

On a straw-colored day came Nooney. Solomon Edwards. NNPUSA p.75; PoNe p.402

On a train in Texas German prisoners eat.* Witter Bynner. PoN p.295; PoNe p.490

On being asked to leave a place of honor for one of comfort, preferably in the norther suburbs. Alice Walker. ONC p.45

On Being Brought From Africa to America. Phillis Wheatley. CNAW p.11; EBAP p.100; KAL p.7; PAL p.92; PPW p.7; TYBP p.205

On Being in Love. Ted Joans. BPW p.56

On Blake's Song of Innocence. William S. Braithwaite. HFL p.97; SPWSB p.87

On Broadway. Claude McKay. FNP p.8; HaS p.12; SPCM p.67

On Calvary's Lonely Hill. Herbert Clark Johnson. PoN p.162; PoNe p.286

On Civil Disorders. Michael S. Harper. DJDC p.81

On Death's Domain Intent I Fix My Eyes. Phillis Wheatley. AVAN p.30; PAL p.68; PPW p.39

On Dreams. Frenchy J. Hodges. B1W p.29

On earth the wise man makes the rules. Countee Cullen. CCC p.60

On Freedom. Thomas S. Sidney. EBAP p.260

On Friendship. Phillis Wheatley. EBAP p.111

On Getting an Afro. Dudley Randall. TGWL p.82

On Going. Countee Cullen. CCC p.105

On Hearing a Robin at Early Dawn. Charles B. Johnson. SOMP p.36

On Hearing James W. Riley Read From a Kentucky Standpoint. Joseph S. Cotter. EBAP p.190; LOF p.44; SPPH p.93

On Hearing of the Intention of a Gentleman to Purchase the Poet's Freedom. George Moses Horton. ANP p.13; EBAP p.23

On Hearing "The Girl with the Flaxen Hair." Nikki Giovanni. BFBTBJ p.4

On Holy Souls is dust of clinging earth. William C. Braithwaite. VER p.103

On Imagination. Phillis Wheatley. AVAN p.28; CNAW p.13; EBAP p.107; PAL p.76; PoN p.7; PoNe p.9; PPW p.29

On Liberty and Slavery. George Moses Horton. ANP p.13; CNAW p.37; ITBLA p.93; KAL p.10; PoN p.9; PoNe p.11

On Listening to the Spirituals. Lance Jeffers. CNAW p.769

On Lookout Mountain. Robert Hayden. BOR p.10

On Major General Lee (1776). Phillis Wheatley. PAL p.53

On morning wings through a trackless sea. Arthur Boze. G1Wo p.4

On Music. William S. Braithwaite. LLL p.56

On my back they've written history, Lord. Owen Dodson. PLL p.15

On my bedroom wall hang a poster. Nikki Giovanni. MyH p.24

On my Blk/ness. Alicia Ley Johnson. CNAW p.769

On natual vanity. J. E. Clare McFarlane. PoN p.321

On ochre walls in ice-formed caves shaggy neanderthrals marked their place in time. Bob Kaufman. KAL p.215; SoS p.30

On one never-to-be-forgotten day, we launched a sky. Ruby Berkley Goodwin. EbR p.70

On Out.   TITLE AND FIRST LINE INDEX

On Out. LeRoi Jones. BMP p.37
On Passing two Negroes (on a dark country road somewhere in Georgia). Conrad
    Kent Rivers. IADB p.78; NNPUSA p.42; SVH p.21
On Philosophy. Barbara Marshall. TNV p.70
On Recollection. Phillis Wheatley. EBAP p.105; PAL p.80; PPW p.28
On Revisiting Newport Beach. William S. Braithwaite. HFL p.108
On Riots. Cy Leslie. NBP p.83
On Rue Jacques Callot. Ted Joans. BPW p.47
On Second sight / the first thoughts of mouth/ Ted Joans. AFR p.13
On seeing Black Journal and watching Negro Leaders "Give Aid and Comfort to
    the Enemy" to Quote Richard Nixon. Nikki Giovanni. MyH p.61
On Seeing Diana Go Maddddddddd. Ben L. Lee. BrT p.109; DSNP p.161; WWW p.37
On Seeing Two Brown Boys in a Catholic Church. Frank Horne. BANP p.276;
    CaD p.112; PoN p.76; PoNe p.146
On Slavery. George R. Allen. EBAP p.260
On such a day as this I think. Joseph S. Cotter, Jr. BOG p.23; CaD p.102
On summer afternoons I sit. Jessie Redmond Fauset. BANP p.205; CaD p.69;
    PoN p.65; PoNe p.67
On that big estate there is no rain. Antonio Jacinto. TYBP p.181
On the appeal from the race of Sheba II. Leopold Sedar Senghor. TYBP p.134
On the back trails in sun glasses and warm air blows cocaine from city to
    river. LeRoi Jones. BMP p.14
On the Birth of my son, Malcolm Coltrane. Julius Lester. SoS p.24
On the bite of a kola nut I was so high the clouds blanketing Africa. Nikki
    Giovanni. MyH p.47
On the Capture of General Lee. Phillis Wheatley. PPW p.97
On the Coast of Maine. Robert Hayden. BOR p.12
On the corner of Newberry and 14th Place. Marion Nicholes. LiS p.11
On the Death of A Child. Edward Silvera. LOP p.45; PoN p.150; PoNe p.260
On the Death of a Young Gentleman. Phillis Wheatley. PAL p.87; PPW p.11
On the Death of a Young Lady of Five Years of Age. Phillis Wheatley. ITBLA
    p.28; PAL p.88; PPW p.10
On the Death of Dr. Samuel Marshall (1771). Phillis Wheatley. PAL p.39;
    PPW p.40
On the Death of J. C. an Infant. Phillis Wheatley. PAL p.64; PPW p.43
On the Death of Dunbar. Charles Fred White. PONS p.101
On the Death of Rev. Dr. Sewell (1769). Phillis Wheatley. PAL p.34; PPW p.7
On the Death of the Rev'd Dr. Sewall 1769. Phillis Wheatley. PPW p.64
On the Death of the Rev. Mr. George Whitefield. (1770). Phillis Wheatley.
    CNAW p.11; EBAP p.101; PAL p.36; PPW p.69
On the Death of Thomas Bailey Aldridge. William S. Braithwaite. HFL p.25
On the Death of W. C. Paul Laurence Dunbar. CPPLD p.469
On the Death of William Edward Burghardt DuBois by African Moonlight and
    Forgotten Shores. Conrad Kent Rivers. NBP p.113
On the Dedication of Dorothy Hall (Tuskegee, Ala.). Paul Laurence Dunbar.
    CPPLD p.348
On the Discovery of Beautiful Black Women. Don L. Lee. DSNP p.55
On the Dismission of a School Term. Ann Plato. ANP p.12
On the dusty earth drum. Joseph S. Cotter, Jr. AVAN p.181; BANP p.188; CaD
    p.100
On the far south side niggers slept in used white folks houses. Marion
    Nicholes. LiS p.12

On the Gift of a Thermometer. Charles Fred White. PONS p.115
On the Gift of a Whisk Broom. Charles Fred White. PONS p.115
On the Mediterranean Sea. Countee Cullen. CpS p.72
On the morning you woke beside me. Alice Walker. ONC p.55
On the River. Paul Laurence Dunbar. CPPLD p.472
On the Road. William C. Braithwaite. VER p.80
On the Road. Paul Laurence Dunbar. CPPLD p.227; LiG p.99
On the Road. Claude McKay. HaS p.41; SPCM p.64
On the sea of the Antilles floats a boat of paper. Nicolas Guillen. MBP
    p.14
On the Sea Wall. Paul Laurence Dunbar. CPPLD p.184
On the sidewalk by the busy flow. William S. Braithwaite. AVAN p.138; HFL
    p.41
On the stairs, in the house on a sheet in the world. LeRoi Jones. BMP p.39
On the train old ladies playing football going for empty seats. Victor Her-
    nandez Cruz. SNA p.47
On the way to the bone orchard, the dirt house of all the gone daddies bones,
    I want to go slump sided. Stanley Crouch. BlSp p.40
On the wide veranda white. Paul Laurence Dunbar. CPPLD p.93; LiG p.54; LOLL
    p.137
On this, thy natal day, O God. Joseph S. Cotter, Sr. CPJSC p.68; WSBO p.41
On vast expanses of the earth it rolls. William S. Braithwaite. SPWSB p.85
On Viewing Death. William L. Morrison. DaR p.44
On Virtue. Phillis Wheatley. PAL p.91; PPW p.4
On Watching a World Series Game. Sonia Sanchez. WABP p.36
On Wearing Ears. William J. Harris. BOL p.70
On when I think of my long-suffering race. Claude McKay. SPCM p.42
On working white liberals. Maya Angelou. JGM p.44
Once. Alice Walker. ONC p.23
Once a snow flake fell on my brow. Nikki Giovanni. MyH p.10
Once der was a meetin' in de wilderness. James Weldon Johnson. FYOP p.8
Once I adopted a little girl child. Langston Hughes. OWT p.16
Once I asked for one lone petal of a rose. Ruth E. J. Sarver. EbR p.128
Once I cried for new songs to sing ... a black rose ... a brown sky. Frank
    Marshall Davis. PoN p.142; PoNe p.252
Once I held my heart's door full wide. Countee Cullen. CpS p.81
Once I made a little poem out of golden hair. William S. Braithwaite. HFL
    p.90
Once I was good like the Virgin Mary and the minister's wife. Fenton Johnson.
    BANP p.145; BLIA p.126; PoN p.61; PoNe p.87
Once in a thousand years a call may ring. Countee Cullen. CpS p.74
Once like a lady. Countee Cullen. B1C p.3; OTIS p.75
Once love grew bold and arrogant of air. Paul Laurence Dunbar. CPPLD p.163
Once more I stand upon these sands and gaze. William S. Braithwaite. HFL
    p.108
Once more, listening to the wind and rain. Arna Bontemps. CaD p.163; CNAW
    p.335; PoN p.114; PoNe p.215
Once riding in old Baltimore. Countee Cullen. BTB p.79; CaD p.187; CNAW
    p.324; CCC p.15; GoS p.138; IADB p.85; ITBLA p.158; MBP p.94; OTIS p.9;
    PoN p.128; PoNe p.232; SoS p.107
Once "The Poets" floated in abstractions called art. Jon Eckels. TGWL p.32

Once there was a happy youth with heart as light and free. Charles Fred
    White. PONS p.86
Once upon a dreary evening in the midst of the world's despair. Gladys Marie
    Parker. EbR p.112
Once upon a time (Il etait une fois ...) on an ease. Ted Joans. AFR p.96
Once upon a time there were three black lines. Kali Grosvenor. BlSp p.105
Once upon the street, when we met that man with the forlorn eye. Gordon
    Parks. InL (unpaged)
One. Langston Hughes. FOW p.17
One a valley among the peaks of humanity. Vernoy E. Hite. TNV p.49
One April. Lucia M. Pitts. EbR p.120
One Blue Note. Ted Joans. AFR p.97
One day a long time ago. Katherine Cuestas. BTB p.75; SoS p.85
One day and a sleep ago few things were on my mind. Frenchy J. Hodges. BlW
    p.14
One day I idled into the field of wheat. Melvin Tolson. RWA p.16
One day I Told My Love.** Countee Cullen. BlC p.54
One day Marilyn marched beside me. Alice Walker. ONC p.37
One day we lay beneath an apple tree. Countee Cullen. CpS p.18
One Day We Played a Game. Countee Cullen. CpS p.18
One day you gonna walk in the house and I'm gonna have on a long African
    gown. Nikki Giovanni. BFBTBJ p.38; BrT p.54
One does such as one will not. James David Corrothers. BANP p.76
One drop of midnight in the dawn of life's pulsating stream. Georgia Douglas
        Johnson. AVAN p.209
One foot down, then hop! Maya Angelou. JGM p.48
125 Ways to Sex or Sexplosion. Ted Joans. AFR p.136
One last deep breath to break the spell. Benjamin Brawley. AVAN p.159
1 letter! 2 letter! 3 letter! 4! Arthur Pfister. BlSp p.162
One Life. Paul Laurence Dunbar. CPPLD p.114; LOLL p.169
One mawn ole marse, he say ter me, "Ike whar you bin las' night. Joseph S.
    Cotter. CPJSC p.74; WSBO p.56
One night in my room still and beamless. Paul Laurence Dunbar. CPPLD p.174
One night while walking 'long the street returning from the choir. Charles
    Fred White. PONS p.78
One night without the usual drowsiness that weights heavily the mind with the
    burdens of the soul. William L. Morrison. DaR p.33
One of Them There School Teachers. John Raven. BFM p.19
One ounce of truth benefits like ripples on a pond. Nikki Giovanni. MyH p.38
One sided shootout (for brothers fred hampton & mark clark murdered 12/4/69
    by chicago police at 4:30 a.m. while they slept). Don L. Lee. DSNP
    p.176; WWW p.52
One Sipped dew, the other one fat, The. Joseph S. Cotter, Sr. SPPH p.71
One still world ago I shared your ripe unfolding. Craig Williamson. AfW p.3
One thing you left with us, Jack Johnson. Sterling A. Brown. KAL p.72; SoR
    p.95; TYBP p.218
One Thousand Nine Hundred & Sixty Eight Winters. Jaci Earley. BlSp p.65;
    MBP p.93; SoS p.127
One thousand saxophones infiltrate the city. Bob Kaufman. TYBP p.252
One Time Henry Dreamed the Number.** Doughtry Long. BrT p.161
One, two, and three. Countee Cullen. ANP p.96; CpS p.84
One Way. Tommy Whitaker. TNV p.135

One-Way Ticket. Langston Hughes. BLIA p.196; ITBLA p.159; OWT p.61
One who sings "Chansons Vulgaires." Langston Hughes. WeB p.28
One Word. Raymond Garfield Dandridge. PAOP p.57; ZaP p.7
One Year Ago. David Llorens. BrT p.22; FoM p.19
One Year After. Claude McKay. HaS p.84; SPCM p.105
One Year Ago. Charles Fred White. PONS p.74
Only a few will really understand. Don L. Lee. DSNP p.176; WWW p.52
Only a little scrap of blue preserved with loving care. Frances Harper.
    PBFH p.19
Only dumb guys fight. Langston Hughes. FCTJ p.33
Only One, The. Don L. Lee. DSNP p.57
Only quiet death brings relief. Waring Cuney. AmNP p.99; BANP p.283; ITBLA
    p.180
Only Song I'm Singing, The. Nikki Giovanni. MyH p.16
Only Successful Heart transplant, The. June Jordan. SCh p.57
Only the deep well. Owen Dodson. PLL p.84
Only the Polished Skeleton. Countee Cullen. MASP p.72
Only the Span of Life.** Charles Fred White. PONS p.170
Only thing we know is the thing we turn out to be, The. LeRoi Jones. BMP
    p.132
Only Woman Blues. Langston Hughes. SIH p.50
Onus Probandi. William S. Braithwaite. BANP p.102
Onward to her destinction o'er the stream the Hannah sped. Frances Harper.
    PBFH p.15
Open dem do's and let me in - free from my sorrer and free from my sin. Eli
    Shepperd. P1S p.114
Open Door. Countee Cullen. CpS p.81
Open Letter. Owen Dodson. PLL p.103
Open Minded. Ted Joans. BPW p.35
Open the face of the ignorant. LeRoi Jones. BMP p.35
Open your ears to spirit sounds. Ed Bullins. BlSp p.38
Opinions of the new Chinese Students. Regina Pedroso. PoN p.372; TYBP p.102
Opportunity. Raymond Garfield Dandridge. PAOP p.32
Opportunity. Paul Laurence Dunbar. CPPLD p.396
Oppression. Langston Hughes. FOW p.112; LUP p.28; PATL p.63
Optimist Mrs., The. J. W. Hammond. ANP p.82
Or. June Jordan. SCh p.34
Or so our cleaning woman tells us. Townsend T. Brewster. TNV p.25
Oranges, The. Abu Dharr. TYBP p.45
Organ Recital, The. Leonidas Gibbs. BTh p.35
Orgle he sounds like he's crowin' today, The. Ray Frederick. FoM p.24
Oriflamme. Jessie Redmond Fauset. ANP p.89; AVAN p.194; BANP p.207
Original. Ragged-round. Rich-robust. Gwendolyn Brooks. FoM p.3; CNAW
    p.523; ITM p.39; TYBP p.247
Oriki Erinle. Anonymous. TYBP p.11
Orishas. Larry Neal. NBP p.92
Orison. Robert Hayden. HSITD p.36
Orison. Conrad Kent Rivers. SVH p.5
O rivulet that trickles through yon clover-scented pass. Joseph S. Cotter,
    Sr. SPPH p.73
Othello Jones dresses for dinner. Ed Roberson. PoNe p.429
Others may Salisbury or Durham praise. William C. Braithwaite. VER p.100

Otis I really love you. Kali Grosvenor. PBK p.48
Otto. Gwendolyn Brooks. ChG p.102
Ouagadougou Ouagadougou. Ted Joans. AFR p.9
Ouagadougou Thelonius Monk salute you. Ted Joans. AFR p.9
Ounce of sunshine, one of rain, An. Raymond Garfield Dandridge. PeP p.20;
    ZaP p.12
Our Aim In Life. Charles Fred White. PONS p.171
Our ancestors are watching us. Ted Joans. AFR p.13
Our Aryan Sires. William C. Braithwaite. VER p.13
Our birth and death are easy hours, like sleep and food and drink. Margaret
    Walker. FMP p.58
Our Black People. Kali Grosvenor. PBK p.21
Our Black people are your and my people. Kali Grosvenor. PBK p.21
Our boys had crossed the ocean. Eloise Culver. GANIV p.74
Our children is restless eyes and their sincere bodies as defense. Clarence
    Major. SAM p.39
Our Days are Numbered. Alicia L. Johnson. BrT p.176
Our Detroit Conference (for Don L. Lee). Nikki Giovanni. BFBTBJ p.8
Our drums were ripped. Sigemonde Kaarius Wimberli. TGWL p.100
Our earth-grit sould grow faint and gaunt and hollow. Joseph S. Cotter, Sr.
    CPJSC p.37; WSBO p.26
Our Flag. Zachary Withers. PAS p.46
Our flesh that was a battle-ground. Countee Cullen. CpS p.13; OTIS p.53
Our Good Knight Ted, girds his broad sword on. Paul Laurence Dunbar. CPPLD
    p.173
Our heart for rent. Tomi Carolyn Tinsley. EbR p.142
Our Here. Frances Harper. PBFH p.15
Our Land. Langston Hughes. FNP p.29; WeB p.99
Our lives are the sweeter because we have sorrowed. Charles Fred White.
    PONS p.156
Our love has dwindled down to this. Countee Cullen. CpS p.45
Our Meeting. Raymond A. Joseph. TGWL p.59
Our Mission. William F. Brooks. LUP p.3
Our moulting days are in their twilight stage. Margaret Danner. AmNP p.153;
    NNPUSA p.29
Our Need. Margaret Walker. FMP p.57
Our park empty, whipped of customers. Michael S. Harper. DJDC p.32
Our paths began at distant points in space.* Rea Lubar Duncan. PoNe p.574
Our Recompense. Charles Fred White. PONS p.156
Our separate winding ways we trod. Georgia Douglas Johnson. HWOP p.12
Our Task. Henrietta Cordelia Ray. AVAN p.152
Our theme this morning is the wounds of Jesus. Anonymous. BLIA p.32
Our World is Our.** Kali Grosvenor. PBK p.39
Our Your Friend Charlie pawnshop was a glorious blaze. Maya Angelou. JGM
    p.34
Ours is the Ancient Story. Countee Cullen. CCC p.64
Out from the plains of Illinois. Charles Fred White. PONS p.130
Out in de night a sad bird moans. Paul Laurence Dunbar. CPPLD p.315; WMS
    p.41
Out in de 'tater field down side de lane. Lucile D. Goodlett. WeB p.22
Out in the night I hear a liquid note. James Edward McCall. BTB p.143
Out in the night thou art the sun. Lucian B. Watkins. BANP p.211

Out in the sky the great dark clouds are massing. Paul Laurence Dunbar.
    BANP p.56; CaD p.7; CPPLD p.10; ITBLA p.95; LOLL p.150
Out in the Still Wet Night.** J. Austin Love. HeD p.29
Out of my heart, one day, I wrote a song. Paul Laurence Dunbar. CPPLD p.187
Out of my heart, one treach'rous winter's day. Paul Laurence Dunbar. CPPLD
    p.163
Out of the dark raw earth. Julia Field. PoNe p.420
Out of the Dingy Alleyways.** J. Henderson Brooks. BTh p.15
Out of the green glooms of Dambassa. Melvin Tolson. RWA p.83
Out of the infinite sea of eternity. FYOP p.49
Out of the land of the burning sun. Marcus B. Christian. GoS p.142
Out of the market place where would I go? June Jordan. SCh p.61
Out of the silence of my dreams. William S. Braithwaite. LLL p.14
Out of the sin of man. Owen Dodson. PLL p.94
Out of the sunshine and out of the heat. Paul Laurence Dunbar. CPPLD p.269
Out of the Sunset's Red.** William S. Braithwaite. LLL p.43
Out of the tense awed darkness my Frangepani comes. Aqua Laluah. CaD p.198
Out of Work. Langston Hughes. SIH p.40
Out on the bush path waits, many high man-hating a bright snake. Craig
    Williamson. AfW p.14
Outcast. Claude McKay. AmNP p.28; HaS p.45; ITBLA p.156; SPCM p.41
Outcast from her home in Syria. Frances Harper. PBFH p.9
Outlawed Spirit, The. Zachary Withers. PAS p.36
Outside the cold, cold night; the dripping rain ... Sterling A. Brown. SoR
    p.128
Outside the high room where the Ohio sprang from two rivers. Gerald W.
    Barrax. AKOR p.30
Outside the rain upon the street. Paul Laurence Dunbar. CPPLD p.414
Outside-wind heavy and wet. Philippe Thoby-Marcelin. PoN p.356
"Ouu gee whiz hey charlie look. Saundra Sharp. MBP p.5
Over & over again to people. Faarah Nuur. MBP p.29; TYBP p.58
Over Guiana Clouds.** A. J. Seymour. PoN p.338
Over Loaded Horse, The. Ted Joans. BPW p.80
Over the eye behind the moon's cloud. Oliver Pitcher. AmNP p.166; KAL
    p.189; NNPUSA p.115
Over the Hills. Paul Laurence Dunbar. CPPLD p.143
Over the hills, and the valleys of dreaming. Paul Laurence Dunbar. CPPLD
    p.143
Over the long, the wide dark seas. William S. Braithwaite. LLL p.57
Over the seas to-night love. William S. Braithwaite. GoS p.91; LLL p.32
Over the warts on the bumpy half-plastered wall. Margaret Danner. BTB p.87;
    KAL p.128
Overbreak. Clarence Major. SAM p.16
Oversea Sister. Ted Joans. AFR p.148
Ox in De Ditch. Lucile D. Goodlett. WGC p.30
Oxford is a Legend.** Margaret Walker. PFND p.13
Oyster man! Oyster man! Anonymous. ITBLA p.125
Oyster Man's Cry. Anonymous. ITBLA p.125

- P -

Paean. J. Henderson Brooks. BTh p.19; CaD p.195
Pagan Isms, The. Claude McKay. CNAW p.325; SPCM p.49
Pagan Prayer. Countee Cullen. CCC p.20; OTIS p.11
Pages From Life. Georgia Douglas Johnson. HWOP p.18
Pain-sharp gnawing comes like a storm-fed mountain flood. Lenora Gillison. EbR p.66
Painful Question, The. Warner B. Wims. TNV p.137
Pains of insecurity surround me. Don L. Lee. BLIA p.419; DSNP p.31
Pains with a light touch. Don L. Lee. BrT p.87
Pawned by the artists and photographers of Oba (8/67). Don L. Lee. BrT p.89; DSNP p.66
Painter. Ted Joans. AFR p.96
Paintings with stiff homuncules. Dudley Randall. BLIA p.338; BrT p.122
Pair in One. Langston Hughes. BTB p.126
Palace. Dorothy Vena Johnson. GoS p.179
Pale Blue Casket, The. Oliver Pitcher. NNPUSA p.114; TYBP p.247
Pale brown Moses went down to Egypt land. Bob Kaufman. PoNe p.412
Pale dressed evening star. Dorothy Vena Johnson. GoS p.185
Palm Tree. Ted Joans. AFR p.11
Pan is not dead, but **sleeping in the brake**. Walter Roberts. PoN p.314
Pansy. Effie Lee Newsome. CaD p.56
Papa John. Jorge De Lima. TYBP p.84
Papa John withered like a rootless stick. Jorge De Lima. TYBP p.84
Pappy's Last Song. Maurine L. Jeffrey. HeD p.24
Paradox. Bernie Casey. LATP p.41
Paradox. Peter Wellington Clark. EbR p.36
Paradox. Paul Laurence Dunbar. CPPLD p.142; KAL p.16
Paradox. Angelina Weld Grimké. CaD p.43
Pardners. Sterling A. Brown. SoR p.81
Pardon Me Do You Have The Time? Arthur Boze. BlWo p.11
Parents: People Like Our Marriage Maxie and Andrew, The. Gwendolyn Brooks. AnA p.6
Part of the Doctrine. LeRoi Jones. BMP p.136
Part of the Doctrine. LeRoi Jones. BMP p.200
Parted. Paul Laurence Dunbar. CPPLD p.234
Parted. Paul Laurence Dunbar. CPPLD p.392; LiG p.115
Party, The. Paul Laurence Dunbar. AmNP p.8; CPPLD p.134; LOLL p.199
Party all the week, go to church on Sunday. John Raven. BFM p.12
Pass Office Song. Anonymous. TYBP p.17
Passed on Blues: Homage to a Poet. Ted Joans. BPW p.2
Passing Couple, The. Ted Joans. AFR p.106
Passing of Mammy, The. Eli Shepperd. P1S p.94
Passion and Love. Paul Laurence Dunbar. CPPLD p.16; LOLL p.21
Passion, Use It. LeRoi Jones. BMP p.167
Past Has Been a Mint, The. Langston Hughes. PATL p.69
Past Memories. Charles Fred White. PONS p.45
Past with all its wrong, The. Joseph S. Cotter, Sr. LOF p.46
Pastorale. Mae V. Cowdery. WLOV p.63
Pastorale. Robert A. Davis. GoS p.178
Pastourelle. Donald Jeffrey Hayes. AmNP p.94

Piano hums again the clear story of our coming, The. Michael S. Harper.
   DJDC p.46
Pick a Bale of Cotton. Anonymous. ITBLA p.121
Picnic historical episode. Clarence Major. SAM p.8
Picnic the liberated. M. Carl Holman. PoNe p.367
Pico Della Mirandola.** Mason Jordan Mason. PoNe p.526
Pictures. Clarence Major. SAM p.36
Pied Noirs, The. Ted Joans. AFR p.33
Pierrot. Langston Hughes. WeB p.67
Pierrot took his heart. Langston Hughes. FOW p.31
Pig will be a pig, A. Katherine Jackson Hunter. BTh p.63
Pigalle: a neon rose. Langston Hughes. BLIA p.198; FOW p.25; KAL p.90
Pilgrimage and staff, The. George Marion McLlelan. EBAP p.135
Pimp's Last Mack: Death Request, A Folk Song. Stanley Crouch. BlSp p.40
Pimps wear their summer hats into late fall, The. Langston Hughes. OWT p.109
Pirouette. Audre Lorde. NNPUSA p.106
Pit of Loud Brother Bullshit, The. Ted Joans. BPW p.15
Pit-vipers are asleep, The. Michael S. Harper. DJDC p.82
Pity me, I said. Countee Cullen. BlC p.48
Pity poor you there, me here wanting to be there. Bernie Casey. LATP p.91
Pity the Deep in Love. Countee Cullen. CpS p.17; OTIS p.54
Pity the rose. Robert Hayden. HSITD p.9
Pity us, the poets. Lucia M. Pitts. EbR p.122
Pity, You There. Bernie Casey. LATP p.91
Place this bunch of mignotte. Paul Laurence Dunbar. CPPLD p.104; LOLL p.155
Place Where the Rainbow Ends, The. Paul Laurence Dunbar. CPPLD p.402
Place your hand into my hand. Ted Joans. AFR p.118
Plainwords come forth as clear and free as notes from chirping linnet. CPJSC
   p.13
Plaint of the Madonna, The. Lucy Mae Turner. BCF p.46
Plan, The. Benjamin Griffith Brawley. AVAN p.157
Planetary Exchange. LeRoi Jones. BMP p.224
Plans. Helen Morgan Brooks. NNPUSA p.107; PoNe p.274
Plant a fence post. Sterling A. Brown. SoR p.19
Plant your toes in the cool swamp mud. Langston Hughes. OWT p.55
Plantain, Burdock, Vetch. Robert Hayden. BOR p.30
Plantation Bacchanal, A. James Weldon Johnson. FYOP p.71
Plantation Child's Lullaby, The. Paul Laurence Dunbar. CPPLD p.393; LiG
   p.13
Plantation Melody, A. Paul Laurence Dunbar. CPPLD p.313
Plantation Portrait, A. Paul Laurence Dunbar. CPPLD p.278; WMS p.71
Plateau, The. Claude McKay. HaS p.19; SPCM p.25
Play de blues for me. Langston Hughes. FCTJ p.19
Play is done, the crowds depart, The. Countee Cullen. CpS p.11; OTIS p.51
Play it once, o, play some more. Langston Hughes. FCTJ p.41
Play of the Imagination. Charles Fred White. PONS p.48
Play Song. Peter Clarke. MBP p.10
Play that thing. Langston Hughes. BANP p.239; FCTJ p.74
Play the St. Louis Blues. Langston Hughes. OWT p.115
Play your guitar boy. Langston Hughes. OWT p.112
Plea, A. Paul Laurence Dunbar. CPPLD p.268; LiG p.63
Please Don't Wites. Kali Grosvenor. PBK p.16
Please. Mae Jackson. BlSp p.90

Please excuse this letter. Beatrice M. Murphy. PoN p.162; PoNe p.287
Pledge. Will Smallwood. EbR p.30
Plenty. LeRoi Jones. BMP p.209
Plowin' Cane. John Wesley Holloway. AVAN p.185
Po' Boy Blues. Langston Hughes. BANP p.237; FCTJ p.23
Poem. Russell Atkins. See Christophe.
Poem. Gerald W. Barrax. AKOR p.14
Poem, A. Elaine Bethel. BTh p.34
Poem. Katherine L. Cuestas. BTB p.75; SoS p.85
Poem. Blanche Taylor Dickinson. ANP p.130; CaD p.107
Poem. Robert Hayden. HSITD p.30
Poem. Langston Hughes. CaD p.150; WeB p.58
Poem. Langston Hughes. DYTB p.24; WeB p.105
Poem. Helene Johnson. AmNP p.100; BANP p.279; CaD p.218
Poem. LeRoi Jones. BMP p.85
Poem Addressed To Women. Frances Harper. ANP p.15
Poem & 1/2 for Black Women. Arthur Pfister. BlSp p.162
Poem At Thirty. Sonia Sanchez. BrT p.136
Poem ... For a Lover. Mae V. Cowdery. WLOV p.51
Poem for a Negro Dancer. Robert Hayden. HSITD p.41
Poem for a Poet, A. Don L. Lee. BrT p.110; DSNP p.67; WWW p.43
Poem for All the Children, A. June Jordan. SCh p.73
Poem (For Anna Hedgeman and Alfreda Duster). Nikki Giovanni. MyH p.53
Poem for Aretha. Nikki Giovanni. BrT p.61
Poem (For BMC No.1). Nikki Giovanni. BFBTBJ p.7; BrT p.48
Poem (For BMC No.2). Nikki Giovanni. BFBTBJ p.10
Poem (For BMC No.3). Nikki Giovanni. BFBTBJ p.13
Poem For Black Hearts. LeRoi Jones. BMP p.12; BrT p.28; FoM p.61;
    IADB p.52
Poem for Black Minds, A. Don L. Lee. BLIA p.421; DSNP p.69
Poem for Black Women. Don L. Lee. DSNP p.34
Poem for Carol, A. Nikki Giovanni. MyH p.8
Poem for Children With Thoughts on Death, A. Jupiter Hammon. JHANP p.37
Poem for Democrats, A. LeRoi Jones. BTB p.136
Poem for Downtown, A. Victor Hernandez Cruz. SNA p.17
Poem (For Dudley Randall). Nikki Giovanni. BFBTBJ p.9
Poem For Etheridge. Sonia Sanchez. WABP p.41
Poem for Halfwhite College Students. LeRoi Jones. BMP p.120
Poem For My Family: Hazel Griffin and Victor Hernandez Cruz. June Jordan.
    SCh p.54
Poem For My Father. Sonia Sanchez. BrT p.139; WABP p.14
Poem For Negro Intellectuals, A. Don L. Lee. DCS p.41; DSNP p.107
Poem (For Nina). Nikki Giovanni. MyH p.46
Poem For Nina Simone to Put Some Music to and Blow Our Niggu/Minds. Sonia
    Sanchez. WABP p.60
Poem for Oswald Spencer. LeRoi Jones. BMP p.71
Poem (For PCH). Nikki Giovanni. BFBTBJ p.12
Poem For Pearl's Dancers. Owen Dodson. PLL p.15
Poem For Religious Fanatics. LeRoi Jones. BMP p.89
Poem for Stacia. Nikki Giovanni. MyH p.14

Poem (For the Portrait of an African Boy After the Manner of Gauguin).
    Langston Hughes. WeB p.102
Poem For Thel--The Very Tops of Trees.   Joseph Major. NBP p.88
Poem (For TW). Nikki Giovanni. BFBTBJ p.6
Poem From Distances, A. Christopher Okigbo. TYBP p.160
Poem From the Empire State. June Jordan. SCh p.65
Poem in Time of War. Robert Hayden. HSITD p.20
Poem Looking For a Reader, A. Don L. Lee. BlSp p.117; DCS p.61; DSNP p.127;
    BrT p.105; SoS p.92
Poem (No Name No.1). Nikki Giovanni. BFBTBJ p.13
Poem (No Name No.2). Nikki Giovanni. BFBTBJ p.19; BOL p.9
Poem (No Name, No.3). Nikki Giovanni. BFBTBJ p.24; BrT p.50
Poem of Angela Yvonne Davis. Nikki Giovanni. BlSp p.74
Poem of the Conscripted Warrior. Rui Nogar. TYBP p.187
Poem of the Future Citizen. Jose Craveirinha. MBP p.106; TYBP p.186
Poem Once Significant Not Happily Not, A. Countee Cullen. CpS p.88
Poem Some People Will Have to Understand, A. LeRoi Jones. BMP p.6
Poem To A Nigger Cop. Bobb Hamilton. TYBP p.255
Poem to Complement Other Poems, A. Don L. Lee. BrT p.99; DCS p.36; DSNP
    p.104
Poem (To F.S.). Langston Hughes. WeB p.95
Poem to Negro and Whites. Maxwell Bodenheim. PoN p.274; PoNe p.511
Poem - To The Black Beloved. Langston Hughes. WeB p.65
Poem to the Hip Generation. Amus Mor. BlSp p.134
Poem to the Mass Communications Media. June Jordan. SCh p.81
Poem Welcoming Jonas Nekas to America, A. LeRoi Jones. BMP p.5
Poem Will Say I Love You Be Full it End. Gerald W. Barrax. AKOR p.74
Poem Written on my 24th Birthday. William L. Morrison. DaR p.15
Poeme D'Automne. Langston Hughes. WeB p.45
Poems. Leon Damas. PoN p.371
Poems. Julius Lester. KAL p.225
Poems are bullshit unless they are teeth or trees or lemons piled on a step.
    LeRoi Jones. BLIA p.306; BMP .p.116
Poems: Birmingham, 1962-1964. Julia Fields. PoNe p.417
Poems for Black Boys (With Special Love to James). Nikki Giovanni. BFBTBJ
    p.50
Poems For My Brother Kenneth. Owen Dodson. IADB p.101; PLL p.65; PoN p.176;
    PoNe p.304
Poems For the Lonely. Mae Jackson. BlSp p.91
Poet, The. Alice D. Anderson. EbR p.1
Poet. Joseph S. Cotter, Sr. SPPH p.11
Poet, The. Joseph S. Cotter. EBAP p.187; LOF p.26; SPPH p.69
Poet, The. Countee Cullen. CpS p.66
Poet, The. Raymond Garfield Dandridge. PAOP p.15; ZaP p.61
Poet. Donald Jeffrey Hayes. AmNP p.92; PoN p.137; PoNe p.242
Poet, The. Adolphus Johnson. ANP p.53
Poet, The. Melvin Tolson. RWA p.28
Poet and His Song, The. Paul Laurence Dunbar. CPPLD p.5; LOLL p.4
Poet and the Baby, The. Paul Laurence Dunbar. AVAN p.89; CPPLD p.182
Poet asks, and Phillis can't refuse, The. Phillis Wheatley. PAL p.93; PPW
    p.60
Poet Cheats us with humility, The. Melvin Tolson. RWA p.28

Possum. Paul Laurence Dunbar. AVAN p.82; CPPLD p.226
'Possum Song (A Warning). James Weldon Johnson. FYOP p.79
Possum Trot. Paul Laurence Dunbar. CPPLD p.236
Post Script. William L. Morrison. DaR p.14
Post War Ballad. Dorothy Vena Johnson. EbR p.91
Postal Clerk Mourns His Lost Love (Who has been going places), The. Gerald
    W. Barrax. AKOR p.77
Postalove Blues. Ted Joans. AFR p.117
Posthumous. Georgia Douglas Johnson. HWOP p.26
Posthumous Recognition. Raymond Dandridge. ZaP p.18
Pot Smokin' Blues. John Raven. BFM p.24
Potter, The. Anonymous. TYBP p.47
Pound of Life. Raymond Garfield Dandridge. PeP p.20; ZaP p.12
Pour o pour that parting soul in song. Jean Toomer. AmNP p.33; BLIA p.164;
    CaD p.96; CNAW p.285; FNP p.12; KAL p.54; PoN p.68; SoS p.32
Poured white powder on the back of a book. LeRoi Jones. BMP p.7
Pow-Wow. Ted Joans. BPW p.98
Power to know the reason why a sad heart must give a sigh. William L. Morri-
    son. DaR p.11
Practices brutality closing doors. James Emanuel. BrT p.46
Practices silence, the way of wind. LeRoi Jones. AmNP p.180
Praise due to Gwen Brooks. Cynthia M. Conley. TGWL p.22
Praise of Creation. George Moses Horton. AVAN p.35
Pray, what can dreams avail. Paul Laurence Dunbar. CPPLD p.166
Pray why are you so bare, so bare. Paul Laurence Dunbar. BANP p.58; CPPLD
    p.356; KAL p.21
Prayer. Isabella Maria Brown. NNPUSA p.61; PoNe p.341
Prayer, A. Joseph S. Cotter, Jr. BANP p.185; BOG p.6
Prayer. Waring Cuney. LUP p.16
Prayer, A. Paul Laurence Dunbar. ANP p.25; CPPLD p.16; LOLL p.20
Prayer, A. Nick Aaron Ford. SFD p.19
Prayer. Langston Hughes. FOW p.70
Prayer. Langston Hughes. CaD p.146; DYTB p.37; FCTJ p.48
Prayer, A. Claude McKay. HaS p.58; SPCM p.55
Prayer, A. George Reginald Margetson. AVAN p.169
Prayer. Jean Toomer. ITBLA p.157
Prayer. Charles Fred White. PONS p.18
Prayer at Sunrise. James Weldon Johnson. FYOP p.51
Prayer for Peace. Leopold Sedar Senghor. TYBP p.135
Prayer Meeting. Langston Hughes. DYTB p.31; FCTJ p.46
Prayer of the Faithful, The. Waverly T. Carmichael. FHOF p.39
Prayer of the Race That God Made Black. Lucian Watkins. ANP p.122
Prayer to God. Placido. TYBP p.99
Prayers of God, The. William E. B. DuBois. BTB p.99
Prayers to the God That. Anonymous. TYBP p.28
Praying Hands, The. William S. Braithwaite. SPWSB p.84
Prayman from Song of myself. Walt Whitman. PoN p.214; PoNe p.469
Preacher, The. Al-Mahdi. TYBP p.45
Precedent, The. Owen Dodson. PLL p.100
Precedent. Paul Laurence Dunbar. CPPLD p.169
Precious Things. Anonymous. TYBP p.198
Precious Curiosity. Linda Brown. BTB p.54

Pure in Heart shall see God, The. Frances Harper. PBFH p.28
Pure speech, such speech that always blends. Joseph S. Cotter, Sr. CPJSC
    p.36
Pushed into the corner of the hobnailed boot. Langston Hughes.   PATL p.19
Put Down. Leon Damas. TYBP p.121
Put my Black father on the penny. Vanessa Howard. SoS p.3
Put on that uniform, my son. Charles Stewart. TNV p.121
Put on yo' red silk stockings. Langston Hughes. FCTJ p.73
"Put out the light!" Raymond Garfield Dandridge. PAOP p.27
Puttin' The Baby Away. Paul Laurence Dunbar. CPPLD p.397
Puzzled. Langston Hughes. CNAW p.308; OWT p.71
Pygmalion. Bobb Hamilton. BTB p.110
Pygmies are pygmies still, though percht on elps, Edward Young. Gwendolyn
    Brooks. AnA p.14; PoNe p.336

- Q -

Quadroon mermaids, afro angels Black Saints. Robert Hayden. AmNP p.109;
    BLIA p.252; BOR p.6; IADB p.32; PoN p.165; PoNe p.29; SPRH p.39
Quaint Lexington, Kentucky. Joseph S. Cotter, Sr. CPJSC p.13
Quality of night that you hate most is its Black and its starteeth eyes.
    LeRoi Jones. BMP p.103
Quarrel, The. Gordon Parks. InL (unpaged)
Quatrains. Gwendolyn B. Bennett. CaD p.155
Quatrains. Joseph S. Cotter, Sr. LOF p.47
Quatrains. Salah Jahin. TYBP p.51
Quavering cry, screech-owl, A? Robert Hayden. SPRH p.25
Queen of your craft, queen of the perfect word and shorthand phrase. Zack
    Gilbert. TGWL p.46
Queens of the Universe. Sonia Sanchez. BlSp p.186
Query. Georgia Douglas Johnson. HWOP p.16
Quest. Georgia Douglas Johnson. HWOP p.11
Quest, A. James E. McGirt. FYSS p.54
Quest and Quarry. Bruce McM. Wright. LUP p.57
Questing. Anne Spencer. CaD p.48
Question. Charles L. Anderson. BTB p.39
Question and Answer. Langston Hughes. PATL p.68
Question is. Warner B. Wims. TNV p.137
Question To a Mob. Lauretta Holman Gooden. HeD p.16
Questions. Sonia Sanchez. WABP p.19
Quick, The. Gerald Barrax. AKOR p.75
Quick night easy warmth the girlmother lies next to me. LeRoi Jones. BMP
    p.193
Quiet afternoon the speaker dull the New Testament washed out. Alice Walker.
    ONC p.47
Quiet and alone she stands. Robert Hayden. HSITD p.54
Quiet fading out of life, The. Langston Hughes. FCTJ p.70
Quiet Has a Hidden Sound. William S. Braithwaite. CNAW p.227; SPWSB p.61
Quiet Ignorant Happiness. Don L. Lee. DSNP p.44
Quiet little space set in, A. William S. Braithwaite. LLL p.41
Quietude. William L. Morrison. DaR p.32
Quilt, The. Effie Lee Newsome. CaD p.58

Quilting, The. Paul Laurence Dunbar. CPPLD p.391
Quo Vadis. Countess W. Twitty. EbR p.149
Quoi Bon, A? Jules Wynn Smith. EbR p.131
Quoits. Effie Lee Newsome. CaD p.59; GoS p.22

- R -

Rabbi, The. Robert Hayden. ITBLA p.219; SPRH p.17
Race. LeRoi Jones. BMP p.222
Race results, U.S.A., 1966. Sarah Webster Fabio. BrT p.171
Race welcomes Dr. W.E.B. Du Bois as its leader, The. Joseph S. Cotter, Sr.
    SPPH p.41
Racist, The. LeRoi Jones. BMP p.126
Radical, The. Waring Cuney. CaD p.212
Radio said FBI uncovered plot to boom boom boom. Clarence Major. SAM p.46
Radish, The. Ibn Quzman. MBA p.31
Radish is a good and doubtless wholesome food, The. Ibn Quzman. MBP p.31
Rag Doll and Summer Birds. Owen Dodson. BLIA p.259; PLL p.29; PoN p.173;
    PoNe p.299
Ragged boys lift sweet. Robert Hayden. BOR p.53; SPRH p.33
Ragged, rumpled, reeking of wine. John Raven. BFM p.26
Raid. Langston Hughes. OWT p.110
Railroad Avenue. Langston Hughes. FCTJ p.27
Rain. Sterling A. Brown. SoR p.128
Rain. Raymond Garfield Dandridge. PAOP p.54
Rain. Frank Marshall Davis. GoS p.100
Rain be praised that trapped you there beneath an arch of city stone, The.
    Gordon Parks. InL (unpaged)
Rain in Summer. William S. Braithwaite. HFL p.54
Rain is falling steadily, The. Georgia Douglas Johnson. HWOP p.17
Rain / Music. Joseph S. Cotter, Jr. AVAN p.181; BANP p.188; CaD p.100
Rain Song, A. Charles Bertram Johnson. AVAN p.189; SOMP p.12
Rain Song, The. Alex Rogers. BANP p.159
Rain-Songs. Paul Laurence Dunbar. CPPLD p.447
Rain steams down like harp-strings from the sky, The. Paul Laurence Dunbar.
    CPPLD p.447
Rain / Wish. Louise Blackman. EbR p.4
Raining Blues. Ted Joans. AFR p.114
Rainy night I went away, The. LeRoi Jones. BMP p.157
Rainy Season Love Song. Aquah Laluah. CaD p.198
Rainy Season, Puerto Vallarta, Jal, Mexico, Aug. 1968, The. Clarence Major.
    SAM p.28
Raise the race raise the rays. LeRoi Jones. BMP p.200
Raison D'etre. Oliver Pitcher. AmNP p.166; KAL p.189; NNPUSA p.115
Ralph Bunche, Nobel Peace Prize Winner (1955) Michigan, 1904-1971. Eloise
    Culver. GANIV p.57
Ramadan - Hot Night. Marion Nicholes. LiS p.12
Rap continues with the bad dude in the lead, The. Mae Jackson. BlSp p.90
Rapidly she jets her thoughts given from the gods. Herman J. D. Carter.
    EbR p.28
Ration. LeRoi Jones. BMP p.68
Rats took over, The. Victor Hernandez Cruz. SNA p.89

Ray Charles is the Black wind of Kilimanjaro. Bob Kaufman, SoS p.36
Ray was D. O. A. John Raven. BFM p.29
Re. Melvin Tolson. LRL p.16
Re-Act For Action (for Brother H. Rap Brown). Don L. Lee. DSNP p.42; NBP
    p.82
Re-act to animals: cage them in zoos. Don L. Lee. DSNP p.42; NBP p.82
Reachin into the depth of the Blk man's soul. Bruce Walton. TGWL p.96
Read yr/ exile i had a mother too. Don L. Lee. BrT p.110; DSNP p.167; WWW
    p.43
Reader listen ere you go. Joseph S. Cotter, Sr. CPJSC p.77
Reading and Weeping. LeRoi Jones. BMP p.86
Ready-noted katy did. Joseph S. Cotter, Sr. LOF p.40
Ready Or Not. LeRoi Jones. BMP p.79
Real cool, the real thing, we are and you. Sarah Webster Fabio. TGWL p.37
Real Question, The. Paul Laurence Dunbar. BLIA p.117; CPPLD p.216
Reality. Peter Wellington Clark. EbR p.37
Reality. Yvette Johnson. TNV p.56
Really I know. Leon Damas. PoN p.371
Reapers. Jean Toomer. CaD p.94; FNP p.13; KAL p.52; SoS p.63
Rebel. Samuel E. Boyd. EbR p.7
Rebel, The. Mari E. Evans. AmNP p.163; IABW p.76; IADB p.4
Rebus, By J. B., A. Phillis Wheatley. PAL p.92
Recall. Georgia Douglas Johnson. HWOP p.19
Recalled Prayer, A. Raymond Garfield Dandridge. PAOP p.17; ZaP p.105
Recapitulations. Karl Shapiro. PoN p.283; PoNe p.563
Recessional. Georgia Douglas Johnson. CaD p.79; PoN p.60; PoNe p.89
Recessional for the class of 1959 of a school for delinquent Negro Girls.
    Joseph R. Cowen. PoNe p.575
Reckoning, The. Naomi Long Madgett. KAL p.177
Recollection. Donald D. Govan. NBP p.55
Recollection For Madrigals. Bruce McM. Wright. LUP p.61
Recollection To Miss A____ M ____, humbly inscribed By the Authoress.
    Phillis Wheatley. PPW p.74
Recompense. Georgia Douglas Johnson. HWOP p.45
Reconnaissance. Arna Bontemps. AmNP p.80; BLIA p.217; KAL p.81
Records. Nikki Giovanni. BFBTBJ p.66
Red. Countee Cullen. CpS p.11; GoS p.116; OTIS p.51
Red Eye. LeRoi Jones. BMP p.72
Red Flower, A. Claude McKay. HaS p.68; SPCM p.94
Red Light. LeRoi Jones. BMP p.132
Red Rose. Raymond Garfield Dandridge. PAOP p.20; ZaP p.102
Red Silk Stockings. Langston Hughes. FCTJ p.73
Red the black and the green, The. S. E. Anderson. BlSp p.10
Red, White, and Blue.** Waverly T. Carmichael. FHOF p.59
Rediscovery. George Awooner Williams. TYBP p.165
Refiner's Gold, The. Frances Harper. PBFH p.58
Reflecting ragged flocks of white upon a background of blue. Raymond Dan-
    dridge. PAOP p.29; ZaP p.64
Reflection. Zachary Withers. PAS p.35
Reflections. Carl Gardner. NNPUSA p.98
Reflections. Vanessa Howard. SoS p.2

Reflections On A Lost Love. Don L. Lee. BrT p.103; DCS p.59; DSNP p.125
Reflections on April 4, 1968. Nikki Giovanni. BFBTBJ p.54
Reflections, Written on Visiting the Grave of a Venerated Friend. Ann Plato.
    EBAP p.115
Refugee. Naomi Long Madgett. PoN p.207; PoNe p.379
Refugee in America. Langston Hughes. BLIA p.194; FOW p.105
Reg wished me to go with him to the field. Claude McKay. HaS p.26; SPCM
    p.22
Regard the first star. Owen Dodson. PLL p.85
Regret. Lucy Mae Turner. BCF p.37
Regretfully Yours. William L. Morrison. DaR p.58
Reign of death was there, The. George Marion McLlelan. EBAP p.129
Reincarnation. Raymond Garfield Dandridge. PeP p.29; ZaP p.95
Religion. Paul Laurence Dunbar. CPPLD p.58; LOLL p.82
Religioso. Robert Hayden. HSITD p.39
Religioso. Robert Hayden. HSITD p.40
Reluctance. Paul Laurence Dunbar. CPPLD p.330; LiG p.83
Remember. Georgia Douglas Johnson. PoN p.57; PoNe p.75
Remember, friend, each harsh word spoken. Raymond Garfield Dandridge. PAOP
    p.44
Remember me. Gordon Parks. InL (unpaged)
Remember Mexico. Michael S. Harper. DJDC p.42
Remember Not. Helene Johnson. BANP p.28; PoN p.153; PoNe p.264
Remember not the promises we made. Helene Johnson. BANP p.281; PoN p.153;
    PoNe p.264
Remember this remember that and don't forget that you're Black. Ted Joans.
    AFR p.63
Remembered. Paul Laurence Dunbar. CPPLD p.194
Remembered Rhythms (The Individuals). Mari Evans. IABW p.88
Remembering. Maya Angelou. JGM p.10
Remembering Nat Turner. Sterling A. Brown. CNAW p.409; PoN p.90; PoNe p.171
Remembrance. J. Henderson Brooks. BTh p.20
Remembrance. Joseph S. Cotter, Jr. BOG p.26
Remembrance. Langston Hughes. FOW p.33
Rencontre. Jessie Fauset. CaD p.70
Rendezvous. Lois Royal Hughes. EbR p.89
Rendezvous with America. Melvin Tolson. RWA p.3
Rendezvous With Life, A. Nick Aaron Ford. SFD p.28
Rendition, The.* John Greenleaf Whittier. ANP p.139
Renewal of Strength. Frances Harper. PBFH p.33
Rent and bleeding upon her knees she cried "Mercy!" Raymond Garfield Dan-
    dridge. PAOP p.24
Rent man knocked, The. Langston Hughes. OWT p.9
Repeal of the Missouri Compromise considered. Elymas Payson Rogers. EBAP
    p.64
Reporting the Sermon. Joseph S. Cotter, Sr. CPJSC p.40; WSBO p.62
Reprise. Langston Hughes. GOW p.115
Reptile. John Raven. BFM p.3; BrT p.134
Repulse. Georgia Douglas Johnson. HWOP p.15
Request. Barbara Marshall. TNV p.71
Request For Requiems. Langston Hughes. OWT p.115
Requiem. Nell Chapman. EbR p.30

Riverbank Blues. Sterling A. Brown. SoR p.99

Rivulet, The. Joseph S. Cotter. SPPH p.73

Roach, The. John Raven. BFM p.4; BrT p.134

Roach came struttin across my bedroom floor, A. John Raven. BFM p.4; BrT p.134

Roaches are winning Mr. Exterminator, The. May Miller. BTB p.152

Road, The. Helene Johnson. AmNP p.100; BANP p.280; CaD p.221; GoS p.176; PoN p.154; PoNe p.266

Road in Kentucky, A. Robert Hayden. BOR p.11; SPRH p.43

Road is like a tomb, The. Conrad Kent Rivers. NNPUSA p.42

Road runs straight with no turning, The. LeRoi Jones. BMP p.199

Road to Anywhere. Dorothy Vena Johnson. EbR p.92

Road to the Bow, The. James David Corrothers. BANP p.75

Road Way, A. Paul Laurence Dunbar. CPPLD p.340

Road winds down through autumn hills, The. Robert Hayden. BLIA p.253; BOR p.9; SPRH p.41

Roar of the Rushing train fearfully rocking. Claude McKay.HaS p.41; SPCM p.64

Robert Burns. Joseph S. Cotter, Sr. LOF p.47

Robert G. Shaw. Henrietta Cordelia Ray. EBAP p.140

Robert Gould Shaw. Paul Laurence Dunbar. CPPLD p.360; KAL p.25

Robert S. Abbott Founder of Chicago Defender Newspaper (1905) 1870-1940, Georgia. Eloise Culver. GANIV p.50

Robert Whitmore. Frank Marshall Davis. KAL p.105; PoNe p.254; PoN p.143

Robin Red Breast. Lula Lowe Weeden. CaD p.228

Robin's Poem, A. Nikki Giovanni. BrT p.68

Rock, for ages, stern and high stood flowing 'gainst the earth and sky, A. Frances Harper. ANP p.16; PBFH p.36

Rock me to sleep, ye waves, and drift my boat. George Marion McLlelan. EBAP p.123

Rocks and the firm roots of trees. Langston Hughes. FOW p.113

Roland Hayes Beaten (Georgia: 1942). Langston Hughes. OWT p.86

Roland Hayes Singer, 1887-   Georgia. Eloise Culver. GANIV p.59

Rolled. John Raven. BFM p.24

Roman Lover in Cathraage, A. William S. Braithwaite. SPWSB p.94

Romance. Claude McKay. HaS p.73; SPCM p.96

Romance of Antar, The. Anonymous. MBP p.66

Rondeau, A. William C. Braithwaite. VER p.72

Rondeau For You. Marie De Andrade. TYBP p.83

Rondeau redouble aux Franc Amis (Double Rondeau to Candid Friends). Nicol Riquet. EBAP p.164; trans. EBAP p.165

Rondeau Write, A? This Afternoon. William C. Braithwaite. VER p.72

Room was a, The. Carolyn M. Rodgers. TNV p.113

Roosevelt. Raymond Garfield Dandridge. PAOP p.27

Rooster, The. Joseph S. Cotter, Sr. CPJSC p.39

Rooser on the fence, with one foot lifted, A. Joseph S. Cotter, Sr. SPPH p.11

Roots. Harold Telemaque. PoN p.348

Rose of neon darkness. Langston Hughes. FOW p.67

Rosemary. Robert Hayden. HSITD p.37

Roses. Paul Laurence Dunbar. CPPLD p.360

Roses After Rain. Georgia Douglas Johnson. HWOP p.45

- S -

S.C. threw S.C. into the railroad yard. Ted Joans. BPW p.81
Sabbath. Charles Fred White. PONS p.47
Sable brother, are you clinging to the penny and the dime? Joseph S. Cotter,
    Sr. SPPH p.88
Sable is my threat. Perient Trott. PoN p.248; PoNe p.548
Sackcloth naked I knew drives of self like cinema. Clarence Major. SAM p.10
Sacrament. Countee Cullen. CCC p.82
Sacramento River. Zachary Withers. PAS p.28
Sacred chant for the Return of Black Spirit and Power. LeRoi Jones. BMP
    p.192
Sacred interpreter, we saw in theee. Joseph S. Cotter, Sr. LOF p.25; SPPH
    p.36
Sacrifice, The. Gerald William Barrax. KAL p.199
Sad Cowboy. LeRoi Jones. BMP p.66
Sadie's Playhouse. Margaret Danner. BTB p.87; KAL p.128
Safari West. John A. Williams. NBP p.132
Sahara I have crossed you with four litres of water. Ted Joans. BPW p.49
Sailing Date. Langston Hughes. FOW p.86
Sailor. Langston Hughes. DYTB p.63; GoS p.102
Sailor's Departure. James E. McGirt. FYSS p.57
Sailors On Leave. Owen Dodson. AmNP p.126
Sailor's Song, A. Paul Laurence Dunbar. CPPLD p.146
St. Bees Head. William C. Braithwaite. VER p.74
St. Bega's Gulls, at Martin-Song. William C. Braithwaite. VER p.74
St. Isaac's Church, Petrograd. Claude McKay. AmNP p.29; KAL p.49; SPCM
    p.84
Saint Peter Relates an Incident of the Resurrection Day. James Weldon John-
    son. KAL p.27
St. Silva's Church. William C. Braithwaite. VER p.98
Sainte Adresse. William C. Braithwaite. VER p.77
Saints. William S. Braithwaite. SPWSB p.21
Sale began - young girls were there, The. Frances Harper. CNAW p.101; EBAP
    p.32; KAL p.13; PoN p.10; PoNe p.14; TYBP p.205
Salia. Lucile D. Goodlett. WGC p.50
Salia totes a white chile. Lucile D. Goodlett. WGC p.50
Salt Water. Joseph S. Cotter, Sr. LOF p.56
Salty air kissed my face, the kisses of the impersonal, the sand ignored my
    presence, The. Bernie Casey. LATP p.57
Salutamus. Sterling A. Brown. CaD p.138; SoR p.123
Salute. Oliver Pitcher. BTB p.161; KAL p.187
Salute to the Sahara. Ted Joans. BPW p.49
Salute to the Tan Yanks. Amos J. Griffin. EbR p.74
Salvation comes by Christ alone. Jupiter Hammon. EBAP p.7; ITBLA p.27; PoN
    p.4; PoNe p.4
Sam Smiley. Sterling A. Brown. SoR p.36
Samantha is My Negro Cat.** William J. Harris. CNAW p.767
Same air purifies my blood, The. Charles Fred White. PONS p.166
Same In Blues. Langston Hughes. BLIA p.199
Samuel Chapman Armstrong. Owen Dodson. PLL p.23
San Francisco. Walter Adolphe Roberts. PoN p.313; PoNe p.82

San Gloria. Tom Redlam. PoNe p.309
San Juan. June Jordan. SCh p.38
Sancturary. Dudley Randall. LoY p.16
Sand. Ted Joans. AFR p.56
Sand in My Rice. Ted Joans. AFR p.56
Sand-man, The. Paul Laurence Dunbar. CPPLD p.382
Sand-man he's a jolly old fellow, The. Paul Laurence Dunbar. CPPLD p.382
Sandy. Raymond Garfield Dandridge. PAOP p.64
Sandy Star. William S. Braithwaite. ANP p.50; AVAN p.144; BANP p.100
Sandy Star and Willie Gee. William S. Braithwaite. BANP p.100; SPWSB p.73
Sank through easeful. Robert Hayden. BTB p.122; CNAW p.385; KAL p.109;
    SPRH p.11
Santa Claws. Ted Joans. BPW p.54
Sapling. Yvette Johnson. TNV p.57
Sapphire. Bernie Casey. LATP p.78
Sapricius. William C. Braithwaite. VER p.18
Sarcasmes. Bruce McM. Wright. LUP p.59
Sassafras Tea. Effie Lee Newsome. CaD p.56; GoS p.8
Sassafras tea is read and clear, The. Effie Lee Newsome. CaD p.56; GoS p.8
Sassy. Lucy Mae Turner. BCF p.11
Satan's Dream. Charles Fred White. PONS p.105
Satisfied now I am content. William S. Braithwaite. SPWSB p.22
Satori. Gayl Jones. SoS p.15
Saturday. Jon Woodson. CNAW p.775
Saturday morning & i would just be going to the pharmacy. Jon Woodson. CNAW
    p.775
Saturday Night. Langston Hughes. FCTJ p.41
Saturday Night in Harlem.** William Browne. BTB p.66
Saturday's Child. Countee Cullen. BLIA p.157; CCC p.18; KAL p.98; OTIS p.10;
    PoN p.128
Savage. Michael S. Harper. DJDC p.40
Savage broke the walls out, The. Michael S. Harper. DJDC p.40
Save the Boys. Frances Harper. PBFH p.40
Saxophone turned into a dolphin. Stanley Crouch. BlSp p.42
Say a mass for my soul's repose, my brother. Paul Laurence Dunbar. CPPLD
    p.345
Say, bud, ya got a cigarette? Naomi Long Madgett. PoN p.207; PoNe p.379
Say day lay day may fay come some bum'll take break. LeRoi Jones. BMP p.169
Say did you go to Mae's rent party? Ernest J. Wilson, Jr. PoNe p.371
Say good-bye to Big Daddy.** Randall Jarrell. PoNe p.567
Say, heav'nly muse, what king, or mighty God. Phillis Wheatley. PAL p.82
Say it and cry aloud. Muhammad Al-Fituri. TYBP p.54
Say, muse divine, can hostile scenes delight. Phillis Wheatley. PAL p.74;
    PPW p.32
Say not the age is hard and cold. Frances Harper. PBFH p.6
Say to them, say to the down-keepers. Gwendolyn Brooks. FaP p.23
Say you brother! Barbara Marshall. TNV p.68
Says so is in a woe of shuddered leaves. Russell Atkins. AmNP p.170
Scabby walls of tenements, The. Melvin Tolson. GoS p.38
Scamp. Paul Laurence Dunbar. BLIA p.115; CPPLD p.388
Scandal and Gossip. Countee Cullen. CpS p.61
Scandal is a stately lady. Countee Cullen. CpS p.61

Sergeant Jerk. Deborah Fuller Wess. EbR p.159
Sermon on the Warpland, The. Gwendolyn Brooks. ITM p.49
Serried host stood man to man. Abu Dharr. TYBP p.45
Service. Georgia Douglas Johnson. CaD p.75
Service, Please. Myrtle Campbell Gorham. EbR p.71
Serving Girl, The. Aquah Laluah. CaD p.200; GoS p.27; PoN p.385
Seven. Ted Joans. BPW p.103
7:25 Trolley, The. Mari Evans. IABW p.55
Seventh Avenue Poem. Ed Bullins. BlSp p.36
Seventy years! the magic of youth. William S. Braithwaite. HFL p.83
Sewanee Hills of Dear Delight. George Marion McClellan. BANP p.95
Sex finger toes in the market place. Michael S. Harper. DJDC p.74
Sexpot. John Raven. BFM p.19
Schackles rend, your hands are free, The. Raymond Garfield Dandridge. PAOP
    p.32
Shadder in de valley. Paul Laurence Dunbar. CPPLD p.368
Shades of Ebony. William L. Morrison. DaR p.37
Shades of the gloaming around me are stealing, The. Georgia D. Johnson.
    HWOP p.55
Shadow. Richard Bruce. CaD p.206
Shadows. Helen F. Clarke. EbR p.40
Shadows. James Edgar Smith. EbR p.131
Shadows of the fixed saints. Bruce McM. Wright. LUP p.63
Shadows of too many nights of love, The. Langston Hughes. WeB p.89
Shadows of trees at night draw pictures on the ground. James Edgar Smith.
    EbR p.131
Shaka, King of the Zulus. A. C. Jordan. TYBP p.16
Shake your brown feet, honey. Langston Hughes. WeB p.36
Shakespeare. Henrietta Cordelia Ray. EBAP p.140
Shakespeare in Harlem. Langston Hughes. SIH p.111
Shakespeare Modernized. Charles Fred White. PONS p.165
Shakespeare's Sonnet. Joseph S. Cotter, Sr. CPJSC p.38
Shall I compare thee, fair creature of an hour. Ernest Attah. MBP p.24
Shall i die shall i die a sweet / death. Sonia Sanchez. BrT p.142; WABP
    p.55
Shall I go all my bright days singing. Countee Cullen. BlC p.38; OTIS p.90
Shame on you. Dorothy C. Parrish. TNV p.89
Shango is an animal like the gorilla. Anonymous. TYBP p.12
Shango is the death who kills money with a big stick. Anonymous. TYBP p.12
Shango I. Anonymous. TYBP p.12
Shango II. Anonymous. TYBP p.12
Share-Croppers. Langston Hughes. SIH p.77
Sharecroppers sat in the delta night, The. Melvin Tolson. RWA p.53
Shattered Dreams. Frenchy J. Hodges. BlW p.75
Shattered Mirror. Mae V. Cowdery. WLOV p.55
Shave & a haircut & a circumcision. Ted Joans. AFR p.32
She aint got no she aint got no man. Ted Joans. BPW p.31
She always has two black eyes. John Raven. BFM p.30
She and I. Bernie Casey. LATP p.39
She and me went to Belgium. Ted Joans. BPW p.116
She came from the East a fair young bride. Frances Harper. PBFH p.63
She came home running. Maya Angelou. JGM p.18

She came pale hands, fair blushes like spring dawn to bring a sheaf for
   stone-crushed bread ... Oliver LaGrone. BTB p.138
She caught a butterfly. Gerald W. Barrax. KAL p.201
She couldn't quote French poetry. Don L. Lee. DSNP p.159; WWW p.35
She danced, near nude, to tom-tom beat. Raymond Garfield Dandridge. AVAN
   p.191; PAOP p.33; ZaP p.1
She didn't know she was beautiful. Dudley Randall. TGWL p.82
She does not know her beauty. Waring Cuney. AmNP p.98; BANP p.283; CaD
   p.212; CNAW p.377; GoS p.28; LUP p.9; TYBP p.237; PoN p.145
She doesn't wear costume jewelry. Don L. Lee. DCS p.19; DSNP p.89; TGWL
   p.68
She dreams after string of episodes. Michael S. Harper. DJDC p.39
She even thinks that up in heaven her class lies late and snores. Countee
   Cullen. CaD p.187; CCC p.50; CNAW p.326; FNP p.19; IADB p.84; KAL p.100;
   MBP p.27; OTIS p.33; PoN p.128; PoNe p.231
She fled to France and bared her Black soul. Ted Joans. BPW p.27
She gave her body for my meat. Countee Cullen. CCC p.82
She Gave Me a Rose.** Paul Laurence Dunbar. CPPLD p.165
She grew up in bedeviled southern wilderness. Robert Hayden. KAL p.113;
   SPRH p.21
She had not found herself a hard pillow. Angeline W. Grimké. AmNP p.15
She is naked now. Ted Joans. BPW p.49
She is somebody quiet, solid this self at the pith of you. Clarence Major.
   SAM p.62
She kneeled before me begging. Donald Jeffrey Hayes. CaD p.190
She knew not why. William Allyn Hill. LUP p.21
She lays beside him. Ted Joans. AFR p.147
She leaned her head upon her head. Frances Harper. EBAP p.34; PBFH p.44
She leans across a garden table. Countee Cullen. CpS p.60
She leaps still after happiness in a flaming flowered dress. James Morrison.
   TGWL p.71
She lived in sinful happiness. Langston Hughes. FOW p.35
She mounts no heights on spreading wings. Raymond Dandridge. ZaP p.56
She of the dancing feet sing. Countee Cullen. CCC p.89; FNP p.18; OTIS p.39
She opened her eyes and she saw me. Ted Joans. BPW p.35
She said ... J. Henderson Brooks. PoN p.136; PoNe p.241
She said, "not only music," brave men marching. J. Henderson Brooks. PoN
   p.136; PoNe p.241
She sang and I listened the whole song thro. Paul Laurence Dunbar. CPPLD
   p.194
She sees the little things that you'd pass by. Alice D. Anderson. EbR p.1
She showed me assholes. Ted Joans. AFR p.95
She Sleeps Beneath the Winter Snow.** William S. Braithwaite. LLL p.47
She spoke out against a Brother. Ted Joans. BPW p.64
She stands in the quiet darkness. Langston Hughes. BLIA p.195; DYTB p.10;
   ITBLA p.159; WeB p.86
She stood before the multitude. Eloise Culver. GANIV p.71
She stood hanging wash before sun and occasionally watched the kids. Carole
   Gregory. NBP p.56
She stood nakedly nakedly against the window's cool. Don L. Lee. WWW p.36
She-Sun Leaving. Craig Williamson. AfW p.17

Sins of a helpless father born fearful and sunburnt. Conrad Kent Rivers.
    SVH p.5
Sir I read of late you have tired of roses. James P. Vaughn. AmNP p.167
Sir Walter Raleigh. William S. Braithwaite. HFL p.96; SPWSB p.88
Siren cries that ran like mad and naked screaming women, The. Robert Hayden.
    BOR p.34; PoN p.167
Sis Hannah may Liza so Emphraim sayed. Raymond Garfield Dandridge. PAOP p.
    p.17; ZaP p.105
Sissy Gal. Ted Joans. BPW p.104
Sister. Marion Nicholes. LiS p.14
Sister Lou. Sterling A. Brown. AmNP p.53; BLIA p.218; BTB p.56; CNAW p.404;
    GoS p.159; PoN p.174; PoNe p.174; SoR p.481
Sister Mandy Attends The Business League. Richard T. Hamilton. HeD p.18
Sister Matilda. William S. Braithwaite. SPWSB p.22
Sister, when at the grassy mound I stand. Joseph S. Cotter, Jr. BOG p.28
/Sisters/ Victor Hernandez Cruz. SNA p.57
Sisters, I saw it to day. Sonia Sanchez. BlSp p.186
Sisters in the Fog. LeRoi Jones. BMP p.221
Sisters its time to be veiled again. Marion Nicholes. LiS p.17
Sit Down Chillun. J. Farley Ragland. BTB p.163
Sit here before my grate. Charles Bertram Johnson. ANP p.37
Sit-Ins. Margaret Walker. PFND p.10
Sit where the light corrups your face. Gwendolyn Brooks. ITM p.5
Sittin' by de windo' gazin' at de snow. James E. McGirt. FYSS p.4
Sitting in a candle lit room warm from **tip top top.** Carolyn Rodgers. BlSp
    p.176
Six-Bits Blues. Langston Hughes. SIH p.37
Six cents on a dollar. John Raven. BFM p.31
Six foot tall, once President United States small letters for 10 years.
    LeRoi Jones. BMP p.64
Six in Deportment. Joseph S. Cotter, Sr. LOF p.61; SPPH p.30
Six O'Clock. Owen Dodson. PoN p.172; PoNe p.298
Six Sunday. Hart LeRoi Bibbs. NBP p.28
Sixteen, Yeah. James Emanuel. BrT p.46
lxvxii. Julius Lester. SoS p.70
Sixty years! How silently those years have crept over your soul, mother dear.
    Nick Aaron Ford. SFD p.17
Sketch. Delores Kendrick. TGWL p.60
Sketch of a Varying Evening Sky. John Boyd. EBAP p.152
Sketches of Harlem. David Henderson. ITBLA p.173; KAL p.223; NNPUSA p.76;
    PoNe p.437
Skiers, The. Michael S. Harper. DJDC p.35
Skies are hung with sullen clouds, The. Raymond Garfield Dandridge. PAOP
    p.48
Skin as Black an' jes as sof' as a velvet dress. James Weldon Johnson. FYOP
    p.77
Sky, The. Anonymous. MBP p.6; TYBP p.8
Sky at night is like a big city, The. Anonymous. MBP p.6; TYBP p.8
Sky hangs heavy tonight, The. Lewis Alexander. CaD p.122
Sky is angry, The. Herman J. D. Carter. EbR p.29
Sky is heavy, it is raining stars, The. Anonymous. TYBP p.24
Sky King. LeRoi Jones. BMP p.56

Sky, lazily disdaining to pursue, The. Jean Toomer. AmNP p.32; BLIA p.163; CaD p.95; FNP p.14; KAL p.55; PoN p.70; SoS p.102
Sky of brightest gray seems dark, The. Paul Laurence Dunbar. CPPLD p.92; LOLL p.137
Sky Pictures. Effie Lee Newsome. CaD p.57; GoS p.177
Sky was blue, so blue, that day, The. Angelina Weld Grimke. CaD p.45; PoN p.97; PoNe p.55
Skyline of New York does not excite me, The. G. C. Oden. KAL p.182; ITBLA p.275; NNPUSA p.90
Slanting gleam upon the wing, The. William S. Braithwaite. HFL p.43
Slave. Langston Hughes. PATL p.77
Slave, The.* James Oppenheim. ANP p.135
Slave and the Iron Lace, The. Margaret Danner. AmNP p.157
Slave Aution, The. Frances Harper. CNAW p.101; EBAP p.32; KAL p.13; PoN p.10; PoNe p.14; TYBP p.205
Slave Mother, The. Frances Harper. AVAN p.41; EBAP p.31
Slave Story.* Hodding Carter. PoNe p.540
Slavery. George Moses Horton. EBAP p.21
Slavery! Oh, thou cruel stain. George R. Allen. EBAP p.260
Slave's Complaint, The. George Moses Horton. EBAP p.22
Slaves couldn't go to school. Eloise Culver. GANIV p.30
Slave's Dream.* Henry Wadsworth Longfellow. PoN p.234; PoNe p.459
Slay fowl and beast; pluck clean the vine. Richard Bruce. CaD p.207
Sleek Black boys in a cabaret. Langston Hughes. WeB p.32
Sleep. Countee Cullen. MASP p.75
Sleep. Langston Hughes. FOW p.51
Sleep. James Weldon Johnson. FYOP p.50
Sleep. Lucy Mae Turner. BCP p.57
Sleep Bitter, Brother. James Worley. FoM p.23
Sleep builds the picture world. LeRoi Jones. BMP p.34
Sleep late with your dream. Owen Dodson. IADB p.101; PLL p.68; PoNe p.304
Sleep, little one, sleep for me. Bob Kaufman. BOL p.76; KAL p.219
Sleep, Love, Sleep. Quandra Prettyman. BOL p.75
Sleep on ye Happy Sons.* Waverly T. Carmichael. FHOF p.16
Sleep, restful sleep. Lucy Mae Turner. BCP p.57
Slender, shy and sensitive young girl is woman now, The. Margaret Walker. TGWL p.95
Slick. Victor Hernandez Cruz. SNA p.107
Slight-boned animal young, what jungle fruit droops with such grace as you in the subway corner in your Saturday suit, A?* Babette Deutsch. PoNe p.513
Slim dragon fly too rapid for the eye to cage.* Marianne Moore. PoNe p.506
Slim Greer. Sterling A. Brown. BANP p.256; SoR p.83
Slim In Atlanta. Sterling A. Brown. CNAW p.407; SoR p.88
Slim lands a job? Sterling A. Brown. SoR p.86
Slit his throat in the March afternoon. Victor Hernandez Cruz. SNA p.15
Slothful Youth, A. James E. McGirt. FYSS p.53
Slow de' night's a fallin'. Paul Laurence Dunbar. CPPLD p.301; LiG p.76
Slow moves the pageant of a climbing-rare. Paul Laurence Dunbar. AVAN p.66; BLIA p.12
Slow through the Dark. Paul Laurence Dunbar. AVAN p.66; BLIA p.112; CPPLD p.344

Slow wand'ring came the sightless sire and she. Henrietta Cordelia Ray.
  EBAP p.141
Slowly down this grimy street I drift lovestruck. Gordon Parks. InL (un-
  paged)
Slowly the night blooms unfurling. Frank Marshall Davis. AmNP p.96; IADB
  p.12; PoN p.143; PoNe p.255
Slowly we learn; the oft repeated line. J. E. Clare McFarlane. PoN p.321
Slums Dreams. Langston Hughes. PATL p.95
Small Bells of Benin, The. Margaret Danner. BrT p.39
Small brown girl began to sing, A. Eloise Culver. GANIV p.69
Small colored boy in the subway.* Babette Deutsch. PoNe p.513
Small Comment. Sonia Sanchez. NBP p.114
Small sounds come from outside the window. Julia Alvarez. SoS p.11
Smell of Lebanon, The. Alice Walker. ONC p.66
Smell of the sea in my nostrils, The. Paul Laurence Dunbar. CPPLD p.145
Smile, A. William L. Morrison. DaR p.43
Smile for me real soon. William L. Morrison. DaR p.51
Smiles do not always echo cheer. Georgia Douglas Johnson. HWOP p.51
Smiling, smiling kiddies we. Joseph S. Cotter, Sr. SPPH p.19
Smoke Screen. Clarence Major. SAM p.50
Smoke seeping from my veins. LeRoi Jones. BMP p.27
Smoking Out the Bees. Joseph S. Cotter, Sr. CPJSC p.65
Smooths and burden. Robert Hayden. SPRH p.20
Smothered Fires. Georgia D. Johnson. HWOP p.32
Snag. Victor Hernandez Cruz. SNA p.43
Snail, The. Langston Hughes. DYTB p.47; FOW p.4; GoS p.149; MBP p.36
Snake. Langston Hughes. FOW p.7
Snake, The. Craig Williamson. AfW p.14
Snake Eyes. LeRoi Jones. KAL p.212
Snake-That-Walked-Upon-His-Tail, The. Countee Cullen. OTIS p.189
Snake's head twained the water's surface, The. Joseph S. Cotter, Sr. CPJSC
  p.36
Snaps. Victor Hernandez Cruz. SNA p.97
Sniffed, dilating, my nostrils, the cocaine creeps up my leg, smacks into my
  groin. Michael S. Harper. DJDC p.12
Snob. Langston Hughes. SIH p.27
Snooker Toots. Raymond Garfield Dandridge. ZaP p.55
Snow. Robert Hayden. SPRH p.20
Snow cannot melt too soon for the birds left behind, The. Owen Dodson. PLL
  p.29; PoN p.173; PoNe p.299
Snow Fairy, The. Claude McKay. HaS p.76; SPCM p.98
Snow has ceased its fluttering flight, The. James Weldon Johnson. FYOP p.42
Snow has left Mount Mitchell, The. Audrey Johnson. BTh p.39
Snow Hill. Waverly T. Carmichael. FHOF p.21
Snow in October. Alice Dunbar Nelson. CaD p.71; ANP p.85
Snow lies deep upon the ground, The. Paul Laurence Dunbar. CPPLD p.167
Snow-White Rosebud, The. Raymond Dandridge. ZaP p.29
Snowin'. Paul Laurence Dunbar. CPPLD p.271
So? James P. Vaughn. AmNP p.168
So Boston was like that. Victor Hernandez Cruz. SNA p.95
So detached and cool she is. Clarissa Scott Delany. CaD p.143; PoN p.94;
  PoNe p.177

So goes the busy jolly day till skies are red, then gold, then gray. Eli
    Shepperd. P1S p.91
So I met this man who was a publisher when he was young. Nikki Giovanni.
    BFBTBJ p.9
So I would hear out those lungs.* James Dickey. PoNe p.579
So joke on, niggers, who gwine keer? Eli Shepperd. P1S p.68
So long, O hermit muse, so long. Joseph S. Cotter. WSBO p.15; SPJSC p.29
So long so far away is Africa. Langston Hughes. PoN p.102
So low down bummin' cut plug from de passers by. Sterling A. Brown. SoR
    p.72
So many cares to vex the day. Leslie Pinckney Hill. BANP p.155
So many little flowers. Langston Hughes. GoS p.180
So many weary years I've crept. Lucy Mae Turner. BCF p.40
So Much. Charles B. Johnson. ANP p.38; SOMP p.33
So much have I forgotten in ten years. Claude McKay. AmNP p.30; BANP p.174;
    CaD p.85; HaS p.9; ITBLA p.156; PoN p.334; PoNe p.104; SPCM p.13
So much of love I need. Charles B. Johnson. ANP p.38; SOMP p.33
So New Year / Come in! Ted Joans. AFR p.19
So now we have come to silence. Michael S. Harper. DJDC p.38
So oft I've read what poets sang of love. James E. McGirt. FYSS p.49
So oft our hearts, beloved lute. James David Corrothers. AVAN p.16; BANP
    p.79
So Quietly. Leslie Pinckney Hill. BANP p.156; IADB p.65
So quietly they stole upon their prey. Leslie Pinckney Hill. AVAN p.197;
    BANP p.157; IADB p.65
So that you will know where the sun was too cold to look up but going down-
    hill home. Gerald W. Barrax. AKOR p.43
So This is Our Revolution. Sonia Sanchez. BrT p.146; WABP p.63
So we, who've supped the self same cup. Paul Laurence Dunbar. CaD p.5;
    CPPLD p.62; LOLL p.88
So we've come at last to Freud. Alice Walker. ONC p.61
So you be'n to ole Kentucky. Joseph S. Cotter. EBAP p.189; LOF p.42; SPPH
    p.56
So you did instant revolution. Clarence Major. B1Sp p.128
Soapship went a-rocking, A. James A. Emanuel. AmNP p.174; NNPUSA p.97
Socks and gloves the medal of honor ablaze in twin fists. Michael S. Harper.
    DJDC p.85
Soft answers turn away, they say, wrath. James Worley. FoM p.5
Soft gray hands of sleep, The. Edward Silvera. LUP p.42; PoN p.150; PoNe
    p.260
Soft night comes back. LeRoi Jones. BMP p.44
Soft Soap. Lucile D. Goodlet. WGC p.24
Soft you day, be velvet, soft. Maya Angelou. JGM p.4
Softly blow lightly. Donald Jeffrey Hayes. CaD p.190
Softly, now, or mammy'll ketch us round. Lucy Mae Turner. BCF p.35
Softly the shades of evening fall. Waverly T. Carmichael. FHOF p.56
Soil of man's escape provides his doom, The. PoNe p.408
Soiled and stained, a page in life's book, I tore from its place. Raymond
    Garfield Dandridge. PeP p.29
Sojourner Truth, Freedom Fighter, 1797-1883, New York. Eloise Culver. GANIV
    p.25
"Sojourner Truth," she named herself. Eloise Culver. GANIV p.25

Song For a Banjo Dance. Langston Hughes. WeB p.36
Song For a Dark Girl. Langston Hughes. CaD p.147; FNP p.28; FCTJ p.75; IADB
   p.67; PoN p.103
Song For A Love That Is Dead. J. Henderson Brooks. BTh p.18
Song For A Suicide. Langston Hughes. PoNe p.198
Song For Billie Holiday. Langston Hughes. OWT p.47
Song For Myself, A. Melvin Tolson. RWA p.45
Song for the Dead, III. Anonymous. TYBP p.13
Song for the First of August. James Madison Bell. ANP p.19; AVAN p.38
Song for the Sisters. A. B. Spellman. TGWL p.91
Song For the Sun That Disappeared Behind the Rain Clouds. Anonymous. TYBP
   p.5
Song for the Unsung Heroes Who Rose in the Country's Need, A. Paul Laurence
   Dunbar. CPPLD p.318
Song Form. LeRoi Jones. BMP p.107
Song I sing a blessing so divine, A. James E. McGirt. FYSS p.45
Song in spite of myself. Countee Cullen. BlC p.51; OTIS p.98
Song in the Front Yard, A. Gwendolyn Brooks. IADB p.11
Song is but a little thing, A. Paul Laurence Dunbar. CPPLD p.5; LOLL p.4
Song No Gentleman Would Sing to Any Lady, A. Countee Cullen. BlC p.37
Song of a Common Lover. Flavien Ranaivo. TYBP p.154
Song of a Summer Breeze. Charles Fred White. PONS p.32
Song of a Syrian Lace Seller. William S. Braithwaite. AVAN p.138; HFL p.41
Song of Ditta. Gylan Kain. BlSp p.100
Song of Hannibal: Rome (Near the Gates of Rome). Marcus B. Christian. GoS
   p.142
Song of Living, A. William S. Braithwaite. ANP p.52; AVAN p.139; HFL p.48
Song of Love, A. James E. McGirt. FYSS p.45
Song of Praise. Countee Cullen. BlC p.66; OTIS p.102
Song of Praise, A. Countee Cullen. BLIA p.158; CCC p.4; FNP p.18; OTIS p.4
Song of Sour Grapes, A. Countee Cullen. CpS p.26; OTIS p.57
Song of Summer. Paul Laurence Dunbar. CPPLD p.40; CLT p.101; LOLL p.56
Song of Thanks, A. Edward Smyth Jones. AVAN p.154; BANP p.148
Song of the Little Children. Eli Shepperd. PlS p.118
Song of the Moon, A. Claude McKay. PoN p.320; PoNe p.98; SPCM p.69
Song of the Negro, A. Nick Aaron Ford. SFD p.38
Song of the Poor Man. Anonymous. TYBP p.49
Song of the Rejected Lover. Countee Cullen. CpS p.31
Song of the Sea. Eli Shepperd, PlS p.135
Song of the Seeker. Eli Shepperd. PlS p.124
Song of the Sixth Month, A. William S. Braithwaite. HFL p.62
Song of the Son. Jean Toomer. AmNP p.33; BLIA p.164; CaD p.96; CNAW p.285;
   FNP p.12; PoN p.66; SoS p.32; KAL p.54
Song of the Storm. Eli Shepperd. PlS p.12
Song: The Rev. Mu Bugwu Dickinson ruminates behind the sermon. Gwendolyn
   Brooks. FaP p.22
Song: The Trail of Stars. William S. Braithwaite. HFL p.81
Song To A Negro Wash-Woman. Langston Hughes. GoS p.41
Song to Christina. Craig Williamson. AfW p.45
Song to Jackie Robinson, Baseball Hall of Fame, Cairo, Georgia, 1919-1972.
   Eloise Culver. GANIV p.73

Sorry you are dead. Michael S. Harper. DJDC p.80
SOS. LeRoi Jones. BMP p.115
Souk. Ted Joans. AFR p.12; MBP p.47
Soul! Austin Black. NBP p.29
Soul. Bernie Casey. LATP p.83
Soul. D. L. Graham. KAL p.231
Soul is a beautiful thing, The. Victor Hernandez Cruz. SNA p.81
Soul: there is no stronger thing than song. Countee Cullen. CCC p.97
Soul-troubled at the febrile ways of breath. Countee Cullen. CCC p.69
Souls of Black and white. Aquah Laluah. PoN p.385
Sound of Afro-American music, The. S. E. Anderson. BlSp p.6
Sound of Black music, The. Ted Joans. BPW p.2
Sounds assault your senses. Bernie Casey. LATP p.67
Sounds Like Pearls. Maya Angelou. JGM p.22
Sounds of the Harlem night drop one by one into stillness, The. Langston
    Hughes. WeB p.103
Source, The. Ted Joans. AFR p.105
South, The. Langston Hughes. WeB p.54
South Atlantic clouds rode low, The. John A. Williams. NBP p.132
South Carolina Chain Gang Song. Anonymous. ITBLA p.121
South is green with coming spring, The. Muriel Rukeyser. PoN p.280; PoNe
    p.560
South Street. Edward Silvera. CaD p.214; LUP p.43
South Street is not Beautiful. Edward Silvera. CaD p.214; LUP p.43
South: The Name of Home. Alice Walker. ONC p.39
Southern Africa where white oppressors play their trick on unarmed Blacks.
    Ted Joans. AFR p.29
Southern Blues. Anonymous. BLIA p.48; ITBLA p.124
Southern gentle lady, do not swoon. Langston Hughes. BLIA p.195; OWT p.56
Southern Justice. Ritten Edward Lee. EbR p.100
Southern Landscape Don' changed, The, Jim. Ted Joans. BPW p.106
Southern Landscapers. Ted Joans. BPW p.106
Southern Mammy Sings. Langston Hughes. SIH p.75
Southern Mansion. Arna Bontemps. AmNP p.80; BANP p.263; BTB p.49; BLIA
    p.217; CNAW p.335; IADB p.25; ITBLA p.161; KAL p.80; PoN p.113; PoNe
    p.214; TYBP p.224
Soutern mob upon a lynching bent, A. Charles Fred White. PONS p.150
Southern Moonlight. Robert E. Hayden. CaD p.16
Southern Reaper. Conrad Kent Rivers. SVH p.4
Southern Road. Sterling A. Brown. BANP p.250; SoR p.46
Southern Road, The. Dudley Randall. BrT p.125; NNPUSA p.41
Southern Song. Margaret Walker. FMP p.18
Southerner, The. Karl Shapiro. PoN p.284; PoNe p.565
South's the sin, The? The North's the glory? Joseph S. Cotter, Sr. CPJSC
    p.73; WSBO p.13
South's Ungolden Rule, Or An American Riddle, The. Charles Fred White.
    PONS p.19
Souvenir. Georgia Douglas Johnson. HWOP p.49
Souvenirs. Dudley Randall. KAL p.135
Spade is Just a Spade, A. Walter Everette Hawkins. AVAN p.149
Spake adventure pacts boys and dogs. LeRoi Jones. BMP p.128
Spanish Needle, The. Claude McKay. GoS p.147; HaS p.24; SPCM p.24

Stop again! This engine must have a bit of oil. Eloise Culver. GANIV p.40
Stop dat racket! Raymond Garfield Dandridge. PeP p.12; ZaP p.64
Stopped. Allen Polite. NNPUSA p.72
Storage. LeRoi Jones. BMP p.73
Storm. Craig Williamson. AfW p.8
Storm and strife and stress. Paul Laurence Dunbar. CPPLD p.370
Storm Ending. Jean Toomer. BLIA p.165
Storms slug its head. Melvin B. Tolson. LUP p.46; RWA p.56
Storms that break and sweep about my feet, The. Charles B. Johnson. SOMP
    p.7
Stormy Monday Girls. Ted Joans. BPW p.59
Story Hour. Joseph S. Cotter, Sr. CPJSC p.51
Story of the Rebellion, A. Frances Harper. PBFH p.60
Straight in the heart of the April meadows. William S. Braithwaite. HFL p.47
Straight Talk. Nikki Giovanni. MyH p.31
Straight, the swift, the debonair, The. Countee Cullen. MASP p.69; OTIS
    p.143
Strain of Music. Mae V. Cowdery. WLOV p.24
Strange atoms we unto ourselves. Georgia Douglas Johnson. AmNP p.23
Strange corpses the one who still talk. LeRoi Jones. BMP p.67
Strange Hurt. Langston Hughes. FOW p.80
Strange Legacies. Sterling A. Brown. KAL p.72; SoR p.95; TYBP p.218
Strange Man, The. Joseph S. Cotter, Sr. LOF p.32; RHY p.10; SPPH p.81
Strange Song. Michael S. Harper. DJDC p.52
Strange summer sun shines round our globe of circumstances. Margaret Walker.
    PFND p.31
Strange, that in this nigger place. Langston Hughes. BANP p.239
Strangeness and the strange walk ambiently body-rounded. Langston Hughes.
    BTB p.126
Stranger in Town. Langston Hughes. OWT p.41
Strategies. Welton Smith. NBP p.124
Stream, The. Lula Lowe Weeden. CaD p.228
Stream flowing steadily over a stone does not wet its core. Abdillahi Muuse.
    TYBP p.57
Stream's Breath tastes of the wood's perfume, The. William S. Braithwaite.
    LLL p.55
Street called crooked (LeHavre, Aug. 1928). Countee Cullen. B1C p.56
Street Called Straight. Melvin Tolson. RWA p.90
Street Demonstration. Margaret Walker. PFND p.7
Street Light, The. Langston Hughes. KAL p.93
Street Scene - 1946.* Kenneth Porter. PoN p.299; PoNe p.539
Street Scene #1. Victor Hernandez Cruz. SNA p.31
Streets of Bronzeville seem more beautiful because you gave them honesty.
    Eugene Perkins. TGWL p.787
Strength. William L. Morrison. DaR p.11
Stretching from length to breadth. William L. Morrison. DaR p.10
Strictly Speaking. J. Farley Ragland. EbR p.124
Stri-i-ke One! the call comes through the air. Lucy Mae Turner. BCF p.10
Strong Men. Sterling A. Brown. ANP p.104; BANP p.258; SoR p.51; TYBP p.219
Strong Men, Riding Horses.** Gwendolyn Brooks. KAL p.158
Stripling Thames, The. William C. Braithwaite. VER p.107
Strive for the highest what avails the May. William C. Braithwaite. VER p.39

Strong Swimmer, The.* William Rose Benet. PoN p.295; PoNe p.500
Structure of man is wroght upon time's anvil. Raymond Dandridge. ZaP p.16
Struggle Staggers Us, The. Margaret Walker. FMP p.58
Struggle With Temptation. Charles Fred White. PONS p.77
Strong up in three major explorations your stomach is American roadwork.
    Michael S. Harper. DJDC p.70
Strut and wiggle. Langston Hughes. WeB p.30
Student I Know, A. J. Henderson Brooks. BTh p.14
Student's Christmas Parting, A. Charles Fred White. PONS p.83
Style. Joseph S. Cotter, Sr. CPJSC p.13
Style. Raymond Garfield Dandridge. ZaP p.2
Stymied in my leave taking I ponder the two vacant days. Michael S. Harper.
    DJDC p.21
Sub Specie Aeternitatis. Robert Hayden. BOR p.52; SPRH p.32
Substitution. Anne Spencer. CaD p.46
Subterfuge. Countess W. Twitty. EbR p.147
Suburbia. Maurice Martinez. PoNe p.408
Subway, The. Conrad Kent Rivers. KAL p.207
Subway in subway out. Victor Hernandez Cruz. SNA p.63
Subway Wind. Claude McKay. HaS p.54; SPCM p.75
Success. Nick Aaron Ford. SFD p.35
Success. Dorothy Vena Johnson. EbR p.92
Success. LeRoi Jones. BMP p.21
Success. James E. McGirt. FYSS p.41
Success does not seem to have spoiled Gwen Brooks. Cynthia M. Conley. TGWL
    p.22
Success is a light upon the farther shore. James E. McGirt. FYSS p.41
Success is like a blazing flame of meteoric light. Dorothy Vena Johnson.
    EbR p.92
Such a pretty little lovely you. Bernie Casey. LATP p.62
Such big lovely eyes, you watched me so intensely. Bernie Casey. LATP p.29
Such simple things can make me know a deep exultant joy. Mae V. Cowdery.
    WLOV p.63
Such trivial things. Beatrice M. Murphy. TNV p.141
Sufferance of her race is shown, The.* Herman Melville. PoN p.247; PoNe
    p.466
Suicide. Langston Hughes. FCTJ p.20
Suicide. Alice Walker. ONC p.74
Suicide Chant. Countee Cullen. CCC p.87
Suicide's Note. Langston Hughes. CaD p.151; DYTB p.57; WeB p.87
Sukee River. Claude McKay. SPCM p.17
Sultry Day, A. William L. Morrison. DaR p.58
Sum, The. Paul Laurence Dunbar. AVAN p.88; CPPLD p.183
Summah is De Lovin' Time. Paul Laurence Dunbar. CPPLD p.434
Summah night an' sighin' breeze. Paul Laurence Dunbar. CPPLD p.211; LiG
    p.106
Summah's nice, wif sun a-shinin'. Paul Laurence Dunbar. CPPLD p.215
Summary. Sonia Sanchez. BrT p.138
Summer. Waring Cuney. BTB p.85
Summer comes. Helene Johnson. CaD p.223; PoN p.152; PoNe p.263
Summer comes on back home. Waring Cuney. BTB p.85
Summer Evening. Langston Hughes. OWT p.123

Summer in Harlem in bright tropical colors. Askia Muhammad Toure. BlSp
   p.223
Summer is coming, The. Don L. Lee. DSNP p.52
Summer Magic. Leslie Pinckney Hill. BANP p.155
Summer Matures. Helene Johnson. CaD p.217; PoN p.150; PoNe p.261
Summer matures, brilliant scorpion appears. Helene Johnson. CaD p.217; PoN
   p.150; PoNe p.261
Summer Morn in New Hampshire. Claude McKay. HaS p.66; SPCM p.16
Summer Night, A. Paul Laurence Dunbar. CPPLD p.434; LOLL p.149
Summer Night. Langston Hughes. WeB p.103
Summer Night's Enchantment, A. William S. Braithwaite. LLL p.78
Summer Oracle. Audre Lorde. SoS p.88
Summer outdoor beer party. Clarence Major. SAM p.11
Summer Pastoral, A. Paul Laurence Dunbar. CPPLD p.460
Summer / time T.V. / (is witer than ever). Sonia Sanchez. WABP p.30
Summer Twilight. William L. Morrison. DaR p.46
Summer Words of a Sistuh Addict. Sonia Sanchez. WABP p.35
Summer's Night, A. Paul Laurence Dunbar. CPPLD p.101
Summertime and the Living. Robert Hayden. BOR p.26; KAL p.115; SPRH p.53
Summing Up By the Defendant. Owen Dodson. BTB p.98
Sun and Softness. Langston Hughes. DYTB p.5; FCTJ p.69; FNP p.28
Sun Came, The. Etheridge Knight. BrT p.84; FoM p.73; TGWL p.64
Sun came, Miss Brooks, The. Etheridge Knight. BrT p.84; FoM p.73; TGWL p.64
Sun has slipped his tether, The. Paul Laurence Dunbar. CPPLD p.160
Sun hath shed its kindly light, The. Paul Laurence Dunbar. CPPLD p.464
Sun House (a living legend). Don L. Lee. DSNP p.175; WWW p.51
Sun is folding, cars stall and rise beyond the window, The. LeRoi Jones.
   BMP p.22
Sun is Low, The. Paul Laurence Dunbar. CPPLD p.472
Sun makes shadow following a hung man's stick. LeRoi Jones. BMP p.78
Sun My Son, The. Ted Joans. BPW p.128
Sun Song. Langston Hughes. DYTB p.5; FCTJ p.69; FNP p.28
Sun sought thy dim bed and brought forth light, The. Claude McKay. BTB
   p.146; FNP p.10; HaS p.35; SPCM p.40
Sun to the earth beams all the while, The. William L. Morrison. DaR p.10
Sun was shining down on a cabin dull and gray, The. Eloise Culver. GANIV
   p.52
Sun went Down in Beauty, The.** George Marion McLlelan. EBAP p.128
Sunday. Langston Hughes. SIH p.7
Sunday afternoon, and couples, walk the breakwater. Robert Hayden. BOR p.47;
   SPRH p.29
Sunday afternoon in the Philippines on Clark AFB in '57 I remember how the
   sun was like. Gerald W. Barrax. AKOR p.36
Sunday Chicken. Gwendolyn Brooks. AnA p.7
Sunday / Evening at Gwen's. Sonia Sanchez. TGWL p.86; WABP p.58
Sunday go to meetin' Folk. John Raven. BFM p.12
Sunday Morning Prophecy. Langston Hughes. OWT p.35
Sunday Morning Song. Anonymous. MBP p.55
Sundays of Satin-Legs Smith, The. Gwendolyn Brooks. CNAW p.516
Sundays too my father got up early. Robert Hayden. BOR p.29; IADB p.10;
   SoS p.21; SPRH p.55
Sundered were our paths on an April morning. Joseph S. Cotter, Sr. SPPH p.60

Sweet on the house top falls the gentle shower. George Moses Horton. AVAN
    p.34
Sweet Potato Man. Anonymous. ITBLA p.125
Sweet Potato Pie. Ted Joans. AFR p.120
Sweet Sally took a cardboard box. Gwendolyn Brooks. AnA p.41
Sweet-scented winds move inward from the shore. George Marion McClellan.
    AVAN p.92
Sweet singer, how I envy you. Raymond Garfield Dandridge. PAOP p.26; ZaP
    p.103
Sweet Timber Land. Arna Bontemps. CaD p.172
Sweet words on Race. Langston Hughes. PATL p.75
Sweet words that take them own sweetime to flower. Langston Hughes. PATL
    p.75
Sweeten' 'Tatahs. James Corrothers. EBAP p.238
Sweetest of the flowers a-blooming. Paul Laurence Dunbar. CPPLD p.386
Sweeter far than lyric rune. Georgia D. Johnson. HWOP p.61
Sweetest Thing, The. Anonymous. MBP p.102; TYBP p.7
Sweetheart, for love of you, I'd give up all the pleasures of this life.
    Charles Fred White. PONS p.104
Sweetly. William Lorenzo Morrison. DaR p.8
Sweetness of poverty like this. Marie De Andrade. TYBP p.82
Swift little-thoughts come a-nesting in my brain. Frenchy J. Hodges. BlW
    p.7
Swift swallows sailing from the Spanish Main. Claude McKay. HaS p.15; SPCM
    p.18
Swing dat hammer - huhn. Sterling A. Brown. BANP p.250; SoR p.46
Swing high, Iscariot. Gerald W. Barrax. KAL p.199
Swing Low, Sweet Chariot. Anonymous. GoS p.61
Swing of Life, The. Jamye H. Coleman. EbR p.52
Swing out, time, use the arrow for the arc. Marion Cuthbert. SOC p.43
Swing sweet rhythm charcoal toes. Mari Evans. BlSp p.71; IABW p.81
Swing, swing, swinging wild animals swinging. Ahmed A. Alhamisi. GuW p.8
Swing swinging thou cotton fields. Don L. Lee. DSNP p.64
Swing yo' lady roun' an' roun'. Paul Laurence Dunbar. CPPLD p.325; AVAN p.75
Sword, The. Abu Bakr. TYBP p.44
Sylvester's Dying Bed. Langston Hughes. SIH p.67
Sympathy. Georgia Douglas Johnson. HWOP p.4
Sympathy. Paul Laurence Dunbar. CaD p.8; CPPLD p.162; IADB p.81; ITBLA p.96;
    PoN p.33; PoNe p.34; AmNP p.13
Symphony. Frank Horne. AmNP p.51
Symphony. Leslie Pinckney Hill. AVAN p.202
Syncopating Rhythm. Frenchy J. Hodges. BlW p.20
Syncopating rhythm please echo home to me. Frenchy J. Hodges. BlW p.20

- T -

T.C. Walter Bradford. BrT p.177
TCB. Sonia Sanchez. WABP p.59
T.T. Jackson Sings. LeRoi Jones. BMP p.105
T.V. Kali Grosvenor. PBK p.34
T.V. is a Fake. Kali Grosvenor. PBK p.34

Teacher was a bad man, The. Margaret Walker. FMP p.44

Tears. Maya Angelou. JGM p.12

Tears. William S. Braithwaite. HFL p.78

Tears and a Dream. Marsha Ann Jackson. TNV p.53

Tears and Kisses. Georgia Douglas Johnson. HWOP p.28

Tears are falling, I am sad. Raymond Garfield Dandridge. PeP p.45

Tears hiding behind a doomed god no longer define the soul. Keorapetse W. Kgositsile. BrT p.77

Tears the crystal rags viscious tatters of a worn-through soul. Maya Angelou. JGM p.12

Teestay. James W. Johnson. FYOP p.32

Tek a cool night, good an' cleah. Paul Laurence Dunbar. CPPLD p.242

Telephone Book. Ted Joans. BPW p.52

Telephone Conversation. Wole Soyinka. TYBP p.161

Tele / vision. LeRoi Jones. BMP p.207

Television Lovers Cannot Help Me. LeRoi Jones. BMP p.195

Television / poem. Sonia Sanchez. WABP p.24

Television / radio Sunday benevolent sundown, Malcolm X assissinated. I am watching sports on network TV. David Henderson. FoM p.46

Tell again the Christmas story: Christ is born in all His glory! Langston Hughes. ChG p.78

Tell all my mourners to mourn in red. Langston Hughes. SIH p.65

"Tell me a story, father, please." Ann Plato. EBAP p.118

Tell me, Deep Ocean. James E. McGirt. FYSS p.73

Tell me is there anything lovelier. Angelina Weld Grimke. CaD p.36; ANP p.86

Tell me, is there peace. Langston Hughes. FOW p.22

Tell me my marks, examiner. Owen Dodson. BTB p.98

Tell me, my soul, tell me, I pine to know, some future day, known as the harvest time. James McGirt. FYSS p.54

Tell Rachel, He Whispered. Owen Dodson. BTB p.91; CNAW p.395

Tell you, love where the roses blow. Paul Laurence Dunbar. CPPLD p.388

Tell you what, men, ah'm discovered. John Wesley Holloway. AVAN p.184

Telling Fortunes. Sterling A. Brown. SoR p.127

Temperate Belt. Durward Collins, Jr. BTB p.68

Temples he built and palaces of air. Paul Laurence Dunbar. CPPLD p.159

Temptation. Joseph S. Cotter, Sr. LOF p.36

Temptation. Paul Laurence Dunbar. AVAN p.83; CPPLD p.235

Temptation. James E. McGirt. FYSS p.76

Temptress, The. James Weldon Johnson. FYOP p.41

10:15 A.M. - April 29, 1969 Poem. Sonia Sanchez. WASP p.39

10 - 9 - 8 - 7 - 6 - 5 - 4 - 3 - 2 - 1 - Death. Roscoe Lee Browne. BTB p.63

Ten Thousand millhands are still today. Peter Wellington Clark. EbR p.38

Tenebris. Angelina Weld Grimké. CaD p.40; PoN p.49; PoNe p.58

Tenement Room: Chicago. Frank Marshall Davis. GoS p.136

Tented City, The. Joseph S. Cotter, Sr. SPPH p.76

Tented eye with distance weds, The. Joseph S. Cotter, Sr. SPPH p.76

Terror does not belong to open day. Owen Dodson. BLIA p.260; PLL p.97; PoN p.174; PoNe p.300; SoS p.59

Test, The. LeRoi Jones. BMP p.188

Test of Love, A. James E. McGirt. FYSS p.59

Tetuan. Claude McKay. SPCM p.87

Teutonic maid with features so sharp that one could thread needles with them.
    Ted Joans. AFR p.38
Thank God for Little Children.** Frances Harper. PBFH p.47
Thanks for the lovely time. Ibn Sharaf. MBP p.32
Thanksgiving. William S. Braithwaite. LLL p.61
Thanksgiving day is coming soon. Charles Fred White. PONS p.41
Thanksgiving 1923. Raymond Dandridge. ZaP p.50
Thanksgiving 1925. Raymond Dandridge. ZaP p.40
Thanksgiving 1969. Dear God I thank you for the problems that are mine and
    evidently mine alone. June Jordan. SCh p.82
Thanksgiving Poem, A. Paul Laurence Dunbar. CPPLD p.464
Thanksgiving Prayer. James E. McGirt. FYSS p.47
That Black bitch of a muse I had refused. Gerald W. Barrax. AKOR p.14
That Bright Chimeric Beast. Countee Cullen. AmNP p.86; B1C p.10; OTIS p.82;
    PoN p.126
That brown girl's swagger gives a twitch. Countee Cullen. CCC p.8
That force is lost. LeRoi Jones. KAL p.212
That Gaiety, Oh. Robert Hayden. BOR p.39
That Hill. Blanche Taylor Dickinson. CaD p.109
That is the way God made you. Gwendolyn Brooks. ITM p.35
That it should seem an age since I unrolled. Barefield Gordon. LUP p.19
That justice is a blind goddess is a thing to which we Black are wise. Lang-
    ston Hughes. PATL p.45
That little yaller gal wid blue-green eyes. Langston Hughes. FCTJ p.31
That lively organ, palpitant and red. Countee Cullen. B1C p.40; OTIS p.92
That Mighty Flight. LeRoi Jones. BMP p.161
That night my angel stooped and strained. Jonathan Henderson Brooks. PoN
    p.134; PoNe p.238
That night she felt those searching hands. Countee Cullen. CCC p.96
That ol sapphire sister encased in & looking outta her twisted broken window.
    Clarence Major. SAM p.43
That old gal ain't she a mess. John Raven. BFM p.19
That Stagelee was an all-right lad. Margaret Walker. FMP p.35
That Star. Owen Dodson. PLL p.85
That time we all heard it. Gwendolyn Brooks. BrT p.38; FaP p.19
That Vengeance gathers. Theodore Stanford. EbR p.132
That weaver of words the poet. Countee Cullen. CpS p.72
Theatre (humans in it). Clarence Major. SAM p.51
Theft of Wishes, A. A. B. Spellman. BTB p.170
Their hair, pomaded, faces jaded. Maya Angelou. JGM p.45
Their hearts are cities and away from them they are old witches. LeRoi Jones.
    BMP p.57
Their Poem. Victor Hernandez Cruz. SNA p.51
Their shadow dims the sunshine of our day. Claude McKay. HaS p.47
Their shoulders you shook. Al-Mahdi. TYBP p.45
Them oldies say it was fear that drove you away. Victor Hernandez Cruz.
    SNA p.101
Theme and Variation (For Erma). Robert Hayden. BOR p.40; SPRH p.59
Theme Brown Girl. Elton Hill-Abu Ishak. NBP p.71
Theme For English. Langston Hughes. CNAW p.305
Then and Now. Joseph S. Cotter, Sr. SPPH p.86
Then and Now. Paul Laurence Dunbar. CPPLD p.205

Then and Now. Frances Harper. PBFH p.75
Then as the crowd up to go Jeb takes again his own banjo. Eli Shepperd. PlS
    p.24
Then call me traitor if you want. Countee Cullen. BlC p.63; CNAW p.331;
    OTIS p.100
Then fled the mellews the wicked Juba. Robert Hayden. BOR p.68; SPRH p.72
Then he slammed on the brakes. Phil W. Petrie. MBP p.86
Then I Met You.** Jack Calvert Wells. EbR p.158
Then I would love you. Joseph S. Cotter, Jr. BOG p.11
Then It Was. June Jordan. SCh p.37
Then it was our eyes locked slowly on the pebble wash. June Jordan. SCh p.37
Then the crude minstrel pressed for more, draws out from his melodious store.
    Eli Shepperd. PlS p.19
Then the golden hour will tick its last. Arna Bontemps. BTB p.49; CaD p.168;
    PoN p.114; PoNe p.214
Theordore R, the III finally got past Aunt Clelia Uncle Dan and the heavy
    glassed front door. Mari Evans. IABW p.42
Theology. Paul Laurence Dunbar. CPPLD p.169
Ther' ain't no use in all this trife. Paul Laurence Dunbar. CPPLD p.74;
    LOLL p.109
There. Langston Hughes. FOW p.88
There Are Blk / Puritans.** Sonia Sanchez. WABP p.17
There are facts lodged in our world. LeRoi Jones. BMP p.168
There are four lions at Trafalgar square. Ted Joans. BLIA p.387; BPW p.25
There are highways in the soul. Georgia Douglas Johnson. HWOP p.8
There are many who deny themselves; you are one. James Thompson. BlSp p.210
There are no beaten paths to glory's height. Paul Laurence Dunbar. ANP p.24;
    CPPLD p.33; LOLL p.46
There are no clocks on the wall. Langston Hughes. FOW p.28
There are no hollows any more. William S. Braithwaite. BANP p.104
There are no reservations for the revolution. Nikki Giovanni. BrT p.64
There are no stars which fell on Alabama, Georgia, Mississippi, New York.
    Calvin C. Hernton. NBP p.64
There are no statistics. Waring Cuney. LUP p.13
There are palm trees in my homeland. Antonio Goncaleves Dias. TYBP p.78
There Are Seeds to Sow. Bernette Golden. TNV p.40
There are still birds. Gwen Marshall. PLL p.100
There are tears sweet, refreshing like dewdrops that rise. Georgia Douglas
    Johnson. HWOP p.28
There are those. Ted Joans. BPW p.58
There are those that say that people are people. Ted Joans. BPW p.58
There are wonder and pain. Langston Hughes. FOW p.58
There are words like freedom. Langston Hughes. BLIA p.194; FOW p.105
There are words like freedom sweet and wonderful to say. Langston Hughes.
    PATL p.33
There he goes with his hat in his hand. J. Farley Ragland. EbR p.123
There is a coarseness. Edward S. Silvera. CaD p.214
There is a gin mill on the avenue. Langston Hughes. OWT p.67
There is a girl I used to go with. Clarence Major. SAM p.47
There is a heaven for ever, day by day. Paul Laurence Dunbar. CPPLD p.169
There is a hunger after associated with pain. Nikki Giovanni. MyH p.2
There is a lovely noise about your name. Claude McKay. HaS p.57

There was grief within our household because of a vacant chair. Frances Harper. PBFH p.34

There was never a life so rich and free as a tiny raindrop starting back to sea. Nick Aaron Ford. SFD p.32

There was profusion in the gift. George Marion McLlelan. EBAP p.122

There Was Seven. Ted Joans. BPW p.103

There were bizarre beginnings in old lands for the making of me. Margaret Walker. FMP p.15

There were Black Cowboys in the west. Arthur Boze. BlW p.17

There were fair ladies three and a gentleman who came to tea. William L. Morrison. DaR p.53

There were fields where once we walked among the clover. Nikki Giovanni. BFBTBJ p.10

There were hours and many of valor and many were those of suspense. Emily Jane Greene. EbR p.73

There were mountains in that place. Robert Hayden. HSITD p.25

There were no lovers bowed before my time. Countee Cullen. MASP p.73

There were properly more Indians. June Jordan. SCh p.66

There were some things I might not know. Countee Cullen. BlC p.37

There You Were. Bernie Casey. LATP p.68

There you were sitting upon that stool. Bernie Casey. LATP p.68

Therefore, Adieu. Countee Cullen. BlC p.44; OTIS p.93

There's a fabulous story. Paul Laurence Dunbar. CPPLD p.402

There's a long, black line o' waiting for freedom. L. Zack Gilbert. EbR p.65

There's a memory keep a-runnin'. Paul Laurence Dunbar. CPPLD p.13; LOLL p.17

There's a new young moon. Langston Hughes. FOW p.8

There's a soft rosy glow o'er the whole world to-day. Georgia Douglas Johnson. HWOP p.25

There's a star in the East on Christmas morn. Anonymous. ChG p.97

There's a tender bud I'm saving. W. Blanche Nivens. BTh p.60

There's a way to happiness. William S. Braithwaite. LLL p.30

There's cold slush in the streets. LeRoi Jones. BMP p.83

There's Fire. Theodore Horne. FoM p.70

There's gladness in the sunshine. Raymond Dandridge. PeP p.10

There's hang'nd moss. Langston Hughes. FOW p.48

There's laughter that comes tumbling out. Portia Lucas. BTh p.37

There's momma, sitting at the window. John Raven. BFM p.6

There's nothing in the world that clings. Georgia Douglas Johnson. HWOP p.34

These Are My People. Robert Hayden. HSITD p.56

These Are My People.** Fenton Johnson. ANP p.40

These are no wind-blown rumors, soft say-sos. Countee Cullen. MASP p.85; OTIS p.154

These are not words set down for the rejected. Kay Boyle. PoN p.275; PoNe p.530

These are the blues. James C. Morris. BTB p.155

These are the days of elfs and fays. Paul Laurence Dunbar. CPPLD p.412

These are your Basic Weapons: hand gun, shot gun, rifle. Ahmed Akinwole Alhamisi. GuW p.4

These Beasts and the Benin Bronze. Margaret Danner. KAL p.126

These Cats Rolling on a Cardboard Box. LeRoi Jones. BMP p.143
These came, hallelujah queen worshipping down the sun star. Craig Williamson.
    AfW p.21
These tell miasmic rings of mist. Georgia Douglas Turner. AmNP p.24
These hands were born with streaks of sunset. Craig Williamson. AfW p.5
These have no **Christ to spit and stoop. Countee Cullen. BANP p.230; CCC p.9;
    BLIA p.158; OTIS p.6
These know fear: for all their singing. Sterling A. Brown. BLIA p.220; SoR
    p.67
These men were kings, albeit they were Black. Countee Cullen. B1C p.64;
    OTIS p.101
These men who do not die, but send to death. Countee Cullen. B1C p.36; OTIS
    p.103
These new night babie flying on ivory wings dig the beginning. Keorapetse W.
    Kgositsile. BrT p.75
These stately trees in majesty proclaim. Ben Nnamdi Azikiwe. LUP p.1
These streets / these wire boulevards / and long avenues. Ted Joans. BPW
    p.19
These the dread days which the seers have foretold. Walter Everette Hawkins.
    AVAN p.150
These things I hold for all the world to see. Katharine Beverly. EbR p.3
These truly are the brave. Roscoe Conkling Jamison. ANP p.109; BANP p.195
These were our fields. Robert A. Davis. FoS p.151; IADG p.31
Thespian. Calvin C. Hernton. BTB p.117
Theta. Melvin Tolson. HaG p.48
They adorn themselves lovingly and go forth. Mari Evans. IABW p.86
They ain't gonna never get rap. Nikki Giovanni. BrT p.68
They all came out that stormy Monday. Ted Joans. BPW p.59
They are embosed in the sod. Georgia Douglas Johnson. AVAN p.209
They are gone. Ted Joans. AFR p.33
They are killing all the young men. David Henderson. FoM p.46
They are not free, whose wine of life is spent. William C. Braithwaite. VER
    p.11
They are ours.* A. B. Magil. PoN p.282; PoNe p.533
They are ours; we claim them and we claim what they have suffered.* A. B.
    Magil. PoN p.282; PoNe p.533
They are upon the slopes. Michael S. Harper. DJDC p.35
They ask: what is Africa like? Ted Joans. BPW p.73
They Black as Black Me They Dig Black Art (For Free).** Ted Joans. BPW p.55
They brought me, tempting - red, life's richest wine. Charles B. Johnson.
    SOMP p.28
They call him strange and certainly he is. J. Henderson Brooks. BTh p.45
They call themselves Black Upper Class. Ted Joans. BPW p.15
They called grateful meetings did grateful dances to the pulse of grateful
    drums. Mari Evans. IABW p.66
They came from Persia to the sacred way. Walter Adolphe Roberts. PoN p.315
They came out of Neanderthalis caves. Ted Joans. BPW p.13
They Came This Evening.** Leon Damas. TYBP p.120
They came to catch the stars. Helen G. Quigless. TNV p.94
They carry on. Askia Muhammad Toure. PoNe p.424
They chain you to a bed and leave your body to sweat upon white sheets.
    Conrad Kent Rivers. SVH p.23

They say La Jac Brite pink skin bleach avails not. Josephine Miles. PoN
    p.300; PoNe p.554
They say that a poem is a beautiful thought expressed. Elaine Bethel. BTh
    p.34
They say that when they burned young Shelley's corpose. Frank Yerby. AmNP
    p.134; PoNe p.332
They say when virtue slipped from her. Countee Cullen. B1C p.24
They say you smile like a woman. Conrad Kent Rivers. BLIA p.357; SVH p.6
They set the slave free.* James Oppenheim. ANP p.135
They shall go down unto life's borderland. Joseph S. Cotter, Jr. AVAN p.182;
    BOG p.17
They shall see Him the crimson flush. Frances Harper. PBFH p.28
They sit alone at a table for two. Dudley Randall. LoY p.13
They stood, these two, against a mammoth well ... Ariel Williams. BTh p.16
They take stations in the broken doorways. Mari Evans. IABW p.49
They tell me I have lived before. Raymond Dandridge. PeP p.29; ZaP p.95
They tell me that I'm beautiful. Nikki Giovanni. MyH p.16
They tell me you are a far-away God who acts as a recorder and a judge.
    Etholia Arthur Robinson. EbR p.127
They told me that the path I took was hard, that many a time my weary feet
    would bleed. James E. McGirt. FYSS p.40
They told me - the voices of hates in the land. Melvin Tolson. RWA p.25
They took me out to some lonesome place. Langston Hughes. PATL p.44; SIH
    p.81
They wait like darkness not becoming stars. June Jordan. SCh p.5
They walk together like strangers. Ted Joans. AFR p.78
They Went Home.** Maya Angelou. JGM p.3
They were Blk / revolutionist. Don L. Lee. DCS p. 55; DSNP p.122
They white & they always say: make money. Ted Joans. BPW p.70
They Who Feel Death.** Alice Walker. ONC p.44
They who of bravery boast, are slave. Zachary Withers. PAS p.40
They'll Put You Up - - - Tight. Ted Joans. BPW p.28
They's somethin sort o' holy goes abeatin' thru my heart. Charles B. Johnson.
    SOMP p.45
Thick eyes dark - staring. Craig Williamson. AfW p.8
Thick lips 3 natural wide nose. Ted Joans. BPW p.53
Thief in me is running a round in circles, The. Alfred B. Spellman. NNPUSA
    p.60
Thin-Sliced. Mari Evans. IABW p.24
Thine, freedom, is a land of distances. William C. Braithwaite. VER p.10
Thing Burn of Darkness, A. Martha E. Lyons. EbR p.103
Things Is Changing. Mari Evans. IABW p.74
Things of the spirit.* Mason Jordan Mason. PoNe p.527
Think how many men have bluntly died. James Worley. FoM p.26
Think not, my friend, if right be crushed today, that violent wrong will ever
    hold the day. James McGirt. FYSS p.50
Think of sweet and choocolate. Gwendolyn Brooks. AnA p.19
Think Twice and Be Nice. Ted Joans. BTB p.131
Think you I am not fiend and savage too? Claude McKay. BANP p.169; SPCM p.38
Thinkin' Spooks. Raymond Garfield Dandridge. PeP p.21; ZaP p.87
Thinning hair estee laundered deliberate sentences. Nikki Giovanni. MyH p.53
Third Avenue, Early Winter. LeRoi Jones. BMP p.77

Third dance poem: in slow motion on a split screen. Gerald W. Barrax. AKOR
    p.65
Third degree. Langston Hughes. OWT p.130; PATL p.18
Third World Bond (for my sisters & their sisters). Don L. Lee. DCS p.55;
    DSNP p.122
Thirst. Claude McKay. HaS p.92; SPCM p.108
Thirteens, the (Black). Maya Angelou. JGM p.46
Thirteens, The (White). Maya Angelou. JGM p.47
.38, The. Ted Joans. BPW p.9; NNPUSA p.83
This Age. Raymond Patterson. SoS p.79
This ain't Torquemada. Marcus B. Christian. AmNP p.53
This and That. William C. Braithwaite. VER p.116
This cannot be the hour for oral speech. Owen Dodson. PLL p.78
This city is the child of France and Spain. Walter Adolphe Roberts. PoN
    p.316; PoNe p.84
This clinging vest of verdure, closely woven. William C. Braithwaite. VER
    p.124
This cool night is strange. Gwendolyn Bennett. BANP p.244; ANP p.128
This could be the way the fire comes. Gerald W. Barrax. AKOR p.13
This country might have been a pioneer land once. Sonia Sanchez. BOL p.42;
    SoS p.104; WABP p.27
This Day. Elroy Douglas. EbR p.59
This day is mine. Elroy Douglas. EbR p.59
This earth is but a semblance and a form. William S. Braithwaite. AVAN
    p.141; HFL p.50
This garden too pleasant the moon too near pools of water a void. Helen
    Quigless. NBP p.102
This gold watch and chain that belonged to my father? Langston Hughes. SIH
    p.95
This Grief. Robert Hayden. HSITD p.34
This grief will perish. Robert Hayden. HSITD p.34
This here's a tale of a sho-nuff man. Margaret Walker. FMP p.49
This Hour. Oliver La Grone. NNPUSA p.47; PoNe p.327
This house where love a little while abode. Countee Cullen. CpS p.24; OTIS
    p.55
This is a land in which you never were. Countee Cullen. OTIS p.152
This is a song for the genius child. Langston Hughes. FOW p.78
This is earthquake. Langston Hughes. FOW p.111
This Is For Freedom, My Son. Charles Stewart. TNV p.121
This Is For You.** Linwood Smith. TGWL p.90
This is has to be here because I am disconsolate. Clarence Major. SAM p.9
This is heavy electric thunder speaking on the hero's chest in gold. LeRoi
    Jones. BMP p.157
This is my country. Mary Wilkerson Cleaves. EbR p.46
This is my Life. William S. Braithwaite. AVAN p.143; HFL p.101
This is my mother, America. Hazel L. Washington. EbR p.151
This is no dream world, no nightmare country, no landscape. Robert Hayden.
    PoN p.164
This is not water running here. Countee Cullen. CCC p.13
This is the circle fairies drew. Countee Cullen. CpS p.82
This is The City. Yvette Johnson. TNV p.58

This is the debt I pay. Paul Laurence Dunbar. AmNP p.5; BANP p.58; CaD p.9;
    CPPLD p.348; KAL p.24

This   TITLE AND FIRST LINE INDEX

This vestige of woman's animalness is the open secret that riddles & ruins me. Gerald W. Barrax. AKOR p.18

This was the song of the wake up world. Countee Cullen. GoS p.103; OTIS p.185

This whole pay check's just for me. Langston Hughes. SIH p.8

This wound will be effaced as others have. Countee Cullen. B1C p.53

This year (so I hear). Mance Williams. NNPUSA p.68

Thomas Mock. Joseph S. Cotter, Sr. SPPH p.43; WSBO p.27

Thomas Wentworth Higginson (For his eighty-third birthday). William S. Braithwaite. HFL p.82

Thorn Forever in the Breast. Countee Cullen. B1C p.39; OTIS p.91

Thorns have the points, The. Ted Joans. BPW p.95

Thorny. Ted Joans. BPW p.95

Those black out lines in living flesh every day pressed to the window panes. Sarah Wright. BTB p.184

Those days of childish thought and joy will never come to me again. Charles Fred White. PONS p.135

Those days when it was all right to be a criminal or die, a postman's son. LeRoi Jones. BMP p.9

Those four Black girls blown up in that Alabama church. Michael S. Harper. DJDC p.62

Those things which you so laughing call hands. Nikki Giovanni. MyH p.18

Those Winter Sundays. Robert Hayden. BOR p.29; IADB p.10; SoS p.21; SPRH p.55

Thou arrant rubber, death! Paul Laurence Dunbar. CPPLD p.469

"Thou art a fool," said my head to my heart. Paul Laurence Dunbar. CPPLD p.6; LOLL p.6

Thou art far more to me than blight and bane. Leslie Pinckney Hill. AVAN p.199

Thou Art My Lute.** Paul Laurence Dunbar. CPPLD p.174

Thou art not dead, although the spoiler's hand. Lewis Alexander. ANP p.130; CaD p.123

Thou art the days man of the human soul. Joseph S. Cotter, Sr. LOF p.53

Thou art the soul of a summer's day. Paul Laurence Dunbar. AmNP p.13; CPPLD p.450

Thou little bird of happy song! Leslie Pinckney Hill. ANP p.76

Thou sweet-voiced stream that first gavest me drink. Claude McKay. SPCM p.17

Thou Too, Death! Nick Aaron Ford. SFD p.33

Thou who didst bid the fellow man. Joseph S. Cotter, Sr. RHY p.16

Thou who gave Homer, for his lack of sight a gift of song such as no other knew. Walter G. Arnold. EbR p.2

Thou. woman, art a jewel of great worth. Charles Fred White. PONS p.159

Though burdensome, your well-borne cross was life's own kiln. Raymond Dandridge. ZaP p.49

Though he hung dumb upon her wall. J. Henderson Brooks. BTh p.21; PoN p.135; PoNe p.239

Though I am not the first in **English** terms to name you of the earth's great nation's Queen. Countee Cullen. MASP p.74

Though I be cast by war onto the rat, the dark. Robert Hayden. HSITD p.20

Though I go drunken. Langston Hughes. FOW p.85

Though I score you with my best. Countee Cullen. CCC p.23
Though many are the dreams I dream. PAOP p.30; ZaP p.35
Though no more we hear the voice. Joseph S. Cotter, Sr. RHY p.17
Though the soil be e'er so fertile it will not yield up its fruit. Charles
    Fred White. PONS p.156
Though the winds be dank. Paul Laurence Dunbar. CPPLD p.113; LOLL p.168
Though thou did'st hear the tempest from a far. Phillis Wheatley. PAL p.70;
    PPW p.37
Though you have hurt your precious name. J. Henderson Brooks. BTh p.58
Though you refused a kiss I've known lesser things I've missed. William L.
    Morrison. DaR p.8
Though your love claims me. Mae V. Cowdery. WLOV p.53
Thought and Feeling. Joseph S. Cotter, Sr. LOF p.57
Thoughts. Raymond Dandridge. ZaP p.16
Thoughts. William L. Morrison. DaR p.62
Thoughts In a Zoo. Countee Cullen. CpS p.42
Thoughts of a Best Man While Standing Up for a Pal and Gal. John Raven. BFM
    p.16
Thoughts of Thanksgiving. Charles Fred White. PONS p.41
Thoughts on Death.** Sterling A. Brown. SoR p.131
Thoughts On the Works of Providence. Phillis Wheatley. EBAP p.101; PAL p.42;
    PPW p.19
Thrall. Georgia Douglas Johnson. HWOP p.23
Three Brown Girls Singing. H. Carl Holman. KAL p.165
Three days / out of Franklin. Victor Hernandez Cruz. SNA p.81
Three faces ... mirrored in the muddy stream of life. Margaret Walker. BrT
    p.152
Three For the Old Man. Albert Aubert. ATB p.21
Three from seven I've seen. Clifford Miller. BTB p.150
Three gray boys tracked us to an old house. LeRoi Jones. BMP p.106
Three Kings, The. Ruben Dario. MBP p.74
Three Kings. James P. Vaughn. NNPUSA p.24; PoNe p.399
Three kings went down to the soul of the sea. James P. Vaughn. NNPUSA p.24;
    PoNe p.399
Three Leaves. Robert Hayden. HSITD p.35
Three Modes of History and Culture. LeRoi Jones. MBP p.3
Three Movements and a Coda. LeRoi Jones. BMP p.103
Three Musicians. Joseph S. Cotter, Sr. SPPH p.73
Three Nonsense Rhymes For My Three Goddaughters. Countee Cullen. MASP p.78
Three northern sons of dixie forgot the earth Mississippi's history. Conrad
    Kent Rivers. SVH p.16
Three O'clock Love Song. Michael S. Harper. DJDC p.32
Three of us went to the top of the city a friend, my son, and I. June Jordan.
    SCh p.65
Three Poems For Gwendolyn Brooks. Delores Kendrick. TGWL p.60
Three poems for my daughter. Mae V. Cowdery. WLOV p.47
Three Sons. Conrad Kent Rivers. SVH p.16
Three students once tarried over the Rhine. James Weldon Johnson. CaD p.17;
    FYOP p.17
Threnody. Waring Cuney. AmNP p.99; BANP p.283; ITBLA p.160
Threnody. Donald Jeffrey Hayes. AmNP p.93
Threnody For a Brown Girl. Countee Cullen. GoS p.4; OTIS p.48

"Threshing Floor, The." Joseph S. Cotter, Sr. CPJSC p.49; LOF p.38
Thrice blessed is he who wields the flail. Joseph S. Cotter, Sr. CPJSC p.49;
    LOF p.38
Throned Upon Straw. William S. Braithwaite. SPWSB p.91
Through ages down time's ceaseless span. Raymond Dandridge. PAOP p.61
Through Agony. Claude McKay. HaS p.94; SPCM p.107
Through airy roads he wings his instant flight. Phillis Wheatley. PAL p.75;
    PPW p.31
Through by the glory of your lady's face. Countee Cullen. B1C p.23
Through the Holly Wreath. Effie Lee Newsome. ChG p.68
Through the long winter. Audre Lorde. NNPUSA p.20
Through the pregnant universe rumbles life's terrific thunder. Claude McKay.
    CaD p.84; HaS p.49
Through the Varied Patterned Lace. Owen Dodson. KAL p.129
Through thickest glooms look back, immortal shade. Phillis Wheatley. PAL
    p.39; PPW p.40
Throughout the afternoon I watched them there. Claude McKay. HaS p.76; SPCM
    p.98
Throwing out the flowers. Gwendolyn Brooks. AnA p.11
Thunder blossoms gorgeously above our heads. Jean Toomer. BLIA p.165
Thunder of the rain God. Langston Hughes. CaD p.152; FOW p.73; LUP p.30
Thunder Showers. Bernie Casey. LATP p.23
Thunder showers are forecast for the moment. Bernie Casey. LATP p.23
Thunderstorm. Dudley Randall. LoY p.8
Thurid. Bernie Casey. LATP p.87
Thurid what a strange and interesting name. Bernie Casey. LATP p.87
Thy omnipresence, Lord of Hosts, will be my fort throughout the year. Ray-
    mond Dandridge. ZaP p.51
Thy tones are silver melted into sound. Paul Laurence Dunbar. CPPLD p.186
Thy various works imperial queen, we see. Phillis Wheatley. AVAN p.28; CNAW
    p.13; EBAP p.107; PAL p.76; PoN p.7; PoNe p.9; PPW p.29
"Thy Works Shall Praise Thee." Charles R. Dinkins. AVAN p.113
Ti. Melvin Tolson. LRL p.30
Ticket Sellin. John Raven. BFM p.29
Tide of March. Ted Joans. AFR p.10
Tiger. Claude McKay. BLIA p.168; SPCM p.47
Tight grip but loose reins hold in harness. Sarah Webster Fabio. TGWL p.34
Tight Rope. LeRoi Jones. BMP p.13
Till the Sun Goes Down. Marvin X. BrT p.155
Till the Wind gets Right. Paul Laurence Dunbar. CPPLD p.433
Tim Muphy's gon' walkin' wie Maggie O'Neill. Paul Laurence Dunbar. CPPLD
    p.431
Timbuctu? They snigger in London. Ted Joans. BPW p.82
Time. Dio Lewis. EbR p.102
Time. George Reginald Margetson. ANP p.57; AVAN p.169
Time and Tide. Hazel Washington Lamarre. PoNe p.360
Time Capsule. Robert Hayden. HSITD p.48
Time is swift and the days step upon one another's heels. Countee Cullen.
    EbR p.149
Time is Young. William C. Braithwaite. VER p.108
Time Poem. Quentin Hill. NBP p.68

Time Sitting on the Throne of Memory. William S. Braithwaite. CaD p.32; HFL
    p.40; SPWSB p.83
Time to Die. Raymond Dandridge. ANP p.91; BANP p.190; PAOP p.16; ZaP p.23
Time to Tinker 'Roun! Paul Laurence Dunbar. CPPLD p.215
Time to wipe away the slime from inner rooms of thinking. Margaret Walker.
    PFND p.9
Time unhinged the gates of Plymouth Rock and Jamestown and Ellis Island.
    Melvin Tolson. RWA p.3
Time would not wait on me. Hazel Washington Lamarre. PoNe p.360
Times - Square - Shoeshine - Composition. Maya Angelou. JGM p.30
Timid Lover. Countee Cullen. CpS p.20
Tired. Fenton Johnson. BANP p.144; BLIA p.125; IADB p.80; KAL p.41; PoN
    p.62; PoNe p.88; TYBP p.210
Tired. Georgia Douglas Johnson. HWOP p.31
Tired cars go grumbling by, The. Claude McKay. GoS p.129; HaS p.60; SPCM
    p.62
Tin Roof Blues. Sterling A. Brown. SoR p.105
Tinabout Eka sell the sick camel and trade skins of gazelles for tobacco.
    Ted Joans. AFR p.44
Tiny firebugs nestle on the avenue. William L. Morrison. DaR p.35
Tired poem / slightly negative / more positive. Carolyn Rodgers. BlSp
    p.178
Tired Worker, The. Claude McKay. BANP p.172; HaS p.44; SPCM p.79
'Tis a pleasant Sunday morning and the sun is shining clear. Charles Fred
    White. PONS p.47
'Tis an old deserted homestead. Paul Laurence Dunbar. CPPLD p.467
'Tis Difficult. Ethel Brown. BTh p.50
'Tis difficult to read man's face aright. Ethel Brown. BTh p.50
'Tis done! the treach'rous deed is done. Elymas Payson Rogers. EBAP p.64
'Tis fine to play. Paul Laurence Dunbar. CPPLD p.381
'Tis not winter time yet. Charles Fred White. PONS p.40
'Tis queer, it is, the ways o' men. Angelina Weld Grimke. CaD p.39
'Tis strange indeed to hear us plead. Joseph S. Cotter, Sr. CPJSC p.71;
    WSBO p.39
'Tis strange that we should fall apart. William S. Braithwaite. LOLL p.15
Title it a smell. LeRoi Jones. BMP p.223
To ___. William S. Braithwaite. LLL p.75
To ___. Raymond Garfield Dandridge. PAOP p.30; ZaP p.35
To ___. Frank Horne. CaD p.118
To a Beauty. Joseph S. Cotter. LOF p.50
To A Bird. Raymond Dandridge. PAOP p.26; ZaP p.103
To a Black Dancer in "The Little Savoy." Langston Hughes. WeB p.35
To a Brown Boy. Countee Cullen. CCC p.8
To a Brown Girl. Ossie Davis. PoNe p.378
To a Brown Girl. Countee Cullen. CCC p.7
To a Brown Lass. V. A. Reese. BTh p.40
To a Brown-Skin Maiden. William L. Morrison. DaR p.18
To a Bunch of Carnations. Charles Fred White. PONS p.117
To a Caged Canary in a Negro Restaurant. Leslie Pinckney Hill. ANP p.76
To a Captious Critic. Paul Laurence Dunbar. CPPLD p.307; KAL p.19; MBP p.33
To a Certain Lady in Her Garden. Sterling A. Brown. SoR p.124; CaD p.136
To a Certain Woman. Albert Rice. CaD p.178

To a Child That Was. Mari Evans. IABW p.43
To a Clergyman on the Death of His Lady. Phillis Wheatley. PAL p.84; PPW
    p.24
To a Creek. William L. Morrison. DaR p.28
To a Dark Girl. Gwendolyn Bennett. ANP p.128; BANP p.243; CaD p.157
To a Dead Friend. Paul Laurence Dunbar. CPPLD p.352
To a Detractor. John Raven. BFM p.31
To a Disease Bearer. John Raven. BFM p.22
To a Fountain. Lucy Mae Turner. BCP p.59
To a Freedom Fighter. Maya Angelou. JGM p.33
To a Friend. Charles Fred White. PONS p.119
To a Friend in D.C. Craig Williamson. AfW p.46
To a Gentleman and Lady on the Death of the Lady's Brother and Sister and a
    Child of the Name of Avis, Aged One Year. Phillis Wheatley. AVAN p.30;
    PAL p.68; PPW p.69
To a Gentleman of the Navy (For the Royal American Magazine). Phillis
    Wheatley. PPW p.81
To a Gentleman on His Voyage to Great Britain for the Recovery of His Health.
    Phillis Wheatley. PAL p.66; PPW p.41
To a Good Wife. Nick Aaron Ford. SFD p.16
To a Husband. Maya Angelou. JGM p.14
To a Lady and Her Children, on the Death of her son and Their Brother.
    Phillis Wheatley. PAL p.69; PPW p.38
To a Lady on her Coming to North America with Her Son, for the Recovery of
    her Health. Phillis Wheatley. PAL p.71; PPW p.36
To a Lady on her Remarkable Preservation in a Hurricane in North Carolina.
    Phillis Wheatley. PAL p.70; PPW p.37
To a Lady on the Death of her Husband. Phillis Wheatley. PAL p.38; PPW p.12
To a Lady on the Death of Three Relations. Phillis Wheatley. PAL p.86; PPW
    p.23
To a Lady Playing the Harp. Paul Laurence Dunbar. CPPLD p.186
To a Little Lover Lass, Dead. Langston Hughes. WeB p.31
To a Man. Maya Angelou. JGM p.6
To a Mountain Laurel. William L. Morrison. DaR p.13
To a Mythical Charlie. Joseph S. Cotter, Sr. SPPH p.12
To a Negro Boy Graduating. Eugene T. Maleska. PoNe p.569
To a Nickel. Lucy Mae Turner. BCP p.57
To a Persian Rose. William S. Braithwaite. LLL p.16
To a Poet. Claude McKay. HaS p.57
To a Persistent Phantom. Frank Horne. AmNP p.50; BANP p.277; CaD p.113
To a Rain Drop. Nick Aaron Ford. SFD p.32
To a Rose. William L. Morrison. DaR p.59
To a Rose at Williston. Charles Fred White. PONS p.108
To a Rosebud. Eva Jesse. ANP p.80
To a Single Shadow Without Pity. Sam Cornish. NBP p.39
To a Skull. Joshua Henry Jones. ANP p.63; BANP p.201
To a Violet Found On All Saints Day! Paul Laurence Dunbar. CPPLD p.288
To a Wild Rose. William Edgar Bailey. ANP p.119
To a Winter Squirrel. Gwendolyn Brooks. ITM p.35
To a Woman Who Wants Darkness and Time. Gerald W. Barrax. AKOR p.20
To a Wounded Bird. Hilda Preer. BTh p.36

To-day the brilliant sunbeam hangs o'er all our joys our cares. Charles Fred
      White. PONS p.103
To Die Before One Wakes Must Be Glad. Alice Walker. ONC p.76
To Don at Salaam. Gwendolyn Brooks. FaP p.16
To dreamy languors and the violet mist. George Marion McClellan. BANP p.96
To E. H. K. Paul Laurence Dunbar. CPPLD p.153
To E.K.E. William S. Braithwaite. SPWSB p.89
To Egypt. Gloria Davis. NBP p.46
To Eliza. George Moses Horton. CNAW p.38; EBAP p.20
To Endymion. Countee Cullen. BTB p.79; CpS p.76; OTIS p.71
To enjoy the spider's web. Joseph S. Cotter, Sr. SPPH p.72
To every man his treehouse. James A. Emanuel. AmNP p.174; BrT p.45; NNPUSA
      p.45
To Fanon. Keorapetse W. Kgositsile. BrT p.77
To Fanon, Culture Meant Only One Thing - an Environment Shaped to Help Us &
      Our Children Grow Shaped by Ourselves in Action Against the System that
      Ensalabes Us. Sonia Sanchez. WABP p.50
To feed my soul with beauty till I die. William S. Braithwaite. AVAN p.143;
      HFL p.101
To Fez Cobra. Ted Joans. AFR p.33
To Fiona. William S. Braithwaite. HFL p.30
To Fiona. Nineteen Months Old. William S. Braithwaite. HFL p.31
To fling my arms wide. Langston Hughes. AmNP p.66; BLIA p.196; CaD p.149;
      DYTB p.40; FNP p.27; IADB p.100; PoN p.97; PoNe p.183; WeB p.43
To Florence. Joseph S. Cotter, Jr. BOG p.28
To France. Countee Cullen. MASP p.74
To France. Countee Cullen. OTIS p.156; MASP p.71
To free every African. Ted Joans. AFR p.34
To Gwen. Tejumola Ologboni. TGWL p.77
To Gwen Brooks. John Chenault. TGWL p.17
To Gwen Brooks. Edward Christmas. TGWL p.6
To Gwen, No Luv. Carolyn M. Rodgers. TGWL p.84
To Gwen With Love. Jon Eckels. TGWL p.32
To Gwendolyn Brooks. R. M. Dennis. TGWL p.30
To Gwendolyn Brooks. Etheridge Knight. TGWL p.65
To Gwendolyn Brooks the Creator in the Beginning - Words. Barbara A.
      Reynolds. TGWL p.83
To H. P. L. Charles Fred White. PONS p.51
To Her. Paul Laurence Dunbar. CPPLD p.440
To him who knoweth not the value of his life nor careth aught for that which
      elevateth him. Charles Fred White. PONS p.60
To His Honor the Lieutenant Governor, On The Death Of His Lady, March 24,
      1773. Phillis Wheatley. PAL p.47; PPW p.55
To hold my own hand in some secret place away from television. Ted Joans.
      AFR p.85
To Hollyhocks. George Marion McClellan. AVAN p.94
To Horace Bumstead. James Weldon Johnson. FYOP p.10
To intoxicate you with the wine of things. Duracine Vaval. PoN p.360
To J. Q. Paul Laurence Dunbar. CPPLD p.387
To James. Frank Horne. BTB p.121; GoS p.94; PoN p.82; PoNe p.82
To James Brown. Michael S. Harper. DJDC p.54
To James Weldon Johnson. Georgia Holloway Jones. EbR p.98

To One Unknown. Charles Fred White. PONS p.166
To one unknown to me. Charles Fred White. PONS p.166
To One Who Said Me Nay. Countee Cullen. CCC p.79
To One Who Was Cruel. Countee Cullen. CpS p.34
To Otis Redding. Kali Grosvenor. PBK p.48
To Our Boys. Irvin W. Underhill. ANP p.108
To Our First Born or the Prophet Arrives. Ebon. BrT p.160
To Our Friends. Lucian B. Watkins. BANP p.212
To Paul Robeson. Jean Brierre. EbR p.12
To Paul Robeson, Opus no. 3. Percy Edward Johnston. CNAW p.772
To Pfrimmer. Paul Laurence Dunbar. CPPLD p.456
To poor and humble farmers, was born near Christmas Night. Eloise Culver.
    GANIV p.55
To Popwell, my Friend, a Black Actor. Arthur Boze. BlWe p.19
To praise the blue whale's crystal jet. Derek Walcott. TYBP p.113
To President Taft's Young Son, Master Charlie on Sending Him a Copy of "The
    Sequel to the Pied Piper of Hamelin. Joseph S. Cotter, Sr. WSBO p.28
To Reggie. Frenchy J. Hodges. BlW p.14
To rest your body to lay it down in bed. Ted Joans. BPW p.28
To Richard Wright. Conrad Kent Rivers. AmNP p.117; IADB p.54
To ride piggy-back to the market of death thence to purchase a slave. Lang-
    ston Hughes. PATL p.77
To Roy Rolfe Gilson. William S. Braithwaite. HFL p.103
To Sallie Walking. Sterling A. Brown. SoR p.39
To Satch (or American Gothic). Samuel Allen. AmNP p.140; BTB p.176; CNAW
    p.616; IADB p.55; KAL p.147; MBP p.86; PoNe p.343; SoS p.58; TYBP p.244
To Scipio Moorhead, a Young African Painter, On Seeing His Works. Phillis
    Wheatley. EBAP p.110; ITBLA p.29; PAL p.58; PPW p.54
To see you standing in the sagging bookstore door. Margaret Danner. NNPUSA
    p.31
To shout / rave / rant / and rage is being militant. Ted Joans. BPW p.34
To show the lab'ring bosom's deep intent. Phillis Wheatley. EBAP p.110;
    ITBLA p.29; PAL p.58; PPW p.54
To sire a Hercules, a Moses or a son of man, keep your feet clean. Alvin
    Aubert. ATB p.30
To Some People. Langston Hughes. FOW p.19
To spin a tale of Africa takes devoted heart and hands. Eloise Culver.
    GANIV p.62
To stand with you at close of day with sunset in our eyes. Will Smallwood.
    EbR p.129
To Strike For Night. Lebert Bethune. NBP p.27
To Telie. Frank Horne. CaD p.118; PoN p.80; PoNe p.152
To Tell the truth, each piece he read. Joseph S. Cotter. EBAP p.190; LOF
    p.44; SPPH p.93
To test himself God spoke the heavens unfurled. Joseph S. Cotter, Sr. WSBO
    p.25
To The Clay. Raymond Dandridge. ZaP p.57
To The Dark Mercedes of "El Palacio De Amor." Langston Hughes. WeB p.90
To The Dunbar High School: a Sonnet. Angelina Grimke. ANP p.87
To the Eastern Shore. Paul Laurence Dunbar. CPPLD p.329; WMS p.121
To the eyes of poets past and the breasted rise of loves bombing. Craig
    Williamson. AfW p.25

To the   TITLE AND FIRST LINE INDEX

To the First of August. Ann Plato. EBAP p.117
To the Freedom Riders. Eloise Culver. GANIV p.78
To the Girls of Kenwood. Charles Fred White. PONS p.53
To the Hon'ble Thomas Hubbard Esq: on the Death of Mrs. Thankfull Leonard
    (1773). Phillis Wheatley. PAL p.59; PPW p.77
To the Honorable T. H. Esq. on the Death of His Daughter. Phillis Wheatley.
    PAL p.61; PPW p.46
To the King's Most Excellent Majesty (1768). Phillis Wheatley. PAL p.34;
    PPW p.6
To the Man in the Yellow Terry. Alice Walker. ONC p.49
To the Memory of Joseph S. Cotter, Jr. Joseph S. Cotter, Sr. SPPH p.44
To the Memory of Mary Young. Paul Laurence Dunbar. CPPLD p.130; LOLL p.193
To the Memory of Mrs. Sallie Brown. Joseph S. Cotter, Sr. SPPH p.39; WSBO
    p.52
To the Memory of the Rev. Andrew Heath. Joseph S. Cotter, Sr. RHY p.17
To the Men of the Soviet Army. H. Binga Dismond. EbR p.58
To the Singer. Helen C. Harris. EbR p.79
To the Men Who Held the Line. Curtis Smith. BTh p.52
To the Miami. Paul Laurence Dunbar. CPPLD p.457
To the Organ. Charles Fred White. PONS p.106
To the Rev. Dr. Thomas Amory, on Reading His Sermons on Daily Devotion in
    Which that Duty is Recommended and Assistence. Phillis Wheatley. PAL
    p.65; PPW p.42
To the Rev. Mr. Pitkin, on the Death of His Lady (1772). Phillis Wheatley.
    PAL p.40; PPW p.76
To the Right Honorable William, Earl of Dartmouths, His Majesty's Principal
    Secretary of State For North America, Etc. Phillis Wheatley. KAL p.4;
    PAL p.73; PPW p.33; TYBP p.204
To the Road. Paul Laurence Dunbar. CPPLD p.262
To the Sea. William S. Braithwaite. AVAN p.145
To the Smartweed. Leslie Pinckney Hill. AVAN p.199
To the South. Paul Laurence Dunbar. CPPLD p.352
To the Student. Alberry A. Whitman. ANP p.21; AVAN p.50
To the Survivors of Hiroshima and Nagasaki. Richard Thomas. BlSp p.200
To the Three for Whom the Book. Countee Cullen. BlC p.3; OTIS p.75
To the University of Cambridge, in New England (1767). Phillis Wheatley.
    CNAW p.10; EBAP p.99; PAL p.33; PPW p.5
To the University of Cambridge, wrote in 1767. Phillis Wheatley. PPW p.63
To the Veterans of Future Wars. Mae V. Cowdery. WLOV p.66
To the White Fiends. Claude McKay. BANP p.169; SPCM p.38
To the White Man. Valerie Tarver. TNV p.130
To the Wind of the Sight. Charles Fred White. PONS p.125
To touch! To burn my palm. Howard Carpenter. EbR p.27
To Toussaint L'Ouverture.* William Wordsworth. PoN p.226; PoNe p.447
To Vanity. Darwin T. Turner. PoNe p.401
To W. A. W. and H. H. William S. Braithwaite. LLL p.60
To walk in the muck of uncertainty. Henrietta C. Parks. TNV p.85
To Wanda. Frank Horne. BTB p.120; CaD p.120; PoN p.81; PoNe p.154
To wander through this living world. Langston Hughes. FOW p.33
To Whittier. Josephine Heard. EBAP p.262
To Williston at parting. Charles Fred White. PONS p.156
To whom should I speak today? Anonymous. TYBP p.26

To Winter. Claude McKay. HaS p.39; SPCM p.72
To write an outasight love poem for your eyes that slant. Ted Joans. AFR
    p.88
To you, who said, "my life is mine." Raymond Dandridge. ZaP p.13
To Yooglec. John Raven. BFM p.22
To you, so far away so cold, and aloof. Frank Horne. BTB p.120; CaD p.120;
    PoN p.81; PoNe p.154
To You Who Read My Book. Countee Cullen. CCC p.xiii; ANP p.97
Toast. Frank Horne. BANP p.277; PoN p.78; PoNe p.150
Today. Langston Hughes. FOW p.111
Today. Margaret Walker. FMP p.28
Today I saw a thing of arresting pignant beauty. Alice Dunbar Nelson. ANP
    p.85; CaD p.71
Today, I will see some empty spaces of people and how they go along. Michael
    Nicholas. NBP p.94
Today is a Day of Great Joy. Victor Hernandez Cruz. SNA p.29; TYBP p.260
Today oh! Oh today oh! Oh today oh! Anonymous. MBP p.55
Today: the Idea Market. Michael Nicholas. NBP p.94
Today the Prince of Peace was laid to rest. Craig Williamson. AfW p.50
Today the rain. Frank Marshall Davis. GoS p.100
Today, white rider, I feel you break through my dody. Craig Williamson.
    AfW p.42
Today's Pimp. Marion Nicholes. LiS p.12
Together. William L. Morrison. DaR p.52
Together. Carolyn Rodgers. BlSp p.176
Together we looked down. James A. Emanuel. KAL p.170; NNPUSA p.81
Toil Created. Raymond G. Dandridge. PAOP p.30; ZaP p.12
Toil, toil, toil, the days goes by, and what have I. Raymond Garfield
    Dandridge. PeP p.41
Toiler, The. Raymond Garfield Dandridge. PeP p.41
Toiling, toiling all day long with his will and might. Charles Fred White.
    PONS p.72
Toll the bell and cover love from head to foot. J. Henderson Brooks. BTh
    p.18
Tom-Tom Echoes. William L. Morrison. DaR p.47
Tom-tom sun awakens day's jungle with heat beats, A. Frank Marshall Davis.
    GoS p.7
Tomorrow's Democracy. William L. Morrison. DaR p.30
Tomorrow's Men. Georgia Douglas Johnson. GoS p.51
Tomorrow's Winds. Samuel E. Boyd. EbR p.8
Tomorrow's winds will blow my brain as clear, as calm, as cool. Samuel E.
    Boyd. EbR p.8
Tone Poem. LeRoi Jones. BMP p.28
Tone Row. LeRoi Jones. BMP p.35
Tonight I push aside my own small dream. Peter Wellington Clark. EbR p.37
Tonight I talked to Jesus. Owen Dodson. BTB p.91; CNAW p.395
Tonight it is the wine. Alice Walker. ONC p.75
Tonight the machinery of shadow moves into the light. June Jordan. SCh p.39
Tonight the waves march in long ranks. Langston Hughes. DYTB p.52; FOW p.6
Tonight when the moon comes out. Nicolas Guillen. MBP p.4; PoN p.380; TYBP
    p.104

Tonight when you spread your pallet of magic I escaped. Maya Angelou. JGM
    p.15
Tonite, thriller was abt an ol woman. Ishmael Reed. SoS p.64
Tongue-tied. Countee Cullen. BlC p.27
Too Blue. Langston Hughes. OWT p.102
Too frail to soar - a feeble thing - it fell to earth with fluttering wing.
    Frances Harper. PBFH p.21
Too green the springing April grass. Claude McKay. BANP p.171; CNAW p.293;
    GoS p.74; HaS p.40; PoN p.329; PoNe p.97; KAL p.46; SPCM p.15
Too many years beatin' at the door. Langston Hughes. PATL p.50
Top Creeps. Ted Joans. BPW p.89
Too often do we voice our ills. Raymond Dandridge. ZaP p.40
Tormented. Claude McKay. HaS p.82; SPCM p.101
Totality. Mae V. Cowdery. WLOV p.33
Touch, The. Countee Cullen. AVAN p.210; CpS p.87
Touch me, touch me. Angelina Weld Grimke. CaD p.38
Touch of God like structure, The. LeRoi Jones. BMP p.56
Touch our bodies, wind. Langston Hughes. FOW p.75
Touche. Jessie Fauset. CaD p.66
Toughest gal I ever did see. Margaret Walker. FMP p.38
Tour 5. Robert Hayden. BLIA p.253; BOR p.9; SPRH p.41
Tourists. Bernie Casey. LATP p.79
Tourists in the courtyard. Nicolas Guillen. PoN p.374; TYBP p.106
Toussaint L'Ouverture. Raymond Garfield Dandridge. PAOP p.63
Toussaint L'Ouverture.* Edwin Arlington Robinson. PoN p.227; PoNe p.471
Toussaint sticking out his tongue at Napoleon Bonaparte. Peter Wellington
    Clark. EbR p.39
Toussaint, the most unhappy man of men.* William Wordsworth. PoN p.226;
    PoNe p.447
Toward a Personal Semantics. June Jordan. SCh p.36
Town Fathers, The. Melvin Tolson. BTB p.22; LUP p.47
Toy Poem. Nikki Giovanni. BrT p.69
Tracin' Tales. Raymond Garfield Dandridge. AVAN p.192; PAOP p.51; ZaP p.74
Traffic Signs. Cornelius V. Troup. EbR p.144
Tragedy. Ritten Edward Lee. EbR p.100
Tragedy of Pete. Joseph S. Cotter, Sr. CaD p.11; PoN p.14; SPPH p.53
Trail behind me narrows to a point, The. Michael S. Harper. DJDC p.19
Trail-Breaker. William S. Braithwaite. SPWSB p.22
Train Ride, The. George B. Browne. EbR p.16
Trailing night's sand-sitted stars. Georgia Douglas Johnson. HWOP p.7
Train, The. Anonymous. TYBP p.9
Train Runs Late to Harlem, The. Conrad Kent Rivers. IADB p.89
Training. Demetrio Herreras. TYBP p.108
Traitor, The. Don L. Lee. DSNP p.73
Traitor to France, The. Melvin Tolson. RWA p.64
'Trane. Clarence Reed. BlSp p.172
Transformation. Lewis Alexander. CaD p.124; PoN p.85; PoNe p.160
Transfusion. Arthur Boze. BlWo p.6
Transition and middle passage. Don L. Lee. BrT p.114; DSNP p.180; WWW p.56
Translated furies ring on the page not thoughts bout life. Keorapetse W.
    Kgositsile. BrT p.27; FoM p.55
Translation. Anne Spencer. BANP p.218

T'ward the last of bleak December when the northern fields are bare. Charles
    Fred White. PONS p.30
Twas a fearful night--the tempest raved. Frances Harper. EBAP p.29; PBFH
    p.35
Twas a night of dreadful horror. Frances Harper. PBFH p.52
'Twas at early morning. James W. Johnson. FYOP p.56
'Twas evening, and the wintry white glistened beneath the star-lit sky.
    George Hannibal Temple. AVAN p.104
'Twas kind of the omnipotent to blow his warm breath on the day. Charles
    Fred White. PONS p.138
'Twas mercy brought me from my pagan land. Phillis Wheatley. CNAW p.11;
    EBAP p.100; KAL p.7; PAL p.92; PPW p.7; TYBP p.205
'Twas Mother. Waverly T. Carmichael. FHOF p.49
'Twas the apple that in Eden. Paul Laurence Dunbar. CPPLD p.412
'Twas three an' thirty years ago. Paul Laurence Dunbar. CPPLD p.43; LOLL
    p.61
Twell De Night is Pas'. Paul Laurence Dunbar. CPPLD p.415
Twelve bells **Bennys on the ropes.***   Frank Lima. PoNe p.58
20th-Century Fox. LeRoi Jones. BMP p.84
Twenty-three is Next. Ted Joans. AFR p.99
Twenty years go by on noiseless feet. James Weldon Johnson. FYOP p.25
Twilight. Paul Laurence Dunbar. CPPLD p.394
Twilight and Dreams. William S. Braithwaite. LLL p.44
Twilight Reverie. Langston Hughes. SIH p.3
Twin stars through my prupling pane. Angelina Weld Grimke. CaD p.46
Twinkling Gown. Dorothy Vena Johnson. GoS p.189
Twist, The. Edward Braithwaite. MBP p.13
Twisted and strange their lives with bitter ranges. Langston Hughes. FOW
    p.86
Twitching in the cactus hospital gown. Michael S. Harper. DJDC p.65
'Twixt a Smile and a Tear. Paul Laurence Dunbar. CPPLD p.394
Two-an'six. Claude McKay. BANP p.176; GoS p.45
Two baths in one day! Don L. Lee. DSNP p.158; WWW p.34
Two Countries. Jose Marti. TYBP p.191
Two countries have I, Cub and the night. Jose Marti. TYBP p.101
Two Epitaphs: 1. For the Unknown Soldier (Paris). Countee Cullen. B1C p.14
Two Epitaphs: 2. For a Child Still-Born. Countee Cullen. B1C p.14
Two football teams met one day down on the gridiron gay. Charles Fred White.
    PONS p.162
Two For Malcolm. Patricia. FoM p.31
Two-gun Buster and Trigger Slim. Margaret Walker. FMP p.42
Two-gun Buster was a railroad hand. Margaret Walker. FMP p.42
224 Stoop. Victor Hernandez Cruz. **BOL p.68**
221-1424 (San/ Francisco / Suicide / Number. Sonia Sanchez. WABP p.12
Two Jazz Poems. Carl Wendell Hines, Jr. AmNP p.184; KAL p.227
Two ladies bidding us "Good Morning." James P. Vaughn. NNPUSA p.63
Two Lean Cats ... Myron O'Higgins. PoN p.196; PoNe p.350
Two Little Boots. Paul Laurence Dunbar. CPPLD p.261; WMS p.21
Two little boots, all rough **an' wo',** two little boots! Paul Laurence Dunbar.
    CPPLD p.261; WMS p.23
Two little children sit by my side. Frances Harper. PBFH p.56
Two Love Songs. Craig Williamson. AfW p.12

Vain and defeated each effort of life feeble and hoary sick of the strife.
    James E. McGirt. FYSS p.42
Vale Dice. Charles Fred White. PONS p.99
Valedictory. Countee Cullen. B1C p.58
Valuation. Raymond Dandridge. PAOP p.24
Valued Lesson, A. Charles Fred White. PONS p.96
Values. Georgia Douglas Johnson. ANP p.87
Vanity of vanities. Countee Cullen. CCC p.66
Vari-Colored Song. Langston Hughes. PATL p.98
Variations on a Theme. Countee Cullen. CpS p.24; OTIS p.55
Variety. William Thompson Goss. EbR p.72
Vashti. Frances Harper. EBAP p.34; PBFH p.44
Vashti. James Weldon Johnson. FYOP p.57; PBFH p.44
Vast realm beyond the gate of death. Raymond Dandridge. PAOP p.48; ZaP p.25
Vaticide. Myron Higgins. IADB p.51; KAL p.161
Veiled Again. Marion Nicholes. LiS p.17
Veldt Men pray, The. Melvin Tolson. RWA p.87
Venereal moon draws six women to the Missouri River, The. Michael S. Harper.
    DJDC p.36
Vengeance is Sweet. Paul Laurence Dunbar. CPPLD p.155
Venus in a Garden. James Weldon Johnson. FYOP p.56
Venusberg, The. George Marion McLlelan. EBAP p.130
Vera Cruz. Robert Hayden. AmNP p.119; BOR p.47; SPRH p.29
Verdict, The. Owen Dodson. PLL p.83
Verse, as a form is artificial. LeRoi Jones. BMP p.41
Verse upon verse has been written. Zachary Withers. PAS p.17
Verse written in the Album of Mademoiselle. Pierre Dalcour. MBP p.24; PoN
    p.12; PoNe p.16; TYBP p.97
Verses to the Lady of the Pearls. Alexandre Dumas. TYBP p.70
Very acme of my woe, The. Georgia Douglas Johnson. AVAN p.209; CaD p.76
Very Fine. LeRoi Jones. BMP p.139
Very friendly prison this is, A. Gayl Jones. SoS p.13
Very proud he barely asked directions to a nearby hotel. Alice Walker. ONC
    p.69
Very soon the Yankee teachers. Frances Harper. CNAW p.106; EBAP p.37
Vesuvius. Melvin Tolson. RWA p.73
Veteran, The. Paul Laurence Dunbar. CPPLD p.422
Vicious Negro, The. Joseph S. Cotter, Sr. CPJSC p.22; WSBO p.53
Victor of today is the vanquished of tomorrow, The. Ahmed A. Alhamisi. GuW
    p.9
Victoria the Queen. James E. McGirt. FYSS p.51
Vie c'est La Vie, La. Jessie Fauset. BANP p.205; CaD p.69; PoN p.65; PoNe
    p.67
Vietnam: I Need More Than This Crust of Salt. Lance Jeffers. BrT p.72
Vietnam is muddy. Julius Lester. SoS p.66
Vietnam #4. Clarence Major. BOL p.48
Vieux Carre. Walter Adolphe Roberts. PoN p.316; PoNe p.84
View From the Corner. Samuel Allen. BrT p.159
Views. Melvin Tolson. RWA p.32
Vignette. John W. Burton. EbR p.19
Village Blues (After a story by John O. Stewart). Michael S. Harper. DJDC
    p.9

Village Voice, The. Ted Joans. BPW p.63
Villages of high quality merchandise. Michael S. Harper. DJDC p.42
Villanelle of the living pan. Walter Adolphe Roberts. PoN p.314
Villanelle of Washington Square. Walter Adolphe Roberts. PoN p.313; PoNe
    p.83
Villain show his indiscretion. Paul Laurence Dunbar. CPPLD p.65; LOLL p.93
Violent Space, The. Etheridge Knight. BLIA p.423; BrT p.81
Violetta you beauty revives the splendor of the Indian Age. Jean Brierre.
    EbR p.9
Virgin Field. Arthur Braziel. EbR p.9
Virgin Mary had a Baby Boy, The.** Anonymous. BLIA p.41; ChG p.95
Virginia Portrait. Sterling A. Brown. SoR p.27
Vision, A. Sarah Collins Fernandis. AVAN p.212
Vision a Poem in Blank Verse. John Boyd. EBAP p.148
Vision of a scion of a despised and rejected race, The. Kelly Miller. ANP
    p.110
Visit, The. LeRoi Jones. BMP p.40
Visit of the Professor of Aesthetics, The. Margaret Danner. NNPUSA p.31
Visit to Oak-Lodge, A. William S. Braithwaite. HFL p.80
Visitor, The. Paul Laurence Dunbar. CPPLD p.284; WMS p.97
Visitors. John Raven. BFM p.16
Visitors to the Black Belt. Langston Hughes. OWT p.65
Vive Noir. Mari Evans. BOL p.50; CNAW p.765; IABW p.70
Vivid grass with visible delight springing triumphant from the pregnant earth,
    The. Claude McKay. HaS p.48; SPCM p.73
Voice above the wind, A. Gus Bertha. TGWL p.13
Voice cries from the wilderness saying "now must you try yourselves." J. Hen-
    derson Brooks. BTh p.67
Voice has gone out of the wilderness, The. Julia Fields. FoM p.33.
Voice in the Crowd. Ted Joans. AmNP p.172; BOL p.14; BPW p.1; KAL p.191;
    TYBP p.247
Voice of the Banjo, The. Paul Laurence Dunbar, CPPLD p.199
Voice of the Hill. Herman J. D. Carter. EbR p.27
Voice of the Ocean, The. Joseph S. Cotter, Sr. LOF p.48
Voice of the Sea.** William S. Braithwaite. LLL p.54
Voice of the Wreck, The. Raymond Dandridge. ZaP p.19
Voice speaks often words which are not uttered. Charles Fred White. PONS
    p.73
Void. William Morrison. DaR p.48
Void. Gordon Parks. InL (unpaged)
Voluptas. James Weldon Johnson. FYOP p.47
Vowels 2. LeRoi Jones. BMP p.189
Voyage of Jimmy Poo, The. James A. Emanuel. AmNP p.174; NNPUSA p.97
Vultures, The. David Diop. TYBP p.138
Vultures hover wheel and hover, The. Robert Hayden. BOR p.46; SPRH p.27

- W -

W. W. LeRoi Jones. BMP p.137; NBP p.78
Wading in de Crick. Paul Laurence Dunbar. CPPLD p.390; WMS p.129
Wah-hoo Mama-tits pluck me when its over my mind is a dying hawd. Gylan
    Kain. BlSp p.100

Waiting. Paul Laurence Dunbar. CPPLD p.160

Wakamba in the East. Ted Joans. AFR p.28

Wake. Langston Hughes. SIH p.65

Wake Cry. Waring Cuney. BANP p.285

Wake For Papa Montero. Nicolas Guillen. PoN p.377

Wake, for the day-spring thrills the landscape through. William C. Braith-
waite. VER p.110

Wake up, boy, and tell me how you died. Owen Dodson. PLL p.3

Wake-up Niggers (you aint part Indian). Don L. Lee. DSNP p.40

Wakeupworld, The. Countee Cullen. GoS p.103; OTIS p.185

Walk, God's Chillun. Lucile D. Goodlett. WGC p.37

Walk out into your country. James Randall. BrT p.131

Walk right in, **Brother** Wilson--how you feelin' today? Alex Rogers. BANP
p.159

Walk self-conscious without a sky. James Cunningham. TGWL p.23

Walk this mile in silence. Donald Jeffrey Hayes. AmNP p.94

Walk with the mayor of Harlem. David Henderson. BlSp p.82

Walk with the sun. Lewis Alexander. PoN p.85; PoNe p.159

Walk within thy own heart's temple, child, and rest. Georgia Douglas Johnson.
HWOP p.38

Walkers with the Dawn. Langston Hughes. DYTB p.26

Walking on the lips of the Bronz. Victor Hernandez Cruz. SNA p.115

Wall, The. Don L. Lee. BrT p.89; DSNP p.66

Wall, The. For Edward Christmas. Gwendolyn Brooks. CNAW p.524; ITM p.42;
PoNe p.338

Wall of the newborn, cry of the dying. Robert Hayden. SPRH p.31

Wallace for president his momma for vice-president. Don L. Lee. DCS p.34;
DSNP p.102

Walls. Langston Hughes. FOW p.66

Walls. Ted Joans. BPW p.68

Walls are made of rain, The. LeRoi Jones. BMP p.33

Walls of Jericho, The. Blanche Taylor Dickinson. CaD p.106

Walls too crampy an' too narrer. Charles B. Johnson. SOMP p.42 ·

Walter Bradford. Gwendolyn Brooks. FaP p.17

Wandering in the dusk. Langston Hughes. FOW p.108

Want to trade me, do you mistah? oh well, now I reckon not. Paul Laurence
Dunbar. CPPLD p.306; CLT p.25

War. Langston Hughes. PATL p.59

War. William Alfred McLean, Jr. BOC p.53

War. Jesse Franklin Patterson. EbR p.113

War war why do God's children fight among each other like animals. Michael
Goode. SoS p.6

Warm day in Winter, A. Paul Laurence Dunbar. CPPLD p.269; WMS p.89

Warm me with your fingertips. Mari Evans. IABW p.24

Warnin' Hymn. Eli Shepperd. P1S p.119

Warning. Samuel A. Haynes. EbR p.80

Warning. Langston Hughes. PATL p.100

Warning. Alice Walker. ONC p.68

Warrior stood before his master, A. James E. McGirt. FYSS p.15

Warrior's Judgment, A. James E. McGirt. FYSS p.15

Warriors Prancing Women Dancing ...****** Nioma Rashidd. NBP p.107

Warrior's Prayer, The. Paul Laurence Dunbar. CPPLD p.197; AVAN p.63

Wars. Bernie Casey. LATP p.17
Wars are for killing. Bernie Casey. LATP p.16
War's Inspiration. Charles Fred White. PONS p.50
Was he 17 years a boy started the dove in mind. Clarence Major. SAM p.15
Was it because you went. William S. Braithwaite. SPWSB p.31
Was it you in Detroit. Michael S. Harper. DJDC p.52
Wash Baby. Harold Taylor. BTh p.41
Washer-Woman, The. Otto Leland Bohanan. BANP p.204
Washing hangs upon the line. Elizabeth Bishop. PoN p.288; PoNe p.550
Washington, true noble son of Ethiopia's pride. Waverly T. Carmichael. FHOF
    p.24
Washiri (poet). Kattie M. Cumbo. BOL p.12
Wasn't That a Mighty Day.** Anonymous. ChG p.94
Wass sat ..., Nonnie. Linda Brown. BTB p.54
"Watch and Pray." William C. Braithwaite. VER p.123
Watch out, Nigger man, what you 'bout, you'll sholy wear dat banjo out. Eli
    Shepperd. PlS p.37
Watch to Keep, A. Raymond Dandridge. ZaP p.28
Watchers, The. William S. Braithwaite. CNAW p.226; PoN p.42; PoNe p.48; LLL
    p.28; SPWSB p.57
Watching, The. Owen Dodson. PLL p.98
Watching you frown at your feet in the mirror. Alice Walker. ONC p.56
Water. William S. Braithwaite. SPWSB p.85
Water-Front Streets. Langston Hughes. DYTB p.60; WeB p.71
Waterbowl, The. Michael S. Harper. DJDC p.14
Watermelon. Ted Joans. BPW p.40
Watermelon. G. T. Smith. HeD p.38
Watermelon in de night. G. T. Smith. HeD p.38
Watermelon Vendor's. Anonymous. ITBLA p.125
Watermelon! Watermelon! red to the rind. Anonymous. ITBLA p.125
W'ats de matter wid you boy. Waverly Turner Carmichael. FHOF p.12
Watts. Conrad Kent Rivers. BOL p.41; SVH p.15
Wave of Sorrow, do not drown me now. Langston Hughes. DYTB p.58
Wave-Song, A. William C. Braithwaite. VER p.55
Waves dashed high! the thunders echoes far, The. Timothy Thomas Fortune.
    AVAN p.115
Way, The. William S. Braithwaite. BANP p.102
Way doun South where de wild rose grows by de stream as de water flows.
    Waverly T. Carmichael. FHOF p.30
Way down South in Dixie. Langston Hughes. CaD p.147; FCTJ p.75; FNP p.28;
    IADB p.67; PoN p.103
Way down South, there's an old, old Blackman. Ariel Williams. BTh p.31
Way Down Yonder. Ted Joans. AFR p.25
Way It Went Down, The. Larry Neal. BlSp p.149
Way-Side Well, The. Joseph S. Cotter, Sr. ANP p.33; CaD p.15; CPJSC p.44
    PoN p.14; PoNe p.18
Ways O' Men, The. Angelina Weld Grimké. CaD p.39
Ways of Black Folks, The. Joseph S. Cotter, Sr. CPJSC p.52
Wayward Child. David Llorens. TNV p.61
We. Nikki Giovanni. MyH p.65
We a Bad People. Sonia Sanchez. TGWL p.87
We a BadddDDD People. Sonia Sanchez. BrT p.141; WABP p.52

We all came screaming into the world. Herman L. McMillan.
We All Is. Ted Joans. AFR p.27
We all should endeavor to make others happy. Charles Fred White. PONS p.171
We are a host that every year drops in upon some city. Joseph S. Cotter, Sr.
    CPJSC p.71
We are all a part of the self same tree--the bark and the limbs are all skin.
    Eve Lynn. ChG p.98
We are all imprisoned in the castle of our skins. Nikki Giovanni. MyH p.46
We are among the skyscrapers. Langston Hughes. WeB p.101
We are Black But we are Men. George R. Dinkins. AVAN p.111
We are but a bleary blink of a bloodshot eye. Joseph R. Cowen. PoNe p.575
We are declare for liberty, Lincoln said. Melvin Tolson. RWA p.70
We are going to do it. Don L. Lee. BrT p.106; DCS p.63; DSNP p.129
We are in the era of imminent brake failure. LeRoi Jones. BMP p.74
We are meat in the air. LeRoi Jones. BMP p.224
We are not come to wage a strife. Arna Bontemps. AmNP p.76; CaD p.171; GoS
    p.181; IADB p.66; PoN p.119; PoNe p.223
We are the children of the sun. Fenton Johnson. ANP p.39; BANP p.141
We are the desperate. Langston Hughes. FOW p.63
"We Are the Hunted."** Robert Hayden. HSITD p.46
We are the screeeeeamers. Sonia Sanchez. WABP p.61
We are things of dry hours and the involuntary plan. Gwendolyn Brooks. PoN
    p.188
We are unfair. LeRoi Jones. BOL p.7
We ask for peace. We at the bound. Angelina Weld Grimke. CaD p.38
We assume: on the death of our son, Reuben Masai Harper. Michael S. Harper.
    DJDC p.63
We assume that in 28 hours, lived in a collapsible isolette, You learned to
    accept pure oxygen as the natural sky. Michael S. Harper. DJDC p.63
We Black People Should. Kali Grosvenor. PBK p.37
We buried him high on a windy hill. Langston Hughes. WeB p.81
We call love somethin blank and longed for. LeRoi Jones. BMP p.131
We can know Surely. Marion Cuthbert. SOC p.11
We caught the racist killer. Arthur Boze. BlWe p.19
We crawled and cried and laughed. Mbella Sonne Dipeke. TYBP p.142
We Dance Like Ella Riffs. Carolyn Rodgers. TNV p.113
We dared to trace yellow streaks of sun powder. Conrad Kent Rivers. SVH
    p.19
We delighted, my Friend.** Leopold Sedar Senghor. TYBP p.133
We die, welcoming bluebeards to our darkening closets. Maya Angelou. JGM
    p.13
We do not care--that much is clear. Langston Hughes. EbR p.88
We eat Better Now. Ahmed Akinwole Alhamisi. GuW p.6
We eat Chinese food on Broadway. Victor Hernandez Cruz. SNA p.57
We falter in our faith and say. William C. Braithwaite. VER p.123
We gave it life, mahogany hands loose in song. Michael S. Harper. DJDC p.58
We Have Been Believers. Margaret Walker. BTB p.179; CNAW p.530; FMP p.16;
    PoN p.180; PoNe p.312; SoS p.130
We have been believers believing in the Black gods of an old land. Margaret
    Walker. BTB p.179; CNAW p.530; FMP p.16; PoN p.180; PoNe p.312; SoS
    p.130

We have been through such pain for each other. William L. Morrison. DaR
 p.59

We have fashioned laughter out of tears and pain. Charles B. Johnson. SOMP
 p.34

We have found you out false faced America. Worth Long. NBP p.84

We have heard from whisperings running on the wind. Owen Dodson. PLL p.49

We have housed my Columbine. William S. Braithwaite. LLL p.39

We have neither summer nor winter. H. D. Carberry. PoN p.336

We have no time--yet time is all we have. George Reginald Margetson. ANP
 p.57; AVAN p.169

"We Have Not Forgotten."** Robert Hayden. HSITD p.10

We Have Tomorrow. Langston Hughes. DYTB p.25; FNP p.30; GoS p.9; LUP p.33
 WeB p.108

We hung from our windows & sat on the steps. Clarence Major. SAM p.42

We is gathahed hyeah my brothas. Paul Laurence Dunbar. CNAW p.206; CPPLD
 p.20; LOLL p.26

We just pushed back from our suppah sweeten taters baked wid poke. Raymond
 Dandridge. PeP p.26

We Know No More. Timothy Thomas Fortune. AVAN p.115

We know others. Don L. Lee. DSNP p.186; WWW p.62

We Launched a Ship. Ruby Berkley Goodwin. EbR p.69

We lay there drained of time. May Miller. CNAW p.361

We lay together, darkness all around. Michael S. Harper. DJDC p.28

We Lift Our Voices. Mae V. Cowdery. WLOV p.67

We live in fragments like speech. LeRoi Jones. BMP p.13

We make crazy lullabies heart pushing. LeRoi Jones. BMP p.65

We may sigh o'er the heavy burdens. Frances Harper. PBFH p.90

We met in the digest. Nikki Giovanni. BFBTBJ p.8

We met when the moon was new. William L. Morrison. DaR p.49

We move to the whispering after the dancing. Victor Hernandez Cruz. SNA
 p.49

We must work well the soil in the garden of life. Raymond Dandridge. PeP
 p.41

We never saw her. John Chenault. TGWL p.17

We Open infant eyes. Countee Cullen. OTIS p.163

We own the Night. LeRoi Jones. BOL p.7

We Pass. Beatrice M. Murphy. TNV p.139

We passed their graves. Langston Hughes. PATL p.56

We plunge through time and feel the westward pull of death. Larry Neal.
 BLIA p.398

We programmed fo death / die / on each day. Sonia Sanchez. WABP p.33

We Real Cool.** Gwendolyn Brooks. BTB p.51; CNAW p.521; IADB p.5; ITBLA
 p.217; MBP p.96; TYBP p.245

We remember Egypt. Robert Hayden. HSITD p.48

We run the dangercourse. Don L. Lee. DSNP p.188; WWW p.64

We saw a bloody sunset over courtland, once Jerusalem. Sterling A. Brown.
 CNAW p.408; PoN p.90; PoNe p.172

We saw Beyond Our Seeming.** Maya Angelou. JGM p.36

We say his is Black. Ted Joans. AFR p.27

We sell it to the rich, we sell it to the poor. Anonymous. ITBLA p.125

We set out yesterday upon a winter drive. Alexandre Dumas. TYBP p.70

We shall go on to the other side of the lake. Clarence Major. SAM p.27

We shall not always plant while other reap. Countee Cullen. ANP p.97; BANP
  p.228; CaD p.183; CpS p.3; IADB p.77; OTIS p.47; KAL p.103; PoN p.132;
  PoNe p.235
We should be as kind and cheerful as we can here on this earth. Charles Fred
  White. PONS p.95
We should have a land of sun. Langston Hughes. FNP p.29; WeB p.99
We sit alone on the pearl-dust couch of the shore. Melvin Tolson. LUP p.48;
  RWA p.18
We sit in our cabin corners waiting for God. Owen Dodson. BLIA p.259; PLL
  p.29
We stand befo u plain of bl / wooomen. Sonia Sanchez. WABP p.45
We stand mute! Georgia Douglas Johnson. HWOP p.5
We stand pinned to the electric mural. Michael S. Harper. DJDC p.44
We stir the unwarmin fire of slavery. Owen Dodson. PLL p.16
We stood there waiting on the corners. Nikki Giovanni. MyH p.65
We, the Black People. Arthur Boze. BlWe p.14
We trace the pow'r of death from tomb to tomb. Phillis Wheatley. PAL p.86;
  PPW p.23
We trekked into a far country. Anne Spencer. BANP p.218
"We use ardena here." Madame Celeste. Gwendolyn Brooks. AnA p.53
We used to gather at the high window. Quandra Prettyman. IADB p.56
We visit bark an unmarked grave. Michael S. Harper. DJDC p.7
We waded in the brook together and drank water from each other's Hands.
  Joseph S. Cotter, Sr. SPPH p.86
We waged a war without a war. Karl Shapiro. PoN p.283; PoNe p.563
We wake on the wrong side of morning. May Miller. BTB p.152
We walk back from the movies. William J. Harris. BOL p.69
We walk the way of the new world. Don L. Lee. DSNP p.188; WWW p.64
We watch the clouds gather in yonder sky. Zachary Withers. PAS p.1
We Wear the Mask That Grins and Lies.** Paul Laurence Dunbar. AmNP p.14;
  BLIA p.116; CaD p.8; CPPLD p.112; IADB p.86; ITBLA p.95; CNAW p.212;
  LOLL p.167; SoS p.134; TYBP p.208
Weather in Spain could ride in a train, The. LeRoi Jones. BMP p.99
We welcome you leader. Joseph S. Cotter, Sr. SPPH p.41
We went there to confer on the possibility of Blackness. BFBTBJ p.30
We were the first dead. Arthur Boze. BlWe p.14
We who have warred incessantly for near a score of years. James C. Morris.
  BTB p.155
We will be no generashuns to cum fer blks r killing r selves. Johari Amini.
  BlSp p.4
We wonder what the horoscope did show. Henrietta Cordelia Ray. EBAP p.140
We would be peaceful. Lucian Watkins. ANP p,122
Weak Dynamite. Clarence Major. SAM p.44
Weak scattered rays of yellow sun, The. John Mbiti. MBP p.49
Wear it like a banner. Langston Hughes. BOL p.3; DYTB p.73; PATL p.67
Wearing his equality like a too-small shoe. Vilma Howard. NNPUSA p.58
Weary Blues, The. Langston Hughes. FNP p.21; PoN p.98; PoNe p.184; WeB p.23
Weary, restless, now fever's minion furnace hot. Countee Cullen. CpS p.47
Weaving between assorted terrors is the Jew who owns the place. Langston
  Hughes. PATL p.10
Web, The. Robert Hayden. BOR p.31; SPRH p.56
We'd like to tell you about the Negro and his songs. Eloise Culver. GANIV p.19

Wed poem before Thanksgiving. Sonia Sanchez. WABP p.18
Weddah. Raymond Dandridge. PAOP p.34; ZaP p.72
Wedding, The. June Jordan. SCh p.6
Wedding Poem For Joseph and Evelyn Jenkins. Owen Dodson. PLL p.92
Wedding Procession. James A. Emanuel. KAL p.170; NNPUSA p.81
Weed and Shell. William C. Braithwaite. VER p.67
Weeds. Robert Hayden. BOR p.30
Week ergo, las' Wednesday night I got an invitation, A. Waverly T. Car-
    michael. FHOF p.22
Weep Not. James E. McGirt. FYSS p.35
Weep not, friend, o'er your condition. James E. McGirt. FYSS p.35
Weep not that the evil are evil. Ahmed A. Alhamisi. GuW p.11
Weep not, weep not. James Weldon Johnson. AmNP p.2; BLIA p.191
Weep not, you who love her. Waring Cuney. BANP p.285; OTIS p.48; PoN p.146
Weeps out of Kansas country something new. Gwendolyn Brooks. PoN p.191;
    PoNe p.335
Weeps out of Western country something new. Gwendolyn Brooks. AnA p.3
Weh down Souf. Daniel Webster Davis. BANP p.81
Weight of mountains is upon you, The. David Wadsworth Cannon, Jr. EbR p.23
Welcome. Michael S. Harper. DJDC p.30
Well, I'll tell you how it is.* James Pipes. AJP p.3
Well may I say my life has been. Gustavus Vassa. EBAP p.14
Well meaning friends often ask, am I not weary of my task. Raymond Dandridge.
    PAOP p.22; ZaP p.104
We'll never live to see the day our great and novle flag swept away. Zachary
    Withers. PAS p.46
Well, old spy. Ray Durem. IADB p.90; NNPUSA p.33; SoS p.26; TYBP p.243
Well, Phillupeeners, how's yo' health? Joseph S. Cotter, Sr. CPJSC p.16;
    WSBO p.54
Well son, I'll tell you. Langston Hughes. AmNP p.67; ANP p.103; CaD p.151;
    CNAW p.306; DYTB p.20; FNP p.26; GoS p.170; ITBLA p.160; LUP p.32; MBP
    p.97; PoN p.104; PoNe p.186; TYBP p.225; SoS p.19; WeB p.107
Well, Uncle Zeb, it seems that you are always peepin "round." Joseph S.
    Cotter, Sr. LOF p.62
Well, white man, are you confused? Valerie Tarver. TNV p.130
Welt. Georgia Douglas Johnson. BANP p.183
Weltschmerz. Paul Laurence Dunbar. CPPLD p.358
Weltschmerz. Frank Yerby. AmNP p.136
W'en a lady gea you bread you say, "Thank you man." Waverly T. Carmichael.
    FHOF p.31
W'en daih's chillun in de house. Paul Laurence Dunbar. CLT p.53; CPPLD p.322
W'en de banjos wuz a-ringin'. James Weldon Johnson. FYOP p.74
W'en de cluds is hangin' heavy in de sky. Paul Laurence Dunbar. CPPLD
    p.282; WMS p.107
W'en de col'ed ban' comes ma'chin' down de street. Paul Laurence Dunbar.
    CPPLD p.286; WMS p.33
W'en de Evenin' shadders. Paul Laurence Dunbar. CPPLD p.298; WMS p.67
W'en de leaves begin to fall. James Weldon Johnson. FYOP p.78
W'en de show's a-fallin'. Paul Laurence Dunbar. CPPLD p.303
W'en de thrushes in de tree 'gins to sing a merry song. Waverly T. Car-
    michael. FHOF p.8

W'en I git up in de mo'nin' an' de cluds is big an' black. Paul Laurence
    Dunbar. CLT p.67; CPPLD p.276
W'en I gits Home. Paul Laurence Dunbar. CPPLD p.316
W'en I wake up in der morn feelin' kind o' tir'd an' sad. Waverly T. Car-
    michael. FHOF p.36
W'en I was a courtin' man, my, I used to dres'. Waverly T. Carmichael. FHOF
    p.29
W'en I wuz jes a little lad on de hill; I cut pranks bof good an' bad on de
    hill. Raymond Dandridge. PeP p.36; ZaP p.32
W'en through life the way seems dark. Waverly T. Carmichael. FHOF p.54
W'en us fellers stomp around, makin' lots o'noise. Paul Laurence Dunbar.
    CPPLD p.437
W'en yo' life is full o' trouble don' complain. Waverly T. Carmichael. FHOF
    p.46
W'en you Full O' Worry. Paul Laurence Dunbar. CPPLD p.409
Were don eagle & gorgeous george sisters. Don L. Lee. DSNP p.40
Were fortune pleased with thy fair grace. Zachary Withers. PAS p.9
We're hoping to be arrested. Margaret Walker. PFND p.7
Were I not Black you would not turn and stare at me. Iola M. Brister. EbR
    p.13
We're in Sistine Chapel, thousand of cranes waiting to feed our fancy Ameri-
    can tongues. Michael S. Harper. DJDC p.59
Were is My Head Going.** Kali Grosvenor. PBK p.62
We're related--you and I. Langston Hughes. DYTB p.77
Were you a leper bathed in wounds. Georgia Douglas Johnson. CaD p.77
Were you to come, with your clear gray eyes. Joseph S. Cotter, Jr. BOG p.11
West Texas. Langston Hughes. SIH p.78
Western Town. David Wadsworth Cannon, Jr. PoN p.160; PoNe p.282
Western Front. LeRoi Jones. BMP p.81
Western Lady, A. LeRoi Jones. BMP p.75
Western Reverie, A. Charles Fred White. PONS p.98
We've got to Live Before We Die. H. A. B. Jones Quartey. LUP p.36
We've kept the faith our souls' high dreams. Lucian B. Watkins. BANP p.212
Whale, His Bulwark, The. Derek Walcott. TYBP p.113
Whar's I bin, who wants to know? Raymond Dandridge. PeP p.18; ZaP p.66
What a balm for the mind's the joyous spring. James E. McGirt. FYSS p.71
"What a waste of a beautiful girl"?! D. T. Ogilvie. NBP p.95
What about that short you saw last week on Frelinghuysen. LeRoi Jones.
    BLIA p.397; BMP p.225
What Am I? Nick A. Ford. SFD p.35
What Am I Offered? LeRoi Jones. BMP p.64
What are the thing, that make life bright. Paul Laurence Dunbar. CPPLD
    p.387
What began that bustle in the village. David Granmer T. Bereng. TYBP p.173
What boots it; poet, that from realms above. Joseph S. Cotter. EBAP p.187;
    LOF p.26
What bright pushbutton? Samuel Allen. PoNe p.344
What bullet killed him? Nicolas Guillen. PoN p.376; TYBP p.105
What can I say. Alicia L. Johnson. BrT p.176
What can punge my heart of the songs and the sadness. Langston Hughes. EbR
    p.87

269

What   TITLE AND FIRST LINE INDEX

What can purge my heart of the song and the sadness? Langston Hughes. OWT
    p.47
What cat is it hides in your face. A. B. Spellman. BTB p.169
What chu care what I feel. James Emanuel. BrT p.47
What-chu gon' do wid dis boy. Welton Smith. BlSp p.194
What! come back from Santiago? Eli Shepperd. PlS p.42
What comer was ever a star again. Owen Dodson. PLL p.55
What dat you whisperin' keepin' from me? Paul Laurence Dunbar. CPPLD p.218
What Declaration. June Jordan. SCh p.29
What declaration can I make to clear this room of strangers leaving quickly
    as an enemy might come? June Jordan. SCh p.29
What desperate nightmare raps me to this land. Dudley Randall. BTB p.166;
    NNPUSA p.43; PoNe p.306
What did you expect to see. Bernie Casey. LATP p.64
What Do I Care For Morning.** Helene Johnson. CaD p.210
What does it matter? Alice Walker. ONC p.52
What does thou here, thou shining, sinless things. George Marion McClellan.
    ANP p.92; BANP p.97
What dreams we have and how they fly. Paul Laurence Dunbar. AVAN p.57;
    CPPLD p.266
What good are words? (For Martin Luther King). Linwood Smith. TNV p.119
What good are words to quench a heart on fire? Linwood D. Smith. TNV p.119
What good deed have I done today. Waverly T. Carmichael. FHOF p.53
What had you to lose? Robert Perry, Jr. EbR p.116
What Happens. June Jordan. SCh p.69
What happens to a dream deferred? Langston Hughes. ITBLA p.158; PATL p.14;
    PoNe p.199
What happens when the dog sits on a tiger. June Jordan. SCh p.69
What Happing To the Heros. Kali Grosvenor. PBK p.33
What Have I Done. Waverly T. Carmichael. FROF p.53
What I am saying now was said before. Countee Cullen. MASP p.84; OTIS p.153
What I growed up dar wor no school. Raymond Dandridge. PeP p.40
What I have sought. Robert Hayden. BOR p.32
What I have written, I cannot unwrite. Norman Jordan. PoNe p.423
What I Need, Is a Dark Woman.** Charles Anderson. BTB p.41
What I never wanted, came back for me to love it. LeRoi Jones. BMP p.40
What I question of night and the day. Charles B. Johnson. SOMP p.32
What if the wind do howl without. Paul Laurence Dunbar. CPPLD p.120; LOFF
    p.178
What if you come. Countee Cullen. CpS p.22
What Invisible Rat.** Jean-Joseph Rebearivelo. TYBP p.153
What Is A Slave? Benjamin Clark. EBAP p.178
What is Africa to me. Countee Cullen. AmNP p.83; ANP p.98; BANP p.221; BLIA
    p.154; CCC p.36; CNAW p.326; FNP p.15; OTIS p.24; PoN p.121; TYBP p.230
What Is God? Ethelia Arthur Robinson. EbR p.127
What Is It. A. B. Spellman. BTB p.169
What Is Life?** Nick Aaron Ford. SFD p.27
What Is Love? Charles Fred White. PONS p.44
What is most precious because it is lost. LeRoi Jones. BLIA p.393
"What Is Precious Is Never To Forget." Robert Hayden. HSITD p.52
What Is The Negro Doing? W. Clarence Jordan. ANP p.126
What is there within this beggar lad. Langston Hughes. WeB p.85

What is this haxe which now I feel. Charles Fred White. PONS p.77
What it means to be an "N." Frenchy J. Hodges. BlW p.25
What jungle tree have you slept under. Langston Hughes. FNP p.22; WeB p.33
What kind of voice wd come to this. LeRoi Jones. BMP p.109
What makes me disinclined. Ibn Rashiq. TYBP p.44
What matters that I stormed and swore? Countee Cullen. CCC p.54
What My Child Learns Of The Sea.** Audre Lorde. NBP p.85
What Need Have I For Memory.** Georgia Douglas Johnson. CaD p.80; HWOP p.47
What Ovid Taught Me. Alice Walker. ONC p.52
What! Roses growing in a meadow. Effie Lee Newsome. CaD p.59
What says the wind to the waving trees? Paul Laurence Dunbar. CPPLD p.108;
    LOLL p.161
What shape has yellow? James Worley. FoM p.65
What should we do when we are alone together. Ted Joans. BPW p.94
What sudden bird will bring us any cheer. William S. Braithwaite. HFL p.25
What was it that caught in our throats that day. James Thompson. BTB p.174
What was not pleasant was the hust that coughed. Gwendolyn Brooks. AnA p.9
What we see in the person of our feeling is driven there. LeRoi Jones. BMP
    p.60
What whim of flesh, what quirk of soul, what cast of the rubicon die. Melvin
    Tolson. RWA p.15
What Would I Do White? June Jordan. SCh p.47
What year is this. Raymond Patterson. SoS p.79
What you Gonna Name That Pretty Little Baby. Anonymous. ChG p.96; ITBLA
    p.97
What you libin' sense you hustled out an' quit de "Cabbage Patch"? Joseph S.
    Cotter, Sr. SPPH p.67
Whatever happens we know we've lived. LeRoi Jones. BlSp p.27
Whatever I have loved has wounded me. Countee Cullen. CpS p.88
Whatever you're given me, whiteface glass to look through, to find another
    there, another what motherfucker? LeRoi Jones. BMP p.55
What's happening to the heroes. Kali Grosvenor. BlSp p.106
What's in this grave is worth your tear. Countee Cullen. CCC p.72
What's that you got tere in your hand. Joseph S. Cotter, Sr. LOF p.61;
    SPPH p.30
What's the boasted creed of color. Charles Dinkins. AVAN p.111
What's The Use.** Paul Laurence Dunbar. CPPLD p.408
Wheel, The. Robert Hayden. BOR p.33; SPPH p.57
When ... Frenchy J. Hodges. BlW p.11
When A Feller's Itchin' To Be Spanked. Paul Laurence Dunbar. CPPLD p.437
When a woman is big and fat with child. Bruce McM. Wright. LUP p.60
When Abel lives again color'll quit dese sons of Cain. Eli Shepperd. PlS
    p.142
When All Is Done. Paul Laurence Dunbar. CPPLD p.181
When all my body has. Gwendolyn Brooks. FaP p.21
When all our hopes are sown on strong ground. Arna Bontemps. PoN p.119;
    PoNe p.222
When all the cards are in. Nikki Giovanni. BrT p.65
When at break of day at a riverside. Gabriel Okara. TYBP p.158
When August days are hot an' dry. Paul Laurence Dunbar. CPPLD p.207
When Bennie was a teen-age boy, each household had a clock. Eloise Culver.
    GANIV p.13

When Black folk's proud dey's mighty proud. Joseph S. Cotter, Sr. CPJSC
    p.52

When Brown is Black. Keorapetse W. Kgositsile. BrT p.73

When buffeted and beaten by life's storms. James Weldon Johnson. FYOP p.55

When can I, a poor Black woman, do to destroy America. Nikki Giovanni.
    BFBTBJ p.54

When Cumbria's wild and gloomy fells lay bound by savage, heaten spells.
    William C. Braithwaite. VER p.22

When dawn Comes to the City. New York. Claude McKay. GoS p.129; HaS p.60;
    SPCM p.62

When de Co'n Pone's Hot. Paul Laurence Dunbar. BANP p.61; CNAW p.210; LiG
    p.47; CPPLD p.89; LOLL p.132

When de dishes rattle like a passel o' cattle. Charles Johnson. SOMP p.41

When de fiddle gits to singin' out a ol' Vahginny reel. Paul Laurence
    Dunbar. AVAN p.72; CPPLD p.220

When De Saints Go Ma'chin' Home. Sterling Brown. AmNP p.55; SoR p.12

When De Sun Shines Hot. James E. McGirt. FYSS p.38

When Dey 'Listed Colored Soldiers. Paul Laurence Dunbar. CPPLD p.293; CLT
    p.77

When face to face we stand. Angelina Weld Grimke. CaD p.43

When first my bosom glowed with hope. George Moses Horton. EBAP p.21

When first of wise old Johnson taught. Paul Laurence Dunbar. CPPLD p.205

When first you sang a song to me. Gwendolyn B. Bennett. CaD p.197

When first your glory shown upon my face. Claude McKay. BANP p.175; HaS
    p.89; SPCM p.103

When fo' yeahs yo've been er trying. James E. McGirt. FYSS p.6

When God said "I'll make me a man." Anonymous. MBP p.7

When Great Does Fight. Melvin Tolson. RWA p.17

When grey skies are round me clinging. William C. Braithwaite. VER p.47

When hard luck overtakes you. Langston Hughes. FCTJ p.18

When he first came from Maui. Owen Dodson. PLL p.23

When he reached the stage drink gave no relief. Albert Aubert. ATB p.24

When i am away from you, and yesterday's wishes spill over into today's for-
    gotten memories. Bernie Casey. LATP p.25

When I Am Dead. Owen Dodson. PLL p.74

When I Am Dead. Georgia Douglas Johnson. CaD p.80; HWOP p.42

When I am Dead, It Will Not Be. Countee Cullen. CpS p.43; OTIS p.60

When I am dead, withould, I pray, your blooming legacy. Georgia Douglas
    Johnson. CaD p.80; HWOP p.42; KAL p.120

When I am in my grave. Waring Cuney. PoN p.148

When I arise each day I always go the way. William L. Morrison. DaR p.36

When I Awoke.** Raymond Patterson. NNPUSA p.113

When I Bid You Good-bye and Go.** William S. Braithwaite. LLL p.65

When I come down to sleep death' endless night. James Weldon Johnson. BANP
    p.125; CaD p.25; PoN p.32; PoNe p.31

When I come in f'om de co'n-fiel' aftah wo'kin' ha'd all day. Paul Laurence
    Dunbar. CLT p.117; CPPLD p.251

When I die. Mari Evans. AmNP p.163; IABW p.76; IADB p.4

When I Die. Fenton Johnson. AVAN p.162; CaD p.62; PoN p.63; PoNe p.90

When I Die. Nikki Giovanni. MyH p.36

When I die, I hope no one who ever hurt me cries. Nikki Giovanni. MyH p.36

When I Die In Dreams.** Craig Williamson. AfW p.30

When I die my song shall be. Fenton Johnson. AVAN p.162; CaD p.62; PoN p.63;
    PoNe p.90
When I gaze at the sun. Samuel Allen. AmNP p.138; CNAWp.615; IADB p.22;
    ITBLA p.220; KAL p.148
When I gaze at the sun I walk to the subway book for change. Samuel Allen.
    AmNP p.138; BTB p.177; CNAW p.615; IADB p.22; ITBLA p.220; KATL p.148
When I get to be a composer. Langston Hughes. DYTB p.78; OWT p.83; PATL
    p.101
When I Grow. Kali Grosvenor. PBK p.59
When I Grow. Kali Grosvenor. PBK p.60
When I **grow** up I went away to work. Margaret Walker. FMP p.54
When I grow up I want the world to be peaceful. Kali Grosvenor. PBK p.60
When I grow up I hope to be just half as great as Booker T. Eloise Culver.
    GANIV p.43
When I grow up I want to see bueuty. Kali Grosvenor. PBK p.59
When I have Passed Away.** Claude McKay. HaS p.31
When I Heard Dat White Man Say.** Zack Gilbert. TGWL p.47
When I move into a neighborhood folds fly. Langston Hughes. OWT p.64
When I return to the block. John Raven. BFM p.17
When I Nap.** Nikki Giovanni. MyH p.23
When I Or Else.** June Jordan. SCh p.32
When I See Black. Kali Grosvenor. PBK p.17
When I Think About Myself.** Maya Angelou. JGM p.25
When I think of it all I am so sad. Oswald Durand. PoN p.350
When I visit Europe & America's zoos I see caged / fenced / and all locked up
    African & Asia animals. Ted Joans. AFR p.19
When I wake up another God-given morning. Frenchy J. Hodges. BlW p.11
When I walked across the Senegal Mali Savannah no Harlem gal tagged along
    with me. Ted Joans. AFR p.25
When I was a boy desiring the title of man. Dudley Randall. BrT p.126; KAL
    p.133
When I Was A Boy. Waring Cuney. LUP p.16
When I was a child I knew red miners. Margaret Walker. BOL p.72; FMP p.53;
    KAL p.145
When I was almost nine months unborn. Ted Joans. AFR p.97
When I was home de sunshine seemed like gold. Langston Hughes. BANP p.237;
    FCTJ p.23
When i was very little though it's still true today there were no sidewalks
    in Lincoln Heights. Nikki Giovanni. MyH p.8
When I was young I longed for love. Paul Laurence Dunbar. CPPLD p.155
When I Went To Paris.** Kali Grosvenor. PBK p.55
When in nineteen-thirty-seven, Etta Moten, sweetheart of our art study group
    kept her promise. Margaret Walker. BrT p.40
When In Rome. Mari Evans. AmNP p.164; BTB p.105; IABW p.56; ITBLA p.274
When in the morning's misty hour. Ann Plato. EBAP p.116
When Israel sate by Babel's stream and wept. Arbery Allson Whitman. EBAP
    p.318
When Israel was in Egypt Lan'. Anonymous. MBP p.79
When it is all over. Hoyt W. Fuller. TGWL p.44
When it is finally ours this freedom, this liberty. Robert Hayden. AmNP
    p.119; CNAW p.392; BOR p.71; IADB p.45; ITBLA p.220; KAL p.117; MBP p.83;
    PoN p.171; PoNe p.296; SoS p.41; SPRH p.78; TYBP p.237

When it was ended and we looked for some meaning. Raymond Patterson. SoS
    p.108
When Jade came he felt the pressure. Victor Hernandez Cruz. SNA p.103
When June comes dancing on the death of May. Claude McKay. HaS p.79; SPCM
    p.99
When labor is light and the morning is fair. Paul Laurence Dunbar. CPPLD
    p.111; LOLL p.165
When life is young, without a care. Georgia Douglas Johnson. HWOP p.52
When life's rapids round you roar. William C. Braithwaite. VER p.122
When love and solitaire within your chamber. Georgia D. Johnson. HWOP p.14
When love is a shimmering curtain. Maya Angelou. JGM p.19
When love's brief dream is done. Georgia Douglas Johnson. PoN p.57; PoNe
    p.75
When ma man looks at me. Langston Hughes. FCTJ p.88
When Ma Rainey comes to town. Sterling A. Brown. BTB p.59; SoR p.62
When Mahalia sings. Quandra Prettyman. IADB p.56
When Malindy Sings. Paul Laurence Dunbar. AVAN p.85; BLIA p.113; CPPLD
    p.131; ITBLA p.95; LOLL p.195; PoN p.35; PoNe p.37; WMS p.9
When midnight came and the child's first cry arose, a hundred beasts awakened
    and the stable became alive. Gabriela Mistral. ChG p.88
When morning shows her first faint flush. James Weldon Johnson. FYOP p.52
When mortals tread the trail of stars. William S. Braithwaite. HFL p.81
When music rises sweet with harmony. Charles Fred White. PONS p.149
When musicians say cookin it is food for soul. LeRoi Jones. BMP p.99
When Ol' Sis' Judy pray.** James Edwin Campbell. BANP p.69
When ole mister sun gits tiah'd a-hangin'. James Weldon Johnson. FYOP p.71
When on life's ocean first I spread my sail. George Moses Horton. ANP p.13;
    EBAP p.23
When on my time of living I reflect. Juan Fransilo Manzano. TYBP p.98
When oppressed on every side, or caught in the receding tide. Raymond Dan-
    dridge. PeP p.15
When our tears are dry on the shore. George Awooner Williams. TYBP p.165
When Phillis sighs and from her eyes. Paul Laurence Dunbar. CPPLD p.282
When Roland sang at concerts he sang of things most dear. Eloise Culver.
    GANIV p.59
When Sam'l Sings. Paul Laurence Dunbar. CPPLD p.339; LiG p.87
When sciene, trembling in the lengthened shade. Arberry Allson Whitman.
    EBAP p.216
When She Spoke Of God. Lance Jeffers. BrT p.72
When sister soul arrives on the other side. Ted Joans. AFR p.148
When Slavery Seems Sweet.** Ed Bullins. NBP p.32
When Southern jailers lose their keys and strange fruit hangs from Southern
    trees. J. Farley Ragland. BTB p.164
When storms arise. Paul Laurence Dunbar. CPPLD p.106; LOLL p.157
When Sue Wears Red. Langston Hughes. BTB p.125; GoS p.111; ITBLA p.158;
    TYBP p.228; WeB p.66
When summer time has come, and all. Paul Laurence Dunbar. CPPLD p.462
When Susanna Jones wears red. Langston Hughes. BTB p.125; GoS p.111; ITBLA
    p.158; TYBP p.228; WeB p.66
When tabes claims my useless frame, and I am with my gather laid. Raymond
    Dandridge. PAOP p.62
When The Armies Passed. Langston Hughes. FOW p.109

When the bees are humming in the honeysuckle vine. Paul Laurence Dunbar.
    CPPLD p.351
When the cold comes. Langston Hughes. KAL p.92; PATL p.97
When the corn's all out and the bright stalks shine. Paul Laurence Dunbar.
    CPPLD p.25; LOLL p.33
When The Different Churches Meet. Waverly T. Carmichael. FHOF p.28
When the fiat of the most high. John Boyd. EBAP p.153
When The Fish Begin To Bite. J. Mord Allen. AVAN p.128
When The Green Lies Over the Earth.** Angelina Grimke. CaD p.41; PoN p.48;
    PoNe p.56
When the ladder to success is broken they all tell you, "use the stairs."
    Helen F. Clarke. EbR p.41
When the lips and the body are done. Langston Hughes. FOW p.51
When The Old Man Smokes. Paul Laurence Dunbar. CPPLD p.150
When the master lived a king and I a starving hutted slave beneath the lash.
    Lance Jeffers. CNAW p.769
When the still somare evening closes down. William S. Braithwaite. LLL p.48
When the sun sets o'er the hills in the desolate wild west. Charles Fred
    White. PONS p.98
When the tom-tom beats ... Jacques Roumain. PONS p.364
When The Way Seems Dark. Waverly T. Carmichael. FHOF p.54
When the white folks get through here come you. Langston Hughes. PATL p.40
When the world goes voodoo.* Walter Lowenfels. PoNe p.516
When there is no longer love. Mae V. Cowdery. WLOV p.59
When they form their white mobs to murder me or shoot me. Ted Joans. AFR
    p.71
When they hear. Sterling A. Brown. SoR p.107
When they shot Malcolm Little down on the Stage of the Audubon Ballroom.
    Raymond Patterson. BrT p.29; FoM p.69; SoS p.37
When they stop poems. Victor Hernandez Cruz. SNA p.29; TYBP p.260
When this great nation, rich and grand with promising youth on every hand.
    Zachary Withers. PAS p.5
When three, he fished these lakes. James Emanuel. BrT p.45
When through the winding cobbled streets of time. Georgia Love. IADB p.103;
    NNPUSA p.69
When Time Has Claimed. Raymond Dandridge. ZaP p.53
When time was laggard in the long ago. Joseph S. Cotter, Sr. CPJSC p.34;
    LOF p.63
When Twilight Comes With Dreams. William S. Braithwaite. LLL p.38
When walking through the woods. Wesley Cartright. GoS p.78
When war's red banner trailed along the sky. Henrietta Cordelia Ray. EBAP
    p.140
When we count out our gold at the end of the day. Georgia Douglas Johnson.
    CaD p.75
When we looked up at the bright evening star. William S. Braithwaite. SPWSB
    p.93
When Wilkes Booth thundered up the aisle of the Audubon Ballroom. Reginald
    Wilson. FoM p.35
When William Blake that day became aware. William S. Braithwaite. SPWSB
    p.89
When winter covering all the ground. Paul Laurence Dunbar. CPPLD p.454
When Winter Darkening All Around. Paul Laurence Dunbar. CPPLD p.454

When work is done, I've got a hunch. William L. Morrison. DaR p.32
When you and I were young, the days. Paul Laurence Dunbar. CPPLD p.37; LOLL
   p.52
When you are gone I'll treasure everything. William L. Morrison. DaR p.29
When you chart your course. Barbara Marshall. TNV p.71
When You Come To Me.** Maya Angelou. JGM p.9
When you dance. Leslie M. Collins. PoN p.172; PoNe p.297
When You Died. Christine C. Johnson. FoM p.71
When you enter strange cities be silent. Nazzam A. Sudan. NBP p.127
When you find yourself in sorrow. Charles Fred White. PONS p.103
When you get up in the morning what the hell do you see? Frenchy J. Hodges.
   BlW p.25
When you Have Gone From Rooms.** Bruce Wright. BTh p.183
When you have seen the ditches and the skies and felt your heart crumble at
   your feet. Eldon George McLean. EbR p.107
When you have soared through dizzy air and cut your name on fame's high
   cliff. Charles Fred White. PONS p.115
When you hear at night de cows, alowin' an' dogs a howlin' out der mournful
   soun'. James E. McGirt. FYSS p.55
When you pored your love like molten flame. Frank Horne. CaD p.116
When you roam the garden over. Joseph S. Cotter, Sr. LOF p.55; RHY p.30
When you see me walkin'. Tommy Whitaker. TNV p.134
When you smile at me anew the sky will be all blue. William L. Morrison.
   DaR p.51
When your talking is murdered, and only very old women will think to give you
   flowers. LeRoi Jones. BMP p.12
When you told of Paul and his letter to Roman Christians. Frenchy J. Hodges.
   BlW p.15
When you turn the corner and you run into yourself. Langston Hughes. OWT
   p.118
When you were but a little child with many faults to cover. Raymond Dan-
   dridge. PeP p.9
When your brave eyes are stopped with dust. Sterling A. Brown. SoR p.132
When your eyes gaze seaward. William S. Braithwaite. AVAN p.142
When you're lonely or in sorrow, wipe away your burning tears. Charles Fred
   White. PONS p.112
Whence. Melvin Tolson. RWA p.21
Whenever I Lift My Eyes To Bliss.** Georgia D. Johnson. HWOP p.40
Whenever skies be blue or dusk, thy matins pierce the twilight grey. Charles
   B. Johnson. SOMP p.36
Where? Georgia D. Johnson. HWOP p.30
Where are my people? Gloria Davis. NBP p.46
Where Are The Men Seized In This Wind Of Madness? Aldo De Espirito Santo.
   TYBP p.183
Where are the ships of long ago. William C. Braithwaite. VER p.60
Where are the swarthy soldiers. William L. Morrison. DaR p.55
Where are the warriors, the young men? Askia Muhammed Toure. BrT p.172
Where are we to go when this is done? Alfred A. Duckett. AmNP p.145; PoN
   p.202; PoNe p.359
Where are you going barefoot boy. Marion Nicholes. LiS p.16
Where are you in the snow. LeRoi Jones. BMP p.172
Where are your heroes. Nikki Giovanni. BFBTBJ p.50

"Where Avon winds."** William C. Braithwaite. VER p.96
Where contemplation finds her sacred spring. Phillis Wheatley. PAL p.40;
    PPW p.76
Where contemplation finds her sacred spring. Phillis Wheatley. PAL p.84;
    PPW p.24
Where death stretches its wide horizons. Langston Hughes. FOW p.88
Where did you come from, mother and why. Yvonne Gregory. AmNP p.153
Where do they go when they leave the love of a poet. Ted Joans. AFR p.142
Where God stands is always morning. Marion Cuthbert. SOC p.17
Where Have You Gone?** Mari Evans. BlSp. p.68; IABW p.35; ITBLA p.274; NNPUSA
    p.105; PoNe p.30; TYBP p.254
Where Hearts Are Gay. Waverly T. Carmichael. FHOF p.30
Where I grew up, I used to see. Robert Hayden. ITBLA p.219; SPRH p.17
Where I was before here I came, I know not. Raymond Dandridge. PeP p.39
Where Is My Woman Now: For Billie Holiday. Michael S. Harper. DJDC p.6
Where is that sugar, Hammond. Langston Hughes. SIH p.113
Where is the hand that first sex thee a-ringing? Joseph S. Cotter, Sr. SPPH
    p.64
Where is the Jim Crow section. Langston Hughes. DYTB p.72; ITBLA p.158;
    PATL p.92; MBP p.94; PoN p.104; PoNe p.192
Where is the romantic life? LeRoi Jones. BMP p.83
Where is the star of Bethlehem? Gerald Barrax. KAL p.200; SIH. p.80
Where is there food for a savage. William L. Morrison. DaR p.56
Where light is where your body is blacker. Gerald W. Barrax. AKOR p.20
Where my grandmother lived. Doughtery (Doc) Long, Jr. TNV p.63
Where now shall I lay my head? John Henrik Clarke. EbR p.43
Where sinks deep my love, dead love. Fenton Johnson. AVAN p.161
"Where Thames, is born." William C. Braithwaite. VER p.101
Where the great road leads to the shining west. William C. Braithwaite. VER
    p.101
Where The Rainbow Ends.** Richard Blue. MBP p.107; TYBP p.180
Where there was some hole to show where you was. Victor Hernandez Cruz. SNA
    p.105
Where to go when i have already been there and aback again. Sonia Sanchez.
    WABP p.18
Where was your lover when the sad sad sun went down? Ted Joans. BPW p.90
Where? When? Which? Langston Hughes. KAL p.92; PATL p.97
Where is Judas hung himself I despise bravura. June Jordan. SCh p.33
Whereas. June Jordan. SCh p.32
Wherefore this busy labor without rest? Leslie Pinckney Hill. ANP p.78;
    AVAN p.196; BANP p.153; PoN p.46; PoNe p.53
Wherein are words sublime or noble? Countee Cullen. OTIS p.167
Where's there the missing of it. LeRoi Jones. BMP p.143
Which calls forth the muse? Leanna F. Johnson. EbR p.95
While all Africa is here in the sun. Ted Joans. AFR p.34
While an intrinsic ardor bids me write. Phillis Wheatley. PPW p.63
While an intrinsic ardor prompts to write. Phillis Wheatley. CNAW p.10;
    EBAP p.99; PAL p.33; PPW p.5
While Avon flows by Brendon Hill. William C. Braithwaite. VER p.89
While deep you morn beneath the cypress-shade. Phillis Wheatley. PAL p.61;
    PPW p.46
While Henry was painting or modeling with clay. Eloise Culver. GANIV p.49

While hireling scribblers prostitute their pen. Phillis Wheatley. EBAP
    p.111
While I search your face for forgiveness your tears are transparent pearls.
    Will Smallwood. EbR p.130
While it is true (though only in a factual sense). Nikki Giovanni. BFBTBJ
    p.16
While others chant of gay elysian scenes. Phillis Wheatley. PAL p.66; PPW
    p.4
While raging tempests shake the shore. Phillis Wheatley. PAL p.46; PPW p.35
While thus you mourn beneath the cypress shade. Phillis Wheatley. PAL p.59;
    PPW p.77
Whim is all it takes and there's the race, A. Gerald W. Barrax. AKOR p.46
Whimper Baby. Lucile D. Goodlett. WGC p.56
Whimsy. William L. Morrison. DaR p.12
Whin yeah corns an' bunions achin an' yoah body's full o' pain. James McGirt.
    FYSS p.26
Whip-Poor Will and Katy-Did. Paul Laurence Dunbar. CPPLD p.301; LiG p.75
Whipping, The. Robert Hayden. BOR p.28; IADB p.8; SPRH p.54
Whisper at twilight, a sigh through the night, A. Georgia D. Johnson. HWOP
    p.57
Whisper Together Brethren.** Mari Evans. IABW p.89
Whispers In a Country Church. Albert Aubert. ATB p.9
Whispers of springtime. Langston Hughes. FOW p.26
Whistling Sam. Paul Laurence Dunbar. CPPLD p.252
White America comfortable and disillusioned. Tony Rutherford. BrT p.174
White America is saying stand up & be counted. Sonia Sanchez. WABP p.26
White ants come out without their shells. Michael S. Harper. DJDC p.61
White Ban, The. Ted Joans. BPW p.67
White Bird, The. Bernie Casey. LATP p.51
White boy, Black boy, you have played black jack with Tycho. Melvin Tolson.
    HaG p.148
White City, The. Claude McKay. HaS p.23; SPCM p.74
White coats white aprons white dresses white shoes. Langston Hughes. OWT
    p.134
White communism white capitalism have joined forces together this hour. Ted
    Joans. AFR p.15
White Fear. Nannie M. Travis. EbR p.142
White felts in Fall. Langston Hughes. OWT p.109
White cowboys carry guns to do violence. Ted Joans. BPW p.93
White folks is white, says Uncle Jim. Countee Cullen. BANP p.229; CpS p.9
White House. Claude McKay. AmNP p.31; CNAW p.294; FNP p.9; ITBLA p.155;
    PoN p.332; PoNe p.101; SoS p.119; SPCM p.78
White Knight. Gordon Parks. InL (unpaged)
White Lace. Ted Joans. AFR p.115
White lady has asked me to dance, The. Gerald Barrax. AKOR p.78
White Magic: an Ode. William S. Braithwaite. HFL p.104; PoN p.43; PoNe p.49
White magic of the silences of snow. William S. Braithwaite. HFL p.104;
    PoN p.43; PoNe p.49
White man at least is corny, The. LeRoi Jones. BMP p.162
White man, grooving I feel you. Craig Williamson. AfW p.12
White man in blackface walking. Arthur Boze. BlWo p.21

White man is a tiger at my throat, The. Claude McKay. BLIA p.168; SPCM p.47
White Mice of the Parcel-Post Window. Waring Cuney. LUP p.15
White Ones, The. Langston Hughes. WeB p.106
White ones stole my babies. Ted Joans. AFR p.149
White pilgrims turn your trumpets west! Melvin Tolson. LRL p.23
White Powder! Victor Hernandez Cruz. SNA p.23
White Road, A. William S. Braithwaite. HFL p.22
White road between sea and land, A. William S. Braithwaite. HFL p.22
White terrace stretching far over the sea, A. Emile Roumer. MBP p.48
White Weekend (April 5-8, 1969). Quincy Troupe. NBP p.128
White Whale, The. Michael L. Harper. DJDC p.50
White witch, The. James Weldon Johnson. BANP p.120; CaD p.22; FYOP p.19
White Woman. Ted Joans. BPW p.126
Whites had taught him how to rip, The. Sterling A. Brown. SoR p.36
Whitey, Baby. James Emanuel. BrT p.47
Whiteyes On Black Thighs. Ted Joans. BPW p.24
Whither? Georgia Douglas Johnson. HWOP p.10
Whittier. Paul Laurence Dunbar. CPPLD p.28; LOLL p.38
Who Am I. Kali Grosvenor. PBK p.18
Who are these among you? Owen Dodson. PLL p.96; PoN p.175; PoNe p.302
Who are you? LeRoi Jones. BMP p.134
Who are you dusky woman, so ancient hardly human.* Walt Whitman. PoN p.214;
    PoNe p.470
Who are you, listening to yourself. LeRoi Jones. BMP p.120
Who built the ark? Eli Shepperd. PlS p.123
Who But the Lord? Langston Hughes. OWT p.73; PATL p.16
Who Can Be Born Black.** Mari Evans. IABW p.93
Who can hold up the intellect and say. Joseph S. Cotter. EBAP p.191; LOF
    p.49; RHY p.15; SPPH p.42
Who collects the pain screamed. Stephany. BrT p.149
Who danced Saturday mornings. PoN p.348
Who dances? Owen Dodson. PLL p.14
Who dat knockin' at de do'? Paul Laurence Dunbar. CPPLD p.296
Who flees the regions of the lower mind. Alberry A. Whitman. ANP p.21;
    AVAN p.50
Who Has Seen the Wind? Bob Kaufman. KAL p.218
Who has strangled the tired voice. Noemia De Sousa. TYBP p.188
Who hath not built his castles in the free and open air. Georgia D. Johnson.
    HWOP p.50
Who I am. Luis Gonzaga Pinto Da Gama. TYBP p.79
Who I break my head against. Victor Hernandez Cruz. SNA p.5
Who is not a stranger still even after making love, or the morning after?
    Stephany. BrT p.148
Who is that a-walking in the corn? Fenton Johnson. GoS p.65; PoN p.64;
    PoNe p.92
Who Knows. A. L. Milner-Brown. TYBP p.167
Who knows? This Africa so richly blest. A. L. Milner-Brown. TYBP p.167
Who leads hither what he finds? Everett Hoagland. BrT p.70
Who lies with his milk white maiden. Countee Cullen. BlC p.66; OTIS p.102
Who lynches me maims but this modeled clay. Charles White. PONS p.165
Who makes a law may force a means to curse. Joseph S. Cotter, Sr. SPPH p.34;
    WSBO p.12

Who rock'd me w'en I was a babe. Waverly T. Carmichael. FHOF p.49

Who say my hea't ain't true to you? Paul Laurence Dunbar. CPPLD p.212

Who Shall Die. James Randall. BrT p.131

Who taught thee conflict with the pow'rs of night. Phillis Wheatley. PAL
    p.87; PPW p.11

Who To? Ted Joans. BPW p.43

Who were the guys who wrote, who wined around and thought about things?
    LeRoi Jones. BMP p.187

Who will know Bessie now of those who loved her. Sterling A. Brown. SoR
    p.41

Who would have the sky any color but blue. Mrs. J. W. Hammond. ANP p.82

Who would not sit with kindled eyes, hid in the hillside moss and brake.
    William C. Braithwaite. VER p.45

Who would who could understand. Carolyn M. Rodgers. BrT p.180

Whoever it was who brought the first wood and coal. Jean Toomer. PoNe p.106

Whole hog or none is de word I sing! Eli Shepperd. P1S p.86

Whole point of writing you is pointless, The. Nikki Giovanni. BFBTBJ p.29

Who'll be ready? Eli Shepperd. P1S p.133

Whom can I confess to? Don L. Lee. BrT p.88; DSNP p.58

Whores. Margaret Walker. FMP p.54

Who's gonna make all that beautiful blk / rhetoric mean something. Sonia
    Sanchez. WABP p.15

Who's that dark woman sittin' next to the preacher eyeing his feet? Albert
    Aubert. ATB p.9

Who's that monster in my bed? John Raven. BFM p.15

Whose broken window is a cry of art. Gwendolyn Brooks. ITM p.36

Whose little lady is you, chile. Paul Laurence Dunbar. CPPLD p.320

Whuh folks, whuh folks don' wuh muh brown too hahd. Sterling A. Brown. SoR
    p.23

Whut time'd dat clock strike? nine? no--eight. Paul Laurence Dunbar. CPPLD
    p.418

Whut you say, dah? huh, uh! chile. Paul Laurence Dunbar. CPPLD p.247

Whut's use wukin' when you kin libe lak white folks 'ont dey care? Joseph S.
    Cotter, Sr. CPJSC p.33; WSBO p.47

Why Adam sinned. Alex Rogers. BANP p.158

Why am I alone? Katherine L. Cuestas. BTB p.76

Why are they Mean? Kali Grosvenor. PBK p.27

Why are white folks so mean. Kali Grosvenor. PBK p.27

Why are you dusky woman, so ancient hardly human.* Walt Whitman. ANP p.134;
    PoN p.214; PoNe p.470

Why chafe you so, my brothers, o, my brothers. Joseph S. Cotter, Sr. CPJSC
    p.76

Why Cry. Ted Joans. AFR p.89

Why did the pilgrems discouver this country? Kali Grosvenor. PBK p.37

Why do I Love This Country? Mary Wilkerson Cleaves. EbR p.46

Why do men smile when I speak? Joseph S. Cotter, Jr. BANP p.187; BOG p.14

Why do poets like to die. Frank Horne. BANP p.270

Why do they walk so tragical. Sterling A. Brown. SoR p.12

Why do you wish to give me over to someone else? Alice Walker. ONC p.58

Why don't we rock the casket here in the moonlight. Oliver Pitcher. NNPUSA
    p.114; TYBP p.247

Why Elizabeth. Craig Williamson. AfW p.41

Why Elizabeth do you reach to twenty. Craig Williamson. AfW p.41
Why Else? Ted Joans. BPW p.48
Why Fades a Dream? Paul Laurence Dunbar. BLIA p.116; CPPLD p.124; LOLL
    p.184
Why i don't get high on shit. Sonia Sanchez. WABP p.57
Why I rebel. Robert J. Sye. TNV p.123
Why must a man who loves his country well. Walter G. Arnold. EbR p.3
Why they closing down Alcatraz & considering closing Sing Sing. Sonia
    Sanchez. WABP p.19
Why this preoccupation, soul, with death. Countee Cullen. MASP p.86; OTIS
    p.155
Why Try. Ted Joans. BPW p.79; BTB p.132
Why was it that the thunder voice of fate. Paul Laurence Dunbar. CPPLD
    p.360; KAL p.25
Why's you tryin' to kick ole Robah. Raymond Dandridge. PeP p.8; ZaP p.14
Widow. Clarence Major. BlSp p.131
Widow Woman. Langston Hughes. SIH p.107
Widow Walk, The. Owen Dodson. BTB p.92
Wife-woman, The. Anne Spencer. ANP p.123; BANP p.216
Wild Goat, The. Claude McKay. CaD p.87; SPCM p.28
Wild May. Claude McKay. HaS p.18; SPCM p.26
Wild poppy-flower withered and dies. Langston Hughes. FOW p.23
Wild rose silently peeps from its uncouth habitation. William Edgar Bailey.
    ANP p.119
Wild Roses. Effie Lee Newsome. CaD p.59
Wild West Savages. Ted Joans. AFR p.22
Wildness of haggared flights. Roussan Camille. TYBP p.95
W'ile doun de narrow path o' life I march wid hop to reach de goal. Waverly
    T. Carmichael. FHOF p.58
Will define herself naturally. Don L. Lee. DCS p.50; DSNP p.121
Will I have some mo' dat pie? Paul Laurence Dunbar. CPPLD p.330; LiG p.84
Will they cry when you're gone, you bet. LeRoi Jones. BMP p.63
Will you think of me my dear, w'ile I am erway? Waverly T. Carmichael.
    FHOF p.34
William D. Gallagher. Joseph S. Cotter, Sr. RHY p.16
William Dean Howells (For his seventieth birthday). William S. Braithwaite.
    HFL p.83
William Leon Hansberry Historian of Ancient Africa, 1894-1965, Mississippi.
    Eloise Culver. GANIV p.62
William Lloyd Garrison. Joseph S. Cotter, Sr. CPJSC p.45; WSBO p.19
Williston Battle Song. Charles Fred White. PONS p.162
Willow, The. Georgia Douglas Johnson. HWOP p.52
Willow bend and weep. Herbert Clark Johnson. PoN p.161; PoNe p.285
Willow tree leans far over the brook. Robert Davis. GoS p.178
Wilma Rudolph, Olympic Star, 1940-   , Tennessee. Eloise Culver. GANIV
    p.75
Wilmington, Delaware. Nikki Giovanni. BFBTBJ p.26; BrT p.51
Wilmington is a funni Negro. Nikki Giovanni. BFBTBJ p.26; BrT p.51
Win' a blowin' gentle so de sun lay low. Paul Laurence Dunbar. CPPLD p.310;
    LiG p.80
Wind. Langston Hughes. FOW p.75
Wind, The. L. Doretta Lowery. BTh p.51

Wind, a jolly old lady in brown, The. L. Doretta Lowery. BTh p.51
Wind and the Sea, The. Paul Laurence Dunbar. CPPLD p.109; LOLL p.162
Wind and the Weather, The. Countee Cullen. BlC p.19
Wind Bloweth Where It Listeth, The. Countee Cullen. CpS p.39
Wind Blows, The.** Mae V. Cowdery. WLOV p.5
Wind gallop up maiden lane, The.** Mason Jordan Mason. PoNe p.521
Wind is blowing from the hill, The. H. A. Vaughan. PoN p.346
Wind is out in the rage to-night, The. Paul Laurence Dunbar. CPPLD p.399
Wind is in the cane come along. Jean Toomer. KAL p.53
Wind is ruffling the tawny pelt, A. Derek Walcott. TYBP p.114
Wind kissed the rose, The. Olivia M. Hunter. BTh p.33
Wind of the night, thou silent guardian. Charles Fred White. PONS p.125
Wind ran black, The. Robert Hayden. HSITD p.22
Wind the Weather Cock and the Warrior's Ghost, The. Robert Hayden. HSITD
    p.22
Wind told the little leaves to hurry, The.** Paul Laurence Dunbar. CPPLD
    p.425
Window is stuffed with newspaper. A. B. Spellman. BTB p.170
Window Pictures. Sarah E. Wright. BTB p.184
Window Washer. Ricardo Weeks. EbR p.156
Winds are still.** William C. Braithwaite. VER p.64
Windy Rain. Kali Grosvenor. PBK p.54
Windy rain my old silly umbrella tries walking backwards. Kali Grosvenor.
    PBK p.54
Wine-maiden of the Zazz-tuned night. Langston Hughes. WeB p.35
Wings of Genesis, The. Craig Williamson. AfW p.25
Wings of Oppression, The. Leslie Pinckney Hill. AVAN p.195
Win's are blowin' on ahaid us. Waverly T. Carmichael. FHOF p.38
Wintah, summah, snow or shine. Paul Laurence Dunbar. CPPLD p.286
Wintah time hit comin'. Paul Laurence Dunbar. CPPLD p.393; FNP p.14
Winter. James E. McGirt. FYSS p.21
Winter--aback sweeps the inward eye. Georgia D. Johnson. HWOP p.19
Winter Chorus. Owen Dodson. PLL p.33
Winter has gone to land-no-end, The. William L. Morrison. DaR p.39
Winter Hawk in Harlem. Ted Joans. BPW p.69
Winter in the Country. Claude McKay. HaS p.37; SPCM p.71
Winter is an old man. Robert Perry, Jr. EbR p.114
Winter is coming. Waverly Turner Carmichael. BANP p.163; FROF p.57
Winter is settling on the place; the sedge. Sterling A. Brown, SoR p.27
Winter Moon. Langston Hughes. DYTB p.55; MBP p.4; WeB p.44
Winter Poem. Nikki Giovanni. MyH p.10
Winter Retreat. Michael S. Harper. DJDC p.19
Winter Rode Away. J. Henderson Brooks. BTh p.38
Winter-Song. Paul Laurence Dunbar. CPPLD p.383
Winter Sweetness. Langston Hughes. GoS p.182
Winter Thoughts. William L. Morrison. DaR p.23
Winter twilight, A. Angelina W. Grimke. CaD p.46; PoN p.47; PoNe p.54
Winter's Approach. Paul Laurence Dunbar. CPPLD p.421
Winter's Day, A. Paul Laurence Dunbar. CPPLD p.192
Wisdom. Langston Hughes. FOW p.107
Wisdom. Frank Yerby. AmNP p.136
Wisdom and War. Langston Hughes. EbR p.88

Wisdom Cometh With the Years. Countee Cullen. CCC p.22; KAL p.99; OTIS p.13
Wise, The. Countee Cullen. CCC p.95; OTIS p.40; PoN p.126; PoNe p.230
Wise guys tell me that Christmas is kid stuff. Frank Horne. AmNP p.41; BTB
    p.119; ChG p.70; ITBLA p.157; KAL p.67; MBP p.76; PoN p.77; PoNe p.148
Wise Men of the East, The. Claude McKay. SPCM p.48
Wish, A. Countee Cullen. B1C p.31
Wish, A. Eleanor A. Thompson. BTh p.47
Wit and laughter thy tears cannot shatter the remorse of years. Jamye H.
    Coleman. EbR p.52
Witch Doctor. Robert Hayden. AmNP p.110; BOR p.18; SPRH p.47
Witches and devils. LeRoi Jones. BMP p.51
Wite / motha / fucka wite / motha / fucka wite / motha fucka whitey. Sonia
    Sanchez. WABP p.59
With a rope of glass I am bound to time. Joseph S. Cotter, Sr. CPJSC p.28;
    WSBO p.22
With all deliberate speed (for the children of our world). Don L. Lee. DSNP
    p.201
With button eyes and cotton skin. Effie Lee Newsome. GoS p.99
With cheerful hearts we've come. James Madison Bell. ANP p.19; AVAN p.38
With "Desire Me" and all that stuff how can women fail. John Raven. BFM
    p.15
With dusky hands through ivory keys unfold the thoughts to them beyond all
    writ or word. William Powell. EbR p.122
With flying rein, a frothing steed, bearing an empty saddle. Raymond Dan-
    dridge. PeP p.7; ZaP p.4
With Freedom's Seed.** Alexander Pushkin. TYBP p.67
With grace she rose when her name was called. Arlena Howard Benton. BTh
    p.61
With gypsies and sailors wanderers of the hills and seas. Langston Hughes.
    WeB p.72
With its fog-shroud. Julius Lester. KAL p.225
With my multi-colored baloon I feel just like I'm a rainbow. Herbert D.
    Greggs. MBP p.16
With open knife he walked the streets. Ted Joans. BPW p.37
With silver ball scarce sounding at the pace. Countee Cullen. CpS p.33
With searing fingers of flame you descended from Black Olumpus. Quincy
    Troupe. BlSp p.236
With sombre mien, the evening gray. Paul Laurence Dunbar. CPPLD p.198
With subtle poise he grips his tray. Countee Cullen. CCC p.10
With the first blush of morning, my soul is a wing. Georgia Douglas Johnson.
    HWOP p.44
With the hooves of a doe my eye has wandered into this strange forest.
    Sidney Alexander. PoN p.304; PoNe p.556
With The Lark. Paul Laurence Dunbar. CPPLD p.143
With the last whippoorwill will call of evening settling over mountains.
    Margaret Walker. PFND p.14
With two white roses on her breasts. Countee Cullen. CCC p.6; FNP p.20; KAL
    p.96; OTIS p.5
With wailing souls and protests came our fathers to this virgin soul.
    Charles Fred White. PONS p.132
With what angelic countenance. William S. Braithwaite. LLL p.59
With what thou gavest me, o master. Paul Laurence Dunbar. CPPLD p.455

With you in that bed no wondering about the wonder of life. Bernie Casey.
    LATP p.55
With your breath upon my cheek there is no spring nor autumn. Mae V. Cowdery.
    WLOV p.52
Within a London garret high. Paul Laurence Dunbar. CPPLD p.152
Within a native hut, are stirred the dawn. Aquah Laluah. CaD p.19; ChG p.20;
    PoN p.384; TYBP p.164
Within my casement came one night. Henrietta Cordelia Ray. EBAP p.142
Within our house of flesh we wear a web of time. Margaret Walker. PFND p.31
Within the cage he ramped and raged. Constance Holley. PoN p.322
Within the day a seventh time I touch the pale wood antelope. May Miller.
    CNAW p.359
Within this Black hive to-night. Jean Toomer. IADB p.79; PoN p.69; TYBP
    p.211
Without a doubt rome did the white thing when it killed christ. Don L. Lee.
    DSNP p.60
Without Benefit of Declaration. Langston Hughes. AmNP p.72; PATL p.54; TYBP
    p.229
Without expectation there is no end. Audre Lorde. SoS p.88
Without Name. Pauli Murray. AmNP p.106; PoN p.159; PoNe p.279
We, his purple an' linen, too. Anonymous. TYBP p.197
Woden-Stone, The. William C. Braithwaite. VER p.22
Woman. Valente Goenha Malangatana. TYBP p.190
Woman. Charles Fred White. PONS p.159
Woman and Eternity. William L. Morrison. DaR p.21
Woman At War, A. Hazel L. Washington. EbR p.152
Woman Power. Nikki Giovanni. BFBTBJ p.78
Woman Thing, The. LeRoi Jones. BMP p.131
Woman with a burning flame, A. Georgia Douglas Johnson. HWOP p.32
Woman with the mirror laugh. Michael S. Harper. DJDC p.24
Woman's **sho a cur'ous** critter, an' dey ain't no doubtin' dat. Paul Laurence
    Dunbar. CPPLD p.273; LiG p.34
Women and Kitchens. Waring Cuney. CNAW p.376; LUP p.15
Wondah whut on earf tiz ails me. Raymond Dandridge. PAOP p.43; ZaP p.79
Wonder. Langston Hughes. DYTB p.59
Wonder of the Modern Age. Clifford Miller. BTB p.150
Wonder why is it I still smell smoke. Theodore Horne. FoM p.70
Wonder Woman, The. Nikki Giovanni. MyH p.28
Wooded Path, The. Joseph S. Cotter, Sr. SPPH p.61
Woods stretch wild to the mountain side, The. Madison Cawein. ANP p.131
Wooing, The. Paul Laurence Dunbar. CPPLD p.86; LOLL p.128
Word From the Right Wing. LeRoi Jones. BMP p.93
Word is writ that he who runs may read, The. Paul Laurence Dunbar. CPPLD
    p.341
Word like the earth / creating. Joe Goncalves. TGWL p.49
Word of An Engineer, The. James Weldon Johnson. FYOP p.48
Word Poem (Perhaps Worth Considering). Nikki Giovanni. BOL p.9; BFBTBJ p.39
Word Raaaaaaaaaaaaaaaaaaaaaaaaaaaaaaaaaaaaaaaaaaaaaaaaaaaaaaaaa, in all its per muta-
    tions. LeRoi Jones. BMP p.155
Word to Ethiopia, A. Waverly Carmichael. FHOF p.23
Wordless kiss, a stifled sigh, A. Georgia D. Johnson. HWOP p.13
Words. Helen Morgan Brooks. NNPUSA p.104; PoNe p.278

You can   TITLE AND FIRST LINE INDEX

You can catch the wind. Langston Hughes. SIH p.31
You Can Finish It (I loved, I love). Don L. Lee. DSNP p.33
You can sigh o'er the sad-eyed Armenian. Frances Harper. ANP p.15; PBFH
    p.72
You cannot hurt Muhammed Ali, and stay alive. LeRoi Jones. BMP p.178
You cannot recall. Bruce McM. Wright. LUP p.61
You can talk about across the railroad tracks. Langston Hughes. OWT p.65
You Cared. Ted Joans. BPW p.91
You charged in here today spewing your woman hurt. Gordon Parks. InL (un-
    paged)
You chatter of your "white supremacy." Leanna F. Johnson. EbR p.95
You dig instant revolution against rotten meat. Clarence Major. NBP p.86
You don't know me because instead of looking at me you hid. Bobb Hamilton.
    BTB p.110
You drink a bitter draught. Maya Angelou. JGM p.33
You drop the cold, wet tugboats' lines. Fleetwood M. McCoy, Jr. EbR p.105
You feeble few that hold me somewhat more. Countee Cullen. CCC p.100
You fought like dogs during courtship. John Raven. BFM p.16
You have been good to me I give you this. Arna Bontemps. AmNP p.79; ITBLA
    p.161; PoN p.116; PoNe p.217
You have borne full well the burden of my friendship. Frank Horne. CaD
    p.115
You have freed me. Frank Horne. CaD p.116
You have known what love can be. William L. Morrison. DaR p.12
You have known what love can be. William L. Morrison. DaR p.60; EbR p.109
You have made my voice a rippling laugh. Frank Horne. CaD p.118; PoN p.80;
    PoNe p.152
You have not heard my love's dark threat. Countee Cullen. BLIA p.158; CCC
    p.4; FNP p.18; OTIS p.4
You kin talk about yer anthems. Paul Laurence Dunbar. CPPLD p.82; LOLL p.122
You Know Joe.** Ray Durem. BOL p.47; PoNe p.330; BTB p.104
You know you can't tell these people anything. Michael S. Harper. DaR p.81
You leave dead friends in a desert. LeRoi Jones. BMP p.63
You lie now in many coffins. Gerald W. Barrax. AKOR p.85
You look at me with children in your eyes. Alice Walker. ONC p.62
You lovely creature of the sky. Hilda Preer. BTh p.36
You made me a slave and kept me a slave. Dorothy Parrish. TNV p.87
You meet a human being who could be a playmate. Ted Joans. AFR p.92
You meet Chicago ere you meet it. Joseph S. Cotter, Sr. SPJSC p.15; WSBO
    p.26
You mind me of the winter's eve. Mae Smith Johnson. ANP p.112
You must remember structure beyond cotton plains. Conrad Kent Rivers. FoM
    p.27; BrT p.24
You need the untranslatable ice to watch. Gwendolyn Brooks. AnA p.30
You Never Can Tell. Milas Love. BTh p.50
You only fucked with my mind, Charlie. Arthur Boze. BlWe p.4
You opened my eyes. Katie M. Cumbo. BOL p.34
You opened our eyes, you taught us to see the beauty of Blackness, of Black
    unity. George Norman. FoM p.23
You phony white bitch. Arthur Boze. BlWo p.10
You probably could put their names to them. G. C. Oden. AmNP p.160; KAL
    p.183

You pushed me down the gutter. Eldon George McLean. EbR p.106
You put me down. Ted Joans. BPW p.85
You ragged rocks, bleak and forlorn, are sparsely strewn with wrecks of those who came to grief. Raymond Dandridge. ZaP p.19
You rock in your rocking chair. Clarence Major. SAM p.68
You said that your people. Conrad Kent Rivers. AmNP p.177; IADB p.59
You said you're crying. Tomi Carolyn Tinsley. EbR p.142
You sat upon the grass and I beside you. William S. Braithwaite. SPWSB p.91
You say I o.k. ed long distance? Langston Hughes. OWT p.13
You say that mammy is dying? Eli Shepperd. P1S p.94
You say "That man was made to mourn." Raymond Dandridge. PAOP p.52; ZaP p.48
You say that virtue is its own reward. Charles Fred White. PONS p.84
You say yes and I say yes ... alas. Mari Evans. NNPUSA p.19
You see boy is universal. Nikki Giovanni. BFBTBJ p.64
You see, my whole life is tied up to unhappiness. Nikki Giovanni. BFBTBJ p.78
You sez dat ale frens am de best. Raymond Dandridge. ZaP p.44; PAOP p.22
You should live naked. Robert Hayden. HSITD p.41
You sportin' tonight? Arthur Boze. BlWo p.7
You talkin' 'bout a time in toun. Waverly T. Carmichael. FHOF p.28
You talkin real bad. John Raven. BFM p.29
You Taught Me Love.** Frederica Katheryne Bunton. EbR p.17
You! the great America. Tommy Whitaker. TNV p.135
You toptoes naked into the jungle of my soul. Eugene Redmond. TNV p.102
You to me and I to you have returned. Gordon Parks. InL (unpaged)
You told me, you told me a thousand years ago. LeRoi Jones. BMP p.153
You too listless to examine. Countee Cullen. CpS p.65
You took it all so casually. John Burton. EbR p.19
You took this World Away From Us. Kali Grosvenor. PBK p.25
You visit Europe on five dollars a day? Ted Joans. BPW p.23
You want a lake. Gerald W. Barrax. AKOR p.81
You want to integrate me into your anonymity. Gerald Barrax. KAL p.203
You want to know what it's like being colored. Waring Cuney. CNAW p.374
You were a sophist. Gwendolyn B. Bennett. CaD p.156
You were born with ecstasy. V. A. Reese. BTh p.40
You were our first brave ones to defy their dissonance of hate with your silence. Margaret Walker. PFND p.11
You were the path I had to take. Countee Cullen. CpS p.27
You who descend river by river. Anonymous. MBP p.39
You will come back to me. Nicolas Guillen. PoN p.380
You with your bullshit niggerish ways want to destroy me. Nikki Giovanni. BFBTBJ p.98; BrT p.60
You would not recognize yourself if I should tell you. Naomi Long Madgett. KAL p.178
You--you are a forest, cool, lush and green. David Wadsworth Cannon, Jr. EbR p.24
You'd be strange too if you lived in a nation of ashamed homosexuals. LeRoi Jones. BMP p.79
You'd better watch out. Ted Joans. AFR p.13
You'll be wonderin' whar's de reason. Paul Laurence Dunbar. AVAN p.74; CPPLD p.210; LiG p.94
You'll Reap What You Sow. Waverly T. Carmichael. FROF p.45

Young Africans. Gwendolyn Brooks. BrT p.37; FaP p.18
Young ash craven never near to gold and further still from blood. June Jordan. SCh p.12
Young Black Soldiers. Bernie Casey. LATP p.49
Young Black soldiers eyeing the flesh. Bernie Casey. LATP p.49
Young Blackland Beautiful in Pursuit of Ancient Freedom Dreams. Mari Evans. IABW p.85
Young Bride. Langston Hughes. WeB p.93
Young David: Birmingham, A. Helen Morgan Brooks. PoNe p.276
Young Gal's Blues. Langston Hughes. FCTJ p.83; FNP p.24
Young Katy's heart was breaking. Eloise Culver. GANIV p.36
Young man--young man--your arm's too short to box with God. James Weldon Johnson. CNAW p.253; GoT p.21
Young Negro Girl. Langston Hughes. SIH p.17
Young Negro Poet.** Calvin Hernton. KAL p.195
Your niggers die old. Lloyd Corbin. SoS p.12
Young ones, Flip Side, The. James Emanuel. MBP p.17; KAL p.169
Young Poet. Myron O'Higgins. PoN p.196; PoNe p.351
Young Prostitute. Langston Hughes. WeB p.34
Young queen nature, ever sweet and fair, The. Paul Laurence Dunbar. CPPLD p.80; LOLL p.118
Young Sailor. Langston Hughes. WeB p.77
Young Singer. Langston Hughes. WeB p.28
Young Soul. LeRoi Jones. BMP p.49
Young Voices Cry, The. Mae V. Cowdery. WLOV p.9
Young Warrior, The. James Weldon Johnson. FYOP p.23
Young Wisdom. Mae V. Cowdery. WLOV p.32
Your beauty is a thunder. Maya Angelou. JGM p.37
Your Big Eyes. Bernie Casey. LATP p.29
Your body was a sacred cell always. Claude McKay. HaS p.90; SPCM p.104
Your door is shut against my tightened face. Claude McKay. AmNP p.31; CNAW p.299; FNP p.9; ITBLA p.155; PoN p.332; PoNe p.101; SoS p.119; SPCM p.78
Your Eyes Have Their Silence.** Gerald Barrax. AKOR p.42
Your face is pale. Ted Joans. BPW p.126
Your face sent a thousand ships to sea. John Raven. BFM p.22
Your good-by was given with chilly grace. Gordon Parks. InL (unpaged)
Your hand in mine for a space. William S. Braithwaite. LLL p.26
Your hand in my hand. Lucy Mae Turner. BCF p.36
Your Hands. Angelina Weld Grimke. CaD p.44
Your head is held high with eyes that sparkle like diamonds on a sunny day. Alfred Diggs. TGWL p.31
Your heart trembles in the shadows like a face. Jacques Roumain. PoN p.364
Your Just Reward. Bernie Casey. LATP p.80
Your knees are as thin. William Allyn Hill. LUP p.22
Your letter came today. Gordon Parks. InL (unpaged)
Your lips are like a Southern lily red. Claude McKay. SPCM p.94
Your love to me was like an unread book. Countee Cullen. BlC p.49; OTIS p.96
Your manners, dear ancestor aryan, in history lost without race. William C. Braithwaite. VER p.13
Your night is here so sleep little one. Marion Nicholes. LiS p.18
Your momma kissed the chauffeur. Maya Angelou. JGM p.47

Your momma took to shouting. Maya Angelou. JGM p.46
Your park's like a gothic cathedral to me. Louis Mordeay. PoN p.354
Your presence like a benison to me. Paul Laurence Dunbar. CPPLD p.440
Your scent is in the room. Claude McKay. BLIA p.167; HaS p.88; SPCM p.102
Your Songs. Gwendolyn Bennett. CaD p.197
Your soul isn't happy and your conscience isn't free. Ritten Edward Lee.
    EbR p.99
Your spoken words are roses fine and sweet. Paul Laurence Dunbar. CPPLD
    p.447
Your subjects hope, dread sire. Phillis Wheatley. PAL p.34; PPW p.6
Your sunsets. Edward Silvera. LUP p.42
Your tombstone, lout, as you lie stark below. Joseph S. Cotter, Sr. SPPH
    p.68
Your top is more popular than your legs. Ted Joans. AFR p.149
Your vividness Grants color where. Sterling Brown. SoR p.39
Your voice is the color of a robin's breast. Claude McKay. BANP p.173; PoN
    p.429; SPCM p.95
Your voice at times a fist. Maya Angelou. JGM p.14
Your walk sacerdotal and slow, undulant. Emile Roumer. TYBP p.91
Your words dropped into my heart like pepples into a pool. Claude McKay.
    CaD p.91; AVAN p.207; HaS p.64; SPCM p.93
Your World. Georgia Douglas Johnson. AmNP p.23
Your world is as big as you make it. Georgia Douglas Johnson. AmNP p.23
Your world is unimportant to me. Conrad Kent Rivers. BTB p.168; KAL p.205
You're a Black man with pride. Arthur Boze. BlWo p.19
You're Black but not yet beautiful. Ted Joans. BPW p.38
You're suppose to be hip. Ted Joans. BPW p.45
Yours is not a beauty to be unobserved. John W. Burton. EbR p.18
Yours was a little glass. William Allyn Hill. LUP p.21
You's Sweet To Yo' Mammy Jes De Same (Lullaby). James Weldon Johnson. FYOP
    p.70
Youth. Langston Hughes. DYTB p.25; GoS p.9; FNP p.30; LUP p.33
Youth. Georgia Douglas Johnson. BANP p.182; GoS p.77; PoN p.57; PoNe p.74;
    HWOP p.24
Youth. Zachary Withers. PAS p.5
Youth and the Moon. William L. Morrison. DaR p.49
Youth sings a song of rosebuds. Countee Cullen. BANP p.226; CpS p.63; PoN
    p.130; PoNe p.234
Youth there was of not great education who thought to raise himself above his
    station, A. Charles Fred White. PONS p.128
Youth went faring up and down. Paul Laurence Dunbar. CPPLD p.86; LOLL p.128
You've heard about this railroad; its runs were late at night. Eloise Culver.
    GANIV p.27
You've just got to dig Sly and the Family Stone. Nikki Giovanni. BFBTBJ
    p.75; BrT p.55
You've never seen such a flat black ocean. Clarence Major. SAM p.28
You're nothing but a Spanish colored kid. Felipe Luciano. BlSp p.123
You've taken my blues and gone. Langston Hughes. OWT p.81
Yule Song: A Memory. William S. Braithwaite. LLL p.53

AUTHOR INDEX

ABRAMS, ROBERTS J.
  Circles in Sand (Fragment)
  Two Poems

ABU BAKR (Moorish)
  Sword, The. A. J. Arberry, tr.

ABU DHARR (Moorish)
  Oranges, The. A. J. Arberry,
    tr.

ABU DOLAMA (Arabic)
  Humorous Verse. Raoul Abdul,
    tr.

ADDISON, LLOYD
  Carpentry

ALBA, NANINA
  For Malcolm X

ALBA, NINA
  Be Daedalus

ALEXANDER, LEWIS
  Africa
  Dark Brother, The
  Day and Night
  Dream Song
  Japanese
  Kokku
  Negro Woman
  Nocturne Varial
  Tanka I-VIII
  Transformation

ALEXANDER, SIDNEY*
  Castle, The
  Lenox Avenue

AL-FITURI, MUHAMMAD (Sudanese)
  I Am A Negro. Samir Zoghby, tr.
  Knell, The. Samir Zoghby, tr.

ALHAMISI, AHMED AKINWOLE
  Across the Ho Chi Minh Trail
  Ayobunmi
  Battle of Algiers
  Guerilla Warfare: an Aftermath
  Look for me Dear Mother
  O African Children of the Afric
    Tribe
  O Mothers O Fathers, of newer
    spirits
  Poet's Survival Kit
  Prophecy (For Afeni Fatima)
  Spiritual Cleanliness

ALLEN, GEORGE LEONARD
  Portrait
  To Melody

ALLEN, GEORGE R.
  On Slavery

ALLEN, HERVEY*
  Upstairs Downstairs

ALLEN, J. MORD
  Counting Out
  Devil and Sis' Viney, The
  Psalm of the Uplift, The
  Shine on, Mr. Sun
  When the Fish Begin to Bite

ALLEN, SAMUEL
  If the Stars Should Fall
  Love Song
  Moment, Please, A
  To Chessman and Associates
  To Satch (or American Gothic)

Death as a Lotus-Flower. Ulli
    Beier, tr.
Dispute Over Suicide, A
    T. Eric Peet, tr.
Hymn to the Sun, The
    J. E. Manchip White, tr.
Love Song. J. E. Manchip White,
    tr.
Love Song (1320-1200 B.C. 19th
    Dynasty. J. E. Manchip
    White, tr.
Magic of Black Poetry
Prayer to the God Thot. Ulli
    Beier, tr.

ANONYMOUS (Ethiopia)
    Potter, The. Halim·El-Dabh, tr.
    Trousers of Wind. Sylvia Pank-
        hurst, tr.

ANONYMOUS (Ewe)
    Sky, The. Ulli Beier, tr.

ANONYMOUS (Gabon)
    All Lives, All Dances, and All
        is Loud

ANONYMOUS (Gabon Pigmy)
    Death Rites II. C. M. Brown,
        tr.
    Elephant II, The. C. M. Brown,
        tr.

ANONYMOUS (Guinea)
    Moon, The

ANONYMOUS (Haiti)
    Sunday Morning Song
    Work Song

ANONYMOUS (Hottentot)
    How Death Came. W. H. I. Bleek,
        tr.
    Song for the Sun that Dis-
        appeared Behind the Rain-
        cloud. Ulli Beier, tr.

ANONYMOUS (Hurutsche)
    Hyena. George Economou, tr.
    Train, The. D. F. Merwe, tr.

ANONYMOUS (Nigeria)
    Hunger. Ulli Beier, tr.

ANONYMOUS (Somaliland)
    Modern Song

ANONYMOUS (South Africa)
    Giraffe
    Pass Office Song. Peggy Ruther-
        ford, tr.

ANONYMOUS (Susu)
    Sweetest Thing, The. Ulli Beier,
        tr.

ANONYMOUS (Trinidad)
    Cordelia Brown

ANONYMOUS (Twi)
    Prelude to Akwasidae. Halim El-
        dabh, tr.

ANONYMOUS (U.S.A.)
    Anonymous verse (from a Puerto
        Rican Christmas card)
    Ballit of de Boll Weevil, De
    Bedbug
    Cala Vendor's Cry
    "Crab Man"
    Creation of Man, The
    Deep River
    Did You Feed my Cow?
    Disgrace
    Dives and Laz'us
    Go Down Moses
    Go Down, Old Hannah
    Go Tell it on the Mountain
    Go' Way From my Window
    God (A Folk Sermon)
    God's Gonna Set Dis World on Fire
    Good Mornin' Blues
    Good Morning, Captain
    Gospel Train, The
    How Long Blues
    I am a Spiritual Alcoholic
    I Got a Home in Dat Rock
    I Got the Blues
    I Vision God
    I'm a Round-Town Gent
    John Henry
    Juba Dance
    Little David, Play on Yo' Harp

Southern Mansion
To a Young Girl Leaving the
    Hill Country
Tree Design, A

BOUNDZEKEI-DON GALA, EMMANUEL
    (Congo)
    Fantasy Under the Moon
        Gerald Moore & Ulli Beier,
        _tr._

BOYD, FRANCIS A.
    Dream, The
    Soliloquy, The

BOYD, JOHN
    Ocean
    Sketch of a Varying Evening Sky
    Vision/ A Poem in Blank Verse,
        The

BOYD, SAMUEL E.
    And So Tomorrow
    Dance Finale
    Rebel
    Tomorrow's Winds

BOYLE, KAY*
    Communication to Nancy Cunard,
        A

BOZE, ARTHUR
    Black Cowboys
    Black 99th, The
    Black Women
    Chained and Sold, The
    Colors
    Doper
    Four Little Girls
    He Had a Dream
    Headline, The
    Myth, The
    Ode to John Howard Griffin
    Pardon Me, do you have the
        Time?
    Revenge
    Sportin'
    To My Black Brothers in South
        Africa
    To Popwell, My Friend, A Black
        Actor
    Transfusion

We, the Black People
You Only Fucked With my Mind,
    Charlie

BRADFORD, WALTER
    T.C.
    Untitled (To Gwendolyn Brooks)

BRAITHWAITE, EDWARD
    Leopard
    Twist, The

BRAITHWAITE, WILLIAM C.
    Across the Sea
    Along the Shore
    Ampler Clime
    At Rest From his Works
    Athlete's Tomb, The
    Autumn Leaf, The
    Ballade of Mackeral
    Ballade of the Ships
    Bank Holiday
    Banbury Bells
    Belfry of Isone, The
    Benedicite
    Berck-Plage
    Blockley Hill
    Borcovicus
    Brother Jucundus
    Brothers and Sisters of the Light
    Chant Royal
    Coast-Guard Path, The
    Comrades in Service
    Cotswold Edge
    Cotswold Sonnets
    Death's Aftermath
    Declining Years
    "Deem Me Not Less The Liege of Thy
        Behest"
    Duddon Calling
    Etretat
    Fairfold Windows
    "Fellows are learning to Swim, The"
    Fellowship
    Fellside, The
    Five Sonnets of Freedom
    Florence to her Cathedral-Builders
    For a Spin
    "From Some Far Fringing Wood"
    Gallant Castle-Builder
    God in his Garden
    Haunting Music of the Ocean's Call

"Hour to Spend, An"
"I Have Escaped"
Imitation of Horace
"In Bounds Confined"
In Flying Coach
In Thronging Town no Longer
    Dwell
In Whichford Wood
King of Chit, The
Land Twixt Severn and Cotswold
Lanthwaite Green
Llyn Barfog
Lowly Grasses and Little Hills,
    The
Man's Pilgrimage
Maxims
Mazzini at Rome
Morning Hymn, A
Mountain Song, A
My Baby-Boy
North Gloster Song
"Oh, Sail With Me"
On the Road
Our Aryan Sires
Pershore
Rondeau, A
Roses Red
Rue
Rue To Berck
St. Bees Head
St. Silva's Church
Sainte Apresse
Sapricius
Shell, The
Spindrift
Stripling Thames, The
Taston
This and That
Time is Young
To My Friends
"Under the Elm"
Upon the Deck
Uses of the Halo, The
"Watch and Pray"
Wave-Song, A
Weed and Shell
"Where Avon Winds"
"Where Thames is Born"
"Winds are Still, The"
Woden-Stone, The
World has Fetters, The
Yule Song: a Memory

BRAITHWAITE, WILLIAM STANLEY
    After Harvest
    "All Heaven in a Grain of Sand"
    Annunciation of the Virgin, The
    April
    Aprilian Rhapsody
    April's Dream
    Arsenal of the Lord, The
    As Silent Through the World She
        Goes
    Ascension
    At Newport
    Ave and Vale
    Beacon Hill
    Book of Love, The
    By an Inland Lake
    Child Elsie
    City Garden, A
    Del Cascar
    Departure of Pierrott, The
    Distances
    Divided
    Dove's Nest
    Dream and a Song, A
    Enigmas
    Epilogue (To the Browning Cen-
        tenary May 12, 1912)
    Eternal Self, The
    Evening
    Exit
    First Born, The
    Flower and Root
    Fragment: Biographic, A
    From the Crowd
    Fugue in Gardenia
    Full Hope, The
    Golden Hair
    Golden Moonrise
    Grey Dawn
    Heart-Song
    Hoc Erat in Votis
    Holly Berry and Mistletoe
    House of Death, The
    House of Falling Leaves, The
    Hymn for the Slain in Battle
    I am Glad Daylong
    I Blow you a Kiss
    If I could Touch
    In a Grave-Yard
    In a Sunken Pool
    In my Lady's Praise

Memorial to Ed Bland
Mentors
My own Sweet Good
Negro Hero
Of De Wit Williams on his way to
    Lincoln Cemetery
Old Laughter
Old-Marrieds, The
Old Relative
Otto
Parents: People like our Mar-
    riage Maxie and Andrew
Piano after War
Pygmies are pygmies Still,
    though, percht on Alps
Rites for Cousin Vit, The
Second Sermon on the War-
    pland, The
Sermon on the War Pland
Song in the Front Yard
Song: the Rev. Mo Bugwu Dick-
    inson Ruminates Behind
    the Sermon
Sonnet Ballad, The
Speech to the Young. Speech to
    the Progress-Toward
Strong Men, Riding Horses
Sun came, The
Sunday Chicken
Sundays of Satin-Legs Smith
Throwing Out the Flowers
To a Winter Squirrel
To Don at Salaam
To Keorapetse Kgositsile
    (Willie)
Truth
Wall, The
Walter Bradford
We Real Cool
Young Africans

BROOKS, HELEN MORGAN
    Plans
    Words
    Young David: Birmingham, A

BROOKS, J. HENDERSON
    And one Shall Live in Two
    Beggars' Will
    Brown Aesthete Speaks, A
    Caucasian, The
    Comfort Ye my People

Disillusion
God's Masterpiece
Gulf, The
Last Quarter Moon of the Dying
    Year
Muse in Late November
My Angel
Out of the Dingy Alleyways
Paean
Remembrance
Resurection
Self-Indictment
She Said ...
Song for a Love That is Dead
Sonnets
Still I am Marveling
Student I Know, A
Winter Rode Away

BROOKS, WILLIAM F.
    Our Mission

BROWN, DELORES A.
    Upon Looking at Love

BROWN, ETHEL
    'Tis Difficult

BROWN, FRANK LONDON
    Jazz

BROWN, ISABELLA MARIA
    Another Day
    Prayer

BROWN, JOE C.
    Signs of Sleep

BROWN, LINDA
    Little Poem, A
    Precocious Curiosity

BROWN, STERLING A.
    After Winter
    Against That Day
    Bessie
    Cabret
    Challenge
    Checkers
    Children of the Mississippi
    Children's Children
    Chillen Get Shoes

Young Voices Cry, The
Young Wisdom

COWEN, JOSEPH R.*
Recessional for the Class of
1959 of a School for De-
linquent Negro Girls

COX, THELMA PARKER
Evolution
Frustration, a Heritage

CRANE, HART*
Black Tambourine

CRAVEIRINHA, JOSE
Poem of the future citizen;
Dorothy Guedes, tr.

CROUCH, STANLEY
Albert Ayler: Eulogy for a De-
composed Saxophone Player
Chops are Flyin
Pimp's Last Make: Death re-
quest a folk song.

CRUZ, VICTOR HERNANDEZ
Advice to a Painter
After the Dancing for Pamela
Alone /December/ Night
& Stuff like That
Back to/ Back To
Boston Roller Coaster, The
Born to be Burned
Cities
Coming Down
Day with Bo, A
Descarga
Descarga en Cueros
Drive, The
Education, The
Energy
Eye Uptown and Downtown (three
days), The
First Claims Poem
For Tiny
Free Spirit
From: Cities #8
Going Uptown to Visit Miriam
Group, The
Half a Page from Square Busi-
ness

How you Feel
Is a Dead Man
Ladies' Poem
Latin & Soul
Man I Thought you was Talking An-
other Language That Day
Megalopolis
Moving
Phase 214 Hours
Poem for Downtown, A
Ritmo 1
Ruskie's Boy
/Sisters/
Slick
Snag
Snaps
Sometimes on my way Back Down to
the Block
Spirits
Street Scene #1
Their Poem
Three Days / Out of Franklin
Today is a Day of Great Joy
224 Stoop
Under me Sometime. Under Mc Walls
& Paint. 1967
Urban Dream
Walking on the Lips of the Bronx
White Powder 1

CUESTAS, KATHERINE L.
I Seek
Mea Culpa
Poem

CULLEN, COUNTEE
Advice to a Beauty
Advice to Youth
After a Visit
All the Dead
And When I Think
Any Human to Another
Asked and Answered
At a Parting
At the Etoile (at the unknown Sol-
dier's Grave in Paris)
At the Wailing Wall in Jerusalem
Atlantic City Waiter
Ballad of the Brown Girl, The
Bilitis Song
Black
Black Magdalens

311

Cullen

AUTHOR INDEX

CUTHBERT, MARIAN
    Great Laws, The
    Great Truths
    I and Me
    Immortality
    Life of God, The
    We can Know Surely

DADIE, BERNARD
    Dry your Tears, Africa
    I Give you Thanks, my God
        Donatus the Nwaga, tr.

DA GAMA, LUIS GONZAGA
    Who I am. Alan Lomax, tr.

DALCOUR, PIERRE
    Verse written in the Album of
        Mademoiselle

DAMAS, LEON
    Poems
    Put Down. Seth L. Wolitz, tr.
    They Came This Evening

DANDRIDGE, RAYMOND GARFIELD
    A. L. Ames
    Abraham Lincoln
    Almighty God
    Angel Incognita, An
    Ante Bellum Symphony
    Appeal, An
    Arise
    Ashes of Love
    At the Bier of Hope
    Awake
    Bachelors
    Best of It, The
    Between Lines (In a little
        Book p.p.)
    Blacks in Blue
    Booker T. Washington
    Braggard, The
    Brook, A
    Brother Mine
    Cardinal Mercier
    Censored
    Christian, A
    Close Mouf
    Coffee Groun' Chloe
    Color Blind
    Days

De Drum Majah
De Innah Part
De Tes'
Deceit
De Creed (Matthew 2:15)
Disagreement, A
Dr. Mason
Down Road, The
Dumb Soldier, The
Ease
Easter
Easter Morn'
Emancipators
Eternity
Everywhere
Facts
Faith
Fifty-Fifty
Fighting Time
Fo Yoreself
Forward
Frenship
Garden of Life, The
Ghost Story, A
Ginoligy
Gone West
Good Everywhere
Grammah
Gratitude
Gray Day, A
Hahd Cidah
Heart Broken
Heritage
Home
Home and Mother
In Ole Kentucky
In Stripes
It is no Longer Night
'Ittle Touzle Head
January First
Jello
Judge Ye Not
Kassel B'ildin
Late Day Chillen
Leader, A
Letter, A
Life's Circus
Little Girl
Little Things
Lure, The
Love
Mah Dawg

DIOP, DAVID
  Africa. Ulli Beier, tr.
  He Who Has Lost All. Anne Atik,
      tr.
  Vultures, The. Ulli Beier, tr.

DIPOKI, MBELLA SONNG
  Autobiography

DISMOND, BINGA
  At Early Morn
  Dominicaine, The
  Revolt in the South
  Status Quo
  To the Men of the Soviet Army

DJANGATOLUM see CORBIN, LLOYD M.
          JR.

DODSON, OWEN
  All this Review
  Autumn Chorus
  Black Mother Praying
  Circle One
  Circle Two
  Confession Stone, The
  Counterpoint
  Conversation on V
  Countee Cullen
  Decision
  Definition
  Drunken Lover
  Engagement
  Epitah for a Negro Woman
  From "The Confession Stone"
  Guitar
  Hymn Written after Jeremiah
      Preached to me in a Dream
  I Break the Sky
  Ignore Those Seal
  Iphigenia
  Jonathan's Sons
  Lament
  Martha Graham
  Midnight Bell
  Miss Packard and Miss Giles
  Open Letter
  Pearl Primus
  Poem for Pearl's Dancers
  Poems for my Brother Kenneth
  Precedent, The
  Rag doll and Summer Birds

  Reunion
  Sailors on leave
  Samuel Chapman Armstrong
  Sickle Pears (for Glidden Parker)
  Signifying Darkness
  Six O'Clock
  Someday We're gonna Tear Them
      Pillars Down
  Sorrow is the Only Faithful One
  Star Chorus
  Summing Up by the Defendant
  That Star
  Tell Rachel, He Whispered
  That Star
  Through the Varied Patterned Lace
  Verdict
  Watching, The
  Wedding Poem for Joseph and Evelyn
      Jenkins
  When I am Dead
  Widow's Walk, The
  Winter Chorus
  Yardbird's Skull (for Charlie
      Parker)

DOUGLAS, ELROY
  This Day

DU BOIS, WILLIAM EDWARD BURGHARDT
  Litany at Atlanta, A
  Prayers of God, The
  Riddle of the Spinx, The

DUBONEE, YLESSA
  Departure
  Nocturne

DUCKETT, ALFRED A.
  Portrait Philippines
  Sonnet

DUMAS, ALEXANDRE, 1824-1895
  Verses to the Lady of the Pearls.
      Gerard Hopkins, tr.

DUMAS, HENRY
  America
  Image

Love's Phases
Love's Pictures
Love's Seasons
Lullaby
Lyric, A
Madrigal, A
Mare Rubrum
Master-Player, The
Masters, The
Meadow Lark
Melancholia
Memory of Martha, The
Merry Autumn
Misapprehension
Misty Day, A
Monk's Walk, The
Morning
Morning Song of Love
Mortality
Murdered Lover, The
Musical, A
My Corn-Cob Pipe
My Lady of Castle Grand
My Little March Girl
My Sort O' Man
My Sweet Brown Gal
Mystery, The
Mystic Sea, The
Nature and Art
Negro Love Song, A
News, The
Night
Night, Dim Night
Night of Love
Noddin' by de Fire
Noon
Nora: a Serenade
Not they who Soar
Nutting Song
October
Ode for Memorial Day
Ode to Ethiopia
Old Apple Tree, The
Old Cabin, The
Old Front Gate, The
Old Homestead, The
Old Memory, An
Ol' Tunes, The
On a Clean Book
On the Death of W.C.
On the Dedication of Dorothy Hall
On the River

On the Road
On the Sea Wall
One Life
Opportunity
Over the Hills
Paradox, The
Parted
Parted
Party, The
Passion and Love
Path, The
Phantom Kiss, The
Philosophy
Photograph
Phyllis
Place Where the Rainbow Ends, The
Plantation Child's Lullaby
Plantation Melody, A
Plantation Portrait, A
Plea, A
Poet, The
Poet and His Song, The
Poet and the Baby, The
Pool, The
Poor Withered Rose
Possession
Possum
Possum Trot
Prayer, A
Precedent
Preference, A
Premonition
Preparation
Prometheus
Promise
Protest
Puttin' the Baby Away
Quilting, The
Rain-Songs
Real Question, The
Religion
Reluctance
Remembered
Resignation
Response
Retort
Retrospection
Riding to Town
Right to Die, The
Right's Security
Rising of the Storm, The
Rivals

River of Ruin, The
Roadway, A
Robert Gould Shaw
Roses
Roses and Pearls
Sailor's Song, A
Sand-Man, The
Scamp
Secret, The
Seedling, The
She Gave me a Rose
She told her Beads
Ships that Pass in the Night
Signs of the Times
Silence
Slow Through the Dark
Snowin'
Soliloquy of a Turkey
Song
Song
Song, A
Song, A
Song, The
Song of Summer
Sonnet
Sparrow, The
Speakin' at de Cou't House
Speakin' O' Christmas
Spellin' Bee, The
Spiritual
Spring Fever
Spring Song
Spring Wooing, A
Starry Night, A
Stirrup Cup, The
Sum, The
Summer Night, A
Summer Pastoral, A
Summer's Night, A
Sunset
Suppose
Sympathy
Temptation
Thanksgiving Poem, A
Then and Now
Theology
Thou art my Love
Till the Wind Gets Right
Time to Tinker 'Roun!
To a Captious Critic
To a Dead Friend
To a Lady Playing the Harp

To a Violet Found on All Saints'
    Day
To an Ingrate
To Dan
To E. H. K.
To Her
To J. Q.
To Louise
To Perimmer
To the Eastern Shore
To the Memory of Mary Young
To the Miami
To the Road
To the South
Trouble in de Kitchen
Tryst, The
Turning of the Babies in the Bed
Twell de Night is Pas'
Twilight
Two Little Boots
Two Songs
Unexpressed
Unlucky Apply, The
Unsung Heroes, The
Vagrants
Valse, The
Vengeance is Sweet
Veteran, The
Visitor, The
Voice of the Banjo, The
Wadin' in de Crick
Waiting
Warm Day in Winter, A
Warrior's Prayer, The
We Wear the Mask
Weltschmerz
W'en I Gits Home
What's the Use
When a Feller's Itchin' to be
    Spanked
When All is Done
When de Co'n Pone's Hot
When Dey Listed Colored Soldiers
When Malindy Sings
When Sam'l Sings
When the Old Man Smokes
When Winter Darkening All Around
Whip-Poor-Will and Katy-Did
Whistling Sam
Whittier
Why Fades a Dream
Wind and the Sea, The

Miss Nancy's Geo'ge
Moanin' Moanin'
Novembah Dusk
Ole Man Jollie
Ox in de Ditch
Rivah's a Black Mare
Salia
Siam at de Radio
Soft Soap
Soliloguy
Susie Lou
'Tater Field
Unk' Enoch Mann
Walk, God's Chillun
Whimper, Baby
Yalla Gal

GOODWIN, RUBY BERKLEY
Guilty
If this be Good-bye
New Year's Prayer
We Launched a Ship

GORDON, BAREFIELD
To Lincoln University--1923-
1924

GORDON, CHARLES F.
Long Night Home, The

GORHAM, MYRTLE CAMPBELL
Service, Please

GOSS, WILLIAM THOMPSON
Man to Man
Variety

GOULBOURNE, CARMIN AULD
Letter for El-Hajj Malik El-
Shabazz

GOVAN, DONALD D.
Recollection

GRAHAM, LE
Black Shining Prince, The

GRAHAM, LORENZ
Every man Heart Lay Day

GRAHAM, P. L.
Soul

GRAHAM, RUDY BEE
Memorandum

GREEN, WILLIAM H.
I am Happy Today

GREENE, EMILY JANE
He's Coming Home at Last

GREER, ROSLYN
Triangle

GREGGS, HERBERT P.
Multi-Colored Balloon

GREGORY, CAROLE
Ghetto Lovesong--Migration

GREGORY, YVONNE
Christmas Lullaby for a New-born
Child

GRIFFIN, AMOS J.
Salute to the Tan Yanks

GRIMARD, LUC
Amitié Amoureuse

GRIMKE, ANGELINA WELD
Black Fingers, The
Dusk
Eyes of Regret, The
For the Candle Light
Grass Fingers
Greeness
Hushed by the Hands of Sleep
I Weep
Mona Lisa, A
Paradox
Puppet Player, The
Surrender
Tenebris
To Clarissa Scott Delany
To the Dunbar High School: a
Sonnet
Ways o' Men, The
When the Green lies over the Earth
Winter Twilight, A
Your Hands

Old Song, An
Old Woman with Violets
Ole Jim Crow
On Lookout Mountain
On the Coast of Maine
Orison
Perseus
Photograph of Isadora Duncan, A
Poem for a Negro Dancer
Poem in Time of War
Primaveral
Prophecy
Prophet, The
Rabbi, The
Religioso
Road in Kentucky, A
Rosemary
Runagate Runagate
School Integration Riot
Shine, Mister?
Snow
Sol Y Sombra
Sonnet Toe
Southern Moonlight
Speech
Spring Offensive
Sub Specie Aeternitatis
Summer Time and the Living
Sunflowers: Beaubien Street
Theme and Variation
These are Our People
This Grief
Those Winter Sundays
Three Leaves
Time Capsule
To a Young Negro Poet
Tour 5
Vera Cruz
"We are the Hunted"
"We Have not Forgotten"
Web, The
Weeds
"What is Precious is Never to
    Forget"
Wheel, The
Whipping, The
Wind, the Weathercock and the
    Warrior's Ghost, The
Witch Doctor
Words this Spring
World's Fair

HAYES, DONALD JEFFREY
    After All
    Alien
    Approggiatura
    Auf Wiedersehen
    Benediction
    Confession
    Haven
    Inscription
    Night
    Pastourelle
    Poet
    Prescience
    Threnody

HAYES, ERSKINE
    Child, The

HAYFORD, GLADYS MAE   see   LALUAH,
    AQUAH

HAYNES, ALBERT
    Law, The

HAYNES, SAMUEL A.
    Challenge, The
    Warning

HEARD, JOSEPHINE D. (HENDERSON)
    To Whittier

HEATH, GORDON
    Two Songs of Love

HENDERSON, DAVID
    Downtown-Boy-Uptown
    Five Winters Age
    4th Dimension
    Handing out in the Music
    Louisiana Weekly #4
    Number 5--December
    Psychedelic Firemen
    Riot Lauch & I Talk
    Sketches of Harlem
    They are Killing all the Young Men
    Walk with the Mayor of Harlem

HENDERSON, ELLIOT B.
    Git on Board, Chillun
    Good Bye, Honey--Good Bye

Picnic: the Liberated
Song
Three Brown Girls Singing

HOLMES, GENE
Golden Stool, The

HORNE, FRANK
Immortality
Kid Stuff
Letters Found Near a Suicide
More Letters found Near a
    Suicide
Nigger
Notes Found Near a Suicide
On Seeing Two Brown Boys in a
    Catholic Church
Symphony
To a Presistent Phantom
To James
To Wanda
Toast

HORNE, THEODORE
Malcolm Exsiccated
There's Fire

HORTON, GEORGE MOSES
Acrostic for Julia Shepard, An
Creditor to His Proud Debtor,
    The
George Moses Horton, Myself
Jefferson in a Tight Phase
Like Brothers we Meet
Lover's Farewell, The
Meditation on a Cold, Dark,
    and Rainy Night
On Hearing of the Intention
    of a Gentleman to Pur-
    chase the Poet's Freedom
On Liberty and Slavery
Praise of Creation
Slavery
Slave's Complaint, The
To Eliza

HOWARD, VANESSA
Monument in Black
Feflections

HOWARD, VILMA
Citizen, The

HUGHES, JAMES C.
Aspiration

HUGHES, LANGSTON
Afraid
Afro-American fragment
After Many Spring
Alabama Earth (at Booker Washing-
    ton's Grave)
American Heart Break
Angel's Wings
Angola Question Mark
Announcement
April Rain Song
Ardella
As I Grew Older
Aspiration
Aunt Sue's Stories
Azikiwe in Jail
Baby
Backlash Blues, The
Bad Luck Card
Bad Man
Bad Morning
Ballad of Gin Mary
Ballad of Margie Polite
Ballad of the Fortune-Teller
Ballad of the Girl Whose Name is
    Mud
Ballad of the Gypsy
Ballad of the Killer Boy
Ballad of the Man Who's Gone
Ballad of the Pawnbroker
Ballad of the Sinner
Beale Street
Beale Street Love
Bed Time
Beggar Boy
Bible Belt
Big Sur
Birmingham Sunday (September 15,
    1963)
Birth
Black Gal
Black Maria
Black Panther
Black Pierrot, A
Blue Bayou
Blues Fantasy
Blues on a Box
Boarding House
Bombings in Dixie

Border Line
Bound No'th Blues
Brass Spittoons
Brief Encounter
Brothers
Burden
Cabaret
Cabaret Girl Dies on Welfare
    Island
Caribbean Sunset
Carol of the Brown King
Carolina Cabin
Cat and the Saxophone
Children's Rhymes
Chippy
Christ in Alabama
Christmas Story, The
Circles
City Called Heaven, The
City: San Francisco
Closing Time
College Formal
Color
Communion
Convent
Cora
Corner Meeting
Could Be
Crap Game
Cross
Crossing
Crowns and Garlands
Cultural Exchange
Curious
Cycle
Dancers
Danse Africaine
Daybreak
Daybreak in Alabama
Death Chants
Death in Harlem
Death in Yorkville
Death of an Old Seaman
Death of Do Dirty; a Rounder
    Song
Deceased
Declaration
Democracy
Desert
Desire
Dimout in Harlem
Dinner Guest: Me

Disillusion
Dole, The
Down and Out
Down Where I am
Draftees
Dream
Dream Dust
Dream Keeper, The
Dream Variation
Dreams
Dressed Up
Dusk
Dustbown
Early Evening Quarrel
Earth Song
Elderly Leaders
End
Ennui
Epigram, tr.
Epilogue
Esthete in Harlem
Evening' Air Blues
Evil
Evil Morning
Evil Woman
Exits
Faithful One
Fantasy in Purple
Farewell, A
Feet O' Jesus
50-50
Final Call
Final Curve
Fire
Fired
Flight
Florida Road Workers
For Billie Holiday
For Dead Mimes
Fragments
Frederick Douglass: 1817-1895
Free Man
Freedom
From Selma
Frosting
Fulfilment
Funeral
Gal's Cry for a Dying Lover
Garmet
Genius Child
Georgia Dusk
Ghosts of 1619

Sinner
Six-Bits Blues
Slave
Sleep
Slum Dreams
Snail, The
Snake
Snob
Soledad
Song
Song for a Banjo Dance
Song for a Dark Girl
Song for a Suicide
Song for Billie Holiday
Song to a Negro Wash-Woman
Songs
Songs to the Dark Virgin
South, The
Southern Mammy Sings
Special Bulletin
Spirituals
Spirit
S-sss-ss-sh!
Stars
Statement
Still Here
Stokely Malcolm Me
Strange Hurt
Stranger in Town
Suicide
Suicide's Note
Summer Evening
Summer Night
Sun Song
Sunday
Sunday Morning Prophecy
Supper Time
Sweet Words on Race
Sylvester's Dying Bed
Tambourine
Theme for English 8
There
Third Degree
To a Black Dancer in "The
    Little Savoy"
To a Little Lover Lass, Dead
To Midnight Nan at Leroy's
To the Dark Mercedes of
    "El Palacio De Amor"
Today
Too Blue
Trip: San Francisco

Troubled Woman
Trumpet Player
Trumpet Player: 52nd Street
Twilight Reverie
Two Somewhat Different Epigrams
Un-American Investigators
Undertow
Vagabonds
Vari-Colored Song
Verse Written in the Album of
    Mademoiselle, tr.
Visitors to the Black Belt
Wake
Walkers with the Dawn
Walls
War
Warning
Water-Front Street
Weary Blues, The
West Texas
When Sue Wears Red
When the Armies Passed
Where? When? Which?
White Felts in Fall
White Ones, The
Who But the Lord?
Widow Woman
Wind
Winter Moon
Winter Sweetness
Wisdom
Wisdom and War
Without Benefit of Declaration
Wonder
Words Like Freedom
Workin' Man
Yesterday and Today
Young Bride
Young Gal's Blues
Young Negro Girl
Young Prostitute
Young Sailor
Young Singer
Youth

HUGHES, LOIS ROYAL
    I Could not Know
    Like Unto a Rose
    Rendezvous

HUNTER, KATHERINE JACKSON
    Congenital

Johnson, Georgia Douglas   AUTHOR INDEX

With all Deliberate Speed (for
    the Children of our World)
You Finish it

LEE, RITTEN EDWARD
    Blend
    Freedom's Snare
    Man
    Southern Justice
    Tragedy

LENNON, FLORENCE BECKER*
    Little White School House Blues

LEONARD, WILLIAM ELLERY
    Lynching Bee, The

LESLIE, CY
    On Riots

LESTER, JULIUS
    Poems
    lxvxii
    Mud of Vietnam
    On the Birth of my Son, Mal-
        colm Coltrane

LEWIS, DIO
    Malcontents, The
    Time

LEWIS, LILLIAN TUCKER
    Longing

LIMA, FRANK*
    Memory of Boxer Benny (kid)
        Paret, The

LINDSAY, VACHEL*
    Congo, The

LLORENS, DAVID
    Of a Woman Turns Rivers
    One Year Ago
    Resonant Silence, A
    Wayward Child

LONG, DOUGHTRY (DOC), JR.
    #4
    #20
    #25
    #28

One Time Henry Dreamed the Number

LONG, WORTH
    Arson and Cold Lace

LONGFELLOW, HENRY WADSWORTH*
    Slave's Dream, The

LORDE, AUDRE
    And Fall Shall sit in Judgment
    Coal
    Father, Son and Holy Ghost
    Naturally
    Summer Oracle
    What my Child Learns of the Sea

LOVE, GEORGE
    Noonday April Sun, The

LOVE, J. AUSTIN
    Down Fish Trap Lane
    Out in the Still Wet Night

LOVE, MILAS
    She was Gone
    You Never Can Tell

LOWELL, JAMES RUSSELL*
    Stanzas on Freedom

LOWENFELS, WALTER*
    Creed

LOWERY, L. DORETTA
    As a Goldfish see the World
    Wind, The

LUCAS, JAMES R.
    Caution

LUCAS, PORTIA
    Laughter

LUCIANO, FELIPE
    Hot Blood/ Bad Blood
    You're Nothing But a Spanish
        Colored Kid

LUMUMBA, PATRICE EMERY
    Dawn in the Heart of Africa

LUPER, LUTHER GEORGE, JR.
    Sonnet Spiritual

LYNN, EVE (EVELYN C. REYNOLDS)
    God's Christmas Tree

LYONS, MARTHA E.
    Thing Born of Darkness, A

MC BROWN, GERTRUDE
    Lilacs

MC CALL, JAMES EDWARD
    New Negro, The
    Tribute to Countee Cullen

MC CLELLAN, GEORGE MARION
    Belated Oriole, A
    Ephemera, The
    Path of Dreams, The
    To Holly Hocks

MC COY, FLEETWOOD M., JR.
    Underway

MC FARLANE, BASIL
    Final Man, The

MC FARLANE, J. E. CLARE
    On National Vanity   ·

MC GAUGH, LAWRENCE
    From Glimpses #xii

MC GIRT, JAMES E.
    Anna, Won't you Marry Me?
    Palm for Weary Minds, A
    Born Like the Pines
    Century's Prayer, The
    Defeated
    Des Fo' Day
    Experience
    God Bless our Country
    "Home Sick"
    I Shall Succeed
    If Love Could See
    If Loving Were Wooing
    Inspiration
    Life and Love
    Love
    Lullaby, Go to Sleep
    Memory of W. W. Brown

My Soul's at Rest
Mystery, A
No Use in Signs
Quest, A
Right Will Win
Rosy Dawn, The
Sailor's Departure, A
Seige of Manila, The
Should I Spy Love
Signs O' Rain
Signs of Death
Slothful Youth, A
Slong of Love, A
Spirit of the Oak, The
Spring
Success
Tell me, Deep Ocean
Temptation
Test of Love, A
Thanksgivin Prayer
True Love
Uncle Is'rel
Victoria the Queen
Warrior's Judgment, A
Weep Not
When de Sun Shines Hot
Winter

MC KAY, CLAUDE
    Absence
    Adolescence
    Africa
    After the Winter
    Alfonso, Dressing to wait at Table
    America
    Baptism
    Barcelona
    Barrier, The
    Birds of Prey
    Castaways, The
    City's Love, The
    Commemoration
    Courage
    Dawn in New York
    December, 1919
    Desolate
    Easter Flower, The
    Enslaved
    Exhortation: Summer, 1919
    Farewell to Morocco, A
    Flame-Heart
    Flirtation

Flower of Love
French Leave
Futility
Harlem Dancer, The
Harlem Shadows
Heritage
Home Thoughts
Homing Swallows
I Know my Soul
I Shall Return
If we Must Die
In Bondage
Jasmines
La Paloma in London
Like a Strong Tree
Look Within
Lynching, The
Memorial
Memory of June
Morning Joy
Moscow
My House
My Mother
Negro's Friend, The
Negro's Tragedy
Night Fire, The
North and South
O Word I Love to Sing
On a Primitive Canoe
On Broadway
On the Road
One Year After
Outcast
Paganisms, The
Poetry
Polarity
Prayer, A
Red Flower, A
Rest in Peace
Romance
Russian Cathedral
St. Isaac's Church, Petrograd
Snow Fairy, The
Song of the Moon, A
Spanish Needle, The
Spring in New Hampshire
Subway Wind
Sukee River
Summer Morn in New Hampshire
Tetuan
Thirst
Through Agony

Tiger
Tired Worker, The
To a Poet
To O.E.A.
To one Coming North
To the White Fiends
To Winter
Tormented
Tropics in New York, The
Truth
Two-An'-Six
When Dawn Comes to the City: New
    York
When I Have Passed Away
White City
White House
Wild Goats, The
Wild May
Winter in the Country
Wise Men of the East

MC KELWAY, ST. CLAIR*
    Boogie-Woogie Ballads

MC LEAN, ELDON GEORGE
    Bitterness
    Experience
    Gutter Rats
    Inevitable Road, The
    Retrospection

MC LEAN, WILLIAM ALFRED, JR.
    War

MC LLELAN, GEORGE MARION
    April of Alabama, The
    Butterfly in Church, A
    Color Bane, The
    Day Break (from Path of Dreams,
        1916)
    Decoration Day, A
    Dogwood Blossoms
    Eternity
    Feet of Judas, The
    Hills of Sewanee, The
    In the Heart of a Rose
    January Dandelion, A
    September Night, A
    Sun Went Down in Beauty, The

MANZANO, JUAN FRANCISCO
    My Thirty Years. Oliver Cobarn
        & Ursula Lehrburger, <u>tr</u>.

MARAN, RENE
    Human Soul. Mercer Cook, <u>tr</u>.

MARGETSON, GEORGE REGINALD
    Fledging Bard and the Poetry
        Society
    Light of Victory, The
    Prayer, A
    Resurrection
    Time

MARKWEI, MATEI
    Life in our Village

MARSHALL, BARBARA
    Colonized Mind
    Little Black Boy
    On Philosophy
    Request

MARSON, UNA
    Hunted
    Nightfall

MARTI, JOSE
    Simple Verses. Seymour Remick,
        <u>tr</u>.
    Two Countries. Mona Hinton,
        <u>tr</u>.

MARTINEZ, MAURICE
    Suburbia

MARVIN X
    Proverbs
    Till the Sun Comes Down

MASON, MASON JORDAN*
    Big Man
    In War
    Last Impression of New York
    Pen Hy Cane
    Pico Della Mirandola
    Things of the Spirit

MATHEUS, JOHN FREDERICK
    Requiem

MAXWELL-HALL, AGNES
    Jamaica Market
    Lizard

MBITI, JOHN
    New York Skyscrappers

MELVILLE, HERMAN*
    "Formerly a Slave"

MENDES, CATULLE
    At early Morn; from the French of
        Catulle Mende

MEYER, JUNE
    All the World Moved

MICKELWAY, ST. CLAIR*
    Boogie-Woogie Ballads

MILES, JOSEPHINE*
    Government Injunction

MILLER, CLIFFORD L.
    Springtime
    Wonder of the Modern Age
    World Wonders

MILLER, KELLY
    I see and am Satisfied

MILLER, MAY
    Calvary Way
    Gift from Kenya
    Last Warehouse, The
    Procession
    Tally
    Wrong Side of Morning

MILNER-BROWN, A. L.
    Who Knows?

MISTRAL, GABRIELA
    Indian Christmas
    Stable, The

MKALIMOTO, ERNIE
    Energy for a New Thang

MOORE, MARIANNE*
    Arthur Mitchell

MUNGIN, HORACE
  Blues
  Of man and Nature

MURAPA, RUKUDZO
  Gwen Brooks--Our Inspirer

MURPHY, BEATRICE M.
  Evicted
  Letter, The
  Signs
  Trivia
  We Pass

MURRAY, PAULI
  Dark Testament
  Without Name

MUUSE, ABDILAAHI
  Eler's Reproof to His Wife, An.
    B. W. Andrzjewski & J. M.
    Lewis, tr.

MYLES, GLENN
  Percy / 68

NAU, IGNACE
  Belle-De-Nuit

NEAL, LARRY
  Garvey's Ghost
  Holy Days
  Jive Eschatology, A
  Love Song in Middle Passage
  Malcolm X--An Autobiography
  Morning Raga for Malcolm
  Orishas
  Rhythm is a Groove (#2)
  Way it went Down, The

NELSON, ALICE DUNBAR
  I sit and Sew
  Snow in October
  Sonnet

NELSON, DAVID
  Essie Mae

NEWMAN, LOUIS*
  World Looks On, The

NEWSOME, EFFIE LEE
  Artic Tern in a Museum
  Baker's Boy
  Bats
  Cotton Cat, The
  Cricket and the Star, The
  Little Birches
  Magi Call Him King, a Christmas
    Song
  Morning Light, the Dewdrier
  Pansy
  Peppermint Candy March, The
  Quilt
  Quoits
  Sassafras Tea
  Sky Pictures
  Wild Roses

NICHOLAS, MICHAEL
  Today: the Idea Market

NICHOLES, MARION
  Blacktop Black to Blacktop Top
    Black Black Top
  Bridge Part, or Gaps in Teeth aint
    new
  Brother of the Hour
  Chakara
  Darlene Blackburn
  Definition
  Food Poisoning
  Fruit of Love
  Healer of the New Day
  Leader of the Pack
  Life Styles
  Lullaby
  No Love
  No Time
  Ramadan--Hot Night
  Rescue Mission
  Sister
  Today's Pimp
  Utility
  Vieled Again

NICHOLS, CONSTANCE
  Baby Hair
  Civil Service
  Desire

Indictment
Soliloguy

PATCHEN, KENNETH*
Nice Day for a Lynching

PATRICIA
Two for Malcolm

PATTERSON, CHARLES
Listen

PATTERSON, JAMES
Ballada O Neizvestnosti
Ballad to the Anonymous

PATTERSON, JESSE FRANKLIN
Grill Room War

PATTERSON, RAYMOND
At That Moment
Black All Day
Envoi
Forgotten, The
From Riot Rimes: U.S.A.
From 26 Ways of Looking at a
Blackman
In Time of Crisis
I've Got a Home in That Rock
Love Song, A
Second Avenue Encounter
This Age
When I Awoke
You are the Brave

PAYNE, ANTOINETTE
Oh! Lord

PAYNE, DANIEL A.
From the Pleasures
May I Not Love?
Mournful Lute or the Precep-
tor's Farewell, The

PEDROSO, REGINO
Opinions of the New Chinese
Students

PERKINS, EUGENE
Bronzeville Poet

PERRY, ROBERT N., JR.
Inevitability
Of Dictators
Seasons, The

PETERS, LENNIE
After They Put Down Their Overalls

PETRIE, PHIL W.
It Happened in Montgomery

PFISTER, ARTHUR
Funny Company (or Why Ain't Him
and His Girls on t.v.?), The
Granny Blak Poet
Poem & 1/2 for Blackwomen

PICKETT, HERBERT G.
Hard is a Horse to Ride

PIPES, JAMES*
Angels in Overalls
Big Iron
Freedom is a Word
Jaw-Bone Town
Mule Mountain
North Yank
Rich Stud
Ziba

PITCHER OLIVER
Harlem: Sidewalk Icons
Pale Blue Casket, The
Raison d'Etre
Salute

PITTS, LUCIA M.
Afternoon Off
If Ever You Should Walk Away
Let Them Come to Us
Never, Never, Never
One April
Poets

PLACIDO
Farewell to His Mother
Prayer to God. Raoul Abdul, tr.
Sonnet to His Mother Pespida A Mi
Madre

REDCAM, TOM
    San Gloria

REDMOND, EUGENE
    Evanescent Love
    God's in Vietnam
    Rush City--The Hole
    Spring in the Jungle

REED, CLARENCE
    Cosa Nostra Economics
    Lemme Tell You What my Black
        is All About
    Lord Girl She Dance, She Dance
    'Trane

REED, ISHMAEL
    Beware: do not Read This Poem
    Feral Pioneers, The
    I am a Cowboy in the Boat of Ra

REEDBURG, ROBERT
    Epitaph to a Man
    Yesterday's Child

REESE, S. CAROLYN
    Letter from a Wife

REESE, V. A.
    Songs of the Dusky Worker
    To a Brown Lass

REYNOLDS, BARBARA A.
    To Gwendolyn Brooks the Crea-
        tor in the Beginning--
        Words

RICE, ALBERT
    Black Madonna, The
    To a Certain Woman

RICHARDS, EDWARD
    Fear

RICHER, EDWARD
    Some Whites Mourn Malcolm,
        As if

RIDGELY, TORRENCE*
    Bird and the Tree, The

RIDHIANA
    Tricked Again

RILEY, CONSTANTIA E.
    Adieu

RIQUETS, NICOL
    Rondeay Redouble (Double Round)

RIVE, RICHARD
    Where the Rainbow Ends

RIVERS, CONRAD KENT
    Africa
    Asylum
    Death of a Negro Poet, The
    Four Sheets to the Wind and A One-
        Way Ticket to France
    Games
    Hemingway
    If Blood is Black then Spirit Neg-
        lects my Unborn Son
    In Defense of Black Poets
    Invisible Man, The
    Journey to Versailles
    Long Gone
    Look Homeward Malcolm
    Mournful Letter from Paris, A
    Note on Black Women
    On Passing two Negroes on a Dark
        Country Road Somewhere in
        Georgia
    On the Death of William Edward
        Burghardt Du Bois
    Orison
    Prelude
    Southern Reaper, The
    Still Voice of Harlem, The
    Subway, The
    Three Sons
    To Richard Wright
    Train Runs Late to Harlem, The
    Underground
    Wordsworth for a Native Son

ROBERSON, ED
    Eclipse
    18,000 Feet
    Othello Jones Dresses for Dinner

ROBERTS, WALTER ADOLPHE
    Boyhood Etchings
    Captains, The
    Maroon Girl, The
    On a Monument to Marti

Peacocks
San Francisco
Vieux Carre
Villanelle of the Living Pan
Villanelle of Washington
   Square

ROBINSON, ALICE
How Can I Forget

ROBINSON, EDWIN ARLINGTON*
Toussaint L'Ouverture

ROBINSON, ETHOLIA ARTHUR
What is God?

RODGERS, CAROLYN
All the Clocks
For O.--Two Hung-Up
Now Aint That Love?
Tired Poem / Slightly Negative /
   More Positive
Two Gwen, Mo Luv
Together
U Name This One
We Dance Like Ella Riffs

RODMAN, SELDEN*
Daphane
Harper's Ferry
On a Picture by Pippin,
   Called "The Den"

ROGERS, ALEX
Rain Song, The
Why Adam Sinned

ROGERS, ELYMAS PAYSON
From on the Fugutive Slave Law

ROLLINS, CHARLEMAE
Through the Holly Wreath

ROSENBERG, DOROTHY*
Bim Bam

ROUMAIN, JACQUES
Guinea
Langston Hughes
When the Tom-Toms Beats

ROUMER, EMILE
Black Girl Goes By. Edna Worthley
   Underwood, tr.
Evening in Haiti
Peasant Declares His Love, The

ROWAN, M. CARL
And on this Shore

RUKEYSER, MURIEL*
Trial, The

RUTHERFORD, TONY
Black and White

SANCHEZ, SONIA
Answer to Yo/ Question of am I not
   Yo / Woman even if U Went on
   Shit Again
Ballad for Sterling Street, A
Blk/ Chant (to be Said Everyday
   Slowly)
Black Magic
Blk/ Rhetoric (for Killebrew Keeby,
   Icewater Baker, Gary Adams and
   Omar Shabazz)
Blk / Woooomen / Chant
Change Us
Chant for Young Brutahs
Coltrane / Poem, A
Don't Wanna Be
For Our Lady
Hospital / Poem (for Etheridge,
   9/26/69
In the Court Room
Indianapolis / Summer / 1969/ Poem
Last Poem I'm Gonna Write About Us
Let us Begin the Real Work
Liberation / Poem
Life / 1/4 pe,
Listenen to Big Black at s. f.
   state
Malcolm
/ Needed/ Poem / for my Salvation,
   A
Poem at Thirty
Poem for my Father, A
Now poem for us
On Watching a World Series Game
Personal Letter no. 3
Poem for Etheridge

On the Death of Dunbar
On the Gift of a Thermometer
On the Gift of a Whiskbroom
One Year Ago
Only the Span of a Life
Our Aim in Life
Our Recompense
Past Memories
Play of the Imagination
Plea of the Negro Soldier
Prayer
Presentation Poem
Sabbath
Satan's Dream
Shakespeare Modernized
Song of a Summer Breeze
South's Ungolden Rule or an
    American Riddle
Spring
Struggle with Temptation
Student's Christmas Parting, A
Tale of a Youth of Brown, A
Tale of Hearts, A
Thoughts of Thanksgiving
To a Bunch of Carnations
To a Friend
To a Rose
To Chicago
To H.P.L.
To Lillian
To One Unknown
To the Girls of Kenwood
To the Organ
To the Wind of the Night
To Williston at Parting
War's Inspiration
Vale Dico
Valued Lesson, A
Western Reverie, A
What is Love?
Williston Battle Song
Woman
Written at the Request of a
    Skeptic
Written in an Album
Written on a Christmas Card
Written on a Christmas Gift

WHITE, JOSEPH
    Black is a Soul

WHITFIELD, JAMES M.
    From America
    Misanthropist, The
    To Cinque
    Stanzas for the First of August

WHITMAN, ARBERY A.
    Custer's Last Ride
    From Leelah Misled
    From Miscellaneous Poems Hymn to
        the Nation
    From the Southland Charms and Free-
        dom's Magnitude
    From Twasinta's Seminoles: or Rape
        of Florida
    Lute of Afric's Tribe
    Stonewall Jackson
    To the Student
    Ye Bards of England

WHITMAN, WALT*
    Drayman, The
    Ethiopia Saluting the Colors
    I Sing the Body Electric
    Runaway Slave
    Wounded Person, The

WHITTIER, JOHN GREENLEAF*
    Christian Slave, The
    Farewell, The
    Rendition, The

WIGGINS, BERNICE LOVE
    Church Folks

WILLIAMS, FRANCIS
    Ode, An

WILLIAMS, JOHN A.
    Safari West

WILLIAMS, LUCY ARIEL see HOLLOWAY,
LUCY ARIEL WILLIAMS

WILLIAMS, MANCE
    For Lover Man, and all the Other
        Young Men who Failed to Return
        From World War II
    Year Without Seasons, A

SUBJECT INDEX

Africa to Me. Samuel W. Allen
African Affair, An. Bruce McM. Wright
African China. Melvin B. Tolson
African Images. Alice Walker
African Love History. LeRoi Jones
Africa's Lament. William L. Morrison
Africa's Plea. Roland Tombekai Dempster
Afrique Accidentale. Ted Joans
Afro-American Fragment. Langston Hughes
Alpha. Melvin Tolson
Angela Question Mark. Langston Hughes
As Don Took Off at Dawn. Ted Joans
Buckle. Ted Joans
Change is Not Always Progress. Don L. Lee
Congo, The. Vachel Lindsay*
Danse Africaine. Langston Hughes
Dawn in the Heart of Africa. Patrice Emery Lumumba
Dry Your Tears Africa. Bernard Dadié
Exhortation: Summer, 1919. Claude McKay
Far Cry From Africa. Derek Walcott
Far From Africa: Four Poems. Margaret Danner
Golden Stool, The. Gene Holmes
Heritage. Countee Cullen
I am a Negro. Muhammad Al-Fituri
Ka-Choo! Ted Joans
Like Me. Ted Joans
Motherland. Langston Hughes
My Trip. Ted Joans
Nativity. Aquah Laluah
No More Talk. Ted Joans
Notice. Ted Joans
O Daedalus Fly Away Home. Robert Hayden
Okay, You are Afraid of Africa. Ted Joans
Old Laughter. Gwendolyn Brooks
Primitive, The. Don L. Lee
Reward, The. Ted Joans.
Spare the Flies But Kill the Lies. Ted Joans
Tangerine Scene. Ted Joans
They Clapped. Nikki Giovanni
To S. M., A Young African Painter, On Seeing His Works. Phillis Wheatley
Way Down Yonder. Ted Joans
We Delighted, my Friend. Leopold Sedar Senghor
Who Knows? A. L. Milner-Brown
William Lee Hansberry. Eloise Culver

AFRICA, SOUTH
Pass Office Song. Anonymous
To My Black Brothers in South Africa. Arthur Boze

AGRICULTURE
Disappointed. Paul Laurence Dunbar
Black Man Talks of Reaping, A. Arna Bontemps

Farm Child's Lullaby, The. Paul Laurence Dunbar
Floodtide. Askia Muhammad Toure
I'm around-town Gent. Anonymous
Iowa Farmer. Margaret Walker
Meditations of a Europe Farmer. John Henrik Clarke

AIR
    Air. Clarence Major
    Air is Dirty, The. Glen Thompson

AIR PILOTS
    Black 99th, The. Arthur Boze

ALABAMA
    Alabama. Julia Fields
    Alabama Earth (At Booker Washington's Grave). Langston Hughes
    April of Alabama, The. George Marion McLlelan
    Birmingham. **Margaret Walker**
    Blues Alabama. Michael S. Harper
    Daybreak in Alabama. Langston Hughes
    Christ in Alabama. Langston Hughes
    Sarcasmes. Bruce McM. Wright
    Tragedy. Ritten Edward Lee

ALCOHOLISM
    At the Tavern. Paul Laurence Dunbar
    Bacchanale. Robert Hayden
    Ballad of Gin Mary. Langston Hughes
    Brother Jucundus. William C. Braithwaite
    De Profundis. Albert Aubert
    Ex-Judge at the Bar, An. Melvin Tolson
    Gin. John Raven
    Uncle Bill. Albert Aubert

ALDRIDGE, IRA
    Ira Aldridge. Eloise Culver

ALDRIDGE, THOMAS BAILEY
    On the Death of Thomas Bailey Aldridge

ALGIERS
    Battle of Algiers. Ahmed A. Alhamisi

ALGIERS MOTEL, INCIDENT
    Mother Speaks: The Algiers Motel Incident, Detroit, A. Michael S. Harper

ALI
    Ali. Lloyd M. Corbin, Jr
    Note to America. LeRoi Jones

ALLEN, RICHARD
    Richard Allen. Eloise Culver

ALONE
Alone. Nikki Giovanni
Alone / December / Night. Victor Hernandez Cruz
Certain Peace, A. Nikki Giovanni
World is Not a Pleasant Place to Be, The. Nikki Giovanni

AMBITION
We Know no More. Timothy Thomas Fortune

AMERICA
Advice Alphabeticamerica. Ted Joans
Afro-America. Charles Fred White
America. John Henrik Clarke
America Negra. Anita Scott Coleman
America to England, 1895. Joseph S. Cotter, Sr.
Black Memorial Day, A. Frenchy J. Hodges
Blend. Ritten Edward Lee
Dear Miss America. Ted Joans
Emigrant, The. Benjamin Clark
Farewell to America (1773) To Mrs. S. W., A. Phillis Wheatley
From America. James M. Whitfield
God Blame America. Ted Joans
Hearts of America, The. Charles Fred White
How Do You Want Yours? Ted Joans
In America. Bernie Casey
Inquiry. John Henrik Clarke
My America. Olive La Grone
Natives of America, The. Ann Plato
Negro in America, The. Robert Hayden
Rendezvous With America. Melvin Tolson
Soliloqui. Leslie M. Collins
These are my People. Robert Hayden
To America. James Weldon Johnson

AMISTAD (SHIP)
Middle Passage. Robert Hayden

ANARCHISM AND ANARCHISTS
Anarchist, The. Zachary Withers

ANCHORED
Anchored. Paul Laurence Dunbar

ANDERSON, MARIAN
Marian Anderson. Eloise Culver
Marian Anderson. William L. Morrison
We Launched a Ship. Ruby Berkley Goodwin

ANGELS
Angels Wings. Langston Hughes
My Angel. J. Henderson Brooks

ANIMALS
    Alley Cat Brushed His Whiskers, The. Waring Cuney
    Beast with Chrome Teeth, The. Thrumond Snyder
    Black Mane. Ted Joans
    Brer Rabbit, You's de Cutes' of 'em All. James Weldon Johnson
    Dat Ol' Mare O' Mine. Paul Laurence Dunbar
    De Critters' Dance. Paul Laurence Dunbar
    Economics. Albert Aubert
    In Stripes. Raymond Dandridge
    Up Out of the African. Ted Joans
    Zoo You Too! Ted Joans

ANNIAD
    Anniad, The. Gwendolyn Brooks
    Appendix to the Anniad (Leaves from a Loose-leaf War Diary). Gwendolyn
      Brooks

ANNIVERSARY
    One April. Lucia M. Pitts

ANTIGONE
    Antigone and Oedipus. Henrietta Cordelia Ray

ANTS
    Ant, The. Bernie Casey
    Ants, The Insects, The. Michael S. Harper

APARTMENT HOUSES
    Efficiency Apartment. Gerald W. Barrax

APPLES
    Apple trees by the River. Lucy Mae Turner
    Apples. Ariel Williams
    Unlucky Apple, The. Paul Laurence Dunbar

APRIL
    April. William S. Braithwaite
    April Day, An. Joseph S. Cotter, Jr.
    April Longing. Mary Wilkerson Cleaves
    April of Alabama, The. George Marion McLlelan
    April Rain Song. Langston Hughes
    April Rhymes and Rigmaroles. Eli Shepperd
    Aprilian Rhapsody. William S. Braithwaite
    April's Dream. William S. Braithwaite
    Near the End of April. William S. Braithwaite
    Paths. Joseph S. Cotter, Sr.

ARABS
    To Her. Paul Laurence Dunbar

ARCADIA
    Ballade. Paul Laurence Dunbar
    Farewell to Arcady. Paul Laurence Dunbar

ARMSTRONG, SAMUEL CHAPMAN
    Samuel Chapman Armstrong. Owen Dodson

ARSON
    Arson and Cold Lace. Worth Long
    Beginning of a Long Poem on Why I Burned the City. Lawrence Benford

ART
    Before a Painting. James Weldon Johnson
    Beta. Melvin Tolson
    Chicago Picasso, The. Gwendolyn Brooks
    Delta. Melvin Tolson
    Desire. Constance Nichols
    I Would be a Painter Most of all. Len Chandler
    Nature and Art. Paul Laurence Dunbar
    Niobe in Distress for her Children Slain by Apollo, From Ovid's Metamor-
        phoses, Book VI, and From a View of the Painting of Mr. Richard
        Wilson. Phillis Wheatley
    Notes From a Guerilla Diary. Askia Muhammad Toure
    Omicron. Melvin Tolson
    Painter. Ted Joans
    Theta. Melvin Tolson
    To S. M., a Young African Painter, on Seeing His Works. Phillis Wheatley
    Wall, The. Don L. Lee

ART, AFRICAN
    Convert, The. Margaret Danner
    Etta Moten's Attic. Margaret Danner

ASPIRATION
    Aspiration. Langston Hughes
    Chant Royal. William C. Braithwaite

ASYLUM
    Asylum. Conrad Kent Rivers

ATHEISM
    Infidel's Creed, The. Joseph S. Cotter, Sr.
    Student I Know, A. J. Henderson Brooks

ATHLETICS
    Athlete, The. Ted Joans
    Athlete's Tomb, The. William C. Braithwaite

ATLANTA
    Litany at Atlanta, A. William Edward Burghardt DuBois
    Slim in Atlanta. Sterling A. Brown

ATLANTIC CITY, NEW JERSEY
  Seashore Through Dark Glasses (Atlantic City). Langston Hughes

ATROCITIES
  Atrocities. Nikki Giovanni

ATTUCKS, CRISPUS
  Crispus Attucks. Eloise Culver
  Crispus Attucks. George Hannibal Temple
  Post War Ballad. Dorothy Vena Johnson

AUGUST
  In August. Paul Laurence Dunbar
  Late August. William S. Braithwaite
  Song for the First of August. James Madison Bell

AUNTS
  Appreciation. Paul Laurence Dunbar

AUTOMOBILES
  Chilly Willie. John Raven
  Drive, The. Victor Hernandez Cruz
  Shift of Gears, The. Melvin Tolson

AUTUMN
  And Fall Shall Sit in Judgment. Audre Lorde
  Autumn Leaf, The. William C. Braithwaite
  Autumn Song. William Allyn Hill
  House of Falling Leaves. Robert Hayden
  Lost Love. Herman L. McMillan
  Lyric of Autumn, A. William S. Braithwaite
  Merry Autumn. Paul Laurence Dunbar
  Poeme D'Autumne. Langston Hughes

AVON, FRANCE
  Where Avon Winds. William C. Braithwaite

AWARENESS
  Awareness. Don L. Lee

– B –

BABIES see INFANTS

BABYLON
  Babylon. Melvin Tolson

BACHELORS
  Bachelor, The. Joseph S. Cotter, Sr.

BACON, SIR FRANCIS
  Bacon. Joseph S. Cotter, Sr.

BACTERIOLOGY
    To a Disease Bearer. John Raven.

BALANCES
    Balances. Nikki Giovanni

BALLADS
    De Ballit of de Boll Weevil. Anonymous
    John Henry. Anonymous
    Stackalee. Anonymous

BALLOONS
    Multi-Colored Balloon. Herbert D. Greggs

BALTIMORE, MARYLAND
    Incident. Countee Cullen

BANDS (MUSIC)
    Colored Band, The. Paul Laurence Dunbar

BANJOS
    Banjo Song, A. Paul Laurence Dunbar
    Banjo Song, A. James Weldon Johnson
    My Soul's at Rest. James E. McGirt
    Song for a Banjo Dance. Langston Hughes
    Songs for my Lady's Banjo. Eli Shepperd
    Uncle Eph's Banjo Song. James Edwin Campbell
    Voice of the Banjo, The. Paul Laurence Dunbar

BANNEKER, BENJAMIN
    Benjamin Banneker. Eloise Culver

BARBERS, AFRICAN
    Shave & a Haircut & a Circumcision. Ted Joans

BARCELONA
    Barcelona. Claude McKay

BARS
    Bars Fight. Lucy Terry.
    Lenox Avenue Bar. Langston Hughes

BASEBALL
    On Watching a World Series Game. Sonia Sanchez
    Stri-i-ke One! Lucy Mae Turner

BASKETS
    Little Christmas Basket, A. Paul Laurence Dunbar

BATS
    Bats. Effie Lee Newsome

BATTLE OF SAN JUAN HILL
    Color Sergeant, The. James Weldon Johnson

BEACHES   see SEASHORE

BEADS
    Beads. Ted Joans

BEALE STREET, MEMPHIS
    Beale Street, Memphis. Thurmond Snyder

BEANS
    Bean Eaters, The. Gwendolyn Brooks

BEARS
    At Bear Mountain. Michael S. Harper

BEAUTY
    Beauty. Delmar Bobo
    Beauty. Ted Joans
    Black Camel on Pink Quartz. John W. Burton
    Essay on Beauty. Robert Hayden
    I sit and Wait for Beauty. Mae V. Cowdery
    Love Beauty Always. William S. Braithwaite
    Loving Beauty is Loving God. Isabelle McClellan Taylor
    To a Beauty. Joseph S. Cotter, Sr.
    To Beauty. William S. Braithwaite
    When I Grop. Kali Grosvenor

BEAUTY SHOPS
    Beauty Shoppe. Gwendolyn Brooks

BED TIME
    Bed Time. Langston Hughes

BEDS
    Crawl into Bed. Quandra Prettyman
    Bed. Ted Joans

BEES
    Beehive. Jean Toomer
    Smoking Out the Bees. Joseph S. Cotter, Sr.
    Songs for my Lady's Banjo. Eli Shepperd
    Two Songs. Paul Laurence Dunbar

BELLS
    Banbury Bells. William C. Braithwaite
    Belfry of Isone, The. William C. Braithwaite
    Endless Chant, The. Eli Shepperd
    Small Bells of Benin, The. Margaret Danner
    To an Old Farm Dinner Bell. Joseph S. Cotter, Sr.

BENEDICTION
      Benediction. Donald Jeffrey Hayes
      Benediction. Georgia Douglas Johnson
      Benediction. Bob Kaufman

BERCK, FRANCE
      Rue to Berck. William C. Braithwaite

BERCK-PLAGE, FRANCE
      Berck-Plage. William C. Braithwaite

BETHUNE, MARY MCLEOD
      Dr. Mary M. Bethune. Eloise Culver
      Mary McLeod Bethune. Margaret Walker

BIAFRA
      Biafra Blues. Michael S. Harper

BIBLE-HISTORY
      At the Lincoln Monument in Washington, August 28, 1963. Margaret Walker
      Prophets for a New Day. Margaret Walker
      Who Built the Ark? Eli Shepperd
      Ziba. James Pipes*

BICYCLES AND BICYCLING
      For a Spin. William C. Braithwaite

BIGOTRY see TOLERATION

BILLIARDS
      Rotation. Julian Bond

BIRDS
      After. Naomi Long Madgett
      Allegory. Robert Hayden
      Artic Tern in a Museum. Effie Lee Newsome
      Ballad of the Light-eyed Little Girl, The. Gwendolyn Brooks
      Bird Catcher, The. Anonymous
      Belated Oriole, A. George Marion McClellan
      Birdie That Has Flown, The. Charles Fred White
      Birds of Prey. Claude McKay
      Clairvoyance. Norman Jordan
      Dove, The. Paul Laurence Dunbar
      Falcon, The. Robert Hayden
      Homing Swallows. Claude McKay
      Lady Bird. Kali Grosvenor
      Man O' War Bird. Derek Walcott
      Maybe the Birds. June Jordan
      Peacocks. Walter Adolphe Roberts
      Mockinbirds. Bernie Casey
      Preparation. Paul Laurence Dunbar
      Rag Doll and Summer Birds. Owen Dodson

Robin Red Breast. Lula Lowe Weeden
Robin's Poem, A. Nikki Giovanni
St. Bees Head. William C. Braithwaite
Sparrow, The. Paul Laurence Dunbar
Sparrow's Fall, The. Frances Harper
To a Bird. Raymond Dandridge
To a Caged Canary in a Negro Restaurant. Leslie Pinckney Hill
To a Wounded Bird. Hilda Preer
Two Songs. Paul Laurence Dunbar
Uncle Ned an' de Mockin' Bird. James D. Corrothers
Whip-Poor-Will and Katy-Did. Paul Laurence Dunbar
With the Lark. Paul Laurence Dunbar

BIRMINGHAM, ALABAMA
     Ballad of Birmingham. Dudley Randall
     Birmingham. Margaret Walker

BIRTH
     For a Cynic. Countee Cullen
     Nativity. Aquah Laluah
     Supremacy. Leonora Gillison
     To our First Born or the Prophet Arrives. Ebon

BITTERNESS
     Bitterness. Eldon George McLean

BLACK (PEOPLE)
     Black All Day. Raymond Richard Patterson
     Black Gauntlet. William Cousins
     Black Is. Kali Grosvenor
     Black is Beautiful. Townsend T. Brewster
     Black is Best. Larry Thompson
     Black Narcissus. Gerald Barrax
     Black is Black. Kali Grosvenor
     Blackberry Sweet. Dudley Randall
     Black People. Ted Joans
     Black Repeater. Ted Joans
     Borne. Daniel Walter Owens
     'Bout Cullud Folkses. Lucy Mae Turner
     Colors. Arthur Boze
     Dark Brother, The. Lewis Alexander
     Demystify. Ted Joans
     For a Child. Noami Long Madgett
     From a Bus. Malaika Ayo Wangara
     Gospel Truth, The. Jackie Earley
     I Love You Don't. Kali Grosvenor
     In a Period of Growth. Don L. Lee
     Is it Because I am Black? Joseph S. Cotter, Jr.
     Ka'Ba. LeRoi Jones
     Lemmen Tell You What my Black Is All About. Clarence Reed
     Love. Kali Grosvenor
     Man Inside, The. Melvin Tolson

Black (People)   SUBJECT INDEX

BLOSSOMS
    Spring Blossom. Ernest Attah

BLUES
    Back Lash Blues, The. Langston Hughes
    Blue. Paul Laurence Dunbar
    Blue John. John Raven
    Blues, The. James C. Morris
    Blues. Horace Mungin
    Blues. Quandra Prettyman
    Blues and Bitterness. Lerone Bennett
    Blues Fantasy. Langston Hughes
    Blues For Momma. John Raven
    Blues, Get Away. John Raven
    Blues is a Woman, The. John Raven
    Blues on a Box. Langston Hughes
    Blues Singer. John Raven
    Blues Today, The. Mae Jackson
    Colored Blues Singer. Countee Cullen
    Elvin's Blues. Michael S. Harper
    Evenin' Air Blues. Langston Hughes
    Get Up, Blues. James Emanuel
    Good Mornin' Blues. Anonymous
    Hard Daddy. Langston Hughes
    Hard Time Blues. Waring Cuney
    Hesitating Blues, The. W. C. Handy
    Hey! Langston Hughes
    Hey! Hey! Langston Hughes
    Hey-Hey Blues. Langston Hughes
    Homage to the Empress of the Blues. Robert Hayden
    Homesick Blues. Langston Hughes
    How Long Blues. Anonymous
    I Got the Blues. Anonymous
    Kentucky Blues. Sterling A. Brown
    Listen Here Blues. Langston Hughes.
    Little Green Tree Blues. Langston Hughes
    Long Gone Lover Blues. Ted Joans
    Love Again Blues. Langston Hughes
    Low Down Blues. Lucile D. Goodlett
    Low Down. Sterling A. Brown
    Memphis Blues. Sterling A. Brown
    Midwinter Blues. Langston Hughes
    Minnie Sings Her Blues. Langston Hughes
    Misery. Langston Hughes
    Monroe's Blues. Langston Hughes
    New St. Louis Blues. Sterling A. Brown
    No Blues With Eros. Ted Joans
    Passed on Blues. Ted Joans
    Po' Boy Blues. Langston Hughes
    Riverbank Blues. Sterling A. Brown
    Six-Bits Blues. Langston Hughes
    Southern Blues. Anonymous

387

Blues   SUBJECT INDEX

    Syncopating Rhythm. Frenchy J. Hodges
    Tin Roof Blues. **Sterling A. Brown**
    Too Blues. Langston Hughes
    Visitor. John Raven
    Weary Blues, The. Langston Hughes
    Young Gal's Blues. Langston Hughes

BOLL WEEVILS
    De Ballit of De Boll Weevil. Anonymous

BOMBINGS
    American History. Michael S. Harper
    Ballad of Birmingham. Dudley Randall
    Birmingham Sunday (Sept. 15, 1963). Langston Hughes
    Bombings in Dixie. Langston Hughes
    Four Little Girls. Arthur Boze
    Respectful Request. Ray Durem
    To the Survivors of Hiroshima and Nagasaki. Richard Thomas

BONAPARTE, NAPOLEON
    Le Retour de Napoleon. Victor Sejour

BOOKS
    Between Lines (In a Little Book P.P.). Raymond Dandridge
    Bright Bindings. Countee Cullen
    End of the Chapter. Paul Laurence Dunbar
    Negro Child and the Story Book. Joseph S. Cotter, Sr.
    Sonnet. Paul Laurence Dunbar
    Tau. Melvin Tolson
    Telephone Book. Ted Joans
    To One Unknown. Charles Fred White
    Visit of the Professor of Aesthetics. Margaret Danner

BOOTHS
    I Love Those Little Booths at Benvenuti's. Gwendolyn Brooks

BOOTS   see SHOE AND SHOE INDUSTRY

BOSTON, MASSACHUSETTS
    Boston Roller Coaster, The. Victor Hernandez Cruz
    Boston Tea. David Wadsworth Cannon, Jr.

BOXING
    Memory of Boxer Benny (Kid) Paret. Frank Lima
    Prize Fighter. Langston Hughes
    This is the Way it Goes. Carl Killebrew

BOYS
    Alfonso, Dressing To Wait at Table. Claude McKay
    Baby. Langston Hughes
    Blacktop Black Top Blacktop Top Black Black Top. Marion Nicholas
    Boy Breaking Glass. Gwendolyn Brooks

Boy's Summer Song. Paul Laurence Dunbar
Baker's Boy, The. Effie Lee Newsome
Beggar Boy. Langston Hughes
Black Muslim Boy in a Hospital. James Emanuel
Boy's Need, A. Herbert Clark Johnson
Brass Spittoons. Langston Hughes
Brown Boy to Brown Girl. Countee Cullen
"Cool" to Gene. John Raven
Economics. Albert Aubert
Elevator Boy. Langston Hughes
Eligia, the Bad Boy. Waverly Turner Carmichael
For Christopher. June Jordan
From a Bus. Malaika Ayo Wangara
Hey Boy. Bernie Casey
In One Battle. LeRoi Jones
Johnny's Dream of Santa Claus. Joseph S. Cotter, Sr.
Kid (Cuernavaca). Robert Hayden
Lad and Lass. Joseph S. Cotter, Sr.
Last Impression of New York. Mason Jason Mason*
Life of Lincoln West, The. Gwendolyn Brooks
Little Black Boy. Barbara Marshall
Little Black Boy, The. William Blake*
Little Brown Boys. Helene Johnson
Little David Play on Yo' Harp. Anonymous
Little Son. Georgia Douglas Johnson
Lullaby. Paul Laurence Dunbar
Martyr of Alabama, The. Frances Harper
Miles' Delight. Ted Joans
Mistah Me! Lucy Mae Turner
Morning Light; the Dew-drier. Effie Lee Newsome
My Baby-Boy. William C. Braithwaite
My Lad. Joseph S. Cotter, Sr.
O Little David, Play on Your Harp. Joseph S. Cotter, Jr.
Odyssey of Big Boy. Sterling A. Brown
Of De Wit Williams on His Way to Lincoln Cemetery. Gwendolyn Brooks
Omega. Melvin Tolson
On Seeing Two Brown Boys in a Catholic Church. Frank Horne
Otto. Gwendolyn Brooks
Pearl Primus. Owen Dodson
Poem. Helene Johnson
Psi. Melvin Tolson
Ruskie's Boy. Victor Hernandez Cruz
Save the Boys. Frances Harper
Scolding Baby Boy. Waverly Turner Carmichael
Sequence from the Roach Riders, A Play. Welton Smith
Small Colored Boy in the Subway. Babette Deutsch*
Son. James Emanuel
Tale of a Youth of Brown, A. Charles Fred White
To a Brown Boy. Countee Cullen
To Our Boys. Irvin W. Underhill
Tunk. (A Lecture on Modern Education). James Weldon Johnson
Young David: Birmingham, A. Helen Morgan Brooks

BRADFORD, WALTER
    Walter Bradford. Gwendolyn Brooks

BRAGGARD
    Braggard, The. Raymond Dandridge

BRAVERY see COURAGE

BRAZIL
    Private Letter to Brazil, A. G. C. Oden

BREAD
    When De Co'n Pone's Hot. Paul Laurence Dunbar
    Of Bread and Wine. Oliver La Grone

BREAKFAST
    Breakfast Time. Charles B. Johnson

BRECKINRIDGE, COL. W. C. P.
    Col. W. C. P. Breckinridge. Joseph S. Cotter, Sr.

BREEZES
    June Breezes and Roses. Joseph S. Cotter, Sr.
    Song of a Summer Breeze. Charles Fred White

BRIDGE (CARD GAME)
    Bridge Party of Gap in Teeth Aint New. Marion Nicholes

BRIDGES
    Trip: San Francisco. Langston Hughes

BROADUS, REV. DR. JOHN A.
    Rev. Dr. John A. Broadus. Joseph S. Cotter, Sr.

BROADWAY
    On Broadway. Claude McKay

BRONX (NEW YORK)
    Walking on the Lips of The Bronx. Victor Hernandez Cruz

BROOKS
    Brook, The. Joseph S. Cotter, Sr.
    Brook, A. Raymond Dandridge

BROOKS, GWENDOLYN
    Afterword: for Gwen Brooks, An. (The Search for the New-Song Begins with
        the Old). Don L. Lee
    As Critic. Margaret Danner
    Black Children. Carole Gregory Clemmons
    Black Consciousness. Bruce Walton
    Black Lady's Inspiration. Alfred Diggs
    Bronzeville Breakthrough. Sarah Webster Fabio

Bronzeville Poet. Eugene Perkins
Dedicated to the Living Memory of Miss Gwendolyn Brooks.
    Clemmons
Drum Song Sister. Sigemonde Kharies Wimberly
Fishing. James Cunningham
For Eusi, Ahy Kwei & Gwen Brooks. Keorapetse Kgositsile
For Gwen--1969. Margaret Walker
For Gwen. Sharon Scott
For Gwendolyn Brooks. Zack Gilbert
For Gwendolyn Brooks. Nikki Giovanni
For Gwendolyn Brooks. Helen H. King
For Gwendolyn Brooks--A Whole & Beautiful Spirit. Johari Amini
For the Honeybee Queen and her Poets. W. D. Wandick
Gathering of Artists, A. Alicia Johnson
Gwen Brooks, A Pyramid. Val Gray Ward
Gwen Brooks--Our Inspirer. Dududzo Murapa
Gwendolyn Brooks. Don L. Lee
Live Celebrations. Sarah Webster Fabio
Lost Moment. Hoyt W. Fuller
Madimba: Gwendolyn Brooks. Michael S. Harper
Of a Woman Who Turns Rivers. David Llorens
Our Meeting. Raymond A. Joseph
Praise Due to Gwen Brooks. Cynthia M. Conley
Significant Other, A. Joe Todd
Spiritual Cleanliness. Ahmed Akinwole Alhamisi
Sun Came, The. Etheridge Knight
Sunday / Evening at Gwen's. Sonia Sanchez
Three Poems for Gwendolyn Brooks. Dolores Kendrick
Tree Poem, The. Paulette Jones
To Gwen. Tejumela Oleghoni
To Gwen Brooks. John Chenault
To Gwen Brooks. Edward Christmas
To Gwen, Mo Luv. Carolyn M. Rodgers
To Gwen With Love. Jon Eckels
To Gwendolyn Brooks. R. M. Dennis
To Gwendolyn Brooks. Etheridge Knight
To Gwendolyn Brooks the Creator in the Beginning--Words. Barbara Rey-
    nolds
Untitled. Walter Bradford
Voice Above the Wind, A. Gus Bertha
When I Heard Dat White Man Say. Zack Gilbert
Words. Joe Concalves

BROTHERHOOD
    God's Christmas Tree. Eve Lynn
    Man to Man. William Thompson Goss

BROTHERS
    Brother Mine. Raymond Dandridge
    Brothers. Solomon Edwards
    Brothers. Langston Hughes
    Brothers and Sisters of the Light. William C. Braithwaite

Brothers   SUBJECT INDEX

    Envoi. Raymond Patterson
    My Brother. Eloise Culver

BROWN, H. RAP
    Re-Act for Action. Don L. Lee
    When Brown is Black. Keorapetse Kgositsile

BROWN, JAMES
    To James Brown. Michael S. Harper

BROWN, JOHN
    Harper's Ferry. Seldon Rodman*
    How Old Brown Took Harper's Ferry. Edmond Clarence Stedman*
    John Browns Prayer. Stephen Vincent Benet*
    October 16: The Raid. Langston Hughes

BROWN, MARY
    For Beautiful Mary Brown Chicago Rent Strike Leader. June Jordan

BROWN, WILLIAM WELLS
    Memory of W. W. Brown. James E. McGirt

BROWNING, ROBERT
    Epilogue (To the Browning Centenary, May 12, 1912). William S. Braith-
        waite
    Life-Long, Poor Browning. Anne Spencer

BRUSHES
    On a Clothes Brush. Charles Fred White

BUGS see INSECTS

BUILDINGS
    Building, The. Frances Harper
    New York Sky Scrapers. John Mbiti.
    On the Dedication of Dorothy Hall. Paul Laurence Dunbar

BULLFIGHTS
    El Toro. Robert Hayden
    El Matador. Robert Hayden
    Sol Y Sombra. Robert Hayden

BUMSTEAD, HORACE
    To Horace Bumstead. James Weldon Johnson

BUNCHE, RALPH
    Ralph Bunche. Eloise Culver

BURDENS
    Burden. Langston Hughes

BURNS, ROBERT
    Robert Burns. Joseph S. Cotter, Sr.

BUSES
    Things is Changing. Mari Evans

BUSINESS
    Dr. Booker T. Washington to the National Negro Business League. Joseph
        S. Cotter, Sr.
    Taken Care of Business. Ted Joans

BUTTERFLIES
    Butterfly in Church, A. George Marion McClellan
    Patroness. Gerald Barrax

BUZZARDS
    Buzzard, The. Joseph S. Cotter, Sr.

- C -

CABARET
    Cabaret. Langston Hughes
    Cabaret (1927, Black & Tan Chicago). Sterling A. Brown
    Harlem Night Club. Langston Hughes
    Minnie Sings Her Blues. Langston Hughes
    Perils of the Cabbage Patch. Joseph S. Cotter, Sr.

CABINS
    Carolina Cabin. Langston Hughes
    Deserted Cabin, The. Lucy Mae Turner
    Little Cabin, A. Charles Bertram Johnson
    My Little Cabin Home. Waverly T. Carmichael
    Old Cabin, The. Paul Laurence Dunbar

CAKE WALK
    Songs for My Lady's Banjo. Eli Shepperd

CALIFORNIA
    Golden State, The. Zachary Withers

CALLS, BIRD
    Bird Call and Apology. William L. Morrison

CAMBRIDGE, MASSACHUSETTS
    Cambridge, Massachusetts. Julian Bond

CANDLES
    For the Candle Light. Angelina Weld Grimke

CANDY
    At Candle-Lightin' Time. Paul Laurence Dunbar
    Peppermint Candy March, The. Effie Lee Newsome

393

CANE
    Plowin' Cane. John Wesley Holloway
    North Yank. James Pipes*

CANNIBALS
    Cannibal Hymn, The. Anonymous

CANOES AND CANOEING
    On a Primitive Canoe. Claude McKay

CAPITAL PUNISHMENT
    Execution. James Randall
    Frankie and Johnny. Sterling A. Brown
    Sam Smiley. Sterling A. Brown
    Silhouette. Langston Hughes
    To Chessman and Associates. Samuel Allen

CAPITALISM
    C-- C-- Raiders. Ted Joans

CARDS
    Bad Luck Card. Langston Hughes
    Madam's Calling Cards. Langston Hughes

CARIBBEAN
    Caribbean Sunset. Langston Hughes

CARMICHAEL, MIRIAM MIKEBA
    Chick Chick, The. Ted Joans

CARNATIONS
    To a Bunch of Carnations. Charles Fred White

CARNIVAL
    At the Carnival. Anne Spencer
    Merry-Go-Round. Langston Hughes

CAROUSEL
    Carnival, The. G. C. Oden

CARPENTERS
    Carpentry. Lloyd Addison

CARVER, GEORGE WASHINGTON
    Dr. George Washington Carver. Eloise Culver

CASTLES
    Gallant Castle Builders. William S. Braithwaite

CATHEDRALS
    Florence to Her Cathedral-Builders. William S. Braithwaite

CATS
    Alley Cat Brushed His Whiskers, The. Waring Cuney
    Cat, The. Countee Cullen
    Cats. Countee Cullen
    Cotton Cat, The. Effie Lee Newsome
    Poem for Carol, A. Nikki Giovanni
    Samantha is My Negro Cat. William J. Harris

CAUCASIANS
    Caucasian, The. J. Henderson Brooks
    Cracker Man. Charles L. Anderson
    Non-John Browns, The. Ted Joans
    Seven. Ted Joans
    TCB. Sonia Sanchez
    Ugly Honkies, or The Election Game and How to Win it. Nikki Giovanni
    White, Baby. James Emanuel
    White Ones, The. Langston Hughes
    White Woman. Ted Joans
    Whiteeyes on Black Thighs. Ted Joans
    Wild West Savages. Ted Joans
    Why are They Mean. Kali Grosvenor
    Yeahh I Dig. Ted Joans
    You Took This World Away From Us. Kali Grosvenor

CAUTION
    Caution. Charles Fred White

CEMETERIES
    Boarding House. Langston Hughes
    Grave-Yard. Langston Hughes

CENSUS
    Madam and the Census Man. Langston Hughes

CENTRAL INTELLIGENCE AGENCY
    Top Creep. Ted Joans

CHAIN GANG
    South Carolina Chain Gang Song. Anonymous
    Southern Road. Sterling A. Brown

CHALLENGE
    Challenge, The. Samuel A. Haynes

CHAMELEONS
    Chameleon is Everywhere, The. H. A. B. Jones-Quartey

CHANEY, JAMES
    For Andy Goodman--Michael Schwerner--and James Chaney. Margaret Walker

CHANGES
    How to Change the U.S.A. Harry Edwards

It is Time. Ted Joans
Poem to Complement Other Poems. Don L. Lee
Primer for Today. Melvin Tolson
To You Who Read My Book. Countee Cullen

CHANTS
Death Chants. Langston Hughes
Nigger. Frank Horne
Suicide Chant. Countee Cullen
These Are My People. Robert Hayden

CHAPALA, JAL
In Chapala, Jal. Clarence Major

CHAPEL
Compulsory Chapel. Alice Walker

CHARACTER
De Innah Part. Raymond Dandridge

CHARITY
Triple Benison, The. Henrietta Cordelia Ray

CHARLES, RAY
Bishop of Atlanta: Ray Charles. Julian Bond
Blues Note. Bob Kaufman

CHAUCER, GEOFFREY
Chaucer. Benjamin Brawley

CHECKERS
Checkers. Sterling A. Brown

CHEERFULNESS
Cheery Good-Day. William L. Morrison

CHICAGO
Beverly Hills, Chicago. Gwendolyn Brooks
Cabaret (1928, Black & Tan Chicago). Sterling A. Brown
Chicago, Ill. Joseph S. Cotter, Sr.
Chicago Picasso, The. Gwendolyn Brooks
Dawn Patrol: Chicago. Richard V. Durham
Tenement Room: Chicago. Frank Marshall Davis
To Chicago. Charles Fred White

CHILDREN
Anonymous Verse (From a Puerto Rican Christmas Card), An. Anonymous
Another Season. Michael S. Harper
Child, The. Joseph S. Cotter, Sr.
Child, The. Erskine Hayes
Childhood. Margaret Walker
Children of the Poor, The. Gwendolyn Brooks

Child Elsie. William S. Braithwaite
Christmas Lullaby for a New-Born Child. Yvonne Gregory
De Little Pickaninny's Gone To Sleep. James Weldon Johnson
Escape. Mari Evans
For a Child. Naomi Long Madgett
Genius Child. Langston Hughes
I and He. Marion Cuthbert
'Ittle Touzle Head. Raymond Dandridge
Kiddies and the Christmas Tree. Joseph S. Cotter, Sr.
Kidsnatchers. Ted Joans
Late Day Chillen. Raymond Dandridge
Lines on the School Fair. Andrew R. Smith
Little Child Shall Lead Them. Frances Harper
Little Child That Leads, The. Joseph S. Cotter, Sr.
Memorial of Childhood, A. Charles Fred White
Motherless Child. Anonymous
My Baby-Boy. William C. Braithwaite
My Childhood. James Randall
Nation's Neglected Child, The. Joseph S. Cotter, Sr.
Negro Child, The. Joseph S. Cotter, Sr.
Negro Child and the Story Book, The. Joseph S. Cotter, Sr.
Nikki-Reasa. Nikki Giovanni
Oh! Lord. Antoinette T. Payne
On the Death of a Child. Edward Silvera
Poem for all the Children, A. June Jordan
Poem for Children with Thoughts on Death, A. Jupiter Hammon
Possession. Paul Laurence Dunbar
Salia. Lucile D. Goodlett
Saturday's Child. Countee Cullen
Scamp. Paul Laurence Dunbar
Six in Deportment. Joseph S. Cotter, Sr.
Song of the Little Children. Eli Shepperd
Thank God for Little Children. Frances Harper
Their Poem. Victor Hernandez Cruz
Why Else. Ted Joans
Yesterday's Child. Robert Reedburg

CHINA
Triumph Aster, The. Melvin Tolson

CHRISTMAS
Anonymous Verse (From a Puerto Rican Christmas Card), An. Anonymous
Back-Log Song, A. Paul Laurence Dunbar
Br'er Rabbit's Christmas Trick. Charles B. Johnson
Chrismus is A-comin'. Paul Laurence Dunbar
Chrismus on the Plantation. Paul Laurence Dunbar
Christmas. Paul Laurence Dunbar
Christmas Carol. Paul Laurence Dunbar
Christmas at Melrose. Leslie Pinckney Hill
Christmas Eve in France. Jessie Redmond Fauset
Christmas Folk Song, A. Paul Laurence Dunbar
Christmas in the Heart. Paul Laurence Dunbar

Christmas Morning I. Carol Freeman
Christmas 1959 Et Cetera. Gerald Barrax
Christmas Story, The. Langston Hughes
Christmas Tree, The. Joseph S. Cotter, Sr.
Christus Natus Est. Countee Cullen
Gift. Carol Freeman
Her Christmas Gift. Charles B. Johnson
Holidays, The. Charles Fred White
Indian Christmas. Gabriela Mistral
Kiddies and the Christmas Tree, The. Joseph S. Cotter, Sr.
Little Christmas Basket, A. Paul Laurence Dunbar
Magi Call Him King, The. Effie Lee Newsome
Memory in Winter, A. Craig Williamson
Negro's Christmas Prayer, The. Joseph S. Cotter, Sr.
On a Christmas Night. Langston Hughes
Otto. Gwendolyn Brooks
Proposition 15. Michael S. Harper
Shepherd's Song at Christmas. Langston Hughes
Sonnets at Christmas. Allen Tate
Speakin' O' Christmas. Paul Laurence Dunbar
Student's Christmas Parting, A. Charles Fred White
Through the Holly Wreath. Charlemae Rollins
Yule-Song. A Memory. William S. Braithwaite

CHRISTMAS, EDWARD
Wall, Thee (For Edward Christmas). Gwendolyn Brooks

CHRISTOPHE, HENRI
Black Majesty. Countee Cullen
Christophe. Russell Atkins

CHURCHES
Butterfly in Church, A. George Marion McClellan
Church Burning: Mississippi. James Emanuel
Church Folks. Bernice Love Wiggins
Inscription For the 1st Baptist Church as it comes out of Saturday to
    Park. Clarence Major
Negro Church, A. Nick Aaron Ford
Night I Went to Church, The. Waverly T. Carmichael
St. Isaac's Church, Petrograd. Claude McKay
St. Silva's Church. William C. Braithwaite
When Mahalia Sings. Quandra Prettyman
When the Different Churches Meet. Waverly T. Carmichael
Whispers in a Country Church. Albert Aubert

CIDER
Hahd Cidah. Raymond Dandridge

CINQUE, JOSEPH
To Cinque. James M. Whitfield

SUBJECT INDEX

CIRCLES
   Circles. Kali Grosvenor
   Circles. Langston Hughes

CITIES AND TOWNS
   Bottled: New York. Helene Johnson
   Cities. Victor Hernandez Cruz
   Cities and Seas. Norman Jordan
   City and Country. Joseph S. Cotter, Sr.
   City: San Francisco. Langston Hughes
   City's Love, The. Claude McKay
   Dawn Cities. Mae V. Cowdery
   Dawn Patrol: Chicago. Richard V. Durham
   Megalopolis. Victor Cruz
   My City. James Weldon Johnson
   Riding to Town. Paul Laurence Dunbar
   Rush City--The Hole, The. Eugene Redmond
   Tenement Room: Chicago. Frank Marshall Davis
   This is the City. Yvette Johnson
   Trip: San Francisco. Langston Hughes
   When Dawn Comes to the City: New York. Claude McKay
   White City, The. Claude McKay
   Zulu King: New Orleans (At Mardi Gras), The. Josephine Copeland

CITIZENSHIP
   Citizen, The. Vilma Howard

CIVIL RIGHTS
   Great Civil Rights Law (A.D. 1964), The. Mari Evans
   Hey Boy. Bernie Casey

CIVIL RIGHTS WORKERS
   For Andy Goodman--Michael Schwerner--and James Chaney. Margaret Walker

CLAY, GEN. CASSIUS M.
   Gen. Cassius M. Clay. Joseph S. Cotter, Sr.

CLEANING
   Housecleaning. Nikki Giovanni
   Office Building Evening. Langston Hughes
   Old Houses. Melvin Tolson

CLERGY
   Called to Preach. Charles B. Johnson
   De Preacher Kyo Siam. Lucile D. Goodlett
   De Reverend is Gwine to de Big 'Soc'ation. Lucy Mae Turner
   Madam and the Minister. Langston Hughes
   Negro Preacher, The. Joseph S. Cotter, Sr.
   Reporting the Sermon. Joseph S. Cotter, Sr.
   Teacher Pre-emminent, The. Joseph S. Cotter, Sr.

CLOCKS AND WATCHES
    All the Clocks. Carolyn Rodgers

CLOTHING AND DRESS
    Dressed Up. Langston Hughes
    I Use to Dress. Waverly T. Carmichael
    Style. Raymond Dandridge

CLOUDS
    Garmet. Langston Hughes
    Sky Pictures. Effie Lee Newsome

CLOVER, FOUR-LEAF
    Four-Leaf Clover. Wesley Cartright

CLOWNS
    Leviticus Tate. Lloyd Warren

CLUBS
    Clubwoman. Mary Carter Smith
    Juice Joint: Northern City. Langston Hughes

COAL
    Coal. Audre Lord

COBRA
    To Fez Cobra. Ted Joans

COBWEBS
    Gossamer. Georgia Douglas Johnson

COCAINE
    Cocaine Galore I. Victor Cruz

COCHRAN, GAVIN H.
    Gavin H. Cochran, the Children's Friend. Joseph S. Cotter, Sr.

COLD
    Cold. Ted Joans

COLOR
    Color. Langston Hughes
    Desire. Constance Nichols
    Epigram. Iola M. Brister
    Nice Colored Man, The. Ted Joans
    Shroud of Color, The. Countee Cullen
    To Anita. Sonia Sanchez
    Who Am I. Kali Grosvenor
    Who To? Ted Joans

COLOR, LIBERATION
    Red, the Black & the Green, The. S. E. Anderson

COLTRANE, JOHN
    Brother John. Michael S. Harper
    Coltrane / Poem, A. Sonia Sanchez
    Coming of John, The. Amos Mor
    Dear John, Dear Coltrane. Michael S. Harper
    Dirge for Trane. Michael S. Harper
    Don't Cry Scream. Don L. Lee
    John Coltrane. Alfred B. Spellman

COLUMBUS, CHRISTOPHER
    Colmbes Didn't Discover This World. Kali Grosvenor
    Columbian Ode. Paul Laurence Dunbar
    To Columbus. Ruben Dario

COMIC BOOKS, STRIPS, ETC.
    C for Charlie. Gerald W. Barrax

COMMENCEMENT
    Graduation. Langston Hughes

COMMUNICATION
    Together. Carolyn Rodgers

COMMUNISM
    C-- C-- Raiders. Ted Joans
    To the Men of the Soviet Army. D. Binga Dismond

COMPENSATION
    Compensation. James Edwin Campbell
    Compensation. Paul Laurence Dunbar
    Compensation, The. Ruth E. J. Sarver

CONFEDERATE STATES OF AMERICA
    Confederate Veteran and the Old Time Negro. Joseph S. Cotter, Sr.

CONGRESSES AND CONVENTION
    Detroit Conference of Unity and Art (For HRB). Nikki Giovanni

CONFESSION see CREEDS

CONJURE see MAGIC

CONRAD, JOSEPH
    For Joseph Conrad. Countee Cullen

CONSCIENCE
    Conscience and Remorse. Paul Laurence Dunbar

CONSOLATION see SYMPATHY

CONTENT
    Content. Charles Fred White

CONTRADICTION
   Contradiction. Joseph S. Cotter
   Contradiction. Don L. Lee

CONTRAST
   Mister Samuel and Sam. Sterling A. Brown

CONVENTS
   Convent. Langston Hughes

CONVERSATION
   Conversation. Nikki Giovanni
   Telephone Conversation. Wole Soyinka

CONVICTS
   Convict. Sterling A. Brown

COOKERY
   Capture, The. Paul Laurence Dunbar
   Curiosity. Paul Laurence Dunbar

COOPERATION
   Man to Man. William Thompson Goss

CORDS
   Cords. Ruth Brownlee Johnson

CORN
   Corn Song, A. Paul Laurence Dunbar
   Corn-Stalk Fiddle, The. Paul Laurence Dunbar

CORNERS
   Lonesome Corner. Langston Hughes

COTTER, JOSEPH S., JR.
   To the Memory of Joseph S. Cotter, Jr. Joseph S. Cotter, Sr.

COTTON
   Cotton Pickin'. Lucile D. Goodlett
   Cotton Song. Jean Toomer
   November Cotton Flower. Jean Toomer
   Old King Cotton. Sterling A. Brown
   Pick a Bale of Cotton. Anonymous
   Secon' Pickin'. J. Mason Brewer

COUNTING
   Counting Out. J. Mord Allen

COUNTRY LIFE
   At Loafing-Holt. Paul Laurence Dunbar
   City and Country. Joseph S. Cotter, Sr.

CRIMES AND CRIMINALS
    Move! LeRoi Jones

CRITICISM
    To a Captious Critic. Paul Laurence Dunbar

CROCUSES
    Crocuses, The. Frances Harper

CROSS
    Late Corner. Langston Hughes

CROWDS
    From the Crowd. William S. Braithwaite
    Question to a Mob. Lauretta Holman Gooden

CROWS
    In Air. Peter Clarke

CRUELTY
    To One Who Was Cruel. Countee Cullen

CRYING
    I Weep. Angelina Weld Grimke
    Oh, Mary, Don't You Weep. Anonymous
    Weep Not. James E. McGirt
    When You Come to See Me. Maya Angelou

CUBA
    Conquerors, The. Paul Laurence Dunbar
    Two Countries. Jose Marti

CULLEN, COUNTEE
    Countee Cullen. Owen Dodson
    Countee Cullen. Eugene T. Maleska
    Tribute to Countee Cullen, 1928. James Edward McCall

CULTURE
    Customs and Culture? Ted Joans

CURIOSITY
    Curiosity. Lucy Mae Turner

CUSTER, GEORGE ARMSTRONG
    Custer's Last Stand. Albery A. Whitman

CYNICISM
    Cynic. Tomi Carolyn Tinsley

- D -

Dating   SUBJECT INDEX

    Tryst, The. Paul Laurence Dunbar
    Wooing, The. Paul Laurence Dunbar

DAYS
    Close of Day, The. Wesley Curtwright
    Day. Paul Laurence Dunbar
    Day and Night. Lewis Alexander
    Daybreak in Alabama. Langston Hughes
    Days. Raymond Dandridge
    Difference was a Day, The. William L. Morrison
    Drowsy Day, A. Paul Laurence Dunbar
    Golden Day, A. Paul Laurence Dunbar
    Gray Day, A. Raymond Dandridge
    Judgment Day. Langston Hughes
    Lazy Day, A. Paul Laurence Dunbar
    Misty Day, A. Paul Laurence Dunbar
    Sultry Day, A. William L. Morrison
    This Day. Elroy Douglas

DEATH
    Against That Day. Sterling A. Brown
    Albert Ayler: Eulogy for a Decomposed Sexaphone Player. Stanley Crouch
    Alexander Crummel--Dead. Paul Laurence Dunbar
    All the Dead. Countee Cullen
    All White on Europe Sixty-Nine Western Front. Ted Joans
    Another way of Dying. Gerald W. Barrax
    Approximations. Robert Hayden
    As the Old Year Passed. William Moore
    At A Parting. Countee Cullen
    At Sea. Vera Guerard
    At the Etoile (At the Unknown Soldier's Grave in Paris). Countee Cullen
    Athlete's Tomb, The. William C. Braithwaite
    Aunt Jane Allen. Fenton Johnson
    Ballad of Late Annie, The. Gwendolyn Brooks
    Ballad of the Brown Girl, The. Countee Cullen
    Ballad of the Light-Eyed Little Girl, The. Gwendolyn Brooks
    Ballad of the Man Who's Gone. Langston Hughes
    Ballade of One Who Died Before His Time. Benjamin Brawley
    Barred. Naomi Evans Vaughn
    Behind the Arras. Paul Laurence Dunbar
    Bessie Smith's Funeral. Albert Aubert
    Blk / Chant (to be said everyday slowly). Sonia Sanchez
    Black Maria. Langston Hughes
    Boarding House. Langston Hughes
    Border Ballad, A. Paul Laurence Dunbar
    Border Line. Langston Hughes
    Breakthrough. John Sinclair
    Breaths. Birago Diop
    Brown Girl Dead. Countee Cullen
    Burial of Sarah. Frances Harper
    Burial of the Young Love. Waring Cuney
    Bury me in a Free Land. Frances Harper

Cabaret Girl Dies on Welfare Island. Langston Hughes
Cardinal Mercier. Raymond Dandridge
Cavalier. Richard Bruce
Challenge. Sterling A. Brown
Circles in Sand (Fragments). Robert J. Abrams
Closing Time. Langston Hughes
Common Dust. Georgia Douglas Johnson
Communion. Paul Laurence Dunbar
Contradiction. Joseph S. Cotter
Cor Cordium. Countee Cullen
Country Graveyard. Charles F. Pressoir
Dance Finale. Samuel E. Boyd
David Morton Sonnet Analyzed, A. Joseph S. Cotter, Sr.
Day of the Dead. Robert Hayden
Daybreak. Langston Hughes
De Sight of Unc' Sol. Eli Shepperd
Death Chant. Langston Hughes
Death In Harlem. Langston Hughes
Death in Yorkville. Langston Hughes
Death is Not as Natural as You Fags Seem to Think. LeRoi Jones
Death of an Old Sea Man. Langston Hughes
Death Prosecuting. Linda Curry
Deceased. Langston Hughes
Dead. Paul Laurence Dunbar
Dead Soldier. Nicolas Guillen
Death. Paul Laurence Dunbar
Death as a Lotus Flower. Anonymous
Death Bed, The. Waring Cuney
Death of a Negro Poet, The. Conrad Kent Rivers
Death of De Dirty A Rounder Song. Langston Hughes
Death of the First Born, The. Paul Laurence Dunbar
Death of the Old Sea King. Frances Harper
Death Rites II. Anonymous
Death Scene. Joseph McMillan
Death Song, A. Paul Laurence Dunbar
Death to the Poor. Countee Cullen
Death's Aftermath. William C. Braithwaite
Deathwatch. Michael S. Harper
Despair. Georgia D. Johnson
Destiny. Joseph S. Cotter, Sr.
Detached, The. Maya Angelou
Dirge. Paul Laurence Dunbar
Dirge For a Soldier. Paul Laurence Dunbar
Dispute Over Suicide, A. Anonymous
Dowager's Death, The. Carl Gardner
Dying Bondman, The. Frances Harper
Dylan, Who is Dead. Samuel W. Allen
Each Night. Mae V. Cowdery
Eclipse. Amir Rashidd
Effie. Sterling A. Brown

Death   SUBJECT INDEX

Nat Turner, an Epitaph. Lucy Mae Turner
News, The. Paul Laurence Dunbar
Night, Death, Mississippi. Robert Hayden
Night of Death. Frances Harper
Niobe in Distress For Her Children Slain by Apollo, From Ovid's Metamor-
    phoses of the Painting of Mr. Richard Wilson. Phillis Wheatley
Nocturne. Countee Cullen
Note, The. Melvin Tolson
Notes Found Near a Suicide. Frank Horne
Obits. Gerald Barrax
Obituary. Robert Hayden
Oblivion. Jessie Redmond Fauset
Ode For Memorial Day. Paul Laurence Dunbar.
Ode of Verses on the Much Lamented Death of The Rev. Mr. George White-
    field, An. Phillis Wheatley
Official Notice. Langston Hughes
Oh, I Have Asked. William S. Braithwaite
Old Relative. Gwendolyn Brooks
On a Suicide. Joseph S. Cotter, Sr.
On Going. Countee Cullen
On the Death of a Child. Edward Silvera
On the Death of a Young Gentleman. Phillis Wheatley
On the Death of a Young Lady of Five Years Old. Phillis Wheatley
On the Death of Dr. Samuel Marshall (1771). Phillis Wheatley
On the Death of Dunbar. Charles Fred White
On the Death of J. C. an Infant. Phillis Wheatley
On the Death of Rev. Dr. Sewell (1769). Phillis Wheatley
On the Death of the Rev. Mr. George Whitefield (1770). Phillis Wheatley
On the Death of the Rev'd Dr. Sewall 1769. Phillis Wheatley
On the Death of Thomas Bailey Aldridge. William S. Braithwaite
On the Death of W. C. Paul Laurence Dunbar
On Viewing Death. William L. Morrison
One Life. Paul Laurence Dunbar
Ox in De Ditch. Lucile D. Goodlett
Pale Blue Casket, The. Oliver Pitcher
Paradox, The. Paul Laurence Dunbar
Passing of Mammy, The. Eli Shepperd
Paupers's Grave, The. Benjamin Clark
Peace. Langston Hughes
Pellets of May 2, 1960. Roscoe Lee Browne
Pimp's Last Mack: Death Request a Folk Song. Stanley Crouch
Poem for Children With Thoughts on Death. Jupiter Hammon
Poem From Distances, A. Christopher Origbo
Poems for My Brother Kenneth. Owen Dodson
Poor Renaldo. Naomi Long Madgett
Posthumous. Georgia Douglas Johnson
Posthumous Recognition. Raymond Dandridge
Prescience. Donald Jeffrey Hayes
Proud Heart, The. Countee Cullen
Psalm of the Uplift, The. Timothy Thomas Fortune
Puttin' the Baby Away. Paul Laurence Dunbar
Quatrains. Salah Tahin

Death   SUBJECT INDEX

To a Gentleman and Lady on the Death of the Lady's Brother and Sister,
    and Child of the Name of Avis, Aged One Year. Phillis Wheatley
To a Lady and Her Children, on the Death of Her son and Their Brother.
    Phillis Wheatley
To a Lady on the Death of Her Husband. Phillis Wheatley
To a Lady on the Death of Three Relations. Phillis Wheatley
To a Little Lover-Lass, Dead. Langston Hughes
To Die Before One Wakes Must Be Glad. Alice Walker
To Florence. Jôseph S. Cotter, Jr.
To His Honor the Lieutenant Governor, on the Death of His Lady, March 24,
    1773. Phillis Wheatley
To Mrs. Leonard on the Death of Her Husband. Phillis Wheatley
To Mr. and Mrs. --,   on the Death of Their Infant Son. Phillis Wheatley
To Strike for Night. Lebert Bethune
To the Clay. Raymond Dandridge
To the Hon'ble Thomas Hubbard Esq. on the Death of Mrs. Thankfull Leonard
    (1773). Phillis Wheatley
To the Honorable T. H. Esq. on the Death of His Daughter. Phillis Wheat-
    ley
To the Memory of Mary Young. Paul Laurence Dunbar
To the Rev. Mr. Pitkin, on the Death of his Lady (1772). Phillis Wheat-
    ley
To Wanda. Frank Horne
Triviality, A. Waring Cuney
Tulips From Their Blood. Edwin Brooks
Two Tpitaphs. Countee Cullen
Two Poems. Don L. Lee
2 Poems for Black Relocation Centers. Etheridge Knight
Two Thoughts of Death. Countee Cullen
Ultima Verba. Countee Cullen
Uncle Bill. Albert Aubert
Unholy Mission. Bob Kaufman
Virginia Portrait. Sterling A. Brown
Wake. Langston Hughes
Wake Cry. Waring Cuney
Wake for Papa Montero. Nicolas Guillen
We Assume: on the Death of our Son Reuben Masai Harper. Michael S.
    Harper
We Real Cool. Gwendolyn Brooks
We've Got to Live Before We Die. H. A. B. Jones-Quartey
When all is Done. Paul Laurence Dunbar
When I Am Dead. Owen Dodson
When I am Dead. Georgia Douglas Johnson
When I Awoke. Raymond Patterson
When I Die. Nikki Giovanni
When I Die. Fenton Johnson
When I Die in Dreams. Craig Williamson
W'en I Gits Home. Paul Laurence Dunbar
Where are the Men Seized in this Wind of Madness? Aldo De Espirito Santo
When I Have Passed Away. Claude McKay
Widow Woman. Langston Hughes
Will They Cry When You're Gone, You Bet. LeRoi Jones

Wise, The. Countee Cullen
Without Benefit of Declaration. Langston Hughes
Young Bride. Langston Hughes

DEBTS
Debt. Paul Laurence Dunbar
Debt I Cannot Pay, A. William L. Morrison

DECEIT
Deceit. Raymond Dandridge
Only the Polished Skeleton. Countee Cullen

DECEMBER
December. Charles Fred White

DECISIONS
Decision, The. Owen Dodson

DECK
Upon the Deck. William C. Braithwaite

DEEDS
What Have I Done. Waverly T. Carmichael

DEFEAT
Defeat. James A. Emanuel
Defeat. Countess W. Twitty
Defeated. James E. McGirt
Road to Anywhere. Dorothy Vena Johnson

DEGRADATION
Hey, Boy! Alexander Young

DELANY, CLARISSA SCOTT
To Clarissa Scott Delany. Angelina Weld Grimke

DELAY
Delay and Truth. Joseph S. Cotter, Sr.

DELTA
Delta. Margaret Walker

DEMOCRACY
Democracy. Langston Hughes
Tomorrow's Democracy. William L. Morrison

DEMONSTRATIONS
Street Demonstration. Margaret Walker

DEPARTURE
Adieu. Constantia E. Riley
As You Leave Me. Etheridge Knight

Sunday Morning Prophecy. Langston Hughes
Temptress, The. James Weldon Johnson

DEW
    Dew. J. Mason Brewer
    Dew. William L. Morrison
    Poem. Robert Hayden

DICKINSON, REV. MU BUGWU
    Song: the Rev. Mu Bugwu Dickinson Ruminates Behind Sermon. Gwendolyn
        Brooks

DICTATORS
    Of Dictators. Robert Perry, Jr.

DIFFERENCES
    Differences. Paul Laurence Dunbar
    Differences. Valerie Tarver
    Growing Up. Arthur Boze
    Retaliation. Tomi Carolyn Tinsley
    Revelation. Blanche Taylor Dickinson
    Trivia. Beatrice M. Murphy

DINNERS AND DINING
    Beatrice Does The Dinner. Mari Evans
    Indignation Dinner, An. James David Corrothers

DIONYSOS
    Hail, Dionysos. Dudley Randall

DISCOURAGED
    Discouraged. John Wesley Holloway
    Trapped. Vernoy E. Hite

DISCRIMINATION

    America. Bobb Hamilton
    Angela Question Mark. Langston Hughes
    At the Closed Gate of Justice. James David Corrothers
    Beginning of a Long Poem on Why I Burned the City, The. Lawrence Benford
    Black Memorial Day, A. Frenchy J. Hodges
    Boogie-Woogie Ballads. St. Clair McKelway
    Brothers. James Weldon Johnson
    Children's Rhymes. Langston Hughes
    Circled By a Horsefly. Helen Quigless
    Color Bane, The. George Marion McLlelan
    Dark People. Kattie M. Cumbo
    etc. etc. etc. Dorothy C. Parrish
    Finger Poppin', August 1961. Charles L. Anderson
    Frustration, A Heritage. Thelma Parker Cox.
    I, Too. Langston Hughes
    Idle Chatter. Charles Cooper

DIVISION OF RACES
    Speech. Robert E. Hayden

DIXIE
    Take Me Home. Waverly T. Carmichael

DOG CATCHER
    Dog Catcher, The. Lucy Mae Turner

DOGS
    Alley Cat Brushed His Whiskers, The. Waring Cuney
    Dog Catcher, The. Lucy Mae Turner
    Mah Dawg. Raymond Dandridge
    On Seeing Diana Go Maddddddddd. Don L. Lee
    When Great Dogs Fight. Melvin Tolson

DOLLS
    I Used to Wrap My White Doll Up In. Mae Jackson

DOMINICANS
    Dominicaine, The. M. Binga Dismond

DOUGH
    Dinah Kneading Dough. Paul Laurence Dunbar

DOUGLASS, FREDERICK
    Douglass. Paul Laurence Dunbar
    Frederick Douglass. Joseph S. Cotter
    Frederick Douglass. Eloise Culver
    Frederick Douglass. Paul Laurence Dunbar
    Frederick Douglass. Robert Hayden
    Frederick Douglass: 1817-1895. Langston Hughes

DOVES
    After. Naomi Long Madgett
    Dove, The. Paul Laurence Dunbar
    Dove, The. Langston Hughes
    Dove's Nest. William S. Braithwaite

DOWNTOWN
    Poem for Downtown, A. Victor Hernandez Cruz

DRAMA
    Prologue to a Supposed Play. Joseph S. Cotter
    Thespian. Calvin C. Hernton

DRAWINGS
    Life in the Art of Drawing. Carolyn Ogletree

DREAMS
    As I Grow Older. Langston Hughes
    Awakening, The. James Weldon Johnson

Dreams   SUBJECT INDEX

Slave's Dream, The. Henry Wadsworth Longfellow
Slum Dreams. Langston Hughes
Spin Me a Dream. Helen C. Harris
To-Night Across the Sea. William S. Braithwaite
Twilight and Dreams. William S. Braithwaite
Two Poems From Trinity: A Dream Sequence. Naomi Long Madgett
When I Die in Dreams. Craig Williamson
Why Fades a Dream? Paul Laurence Dunbar
Wonder Woman, The. Nikki Giovanni

DREW, CHARLES R.
    Dr. Charles R. Drew. Eloise Culver

DRIFTWOOD
    To Pfrimmer. Paul Laurence Dunbar

DROPOUTS
    "Cool" To Gene. John Raven
    We Real Cool. Gwendolyn Brooks

DROUGHTS
    Drought. Gerald W. Barrax

DROWNINGS
    Life is Fine. Langston Hughes
    Scuba Diver Receovers the Body of a Drowned Child, The. Gerald W. Barrax

DRUM MAJORS
    De Drum Majah. Raymond Dandridge

DRUMS
    Drums of Haiti. Marcus B. Christian
    Mama Drum. Ted Joans
    Mystic Drum. Gabriel Okara
    Piano and Drums. Gabriel Okara
    Ritmo I. Victor Hernandez Cruz

DUBOIS, WILLIAM EDWARD
    Booker T. and W. E. B. Dudley Randall
    Dr. W. E. B. DuBois. Eloise Culver
    For William Edward Burghardt DuBois on his Eightieth Birthday. Bettie
        Darcie Latimer
    Newest Star, The. Eloise Culver
    On the Death of William Edward Burghardt DuBois, By African Moonlight
        and Forgotten Shores. Conrad Kent Rivers
    Race Welcome, Dr. W. E. B. DuBois as its Leader. Joseph S. Cotter, Sr.

DUDDON RIVER
    Duddon Calling. William C. Braithwaite

DUMAS, ALEXANDRE
    Lines Written at the Grave of Alexandre Dumas. Gwendolyn Bennett

DUNBAR, PAUL LAURENCE
        Answer to Dunbar's "A Choice." Joseph S. Cotter
        Answer to Dunbar's "After a Visit." Joseph S. Cotter
        Dunbar. Anne Spencer
        For Paul Laurence Dunbar. Countee Cullen
        Mantle of Dunbar. Charles B. Johnson
        On the Death of Dunbar. Charles Fred White
        Paul Lawrence Dunbar. Waverly T. Carmichael
        Paul Laurence Dunbar. James David Corrothers

DUNCAN, ISADORA
        Photograph of Isadora Duncan, A. Robert Hayden

DUSK
        Dusk. Mae V. Cowdery
        Dusk. Angelina Weld Grimke
        Dusk. Langston Hughes
        Georgia Dusk. Langston Hughes

DUST
        Dust. Waring Cuney
        Dust Bowl. Robert A. Davis

DUTY
        Duty. Zachary Withers

DYNAMITE
        Dynamite Transported From Canada to New York City. Clarence Major

- E -

EAGLES
        Allegory. Robert Hayden

EAR
        On Wearing Ears. William J. Harris

EARTH
        Earth Song. Langston Hughes
        Of Earth. Mae V. Cowdery
        Pearl Primus. Owen Dodson
        To Lovers of Earth: Fair Warning. Countee Cullen

EARTHQUAKE
        Earth-quake. Waring Cuney

EASE
        Ease. Raymond Dandridge

EAST
        Going East. Frances Harper
        To the Eastern Shore. Paul Laurence Dunbar

EASTER
 Easter. Raymond Dandridge
 Easter Flower, The. Claude McKay
 Easter Morn. Raymond Dandridge
 Easter Morn, An. Charles Fred White
 For Jim, Easter Eve. Anne Spencer

EASY-GOING
 Easy-Goin' Feller, An. Paul Laurence Dunbar

EBONY
 In Shades of Ebony. William L. Morrison

ECHO
 Echo. Dorothy F. Blackwell

ECONOMICS
 Indianapolis / Summer / 1969 / Poem. Sonia Sanchez

EDUCATION
 Chicago Defender Sends a Man to Little Rock, Fall 1957. Gwendolyn Brooks
 Giles Johnson, PHD. Frank Marshall Davis
 Learning to Read. Frances Harper
 Little White Schoolhouse Blues. Florence Becker Lennon*
 Negro's Educational Creed, The. Joseph S. Cotter, Sr.
 School Integration Riot. Robert Hayden
 To the University of Cambridge, Wrote in 1767. Phillis Wheatley
 Tunk (A Lecture on Modern Education). James Weldon Johnson

EGGS
 Egg Boiler, The. Gwendolyn Brooks

EGYPT
 Riddle of the Sphinx. William E. B. DuBois
 To Egypt. Gloria Davis

ELEPHANTS
 Elephant I, The. Anonymous
 Elephant II, The. Anonymous

ELEVATORS
 Elevator Boy. Langston Hughes

ELLINGTON, DUKE
 Duke's Advice. Ted Joans

ELLISON, RALPH
 Invisible Man, The. Conrad Kent Rivers

ELM
 "Under the Elm." William C. Braithwaite

EMERSON, RALPH WALDO
    Emerson. Joseph S. Cotter

EMOTIONS
    Frustration, a Heritage. Thelma Parker Cox

ENCHANTMENT
    Enchantment. Georgia Holloway Jones

ENCOURAGEMENT
    Best of It. Raymond Garfield Dandridge
    Des Fo' Day. James E. McGirt
    Encouragement. Charles Fred White
    Good After Ill. Waverly T. Carmichael
    Move On. Waverly T. Carmichael

ENEMIES
    Love Your Enemy. Yusef Iman
    No Enemies. Benjamin Clark

ENGLAND
    Ye Bards of England. Arbery Allson Whitman
    America to England. Joseph S. Cotter, Sr.

ENIGMAS
    Enigmas. William S. Braithwaite

ENTERTAINING
    Dinner Guest: Me. Langston Hughes
    Mae's Rent Party. Ernest J. Wilson, Jr.
    Party, The. Paul Laurence Dunbar

EPHEMERA
    Ephemera, The. George Marion McClellan

EPITAPHS
    All the Dead. Countee Cullen
    Epitaph for a Badman. John Raven
    For a Cynic. Countee Cullen
    For a Fatalist. Countee Cullen
    For a Fool. Countee Cullen
    For a Lady I Know. Countee Cullen
    For a Lovely Lady. Countee Cullen
    For a Magician. Countee Cullen
    For a Mouthy Woman. Countee Cullen
    For a Pessimist. Countee Cullen
    For a Philosopher. Countee Cullen
    For a Poet. Countee Cullen
    For a Preacher. Countee Cullen
    For a Singer. Countee Cullen
    For a Skeptic. Countee Cullen
    For a Virgin. Countee Cullen

    For a Wanton. Countee Cullen
    For An Anarchist. Countee Cullen
    For An Atheist. Countee Cullen
    For an Evolutionist and His Opponent. Countee Cullen
    For An Unsuccessful Sinner. Countee Cullen
    For Daughters of Magdalen. Countee Cullen
    For Hazel Hall American Poet. Countee Cullen
    For John Keats, Apostle of Beauty. Countee Cullen
    For Joseph Conrad. Countee Cullen
    For My Grandmother. Countee Cullen
    For Myself. Countee Cullen
    For One Who Died Singing of Death. Countee Cullen
    For One Who Gayly Sowed His Oats. Countee Cullen
    For Paul Lawrence Dunbar. Countee Cullen
    Nat Turner, An Epitaph. Lucy Mae Turner

EQUALITY
    Equality. Herman L. McMillan
    Looking For Equality. Herman L. McMillan

ERRORS
    I Think I Thought A Lie. David Gatewood Thomas
    Fallacy. Ricardo Weeks
    Mistakes. Naomi Evans Vaughn

ETERNITY
    Eternity. Raymond Dandridge

ETHIOPIA
    Ethiopian Sonnet. William L. Morrison
    Ode to Ethiopia. Paul Laurence Dunbar
    Word to Ethiopia. Waverly T. Carmichael

EUROPE
    Europe on Five Dollars a Day. Ted Joans

EVENING
    At Evening. Charles Fred White
    City: San Francisco. Langston Hughes
    Evening. William S. Braithwaite
    Evening. Paul Laurence Dunbar
    Evening in Haiti. Emile Reumer
    Evening Song. Jean Toomer
    Evening Thought, An. Jupiter Hammon
    Evening. Waverly T. Carmichael
    Hymn to the Evening, An. Phillis Wheatley
    In the Evening. Fenton Johnson
    Lyric: When the Still Sombre Evening Closes Down. William S. Braithwaite
    Sketch of a Varying Evening Sky. John Boyd

EVERS, CHARLES
    Medgar Evers. Gwendolyn Brooks

EVERS, MEDGAR
      Medgar Evers. Gwendolyn Brooks
      Micah. Margaret Walker

EVICTION
      Broke. John Raven
      Evicted. Beatrice M. Murphy

EVIL see GOOD AND EVIL

EVOLUTION
      Evolution. Thelma Parker Cox

EXILES
      From Song of Exile. Antonio Goncalves Dias

EXPERIENCE
      Experience. James E. McGirt

EYE
      Her Eyes Twin Pools. James Weldon Johnson
      Inconstancy. Joseph S. Cotter, Jr.
      Your Big Eyes. Bernie Casey

- F -

FACE
      Black Faces. Anita Scott Coleman
      Faces. Maya Angelou
      Faces. Dudley Randall
      Faces. Ted Joans
      Face. Jean Toomer

FACIALS
      Beauty Shoppe. Gwendolyn Brooks

FAILURE
      For the Man Who Fails. Paul Laurence Dunbar

FAIRIES
      Discovery, The. Paul Laurence Dunbar
      Disenchantment. Countee Cullen

FAITH
      After While. Paul Laurence Dunbar
      Faith. Joseph S. Cotter, Sr.
      Faith. Raymond Dandridge
      Faith. Paul Laurence Dunbar
      Triple Benison, The. Henrietta Cordelia Ray

FAITHFUL see LOYALTY

FALLACIES see ERRORS

FALCON
    Falcon, The. Robert Hayden

FANON, FRANTZ
    To Fanon. Keorapetse Kgositsile

FANTASY
    Fantasy. Gwendolyn B. Bennett

FASHION SHOWS
    Sepia Fashion Show. Maya Angelou

FATHERS
    Clock on Hancock Street. June Jordan
    Father, Son and Holy Ghost. Audre Lord
    Fruit of the Flower. Countee Cullen
    Lines to My Father. Countee Cullen
    Obituary. Robert E. Hayden
    Pappy's Last Song. Maurine Jeffrey
    Paternal. Ernest J. Wilson, Jr.
    Poem for My Father, A. Sonia Sanchez
    To Father. Henrietta Cordelia Ray
    Worker, The. Richard Thomas

FEAR
    Admonition. Stanley E. Morris, Jr.
    Afraid. Langston Hughes
    White Fear. Nannie M. Travis

FEBRUARY
    Black February Blood Letting. Ted Joans

FEDERAL BUREAU OF INVESTIGATION (FBI)
    Award. Ray Durem
    I Laughed When I Wrote It. Nikki Giovanni
    Top Creep. Ted Joans

FEMALE IMPERSONATION
    Feflections On a Lost Love. Don L. Lee

FERGUSON, KATHERINE
    Katherine Ferguson. Eloise Culver

FETTERS
    World Has Fetters, The. William C. Braithwaite

FIDDLES
    Der Fiddle is my Comfort. Waverly T. Carmichael
    Fiddle in de Win'. Lucile D. Goodlett

FIDELITY
    Fidelity. Charles Fred White

FIGHTS
    Bars Fight. Lucy Turner
    Fighting Time. Ray Garfield Dandridge
    My Lord, What a Morning. Waring Cuney

FILIBUSTERS
    Filibuster, 1964. Gerald Barrax

FINGERS
    Black Finger, The. Angelina Weld Grimke

FILIPINOS
    Dem Phillupeeners. Joseph S. Cotter, Sr.

FIRE FLIES
    Wish, A. Eleanor A. Thompson

FIREARMS
    If I had a Gun That Would Shoot. Mari Evans
    Right On: Wite America 4. Sonia Sanchez
    .38, The. Ted Joans

FIRED
    Fired. Langston Hughes

FIREPLACE
    Fireplace, The. Michael S. Harper

FIRES
    Fire. Langston Hughes
    Fire Next Time Blues, The. Ted Joans

FISHES
    Ballade of Mackeral. William C. Braithwaite
    Down Fish Trap Lane. J. Austin Love

FISHING
    Fishermen. James Emanuel
    Fishin'. Lucile D. Goodlett
    Fishing. Paul Laurence Dunbar
    Fishy Poem, A. Nikki Giovanni
    My Lover is a Fisherman. Gertrude Davenport
    Turn't Errown'. Raymond Dandridge
    When the Fish Begins to Bite. J. Mord Allen

FLAGS
    Flags. Gwendolyn Brooks
    Old Glory. Raymond Dandridge

Our Flag. Zachary Withers
Red, White and Blue. Waverly T. Carmichael

FLANDERS FIELD
Poppies Cannot Grow in Flanders Field. William L. Morrison

FLIES
Blue Fly. Joaquim Maria Machado De Assis

FLIGHT
Flyin'. Lucy Mae Turner
If I Could Fly. Kali Grosvenor

FLORENCE, ITALY
Florence to Her Cathedral-Builders. William C. Braithwaite

FLORIDA
Florida Night, A. Paul Laurence Dunbar
Florida Road Workers. Langston Hughes
From Twasinta's Seminoles; or Rape of Florida. Joseph S. Cotter

FLOWERS
Compensation. Joseph S. Cotter, Jr.
Cycle. Langston Hughes
Death as a Lotus Flower. Anonymous
Easter Flower, The. Claude McKay
Ephemera, The. George Marion McClellan
Flower, The. Waverly T. Carmichael
Fragility. James Edgar Smith
Fugue in Gardenia. William S. Braithwaite
Fulfilment. Paul Laurence Dunbar
Japanese Hokku. Lewis Alexander
Lilacs. Gertrude Parthenia McBrown
Lily of the Valley, The. Paul Laurence Dunbar
Little Dandelion, The. Lula Lowe Weeden
Lonely Tulip Grower. Julia Alvarez
Lure, The. Raymond Dandridge
Magnolia Flowers. Langston Hughes
May Flowers Come and Keep My Watch. William L. Morrison
Narcissus, The. Raymond Dandridge
Old Woman With Violets. Robert Hayden
On a Pressed Flower in My Copy of Keats. William S. Braithwaite
Pansy. Effie Lee Newsome
Poppy Flower. Langston Hughes
Pretty Flowers. Raymond Dandridge
Primrose and Thistle. Alpheus Butler
Promise. Paul Laurence Dunbar
Quoi Bon, A? Jules Wynn Smith
Red Flower, A. Claude McKay
Seedling, The. Paul Laurence Dunbar
Snow-White Rosebud. Raymond Dandridge
Song. Paul Laurence Dunbar

Flowers   SUBJECT INDEX

    Songs for my Lady's Banjo. Eli Shepperd
    Spanish Needle, The. Claude McKay
    Sunflowers: Beaubien Streets. Robert E. Hayden
    Throwing Out the Flowers. Gwendolyn Brooks
    To a Bunch of Carnations. Charles Fred White
    To a Rose at Williston. Charles Fred White
    To a Violet Found on All Saints' Day. Paul Laurence Dunbar
    To a Wild Rose. William Edgar Bailey
    To Hollyhocks. George Marion McClellan
    Tulips. W. Blanche Nivens
    Wild Roses. Effie Lee Newsome

FOOD
    Black Man's Feast. Sarah Webster Fabio
    Choicy. Lawrence Carlyle Tatum
    Favorite Diet, The. Waverly T. Carmichael
    Food Poisoning. Marion Nicholes
    Hod Meat. Daniel Webster Davis
    Opportunity. Paul Laurence Dunbar
    Preference, A. Paul Laurence Dunbar
    Soul. Bernie Casey
    Stealin' Grub. Lucy Mae Turner
    Uncle Eph--Epicure. James Edwin Campbell

FOOTBALL
    To The Men Who Held the Line. Curtis Smith
    Williston Battle Song. Charles Fred White

FOREVER
    Forever. Paul Laurence Dunbar

FORGIVENESS
    Forgiveness. Will Smallwood

FORTUNE TELLING
    Ballad of the Fortune-Teller. Langston Hughes
    Madam and the Fortune Teller. Langston Hughes
    Telling Fortunes. Sterling A. Brown

FOUNDING
    Migrant. Langston Hughes

FOUNT OF TEARS
    Fount of Tears. Paul Laurence Dunbar

FOUNTAINS
    To a Fountain. Lucy Mae Turner

FOXES
    Fugitive. Ricardo Weeks
    Jefferson in a Tight Place. George Moses Horton

FRANCE
    Christmas Eve in France. Jessie Redmond Fauset
    La Belle, La Douce, La Grande. Countee Cullen
    To France. Countee Cullen
    Traitor to France, The. Melvin Tolson

FRANKLIN, ARETHA
    Descarga. Victor Hernandez Cruz
    Poem For Aretha. Nikki Giovanni

FREEDOM see LIBERTY

FREEDOM RIDERS
    Freedom Rider: Washout. James Emanuel

FREUD, SIGMUND
    So We've Come at Last to Freud. Claude McKay

FRIENDSHIP
    After the Quarrel. Paul Laurence Dunbar
    Dear Friends and Gentle Hearts. Countee Cullen
    Frenship. Raymond Dandridge
    How Come Dat? Lucy Mae Turner
    I Have a Friend. Anne Spencer
    Negro's Friend, The. Claude McKay
    Old Friends. Charles Bertram Johnson
    On Friendship. Phillis Wheatley
    Poem (To F.S.). Langston Hughes
    To a Friend. Charles Fred White
    To My Friends. Countee Cullen
    To My Friends. William C. Braithwaite
    Written on a Christmas Card. Charles Fred White

FROWNING
    What's the Use. Paul Laurence Dunbar

FRUIT
    Apples. Ariel Williams

FULFILLMENT
    Fulfillment. Helene Johnson

FUNERAL RITES AND CEREMONIES
    Bessie Smith's Funeral. Albert Aubert
    Funeral. Sterling A. Brown
    Funeral. Langston Hughes
    Ox in De Ditch. Lucile D. Goodlett
    Pimp's Last Mack: Death Request, A Folk Song. Stanley Crouch

FUTILITY
    Futility. Claude McKay

- G -

GAIN
   Gain and Loss. Joseph S. Cotter, Sr.

GALLAGHER, WILLIAM D.
   William D. Gallagher. Joseph S. Cotter, Sr.

CAMBLING
   Crap Game. Langston Hughes
   Rich Stud. James Pipes

GAMES
   Game of Game, The. Nikki Giovanni
   Games. Conrad Kent Rivers
   One Day We Played a Game. Countee Cullen
   Quoits. Anonymous

GANDHI, MOHANDAS
   Vaticide. Myron O'Higgins

GANGS
   Gang Girls. Gwendolyn Brooks

GARDENIA
   Fugue in Gardenia. William S. Braithwaite

GARDENS
   City Garden, A. William S. Braithwaite
   Come Visit My Garden. ' Tom Dent
   Garden City. Albert Aubert
   Garden Sanctuary. William L. Morrison
   In an English Garden. Paul Laurence Dunbar
   In the Public Garden. William S. Braithwaite
   Lapse, The. Paul Laurence Dunbar
   My City Garden Plot. Lucy Mae Turner
   To a Certain Lady, in Her Garden (For Anne Spencer). Sterling A. Brown
   To a Persian Rose. William S. Braithwaite
   Venus in a Garden. James Weldon Johnson

GATES
   Old Front Gate, The. Paul Laurence Dunbar

GARRISON, WILLIAM LLOYD
   William Lloyd Garrison. Joseph S. Cotter, Sr.

GARROWAY, DAVE
   These Beasts and the Benin Bronze. Owen Dodson

GENEALOGY
   Ginoligy. Raymond Dandridge

GENIUS
   Genius Child. Langston Hughes

GEORGIA
   Georgia Dusk. Langston Hughes
   July in Georgy. James Weldon Johnson

GERMAN LANGUAGE
   From the German of Uhland. James Weldon Johnson

GETHSEMANE
   Gethsemane. Arna Bontemps
   Gethsemane. Georgia Johnson

GHETTOS
   Ghetto. Yvette Johnson
   U Name This One. Carolyn M. Rodgers
   Visitors to the Black Belt. Langston Hughes

GHOSTS
   Ghost of Deacon Brown, The. James Weldon Johnson
   Ghost Story, A. Raymond Dandridge
   Ghosts. Countee Cullen
   Ghosts of 1619. Langston Hughes
   Haunted. Mae V. Cowdery
   Spook Village. Lucy Mae Turner
   Thinkin' Spooks. Raymond Dandridge
   Wind, The Weathercock and the Warrior's Ghost. Robert Hayden

GIFTS
   Gift, The. Dudley Randall
   Her Christmas Gift. Charles B. Johnson
   Present. Langston Hughes
   Written on a Christmas Gift. Charles Fred White

GILEAD
   Gilead. Georgia Douglas Johnson

GILSON, ROY ROLFE
   To Roy Rolfe Gilson. William S. Braithwaite

GIRAFFES
   Giraffe. Anonymous

GIRLS
   Ballad of the Brown Girl, The. Countee Cullen
   Ballad of the Brown Girl. Alice Walker
   Ballad of the Girl Whose Name is Mud. Langston Hughes
   Black Gal. Langston Hughes
   Black Girl. Albert Aubert
   Black Girl Goes By, A. Emile Reumer

Song of Praise. Countee Cullen
Theme Brown Girl. Elton Hill
Three Brown Girls Singing. M. Carl Holman
To a Brown Girl. Countee Cullen
To a Brown Girl. Ossie Davis
To a Brown Lass. V. A. Reese
To a Brown-Skin Maiden. William L. Morrison
To a Dark Girl. Gwendolyn Bennett
To a Little Lover-Lass, Dead. Langston Hughes
To a Young Girl Leaving the Hill Country. Arna Bontemps
To Anita. Sonia Sanchez
To Fiona. William S. Braithwaite
To Fiona (Nineteen Months Only). William S. Braithwaite
To Midnight Nan at Leroy's. Langston Hughes
To the Girls of Kenwood. Charles Fred White
20th-Century Fox. LeRoi Jones
Why Try. Ted Joans
Yalla Gal. Lucile D. Goodlett
Young Gal's Blues. Langston Hughes
Young Negro Girl. Langston Hughes

GOATS
Mr. Goody's Goat. Joseph S. Cotter, Sr.
Wild Goats, The. Claude McKay

GOLD
Real Question, The. Paul Laurence Dunbar
Service. Georgia Douglas Johnson
In the Gold Mines. B. W. Vilakazi

GOLIATH
Goliath of Gath. Phillis Wheatley

GOOD AND EVIL
Combat, The. Waverly T. Carmichael
Evil. Langston Hughes
Evil Woman. Langston Hughes
Good Everywhere. Raymond Dandridge

GOSPEL
Gospel Train, The. Anonymous

GOSSIP
Scandal and Gossip, Countee Cullen

GOURD
Gourd, The. Paul Laurence Dunbar

GRADUATION see COMMENCEMENT

GRAMMAR
Grammah. Raymond Dandridge

GRANDMOTHERS
    Grandma. Langston Hughes
    Legacies. Nikki Giovanni

GRANT, ULYSSES
    Grant and Lee.   Joseph S. Cotter, Sr.

GRASSES
    Grass Fingers. Angelina Weld Grimke
    Quatrains. Gwendolyn B. Bennett

GRASSHOPPERS see LOCUSTS

GRAY
    Growin' Gray. Paul Laurence Dunbar

GREAT BRITAIN
    To the First of August. Ann Plato

GREATNESS
    Greatness. Zachary Withers

GREENESS
    Greeness. Angelina Weld Grimke

GRIFFIN, JOHN HOWARD
    Ode to John Howard Griffin. Arthur Boze

GROWTH
    Grow in Hope and Grace. Barbara Anne Baxter

GUADALAJARA
    Guadalajara. Clarence Major

GUITAR
    Guitar. Owen Dodson
    Guitar Music. Waring Cuney

GULLS
    Gulls. Robert Hayden

GUMS AND RESIN
    Disappointment. Arlena Howard Benton

GYPSIES
    Ballad of the Gypsy. Langston Hughes
    Gypsy Man. Langston Hughes

- H -

HAIR
    Baby Hair. Constance Nichols
    Golden Hair. William S. Braithwaite

HAIR STYLES
    On Getting an Afro. Dudley Randall

HAITI
    Drums of Haiti. Marcus B. Christian
    Evening in Haiti. Emile Reumer

HALLOWEEN
    Hallowe'en. Charles Fred White

HALLUCINATIONS AND ILLUSIONS
    Illusion. Georgia Douglas Johnson

HALOS
    Uses of the Halo, The. William C. Braithwaite

HAMPTON, FRED
    One Sided Shootout. Don L. Lee

HAMPTON, LIONEL
    For Lionel Hampton. Olive La Grone

HAMPTON INSTITUTE
    Samuel Chapman Armstrong. Owen Dodson

HANDS
    Butterfly, The. Nikki Giovanni
    Dark Hands. Nannie M. Travis
    Dusk Thoughts. Countee M. Twitty
    Hands. Anita Scott Coleman
    Hands. Glen Thompson
    Here Hold my Hands. Mari Evans
    I Have Seen Black Hands. Richard Wright
    Praying Hands, The. William S. Braithwaite
    Some Hands are Lovelier. Mae V. Cowdery
    Sunset Streaking Hands. Craig Williamson
    Your Hands. Angelina Weld Grimke

HAPPINESS
    Big Spender. James Pipes*
    Happiness is Heaven. Charles Fred White
    I am Happy Today. William H. Green
    Poem. Blanche Taylor Dickinson
    Soliloguy. Dorothy C. Parrish

HARBORS
    Dar Es Salaam. Craig Williamson

HARLEM, NEW YORK
    Alpha. Melvin Tolson
    Death in Harlem. Langston Hughes
    Deceased. Langston Hughes
    Deep Ellum and Central Track. J. Mason Brewer
    Dimout in Harlem. Langston Hughes
    Disillusion. Langston Hughes
    Duke's Advice. Ted Joans
    Esthete in Harlem. Langston Hughes
    Eta. Melvin Tolson
    Harlem. Jean Brierre
    Harlem Dance Hall. Langston Hughes
    Harlem Dopscotch. Maya Angelou
    Harlem Gallery (Fragments). Melvin Tolson
    Harlem Night Club. Langston Hughes
    Harlem Night Song. Langston Hughes
    Harlem Shadows. Claude McKay
    Harlem: Sidewalk Icons. Oliver Pitcher
    Harlem Sounds: Hallelujah Chorus. William Browne
    Harlem Street Walkers. Sterling A. Brown
    Harlem Sweeties. Langston Hughes
    John Henry in Harlem. Melvin Tolson
    Mecca. Sterling A. Brown
    Puzzled. Langston Hughes
    Return of the Native. LeRoi Jones
    Saturday Night in Harlem. William Browne
    Sketches of Harlem. David Henderson
    Sonnet to a Negro in Harlem. Helene Johnson
    Still Voice of Harlem, The. Conrad Kent Rivers
    To Mr. Clean and His Friends. John Raven
    Train Runs Late to Harlem, The. Conrad Kent Rivers
    Walk with the Mayor of Harlem. David Henderson

HARP
    Master-Player, The. Paul Laurence Dunbar
    O Little David, Play on Your Harp. Joseph S. Cotter, Jr.
    To a Lady Playing the Harp. Paul Laurence Dunbar

HARVEST
    After Harvest. William S. Braithwaite
    Harvest, The. Zachary Withers
    Harvest Song. Jean Toomer

HATRED
    Ghost of Hate, The. Zachary Withers
    Great Truths. Marion Cuthbert
    Hatred. Gwendolyn B. Bennett
    Triangle. Roslyn Greer

HATS
    Hat, The. Ted Joans
    Red. Countee Cullen

White Felts in Fall. Langston Hughes

HAYES, JOHN RUSSELL
    Madame of Dreams. William S. Braithwaite

HAYES, ROLAND
    Roland Hayes. Eloise Culver
    Roland Hayes Beaten. Langston Hughes

HEAD
    Retort. Paul Laurence Dunbar
    W'ere is my Head Going. Kali Grosvenor

HEALTH
    To a Lady on Her Coming to North America With Her Son, for the Receevery
       of Her Health. Phillis Wheatley

HEALING
    Healer of the New Day. Marion Nicholes

HEART
    Dear Friends and Gentle Hearts. Countee Cullen
    Foolish Heart, The. Countee Cullen
    Heart. Langston Hughes
    Proud Heart, The. Countee Cullen

HEATH, ANDREW
    To the Memory of the Rev. Andrew Heath. Joseph S. Cotter, Sr.

HEAVEN
    Angels in Overalls. James Pipes*
    City Called Heaven, The. Langston Hughes
    Confessional. Paul Laurence Dunbar
    Fishers of Men. Frances Harper
    For a Mouthy Woman. Countee Cullen
    Free Wine on Communion Day. Linwood D. Smith
    Gone West. Raymond Dandridge
    Heaven. Langston Hughes
    Hunchback Girl: She Thinks of Heaven. Gwendolyn Brooks
    Latent Thought, The. Charles Fred White
    Little Lyric. Langston Hughes
    North Boun'. Ariel Williams Holloway
    Oh, Dem Golden Slippers. James A. Bland
    Renewal of Strength. Frances Harper
    She of the Dancing Feet Sings. Countee Cullen
    Sonnet. Countee Cullen
    Swing Low, Sweet Chariot. Anonymous
    Theology. Paul Laurence Dunbar

HEMINGWAY, ERNEST
    Hemingway. Conrad Kent Rivers

HERITAGE
America Negra. Anita Scott Coleman
Ballad of the Free, The. Margaret Walker
Children's Children. Sterling A. Brown
Dark Blood. Margaret Walker
Dark Heritage. Marcus B. Christian
Frustration, A Heritage. Thelma Parker Cox
Heritage. Naomie Buford
Heritage. Dolores Clinton
Heritage. Claude McKay
Heritage (For Harold Jackman). Countee Cullen
Heritage. Gwendolyn Bennett
How Many Silent Centuries Sleep in my Sultry Veins? Margaret Walker
Idea of Ancestry, The. Etheridge Knight
Lemme Tell You What My Black is All About. Clarence Reed
New Poem For Us. Sonia Sanchez
Our Aryan Sires. William C. Braithwaite
Poem (For the Portrait of an African Boy after the Manner of Gaugauin).
    Langston Hughes
These are my People. Fenton Johnson
We Have Not Forgotten. Robert Hayden
You'd Better Watch Out. Ted Joans
What is Precious is Never to Forget. Robert Hayden

HEROES
Hero. Don L. Lee
My Hero (To Robert Gould Shaw). Benjamin Brawley
Negro Here. Gwendolyn Brooks
Our Hero. Frances Harper
Post War Ballad. Dorothy Vena Johnson
Strange Legacies. Sterling A. Brown
Unsung Heroes, The. Paul Laurence Dunbar
What Happing to the Heroes. Kali Grosvenor

HIGGINSON, THOMAS WENTWORTH
Thomas Wentworth Higginson For His Eighty-Third Birthday. William S.
    Braithwaite

HILLS
Hills, The. Frenchy J. Hodges
Hills of Sewanee, The. George Marion McClellan
In the High Hills. William S. Braithwaite
Lowly Grasses and Little Hills. William C. Braithwaite
Moonlight Amid the Hills. Zachary Withers
Price Hill. Raymond Dandridge
That Hill. Blanche Taylor Dickinson
To a Young Girl Leaving the Hill Country. Arna Bontemps

HOES
Stickin' to the Hoe. Daniel Webster Davis

HOGS
Hawg Killin'. Lucile D. Goodlett
Hog Killin' Times in Dixie Land. Eli Shepperd
Hog Meat. Daniel Webster Davis

HOLIDAY, BILLIE
Elegy for a Lady. Walt Delegall
For Billie Holiday. Langston Hughes
For Our Lady. Sonia Sanchez
Song for Billie Holiday. Langston Hughes

HOLIDAYS
Bank Holiday. William C. Braithwaite
Holidays, The. Charles Fred White
Memorial Day in East-Hampton. Charles Fred White
Ode for Memorial Day. Paul Laurence Dunbar
    See Also
    CHRISTMAS
    EASTER
    HALLOWEEN
    THANKSGIVING

HOLINESS
Holy Day. Larry Neal

HOLLAND
Dutch Treatment. Ted Joans

HOLLY
Holly Berry and Mistletoe. William S. Braithwaite
Through the Holly Wreath. Charlemae Rollins

HOLMES, OLIVER WENDELL
Oliver Wendell Holmes. Joseph S. Cotter

HOME
Bein' Back Home. Paul Laurence Dunbar
Home. Ted Joans
Home and Mother. Raymond Dandridge
Home, Sweet Home. Frances Harper
Home Thoughts. Claude McKay
Take Me Home. Waverly T. Carmichael
They Went Home. Maya Angelou
W'en I Gits Home. Paul Laurence Dunbar

HOME SICKNESS
Home Sick. James E. McGirt

HOME STEAD
Old Homestead, The. Paul Laurence Dunbar

HOME TOWN
    Possum Trot. Paul Laurence Dunbar

HOMOSEXUAL
    Funny Company? or Why Ain't Him and His Girls on T.V., The? Arthur Pfister

HONEY
    Honey and Roses. William L. Morrison
    Smoking out the Bees. Joseph S. Cotter, Sr.

HOPE
    At the Bier of Hope. Raymond Garfield Dandridge
    Dark Testament. Pauli Murray
    Hope. Joseph S. Cotter, Sr.
    Hope. Paul Laurence Dunbar
    It Seems to Me. Edna L. Anderson
    Service, Please. Myrtle Campbell Gorham
    Triple Benison, The. Henrietta Cordelia Ray

HOPE, LAURENCE
    To Laurence Hope. William S. Braithwaite

HOPSCOTCH
    Harlem Hopscotch. Maya Angelou

HORNS
    Loud Jazz Morn. Carter Webster

HORSES
    Dat Ol' Mare O' Mine. Paul Laurence Dunbar
    Hard is a Horse to Ride. Herbert G. Pickett
    Near Colorado. Michael S. Harper
    Over Loaded Horse, The. Ted Joans
    Rivah's a Black Mare. Lucile D. Goodlett
    Strong Men, Riding Horses. Gwendolyn Brooks

HORSES, SEA
    Sea Horse. Anonymous

HOSPITALITY
    Poem (For TW). Nikki Giovanni

HOSPITALS
    Black Muslim Boy in a Hospital. James Emanuel
    Interne at Provident. Langston Hughes

HOUSES
    De Tar Paper Bungalow. Lucy Mae Turner
    Languages We Are, The. F. J. Bryant
    Little Song on Housing. Langston Hughes
    My House. Nikki Giovanni

My House. Claude McKay
Old Houses. Melvin Tolson
Plans. Helen Morgan Brooks

HOWELLS, WILLIAM DEAN
William Dean Howells (For His Seventieth Birthday). William S. Braith-
    waite

HUGHES, LANGSTON
Langston. Mari Evans
Langston Hughes. Eloise Culver
Langston Hughes. Jacques Roumain
Letter to Langston Hughes. Kali Grosvenor
Promised Land. Ted Joans

HUMANITY
Hymn to Humanity (To S.P.G. Esq.), An. Phillis Wheatley

HUMILITY
Humility. Anita Scott Coleman

HUNCHBACK OF NOTRE DAME
Bells of Notre Dame, The. Benjamin Brawley

HUNGER
Hunger. Anonymous
Hunger. Countee Cullen
I am Hungry. Ted Joans

HUNTING
Big Game Hunter, The. Melvin Tolson
Forest Greeting, The. Paul Laurence Dunbar
Hunting Song. Paul Laurence Dunbar

HURRICANE
To a Lady on her Remarkable Preservation in a Hurricane in North Carolina.
    Phillis Wheatley

HUSBANDS
Madam and Her Might-Have-Been. Langston Hughes
To a Husband. Maya Angelou

HYENAS
Hyena. Anonymous

HYMNS
Hymn, A. Paul Laurence Dunbar
Hymn. Alice Walker
Hymn for Zion's Centennial. Joseph S. Cotter, Sr.
Hymns of the Black Belt. Eli Shepperd

- I -

IBADAN, NIGERIA
    Ibadan. John Pepper Clark

ICICLES
    Icicles. Joseph S. Cotter, Sr.
    Icicles on Trees. Catherine L. Findley

IDEALISM
    Shrine to What Should Be. Mari Evans

IMAGINATION
    On Imagination. Phillis Wheatley

IMMORTALITY
    Immortality. Marion Cuthbert
    Immortality. Frank Horne

INDIANS OF NORTH AMERICA
    Combes Didn't Discover This World. Kali Grosvenor
    Custer's Last Stand. Albery Whitman
    From Twasinta's Seminoles or Rape of Florida. Albery A. Whitman
    Seminole, The. Benjamin Clark

INDIANA
    Indiana Deformatory, The. Joseph S. Cotter, Sr.

INFANTS
    And Always. Bruce McM. Wright
    Babe is a Babe, A. Joseph S. Cotter, Sr.
    Baby Cobina. Aquah Laluah
    Baby Hair. Constance Nichols
    First Born, The. William S. Braithwaite
    Hush Now. Dorothy C. Parrish
    Little Brown Baby. Paul Laurence Dunbar
    Liza May. Paul Laurence Dunbar
    Making Friends With Baby. Charles B. Johnson
    Mammy's Baby Scared. Waverly T. Carmichael
    Nativity. Aquah Laluah
    On the Birth of My Son, Malcolm Coltrane. Julius Lester
    Pot and the Baby, The. Paul Laurence Dunbar
    Puttin' the Baby Away. Paul Laurence Dunbar
    Scolding Baby Boy. Waverly T. Carmichael
    Snooker Toots. Raymond Dandridge
    S-sss-ss-Sh! Langston Hughes
    Two Epitaphs. Countee Cullen
    Wash Baby. Harold Taylor
    What You Gonna Name That Pretty Little Baby? Anonymous
    Whimper, Baby. Lucile D. Goodlett

JACKSON, MISSISSIPPI
    Jackson, Mississippi. Margaret Walker

JACKSON, STONEWALL
    Stonewall Jackson. Arbery Allson Whitman

JANUARY
    January Dandelion, A. George Morton McLleLan

JASMINE
    Jasmine. Claude McKay

JAZZ MUSIC
    Battle Report. Bob Kaufman
    Jazz. Frank London Brown
    Jazz Anatomy. Ted Joans
    Jazz Bank in a Parisian Cabaret. Langston Hughes
    Jazz Fantasia. Carl Sandburg*
    Jazz is my Religion. Ted Joans
    Jazz Must be a Woman. Ted Joans
    Jazzonia. Langston Hughes
    Loud Jazz Horns. Carter Webster
    One Blue Note. Ted Joans
    Stormy Monday Girls. Ted Joans
    Two Jazz Poems. Carl Wendell Hines, Jr.

JEALOUSY
    Jealous. Paul Laurence Dunbar
    Jealous. William L. Morrison

JELLO
    Jello. Raymond Dandridge

JEREMIAH
    Hymn Written After Jeremiah Preached to Me in a Dream. Owen Dodson.

JERICHO
    Walls of Jericho, The. Blanche Taylor Dickinson

JERUSALEM
    Lines Written in Jerusalem. Countee Cullen

JESTERS
    Jester, The. Langston Hughes

JESUS CHRIST--CRUCIFIXION
    Crucifixion. Carter Webster
    Crucifixion. Waring Cuney
    Crucifixion, The. James Weldon Johnson

JESUS CHRIST--NATIVITY
    Carol of the Brown King. Langston Hughes

Christmas Story, The. Langston Hughes
Magi Called Him King. Effie Lee Newsome
On a Christmas Night. Langston Hughes
On a Pallet of Straw. Langston Hughes
Rise Up, Shepherd and Follow. Anonymous
Shepherd's Song of Christmas. Langston Hughes
Stable, The. Gabriela Mistral
Virgin Mary Had a Baby Boy, The. Anonymous
Wasn't That a Mighty Day. Anonymous

JEWELS
Jewels. Lucy Mae Turner

JEWS
Jonathan's Song. Owen Dodson

JILTED
Jilted. Paul Laurence Dunbar

JIM CROW
Defeat. Witter Bynner*
Guilty. Ruby Berkley Goodwin
Jim Crow Car. Langston Hughes
Merry-Go-Round. Langston Hughes
Now. Margaret Walker
Ole Jim Crow. Robert Hayden
One-Way Ticket. Langston Hughes
Sit Down, Chillun. J. Farley Ragland
Strictly Speaking. J. Farley Ragland

JOHANNESBURG, SOUTH AFRICA
Eyes of Johanna, The. Craig Williamson

JOHNSON, JACK
My Lord, What a Morning. Waring Cuney

JOHNSON, JAMES WELDON
To James Weldon Johnson. Georgia Holloway Jones

JOHNSON, LYNDON BAINES
LBJ: Rejoinder. June Jordan
Word From the Right Wine. LeRoi Jones

JOY AND GRIEF
Grief. Langston Hughes
Joy. Clarissa Scott Delany
Joy. Georgia D. Johnson
Joy or Sorrow. Leanna F. Johnson
This Grief. Robert Hayden

SUBJECT INDEX

JUDGING
 Judge Ye Not. Raymond Dandridge
 Judgment, The. James Weldon Johnson

JUDGMENT DAY
 Judgment Day. Langston Hughes

JULY
 July in Georgy. James Weldon Johnson

JUNE
 June Breezes and Roses. Joseph S. Cotter, Sr.
 Memory of June, A. Claude McKay
 Song of the Sixth Month. William S. Braithwaite

JUNGLES
 Jungle. Mary Carter Smith
 Jungle Taste. Edward S. Silvera

JUSTICE
 Death of Justice, The. Walter Everette Hawkins
 Ex-Judge at the Bar, An. Melvin Tolson
 Justice. Langston Hughes

- K -

KATY-DID
 Katy-Did, The. Joseph S. Cotter, Sr.

KEATS, JOHN
 For John Keats. Countee Cullen
 October XXIX, 1795. William S. Braithwaite
 Keats Was an Unbeliever. William S. Braithwaite
 On a Pressed Flower in my Copy of Keats. William S. Braithwaite
 To Endymion. Countee Cullen
 To John Keats, Poet, at Springtime. Countee Cullen

KELLER, HELEN
 For Helen Keller. Countee Cullen

KENNEDY, EDWARD (TED)
 Television / Poem. Sonia Sanchez

KENNEDY, JOHN FITZGERALD
 J.F.K. Blues. Ted Joans

KENNEDYS
 Right on: Wite America. Sonia Sanchez

KENTUCKY
 After a Visit. Paul Laurence Dunbar
 Answer to Dunbar's "After a Visit." Joseph S. Cotter

Description of a Kentucky School House.   Joseph S. Cotter, Sr.
In Ole Kentucky. Raymond Dandridge
Kentucky Blues. Sterling A. Brown
Road in Kentucky, A. Robert Hayden
To Kentucky. Joseph S. Cotter, Sr.

KENYA
  Gift From Kenya. May Miller

KGOSITSILE, KEORAPETSE
  To Keorapetse Kgositsile. Gwendolyn Brooks

KING, MARTIN LUTHER, JR.
  Amos--1963. Margaret Walker
  Amos (Postscript-1968). Margaret Walker
  April 4, 1968. Michael Goode
  Assassination. Don L. Lee
  Dreams, Common Sense and Stuff. Frenchy J. Hodges
  Elegy Written in America. Frenchy J. Hodges
  Epitaph in April (1968). Craig Williamson
  Epitaph To a Man. Robert Reedburg
  Funeral of Martin Luther King, Jr. Nikki Giovanni
  Good Assassination Should be Quiet. Mari Evans
  He Had a Dream. Arthur Boze
  In Memoriam: Martin Luther King, Jr. June Jordan
  Innocent Question. Frenchy J. Hodges
  Listen! I'se Talkin' To You, Lawd. Frenchy J. Hodges
  Look at That Gal. Julian Bond
  Martin Luther King, Jr. Gwendolyn Brooks
  Martin Luther King. Eloise Culver
  No Train of Thought, April 4, 1969. June Jordan
  Reflections on April 4, 1968. Nikki Giovanni
  To Reggie. Frenchy J. Hodges
  What Good are Words? Linwood P. Smith
  White Weekend (April 5-8, 1969). Quincy Troupe

KINGS AND RULERS
  Kingdoms and Heirs. William S. Braithwaite
  Rulers. Fenton Johnson
  Three Kings. James P. Vaughn
  To the King's Most Excellent Majesty (1768). Phillis Wheatley

KISSES
  I Blow You a Kiss. William S. Braithwaite
  Kiss, A. William L. Morrison
  Kiss, The. Alice Walker
  My Mother's Kiss. Frances Harper
  Phantom Kiss, The. Paul Laurence Dunbar
  Song. Paul Laurence Dunbar
  Tears and Kisses. Georgia D. Johnson

KITCHENS
    Women and Kitchens. Waring Cuney

KNIGHT, ETHERIDGE
    Poem for Etheridge. Sonia Sanchez

KNIGHTS AND KNIGHTHOOD
    Knight, The. Paul Laurence Dunbar

KNIFINGS
    Statements. Langston Hughes
    Think Twice and Be Nice. Ted Joans

KNOWLEDGE, THEORY OF
    Cup of Knowledge, The. Charles B. Johnson

KNOXVILLE, TENNESSEE
    Knoxville, Tennessee. Nikki Giovanni

KU KLUX KLAN
    Ku Klux. Langston Hughes

- L -

LABOR AND LABORING CLASSES
    E. O. Blues, The. John Raven
    Labor On. Waverly T. Carmichael
    Songs of the Dusky Worker. V. A. Reese

LACE AND LACE MAKING
    Song of a Syrian Lace Seller. William S. Braithwaite

LAKES
    By an Inland Lake. William S. Braithwaite
    Rising of the Storm, The. Paul Laurence Dunbar

LAMENESS
    Ballad of the Lame Man and the Blind Man. Waring Cuney

LAMPS
    Lamps. Mae V. Cowdery

LAND
    Dust Bowl. Langston Hughes
    Our Land. Langston Hughes

LARK
    With the Lark. Paul Laurence Dunbar

LAUGHTER
    Laughers. Langston Hughes
    Laughter. Portia Lucas

Old Laughter. Gwendolyn Brooks
When I Think About Myself. Maya Angelou

LAUREL
To a Mountain Laurel. William L. Morrison

LAWYERS
Lawyer's Ways. Paul Laurence Dunbar

LAZINESS
Lazy. James Weldon Johnson
Lazy Day, A. Paul Laurence Dunbar
Lazy Sam. Joseph S. Cotter, Sr.
Loafing Negro, The. Joseph S. Cotter, Sr.

LEADERSHIP
Leader, A. Raymond Dandridge
Leaders, The. Gwendolyn Brooks
Lines on Leadership. Leslie Pinckney Hill.
Little Child That leads, The. Joseph S. Cotter, Sr.
Town Fathers, The. Melvin Tolson
We Pass. Beatrice M. Murphy

LEAVES
Chase, The. Paul Laurence Dunbar
Autum Leaf, The. William C. Braithwaite
Dead Leaves. Georgia Johnson
Death of the Leaves, The. Charles Fred White
Leaves Blow Backward. June Jordan
Leaves. Countee Cullen
Leaves in the Wind. Robert Hayden
Three Leaves. Robert Hayden

LEBANON
Smell of Lebanon, The. Alice Walker

LEE, DON L.
As Don Took Off at Dawn (To Don L. Lee). Ted Joans

LEE, ROBERT E.
Grant and Lee. Joseph S. Cotter, Sr.

LEGS
Legs. Bernie Casey

LEOPARD
Leopard. Edward Braithwaite

LETTERS
Censored. Raymond Dandridge
Dear John Letter. John Raven
Letter, A. Raymond Dandridge

Words Like Freedom. Langston Hughes
Uhuru Uberalles! (... and the sound of weeping). Mari Evans

LIES

How I Can Lie to You. Maya Angelou
I Think I Thought a Lie. David Gatewood Thomas
If You Should Lie to Me. Melvin Tolson
Remembering. Maya Angelou

LIFE

Border Line. Langston Hughes
De Way T'ings Come. Paul Laurence Dunbar
Garden of Life, The. Raymond Dandridge
I Have a Rendevous With Life. Countee Cullen
Larger Life, A. Charles B. Johnson
Life. Joseph S. Cotter, Sr.
Life. Paul Laurence Dunbar
Life. William L. Morrison
Life and Death. William S. Braithwaite
Life and Death. Joseph S. Cotter, Sr.
Life is Fine. Langston Hughes
Life is the Art of Drawing. Carolyn Ogletree
Life. James Weldon Johnson
Life's Circus. Raymond Dandridge
One Life. Paul Laurence Dunbar
Only the Span of a Life. Charles Fred White
Pound of Life, A. Raymond Dandridge
Rendezvous with Life, A. Nick Aaron Ford
Song of Living, A. William S. Braithwaite
Sum, The. Paul Laurence Dunbar
Swing of Life, The. Jamye M. Coleman
This is my Life. William S. Braithwaite
Two Questions. William S. Braithwaite
What is Life? Nick Aaron Ford

LIGHT

Brothers and Sisters of the Light. William C. Braithwaite
City Lights. William L. Morrison
Let the Light Enter. Frances Harper
Lights. W. Blanche Nivens
This Little Light of Mine. Kali Grosvenor
Turn Out the Light. Joshua Henry Jones
Wonder. Langston Hughes

LIGHTHOUSE

Sainte Adresse. William C. Braithwaite

LILACS

Lilac. Gertrude Parthenia McBrown

LILIES

Easter Flower, The. Claude McKay

LIMITATIONS
Limitations. Paul Laurence Dunbar

LINCOLN, ABRAHAM
Abraham Lincoln. Eloise Culver
Abraham Lincoln. John W. Fentress
Abraham Lincoln. Raymond Dandridge
Cameo No. I. June Jordan
Father, Father Abraham. James Weldon Johnson
In Honor of Lincoln. Charles Fred White
Lincoln. Paul Laurence Dunbar
Lincoln. Timothy Thomas Fortune
Lincoln and Davis. Joseph S. Cotter, Sr.

LINCOLN UNIVERSITY
Alma Mater. A. Denee Bibb
I'll Remember Lincoln. Jack M. Dawley
To Lincoln at Graduation. Edward Silvera
Lincoln University: 1954. Langston Hughes
To Lincoln. Ben Nnamdi Azikiwe

LINE MEN
Gus, the Lineman. Margaret Walker

LIONS
Black Mane. Ted Joans
Ubiquitous Lions, The. Ted Joans

LIPS
Red Flower, A. Claude McKay

LIPSCOMB, GENE (BIG DADDY)
Say Good-Bye to Big Daddy. Randall Jarrell*

LITTLE, MALCOLM
Aarkvark. Julia Fields
At That Moment. Raymond Patterson
Ballad To the Anonymous. James Patterson
Berkley's Blue Black. Edward S. Spriggs
Black Shining Prince, The. LeGraham
Brother Freedom. Margaret Burroughs
Brother Malcolm: Waste Limit. Clarence Major
Brother Malcolm's Echo. Keorapetse W. Kgositsile
Caution. James Lucas
Days After. Helen Quigless
De Gustibus. James Worley
Dead-Day: Malcolm, Feb. 21. Michael S. Harper
Death of the Man. Clarence Major
Destruction of America, The. John Sinclair
        Malik El-Shabazz. Robert Hayden
For Brother Malcolm. Edward Spriggs
For Malcolm. Joyce Whitsitt Lawrence

For Malcolm, A Year After. Etheridge Knight
For Malcolm X. Nanina Alba
For Malcolm X. Julia Fields
For Malcolm X. Margaret Walker
For Malik. Bobb Hamilton
For Our American Cousins. Reginald Wilson
I Remember. Mae Jackson
If Blood is Black Then Spirit Neglects my Unborn Son. Conrad Kent Rivers
It was a Funky Deal. Etheridge Knight
Judgment Day for Big Red the Drawinian Doge R.I.P. Kent Foreman
Jungle Flower. Marcella Caine
Letter For El-Haji Malik El-Shabazz. Carmin Auld Goulbourac
Look Homeward Malcolm. Conrad Kent Rivers
Malcolm. Katie M. Cumbo
Malcolm. Ray Frederick
Malcolm. Sonia Sanchez
Malcolm Exsiccated. Theodore Horne
Malcolm Spoke / Who Listened? Don L. Lee
Malcolm X. Vernoy E. Hite
Malcolm X, a Lover of the Grass Roots. Margaret Danner
Malcolm X--An Autobiography. Larry Neal
Malcolm's Blues. Michael S. Harper
Memorial Day. Bobb Hamilton
Morning Raga for Malcolm. Larry Neal
My Ace of Spades. Ted Joans
My Brother Malcolm. Christine Johnson
One Year Later. David Llorens
Poem for Black Hearts, A. LeRoi Jones
Sleep Bitter, Brother. James Worley
Solitude of Change, The. Jay Wright
Some Whites Mourn Malcolm, as If. Edward Richer
They are Killing All The Young Men. David Henderson
They Feared That He Believed. Clarence Major
True Blues for a Dues Payer. Ted Joans
Two For Malcolm. Patricia
When You Died. Christine Johnson
Written After Thinking of Malcolm. Zack Gilbert

LITTLE ROCK, ARKANSAS, 1957
    Chicago Defender Sends A Man to Little Rock, Fall, 1957. Gwendolyn
        Brooks

LLYN BARFOG
    Llyn Barfog. William C. Braithwaite

LOCUSTS
    Grasshopper World, The. Frenchy J. Hodges
    Locust. Robert Hayden

LODGES
    Visit to Oak-Lodge, A. William S. Braithwaite

LONDON
    Garret, The. Paul Laurence Dunbar

LONELINESS
    Dressed Up. Langston Hughes
    Hope. Langston Hughes
    I'm Not Lonely. Nikki Giovanni
    Little Song. Langston Hughes
    Lonesome. Paul Laurence Dunbar
    One. Langston Hughes
    Soliloguy. Dorothy Parrish

LONG, CORPORAL ARTHUR
    She Said. J. Henderson Brooks

LONGFELLOW, HENRY WADSWORTH
    Henry Wadsworth Longfellow. Eloise Culver

LONGINGS
    Longing. Paul Laurence Dunbar
    Longing. Lillian Tucker Lewis
    Longings. Mae V. Cowdery
LOOK
    They Look at Me. Bernie Casey

LORD'S SUPPER
    Communion. Langston Hughes
    Free Wine on Communion Day. Linwood D. Smith

LOST
    Alien. Bernie Casey
    No Loser, No Weeper. Maya Angelou
    Gain and Loss. Joseph S. Cotter, Sr.
    Mystery, The. William S. Braithwaite

LOTTERY
    Lottery Girl, The. James Weldon Johnson

LOUIS, JOE
    Joe Louis. Eloise Culver

LOYALTY
    Faithful One. Langston Hughes

LOVE
    Absence. Paul Laurence Dunbar
    Absence. Claude McKay
    Advice to the Lovelorn. Mae V. Cowdery
    African Love History. LeRoi Jones
    All This Review. Owen Dodson
    And Fall Shall Sit in Judgment. Audre Lorde

Love   SUBJECT INDEX

Modern Love Songs. Faarah Nuur
Morning Song of Love. Paul Laurence Dunbar
My Love. Ted Joans
My Path is Lighted By a Star. Lucy Mae Turner
Negro Love Song. Joseph S. Cotter, Sr.
Night of Love. Paul Laurence Dunbar
No Love. Marion Nicholes
Noblesse Oblige. Jessie Fauset
Now Ain't That Love? Carolyn M. Rodgers
Old Song, An. Robert Hayden
On Being In Love. Ted Joans
On Diverse Deviations. Maya Angelou
One Day I Told My Love. Countee Cullen
One Year After. Claude McKay
Open Door. Countee Cullen
Our Black People. Kali Grosvenor
Pages From Life. Georgia Douglas Johnson
Passion and Love. Paul Laurence Dunbar
Pierrot. Langston Hughes
Pity the Deep in Love. Countee Cullen
Plea, A. Paul Laurence Dunbar
Poem ... For A Lover. Mae V. Cowdery
Poem Once Significant, Now Happily Not. Countee Cullen
Poem--To the Black Beloved. Langston Hughes
Poet Puts His Heart to School. Countee Cullen
Portrait of a Lover. Countee Cullen
Postal Clerk Mourns His Lost Love (Who Has Been Goin Places). Gerald
    Barrax
Protest. Paul Laurence Dunbar
Premonition. Paul Laurence Dunbar
Profile on the Pillow. Dudley Randall
Proving. Georgia Douglas Johnson
Rainy Season Love Song. Aquah Laluah
Recontre. Jessie Fauset
Regret. Lucy Mae Turner
Rendezvous. Lois Royal Hughes
Resonant Silence, A. David Llorens
Retrospection. Eldon George McLean
Rivalry. Joseph S. Cotter, Sr.
Road in Kentucky, A. Robert Hayden
Roman Lover in Carthage. William S. Braithwaite
Romance. Claude McKay
Roulette. William L. Morrison
Second Thoughts. Gordon Parks
Sentiment. Thelma T. Clement
Sequel. Mae V. Cowdery
Shattered Mirror. Mae V. Cowdery
Should I Spy Love. James E. McGirt
So Much. Charles Johnson
Song. Countee Cullen
Song. Paul Laurence Dunbar
Song. LeRoi Jones

Love   SUBJECT INDEX

- M -

Hard Rock Returns to Prison From the Hospital For the Criminal Insane.
    Etheridge Knight
He is Foredoomed. Robert Hayden
Heart. Langston Hughes
His Excellency General Washington. Phillis Wheatley
I am Man. Tomi Carolyn Tinsley
I Remember. Nikki Giovanni
In the Tents of Akbar. Paul Laurence Dunbar
Invisible Man, The. Conrad Kent Rivers
Is a Dead Man. Victor Hernandez Cruz
Is MacBeth a God in Ruins? Charles Fred White
'Ittle Touzle Head. Raymond Dandridge
Jaime. Langston Hughes
Jessie Rufus. Lucile Goodlett
Johann. Alice Walker
John Henry. Anonymous
John Henry in Harlem. Melvin Tolson
Johnny Speaks. Paul Laurence Dunbar
Johnny Thomas. Sterling A. Brown
Judas Iscariot. Countee Cullen
Judge Robert W. Bingham. Joseph S. Cotter, Sr.
Judgment Day, The. James Weldon Johnson
Kid Sleepy. Langston Hughes
Lame Man and the Blind Man. Waring Cuney
Lazy Sam. Joseph S. Cotter, Sr.
Lear is Gay. Robert Hayden
Let My People Go. James Weldon Johnson
Leviticus Tate. Lloyd Warren
Long John Nelson and Sweetie Pie. Margaret Walker.
Maceo. Frances Harper
Madam and the Census Man. Langston Hughes
Madam and the Number Runner. Langston Hughes
Madam and the Rent Man. Langston Hughes
Madness. LeRoi Jones
Ma Man. Langston Hughes
Man, A. Bernie Casey
Man. Langston Hughes
Man. Ritten Edward Lee
Man and a Woman, A. Gerald Barrax
Man Does Not Know. Joseph S. Cotter, Sr.
Man Hunt, The. Madison Cawein
Man Inside, The. Melvin Tolson
Man Into Men. Langston Hughes
Man's Pilgrimage. William C. Braithwaite
Mecca. Sterling A. Brown
Memorial to Ed Bland. Gwendolyn Brooks
Minstrel Man. Langston Hughes
Miss Nancy's Geo'ge. Lucile D. Goodlett
Mister Banjo. Anonymous
Mister Samuel and Sam. Sterling A. Brown
Mr. Z. M. Carl Holman
Moanin' Moanin'. Lucile D. Goodlett

Sylvester's Dying Bed. Langston Hughes
Taint No Nee O' Women Worrin'. Waverly T. Carmichael
Teacher. Margaret Walker
This Man. June Jordan
Thomas Mack. Joseph S. Cotter, Sr.
Three Sons. Conrad Kent Rivers
Through the Varied Patterned Lace. Owen Dodson.
'Tis Difficult. Ethel Brown
To a Man. Maya Angelou.
To a Mythical Charlie. Joseph S. Cotter, Sr.
To An Unhanged Judas. Raymond Dandridge
To Merani / Mungu. Sonia Sanchez
Tomorrow's Men. Georgia Douglas Johnson
Tragedy of Pete. Joseph S. Cotter, Sr.
'Trane. Clarence Reed
True Man, The. Joseph S. Cotter, Sr.
Trumpet Player. Langston Hughes
Two-Gun Buster and Trigger Slim. Margaret Walker
2 Poems For Black Relocation Centers. Etheridge Knight
Uncle Aaron's Greeting: A Monologue. Eli Shepperd
Uncle Bill. Albert Aubert
Uncle Bullboy. June Jordan
Uncle Eph's Banjo Song. James Edwin Campbell
Uncle Is'rel. James E. McGirt
Uncle Jim. Countee Cullen
Uncle Ned an' D Mockin' Bird. James Corrothers
Uncle Remus to Massa Joel. Joseph S. Cotter, Sr.
Uncle Tom. J. Farley Ragland
Uncle Tom. Eleanor A. Thompson
Uncle Zero. Joseph S. Cotter, Sr.
Unk' Enoch Mann. Lucile D. Goodlett
Upsilon. Melvin Tolson
Voice in the Crowd. Ted Joans
Watermelon Vendor's Cry. Anonymous
Ways o' Men. Angelina Weld Gimke
We are Men But We Are Men. Charles Dinkins
What Am I Offered. LeRoi Jones
When Sam'l Sings. Paul Laurence Dunbar
When the Old Man Smokes. Paul Laurence Dunbar
Whistling Sam. Paul Laurence Dunbar
Wilmington, Delaware. Nikki Giovanni
Winter Hawk in Harlem. Ted Joans
Wise Men of the East, The. Claude McKay
Workin' Man. Langston Hughes
Xi. Melvin Tolson
Yalluh Hammuh. Margaret Walker
Ziba. James Pipes*
Zorro Man, A. Maya Angelou

MANSIONS
     Southern Mansion. Arna Bontemps

MANICURES
      Beauty Shoppe. Gwendolyn Brooks

MANILA
      Seige of Manila. James E. McGirt

MANNERS AND CUSTOMS
      Customs and Culture. Ted Joans
      Home Instructions. Waverly Carmichael

MANNIKIN
      Mannikin Boy of Brussels. Ted Joans

MAPS
      Map, The. G. C. Oden

MARCH
      In March. Charles B. Johnson

MARCH ON WASHINGTON
      At the Lincoln Monument, August 28, 1963. Margaret Walker

MARCHING
      No More Marching. Don L. Lee

MARDI GRAS
      Zulu King: New Orleans (At Mardi Gras), The. Josephine Copeland

MARES
      Dat Ol' Mare O' Mine. Paul Laurence Dunbar

MARKETS
      Market. Robert Hayden
      Souk. Ted Joans
      Soux. Ted Joans
      Two-An' Six. Claude McKay

MARRIAGE
      Anna, Won't You Marry Me? James E. McGirt
      Bridal Measure, A. Paul Laurence Dunbar
      Going East. Frances Harper
      It Just Ain't Right. Theresa Thorpe
      Old Marrieds, The. Gwendolyn Brooks
      Pains With a Light Touch. Don L. Lee
      Song: As a New. William S. Braithwaite

MARTYR
      Martyr of Alabama, The. Frances Harper

MARY, VIRGIN
      Annunciation of the Virgin, The. William S. Braithwaite
      Black Madonna, The. Albert Rice

SUBJECT INDEX

        Inevitably. Georgia D. Johnson
        Memories. Joseph S. Cotter, Jr.
        Memories. Raymond Dandridge
        Memory, A. William S. Braithwaite
        Memory. Charles B. Johnson
        Memory. Margaret Walker
        Old Memory, An. Paul Laurence Dunbar
        Past Memories. Charles Fred White
        Remembrance. J. Henderson Brooks
        Remembrance. Langston Hughes
        Retrospect. Georgia Johnson
        Retrospection. Paul Laurence Dunbar
        What Need Have I For Memory.   Georgia D. Johnson

MEMPHIS, TENNESSEE
        Memphis Blues. Sterling A. Brown

MEREDITH, JAMES
        James Meredith. Eloise Culver

MERMAIDS
        Madness One Monday Evening. Julia Fields

MEXICO
        Remember Mexico. Michael S. Harper

MIAMI, FLORIDA
        To the Miami. Paul Laurence Dunbar

MICE
        White Mice at the Parcel-Post Window. Waring Cuney

MID-DAY
        Mid-day. William L. Morrison

MIDDLE CLASSES
        Black Bourgeoisie. LeRoi Jones
        Sepia Fashion Show. Maya Angelou

MIDNIGHT
        Barrier, The. Paul Laurence Dunbar
        Lenox Avenue: Midnight. Langston Hughes
        Midnight Bell. Owen Dodson
        Midnight Chippie's Lament. Langston Hughes
        Midnight Raffle. Langston Hughes

MIGRATION
        Bound No'th Blues. Langston Hughes
        Ghetto Love Song--Migration. Carole Gregory
        Migration. Langston Hughes

MILITANTS
    Definition. Marion Nicholes
    Making of a Militant. Yillie Boy
    Militant. Langston Hughes

MILITARY SERVICE, COMPULSORY
    Draftees. Langston Hughes

MILLS
    Old Mill, The. Waverly T. Carmichael

MILTON, JOHN
    Milton. Henrietta Cordelia Ray

MIMES
    For Dead Mimes. Langston Hughes

MIND
    Mind and Soul After Dark. Norman Jordan

MINISTERS see CLERGY

MINSTREL
    Minstrel Man. Langston Hughes

MIRACLES
    Miracle Demanded, A. Countee Cullen
    Miracles. Arna Bontemps

MIRRORS
    Beware: Do Not Read This Poem. Ishmael Reed
    Looking-Glass, The. Paul Laurence Dunbar

MISCEGENATION
    Black Man's Son. Oswald Durane
    Bottoms, The. Nick Aaron Ford
    Crees. Langston Hughes
    Mulatto. Langston Hughes
    Near White. Countee Cullen
    Mulatto to His Critic, The. Joseph S. Cotter, Jr.
    Octoroon, The. Georgia Douglas Johnson
    Whiteeyes on Black Thighs. Ted Joans

MISFORTUNE
    Heartbroken. Raymond Dandridge

MISSISSIPPI
    Church Burning: Mississippi. James Emanuel
    Jackson, Mississippi. Margaret Walker
    Mississippi. Langston Hughes
    Mississippi Levee. Langston Hughes

Night, Death, Mississippi. Robert Hayden
Oxford is a Legend. Margaret Walker

MISSOURI COMPROMISE
Repeal of the Missouri Compromise Considered, The. Elymas Payson Rogers

MISTLETOE
Holly Berry and Mistletoe. William S. Braithwaite
Under the Mistletoe. Countee Cullen

MISTRESS
O White Mistress. Don Johnson

MITCHELL, ARTHUR
Arthur Mitchell. Marianne Moore

MOCKING BIRD
Mockingbirds. Bernie Casey

MONASTICISM AND RELIGIOUS ORDERS
Monk's Walk, The. Paul Laurence Dunbar

MONDAY
Back To / Back To. Victor Hernandez Cruz

MONEY
Basic. Ray Durem
Bread. Ted Joans
Friday Ladies of the Pay Envelopes, The. Mari Evans
Real Question, The. Paul Laurence Dunbar
To a Nickel. Lucy Mae Turner

MONK, THELONIUS
Ouagadougou Ouagadougou. Ted Joans

MONKEYS
Disillusion. Lillian G. Brown
These Beats and the Benin Bronze. Owen Dodson

MONUMENT
Before a Monument. Alexander Young
Monument in Black. Vanessa Howard

MOON
'Bout De Moon. Lucile D. Goodlett
Dark of the Moon. Sterling A. Brown
Fantasy Under the Moon. Emanuel Boundzekei-Dongala
Full Moon. Robert Hayden
House in Taos, A. Langston Hughes
Lover and the Moon, The. Paul Laurence Dunbar
March Moon. Langston Hughes
Mill Mountain. Sterling A. Brown

Moon and the Cricket, The. Joseph S. Cotter, Sr.
Moon, The. Anonymous
Moon Poem. Saundra Sharp
Moonlight Night: Carmel. Langston Hughes
New Moon. Langston Hughes
Nobody's Lookin' But De Owl & De Moon. James Weldon Johnson
Song of the Moon, A. Claude McKay
Southern Moon Light. Robert Hayden
Winter Moon. Langston Hughes
Golden Moon Rise. William S. Braithwaite
Moon Drops. William L. Morrison
Moon Light Amid the Hills. Zachary Withers
Youth and the Moon. William L. Morrison

MORNING
    Ballad of the Morning Streets. LeRoi Jones
    City: San Francisco. Langston Hughes
    Evil Morning. Langston Hughes
    Hymn to the Morning, A. Phillis Wheatley
    Hymn to the Morning, An. Phillis Wheatley
    In the Morning. Paul Laurence Dunbar
    Midsummer Morn. Frank Marshall Davis
    Morning. Paul Laurence Dunbar
    Morning Noon and Night. James Weldon Johnson
    Morning After. Langston Hughes
    Morning. Bernette Golden
    Morning Hymn, A. William C. Braithwaite
    Morning Joy. Claude McKay
    Morning Song of Love. Paul Laurence Dunbar
    Spring Morning, A. Raymond Dandridge
    Summer Morn in New Hampshire. Claude McKay
    Sunday Morning. Anonymous
    This Morning. Jay Wright
    What Do I Care for Morning. Helene Johnson

MORRIS, WILLIAM
    Little While Before Farewell, A. William S. Braithwaite

MOROCCO (NORTH AFRICA)
    Farewell to Morocco, A. Claude McKay

MOSCOW
    Moscow. Claude McKay

MOSQUITOES
    Mistah Skeeter. Lucy Mae Turner

MOTEN, ETTA
    Convert, The. Margaret Danner
    Etta Moten's Attic, Margaret Danner

471

MOTHERS
     Appreciation. Paul Laurence Dunbar
     Ballad of the Brown Girl. Countee Cullen
     Black Mother Praying. Owen Dodson
     Blues For Momma. John Raven
     Curiosity. Paul Laurence Dunbar
     December, 1919. Claude McKay
     Dedication Poem. Frances Harper
     Farewell to Mother. Placido
     For a New Mother. Mae V. Cowdery
     For Me Again. Ted Joans
     For Mother in Paradise. Malcolm Christian Conley
     For My Mother. June Jordan
     Fruit of the Flower. Countee Cullen
     Home and Mother. Raymond Dandridge
     Lonely Mother, The. Fenton Johnson
     Mama and Daughter. Langston Hughes
     Mary, Mother of Christ. Countee Cullen
     Mother. Raymond Dandridge
     Mother in Wartime. Langston Hughes
     Mother Speaks: The Algiers Motel Incident, Detroit. Michael S. Harper
     Mother To Son. Langston Hughes
     Motherhood. William S. Braithwaite
     Motherless Child. Anonymous
     Mothers. Waring Cuney
     Mothers. Nikki Giovanni
     Mother's Farewell to Her Son. Waverly T. Carmichael
     Mother's Treasures. Frances Hamilton
     Muddah Wit. Raymond Dandridge
     My Mother. Kali Grosvenor
     My Mother. Claude McKay
     My Mother. Eleanor A. Thompson
     My Mother's Kiss. Frances Harper
     Negro Mother's Lullaby, A. Countee Cullen
     One Word. Raymond Dandridge
     Placido's Sonnet To His Mother. Placido
     Slave Mother, The. Frances Harper
     Snow Hill. Waverly T. Carmichael
     There She Is. Ted Joans
     To Mother on Her Sixtieth Birthday. Nick Aaron Ford
     Tribute (To My Mother). Countee Cullen
     'Twas Mother. Waverly T. Carmichael

MOUNTAIN CLIMBER
     Mountain Climber, The. Melvin Tolson

MOUNTAINS
     Go Tell it on The Mountain. Anonymous
     Mount Shasta. Zachary Withers
     Mountain Song. William C. Braithwaite
     Mountains. David Wadsworth Cannon, Jr.
     Mountains. Robert Hayden

Mountains, The. Robert Hayden
Mountain At Night. Lucy Mae Turner
On Lookout Mountain. Robert Hayden

MOUTH
Mouth. Ted Joans

MULATTO
Mulatto To His Critics. Joseph S. Cotter, Jr.

MULES
Me and the Mule. Langston Hughes
Plowin' Cane. John Wesley Holloway

MURDER
Bad-Man Stagolee. Margaret Walker
Ballad of the Killer Boy. Langston Hughes
Black February Blood Letting. Ted Joans
Brief Encounter. Langston Hughes
Coleman. Robert Hayden
Colonized Mind. Barbara Marshall
For Andy Goodman--Michael Schwerner--and James Chaney. Margaret Walker
Furlough, The. Melvin Tolson
Guilty. Ruby Berkley Goodwin
Martyr of Alabama, The. Frances Harper
On the Birth of My Son, Malcolm Coltrane. Julius Lester
Prelude. Conrad Kent Rivers
Questions. Sonia Sanchez
Three Sons. Conrad Kent Rivers
Traitor, The. Don L. Lee.
True Import of Present Dialogue, Black vs. Negro (For Peppe, Who Will Ul-
    timately Judge Our Efforts), The. Nikki Giovanni
Untitled. Johari Amini

MUSES
My Muse. Joseph S. Cotter, Sr.
On Recollection. Phillis Wheatley
Recollection, to Miss A-- M--, Humbly Inscribed by the Authoress.
    Phillis Wheatley

MUSIC
Ante Bellum Symphony. Raymond Dandridge
Apostolic. J. Mason Brewer
Blackmusic / A Beginning. Don L. Lee
Blue Melody. William Powell
Eerie Music, An. Bernie Casey
Guitar Music. Waring Cuney
Hanging Out in the Music. David Henderson
I Shall Build a Music-Box. Bruce McM. Wright
Lamda. Melvin Tolson
Mr. P.C. Michael S. Harper
Music. William L. Morrison

Music   SUBJECT INDEX

    Musical, A. Paul Laurence Dunbar
    On Music. William S. Braithwaite
    Revolutionary Music. Nikki Giovanni
    Rubenstein Staccato Etude, The. R. Nathaniel Dett
    Soul. D. L. Graham
    Sound of Afro-American Music Chapt. I. S. E. Anderson
    Strain of Music. Mae V. Cowdery

MUSICAL INSTRUMENTS
    Albert Ayley: Eulogy for a Decomposed Saxophone Player. Stanley Crouch
    Battle Report. Bob Kaufman
    Guitar. Owen Dodson
    Little David, Play on Yo' Harp. Anonymous
    Loud Jazz Horns. Carter Webster
    Organ Recital, The. Leonidas Gibbs
    Songs for My Lady's Banjo. Eli Shepperd
    Tambourines. Langston Hughes
    Thou Art My Love. Paul Laurence Dunbar
    To a Lady Playing a Harp. Paul Laurence Dunbar
    To the Organ. Charles Fred White
    Trumpet Player. Langston Hughes
    Trumpet Player: 52nd Street. Langston Hughes

MYTHOLOGY
    Niobe in Distress For Her Children Slain by Apollo, From Ovid's Metamor-
        phoses, Book VI, and From a View of the Painting of Mr. Richard
        Wilson. Phillis Wheatley
    Perseus. Robert Hayden

                            - N -

NAMES
    Calling of Names, The. Maya Angelou
    Debra: An Africanese Name Reading on the Sound of Debra. Ronda Davis
    Names. John Raven
    New Names. Ted Joans

NARCISSUS
    Narcissus, The. Raymond Dandridge

NARCOTIC HABIT
    Answer To You / Question of Am I Not Yo / Woman Even If U Went On Shit
        Again. Sonia Sanchez
    Cocaine Galore. Victor Hernandez Cruz
    Dago Red. Askia Muhammad Toure
    Don't Wanna Be. Sonia Sanchez
    Doper. Arthur Boze
    Houdini. LeRoi Jones
    Junior Addict. Langston Hughes
    Letter to an Aspiring Junkie. Maya Angelou
    O. D. er. John Raven
    Pot Smokin' Blues. John Raven

NEPTUNE
    Ode to Neptune. Phillis Wheatley

NEW ENGLAND
    Off the New England Coast. William S. Braithwaite

NEW HAMPSHIRE
    Spring in New Hampshire. Claude McKay
    Summer Morn in New Hampshire. Claude McKay

NEW ORLEANS, LOUISIANA
    Zulu King: New Orleans (At Mardi Gras). Josephine Copeland

NEW YEAR
    Happy Feel Year. Ted Joans
    January First. Raymond Dandridge
    Negro's New Year Prayer, The. Joseph S. Cotter, Sr.
    New Year's Prayer. Ruby Berkley Goodwin

NEW YORK
    Bottled: New York. Helene Johnson
    Dawn in New York. Claude McKay
    Just a New York Poem. Nikki Giovanni
    New York Skyscrapers. John Mbiti
    Poem From the Empire State. June Jordan
    When Dawn Comes to the City: New York. Claude McKay

NEWARK, NEW JERSEY
    Last Night in Newark. Ted Joans
    Mise En Scene: Newark, 1947. LeRoi Jones
    Newark Later. LeRoi Jones

NEWPORT
    At Newport. William S. Braithwaite

NEWPORT BEACH
    On Revisiting Newport Beach. William S. Braithwaite

NICKELS
    To a Nickel. Lucy Mae Turner

NIGERIA
    Nigerian Unity / or Little Niggers Killing Little Niggers (For Brothers
        Christopher Okigbo & Wole Soyinka). Don L. Lee

NIGGERS
    Dedication to the Final Confrontation. Lloyd Corbin
    Nice Colored Man, The. Ted Joans
    Songs For My Lady's Banjo. Eli Shepperd
    Wake Up Niggers. Don L. Lee

NIGHT
    African Night. Craig Williamson
    At Night. Paul Laurence Dunbar
    Dawn Patrol: Chicago. Richard V. Durham
    Day and Night. Lewis Alexander
    Florida Night, A. Paul Laurence Dunbar
    Flowers of Darkness. Frank Marshall Davis
    Four Glimpses of Night. Frank Marshall Davis
    Harlem Night Song. Langston Hughes
    I Closed My Shutters Late Last Night. Georgia D. Johnson
    Late Last Night. Langston Hughes
    'Long-To'ds Night. Paul Laurence Dunbar
    Meditation on a Cold Dark, and Rainy Night. George Moses Horton
    Morning After. Langston Hughes
    Morning, Noon and Night. James Weldon Johnson
    Mother Night. James Weldon Johnson
    Mountains at Night. Lucy Mae Turner
    Negro Speaks of Night. Iola M. Brister
    Night, The. Bernie Casey
    Night. Paul Laurence Dunbar
    Night. Donald Jeffrey Hayes
    Night. William L. Morrison
    Night. Birdelle Wycoff Ransom
    Night. Sam Duby R. Sutu
    Night and a Child. Nick Aaron Ford
    Night, Death, Mississippi. Robert Hayden
    Night Dim / Night. Paul Laurence Dunbar
    Night: Four Songs. Langston Hughes
    Night Interpreted. Everett Hoagland
    Night of Death, The. Frances Harper
    Night of Love. Paul Laurence Dunbar
    Night on the Ol' Plantashun. Daniel Webster Davis
    Night Slivers. Darwin T. Turner
    Night Song. Langston Hughes
    Night Walks Down the Mountain. William Allyn Hill
    Nocturnal. Hermal L. McMillan
    Nocturne. Gwendolyn Bennett
    Nocturne. Dorothy F. Blackwell
    Nocturne. Roussan Camille
    Nocturne. Ylessa Dubonee
    Nocturne. Donald Jeffrey Hayes
    Noises in the Night. William L. Morrison
    On a Christmas Night. Langston Hughes
    Out in the Still Wet Night. J. Austin Love
    Quilt, The. Effie Lee Newsome
    Ramadan--Hot Night. Marion Nicholes
    Saturday Night. Langston Hughes
    Saturday Night in Harlem. William Brown
    September Night, A. George Marion McLlelan
    Starry Night, A. Paul Laurence Dunbar
    Summer Night, A. Paul Laurence Dunbar
    Summer Night. Langston Hughes

NIGHT (Cont.)
    Summer Night's Enchantment. William S. Braithwaite
    To the Wind of the Night. Charles Fred White
    Twell de Night is Pas'. Paul Laurence Dunbar
    Two Countries. Jose Marti
    White Night. Gordon Parks

NIGHTMARES
    Child's Nightmare, A. Bobb Hamilton
    In Light Half Nightmare and Half Vision. Robert Hayden
    Nightmares Again. Michael S. Harper

NODDING
    Noddin' By De Fire. Paul Laurence Dunbar

NOON
    Morning, Noon and Night. James Weldon Johnson
    Noon. Paul Laurence Dunbar

NORTH
    Boun No'th Blues. Langston Hughes
    Evenin' Air Blues. Langston Hughes
    North and South. Joseph S. Cotter, Sr.
    One-Way Ticket. Langston Hughes
    To One Coming North. Claude McKay

NORTH CAROLINA
    To a Lady on Her Remarkable Preservation in a Hurricane in North Carolina.
        Phillis Wheatley

NOSTALGIA
    Nostalgia. Mae V. Cowdery

NOTRE DAME
    Bells of Notre Dame, The. Benjamin G. Brawley

NOVEMBER
    In the Athenaeum Looking out on the Granary Burying Ground on a Rainy Day
        in November. William S. Braithwaite
    November. Joseph S. Cotter, Jr.
    Novembah Dusk. Lucile D. Goodlett
    November Cotton Flower. Jean Toomer
    November Eventide, A. Charles Fred White
    November Sabbath Morn, A. Charles Fred White

NOW
    Now. Donald E. Bogle

NUDITY
    Bare Beauty. Ted Joans
    Knee Deep. Ted Joans

SUBJECT INDEX

OKLAHOMA
    Girl From Oklahoma. Waring Cuney

OLD
    Old Things. Charles Bertram Johnson

OLD AGE
    Elderly Leaders. Langston Hughes
    Grandma. Langston Hughes
    Growin' Gray. Paul Laurence Dunbar
    Ol' Doc' Hyar. James Edwin Campbell
    Poem (For Anna Hodgeman and Alfreda Duster). Nikki Giovanni

OPERATION
    After the Operations. Michael S. Harper

OPOSSUM
    Expectation. Paul Laurence Dunbar
    Possum. Paul Laurence Dunbar
    'Possum Song. James Weldon Johnson

OPPRESSION
    Oppression. Langston Hughes
    Wings of Oppression, The. Leslie Pinckney Hill

OPTIMISM
    Optimist, The. Mrs. J. W. Hammond

OWLS
    Nobody's Lookin' But De Owl & De Moon. James Weldon Johnson

ORGAN
    To the Organ. Charles Fred White
    Organ Recital, The. Leonidas Gibbs
    Strain of Music. Mae V. Cowdery

ORIOLE
    Belated Oriole, A. George Marion McClellan

ORISON
    Orison. Robert Hayden

OWENS, JESSIE
    Jessie Owens. Eloise Culver

OXEN
    Toil Created. Raymond Dandridge

OXFORD, MISSISSIPPI
    Oxford is a Legend. Margaret Walker

OYSTERS
    Oyster Man's Cry. Anonymous

                        - P -

PACKARD, MISS
    Miss Packard & Miss Giles. Owen Dodson

PAIGE, SATCHELL
    American Gothic see To Satch. Samuel W. Allen
    To Satch (or American Gothic). Samuel Allen

PAIN
    Absolute Pain. Bernie Casey
    And Once Again, Pain. William Browne
    Supremacy. Lenora Gillison

PAINTING
    Advice to a Painter. Victor Hernandez Cruz
    Quatrains. Gwendolyn B. Bennett

PARABLES
    Great Laws. Marian Cuthbert

PARADISE
    It Were as if This World Were Paradise. William C. Braithwaite

PARADOX
    Paradox. Peter Wellington Clark

PARIS, FRANCE
    Big. Ted Joans
    On Rue Jacques Callet. Ted Joans
    When I Went To Paris. Kali Grosvenor

PARKER, CHARLES
    Charles Parker, 1925-1955. Waring Cuney
    Requiem For "Bird" Parker. Gregory Corse
    They Forget to Fast. Ted Joans
    Yardbird's Skull (For Charlie Parker). Owen Dodson

PARKER, GLIDDEN
    Sickle Pears (For Glidden Parker). Owen Dodson

PARKS, ROSA
    It Happened in Montgomery. Phil W. Petrie

PASSION
    Passion and Love. Paul Laurence Dunbar

PAST
    Burial of the Past, The. Charles Fred White

    Long Ago. Paul Laurence Dunbar

PATHS
    Path, The. Paul Laurence Dunbar
    Paths. Joseph S. Cotter, Sr.
    Wooded Path, The. Joseph S. Cotter, Sr.

PAWNBROKER
    Ballad of the Pawnbroker. Langston Hughes

PAY DAY
    Pay Day. Langston Hughes
    Pay Day. Lucy Mae Turner

PEACE
    Liberty and Peace. Phillis Wheatley
    Peace. Langston Hughes
    Sing Out For Peace. Waverly T. Carmichael
    Peace. Nick Aaron Ford
    Peace. James Morris
    Peace and Principle. Isabelle McClellan Taylor
    Peace is a Fragile Cup. Frank Marshall Davis
    Surrender. Angelina Weld Grimke

PEARLS
    Roses and Pearls. Paul Laurence Dunbar

PEARS
    Sickle Pears (For Glidden Parker). Owen Dodson

PEOPLE
    Esperanto. Melvin Tolson
    Kappa. Melvin Tolson
    My People. Langston Hughes
    #28. Doughtry (Doc) Long, Jr.

PERCEPTION
    Perception. Catherine L. Findley

PERFUME
    Perfume. John Raven
    Queens of the Universe. Sonia Sanchez

PERSEUS
    Perseus. Robert Hayden

PESSIMISM
    For a Pessimist. Countee Cullen

PHILADELPHIA, PENNSYLVANIA
    South Street. Edward S. Silvera

PHILIPPINES
    Portrait Philippines. Alfred A. Duckett

PHILOSOPHY
    Philosophy. Paul Laurence Dunbar
    Self-Determination. Leslie Pinckney Hill

PHOTOGRAPHY
    Photo Album. Albert Aubert
    Photograph, The. Paul Laurence Dunbar

PHYSICIANS
    Arthur Ridgewood. Frank Marshall Davis
    Calling the Doctor. John Wesley Holloway
    Interne at Provident. Langston Hughes
    Ol' Doc' Hyar. James Edwin Campbell
    To Dan. Paul Laurence Dunbar

PIANO
    Piano and Drums. Gabriel Okara

PICNICS
    Picnic: the Liberated. M. Carl Holman
    Picnics Historical Episode. Clarence Major

PICASSO, PABLO
    Harlem to Picasso. Ted Joans

PIGEONS
    Ballad of the Light Eyed Little Girl. Gwendolyn Brooks

PIBS
    Congenital. Katherine Jackson Hunter
    Songs for my Lady's Banjo. Eli Shepperd
    Unknown Color, The. Countee Cullen

PILGRIMS
    We Black People Should. Kali Grosvenor

PIMPS
    Don't Wanna Be. Sonia Sanchez
    Pimp's Last Mack: Death Request: a Folk Song. Stanley Crouch
    Poppa Chicken. Margaret Walker
    Today's Pimp. Marion Nicholes

PINE
    TANZANIA Pine. Craig Williamson

PIPER
    Sequel to the "Pied Piper of Hamelin." Joseph S. Cotter, Sr.

Lapse, The. Paul Laurence Dunbar
Magic of Black Poetry, The. Anonymous
Negro Poets. Charles Bertram Johnson
No Time For Poetry. Julia Fields
Poem, A. Elaine Bethel
Poem For a Poet, A. Don L. Lee
Poet, The. Alice D. Anderson
Poet, The. Countee Cullen
Poet, The. Joseph S. Cotter
Poet, The. Raymond Dandridge
Poet, The. Adolphus Johnson
Poet, The. Melvin Tolson
Poet, The. Paul Laurence Dunbar
Poet and His Song, The. Paul Laurence Dunbar
Poet and the Baby, The. Paul Laurence Dunbar
Poet to Bigot. Langston Hughes
Poetess, A. Herman J. D. Carter
Poetry. Georgia D. Johnson
Poets. Lucia M. Pitts
Portrait of a Poet. Alpheus Butler
Rondeau, A. William C. Braithwaite
Still I Am Marveling. J. Henderson Brooks
This Poem Is. Ted Joans
To a Young Negro Poet. Robert Hayden
To a Younger Poet. Alvin Aubert
To An Unknown Poet. Countee Cullen
Today is a Day of Great Joy. Victor Hernandez Cruz
Toy Poem. Nikki Giovanni
Two Poets. Countee Cullen
Two Words. Ted Joans
Voice in the Crowd. Ted Joans
Ye Bards of England. Arbery Allson Whitman
Young Negro Poet. Calvin C. Hernton

POLICE
Dawn Song. Linwood D. Smith
He Spy. Ted Joans
Poem to a Nigger Cop. Bobb Hamilton
Who But the Lord. Langston Hughes

PONIES
Delinquent, The. Paul Laurence Dunbar

POPPIES
Poppies Cannot Grow in Flanders Field. William L. Morrison
Poppy Flower. Langston Hughes

PORTERS
Porter. Langston Hughes

POTATOES
    Hog Killin' Times in Dixie Land. Eli Shepperd
    Sweet Potato Man. Anonymous
    Sweeten Tatahs. James D. Corrothers
    'Tater Field. Lucile D. Goodlett

POTS
    Trouble in De Kitchen. Paul Laurence Dunbar

POTTERY
    Potter, The. Anonymous

POULTRY
    Sunday Chicken. Gwendolyn Brooks

POVERTY
    Aspiration. Mario De Andrade
    Broke. John Raven
    Children of the Poor. Gwendolyn Brooks
    Down and Out. Langston Hughes
    Ennui. Langston Hughes
    Face of Poverty. Lucy Smith
    Inconvenience, An. John Raven
    Kitchenette Building. Gwendolyn Brooks
    My Poverty and Wealth. Joseph S. Cotter
    Precedent. Paul Laurence Dunbar
    Rag Doll and Summer Birds. Owen Dodson
    Song of the Poor Man. Anonymous
    Soul. D. L. Graham

POWELL, ADAM CLAYTON
    Seventy Avenue Poem. Ed Bullins

POWELL, BUD
    For Bud. Michael S. Harper

POWELL, JAMES
    Death in Yorkville. Langston Hughes

PRAYERS
    Answer to Prayer. James Weldon Johnson
    Black Mother Praying. Owen Dodson
    Call to Prayer. Anonymous
    Century's Prayer, The. James McGirt
    Confessional. Paul Laurence Dunbar
    Daily Prayer, A. Waverly T. Carmichael
    Detached, The. Maya Angelou
    Formula. Carolyn Ogletree
    His Answer. Clara Ann Thompson
    John Brown's Prayer. Stephen Vincent Benet*
    Listen, Lord. James Weldon Johnson
    Muhammedan Call to Prayer. Bilal

Negro's Christmas Prayer, The. Joseph S. Cotter, Sr.
Negro's Prayer, A. Richard T. Hamilton
New Year's Prayer. Ruby Berkley Goodwin
Oh! Lord. Antoinette T. Payne
Pagan Prayer. Countee Cullen
Prayer. Isabella Maria Brown
Prayer, A. Joseph S. Cotter, Jr.
Prayer. Waring Cuney
Prayer, A. Paul Laurence Dunbar
Prayer, A. Nick Aaron Ford
Prayer. Langston Hughes
Prayer, A. Claude McKay
Prayer, A. George Reginald Margetson
Prayer. Charles Fred White
Prayer at Sunrise. James Weldon Johnson
Prayer For Peace; II. Leopold Sedar Senghor
Prayer Meeting. Langston Hughes
Prayer of the Faithful, The. Waverly T. Carmichael
Prayer to God. Placido
Prayers of God, The. William E. B. DuBois
Praying Hands, The. William S. Braithwaite
Recalled Prayer, A. Raymond Dandridge
School of Prayer, A. LeRoi Jones
Sea-Prayer, A. William S. Braithwaite
Service Please. Myrtle Campbell Gorham
Singin' An' Prayin'. Raymond Dandridge
Song of Thanks, A. Edward Smyth Jones
Supplication. Raymond Dandridge
To An Ecclesiast I Know. William Allyn Hill
Thanksgiving Prayer. James McGirt
Warrior's Prayer, The. Paul Laurence Dunbar
Watch and Pray. William C. Braithwaite
When Ol' Sis' Judy Pray. James Edwin Campbell

PREFERENCE
   Preference, A. Paul Laurence Dunbar

PREGNANCY
   Fruit of Love. Marion Nicholes
   Nine Month Blues. Ted Joans
   One Blue Note. Ted Joans

PREJUDICES AND ANTIPATHIES
   Chicago Defender Sends a Man to Little Rock, Fall, 1957, The. Gwendolyn
      Brooks
   Civil Service. Constance Nichols
   Cultural Exchange. Langston Hughes
   Incident. Countee Cullen
   Moment Please, A. Samuel Allen
   Pride and Prejudice. Linwood D. Smith
   Signifying Darkness, The. Owen Dodson

PRIDE
    Aren't We All? Norman Hills Stateman
    On a Proud Man. Joseph S. Cotter, Sr.
    Pride. John Raven
    Pride and Prejudice. Linwood D. Smith

PRINCIPLE
    Peace and Principle. Isabelle McClellan Taylor

PRISON
    Azikiwe in Jail. Langston Hughes
    Girl Held Without Bail. Margaret Walker
    Prison. Bernie Casey
    Questions. Sonia Sanchez

PRODIGAL
    Prodigal, The. Raymond Dandridge

PROGRESS
    Century of Progress (1933). Nick Aaron Ford

PROMETHEUS
    Prometheus. Paul Laurence Dunbar

PROPHETS
    Prophet, The. Joseph S. Cotter, Sr.
    Prophet, The. Robert Hayden
    Prophets For a New Day. Margaret Walker

PROSERPINE
    Pearl Primus. Owen Dodson

PROSSER, GABRIEL
    Gabriel. Robert Hayden

PROSTITUTES
    For a Lady of Pleasure Now Retired. Nikki Giovanni
    Natcha. Langston Hughes
    Sportin'. Arthur Boze
    To Mich Who Sometimes Turns a Trick. John Raven
    Violent Space, The. Etheridge Knight
    Young Prostitute. Langston Hughes

PROVERBS
    Maxims. William C. Braithwaite

PUBLIC WELFARE
    Feeding the Lions. Norman Jordan

PUERTO RICO
    You're Nothing But a Spanish Colored Kid. Felipe Luciano

PUNISHMENT
    Whipping, The. Robert Hayden

PUPPETS
    Puppet Player, The. Angelina Weld Grimké

PUSHKIN, ALEXANDER
    I Loved You Once (From the Russian of Alexander Pushkin). Dudley Randall
    Melchisedec and Pushkin. Joseph S. Cotter, Sr.

- Q -

QUARREL
    After the Quarrel. Paul Laurence Dunbar
    Earl Evening Quarrel. Langston Hughes
    Long John Nelson and Sweetie Pie. Margaret Walker
    Quarrel, The. Gordon Parks
    .38, The. Ted Joans
    Words! Words! Jessie Fauset

QUEST
    Quest. Georgia D. Johnson

QUESTIONS
    Little Poem, A. Linda Brown
    Whence? Melvin Tolson

- R -

RABBI
    Rabbi, The. Robert Hayden

RABBITS
    Brer Rabbit You's De Cutes' Of 'em All. James Weldon Johnson
    Der Rabbit's Foot. James D. Corrothers

RACCOONS
    Coon Song. Lucile D. Goodlett

RACISM
    On Civil Disorder. Michael S. Harper

RADICALS
    Radical, The. Waring Cuney

RADISH
    Radish, The. Ibn Quzman

RAFFLES
    Midnight Raffle. Langston Hughes

RAIDS
    Raid. Langston Hughes

RAILROAD WORKERS
    Two-Gun Buster and Trigger Slim. Margaret Walker

RAIN
    April Rain Song. Langston Hughes
    Discovery. Gordon Parks
    Drizzle. Paul Laurence Dunbar
    First Carolina Rain. Gerald W. Barrax
    House in Taos, A. Langston Hughes
    In the Athenaeum Cooking Out on the Granary Burying Ground on a Rainy Day
        in November. William S. Braithwaite
    In Time of Silver Rain. Langston Hughes
    Rain. Sterling A. Brown
    Rain. Raymond Dandridge
    Rain. Frank Marshall Davis
    Rain In Summer. William S. Braithwaite
    Rain Song, A. Charles B. Johnson
    Rain Song, The. Alex Rogers
    Rain-Songs. Paul Laurence Dunbar
    Rain Wish. Louise Blackman
    Raindrop. Nick Aaron Ford
    Raining Blues. Ted Joans
    Rainy Season, The. Clarence Major
    Out in the Still Wet Night. J. Austin Love
    Rainy Season Love Song. Aquah Laluah
    Signs O' Rain. James E. McGirt
    Thunder Showers. Bernie Casey
    Thunderstorm. Dudley Randall
    Time to Tinker 'Round! Paul Laurence Dunbar
    Windy Rain. Kali Grosvenor
    My Rainy Day. Maurine L. Jeffrey

RAINBOWS
    Place Where the Rainbow Ends. Paul Laurence Dunbar
    Where the Rainbow Ends. Richard Rive

RAINEY, "MA"
    Dance For Ma Rainey, A. Al Young
    Ma Rainey. Sterling A. Brown

RALEIGH, SIR WALTER
    Sir Walter Raleigh. William S. Braithwaite

RANDALL, DUDLEY
    Malcolm X (For Dudley Randall). Gwendolyn Brooks

RAPE
    Flight. Langston Hughes

RATS
    Assailant. John Raven
    How You Feel. Victor Hernandez Cruz
    What Invisible Rat. Jean-Joseph Rebearivelo

REALITY
    Reality. Peter Wellington Clark
    Reality. Yvette Johnson

REAPING
    Reaper. Jean Toomer
    You'll Reap What You Sow. Waverly Carmichael

REBELLION
    Revolt in the South. H. Binga Dismond
    Sassy. Lucy Mae Turner
    Strictly Speaking. J. Farley Ragland
    Why I Rebel. Robert J. Sye

RECEPTIONS
    Reception, The. June Jordan

RECOLLECTION
    On Recollection. Phillis Wheatley

RECREATION
    Day's Recreation, A. J. C. Stevenson

RED
    Red. Countee Cullen

REDDING, OTIS
    To Otis Redding. Kali Grosvenor

REFLECTIONS
    Reflections. Carl Gardner

REFORMATORIES see also PRISON
    Indiana Reformatory. Joseph S. Cotter, Sr.

REGRET
    Eyes of Regret, The. Angelina Weld Grimke

REINCARNATION
    Reincarnation. Raymond Dandridge

RELATIVES
    My People. Kali Grosvenor
    Old Relative. Gwendolyn Brooks

RELIGIOUS POETRY
    All the World Moved. June Jordan
    Almighty God. Raymond Dandridge
    Alternative, The. Rev. John Henry Owens
    American Ideals. Malcolm Christian Conley
    Annunciation of the Virgin. William S. Braithwaite
    Answer, The. Rev. John Henry Owens
    Answer to Prayer. James Weldon Johnson
    As It Is. Joseph S. Cotter, Sr.
    Ascension. William S. Braithwaite
    At Rest From His Works. William S. Braithwaite
    At Sea. Vera E. Guerard
    At the Wailing Wall in Jerusalem. Countee Cullen
    Autumn Chorus. Owen Dodson
    Babe is a Babe, A. Joseph S. Cotter, Sr.
    Band of Gideon, The. Joseph S. Cotter, Jr.
    Benediction. Bob Kaufman
    Bible Belt. Langston Hughes
    Bishop Charles E. Woodcock. Joseph S. Cotter, Sr.
    Bishop Thomas U. Dudley. Joseph S. Cotter, Sr.
    Black. Countee Cullen
    Black Christ, The. Don L. Lee
    Black Church on Sunday. Joseph M. Mosley, Jr.
    Black Christ, The. Countee Cullen
    Black Magdalens. Countee Cullen
    Black Mother Praying. Owen Dodson
    Brown Girl's Sacrament. Robert Hayden
    Butterfly in Church, A. George Marion McClellan
    By Rugged Ways. Paul Laurence Dunbar
    Calvary Way. May Miller
    Carol of the Brown King. Langston Hughes
    Chant Royal. Chant Royal. William C. Braithwaite
    Children of the Poor. Gwendolyn Brooks
    Christ in Alabama. Langston Hughes
    Christian, A. Raymond Dandridge
    Christmas Eve in France. Jessie Redmond Fauset
    Christmas 1959 Et Cetera. Gerald Barrax
    Christmas Story, The. Langston Hughes
    Christus Natus Est. Countee Cullen
    Church Burning Mississippi. James Emanuel
    Colorist, The. Anita Scott Coleman
    Come Beloved. Will Smallwood
    Communication to Nancy Cunard. Nancy Boyle*
    Conception. Waring Cuney
    Confession Stone, The. Owen Dodson
    Cotton Son. Jean Toomer
    Creation of God, The. Anonymous
    Creed. Anne Spencer
    Crucifixion. James Weldon Johnson
    Daily Prayer, A. Waverly Carmichael
    Dark Morning. Craig Williamson
    Day. Paul Laurence Dunbar

Day of Repentance, The. Waverly Carmichael
Day of Rest. Charles Fred White
De Lawd! Lucy Mae Turner
De Reverend is Gwine to de Big 'Soc'ation. Lucy Mae Turner
Deacon Jones' Grievance. Paul Laurence Dunbar
De Creed (Matthew 2:15). Raymond Garfield Dandridge
Definition. Owen Dodson
Devil and the Higher Criticism, The. Joseph S. Cotter, Sr.
Dew. J. Mason Brewer
Dialogue. Countee Cullen
Dialogue Intitled the Kind Master and the Dutiful Servant as Follows.
    Jupiter Hammon
Dictum. Countee Cullen
Dives and Laz'us. Anonymous
Earth-Quake. Waring Cuney
Echoes of Childhood. Alice Corbin*
El Cristo. Robert Hayden
Entreaty. Walter G. Arnold
Epitaph, An. Countee Cullen
Equipment. Paul Laurence Dunbar
Every Man Heart Lay Down. Lorenz Graham.
Everywhere. Raymond Dandridge
Faith. Paul Laurence Dunbar
Feet O' Jesus. Langston Hughes
Fellowship. William C. Braithwaite
Fire. Langston Hughes
Florence to Her Cathedral-Builders. William C. Braithwaite
For a Mouthy Woman. Countee Cullen
For a Preacher. Countee Cullen
Free Wine on Communion Day. Linwood D. Smith
Garden Sanctuary. William L. Morrison
Git on Board, Chillun. Elliot B. Henderson
Go Tell It On The Mountain. Anonymous
Go Work in my Vineyard. Frances Harper
Goal, The. Joseph S. Cotter, Jr.
God. Anonymous
God Bless Our Native Land. Frances Harper
God Give to Men. Arna Bontemps
God is Kind. Mae V. Cowdery
God is Tall Trees. Craig Williamson
Gods. Countee Cullen
God's Christmas Tree. Eve Lynn
God's Gonna Set Dis World on Fire. Anonymous
God's Gwine to Take All My Trubbles Away. Lucy Mae Turner
God's Masterpiece. J. Henderson Brooks
Golden Stool, The. Gene Holmes
Golgotha is a Mountain. Arna Bontemps
Goliath of Gath. (I Samuel, Chapter XVII). Phillis Wheatley
Gospel Train, The. Anonymous
Great Laws, The. Marian Cuthbert
Harsh World That Lashest Me. Countee Cullen
He "Had Not Where to Lay His Head." Frances Harper

Religious Poetry　　　　　　　　SUBJECT INDEX

How Lucy Backslid. Paul Laurence Dunbar
Hymn. Paul Laurence Dunbar
Hymn Chune, A. Eli Shepperd
Hymn for Zion's Centennial. Joseph S. Cotter, Sr.
Hymn of Freedom. Eli Shepperd
Hymn of Rejoicing. Eli Shepperd
Hymn of Repentance. Eli Shepperd
Hymn Written After Jeremiah Preached to me in a Dream. Owen Dodson
Hymns of the Black Belt. Eli Shepperd
I am a Spiritual Alcoholic. Anonymous
I and He. Marion Cuthbert
I Give You Thanks my God. Bernard Dadio
I Know Jesus Heard Me. Charles L. Anderson
I Thank Thee, Lord. Charles Fred White
I Think I See Him There. Waring Cuney
I Vision God. Anonymous
Immortality. Marion Cuthbert
Impelled. Georgia D. Johnson
In a Sunken Pool. William S. Braithwaite
Invocation. Charles R. Dinkins
Isaiah LXIII 1-8. Phillis Wheatley
Itching Heels. Paul Laurence Dunbar
John Brown's Prayer. Stephen Vincent Benét*
Judas Iscariot. Countee Cullen
Judgment Day. Langston Hughes
Judgment Day, The. James Weldon Johnson
Katherine Ferguson. Eloise Culver
Keep Me, Jesus Keep Me. Waverly Carmichael
L'Envoi. William S. Braithwaite
Let My People Go. James Weldon Johnson
Life of God, The. Marion Cuthbert
Light Lady. Countee Cullen
Lines From Act III of "Caleb the Degenerate." Joseph S. Cotter, Sr.
Lines From the Vision of Lazarus. Fenton Johnson
Lines Written in Jerusalem. Countee Cullen
Listen Lord. James Weldon Johnson
Litany of the Dark People. Countee Cullen
Loving Beauty Is Loving God. Isabelle Taylor
Ma Lord. Anonymous
Magi Call Him King, The. Effie Lee Newsome
Malcontents, The. Dio Lewis
Mare Rubrum. Paul Laurence Dunbar
Mary, Mother of Christ. Countee Cullen
Mate. Georgia Johnson
Maxie Allen. Gwendolyn Brooks
Meetin' Chant, A. Eli Shepperd
Member's Hymn. Eli Shepperd
Milennial. Countee Cullen
Minister, The. Fenton Johnson
Miracle Demanded. Countee Cullen
Mean. Langston Hughes
Modern Moses, or "My Policy" Man. James Madison Bell.

To the Rev. Dr. Thomas Amory, on Reading His Sermons on Daily Devotion,
     in Which That Duty is Recommended and Assisted. Phillis Wheatley
To the Sea. William S. Braithwaite
To the Univ. of Cambridge in New England (1767)
Trivia. Beatrice M. Murphy
Troubled Jesus. Waring Cuney
Truth. Claude McKay
Two Somewhat Different Epigrams. Langston Hughes
Vagabond Morning. Craig Williamson
Vashti. Frances Harper
Walk, God's Chillun. Lucile D. Goodlett
Warrior's Prayer, The. Paul Laurence Dunbar
Wasn't That a Mighty Day. Anonymous
Watch and Pray. William C. Braithwaite
We Can Know Surely. Marion Cuthbert
What Is God. Etholia Arthur Robinson
What You Gonna Name That Pretty Little Baby? Anonymous
When Ol' Sis' Judy Pray. James Edwin Campbell
When She Spoke of God. Lance Jeffers
When the Day Seems Dark. Waverly T. Carmichael
Who Built the Ark? Eli Shepperd
Who But the Lord? Langston Hughes
Who'll Be Ready? Eli Shepperd
Why Adam Sinned. Alex Rogers
Winter Chorus. Owen Dodson
Wise Men of the East, The. Claude McKay
Wounds of Jesus, The. Anonymous
Yet Do I Marvel. Countee Cullen

REMEMBRANCE
     Remembrance. Joseph S. Cotter, Jr.

RENT
     Little Lyric. Langston Hughes
     Madam and the Rent Man. Langston Hughes

REPARATION
     Ruminations of Luke Johnson. Sterling A. Brown

REPENTANCE
     Unrepentant. Countee W. Twitty

REPTILES
     Reptile. John Raven

REPUTATION
     Snob. Langston Hughes

RESOLUTIONS
     New Year's Resolution. Joseph S. Cotter, Sr.
     New Year's Resolve, The. Waverly T. Carmichael

RESURRECTION
    Resurrection, The. J. Henderson Brooks
    Resurrection. George Reginald Margetson
    Saint Peter Relates an Incident of the Resurrection Day. James Weldon
        Johnson

REVENGE
    Revenge. Arthur Boze
    Revenge. Ted Joans

REVOLUTION, BLACK
    Black Judgment. Nikki Giovanni
    Chain Waves. S. E. Anderson
    Evolution. Thelma Parker Cox
    For Black People. Don L. Lee
    Message All Blackpeople Can Dig, A. Don L. Lee
    No Reservations. Nikki Giovanni
    Revolutionary Screw, The. Don L. Lee
    Roses and Revolutions. Dudley Randall
    So This is Our Revolution. Sonia Sanchez
    There are Seeds to Sow. Bernette Golden
    To the White Man. Valerie Tarver
    U Name This One. Carolyn M. Rodgers

RHETORIC
    Blk / Rhetoric (For Killebrew Keeby, Icewater, Baker, Gary Adams and Omar
        Shabazz. Sonia Sanchez

RHYTHM
    Ebony Rhythm. Hood C. Butler
    Remembered Rhythms. Mari Evans
    Rhythm Is a Groove (#2). Larry Neal

RIGHT
    Right Will Win. James E. McGirt

RILEY, JAMES WHITCOMB
    James Whitcomb Riley. Paul Laurence Dunbar
    On Hearing James W. Riley Read (From a Kentucky Standpoint). Joseph S.
        Cotter

RIOTS
    Aftermath. Michael S. Harper
    Arson and Cold Lace. Worth Long
    From Riot Rimes: USA. Raymond Patterson
    Litany For Peppe, A. Nikki Giovanni
    Molasses and the Three Witches. Michael S. Harper
    On Riots. Cy Leslie
    Riot Lauch & I Talk. David Henderson
    Riot: Gus. Maya Angelou
    Watts. Conrad Kent Rivers
    White Weekend. Quincy Troupe

RIVALS
Rivals, The. Paul Laurence Dunbar
Rivals, The. James Weldon Johnson

RIVERS
Brown River, Smile. Jean Toomer
Children of the Mississippi. Sterling A. Brown
Deep River. Anonymous
Foreclosure. Sterling A. Brown
Lapse. Paul Laurence Dunbar
Negro Speaks of Rivers, The. Langston Hughes
On the River. Paul Laurence Dunbar
Reverie on the Harlem River. Langston Hughes
Rivah's A Black Mare. Lucile D. Goodlett
River of Ruin, The. Paul Laurence Dunbar
Rivulet, The. Joseph S. Cotter, Sr.
Sacramento River. Zachary Withers
Sukee River. Claude McKay
Where Thames is Born. William C. Braithwaite

ROACHES
Last Warehouse, The. May Miller
Roach, A. John Raven

ROADS
Florida Road Workers. Langston Hughes
On the Road. William C. Braithwaite
On the Road. Paul Laurence Dunbar
Road, The. Helene Johnson
Roadway, A. Paul Laurence Dunbar
To the Road. Paul Laurence Dunbar
White Road, A. William S. Braithwaite

ROBBERS AND OUTLAWS
Opportunity. Paul Laurence Dunbar
Pomp's Case Argued. Daniel Webster Davis
Rolled. John Raven
Stealin' Grub. Lucy Mae Turner

ROBESON, PAUL
Paul Robeson. Gwendolyn Brooks
Paul Robeson. Eloise Culver
To Paul Robeson. Jean Brierre
To Paul Robeson, Opus No. 3. Percy Edward Johnston

ROBINS
Little Red Breast. Lula Lowe Weeden
On Hearing a Robin at Early Dawn. Charles B. Johnson
Robin's Poem, A. Nikki Giovanni

ROBINSON, JACKIE
Song to Jackie Robinson. Eloise Culver

ROGERS, JOEL A.
    Joel A. Rogers. Eloise Culver

ROME
    Song of Hannibal: Rome. Marcus B. Christian

ROOMS
    Lonely Room, A. Bernie Casey

ROOSEVELT, ELEANOR
    First Lady. Edna L. Harrison

ROOSEVELT, THEODORE
    Roosevelt. Raymond Dandridge

ROOSTERS
    Rooster, The. Joseph S. Cotter, Sr.

ROSES
    Crimson Rose, A. Thelma T. Clement
    Fragility. James Edgar Smith
    Fulfilment. Paul Laurence Dunbar
    In the Heart of a Rose. George Marion McLlelan
    June Breezes and Roses. Joseph S. Cotter, Sr.
    Like Unto a Rose. Lois Royal Hughes
    Poor Withered Rose. Paul Laurence Dunbar
    Promise. Paul Laurence Dunbar
    Red Rose. Raymond Dandridge
    Roses. Paul Laurence Dunbar
    Roses and Pearls. Paul Laurence Dunbar
    Roses Red. William C. Braithwaite
    She Gave Me a Rose. Paul Laurence Dunbar
    Snow-White Rosebud, A. Raymond Dandridge
    To a Rose. William L. Morrison
    To a Rose At Williston. Charles Fred White
    To A Rosebud. Eva Jessye
    To A Wild Rose. William Edgar Bailey
    Two Questions. William S. Braithwaite
    Wild Roses. Effie Lee Newsome

ROSSETTI, DANTE GABRIEL
    To Dante Gabriel Rossetti. William S. Braithwaite

ROUND
    Round. Ted Joans

ROYALTY
    Black Prince, The. Alice Walker
    Bronze Queen. Gertrude Parthenia McBrown
    Carol of the Brown King. Langston Hughes
    Group, The. Paul Laurence Dunbar
    King is Dead, The. Paul Laurence Dunbar

King's Daughter, The. William S. Braithwaite
Last Prince of the East, Langston Hughes
Me Alone. Lula Lowe Weeden
Shaka, King of the Zulu. Anonymous
Three Kings, The. Ruben Dario
Three Kings. James P. Vaughn
Victoria the Queen. James E. McGirt

RUDOLPH, WILMA
Wilma Rudolph. Eloise Culver

RUMBA
Rumba. Jose Zacarias Tallet

RUNAWAY SLAVES
Bib Bell in Zion, The. Theodore Henry Shackleford

RUNNYMEDE
From the Porch at Runnymede. Paul Laurence Dunbar

- S -

SACCO, NICOLAS
Not Sacco and Vanzetti. Countee Cullen

SADNESS
Melancholia. Paul Laurence Dunbar

SAHARA DESERT
Salute to the Sahara. Ted Joans

SAILING
Oh, Sail With Me. William C. Braithwaite
Sailing Date. Langston Hughes

SAINT LOUIS, MISSOURI
Crisis in the Midlands: St. Louis, Missouri. Michael S. Harper
New St. Louis Blues. Sterling A. Brown

ST. PETER
Saint Peter Relates an Incident of the Resurrection Day. James Weldon
    Johnson

SAINTS
Good Saint Benedict. Anonymous

SALESMEN AND SALESMANSHIP
Song of a Syrian Lace Seller. William S. Braithwaite

SALVATION
Evening Thought, An. Jupiter Hammon

SAMSON
    Watching, The. Owen Dodson

SAN FRANCISCO
    City: San Francisco. Langston Hughes
    San Francisco. Walter Adolphe Roberts
    Trip: San Francisco. Langston Hughes

SAND
    Sand. Ted Joans

SANTA CLAUS
    Johnny's Dream of Santa Claus. Joseph S. Cotter, Sr.
    Santa Claus. Ted Joans

SASSAFRAS TEA
    Sassafras Tea. Effie Lee Newsome

SATURDAY
    Saturday. Jon Woodson
    Saturday Night. Langston Hughes
    Saturday Night in Harlem. William Browne

SAVAGES
    Savage. Michael S. Harper

SAW MILLS
    Jaw Bone Town. James Pipes*

SAXOPHONES
    Albert Ayler: Eulogy for a Decomposed Saxophone Player. Stanley Crouch

SCANDAL
    Scandal and Gossip. Countee Cullen

SCHOOL BUILDINGS
    Description of a Kentucky School-House. Joseph S. Cotter, Sr.

SCHOOLS
    Six in Deportment. Joseph S. Cotter, Sr.
    To the Dunbar High School: A Sonnet. Angelina Weld Grimke

SCHWERNER, MICHAEL
    For Andy Goodman--Michael Schwerner--and James Chaney. Margaret Walker

SCOTTSBORO BOYS
    They Are Ours. A. B. Magil

SCRAPBOOKS
    Scrapbooks. Nikki Giovanni

SERENITY
    Serenity. Charles B. Johnson

SERMONS
    Antebellum Sermon, An. Paul Laurence Dunbar
    Reporting the Sermon. Joseph S. Cotter, Sr.
    Second Sermon on the Warpland, The. Gwendolyn Brooks
    Sermon on the Warpland. Gwendolyn Brooks
    To the Rev. Dr. Thomas Amory, on Reading His Sermon on Daily Devotion, In
        Which That Duty is Recommended and Assisted. Phillis Wheatley
    Dialogue Intitled the Kind Master and the Dutiful Servant as Follow.
        Jupiter Hammon

SERVANTS
    Negro Servant. Langston Hughes
    When in Rome. Mari Evans

SEWANEE
    Hills of Sewanee, The. George Marion McClellan

SEWING
    I Sit and Sew. Alice Dunbar Nelson

SEX
    125 Ways to Sex or Sexplosion. Ted Joans
    Poem & 1/2 For Blackwomen. Arthur Pfister

SHADOWS
    Beyond the Shadows. William L. Morrison
    Shadow. Richard Bruce
    Shadows. Helen F. Clarke
    Shadows. James Edgar Smith

SHAKESPEARE, WILLIAM
    Puck Goes to Court. Fenton Johnson
    Shakespeare. Henrietta Cordelia Ray
    Shakespeare Modernized. Charles Fred White
    Shakespeare's Sonnet. Joseph S. Cotter, Sr.

SHAME
    Indictment. Dorothy C. Parrish

SHARE CROPPERS
    Share-Croppers. Langston Hughes

SHAW, ROBERT GOULD
    My Hero (To Robert Gould Shaw). Benjamin Brawley
    Robert Gould Shaw. Paul Laurence Dunbar
    Robert G. Shaw. Henrietta Cordelia Ray.

SHELLY, PERCY B.
    Fishes and the Poet's Hands, The. Frank Yerby

SHELLS
    Palace. Dorothy Vena Johnson
    Shell, The. William C. Braithwaite
    Weed and Shell. William C. Braithwaite

SHEPHERDS
    Rise Up, Shepherd and Follow. Anonymous
    Shepherd of the Flock of Dreams, The. William S. Braithwaite
    Shepherd's Song at Christmas. Langston Hughes

SHIPS
    Ballade of Ships. William C. Braithwaite
    Odysseus at the Mast. Gerald Barrax
    Ships That Pass in the Night. Paul Laurence Dunbar
    Shipwright, The. Melvin Tolson
    We Launched a Ship. Ruby Berkley Goodwin

SHOES
    Bad Morning. Langston Hughes
    Chillen Got Shoes. Sterling A. Brown
    Oh, Dem Golden Slippers. James A. Bland
    Shine Mister? Robert Hayden
    Shoe Maker (Some of Them in Chicago--the Ole Kind). Clarence Major
    Times-Square-Shoeshine Composition. Maya Angelou
    Two Little Boots. Paul Laurence Dunbar

SHOPLIFTING
    Shoplifter. Solomon Edwards

SICK
    Calling the Doctor. John Wesley Holloway
    De Preacher Kyo Siam. Lucile D. Goodlett
    Lines For a Hospital. Countee Cullen
    Modern Song. Anonymous
    Sick Room. Langston Hughes

SIGHING
    What's the Use. Paul Laurence Dunbar

SIGNS
    No Use in Signs. James E. McGirt

SILENCE
    Silence. Langston Hughes

SILVER
    Real Question, The. Paul Laurence Dunbar

SIMONE, NINA
    For Nina Simone. Kali Grosvenor
    Ivory Masks in Orbit. Keorapetse Kgositsile

Poem for Nina Simone to Put Some Music to and Blow Our Nigguh / Minds.
    Sonia Sanchez

SIN
    Ballad of the Sinner. Langston Hughes
    Sinner. Langston Hughes
    To An Ecclesiast I Know. William Allyn Hill
    Wrath. Paul Laurence Dunbar

SINKS
    Sink, The. Ted Joans

SISTERS
    Brothers and Sisters of the Light. William C. Braithwaite
    Letter to my Sister. Anne Spencer
    My Sister is a Sister. Kali Grosvenor
    My Sisters. Charles Fred White

SIT-INS
    Sit-Ins. Margaret Walker

SKELETONS
    Only the Polished Skeleton. Countee Cullen

SKILLETS
    Trouble in De Kitchen. Paul Laurence Dunbar

SKIN
    Poem (For Nina). Nikki Giovanni

SKING
    Skiers, The. Michael S. Harper

SKULLS
    To a Skull. Joshua Henry Jones

SKY
    I Break the Sky. Owen Dodson
    Sketch of a Varying Evening Sky. John Boyd
    Sky, The. Anonymous

SKYSCRAPERS
    New York Skyscrapers. John Mbiti

SLAVERY
    Arise. Raymond Dandridge
    Aunt Sue's Stories. Langston Hughes
    Awakening, The. Paul Laurence Dunbar
    Big Iron. James Pipes*
    Boat Ride, The. Ted Joans
    'Bout Cullud Folkses. Lucy Mae Turner
    Buy and Buy. Ted Joans

Chained and Sold, The. Arthur Boze
Christian Slave, The. John Greenleaf Whittier*
Do They Miss Me? A Parody. Benjamin Clark
Dying Bondman, The. Frances Harper
Emancipators. Raymond Dandridge
Enslaved. Claude McKay
Essay on Beauty. Robert Hayden
Etc. Etc. Etc. Dorothy C. Parrish
Evolution. Thelma Parker Cox.
Farewell, The. John Greenleaf Whittier*
Fifty Years, 1863-1913. James Weldon Johnson
Formerly a Slave. Herman Melville*
Freedom's Snare. Ritten Edward Lee
From on the Fugitive Slave Law. Elymas Payson Rogers
Gabriel. Robert E. Hayden
He Who Has Lost All. David Diop
I See and Am Satisfied. Kelly Miller
In Bondage. Claude McKay
Indictment. Dorothy C. Parrish
Inevitable Road, The. Eldon George McLean
Lament of the Slave. Anonymous
Long View: Negro. Langston Hughes
Love Song in Middle Passage. Larry Neal
Love Your Enemy. Yusef Iman
Lute of Afric's Tribe, The. Arbery Allson Whitman
Meditations of a Negro's Mind V. Charles Fred White
Middle Pssaage. Robert Hayden
Miscellaneous Verses. Gustavus Vassa
Moral, A. Zachary Withers
My Guilt. Maya Angelou
News, The. Paul Laurence Dunbar
No More Auction Block. Anonymous
Ode to Blackmen. Zachary Withers
On Being Brought From Africa to America. Phillis Wheatley
On Freedom. Thomas S. Sidney
On Liberty and Slavery. George Moses Horton
Parted. Paul Laurence Dunbar
Poem for Pearl's Dancers. Owen Dodson
Prayer For Peace II. Leopold Sedar Senghor
Runagate Runagate. Robert Hayden
Runaway Slave, The. Walt Whitman
Runaway Slave at Pilgrim's Point, The. Elizabeth Barrett Browning*
Safari West. John A. Williams
Slave. Langston Hughes
Slave, The. James Oppenheim*
Slave and the Iron Lace. Margaret Danner
Slave Auction, The. Frances Harper
Slave Mother, The. Frances Harper
Slave Story. Hodding Carter
Slavery. George Moses Horton
Slave's Complaint, The. George Moses Horton
Slave's Dream, The. Henry Wadsworth Longfellow*

Slavery   SUBJECT INDEX

SNAKES
    Battle of the Rattlesnake, The. Melvin Tolson
    Dying Water-Moccasin, The. Joseph S. Cotter
    Snake. Langston Hughes
    Snake, The. Craig Williamson
    Snake-That-Walked-Upon-His-Tail, The. Countee Cullen
    To Fez Cobra. Ted Joans

SNOBBISHNESS
    Snob. Langston Hughes

SNOW
    Grievance, A. Paul Laurence Dunbar
    Poem. Robert Hayden
    Snow. Robert Hayden
    Snow Fairy, The. Claude McKay
    Snow in October. Alice Dunbar Nelson
    Snowin'. Paul Laurence Dunbar
    To One Coming North. Claude McKay
    Winter Poem. Nikki Giovanni
    Winter Sweetness. Langston Hughes

SOAP
    Soft Soap. Lucile D. Goodlett

SOLDIERS
    At the Etoile (At the Unknown Soldier's Grave in Paris). Countee Cullen
    Before Monument. Alexander Young
    Belsen, Day of Liberations. Robert Hayden
    Black Recruit. Georgia Douglas Johnson
    Black Samson of Brandy Wine. Paul Laurence Dunbar
    Black Soldier. May Wilkerson Cleaves
    Blacks in Blue. Raymond Dandridge
    Color Sergeant, The. James Weldon Johnson
    Colored Soldiers, The. Paul Laurence Dunbar
    Conquerors, The. Paul Laurence Dunbar
    Dirge For a Soldier. Paul Laurence Dunbar
    Dumb Soldier, The. Raymond Dandridge
    Eighth Illinois in Cuba, The. Charles Fred White
    Eighth Returning From Cuba, The. Charles Fred White
    Facts. Raymond Garfield
    For John Moses / PFC. Albert Aubert
    For Lover Man, and All the Other Young Men Who Failed to Return From
        World War II. Mance Williams
    He's Coming Home at Last. Emily Jane Greene
    Impressions on Induction. R. Orlando Jackson
    Negro Soldiers, The. Roscoe Conkling Jamison
    Negro Volunteer, The. Charles Fred White
    Old Negro Soldier of the Civil War, The. Joseph S. Cotter, Sr.
    On Major General Lee (1776). Phillis Wheatley
    On the Capture of General Lee. Phillis Wheatley
    One Year Ago. Charles Fred White

Plea Of the Negro Soldier. Charles Fred White
Psalm of the Negro Soldier. Joseph S. Cotter, Sr.
Robert G. Shaw. Henrietta Cordelia Ray
Salute to the Tan Yanks. Amos J. Griffin
Sam Smiley. Sterling A. Brown
Sergeant Jerk. Deborah Fuller Wess
Sonnet to Negro Soldiers. Joseph S. Cotter, Jr.
Speakin' at De Couthose. Paul Laurence Dunbar
This is For Freedom, My Son. Charles Stewart
To Captain H--D, Of the 65th Regiment. Phillis Wheatley
To the Men of the Soviet Army. H. Ginga Dismond
Two Epitaphs. Countee Cullen
Unknown Soldier. Mae V. Cowdery
Unknown Soldier, The. Melvin Tolson
Unsung Heroes, The. Paul Laurence Dunbar
When Dey 'Listed Colored Soldiers. Paul Laurence Dunbar
When the Armies Passed. Langston Hughes
Young Black Soldiers. Bernie Casey
Young Warrior, The. James Weldon Johnson

SOLIDARITY DAY
Solidarity Day, 1968. June Jordan

SOLITUDE
Solitude. Carlyle B. Hall

SONGS
Arbor Singing. Charles B. Johnson
Banjo Song, A. James Weldon Johnson
Birth of American Song, The. Joseph S. Cotter, Sr.
Blues Singer. John Raven
Choice, A. Paul Laurence Dunbar
Colored Blues Singer. Countee Cullen
Corn Song, The. John Wesley Holloway
Compensation. Joseph S. Cotter, Jr.
Dream and a Song. William S. Braithwaite
Dream and the Song. James David Corrothers
Dusk Song. William H. A. Moore
Earth Song. Langston Hughes
For a Singer. Countee Cullen
Gift to Sing, The. James Weldon Johnson
Gypsy Melodies. Langston Hughes
Harlem Night Song. Langston Hughes
Heritage. Mae V. Cowdery
Hymn. Paul Laurence Dunbar
Hymn, A. Paul Laurence Dunbar
I Can No Longer Sing. Mari Evans
I Sing No New Songs. Frank Marshall Davis
I've Learned to Sing. George Douglas Johnson
Juke Box Love Song. Langston Hughes
Keep a Song Up on De Way. Paul Laurence Dunbar
Little Song, A. William S. Braithwaite

Love Song, A. Paul Laurence Dunbar
Love Song, A. Raymond Richard Patterson
Ma Lady's Lips Am Like De Honey (Negro Love Song). James Weldon Johnson
Minnie Sings Her Blues. Langston Hughes
Misapprehension. Paul Laurence Dunbar
More Than a Fool's Song. Countee Cullen
Morning Song of Love. Paul Laurence Dunbar
My Song. Joseph S. Cotter, Sr.
Negro Love Song. Joseph S. Cotter, Sr.
Negro Love Song, A. Paul Laurence Dunbar
Negro Peddler's Song, A. Fenton Johnson
Negro Serenade. James Edwin Campbell
Negro Singer, The. James David Corrothers
Nobody's Lookin' But De Owl and De Moon. James Weldon Johnson
Now and Then. Charles B. Johnson
O Word I Love to Sing. Claude McKay
Ol' Tunes, The. Paul Laurence Dunbar
Out of the Dingy Alleyways. J. Henderson Brooks
Plantation Bacchanal. James Weldon Johnson
Plantation Melody, A. Paul Laurence Dunbar
Poet and His Song, The. Paul Laurence Dunbar
Remembered. Paul Laurence Dunbar
Sailor's Song, A. Paul Laurence Dunbar
Secret. Gwendolyn B. Bennett
Sing Me a New Song. John Henrik Clarke
Sing On to Jesus. Waverly T. Carmichael
Singin' An' Prayin'. Raymond G. Dandridge
Singing At Amen Church. Charles B. Johnson
Song. William S. Braithwaite
Song. William S. Braithwaite
Song. Paul Laurence Dunbar
Song, A. Paul Laurence Dunbar
Song, A. Paul Laurence Dunbar
Song, A. Paul Laurence Dunbar
Song, The. Paul Laurence Dunbar
Song. Charles B. Johnson
Song to a Negro Washwoman. Langston Hughes
Song: To-Night the Stars are Wooing, Love. William S. Braithwaite
Song: As a New Made Bride. William S. Braithwaite
Song of Living. William S. Braithwaite
Song of the Syrian Lace Seller. William S. Braithwaite
Song: the Trail of Stars. William S. Braithwaite
Song To-Day and To-Morrow. William S. Braithwaite
Songs. Langston Hughes
Songs and Smiles. Raymond Dandridge
Songs For the People. Frances Harper
Sonnet Spiritual. Luther George Luper, Jr.
Spirits Enchantment. Ed Bullins
To Melody. George Leonard Allen
To The Singer. Helen C. Harris
Uncle Eph's Banjo Song. James Edwin Campbell
When De Saints Go Machin' Home. Sterling A. Brown

My South. Don West*
North and South. Joseph S. Cotter, Sr.
O Southland! James Weldon Johnson
Sorrow Home. Margaret Walker
South, The. Langston Hughes
South, the Name of Home. Alice Walker
Southern Landscapers. Ted Joans
Southern Reaper, The. Conrad Kent Rivers
Southern Road, The. Dudley Randall
Southern Song. Margaret Walker
Southerner, The. Karl Shapiro*
Sunny South. Lucy Mae Turner
To The South. Paul Laurence Dunbar
Vari-Colored Song. Langston Hughes
Weh Down Souf. Daniel Webster Davis
Where Hearts Are Gay. Waverly T. Carmichael

SOUTH CAROLINA
    South Carolina Chain Gang Song. Anonymous

SOUVENIRS
    Souvenir. Georgia D. Johnson

SOWING
    "You'll Reap What You Sow." Waverly T. Carmichael

SPACE
    One Way. Tommy Whitaker

SPADES
    Spade is Just a Spade, A. Walter Everette Hawkins

SPANISH AMERICAN WAR
    "Do Not Cheer, Men Are Dying," Said Capt. Phillips in the Spanish Ameri-
        can War. Frances Harper

SPANKINGS
    When a Feller's Itchin' To Be Spanked. Paul Laurence Dunbar

SPARROWS
    Sparrows, The. Paul Laurence Dunbar
    Sparrow's Fall, The. Frances Harper

SPELLING BEE
    Spellin' Bee, The. Paul Laurence Dunbar

SPELMAN COLLEGE
    Miss Packard and Miss Giles. Owen Dodson

SPHINX
    Riddle of the Sphinx, The. William E. B. DuBois

Spiders   SUBJECT INDEX

SPIDERS
    Web, The. Robert Hayden

SPIES
    He Spy. Ted Joans

SPINDRIFT
    Spindrift. William C. Braithwaite

SPIRIT
    Desolate. Claude McKay
    Outlawed Spirit, The. Zachary Withers
    Spirit. William L. Morrison
    Spirit Enchantment. Ed Bullins

SPIRITUALS
    Go Tell it on the Mountain. Anonymous
    God's Gonna Set Dis World on Fire. Anonymous
    I Got a Home in Dat Rock. Anonymous
    Negro Spirituals. Eloise Culver
    No More Auction Block. Anonymous
    On Listening to the Spirituals. Lance Jeffers
    Oh, Mary, Don't You Weep. Anonymous
    Rise Up, Shepherd and Follow. Anonymous
    Spiritual, A. Paul Laurence Dunbar
    Spirituals. Langston Hughes
    Steal Away. Anonymous
    Virgin Had a Baby Boy, The. Anonymous
    Wasn't That a Mighty Day. Anonymous
    What You Gonna Name That Pretty Little Baby? Anonymous

SPRING
    Absent in Spring. William S. Braithwaite
    De Signs O' Spring. Waverly T. Carmichael
    Earth Song. Langston Hughes
    Memory. Georgia D. Johnson
    Primaveral. Robert Hayden
    Signs. Beatrice M. Murphy
    Sprin' Fevah. Raymond Dandridge
    Spring. Charles B. Johnson
    Spring. Charles Fred White
    Spring. James McGirt
    Spring Blossom. Ernest Attah
    Spring in Callea. Charles Johnson
    Spring in Carolina. Audrey Johnson
    Spring in New Hampshire. Claude McKay
    Spring in the Jungle. Eugene Redmond
    Spring is Here. Olivia M. Hunter
    Spring Lament. Mae V. Cowdery
    Spring. Leslie Pinckney Hill
    Spring Morning, A. Raymond Dandridge
    Spring 1917. Charles Johnson

STOOLS
    There You Were. Bernie Casey

STORIES
    Aunt Sue's Stories. Langston Hughes
    Cabin Tale, A. Paul Laurence Dunbar
    Story Hour, The. Joseph S. Cotter, Sr.
    Tracin' Tales. Raymond Dandridge

STORMS
    Electrical Storm (For Arna and Alberta). Robert Hayden
    Mountain in a Storm. Herman J. D. Carter
    Ring of the Storm, The. Paul Laurence Dunbar
    Song of the Storm. Eli Shepperd
    Storm. Craig Williamson
    Storm Ending. Jean Toomer
    Typhoon. William L. Morrison

STOWE, HARRIET BEECHER
    Harriet Beecher Stowe. Paul Laurence Dunbar

STRANGERS
    Stranger in Town. Langston Hughes

STREAMS
    Stream, The. Lula Lowe Weeden

STREET CRIES
    Cala Vendor's Cry. Anonymous
    Crab Man. Anonymous
    Oyster Man's Cry. Anonymous
    Sweet Potato Man. Anonymous
    Watermelon Vendor's Cry. Anonymous

STREETS
    Ballad For Sterling Street. Sonia Sanchez
    Beale Street. Waring Cuney
    Beale Street. Langston Hughes
    Beale Street Love. Langston Hughes
    Could Be. Langston Hughes
    Lenox Avenue: Midnight. Langston Hughes
    Railroad Avenue. Langston Hughes
    South Street. Edward Silvera
    Street Scene #1. Victor Hernandez Cruz
    Sunflowers: Beaubin Street. Robert Hayden

STRENGTH
    Strength. William L. Morrison

STRUGGLES
    Struggle Stagger Us, The. Margaret Walker

STUDENTS
Black Students. Julia Fields
Poem for Halfwhite College Students. LeRoi Jones
To the Student. Alberry A. Whitman
To the Univ. of Cambridge in New England (1767). Phillis Wheatley
To the University of Cambridge, Wrote in 1767. Phillis Wheatley

SUBMISSION
Limits of Submission, The. Faarah Nuur

SUBWAYS
De Subways Race. Kali Grosvenor
Subway, The. Conrad Kent Rivers
Subway Wind. Claude McKay
Underground Bitch, The. Ted Joans

SUCCESS
I Shall Succeed. James McGirt
Success. Nick Aaron Ford
Success. Dorothy Vena Johnson
Success. James McGirt

SUFFERING
To be Black is to Suffer. Austin D. Washington

SUICIDE
Ballad of the Brown Girl
Dispute Over Suicide, A. Anonymous
For Black Poets Who Think of Suicide. Etheridge Knight
Life is Fine. Langston Hughes
Note, The. Melvin Tolson
On a Suicide. Joseph S. Cotter, Sr.
Song for a Suicide. Langston Hughes
Letters Found Near a Suicide. Frank Horne
More Letters Found Near a Suicide. Frank Horne
Neighbors Stood on the Corner, The. Waring Cuney
Notes Found Near a Suicide. Frank Horne
Preface to a Twenty Volume Suicide Note. LeRoi Jones
Suicide. Langston Hughes
Suicide, The. James Weldon Johnson
Suicide. Alice Walker
Suicide Chant. Countee Cullen
Suicide's Note. Langston Hughes
To a Young Suicide. William Allyn Hill
To a Youth Contemplating Suicide. Raymond Dandridge
To Wanda. Frank Horne
221-1424 San/Francisco/ Suicide / Number. Sonia Sanchez

SUMMER
Boy's Summer Song, A. Paul Laurence Dunbar
In Summer. Paul Laurence Dunbar
In Summer Time. Paul Laurence Dunbar

Love Song For Summer. Mae V. Cowdery
Rain in Summer. William S. Braithwaite
Song of Summer. Paul Laurence Dunbar
Summer. Waring Cuney
Summer Evening.
Summer Magic. Leslie Pinckney Hill
Summer Matures. Helene Johnson
Summer Morn in New Hampshire. Claude McKay
Summer Night. Langston Hughes
Summer Night, A. Paul Laurence Dunbar
Summer Night's Enchantment, A. William S. Braithwaite
Summer Pastoral, A. Paul Laurence Dunbar
Summer's Night, A. Paul Laurence Dunbar
Summertime and the Living. Robert Hayden

SUN

Barrier, The. Paul Laurence Dunbar
House in Taos, A. Langston Hughes
Hymn to the Sun, The. Anonymous
Shine on, Mr. Sun. J. Mord Allen
Song For the Sun That Disappeared Behind the Rain Clouds. Anonymous
Sun Came, The. Etheridge Knight
Sun Song. Langston Hughes
Sun Went Down in Beauty, The. George Marion McLlelan
Sunset. Raymond Dandridge
Sunset. Paul Laurence Dunbar
Sunset in the Tropics. James Weldon Johnson
Sunset Pastel. William L. Morrison
When De Sun Shines Hot. James McGirt

SUNDAY

Day of Rest, The. Charles Fred White
November Sabbath Morn, A. Charles Fred White
Sabbath. Charles Fred White
Sunday Chicken. Gwendolyn Brooks
Sunday Go to Meetin' Folk. John Raven
Sunday. Langston Hughes
Sunday Morning Prophecy. Langston Hughes
Sunday Morning Song. Anonymous
These Winter Sundays. Robert Hayden

SUN FLOWERS

Sunflowers: Beaubien Street. Robert Hayden

SUPERSTITION

Purcaution. Raymond Dandridge

SUPPER

Supper Time. Langston Hughes

SUPPOSITION

If-ing. Langston Hughes

SUPREMACY
    Supremacy. Leanna F. Johnson

SURFS
    Surf Breaking. William S. Braithwaite

SURVIVAL
    Castaway, The. Claude McKay
    Gospel Truth, The. Jackie Earley
    Mixed Sketches. Don L. Lee
    Poet's Survival Kit. Ahmed Akinwole Alhamisi

SWALLOWS
    Homing Swallows. Claude McKay

SWEAT
    Sweat and Tears. Raymond Dandridge

SWIMMING
    Fellows Are Learning to Swim, The. William C. Braithwaite
    Pool, The. Paul Laurence Dunbar
    Strong Swimmer, The. William Rose Benét*

SWINBURNE, ALGERNON CHARLES
    Algernon Charles Swinburne. Joseph S. Cotter, Sr.

SWORDS
    Sword, The. Abu Bakr

SYMPATHY
    Consolation. Charles Fred White
    Sympathy. Paul Laurence Dunbar
    Sympathy. Georgia Douglas Johnson

SYMPHONY
    Symphony, The. Leslie Pinckney Hill

- T -

TACT
    Tact in Relating. Joseph S. Cotter, Sr.

TALENT, AMATEUR
    Amateur Night. Charles Burbridge

TAMBOURINES
    Tambourines. Langston Hughes

TANNER, HENRY O.
    Henry O. Tanner. Eloise Culver

TENNYSON, ALFRED
      Alfred Tennyson. Joseph S. Cotter, Sr.

TETUAN
      Tetuan. Claude McKay

TEXAS
      West Texas. Langston Hughes

THAMES (RIVER)
      Where Thames is Born. William C. Braithwaite

THANKS
      Gratitude. Raymond Dandridge

THANKSGIVING
      Signs of the Times. Paul Laurence Dunbar
      Thanksgiving. William S. Braithwaite
      Thanksgiving (1923). Raymond Dandridge
      Thanksgiving (1925). Raymond Dandridge
      Thanksgiving Poem, A. Paul Laurence Dunbar
      Thoughts of Thanksgiving. Charles Fred White

THEATRE
      Curtain. Paul Laurence Dunbar
      Lincoln Theatre. Langston Hughes
      Note on Commercial Theatre. Langston Hughes

THERMOMETERS
      On the Gift of a Thermometer. Charles Fred White

THINGS, LITTLE
      Poem For Stacia. Nikki Giovanni

THIRD DEGREE
      Third Degree. Langston Hughes

THIRD WORLD
      Third World Bond (for My Sisters and Their Sisters), The. Don L. Lee

THIRST
      Thirst. Claude McKay

THORNS
      Thorny. Ted Joans

THOUGHTS
      Invitation. Frenchy J. Hodges
      Thoughts. William L. Morrison

TIGHT ROPE
      I'll Walk the Tightrope. Margaret Danner

Toussaint L'Ouverture. Raymond Dandridge
Toussaint L'Ouverture. Edwin Arlington Robinson

TRACK
Black Runners / Black Men or Run Into Blackness. Don L. Lee
To James. Frank Horne

TRAGEDIES
Life's Tragedy. Paul Laurence Dunbar

TRAINS
Going Uptown to Visit Miriam. Victor Hernandez Cruz
On the Road. Claude McKay
Train Ride, The. George B. Browne
Train Runs Late to Harlem, The. Conrad Kent Rivers
Word of an Engineer, The. James Weldon Johnson

TRAITORS
To an Unhanged Judas. Raymond Dandridge

TRANSPLANTS, HEART
Uhuru in the O.R. June Jordan

TRAVEL
Circle Two. Owen Dodson
Emigrant, The. Benjamin Clark
Journey. Ted Joans
Letter From a Traveler. Michael S. Harper
Lonely Traveler. Kwesi Brew
Long Gone. Sterling A. Brown
One Way Ticket. Langston Hughes
Still Traveling. Ted Joans
Tour 5. Robert Hayden

TREASURES
Treasured. William L. Morrison

TREE HOUSE
Tree House, The. James Emanuel

TREES
Apple Trees By the River. Lucy Mae Turner
Bronze Queen. Gertrude Parthenia McBrown
Death of a College Oak. Nick Aaron Ford
Dogwood Blossoms. George Marion McClellan
God is Tall Trees. Craig Williamson
Haunted Oak, The. Paul Laurence Dunbar
Icicles on Trees. Catherine L. Findley
Like a Strong Tree. Claude McKay
Little Birches. Effie Lee Newsome
Little Green Trees. Langston Hughes
Nature's Puzzle. Joseph S. Cotter, Sr.

Trees   SUBJECT INDEX

TURKEYS
      Knowing the Christmas Turkey. Joseph S. Cotter, Sr.
      Soliloquy of a Turkey. Paul Laurence Dunbar

TURNER, NAT
      Ballad of Nat Turner, The. Robert Hayden
      Nat Turner, an Epitaph. Lucy Mae Turner
      Nat Turner in the Clearing. Albert Aubert
      Remembering Nat Turner. Sterling A. Brown

TURTLES
      Emancipation of George Hector (A Colored Turtle). Mari Evans

TUSKEGEE INSTITUTE
      Lewis Adams. Eloise Culver
      On the Dedication of Dorothy Hall. Paul Laurence Dunbar
      Tuskegee. Joseph S. Cotter, Sr.
      Tuskegee. Leslie Pinckney Hill

TWILIGHT
      Summer Twilight. William L. Morrison
      Twilight. Paul Laurence Dunbar
      Twilight and Dreams. William S. Braithwaite
      Twilight Reverie. Langston Hughes

- U -

UGLINESS
      Disgrace. Anonymous

UMBRELLAS
      Windy Rain. Kali Grosvenor

UNCERTAINTY
      Uncertainty. Henrietta C. Parks

UNCLE SAM
      Question. Charles L. Anderson

UNCLE TOM
      He Spy. Ted Joans
      Leviticus Tate. Lloyd Warren
      Uncle Tom Tom. Ted Joans
      Uncle Tom. J. Farley Ragland
      Uncle Tom. Eleanor A. Thompson

UNDERGROUND
      Underground. Conrad Kent Rivers

UNDERGROUND RAILROAD
      Underground Railroad, The. Eloise Culver

UNDERWEAR
    Magic Pants. Ted Joans

UNEMPLOYMENT
    Bacchanale. Robert Hayden
    Commencement. Edna Mae Weiss
    Out of Work. Langston Hughes
    Shine Mister. Robert Hayden

UNEXPRESSED
    Unexpressed. Paul Laurence Dunbar

U. S. AIR FORCE
    Black 99th, The. Arthur Boze

U. S. ARMY
    2 Poems For Black Relocation Centers. Etheridge Knight

U. S. COAST GUARD
    Coast-Guard Path, The. William C. Braithwaite

U. S. HISTORY
    American History. Michael S. Harper
    Ballad of the Free, The. Margaret Walker
    Colonized Mind. Barbara Marshall
    Final Call. Langston Hughes
    From Miscellaneous Poems Hymn to the Nation. Arbery Allson Whitman
    Historic Episodes. Peter Wellington Clark
    Historical Review. Charles Fred White
    History. Langston Hughes
    Modern Moses, or "My Policy Man." James Madison Bell
    Nigger. Frank Horne
    Rendezvous With America. Melvin Tolson

U. S. HISTORY-CIVIL WAR
    Fragment. James Weldon Johnson
    Memorial Wreath. Dudley Randall
    News, The. Paul Laurence Dunbar
    Old Negro Soldier of the Civil War. Joseph S. Cotter, Sr.

U. S. NAVY
    Phillis's Reply to the Answer in our Last by the Gentleman in the Navy.
        Phillis Wheatley
    To a Gentleman of the Navy (For the Royal American Magazine). Phillis
        Wheatley

U. S. POLITICS
    Fifty-Fifty. Raymond Dandridge

UNITY
    Pow-Wow. Ted Joans

SUBJECT INDEX

UPPER CLASS
    Pit of Cold Brother Bull shit. Ted Joans

UPSON, ARTHUR
    To Arthur Upson. William S. Braithwaite

- V -

VAGRANTS
    Vagrants. Paul Laurence Dunbar

VARIETY
    Variety. William Thompson Goss

VASHTI
    Vashti. James Weldon Johnson

VAUDEVILLE
    Downtown Vaudeville. Gwendolyn Brooks

VEGETABLES
    Radish, The. Ibn Quzman

VENGEANCE
    That Vengeance Gathers. Theodore Stanford
    Vengeance is Sweet. Paul Laurence Dunbar

VENUS
    Venus in a Garden. James Weldon Johnson

VANZETTI, BARTOLOMEO
    Not Sacco and Vanzetti. Countee Cullen

VERSAILLES
    Journey to Versailles. Conrad Kent Rivers
    Legend of Versailles, A. Melvin Tolson

VESUVIUS
    Vesuvius. Melvin Tolson

VETERANS
    To the Veterans of Future Wars. Mae V. Cowdery
    Veteran, The. Paul Laurence Dunbar

VIETNAM
    From a Logical Point of View. Nikki Giovanni
    Gods in Vietnam. Eugene Redmond
    Mud of Vietnam. Julius Lester
    Guerrilla-Cong, The. Michael S. Harper
    Under Fire. John Raven
    Vietnam: I Need More Than This Crust of Salt. Lance Jeffers
    Vietnam #4. Clarence Major

VIEWS
    Views. Melvin Tolson

VIOLETS
    Old Woman With Violets. Robert Hayden
    Sonnet. Alice Dunbar Nelson
    To a Violet Found on All Saints Day. Paul Laurence Dunbar

VIOLINS
    Maid and Violinist. Alpheus Butler

VIRGINS
    For a Virgin. Countee Cullen
    Songs to the Dark Virgin. Langston Hughes

VIRGINIA
    Carry Me Back to Old Virginny. James A. Bland
    Life-Long Poor Browning. Anne Spencer·

VIRGINIA REEL
    Angelina. Paul Laurence Dunbar

VIRTUE
    On Virtue. Phillis Wheatley

VISIONS
    Vision, A. Sarah Collins Fernandis

VISITORS
    Visitor, The. Paul Laurence Dunbar

VOTING
    Democratic Order: Such Things in Twenty Years I Understand. Alice Walker

VOYAGES
    To a Gentleman on His Voyage to Great Britain for the Recovery of His
        Health. Phillis Wheatley

- W -

WADING
    Wadin' in De Crick. Paul Laurence Dunbar

WAITERS
    Atlantic City Waiter. Countee Cullen
    Ebony. Lucy Mae Turner

WAITING
    Hour to Spend, An. William C. Braithwaite
    I am Waiting. Michael Goode
    Waiting. Paul Laurence Dunbar

WASHINGTON, BOOKER T.
    Alabama Earth. Langston Hughes
    Booker T. and W.E.B. Dudley Randall
    Booker T. Washington. Waverly T. Carmichael
    Booker T. Washington. Eloise Culver
    Booker T. Washington. Raymond Dandridge
    Booker T. Washington. Paul Laurence Dunbar
    Booker T. Washington. John Wesley Fentress
    Dr. Booker T. Washington to the National Business League. Joseph S.
       Cotter, Sr.
    Ode to Booker Washington. Charles B. Johnson
    We Launched a Ship. Ruby Berkley Goodwin

WASHINGTON, GEORGE
    Cameo No. II. June Jordan
    His Excellency General Washington. Phillis Wheatley

WATCHING
    I Watch. Bernie Casey
    I Watch You. Bernie Casey

WATER
    Salt Water. Joseph S. Cotter, Sr.
    Thirst. Claude McKay
    Water. William S. Braithwaite

WATERMELON
    Watermelon. Ted Joans
    Watermelon. G. T. Smith

WATER-MOCCASIN
    Dying Water-Moccasin. Joseph S. Cotter, Sr.

WATTERSON, HENRY
    "Marse" Henry Watterson. Joseph S. Cotter, Sr.

WATTS, (CALIFORNIA)
    Yesterday's Child. Robert Reedburg

WAVES
    Wave-Song, A. William C. Braithwaite

WEALTH
    My Poverty and Wealth. Joseph S. Cotter
    Precedent. Paul Laurence Dunbar

WEARINESS
    World Weariness. David Wadsworth Cannon, Jr.

WEATHER
    Cold Weather Causes Curses. Ted Joans
    Weddah. Raymond Dandridge

Wind, the Weathercock and the Warrior's Ghost, The. Robert Hayden

WEDDINGS
    Rituals. Nikki Giovanni
    Thoughts of a Best Man While Standing Up For a Pal and a Gal. John Raven
    Wedding, The. June Jordan
    Wedding Procession. James A. Emanuel

WEEDS
    To the Smartweed. Leslie Pinckney Hill
    Weed and Shell. William C. Braithwaite
    Weeds. Robert Hayden

WEEPING
    What's the Use. Paul Laurence Dunbar

WELLS
    Way-Side Well, The. Joseph S. Cotter, Sr.

WEST
    One Way Ticket. Langston Hughes

WEST INDIES
    Guadelupe, W.I. Nicolas Guillen

WHALES
    Whale, His Bulwark, The. Derek Walcott

WHEATLEY, PHILLIS
    Address to Miss Phillis Wheatley (Sic) Ethiopian Poetess, An. Jupiter
        Hammon
    Phillis Wheatley. Eloise Culver

WHISKBROOM
    On the Gift of a Whisk Broom. Charles Fred White

WHISKEY
    Rot Gut Whiskey. John Raven

WHISTLING
    Just a Whistle a Bit. Paul Laurence Dunbar
    Whistling Sam. Paul Laurence Dunbar

WHITTIER, JOHN GREENLEAF
    To Whittier. Josephine D. (Henderson) Heard
    White Magic: an Ode. William S. Braithwaite
    Whittier. Paul Laurence Dunbar

WHORES
    Whores. Margaret Walker

WIDOWS
    Popsicle Cold. Norman Jordan
    Widow. Clarence Major

WILKINS, ROY
    Civil Rights Poem. LeRoi Jones

WILL
    Brute Will. Joseph S. Cotter, Sr.

WILLIAMS, DE WIT
    Of De Wit Williams on His Way to Lincoln Cemetary. Gwendolyn Brooks

WILLIAMS, DR. DANIEL HALE
    Dr. Daniel Hale Williams, Pioneer in Heart Surgery, 1858-1931, Pennsyl-
        vania. Eloise Culver

WILLS
    Beggars' Will. J. Henderson Brooks
    Codicil. Albert Aubert
    Last Will and Testament. Alvin Aubert

WIND
    Chase, The. Paul Laurence Dunbar
    House in Taos, A. Langston Hughes
    Hymn of the Winds. Eli Shepperd
    Leaves in the Wind. Robert Hayden
    Till the Wind Gets Right. Paul Laurence Dunbar
    To the Wind of the Night. Charles Fred White
    Tomorrow's Winds. Samuel E. Boyd
    Unknown Color, The. Countee Cullen
    Who Has Seen the Wind? Bob Kaufman
    Wind. Langston Hughes
    Wind, The. L. Doretta Lowery
    Wind and the Sea, The. Paul Laurence Dunbar
    Wind Blows, The. Mae V. Cowdery
    Wind, the Weathercock and the Warrior's Ghost, The. Robert Hayden
    Winds are Still, The. William C. Braithwaite

WINE
    Bubbling Wine. Abe Zakariya
    Free Wine on Communion Day. Linwood D. Smith
    Harlem Wine. Countee Cullen
    Of Bread and Wine. Olive LaGrone

WINGS
    Angels Wings. Langston Hughes
    If We Had Wings. Nick Aaron Ford

WINTER
    After the Winter. Claude McKay
    After Winter. Sterling A. Brown

And Fall Shall Sit in Judgment. Audre Lorde
Five Winters Age. David Henderson
Land-No-End. William L. Morrison
Midwinter Blues. Langston Hughes
Plantation Child's Lullaby, The. Paul Laurence Dunbar
Spring Poem in Winter. Mae V. Cowdery
These Winter Sundays. Robert Hayden
To Winter. Claude McKay
Warm Day in Winter, A. Paul Laurence Dunbar
When Winter Darkening All Around. Paul Laurence Dunbar
Winter. James McGirt
Winter Chorus. Owen Dodson
Winter in the Country. Claude McKay
Winter is Coming. Waverly Turner Carmichael
Winter Poem. Nikki Giovanni
Winter Retreat. Michael S. Harper
Winter Rode Away. J. Henderson Brooks
Winter-Song. Paul Laurence Dunbar
Winter Sweetness. Langston Hughes
Winter Thoughts. William L. Morrison
Winter Twilight, A. Angelina Weld Grimke
Winter's Approach. Paul Laurence Dunbar
Winter's Day, A. Paul Laurence Dunbar

WINDOWS
Window Washer. Ricardo Weeks

WISDOM
Wisdom. Frank Yerby
Wisdom and War. Langston Hughes
Wisdom Cometh With the Years. Countee Cullen
Wisdom. Langston Hughes

WISHES
Wish, A. Countee Cullen

WIT AND HUMOR
Black Sketches. Don L. Lee
Humor. Charles Johnson
Humorous Verse. Abu Dolame

WITCH DOCTOR
Witch Doctor. Robert Hayden

WITCHES
Molly Means. Margaret Walker
White Witch, The. James Weldon Johnson

WIVES
Letter From a Wife. S. Carolyn Reese
To a Good Wife. Nick Aaron Ford

WOMAN
    About June. John Raven
    Advice to a Beauty. Countee Cullen
    Advice to Young Ladies. Ann Plato
    After Her Man Had Left Her for the Sixth Time That Year (An Uncommon Oc-
        curence). Don L. Lee
    Aint Got. Ted Joans
    Alice. Paul Laurence Dunbar
    And Always. Bruce McM. Wright
    And the Old Women Gathered. Mari Evans
    And There Are Those. James Thompson
    Angelina. Paul Laurence Dunbar
    Angie Saves Her Man. Lucile D. Goodlett
    Anna, Won't You Marry Me? James McGirt
    Announcement. Langston Hughes
    Appeal. Noemia De Sousa
    Ardella. Langston Hughes
    Areytos. Jean Brierre
    Aunt Chloe's Lullaby. James Edwin Campbell
    Aunt Jane Allen. Fenton Johnson
    Aunt Sue's Stories. Langston Hughes
    Ballad of Gin Mary. Langston Hughes
    Ballad of Late Annie, The. Gwendolyn Brooks
    Ballad of Margie Polite, The. Langston Hughes
    Ballad of Sue Ellen Westerfield (For Clyde), The. Robert Hayden
    Ballad of the Killer Boy. Langston Hughes
    Bane Black. Ted Joans
    beATrice does the dinner. Mari Evans
    Beautiful Black Women. LeRoi Jones
    Belle-De-Nuit. Ignace Nau
    Bessie. Sterling A. Brown
    Big Momma. Don L. Lee
    Black Mammies. John Wesley Holloway
    Blackwoman. Don L. Lee
    Black Mammy, The. James Weldon Johnson
    Black Woman. Leopold Sedar Senghor
    Black Women. Arthur Boze
    Blackwoman. Don L. Lee
    Blk/Wooooomen /Chant. Sonia Sanchez
    Blind and Deaf Old Woman. Clarence Major
    Blues For Momma. John Raven
    Breaking the Charm. Paul Laurence Dunbar
    Bridal Measure, A. Paul Laurence Dunbar
    Choucoune. Oswald Durand
    Club Woman. Mary Carter Smith
    Coffee Groun' Chloe. Raymond Dandridge
    Color Bane, The. George Marion McLlelan
    Conjuh Bag. Lucile D. Goodlett
    Cora. Langston Hughes
    Cordelia Brown. Anonymous
    Curious. Langston Hughes
    Daphne. Selden Rodman*

Virginia Portrait. Sterling A. Brown
W.W. LeRoi Jones
Washer-Woman, The. Otto Leland Bohanan
Waterbowl, The. Michael S. Harper
What I Need, Is a Dark Woman. Charles Anderson
When Mahalia Sings. Quandra Prettyman
When Malindy Sing. Paul Laurence Dunbar
When Ol' Sis' Judy Pray. James Edwin Campbell
When Sue Wears Red. Langston Hughes
White Lace. Ted Joans
White Woman. Ted Joans
Widow. Clarence Major
Widow Woman. Langston Hughes
Widow's Walk, The. Owen Dodson
Wife-Woman, The. Anne Spencer
Woman. Valente Goenha Malangatana
Woman. Charles Fred White
Woman at War. Hazel L. Washington
Woman Poem. Nikki Giovanni
Women and Kitchens. Waring Cuney
Wonder Woman, The. Nikki Giovanni
Yes Indeed Blues. Ted Joans
Zalka Peetruza. Raymond Dandridge

WONDERS
    World Wonders. Clifford Miller

WOODS
    Deep in the Quiet Wood. James Weldon Johnson
    Heart of the Woods. Wesley Curtright
    In Whichford Wood. William S. Braithwaite

WOODSON, CARTER
    Dr. Carter G. Woodson. Eloise Culver

WORDS
    Subterfuge. Countess W. Twitty
    Sweet Words on Race. Langston Hughes
    Words. Bernette Golden
    Words Will Resurrect. Jorge De Lima

WORK
    Toiler, The. Raymond Dandridge
    Work Song. Anonymous
    Worker, The. Richard Thomas
    Workin' Man. Langston Hughes

WORLD
    No Way Out. Linda Curry
    Our World Is Ours. Kali Grosvenor
    World I See, The. Mari Evans